TRADE AND AMERICAN LEADERSHIP

From the nation-building of Alexander Hamilton to the trade wars of Donald Trump, trade policy has been a key instrument of American power and wealth. The open trading system that the United States sponsored after the Second World War has served US interests by promoting cooperation and prosperity, but has also allowed the allies to become more independent and China to rise. The case studies in *Trade and American Leadership* examine how the value of preferential trade programs is undercut by the multilateral liberalization that the United States promoted for generations, and how trade sanctions tend to be either too economically costly to impose or too modest to matter. These problems are exacerbated by a domestic political system in which the gains from trade are unevenly distributed, power is fragmented, and strategies are easily undermined. *Trade and American Leadership* places special emphasis on today's challenges and on the rising danger of economic nationalism.

Craig VanGrasstek teaches at the Harvard Kennedy School and has previously taught at American University's School of International Service, Georgetown University's School of Foreign Service, the World Trade Institute, and the University of Barcelona. He is the author of *The History and Future of the World Trade Organization* (2013).

Trade and American Leadership

THE PARADOXES OF POWER AND WEALTH FROM
ALEXANDER HAMILTON TO DONALD TRUMP

CRAIG VANGRASSTEK

Harvard University

CAMBRIDGE
UNIVERSITY PRESS

CAMBRIDGE
UNIVERSITY PRESS

University Printing House, Cambridge CB2 8BS, United Kingdom

One Liberty Plaza, 20th Floor, New York, NY 10006, USA

477 Williamstown Road, Port Melbourne, VIC 3207, Australia

314-321, 3rd Floor, Plot 3, Splendor Forum, Jasola District Centre, New Delhi - 110025, India

79 Anson Road, #06-04/06, Singapore 079906

Cambridge University Press is part of the University of Cambridge.

It furthers the University's mission by disseminating knowledge in the pursuit of education, learning and research at the highest international levels of excellence.

www.cambridge.org
Information on this title: www.cambridge.org/9781108476959
DOI: 10.1017/9781108606141

First published 2019

A catalogue record for this publication is available from the British Library

Library of Congress Cataloging in Publication data
NAMES: VanGrasstek, Craig, author.
TITLE: Trade and American leadership : the paradoxes of power and wealth from Alexander Hamilton to Donald Trump / Craig VanGrasstek, Harvard University, Massachusetts.
DESCRIPTION: Cambridge, United Kingdom ; New York, NY : Cambridge University Press, 2019. | Includes bibliographical references.
IDENTIFIERS: LCCN 2018038865 | ISBN 9781108476959 (hardback)
SUBJECTS: LCSH: United States – Foreign economic relations. | United States – Foreign relations. | United States – Politics and government.
CLASSIFICATION: LCC HF1455 .V26 2019 | DDC 382/.30973–dc23
LC record available at https://lccn.loc.gov/2018038865

ISBN 978-1-108-47695-9 Hardback
ISBN 978-1-108-70179-2 Paperback

For Janet

Contents

Figures

Tables

Foreword

At a time when the esoteric topic of tariffs on trade fills headlines in newspapers, claims clicks on computer screens, and inspires emphatic messages in presidential tweets, there is need for an informed and insightful explanation of how we got to where we are in American trade policy. If we understand how we got here, we can understand better where we should go from here. Whether we Americans should turn inward toward insularity from international trade or turn outward toward more engagement with international trade is one of the most pressing of all questions in the making of American economic and foreign policy. Moreover, it is a question central to whether we see the future of the United States as a more closed or a more open society, with repercussions extending far beyond the commercial matters of trade.

In this book, Craig VanGrasstek provides the information and the insight needed to help answer this question. He is both professor and practitioner, with decades of experience in teaching about trade and in making trade work. Professor VanGrasstek is an Adjunct Lecturer in Public Policy at the John F. Kennedy School of Government at Harvard University, where he teaches courses on the political economy of trade policy. He is also a longtime participant in making and implementing trade policy, having advised such international institutions as the World Trade Organization, the Organization for Economic Cooperation and Development, the United Nations Conference on Trade and Development, and the World Bank, and having consulted for private firms and individual countries. As reflected in his latest book, his dual roles as professor and practitioner combine to shape his thinking on trade and on trade policymaking. The author knows the most subtle of the nuances of textile tariffs – a sure sign of trade expertise.

Previously, Professor VanGrasstek authored a well-received history of the World Trade Organization.[1] In this book, he turns his attention to the history of the trade policy of the United States of America. He does so with fluency and with a flair, wearing the depth and breadth of his learning lightly while telling a tale that demonstrates how American trade policy has changed over time with changing circumstances. He shows us that our current quandary over whether we Americans want our domestic economy to be open to commercial engagement with the wider world is not new but is only the most recent iteration of a long-running dilemma. Together with a wealth of documentation, he mixes in every now and then a felicitous turn of phrase or an apt literary allusion that help communicate his message.

Professor VanGrasstek is clearly on the side of those (like me) who seek more open trade as an essential ingredient of more open societies. He asserts, at the outset, "It is not utopian to hope that states can collaborate in the establishment and maintenance of a more or less open trading system, especially when that system can meet most of the needs (if not all of the demands) of its many and diverse members. This task requires greater imagination and energy in a time when US influence is on the wane." He adds, "I find it impossible to be objective regarding the possible extinction of the trading system as we know it. For all its faults, that system has better served the interests of the United States and its partners than any conceivable alternative."

Yet his personal preference for global cooperation in lowering barriers to global trade does not affect the quality of his historical analysis of American trade policy, which is scrupulously even-handed while ranging far and wide. Indeed, there is not much the author omits in his historical *tour d'horizon* of how we Americans got to where we are as a country on trade. Every region of the world and virtually every major sector of the American economy appear in the explication in this book. From China to Russia, from Japan to the Middle East, from steel to oil to textiles to agriculture, they are all here, and they are all discussed here with considerable authority.

Any number of passages in the book are worthy of highlight.

One is his discussion of how "foreign economic policy begins and ends at home." The author fully understands that, like all politics, trade politics is local. Everyone who has ever served as a trade negotiator for the United States knows that often the most difficult negotiation is not with other countries but with domestic interests and with those members of Congress who speak for domestic interests. There is no point in securing an agreement with another

---

[1] Craig VanGrasstek, *The History and Future of the World Trade Organization* (Geneva: WTO Publications, 2013).

country to reduce barriers to trade if that agreement will not be accepted back home. Thus, in trade, the "contagion of conflict at home and abroad can erect new hurdles to the negotiation, approval, and implementation of trade agreements, making it ever more difficult for the trading system to function effectively."

Another is his discussion of "sociotropism" – meaning a notion of fairness that transcends self-interest to inspire a motivation that proceeds from a concern for the welfare of others. Harking back to fundamental notions of human empathy found in Adam Smith's theory of moral sentiments and in John Donne's poetry, Professor VanGrasstek sees evidence of "domestic sociotropism" emerging in how the American people view trade. Instead of basing their view of trade on how trade may affect them, people who do not feel threatened by trade may nevertheless oppose freer trade "based on the concern that opening the US market to foreign competition might cause other Americans to lose their jobs."

Still another passage deserving highlight is the lengthy chapter on trade between the United States and China. Here the author provides a valuable historical account of how trade with China moved from back stage to center stage in US trade politics. Especially worthwhile is his discussion of something every reader ought to know: the long history of Western trade discrimination and, indeed, humiliation of China leading up to China's gradually opening to the world economy following the death of Mao Tse-Tung. Professor VanGrasstek helps us understand why – although China was a charter member of the General Agreement on Tariffs and Trade (GATT) – Mao withdrew GATT compliance port-by-port as he marched his armies across China in 1949, and his Nationalist antagonists withdrew China from the GATT after he chased them off the mainland. Any attempt to understand the Chinese hesitation about international treaties now must take into account how international treaties were long used by Western countries to oppress China.

Likewise deserving of particular attention is the author's passage explaining clearly the various obscure US trade statutes that have been unearthed by the current president of the United States and his trade advisers to use as unilateral clubs in flaunting multilateral trade commitments – Section 232, Section 301, and more. He tells us why these laws exist. He explains to us why, until the ascendancy of Donald Trump, they were used rarely or not at all. He spells out for us the dire economic implications of using them now. Especially interesting is his narrative of the history of the development in trade law of an exception for national security and his lucid explanation of why it would be far better if countries continued for another seventy years without using this exception and without defining it.

Equally noteworthy is the brief passage on "hegemony and international law" in which Professor VanGrasstek provides us with a variety of historical antecedents for the current American ambivalence over international law. A reliance on international law, he informs us, has always been a challenge for those who have the power to impose their will without law. Hugo Grotius, the great Dutch originator of the use of law to ensure the freedom of the seas, nevertheless "defended a Dutch admiral who took a Portuguese merchantman as a prize even though the two countries were then at peace." Similarly, although they too helped create and establish international law, "the British in hegemony did not always consult the law books before weighing their interests." The United States as well has waxed and waned in its commitment to comply with international law, including in trade. The skeptics of international law in the Trump administration – inclined to employ international law when it suits them and to ignore it when it does not – are not without predecessors.

There is much more in the book: The trade debate between Thomas Jefferson and Alexander Hamilton; the historical antecedents of trade sanctions; the enduring relevance of sea power to trade; the domestic sources of the ebb and flow of the tariffs imposed by the United States over more than two centuries; the effects on trade policy of the gradual shift from Great Britain to the United States as the leading power on the world stage; the key role of the United States in laying the foundations for the WTO-based multilateral trading system; the back and forth on trade between the United States and the Soviet Union during the Cold War; the Arab boycott of Israel. The ins and outs of trade policy on energy; the efforts, increasingly, to reconcile trade liberalization with social goals; the proliferation of free trade agreements and the motivations underlying them; and the implications of the looming threat of a possible withdrawal by the United States under President Trump from membership in the WTO.

Throughout the book, the author emphasizes the need for "economic statecraft" – for fully informed and far-sighted thinking in making trade policy. His book, as he puts it, "mixes scholarly and practical aims." He explains, "This book is premised on the hope that a proper understanding of history may promote a sense of retrospective empathy, remind us of the times when policymakers succeeded in promoting high ambitions, and offer practical observations on what does and does not work." His book fulfills this hope, if only we had more such practical idealists engaged in such an enlightened "economic statecraft" on trade.

James Bacchus
University of Central Florida

Preface

"Discovery commences with the awareness of anomaly,"[1] as Thomas Kuhn trenchantly noted, and two great anomalies have perplexed me for years. Chief among them is the late arrival of a resurgent protectionist movement in the United States, and the consequent abandonment of America's leadership position. Had I written this book just a few years ago, I would have stressed not the lateness but the near-absence of protectionism. The level of protection that the private sector demands, and that politicians supply, had long been lower than one might expect. This was a phenomenon that had puzzled me ever since I was a graduate student in the 1980s, when the theory of hegemonic stability still had that new-paradigm smell. The theory predicted that when the United States inevitably declined it would adopt a more insular policy. These concerns extended well beyond the academy. In the 1980s one could open the *New York Times* – not just to the business section, but the cover story of the Sunday magazine[2] – to find discussions of such books as Paul Kennedy's instant classic, *The Rise and Fall of the Great Powers*. The recognition then accorded to trade nerds was Warholian in its brevity, but helped to shape the tone and direction of the national debate.

While many then took American decline virtually as an article of faith, I was in the minority who thought the case was overblown.[3] In those days I commuted weekly between my classes at Princeton and my fledgling consulting practice on Capitol Hill, and what I saw from the latter perch did not square with what I was told to expect in the former. Presidents still favored

---

[1] Kuhn (1970), p. 52.
[2] See, for example, Schmeisser (1988), Wade (1988), and (in the same vein if not the same place) Brownstein (1988).
[3] See, for example, Russett (1985, p. 231), who correctly concluded that American hegemony (like Mark Twain) would eventually die, but that "in both cases early reports of their demise have been greatly exaggerated."

multilateral liberalization, began to supplement it by negotiating bilateral trade agreements, and rejected protectionist entreaties more often than they appeased them. While I appreciated the broader historical sweep that my professors offered, I began to fear that they might personify how Dante described the shades in Hell: "You see beforehand that which time will bring,/but cannot know what happens in the present."[4] Time and experience made me reassess that impression.

This book starts from the premise that the underlying assumptions of hegemonic stability theory were correct, but that its earlier proponents were precisely that: early. Exploiting the hindsight that is the historian's prerogative, we can now see what they could not anticipate. The theory's original proponents correctly devoted much attention to the transfer of hegemony from London to Washington, but they would have made an even greater contribution if they could foresee who would become the challenger this time around. They looked too far east and too near into the future, failing to anticipate how soon the Japanese challenge would crumble and how, after an interval, China would take Japan's place. This would prove to be a switch not just in role but in type. Whereas Tokyo had foresworn militarism in the constitution that Douglas MacArthur bestowed, Beijing challenges Washington in both the economic and security spheres. This full-spectrum competition will likely make the first half of our own century less predictable and more tumultuous than was the latter half of the twentieth century.

Another, later anomaly concerned the apparent decline of US policymakers' interest in trade. This had been a top-tier issue from the early 1980s through the mid-1990s, but by the dawn of the new millennium it was relegated to the second or third level. My initial perception of that downgrade was only impressionistic, but then I began devising ways to measure the diminishing resources that Washington invested in this subject. Whatever metrics I tried, they all confirmed that the salience of this issue had fallen as quickly as it had risen; readers will find that evidence in Chapter 6. My perplexity was only deepened by countervailing directions in the real economy. Cross-border transactions accounted for a growing share of GDP, and the merchandise trade balance turned progressively more negative. There were only two ways to reconcile the rise in trade's economic significance with its declining political salience. One was to conclude that the trade issue had been solved, with a critical mass of leaders having concurred that globalization was in the national interest. That explanation seemed persuasive for quite some time, to the embarrassment of the theory of hegemonic stability. Another

[4] Dante (c. 1306), *Inferno* canto X, p. 191.

possibility was that those same leaders had fallen out of step with a significant slice of the electorate, and that by sublimating the voters' instinct for economic nationalism they were allowing a dangerous buildup of pressures. If so, something had to give.

Here, too, the early proponents of hegemonic stability theory made the mistake of being right too soon. They did not know how resilient Washington's attachment to trade liberalization would prove, or how adept the executive would be in devising mechanisms to cope with protectionist demands. One was the perennial maneuver of "two steps forward, one step back," allowing presidents to wheedle favors from Congress by making judicious compromises on some demands for protection or a stricter reciprocity policy. More consequentially, they made up for the formerly pro-trade sectors that had gone rogue by adopting new negotiating objectives that spoke to the interests of capital- and knowledge-intensive sectors. Legacy industries might switch from free trade to protection, but they could be replaced by service industries and the owners of intellectual property rights. The move from multilateral to discriminatory liberalization was also critically important, as it injected elements of managed trade into an otherwise liberalizing project. By reforming the form and substance of policy, pro-trade policymakers delayed a reckoning with that portion of the electorate that was on the losing side of globalization and the process of Creative Destruction. That postponement might have been indefinite but for the advent of Donald Trump. We cannot fault either policymakers or analysts for failing to predict a swan so black.

This book aims to resolve those two anomalies. What follows is an extended exploration of the international and domestic political economy of trade, focused primarily on the place of the United States in two successive hegemonies. I argue that Washington behaved as we would expect in both eras, moving from free-rider to leader, but that its options in late hegemony were constrained by the choices it made at earlier stages. To the extent that the United States succeeded in negotiating down its own tariffs, it also diminished its future capacity to use preferences as a tool of foreign policy. To the extent that it succeeded in building up its allies' economies, it also ensured that any future sanctions campaigns would require the cooperation of those countries. And most significant of all, in establishing a more open trading system the hegemon provided the means by which its challengers could rise. I present the evidence and arguments both chronologically and thematically, with sections devoted to overviews and case studies in hegemony, domestic trade policymaking, and the use of discriminatory options (i.e., preferences and sanctions) as tools of commercial and foreign policy.

The sources and methods that I use to explore these issues are deliberately eclectic. "It is astonishing what foolish things one can temporarily believe if one thinks too long alone," Keynes noted, "particularly in economics (along with the other moral sciences)."[5] While reserving judgment as to whether political science may be characterized as moral, I do take to heart the admonition that we ought not to dwell too long within our walled gardens. That has been as true of my professional work as it is of this book, which some readers may find difficult to pigeonhole. I learned long ago that one can quickly carry the division of labor too far, and that in this field the only thing more pathetic than a lawyer who does not understand economics or an economist who does not understand the law is a political scientist who does not understand either. This book might best be described as the work of a political scientist who never got over a youthful dalliance with historiography, and who has tried to mimic the better habits of the economists and lawyers with whom he has worked over the past four decades. My analysis nonetheless gives primacy to politics, and I thus feel obliged to define that term.

The distinction that separates politics from economics, law, and other fields comes down to two related points. We may say that an issue or position has taken on a political hue whenever it amounts to either an exercise of power or an appeal to fairness – two concepts that tend to baffle economists and lawyers. Power can be simply defined as the capacity of one actor to compel another. Or as Dahl so memorably put it, "A has power over B to the extent that he can get B to do something that B would not otherwise do."[6] By fairness I mean a sense of equity, whether expressed in personal or abstract terms. That equity sometimes relates to procedural justice (e.g., B retorts to A that coercion is unfair), but more often concerns distributive justice (e.g., B objects that A has more wealth). Power and distributive justice are alike insofar as each concept is relative (A's share is measured against B's) as well as zero-sum (A's gains are B's losses). Or to let Occam's razor do its parsimonious work, a political perspective will typically involve one form or another of zero-sum conflict.

I share Gilpin's belief that "the fundamental nature of international relations has not changed over the millennia," and that it continues to be "a recurring struggle for wealth and power among independent actors in a state of anarchy."[7] There are means by which we may contain that anarchy, or at least dress it up so as to be more presentable in polite society. Chief among these is

---

[5] Keynes (1935), p. vii.
[6] Dahl (1957), p. 201.
[7] Gilpin (1981), p. 7.

the creation of domestic and international institutions that we task with maintaining order and enforcing property rights. To the extent that these institutions function efficiently and effectively, they may well give the appearance that the world has outgrown its chaotic and violent past. Appearances can easily deceive and lead one to the erroneous conclusion that hard political realities have been softened by the rule of law or the rational pursuit of mutual gain. We still live in a tough neighborhood, and rather than looking for economic cooperation to replace political competition we would do better to consider how they relate to one another.

Recognizing a problem does not mean resigning oneself to it, and in acknowledging these harsh realities I do not mean to imply that progress is impossible. I would not have written this book if I thought that there was no chance of encouraging policymakers to elevate their aims. This book is premised on the hope that a proper understanding of history may promote a sense of retrospective empathy, remind us of times when policymakers succeeded in promoting high ambitions, and offer some practical observations on what does and does not work.

Empathy is a virtue too often in short supply, and it will do current and prospective policymakers no harm to understand their own history. This is especially important when appraising the policies that a smaller, poorer country might adopt, bearing in mind that there was a time when those two words were just as applicable to the United States as they are to any developing country today. A recurring theme of this study concerns the many ways in which the perspectives and objectives of US policymakers changed on the acquisition of hegemony; a similar process is again underway as the country adjusts to circumstances that, if not exactly straitened, are not as grand as they once were. It is entirely understandable when legislators, diplomats, and others approach such issues as political neutrality and trade discrimination according to their country's current level of economic development and political power. Those same persons often fail to acknowledge the evolutionary character of these positions, or to recognize that the views expressed today in other countries are comparable to what their own predecessors had to say. Many developing countries pursue economic policies that would please Alexander Hamilton and foreign policies that echo George Washington or Thomas Jefferson. It is much more unusual to see modern American politicians who are willing to own up to that fact.

While the study of history ought to give us a proper appreciation for the roots of different countries' perspectives on power and wealth, it need not inhibit us from aiming high. When Peter Berger sought a generation ago to reset the debate over economic development he called for the blending of "two attitudes that are usually separate – the attitudes of 'hard-nosed' analysis and utopian imagination."[8] It is hard-nosed to acknowledge the stern realities of a world in which sovereign states are not only economically selfish but also politically narrow-minded and demonstrate a disturbing predilection toward violence. While those states may thus appear self-centered, they may also be persuaded that it is in their interest to cooperate. There are enough historical examples of such cooperation to confirm that "utopian" is not a synonym for "impossible." It is not utopian to hope that states can collaborate in the establishment and maintenance of a more or less open trading system, especially when that system can meet most of the needs (if not all of the demands) of its many and diverse members. That task requires greater imagination and energy in a time when US influence is on the wane. Above all else, it demands that the United States not respond to inexorable economic forces with a fit of pique. However tempting it may be for the United States to pick up its marbles and go home, US interests would be better served by using its influence – diminished though it may be – to adapt the trading system to the shifting realities of a more dynamic world.

Any work that mixes scholarly and practical aims will naturally raise questions regarding the author's objectivity. That is a virtue that historians ideally ought to practice, but I have made a conscious decision to make no false pretense of impartiality. This is no small confession, as I was raised in that intellectual tradition that led Henry Adams to declare that "[n]o honest historian can take part with – or against – the forces he has to study." He went so far as to opine that for an historian "even the extinction of the human race should be merely a fact to be grouped with other vital statistics,"[9] and while I can appreciate that position in the abstract I find it impossible to be objective regarding the possible extinction of the trading system as we know it. For all of its faults, that system has better served the interests of the United States and its partners than any conceivable alternatives. Much of this book is devoted to an explanation of the stresses that must inevitably build in a system that relies so heavily on the leadership of one country, especially when that country is challenged from without by a Law of Uneven Growth and from within by the process of Creative Destruction. It is beyond the scope of this book to propose a specific program by which those challenges might be met and those stresses overcome. It is also beyond the capacity of the author to be indifferent toward the gravity of the problem, or impartial with respect to proposed solutions that are more likely to exacerbate than to solve it.

---

[8]   Berger (1976), p. xiv.
[9]   Quoted in Seldes (1967), p. 474.

Acknowledgments

My first and least payable debt of gratitude is to Sinclair Lewis, a fellow Minnesotan who died eight years before I was born. When I read his novel *Arrowsmith* during my first year of graduate school I saw in it a design for living. His title character longed only to conduct original research and to divorce himself from all the cares of business and office politics, and so he took up a chemist friend's offer of a two-room rural shanty. There he could subsidize his full-time research by making sera for pharmacists. If he spent just "two hours a day on the commercial end, and say about six for sleeping and a couple for feeding and telling dirty stories" he would still have "fourteen hours a day for research (except when you got something special on), with no Director and no Society patrons and no Trustees that you've got to satisfy by making fool reports."[1] Subtracting some dirty stories and adding many more fool reports, that formula admirably captures my approach to the work–life balance.

I can only guess whether the many analyses that I have written from my rural hermitage over these past decades did as much good for my clients and their constituents as Arrowsmith's chemicals did for his customers and their patients, but I gratefully acknowledge that their commissions subsidized my work and allowed me to reconnoiter the issues covered in this book. More than that, these sometimes random assignments have not infrequently sent me down analytical avenues that I might not have thought to explore in a life more ordinary, allowing for some serendipitous discoveries. Chief among these blameless if unwitting patrons have been (in chronological order) Stephen Lande, Miguel Rodriguez Mendoza, Murray Gibbs, Alejandro Jara, and Simon Evenett. I am also grateful to Clem Boonekamp, Evelyn Horowitz, Nicolas Imboden, Stefano Inama, Iza Lejarraga, Douglas Lippoldt, Patrick Low, Christopher Malone, Mario Matus, Roberto Matus, Eduardo

---

[1] Lewis (1925), p. 393.

Mayobre, Hal Northcott, Victor Ognivtsev, Bruno Perron, Carlos Alberto Primo Braga, Maryse Robert, Raed Safadi, Pierre Sauvé, John Simpson, Manuela Tortora, Guillermo Valles, Theresa Wetter, Wayne Wright, and Simonetta Zarrilli.

Martin Arrowsmith also depended on two other blessings. One was the inspiration of his mentor, Max Gottlieb, the professor of bacteriology of whom it "was said that he could create life in the laboratory, that he could talk to the monkeys which he inoculated, that he had been driven out of Germany as a devil-worshiper or an anarchist, and that he secretly drank real champagne every evening at dinner."[2] While I have yet to meet anyone who precisely matches that description, it has been my pleasure to know mentors and colleagues who resemble Gottlieb in one or more of those particulars. I especially appreciate the lessons and opportunities provided by Doug Arnold, William Baumol, Kinley Brauer, Fernando Cepeda Ulloa, Robert Gilpin, Robert Z. Lawrence, Francisco Leal Buitrago, Frances X. Winters, and Gary Wynia on the academic side, and by Arancha Gonzalez, Gary Horlick, Gary Hufbauer, Pascal Lamy, and Rubens Ricupero on the professional side. I am also grateful to those many students in Barcelona, Bern, Cambridge, and Washington with whom I have engaged in reciprocal learning over the past three decades. The questions that they ask have forced me to think about how it all works, and then to rethink it a few times more.

Lewis' hero could not have advanced in life without the support of his wife Leora. "They had that understanding of each other known only to married people, a few married people," he wrote, "wherein for all their differences they were as much indissoluble parts of a whole as are the eye and hand."[3] Hence Arrowsmith's dedication, and my own.

Gary Horlick, Alejandro Jara, Gabrielle Marceau, Victor Ognivtsev, and Manuela Tortora all gave invaluable guidance in helping me to avoid error. I also appreciate the comments that I received from Victor Do Prado, Tim Groser, David Hartridge, Gary Hufbauer, and Steve Meardon. Reitze Gouma of the University of Groningen was helpful in tracking down comparative economic data. I am grateful to those public affairs officers and other officials of US agencies and international organizations who have kindly assisted me in verifying facts or ensuring that my citations are correct. They include Molly Hale of the Central Intelligence Agency and Peg O'Laughlin of the US International Trade Commission. My thanks as well to John Berger of Cambridge University Press, who, together with Danielle Menz and

[2] Ibid., p. 12.
[3] Ibid., p. 262.

Catherine Smith of his editorial staff, have provided patient guidance. I also thank the copyeditor, Theresa Kornak, and the production team for their high professionalism.

An initial version of Chapter 6 came out as a European University Institute Robert Schuman Centre working paper. Portions of that chapter, and of Chapter 3, also appeared in chapter 3 ("Back to the Future: US Trade Policy under the Trump Administration") of *Future of the Global Trade Order* (2nd edn, 2017), edited by Carlos A. Primo Braga and Bernard Hoekman. Portions of Chapter 11 previously appeared as chapter 7 ("Continuity and Change in the Politics of US Trade Relations with Russia") of *The New Economic Diplomacy: Decision-Making and Negotiation in International Economic Relations* (4th edn, 2017), edited by Nicholas Bayne and Stephen Woolcock. Material from those earlier chapters appears here in revised and updated versions with the kind permission of Messrs. Bayne, Hoekman, Primo Braga, and Woolcock. Portions of Chapter 15 previously appeared in "Peace, Security, and Middle East Trade: Is Discrimination the Problem or the Solution?" published in *The Journal of World Investment & Trade* (Volume 4, Issue 5), 2003. Those portions are included here with the kind permission of Koninklijke Brill NV.

Any errors that remain are entirely my own.

Abbreviations

AB	Appellate Body
AD	Antidumping
AFL	American Federation of Labor
AFL-CIO	American Federation of Labor-Congress of Industrial Organizations
AGOA	African Growth and Opportunity Act
AIADA	American International Automobile Dealers Association
APEC	Asia Pacific Economic Cooperation
ASEAN	Association of Southeast Asian Nations
ASP	American selling price
ATPA	Andean Trade Preferences Act
BIT	Bilateral investment treaty
CACRs	Cuban Assets Control Regulations
CAFTA-DR	Free Trade Agreement with Central America and the Dominican Republic
CARS	Consumer Assistance to Recycle and Save
CBC	Congressional Black Caucus
CBI	Caribbean Basin Initiative
CFTA	US-Canada Free Trade Agreement
CIA	Central Intelligence Agency
CIO	Congress of Industrial Organizations
CoCom	Coordinating Committee
CSI	Coalition of Service Industries
CVD	Countervailing duty
DFQF	Duty-free, quota-free
DSB	Dispute Settlement Body
DSU	Dispute Settlement Understanding
EU	European Union

FDR	Franklin Delano Roosevelt
FRUS	Foreign Relations of the United States
FTA	Free Trade Agreement
FTAA	Free Trade Area of the Americas
GATT	General Agreement on Tariffs and Trade
GCC	Gulf Cooperation Council
GDP	Gross domestic product
GM	General Motors Corporation
GSP	Generalized System of Preferences
IDB	Inter-American Development Bank
ISI	Import-substitution industrialization
ITO	International Trade Organization
JFK	John Fitzgerald Kennedy
KGB	*Komitet Gosudarstvennoy Bezopasnosti* (Committee for State Security)
LDC	Least developed country
MAI	Multilateral Agreement on Investment
MFA	Multi-Fibre Arrangement
MFN	Most favored nation
MNNA	Major Non-NATO Ally
MP	Member of Parliament
NAFTA	North American Free Trade Agreement
NAIC	North American Industrial Classification
NATO	North Atlantic Treaty Organization
NME	Nonmarket economy
NSC	National Security Council
NTR	Normal trade relations
OECD	Organisation for Economic Co-operation and Development
OPEC	Organization of Petroleum Exporting Countries
OTCA	Omnibus Trade and Competitiveness Act
PAC	Political action committee
PHP	Preferential handling procedure
PNTR	Permanent normal trade relations
PPP	Public Papers of the Presidents
QIZ	Qualifying Industrial Zone
RTAA	Reciprocal Trade Agreements Act
S&D	Special and differential
SIC	Standard Industrial Classification
TAA	Trade Adjustment Assistance
TPA	Trade Promotion Authority

TPP	Trans-Pacific Partnership
TR	Theodore Roosevelt
TRIPS	Agreement on Trade-Related Aspects of Intellectual Property Rights
TTIP	Transatlantic Trade and Investment Partnership
UAE	United Arab Emirates
UAW	United Auto Workers
UN	United Nations
UNCTAD	United Nations Conference on Trade and Development
UNESCO	United Nations Educational, Scientific, and Cultural Organization
USITC	United States International Trade Commission
USMCA	United States Mexico Canada Agreement
USSR	Union of Soviet Socialist Republics
USTR	United States Trade Representative
VER	Voluntary export restraint
WIPO	World Intellectual Property Organization
WTO	World Trade Organization

PART I

INTRODUCTION AND OVERVIEW

1

The Domestic Diplomacy of Trade and the Paradoxes of Power and Wealth

Foreign economic policy is a major instrument in the conduct of United States foreign relations. It is an instrument which can powerfully influence the world environment in ways favorable to the security and welfare of this country. It is also an instrument which, if unwisely formulated and employed, can do actual harm to our national interests.

National Security Council Report 68 (1950)

INTRODUCTION

The United States demonstrated in the Cold War that it is fully capable of balancing the imperatives of what the National Security Council (NSC) called "security and welfare." Adam Smith preferred the terms "defense" and "opulence" to describe this great dichotomy of foreign policy, just as his nineteenth-century successors distinguished the "high politics" of war and peace from the "low politics" of trade and investment. Herman Goering famously observed that countries must choose between "guns and butter"; talk of "blood and treasure" came back into vogue after 9/11, and in his inaugural address Donald Trump promised to deliver "prosperity and strength." Whatever we choose to call them, power and wealth have always been the principal means and ends of foreign policy. Statesmen must secure the country's borders and ensure the people's safety, and also promote economic opportunity through trade and investment. These two aims are often in tension, and sometimes in conflict, but they are neither wholly distinct nor mutually exclusive. A country that pursues security without regard to its welfare risks stagnation and bankruptcy, and a country that pursues welfare without regard to its security courts indolence and invasion. Finding the right mix, and steadfastly pursuing it, is a supremely difficult task for a democracy in which lawmakers do not habitually defer to the president, government is more often divided than unified, and voters are not fond of taxes or conscription. Yet Harry Truman and his eight successors managed to pull it off.

Economic policy was a critical element in the US grand strategy. "The only sure victory," according to NSC-68, "lies in the frustration of the Kremlin design by the steady development of the moral and material strength of the free world and its projection into the Soviet world in such a way as to bring about an internal change in the Soviet system." To this end, the NSC urged that the doctrine of containment be complemented by "an international economy based on multilateral trade, declining trade barriers, and convertible currencies," aid to Western Europe and other allies, and "assistance in the development of under-developed areas."[1] Americans sacrificed a great deal to implement this plan in the ensuing decades and obliged others to sacrifice even more. There were times that the strategy faltered, sometimes tragically, but containment ultimately delivered exactly what it promised: The growing gap in material prosperity between East and West, coupled with a costly arms race and Moscow's imperial overstretch, precipitated the collapse of Communism.

We would do well to learn both the positive and negative lessons from that experience, but should also heed a warning from NSC-68. Foreign economic policy "is an instrument uniquely suited to our capabilities," according to the NSC strategists, "provided we have the tenacity of purpose and the understanding requisite to a realization of its potentials,"[2] and yet it also has the capacity to harm the national interest. Apart from an outright military attack, there may be no damage that an adversary can wreak upon the United States greater than the self-inflicted wound of an ill-conceived foreign economic policy. Short-sighted pundits and policymakers cannot see that trade is as much about creating value with partners as it is about claiming value for oneself, and that missteps in this field can cripple exporters, stifle innovation, burden consumers, embolden rivals, and make erstwhile allies rethink their ties to an unreliable friend. That is precisely the danger that the United States now faces, as anticipated by a prescient contemporary of NSC-68. "We have met the enemy," said Pogo Possum in 1953, "and he is us."[3]

---

[1] A Report to the National Security Council by the Executive Secretary (Lay), "NSC-68" (April 14, 1950), *FRUS 1950*, Volume I, pp. 259 and 291.

[2] Ibid., p. 258.

[3] Kelly (1953), p. i.

HOW THE PAST CAN INFORM MODERN ECONOMIC STATECRAFT

What follows in this book is an historical review and contemporary critique of how American policymakers balance power and wealth as tools and objectives in foreign policy. This analysis is inspired by a profound concern that an overreaction against the perceived excesses of globalization threatens to over-turn the foundations of an international order that not only worked out well during the Cold War but is also adaptable and scalable to a new world in which the opportunities and the dangers are more widely distributed. Though the critics in the Trump administration cannot be faulted for their recognition that power and wealth are intimately related, they show a remarkable knack for coming up with precisely the wrong answers. By replacing inter-nationalism with protectionism, promoting an "America first" ethos that reduces partners to clients, and taking a wholly transactional and zero-sum view of economic exchange, the radically anachronistic policies that they promote are unlikely to deliver either prosperity or strength. They instead threaten to render the United States economically impotent and politically impoverished.

This is a study of economic statecraft. That term encompasses the universe of practices in international relations by which states either employ their wealth to promote their power or vice versa. Whereas in garden-variety trade policy both the means and the ends are strictly commercial, in economic statecraft some of those same tools are employed in pursuit of larger aims. In addition to trade barriers, as well as agreements to reduce or eliminate them, the instruments of economic statecraft include trade preferences and sanctions, the regulation or promotion of foreign investment, immigration rules, exchange rate policy, foreign assistance, etc., all of which may be directed toward such equally varied ends as peace, victory, regional stability, the strengthening of allies, the weakening of adversaries, security of supply for food and fuel, and promoting positive change in other countries' internal or external policies.

Thinking about economic statecraft requires that we use both sides of the brain, and not shy away from topics just because they are outside our comfort zone. This point is especially relevant whenever we consider the relationship between war – hot or cold, potential or actual – and the trading system. The economics of military conflict remain a surprisingly underdeveloped field, owing to the widespread misconception that war is so abnormal as to constitute a rare and special case (if it is considered at all). Economic models typically make a great many simplifying assumptions that elide past the details of a messy reality, one of them being that countries are in a state of perpetual peace. Intellectual honesty obliges us to recognize that while war is morally abhorrent it is not historically aberrant.

It is a sad but unavoidable fact that most of human history can be divided between those periods in which countries were more often at war than they were at peace and those in which mankind believed it had outgrown armed conflict. Even if one counted only the declared wars, and set aside covert operations, armed interventions, and other forms of low-intensity conflict, the record is sobering. In the years from 1917 to 2017, the United States fought nine declared wars[4] that stretched across forty-one years. It also lived through eighteen recessions that lasted thirty-eight years.[5] With wars being half as frequent but twice as long as recessions, we might expect economists to devote as much attention to these political failures as they routinely do to market failures. Quite to the contrary, the belief that war is rare "has been so powerful as to focus the operation of a substantial body of [economic] theory on the workings of a peacetime economy only."[6] The twentieth century's literature on the economics of war could fill no more than a modest bookshelf. One of these volumes was devoted entirely to showing how and why "economists seem to have turned their attention very little to this area of policy,"[7] and most of the others dealt primarily with war finance.

The problem is worsened by the common assumption that markets offer a sovereign remedy for all afflictions, not least war itself. "If goods don't cross borders," Frédéric Bastiat is often quoted as saying, "armies will." The problem with this sentiment, besides the fact that Bastiat never actually said this,[8] is that lazy minds eagerly treat it as an unassailable verity rather than a testable proposition. It instead offers a good example of what social scientists call a falsifiable statement – a well-formed hypothesis that can be discarded if we find contrary evidence. That evidence is bountiful: Many of history's deadliest wars have been fought between adversaries that traded with one another right up to the day that troops replaced exports. The internal market of the United States was fully open before the Civil War, for example, and the First World War erupted at a time when European markets were closely integrated. This is not to suggest that commerce and conflict are unrelated. Much of this book is devoted to the proposition that trade is an important

---

[4] In this tally I include United Nations Security Council resolutions and authorizations of military force approved by Congress that are associated with the Korean War, the Vietnam War, and the two Gulf wars.

[5] Calculated from National Bureau of Economic Research data at www.nber.org/cycles.html.

[6] Milward (1979), p. 1.

[7] Goodwin (1991b), p. 1.

[8] See Snow (2010).

instrument of foreign policy, providing a versatile set of tools that can serve the needs of aggressors, defenders, or peacemakers. Even when we put a hard edge on soft power, however, we need to acknowledge the tactical limitations of this instrument. That, too, is a recurring theme in this book.

This analysis is built around two sets of problems. The first is what I deem the three paradoxes of power and wealth, each of which concerns difficult choices and trade-offs in the conduct of economic statecraft. Any country that is not a mere price-taker in the global power market, and plans to use the tools of low politics to secure the aims of high politics, must offer a solution to at least one of these three riddles. The second set of problems concerns the domestic diplomacy of foreign economic policy, by which I mean the often difficult task of devising and executing a consistent strategy in a democracy. Policymaking in the United States is special in many respects, and unique in a few. Americans have a well-established aversion to the concentration of power, as reflected in a Constitution that deliberately fragments authority along lines that are horizontal (i.e., the separation of powers) and vertical (i.e., federalism). While these politically centrifugal instincts help to preserve liberty, they also confound coherent policymaking. Taken together, the paradoxes and the challenges of domestic diplomacy make for a system in which both the problems and the solutions are subject to change – sometimes steady and incremental, and sometimes sudden and radical.

THE THREE PARADOXES OF POWER AND WEALTH

The very term "economic statecraft" may seem self-contradictory, conflating as it does the functions of the market and the state. Anyone who explores this territory will come across advocates who hold very different notions, from wide-eyed prophets of the open market to jaded practitioners of power politics. Where the one group typically sees the chief function of the state primarily in negative terms, favoring the negotiation of agreements by which governments mutually agree to get out of the way, security-minded analysts and officials take quite a different view. It is little wonder that paradoxes abound in this field.

The Paradox of Hegemony: A Leader Either Hobbles Itself or Enables Challengers

Much of this book is devoted to the theory and practice of hegemony. A hegemon may be simply described as a country whose power and wealth dwarf those of all other contenders, and is prepared to use these resources to guide and shape the international system. (We might alternatively call such a country a leader, an imperialist, or a bully, but even polemicists can appreciate the utility of neutral terminology.) Hegemony is more of a process than a state of being, and this distinction can pass from one country to another. The nineteenth and early twentieth centuries were dominated by French and then German challenges to British hegemony, followed by a comparatively easy transition to US leadership, just as the rivalry between the United States and China is one of the defining – and most hazardous – characteristics of the twenty-first century.

The theory of hegemonic stability first emerged in the 1970s as a way of explaining why global markets are often closed but sometimes open.[9] It rests upon the importance of public goods and the ability of a hegemon to deliver one of them. As first described by Paul Samuelson in 1954, public goods share two special characteristics: They are nonexcludable (no one can be prevented from enjoying them) and nonrivalrous in consumption (any person's use of that good does not diminish its availability to others). A sidewalk is one such example. Everyone benefits from the sidewalk; I do not exhaust that amenity when I take a stroll, nor can I lawfully push anyone else into the street. A further characteristic shared by most public goods is that they are subject to a free-rider problem, and hence they tend to be underprovided. A rational, self-interested actor sees no advantage in supplying a public good when it expects others to exploit that investment, and the sidewalk may never be built if everyone waits for everyone else to supply it. This market failure offers a rationale for the state to provide what private interests will not. We task municipal governments with building sidewalks, and the federal government is responsible for interstate highways.

Overcoming the free-rider problem is even more difficult when a public good is international. An open world market is, after universal peace, the second greatest of all global public goods. It is also predictably under-provided, with free trade having historically been scarcer than protection-ism. The facile solution is to rely on global government. We have a World Trade Organization (WTO), but just how did the WTO and its predecessor, the General Agreement on Tariffs and Trade (GATT), come to be? According to the theory of hegemonic stability, we would never have produced the GATT in 1947 without US hegemony, just as the more or less open markets of the late nineteenth century depended on the Pax Britannica. Only a hegemon has both the motive and the means to supply an open global market. The motive stems from the hegemon's economic

---

[9]   See, for example, Gilpin (1987), Kindleberger (1973), and Krasner (1976). See Meardon (2014) for the development of Kindleberger's ideas first in practice and then in theory.

United Kingdom = 1

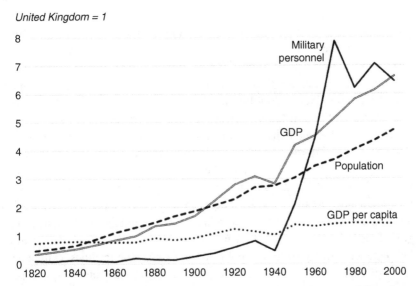

FIGURE 1.1 Power and wealth of the United States vis-à-vis the United Kingdom, 1820–2000.
Source: GDP, population, and GDP per capita from the Maddison Historical GDP Data at www.worldeconomics.com/ Data/MadisonHistoricalGDP/Madison %20Historical%20GDP%20Data.efp. Military personnel from http://correlatesof war.org/ data-sets/national-material-capabilities.

efficiency: It needs access to foreign markets to take full advantage of its competitiveness. As for the means, a hegemon has the market power and political influence to entice or coerce a critical mass of countries to join it at the negotiating table.

The theory explains why markets were generally open during the UK and US hegemonies, and why they were generally closed prior to British hegemony and again from 1918 to 1945. The Great War left England too weak to exercise its old role, and the United States was not prepared for global leadership until we got into the regrettable habit of numbering our world wars. The data illustrated in Figure 1.1 suggest that Washington could have relieved London long before it actually did so. The United States surpassed the United Kingdom in population by 1860, in gross domestic product (GDP) by 1875, and in GDP per capita by 1920. None of that mattered until the nascent hegemon stopped shirking its responsibilities. The gap between American resources and ambitions can best be seen in the relative size of the military, which remained far smaller than its British counterpart until the Second World War was well underway.[10] Prior to that conflict, Washington took only a few, poorly considered steps toward the center of the global stage. The horrors of the First World War and the failures of the Versailles Peace Conference made the American people recoil from a premature foray into leadership, but then the attack on Pearl Harbor and the dawn of the atomic era forced a complacent public to reassess its instinctive insularity. The transatlantic transfer of power was accomplished without a direct confrontation between the old and new hegemons, as the two countries shared culture, interests, and – above all – enemies.

The peaceful transition from British to American hegemony was exceptional. Political thinkers have recognized for millennia that the rivalries between hegemons and their challengers are as perilous as they are perennial, and that conflict is made all the more likely by the tendency of challengers to grow faster than hegemons. It is now fashionable to call this relationship between economic growth and political conflict the Thucydides Trap, after its original proponent.[11] "The real cause" of the Peloponnesian War, according to Thucydides, was that the "growth of the power of Athens" alarmed Sparta and "made war inevitable."[12] Athens owed its growth to mastery of ceramics and commerce, a pair of peaceful and seemingly apolitical arts that the Spartans disdained. Two millennia later, Lenin argued that the power of capitalist countries "does not change to an equal degree," and it was inconceivable "that in ten or twenty years' time the relative strength of the imperialist powers will have remained unchanged."[13] European rivalries led first to competition at the colonial periphery, and then to war in the metropolitan heartland. We should take notice whenever thinkers at the opposing poles of Western thought express essentially the same idea. For all else that divided Thucydides and Lenin, they both perceived a Law of Uneven Growth by which differing rates of economic expansion disturb the status quo, leading to political friction and war. Their only real disagreement concerned the desirability of change: Where the Greek Realist dreaded the instability spawned by unequal growth, the Russian Bolshevik saw an opening. These are not abstract musings from bygone days. China's rapid growth may be just as destabilizing as Thucydides would fear, and disrupt the equilibrium just as much as Lenin would hope. What is most remarkable about Beijing's rise is not only that it is

---

[10]   The Civil War is not captured by the once-a-decade observations shown in Figure 1.1. In 1865 the United States quite temporarily had 3.6 times as many men under arms as the United Kingdom.

[11]   See Allison (2015).

[12]   Thucydides (400 BCE), p. 355.

[13]   Lenin (1916), p. 144.

accelerated by the trading system that Washington worked so hard to establish, but that US policymakers had little choice in the matter. They could not have their cake without China eating it too.

This is the paradox of hegemony: A hegemon must establish an open world market to reap the rewards of competitiveness, but in so doing it facilitates the rise of its challengers. This paradox bedeviled London in its day, and Washington now faces the same dilemma. Just as the British provided Germany with the means to rise, so too has the United States enabled China's growth. But what else could it have done? A generation ago, US policymakers saw much to be gained by encouraging the world's most populous country to emerge from the chaos of the Cultural Revolution and reintegrate into the global community. That was a fateful decision with long-term consequences, even if the implications were not as apparent in the waning days of the Cold War as they are today.

The Paradox of Preferences: Discrimination Expands as Its Value Declines

The choice between openness and closure is the largest strategic decision that the community of states will make for the trading system, and critically depends on a willing and able hegemon, but the exceptions can be just as important as the rule. International society must also decide how much discrimination it will tolerate, whether in the positive form of preferences or the negative form of sanctions. Preferences may be nicer than sanctions, but they are no less an exercise of power. Yet while the benefits that a hegemon expects to derive from both forms of discrimination may grow over time, two more paradoxes constrain its ability to utilize these instruments effectively.

The paradox of preferences is that policymakers will be drawn toward trade discrimination just when the value of that tool is in decline. This paradox is a product of the hegemon's evolving economic and political position. The hegemon may focus on grand strategy and the virtues of multilateralism when its power is unchallenged, but over time the tactical deployment of discriminatory options may figure more prominently in its calculations and actions. American economic efficiency peaked just after the Second World War, which is also when Washington was most insistent that trade liberalization be deep and nondiscriminatory. As time went on and tariffs declined, however, the attractiveness of discrimination rose. One advantage of preferences is that they allow the hegemon to support poorer partners without asking a cash-strapped legislature to approve more foreign aid. The economic appeal of "trade, not aid" also rests on the benefits that it can extend to declining domestic industries. Duty-free treatment for imports of clothing from preferred partners, for example, can be made contingent on their use of American fabric. This encourages the relocation of apparel factories to the partner country while also providing a captive market for the dwindling US textile industry. These schemes have a win–win appeal, but can work only if the overall level of protection remains high enough for preferences to matter.

Preferences offer another example of how this hegemon has followed the same path as its predecessor. The United Kingdom and the United States went through a comparable sequence. Both favored an open form of bilateralism at early stages of their hegemony, and then adopted a more discriminatory approach as their own competitiveness waned. The tariff-reduction treaties that the British started to negotiate in 1860, and the comparable agreements that the United States championed from 1934 to 1946, each included most-favored-nation (MFN) clauses promising their partners that no other country would be granted exclusive preferences. If England reached a bargain with (for example) Sweden in 1875, and the United States did the same in 1935, the tariff reductions that they each extended to Stockholm (and vice versa) would be granted to all other countries to which they accorded MFN status. Both hegemons used nondiscriminatory, bilateral agreements to produce a distributed multilateral system. Britain turned to more discriminatory alternatives when it lost ground to Germany, culminating in the restrictive Imperial Preferences negotiated at the Ottawa Conference in 1932. Prior to the Ottawa Agreements, many of the British dominions operated on an "open door" basis in which they made no distinction between imports from the British Commonwealth, its colonies and territories, and the rest of the world. This reintroduction of discrimination was highly objectionable to Washington, which equated preferences with protection, but what was good for the English goose eventually became equally attractive to the Yankee gander. The United States began to negotiate discriminatory free trade agreements (FTAs) just when serious doubts emerged over its competitive position vis-à-vis Japan in the 1980s, and that process accelerated when China replaced Japan and the Soviet Union as the principal challenger to US wealth and power.

The proliferation of discriminatory programs and agreements since the mid-1970s is politically logical but economically puzzling. It would have been quite valuable for a country to enjoy preferential access to the US market in 1932, when the average tariff on dutiable goods was 59%, but in those days only Cuba and the Philippines were granted this boon. The attraction would still be high at the start of the GATT era, with US tariffs averaging 20% in 1947. Preferences were not an important part of the US trade regime until 1976, however, starting with a Generalized System of Preferences (GSP) that extended duty-free

Percentages and Raw Numbers

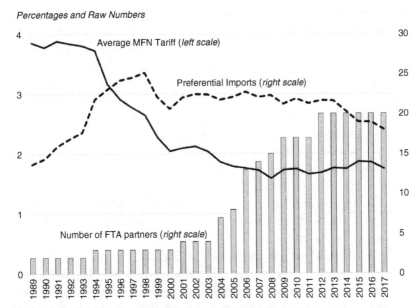

FIGURE 1.2 Discrimination in US merchandise trade, 1989–2017.
Preferential Imports = Share of total US merchandise imports that entered under
the terms of FTAs or preference programs (i.e., GSP and the regional programs for
Andean countries, the Caribbean Basin, and sub-Saharan Africa). Average MFN
Tariff is based on all imports not entering under preferential terms. FTA Partners =
Number of partner countries with which FTAs were in force in the year.
Source: Calculated from US International Trade Commission DataWeb at https://
dataweb.usitc.gov.

treatment to some imports from developing countries. The average US tariff
had fallen by then to just 6%. It was about the same when the United States
negotiated its first FTA in 1985, but by 2016 the average tariff on nonpreferential
imports was a shade below 2%.[14] Exoneration of a nuisance-level tax offers
precious little inducement. The value of discrimination is undercut by preference erosion, with every reduction in MFN rates narrowing the margin of
preference. It is also subject to preference dilution, with the benefits of all prior
programs and agreements diminishing every time a new one is inaugurated.

The net result can be appreciated from the data illustrated in Figure 1.2.
If we looked only at the final decade of the twentieth century it might
appear as if preferences were powerful. The share of imports entering on

[14] Figures for 1932 to 1985 are from unpublished US International Trade Commission data.
Except where otherwise noted, all US trade data in this book are calculated from the
commission's DataWeb at https://dataweb.usitc.gov.

a preferential basis climbed steadily, peaking at about one-quarter of the total just before the turn of the century. The share dropped thereafter, despite all the new, discriminatory arrangements. In addition to the advent of special preferential programs for the Caribbean Basin (since 1984), the Andean countries (1991–2013), and sub-Saharan Africa (since 2000), the number of FTA partners rose from two in the 1980s to twenty by 2012. Why then has the actual share of preferential imports declined? The first and most important explanation is that more products are now duty-free on an MFN basis, making preferences moot for most items. Just before the Uruguay Round tariff cuts began to take effect in 1995, 26% of all imports (by value) were on the free list; by 2017, the share had grown to 63%. That same round of multilateral trade negotiations reduced most remaining tariffs, with the average US rate being halved during the decade of phase-ins (1995–2005).

Why do trading partners place such a high priority on acquiring the small and diminishing advantage of an FTA with the United States? The explanations include the rising importance of global value chains, persistently high levels of protection in a handful of sectors, and the desire of foreign leaders to have photo ops in the Oval Office. Perhaps the most persuasive answer is the simplest: Those officials vastly overestimate the power of preferences. Casual observers – a group that includes most presidents, prime ministers, and trade ministers – often have a grossly distorted sense of just how high the MFN tariffs are, and will erroneously expect tremendous benefits after they knock down a supposedly insuperable tariff wall. These mercantilist misperceptions can work to the benefit of US negotiators, giving them greater leverage not just in a trade agreement but also in any other matters that they link to this initiative. That advantage may not be sustainable over the long term if the prospective partners get cagier about the realities of trade.

While preferences are not nearly as valuable as US partners typically expect, one other consequence of discrimination is undeniable: It is impossible to favor some partners without disadvantaging others. And this may ultimately be the point, even if policymakers do not explicitly acknowledge it. To the extent that the United States now confines its liberalization to discriminatory deals, and makes no new, multilateral commitments of any significance in the WTO, China will be relegated to the status of the least-favored nation. That may prove to be a distinction without a difference, however, as the low tariff wall that remains has not prevented China from capturing ever-larger shares of the US import market.

The Paradox of Sanctions: Political Feasibility versus Economic Effectiveness

Let us suppose, for the sake of argument, that a leading aim of US policy was the economic containment of China. The foregoing discussion implied that positive yet indirect discrimination against China has not achieved this goal, so might American policymakers opt instead for direct, negative discrimination against China? That depends in part on whether they can resolve the third paradox, which posits an inverse relationship between the economic impact and the political feasibility of sanctions. The underlying reason for this paradox is that sanctions impose costs not just on the target state, but also on the sender. That country is typically a pluralist democracy in which interested domestic parties can organize in self-defense. The more economic pain that a given sanction is expected to deliver, the greater the resistance at home; conversely, it is much easier to impose sanctions when symbolism outweighs substance. Here we see the significance of the domestic diplomacy of trade policy in a democracy. Commercial intimidation may be taken more seriously by the target country as the volume of trade increases, but higher volumes also make it less likely that the prospective sender will carry out its threats.

The United States does enjoy some important advantages in the use of trade sanctions. It has the world's largest market, and yet its economy is also one of the least trade-intensive. Exports of goods and services accounted for just 12% of US GDP in 2016, well below the world average of 29%.[15] While it also has a highly diversified portfolio of trading partners, the United States is either the largest or second-largest market for so many of them. In brief, this country matters more to its partners than vice versa, and can pressure them at little cost to itself. It is therefore little wonder that the practitioners of US economic statecraft so often see advantages in leveraging the country's economic position for political ends. The only permanent handicap for the United States is that its antagonists are almost never democracies, and hence they may be better able than Washington to withstand the domestic pressures that sanctions are typically intended to exploit.

Figure 1.3 shows how the relative degree of leverage differs from one partner to another. Washington's ability to apply pressure via sanctions should be high whenever bilateral trade (1) is equivalent to a large share of the partner's economy and (2) accounts for a small share of the US economy. Leaving aside the threshold question of what "large" and "small" mean, it is

---

[15]   World Bank data at http://data.worldbank.org/indicator/NE.EXP.GNFS.ZS.

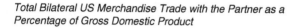

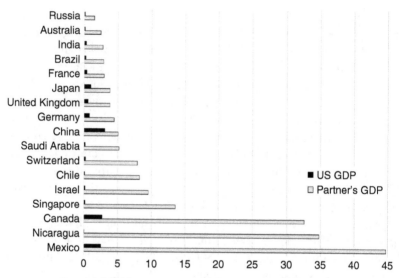

FIGURE 1.3 Potential US leverage in trade with selected partners, 2016.
Sources: Calculated from US import and export data in the US International
Trade Commission DataWeb at https://dataweb.usitc.gov and World Bank GDP
data at http://data.worldbank.org/indicator/NY.GDP.MKTP.CD.

immediately evident that Nicaragua offers an ideal example of a country that
should be vulnerable to pressure. Whereas trade with the United States
amounted to just over one-third of Nicaraguan GDP, that same flow
accounted for a virtually invisible share of the US economy. Were
Washington of a mind to impose sanctions on Managua, as it has in the
past, it could put a considerable slice of the Nicaraguan economy at risk
while inflicting practically no damage on itself. The same might be said,
albeit to a lesser degree, for Chile, Israel, and Singapore. All four of these
countries are FTA partners of the United States, and thus exemplify why
Hufbauer et al. rather cheekily concluded that if policymakers want their
sanctions to be effective they ought to go after allies rather than adversaries.[16]

The data also point to other partners for whom sanctions may be more
problematic. Canada and Mexico are just as wedded as Nicaragua to the
US economy, but although they have more to lose than the United States the

---

[16]   Hufbauer et al. (1990).

stakes for Washington are not trivial. There are real risks to playing hardball with next-door neighbors that account for large shares of trade, especially when they provide more than half of all energy imports. China also represents a special case, with the share of the US economy that might be put in jeopardy by a trade war being on the same order of magnitude as the Chinese share that would be at risk. The Russian case is quite different, with the low level of bilateral trade making for distinct international and domestic calculations. Sanctions were politically feasible against Beijing and Moscow as long as they each accounted for very little trade, and they were both subject to restrictions of varying severity for much of the twentieth century. By 2000, however, China had become second only to Canada as a US trading partner. While it is still easy for the United States to impose or tighten sanctions on Russia, these measures have little commercial impact; they matter more to Moscow for the insult they convey than for the actual damage that they cause. Conversely, sanctions on China are economically more meaningful – and hence the threat to impose and sustain them is less credible. China is also in a much stronger position to respond in kind.

The paradox of sanctions manifests itself not just in domestic policymaking but also at the level of coalition diplomacy. Here the paradox is complemented by a simple corollary: The more that sanctions depend on cooperation among allies, the greater the temptation for any one of them to cheat. A country can act effectively against any adversary for which it is either the monopolistic supplier of vital exports or the monopsonistic purchaser of major imports. In all other cases – which is to say nearly all the time – third parties can undermine sanctions by taking up the slack. Practically the only strategic exports that Washington has been able to control are high-technology weapons and related technologies, and then only in coordination with Western Europe, Japan, and Canada. The transatlantic alliance is strained whenever the partners either disagree on the benefits of a policy, such as when Europeans do not share the US strategic assessment of the target country, or the costs of compliance fall more heavily on the partners. These differences have produced some notable disputes, including those related to the accession of Eastern European countries to the GATT in the 1960s and 1970s, Western European reliance on Soviet or Russian energy exports since the 1980s, and the extraterritorial application of US sanctions on Cuba in the 1990s.

This represents another way in which the hegemon's earlier success at the strategic level may constrain its later efforts to deploy trade for tactical purposes. To the extent that it has promoted stability and prosperity among its allies, it will also have built up their capacity to act as "spoilers" in the enforcement of sanctions. That problem is magnified by the probability that adversaries and allies alike may become more willing and able over time to challenge the hegemon. Managing an alliance becomes even more important as the gap closes between its senior and junior members. That point was already clear in the later years of the Cold War; it became even more evident in the Trump administration, with the widening transatlantic rifts over policies toward Iran and Russia.

The paradoxes of preferences and sanctions suggest that the tactical use of trade has inherent limitations, and that those limitations become more constraining as time passes and hegemony fades. The potential impact of preferences is restricted by quirks of timing, with the hegemon turning to this instrument after it has lost much of its potential punch, and the impact of sanctions is restricted by the operation of domestic and alliance politics. Neither of these points mean that trade policy provides no advantages to the hegemon. What it instead implies is that the principal level at which trade matters in power politics remains grand-strategic, where the effects are felt over decades and generations rather than months or years. It also means that the choices the young hegemon may feel compelled to make will restrict the ability of its later self to make meaningful adjustments at the tactical level.

THE DOMESTIC DIPLOMACY OF POWER AND WEALTH

A statesman who proposes solutions to these paradoxes has completed only half the task. The next step is to move a proposal through the policymaking machinery. The constitutional order and political culture of the United States ensure that the domestic diplomacy of power and wealth is at least as tricky as the international variety, and pose major obstacles to the enactment and maintenance of coherent policies.

This part of the problem stems from the core paradox of classical liberalism. Democracy and the market, respectively, represent the political and economic manifestations of the liberal ideal, being founded upon the hope that when individuals make decisions in their own self-interest they will collectively produce an efficient economy and a responsive government. Yet these twin *desiderata* may collide: Democracy gives narrow-minded interest groups the opportunity to undermine an open market, and that same market may produce disparities in wealth that make a mockery of equal political rights. These problems are made more severe when governmental authority is deliberately fragmented, and when the pluralist tradition invites a bewildering array of parties to participate.

The Consequences of Divided Government

The US government is divided by branch as well as party, often at the same time. It is increasingly rare for both houses of Congress to be controlled by the president's party. While government was divided in just seven of the thirty-four congresses (21%) from 1901 through 1968, the share grew to nineteen of the twenty-six congresses (73%) from 1969 through 2020. Jimmy Carter was the last president to enjoy unified government for the entirety of his mandate, and he served just a single term. Every one of his successors has had to deal with a legislative branch in which the opposition controlled at least one chamber for anywhere from two to eight years.

Divided government complicates all manner of policymaking, but is especially problematic for the approval of treaties. Even when the United States is the chief promoter of a new negotiation, the results may still be trashed at home. President Wilson set that pattern when he signed the Treaty of Versailles in 1919, only to see the Senate gut it with amendments and then disown the mutilated corpse. Harry Truman did no better than Wilson when in 1947 he asked Congress to approve the Havana Charter of the International Trade Organization, although this time the rest of the world did not try to make a rump international institution function without the United States. Put another way, US membership in the Trans-Pacific Partnership – from which Donald Trump withdrew the United States just days after taking office – need not feel lonely. Its bones rest in an elephant graveyard to which domestic US politics have dispatched many an earlier treaty. The only thing that was unusual about this episode is that it was a president who slipped in the knife; that task usually falls to Congress.

Presidential dealings with Capitol Hill are made more difficult by the three hats that all members of Congress wear, any one of which might tilt against cooperation. The most obvious is the partisan hat, but lawmakers are also officers of the legislative branch and representatives of their constituencies. Even when presidents deal with members of their own party, they will run into trouble whenever their initiatives impinge on the constitutional prerogatives of a co-equal branch or are contrary to the economic interests of specific states and districts. This problem is only worsened by the more complex domestic diplomacy of trade in the post-hegemonic period. The connections between economic statesmanship and the rest of foreign policy are more explicit than ever before, now that a broad sense of strategic congruence has given way to a more tactical deployment of preferences and sanctions. Differential treatment invites members of Congress to act as special pleaders on behalf of groups in their constituencies. The rise in discriminatory programs and agreements contributes to the repoliticization of trade at both the international and the domestic levels, and gives the branches and the parties a new set of reasons to fight. The bromide about politics stopping at the water's edge has never been wholly true, and the days have long since passed when it seemed to describe the rule rather than the exception.

The argument here runs counter to a widely held belief that the association between trade policy and foreign policy makes it easier for presidents to win support for their programs. Appeals to the national interest, it is often argued, tend to dampen the partisanship and interbranch rivalry that had once dominated trade politics. Lowi thought so when he reviewed how Congress handled this field in the 1950s, concluding that the outcome of trade debates depended "upon whose *definition of the situation* prevailed," such that "[i]f tariff protection is an instrument of foreign policy and general regulation for international purposes, the anti-protectionists win; if the traditional definition of tariff as an aid to 100,000 individual firms prevails, then the protectionists win."[17] In the decades since Johnson and Nixon, however, the notion of a nonpartisan foreign policy has become as outdated as phonographs, typewriters, and public trust in presidential credibility.

The Consequences of the Economic Transition

Even if the foreign-policy dimension of trade is resolved, we are still left with a domestic policymaking system in which the issues are more divisive today than in the past. What had once been a relatively simple contest between free traders and protectionists is instead dominated by fundamental disputes over issues that have come to be associated with trade, such as labor rights and the environment. The emergence of these trade-related matters is just one of many ways in which the economic transition redefines trade politics. That transition, which had no beginning and will never reach an end, has already seen the United States reinvent itself from an almost exclusively agrarian to a predominantly industrial economy, and from there to a postindustrial society in which services dominate. It is complemented by globalization, which variously takes the form of increased foreign direct investment (inward and outward), greater import competition, and often intricate global supply chains. These economic developments affect not only the interests of the American people but also their political tastes; the median voter's level of tolerance for an unclean environment, and for even dirtier foreign regimes, declines with the passage of time. These economic and political transitions lead to changes in the relative power of the groups that favor or oppose specific initiatives, in the positions of political parties, and in the authority wielded by different government institutions.

Here we find the domestic complement to the Law of Uneven Growth. Just as differing rates of growth destabilize relations between countries, the process

---

[17]   Lowi (1963), pp. 682–683. Emphasis in the original.

of Creative Destruction can reorder the composition of the pro-trade and trade-skeptical coalitions. Like the sighting of a hostile tribe on the horizon, the appearance of competitive imports can provoke a fight-or-flight response from CEOs. A generation ago, when the present form of globalization was in its earlier stages, several large and formerly confident US industries responded to the threat by demanding protection. More recently, the typical response has been to internationalize operations by turning to foreign capital, purchasing imported inputs, or relocating production abroad.

Presidents have responded to the economic transition in two ways. One was to make limited accommodations to demands for protection from troubled industries. That was a major theme from the 1960s through the 1980s. More consequentially, they also brought new issues to the negotiating table in a bid to attract new and more competitive industries into the pro-trade coalition. The net result is that this coalition looks quite different today than it did a few generations ago. In the 1950s, its core members included the automotive and steel industries as well as their associated unions. Those same groups later became prominent members of the opposing camp, whereas the pro-trade coalition is now dominated by the high-tech and capital-intensive sectors in which the United States remains a leader. That shift has, in turn, changed the priorities for trade negotiators. Tariffs are less important to these producers than are the rules affecting investment, trade in services, the protection of intellectual property rights, and other arcane topics that would have flummoxed trade negotiators in the mid-twentieth century.

The trade-skeptical coalition has changed even more than its pro-trade antagonist. Much more is now at stake than the movement of some formerly competitive industries and their unions from Team Trade to Team Protection, as the entire foundation of the policy debate has undergone profound shifts. Traditional fights over free trade versus protection have not disappeared altogether, but they sometimes have a lower profile than disputes over such hot-button topics as labor rights, the environment, and access to medicine. Some of these issues first arose in trade disputes that other countries took to the GATT, complaining that the United States discriminated against imports when it enacted laws to protect the environment. Other groups joined the fight after US negotiators brought new issues to the table on behalf of domestic industries (e.g., patent protection for pharmaceuticals), and still others reflect the demands of social and economic activists (e.g., labor rights). Whatever the economic or legal cause, the political consequences of associating these issues with trade are enormous.

New issues mean new voices, and the diversity of participants produces a clash of economic and social philosophies. This can amount to a geometric rather than an arithmetic rise in the degree of difficulty. The old struggles over narrow, commercial issues such as tariffs and quotas could typically be settled through some difference-splitting bargain or by compensating the losing side. The newest issues are notable for involving not just producers with interests but also consumers and even socially conscious spectators. Groups that are more interested in political causes than in their own economic interests are not easily placated by the usual instruments of cooption. The involvement of consumer groups is especially notable, as they are intended to be the ultimate beneficiaries of the lower prices and wider choices that a free market is supposed to bring. Many of them object instead to trade rules that appear, from the activist's vantage point, as a sneaky means by which foreign and corporate interests can dismantle domestic health, safety, and environmental rules that they fought so hard to establish. These issues also widen the partisan divide. Social issues relate more directly to the ideological divisions between Democrats and Republicans, and their incorporation into trade politics has transformed the word "compromised" from something that pragmatic legislators frequently have done to something that their purist colleagues do not want to be. All of this makes it immensely more difficult to reach accommodations among government and civil society, which in turn complicates any efforts to use trade as an instrument of foreign policy.

THE PLAN OF THIS BOOK

To synthesize, the foregoing argument may be reduced to three principal points. The first is that power and wealth are equally important components of a country's foreign policy, and we ought not to erect artificial barriers between them in our analyses and our policymaking. To the contrary, the most talented thinkers and statesmen have addressed themselves not solely to one or the other of these twin instruments and objectives, but to the complex and even paradoxical ways in which they relate to one another. Second, managing the relationship between power and wealth is especially consequential – but also especially difficult – for a hegemon. That status must inevitably prove transitory, as it falls to the hegemon to sponsor an open world market that may incubate its challengers and make its allies more independent. The third point is that the hegemon will be prone in the later stages of its leadership to deploy power and wealth at tactical rather than strategic levels, marshalling its market power in the form of positive discrimination (preferences) and negative discrimination (sanctions). Its capacity to utilize these instruments will be diminished to the extent that its own early success contributes to its later difficulties. The effectiveness of preferences will be undercut by low overall barriers, and the effectiveness of sanctions depends on coordination with allies. Its ability to pursue a coherent and consistent policy in either of these directions will also be constrained by the operation of a democracy in which many of its own stakeholders are economically tied to nondiscriminatory trade, and others have developed political tastes that privilege social issues over narrowly commercial objectives. The net result is that the hegemon finds it increasingly difficult to devise and execute policy effectively, and may be tempted in its frustration either to abandon its leadership position or to reverse course and find refuge in protectionism.

A pessimist might see here all the makings of a Greek tragedy. A latter-day Sophocles could well portray the United States as a doomed protagonist that is inexorably drawn toward a predetermined end by the workings of destiny and its own fatal flaws. While I do believe that much of the story told in this volume has the whiff of fate about it, I would not go so far as to suggest that this trajectory is inevitable or irreversible. Managing the relationship between power and wealth is clearly more challenging in post-hegemonic times than it was in earlier, headier days, and the extremely limited number of historical cases suggests that that the story will not end well. We would be remiss, however, if we did not try to learn from experience. It is in that spirit that this book is written.

By focusing principally on the trials that we have faced in the past, and still face today, this analysis illustrates the perennial nature of the problem and the peculiar circumstances of our present time. It starts from the premise that the welfare and safety of the United States, and of the world at large, have been well served by an international system in which countries can make the most of their talents and resource endowments, and in which Washington cooperates with its allies to keep the world safe. That system has its costs as well as its benefits, but it has generated more prosperity and security than would the alternatives. And while hegemony is now more a memory than a fact, America remains *primus inter pares* in both the political and the economic spheres. The decline in influence makes it even more vital that the country work with its trading partners – especially, but not exclusively, with its allies – to ensure that markets are relatively open, and that the rules are clear and respected. Failure to do so means further undercutting the country's capacity to use trade as a means of shaping the perceptions and actions of its adversaries.

Introduction and Overview

The book is divided into six parts. These parts are thematic rather than chronological, although there is an underlying structure to their sequence. The first part is primarily historical, and the other parts follow the order in which issues and bilateral relationships reached prominence in US policymaking. The present chapter, and the two that follow, frame the issues by placing them in the context of ideas and history.

Chapter 2 covers the period from independence to the waning days of the Cold War. It stresses that while ideas do not flow directly from conception to concrete policy, as something is usually lost in translation when they are exposed to conflicting interests, interbranch bargaining, and pragmatism, they nonetheless produce recurring themes in policymaking. The chapter explores how policymakers from Alexander Hamilton forward have adapted the ideas of mercantilism, free trade, and Physiocracy to American conditions. In place of "pure" applications of any of these doctrines, US policymakers since pre-hegemonic times have favored the hybrids of selective protectionism and reciprocity. The chapter reviews the evolution of these policies over two centuries, and provides a chronological context for the events and ideas that are explored in the rest of the book.

The next chapter picks up at the point where American hegemony appeared to reach its apogee, with the collapse of Communism and the formation of the WTO, but then entered a period of gradual decline and doubt. Chapter 3 reviews a quarter-century that future historians may see either as the first phase of the post–Cold War, post-hegemonic era, or instead as the final phase of the pre-Trump era. These events were put in motion by the Law of Uneven Growth, a destabilizing process characterized by higher growth for challengers than for the hegemon, and a process of Creative Destruction that disrupts the country's internal equilibrium. Taken together, they require that policymakers adapt to changing economic environments at home and abroad. The principal trend on the negative side was the rise and then the fall of protectionism, as US industries first fought and then accommodated themselves to greater global competition. Presidents also became increasingly prone to pursue discriminatory rather than multilateral liberalization. Both the negative and the positive options encountered rising difficulties over time, with presidents resisting protectionist pressures at the same time that Congress resisted further liberalization. These difficulties foreshadowed the events of 2016, when the United States would unexpectedly send an avowed protectionist to the White House.

The Domestic Diplomacy of Trade

The second part delves more deeply into the domestic diplomacy of trade, examining how public and private institutions might cooperate – but often conflict – to devise and pursue US objectives in the trading system. Two chapters are devoted primarily to describing the policymaking system as it existed prior to the advent of Donald Trump, while the third examines how this protectionist came to win the presidency.

Chapter 4 begins this examination by reviewing the perennial struggle between the executive and legislative branches over control of trade policy, and especially the authorization and approval of trade agreements. After recounting how the Senate traditionally rejected or revised most trade treaties that presidents negotiated before the 1930s, the analysis turns to the inter-branch negotiations that subsequently dominated this field. It explains the accommodations between lawmakers and presidents, especially in the delegation of negotiating authority from Congress to the president, and how this domestic diplomacy affects the international variety. The chapter concludes with evidence on how winning congressional approval for trade agreements has become a heavier lift.

Trade policy was once confined to relatively simple conflicts between competitive and uncompetitive producers of goods, but Chapter 5 explains how and why it has come to encompass a much wider range of topics and stakeholders. New issues have made it into the system in response to the shifting demands of US industry, and through multilateral trade disputes, as well as the changing political preferences of a postindustrial electorate. These processes have expanded the jurisdiction of the trading system to include such matters as labor rights, the environment, and intellectual property protection, all of which attract new stakeholders and change the nature of policy debates. The resulting contagion of conflict has greatly complicated the conduct of domestic diplomacy, making trade agreements trickier to negotiate, more prone to partisan divisions, and considerably less susceptible to the give-and-take that used to characterize policymaking.

These rising difficulties, coupled with the decreasing willingness of professional politicians to address the topic, created an opportunity for a man who promised to cut the Gordian knot. Chapter 6 explains how Donald Trump did just that, and how the traditional issues of free trade versus protectionism made a comeback in the 2016 presidential election. The analysis quantifies and chronicles the evolving salience of trade policy, showing how the attention that politicians devoted to this issue peaked in the early 1990s. Legislators and presidents invested less of their political capital in this issue thereafter, such that by 2016 many of them treated this as a third-tier topic. Trump correctly perceived that the inattention of the political professionals left behind an underserved market, and one that he could effectively exploit by appealing to a neglected constituency that sees globalization as a threat. The chapter also speculates on what Trump's manipulation of this issue may mean for partisanship and policymaking in the years to come.

Trade with Allies

The next three parts take up issues in US relations with allies, adversaries, and developing countries. The review of trade with allies focuses on three partners with which the United States has gone through periods of cooperation and confrontation: the United Kingdom, Japan, and Canada. The principal themes in those three cases concern, respectively, the exercise of hegemony, the management of the economic transition, and the domestic diplomacy of trade agreements.

In Chapter 7 we examine the nexus between trade and security in the transatlantic alliance, focusing on recurring controversies over sea power in Anglo-American relations. While the setting and enforcement of rules was once principally the responsibility of the United Kingdom, with the United States often acting as a free-rider and antagonist, their respective roles have since been reversed. This can be seen in the related topics of the rights of neutrals in wartime and the protection and promotion of maritime shipping. In addition to chronicling the historical role-reversal on these issues, the chapter also highlights how the US approach to hegemony differs from that of its predecessor. Those differences may be traced to a lesser degree of trade dependence, which gives Washington more leeway than London had in privileging power over wealth when devising and enforcing rules.

The analysis in Chapter 8 shows that while the hegemon may indeed be challenged, and that trade often provides a critical vector for the challenger, it is not inevitable that the rival overthrows the leader. In the 1980s Japan posed just as great an economic challenge to the United States as China does now, albeit one that was only indirectly related to security concerns. This chapter explores the rise and fall of that challenge by focusing on bilateral competition in the automotive sector. It stresses how the economic transition in the United States produced an important shift in objectives, leading one president to grant import protection (Reagan in 1981) and another to reject it (Obama in 2009). That change illustrates a broader process by which the clashing interests of the hegemon and the challenger can give way to greater cooperation.

The principal aim of Chapter 9, which focuses on US trade relations with Canada, is to present case studies in the domestic diplomacy of trade agreements. Despite the commercial significance of the US–Canada FTA, which set the terms for the world's largest bilateral trade relationship, members of Congress were more interested in the agreement's extrinsic value – the leverage it gave them for negotiations with the president – than in the intrinsic value of the agreement itself. They took full advantage of the opportunities that this agreement presented in order to pry larger changes in US policy on the reciprocity and trade-remedy laws. That same process was less in evidence when Congress debated the NAFTA agreement, when the intrinsic significance of trade and related issues with Mexico were of much higher importance, but many of the themes from the earlier debate were repeated in that episode.

Trade with Adversaries

Chapter 10 elaborates on how sanctions have been a key element of foreign economic policy even longer than there has been a United States, with merchants in colonial America having effectively used boycotts as an instrument of pressure on London. But while the boycotts of the 1760s were devised to maximize external pressure and minimize the domestic costs, the modern successors to those colonial merchants have had greater difficulty in hitting that sweet spot. Washington finds it easy to impose ineffective sanctions on countries with which economic relations are insignificant, and hard to impose effective sanctions on countries with which those relations are important. The analysis reviews how the theory and practice of US sanctions policy has evolved over time, with special attention to the economic and political trends that have worked against the capacity of the United States to deploy sanctions effectively.

Those difficulties are exemplified by the patterns explored in Chapter 11. Whether one looks at the czarist, Communist, or modern eras, Washington's policies toward Russia have followed the same pattern: The low level of trade has facilitated the imposition of restrictions for political reasons, but also ensured that those sanctions are ineffective. Another recurring element is that confrontations with Russia typically involve the movement of persons, whether it was czarist restrictions on the entry of American Jews, Communist taxes on the exit of Soviet Jews, or targeted US sanctions on the travel of Russian officials who suppress human rights. That was at least the pattern until 2016. The issue now has new twists and urgency, and apparent historical constants seem to have been reversed. Where we once saw low levels of economic ties and correspondingly low-impact sanctions, the bilateral relationship has been redefined by the intense economic interests of a few individuals and by Russia's deployment of what may be the most consequential counter-sanctions in history.

Chapter 12 shows that the pattern of trade relations with China followed quite the opposite pattern of those with pre-2016 Russia. The high economic stakes, together with the power of US business interests and Congress, have made it difficult for American policymakers to carry out broad-based threats against Beijing. In addition to reviewing the evolution of the US-China relationship, with special emphasis on the presidencies of Nixon through Obama, the chapter also examines the current state of play in Sino-American competition. That competition has both a direct and negative side (i.e., trade-remedy laws and disputes) and an indirect and positive side (e.g., the Trans-Pacific Partnership), but the latter half of the formula has now been undone by a president who does not share his predecessors' faith in an alliance to contain China.

Trade with Developing Countries

Chapter 13 reviews the strategy and domestic diplomacy of trade preferences, examining the historic evolution of US policy on discrimination. That meant going from a pre-hegemonic predilection for nondiscriminatory protectionism to becoming the principal advocate of nondiscriminatory liberalization in hegemony, and then shifting in later hegemony from critic to practitioner of discriminatory liberalization. That last policy of discrimination has also moved through stages, with the extension of autonomous, generalized preferences to most developing countries being followed by the creation of more generous and targeted programs for favored regions, and then the negotiation of reciprocal, preferential agreements with specific partners. The analysis shows that while the economic and political attractions of discrimination have risen in recent decades, Washington's capacity to utilize those preferences is undercut by conflicting objectives as well as by the declines in the overall level of protection and the US share of the global market.

Trade relations in the Americas, where generations of statesmen have been frustrated by their inability to achieve lasting economic integration, are taken up in Chapter 14. These efforts go as far back as the 1820s, but have repeatedly encountered the same barriers. Chief among them is Washington's short attention span, in which periodic proposals for new initiatives in the Western Hemisphere typically lose momentum when other regions rise in importance. The chapter examines how the failure of the negotiations for a Free Trade Area of the Americas recapitulated well-established patterns in inter-American relations, as did the subsequent fragmentation of that process into a series of subregional and bilateral FTA negotiations. The chapter elaborates on these points by examining in greater detail the US objectives and accomplishments in the apparel and petroleum sectors, each of which initially enjoyed success but have lately floundered.

Chapter 15 explores trade as an instrument of war and peace in the Middle East, a region that is rife with discriminatory instruments. These encompass sanctions (including the Arab League boycott of Israel and the OPEC oil embargoes) as well as preferences (including regional and extraregional trade agreements). The main focus of the chapter is on President George W. Bush's proposal in 2003 that the United States negotiate an FTA with the entire Middle Eastern region, an initiative that was intended to address security and economic problems all in one. That offer had few takers, and produced even fewer bilateral agreements. The analysis explains why this outcome was entirely predictable, and exemplified the paradox of preferences. The benefits of the proposed agreements were limited by the narrow scope that was left for extending meaningful preferences to US imports from the region, and its perceived costs were amplified by the political demands that the United States made of its prospective partners.

Trade after Trump

The concluding part considers where US policy is in the Trump era, and what may come after it. Chapter 16 takes stock of the many ways in which the administration seeks to redefine the trading system and what the United States seeks from it, as well as the implications of these changes for US power and wealth. The chapter concludes by reviewing the challenges that the United States and its trading partners will face in the years to come, which were already in place before Trump came to power and will remain after he leaves.

2

The Theory and Practice of the Anglo-American Hegemonies

I was brought up, like most Englishmen, to respect free trade not only as an economic doctrine which a rational and instructed person could not doubt, but almost as a part of the moral law. I regarded ordinary departures from it as being at the same time an imbecility and an outrage.

John Maynard Keynes, "National Self-Sufficiency" (1933)

INTRODUCTION

It is now a cliché for economists to repeat the claim of John Maynard Keynes (1883–1946) that practical men "are usually the slaves of some defunct economist," and that the madmen "who hear voices in the air, are distilling their frenzy from some academic scribbler of a few years back."[1] We might forgive the conceit, considering the eloquence with which Keynes placed all of his tribe on a pedestal, but they rarely bother to delve more deeply into this polymath's evolving notions of trade. Keynes was all over the board, having gone from strident support for free markets just after the Great War to deep doubts in the run-up to the next, terrible one. Considering the evanescence of Keynes' own convictions, it is little wonder that many of his peers have had serious doubts about whether truth can get a word in edgewise with power. Count Adam Smith (1723–1790) among those skeptics. He believed that special pleaders drown out philosophers, with the monopolists being so "formidable to the government" that they "intimidate the legislature."[2] That frustration was equally strong on the western side of the Atlantic in 1930. More than a thousand members of the American Economic Association failed that year to deter Congress from

---

[1] Keynes (1935), p. 383.
[2] Smith (1776), p. 471.

enacting the Hawley–Smoot Tariff Act, and could not convince President Hoover to veto it.[3]

While economists and other social scientists have good cause to put more stock in Smith's modesty than in Keynes' grandiloquence, the ideas in which they traffic may nonetheless exercise a subtle and important influence on political entrepreneurs. "It is not markets but ideas that establish the rules of the game," as Goldstein noted, "that demarcate for policy makers the proper form of new programs, that privilege particular constituents."[4] This chapter is devoted to an exploration of the theory and practice of hegemony from US independence to the close of the Cold War, providing an overview of ideas, events, and issues that we will later explore in greater depth. I make no specious assertions here about the irresistible pull that ideas may have on policymakers, but do suggest two more modest points. The first is that these ideas provide useful frameworks that help us to characterize the actual choices that policymakers made in the past, and to understand the options available to them today. And like Goldstein, I believe that ideas help to shape programs and to give policy at least the veneer of consistency.

The attraction that any set of ideas has for interest groups, opinion leaders, and policymakers may depend on where their country fits in the global hierarchy. Realists never tire of quoting Palmerston's truism that nations do not have permanent friends or permanent enemies, only permanent interests. The perpetuity of those interests is presumably founded upon such immutable factors as geography and (somewhat more pliably) international borders. Taking the long view, however, those interests are subject to reinterpretation as a country's power rises or falls. An "ordinary" state would do well to reassess its interests if it becomes a contender for hegemony. A similar self-assessment is in order for a challenger that achieves this status, or a country for which hegemony is only a bittersweet memory. We can see just such a process of reinvention in the British experience, as expressed in the arc of Keynes' thinking; what he professed to believe when London still retained hegemonic pretensions was quite different from the positions that he adopted after those illusions were shattered. And despite distinct political cultures, circumstances, and leadership styles, there are many respects in which

---

[3] See Lake (1988), p. 1. For the 2018 equivalent see www.ntu.org/governmentbytes/page/econo mists-join-ntu-to-voice-opposition-to-tariffs-protectionism.

[4] Goldstein (1993), p. xii. See also Rodrik's point that ideas shape actions as "we don't have 'interests'" but "*ideas* about what our interests are" (2018, p. 163; emphasis in original); and Irwin (2017), pp. 24–25.

Washington has, at each stage in its ascent and descent, generally followed the path that the cousins blazed.

TRADE STRATEGY: FRAGMENTS, ADAPTATIONS,
AND PRAGMATISM

The thirteen former British colonies inherited centuries of practice and a new, revolutionary theory. Their adaptations of these received ideas might be seen as the application of Louis Hartz's "fragment" theory of political ideology to a specific category of public policy. He argued that the intellectual traditions and political cultures of immigrant societies such as the United States begin as fragments from their mother countries, and that these habits of mind may persist even longer in the new societies than they did in the old.[5] The colonies were born and raised in a mercantilist system, but the United States broke away just when Englishmen were developing the rationale and the resources to lead the world into a more open order. The American capacity to modify and adapt these ideas was greater than a literal reading of Hartz might suggest. Public intellectuals played a unique role in the early republic, with the Founders living in a time when the "chasm between men of affairs and men of thought had not yet opened."[6] Trade played a critical role in their thinking. The ideas that they inherited and adapted were further modified by a strong streak of pragmatism in American political culture, which tended to rebel against the wholehearted pursuit of any one trade strategy.

Three developments in 1776 shaped the future in which both hegemons would develop. The Declaration of Independence took six difficult years to transform from wish to fulfillment; the other two developments took longer to blossom. James Watts' invention of the steam engine was to provide the material foundation for Britain's industrial mastery, while the publication of Adam Smith's masterpiece was an equally revolutionary creation that gave intellectual purpose to the country's emerging status.

The Original British Fragment: Mercantilism

In most places and in most times, it is a safe assumption that the median statesman will – in the absence of contrary pressures or an academic intervention – enter public life with a vaguely mercantilist notion that the proper object of foreign economic policy is to promote a trade surplus. This default

---

[5] Hartz (1964).
[6] Dorfman (1946), Volume One, p. xi.

assumption conforms to the understandable (if primitive) beliefs that exports are gains, imports are losses, and trade balances offer a quick and dirty gauge of a country's competitiveness. It represents the elevation of a fallacy of construction into a principle of statecraft, based on the faulty logic that what holds true for private firms is equally applicable to countries. Mercantilism also rests on the intuitive belief that the low politics of trade are interwoven with the high politics of war and peace. This line of thought has marked the views of many policymakers throughout American history, not least Donald Trump.

Classical mercantilism encompassed a mixed bag of thinkers and practitioners, and did not even acquire its present name until the nineteenth century,[7] but its adherents shared some fundamental assumptions. The doctrine's essentials can be reduced to a simple syllogism:

- **Major Premise:** All political and economic relations are hierarchical dealings in which one either dominates or is subordinate. The state is the dominant domestic institution, and the stronger, richer states dominate weaker, poorer states.
- **Minor Premise:** Power and wealth are inextricably linked, being both interchangeable and equal in importance. Each of these *desiderata* is zero-sum, such that any state's gains in power and wealth necessarily come at the expense of other states.
- **Conclusion:** Trade is an essential component in the power relations between states, and to that end the state should intervene to maximize exports (especially of finished goods), minimize imports (except for raw materials), and promote a positive trade balance.

The classical mercantilists believed that wealth could be measured by the specie (i.e., gold and silver) that a country accumulated from trade surpluses, and that the wealth stored in those precious metals could be readily transmuted into power. That bit of political alchemy was easily achieved in an age when practically the only differences between merchant ships and men-of-war were the size of their holds and the number of gun-ports, and when mercenary armies roamed Europe in search of employment. The syllogism also suggests three reasons why countries should not reach binding treaties: A sovereign state will not want to restrict its freedom of action, it should doubt any partner's intent to honor inconvenient commitments, and the only way for a pair of mercantilist states to ensure a positive-sum outcome is through joint predation

---

[7]   Adam Smith called it the "mercantile system." The oldest references to "mercantilism" or "mercantilist" in the *Oxford English History* date to 1854. See also VanGrasstek (2017) on the varieties of mercantilism.

on third parties. Trade diplomacy as we know it was not a feature of the mercantilist era. Apparent exceptions such as the Methuen Treaty between Portugal and England (1703) were just military arrangements with commercial sweeteners.

The Newer British Fragment: Free Trade

It would be a mistake to see Adam Smith strictly as an economist. His major contributions to this field rested on the work of his predecessors, and were perfected by his successors. So while Smith's notions of the division of labor and absolute advantage were persuasive and intellectually accessible, it took David Ricardo (1772–1823) and the more sophisticated construction of comparative advantage to explain why even uncompetitive countries can gain from specialization and trade. It is also important to recognize where Smith agreed with his antagonists. Even though *An Inquiry into the Nature and Causes of the Wealth of Nations* "became the bible ... of the laissez-faire school of nineteenth-century British economic theorists," as Earle noted, Smith "did not really repudiate certain fundamentals of mercantilist doctrine."[8] Yet whatever his ideas lacked in originality or quantitative complexity was more than made up by the quality of their presentation and the sweep of their implications. Smith was a *political* economist who did not refute mercantilism's major premise of perennial conflict, but – as flagged in the full title of his book – he decisively attacked the minor premise by which wealth was equated with power, and reputed to be zero-sum.

In the same way that first-time attendees might think that Shakespeare presents only a string of clichés, a modern reader of Smith may not fully appreciate the innovations of his argument. His principal points can be derived from the topic sentences of the first three chapters: (1) "The greatest improvement in the productive powers" was achieved by "the division of labour," (2) that division was the natural consequence of man's "propensity to truck, barter, and exchange one thing for another," but (3) it is also limited "by the extent of the market." The now-obvious conclusion is that countries can achieve mutual gains by removing the barriers to a truly international market. To accept that conclusion in its entirety, however, one must reject what Smith called "the popular notion" that "wealth consists in money, or in gold and silver."[9] The true wealth of nations lay not in their purses but in their productivity, and productivity could be enhanced through the international

---

[8] Earle (1943), p. 222.
[9] Smith (1776), pp. 13, 25, 31, and 429.

division of labor. In distinguishing wealth from money and power, Smith also showed that it is not zero-sum. As unremarkable as that point may sound today, it was revolutionary in its time. It implied that countries could focus more on the cooperative creation of wealth than on appropriating it all to themselves.

This lion of the Scottish Enlightenment might have followed up these intuitive leaps with yet another, arguing that countries should aim for maximum mutual gains through maximum liberalization, but his strides grew cautious when he moved from analysis to prescription. Smith thought that the chances for free trade were circumscribed by domestic politics, and that its advisability was further limited by the exigencies of national security. This man of his violent times still thought conflict was endemic, viewed adversaries with ambivalence, and believed that while wealth and power were distinct they remained closely related. He acknowledged that the "wealth of a neighbouring nation" was "certainly advantageous in trade," but also warned that it is "dangerous in war and politics."[10] As discussed at greater length in Chapter 7, Smith considered it unsafe for Britain to pursue open markets across-the-board, and advocated a security exception. It was not until London was well into hegemony that Smith's intellectual successors would pursue his ideas to their logical conclusion (or perhaps a bit further). Taking up his premises that wealth is positive-sum and can be expanded through trade, Richard Cobden (1804–1865) and John Stuart Mill (1806–1873) would come close to suggesting that open markets were so advantageous that they might be a substitute for foreign policy.

The French Sliver: Physiocracy

The French school of economists known as the Physiocrats might normally merit no more than a footnote, given the brevity of their existence and the shallowness of their contribution. "*Tout Paris* and still more Versailles talked about [Physiocracy] from 1760 to 1770," as Schumpeter noted, but "everybody (excluding professed economists) had forgotten it by 1780."[11] Their doctrine nonetheless held a natural appeal for one section of the early American republic. Southern planters were seduced by their view that all national wealth was derived from land and agricultural production, and that everything else was derivative or parasitic. François Quesnay (1694–1774), father of this school and physician to Louis XV, was also an early advocate of free trade, a critic of

---

[10] Smith (1776), p. 494.
[11] Schumpeter (1954), p. 228. On the reception of the Physiocrats in America see Hartz (1955), pp. 45–55.

privileges and monopolies, and an important influence on Adam Smith. He contradicted the mercantilists, preaching that "exporting raw materials and agricultural goods and importing manufactured goods was much more desirable than the reverse."[12]

To rural Americans, this paean to agriculture was an affirmation of common sense. Although the Physiocratic doctrine withered, its underlying sentiment had staying power in a country where the internal frontier mattered more than the oceans until 1890, and where rural voters were in the majority until 1920. Politicians such as Thomas Jefferson (1743–1826) were on safe ground when they flattered their electors (and themselves) with bucolic hyperbole. "Those who labor in the earth are the chosen people of God,"[13] he asserted, and this third president preferred that the republic of agrarian virtue produce raw materials so as to leave the shabbier industrial, commercial, and financial operations to the money-grubbers across the sea. And also like the Greeks and Romans whom they so admired, Jefferson and his fellows were content to rest this virtuous society upon a foundation of slavery. The Civil War put an end to that last element of their program, but one can still find remnants of the Physiocratic doctrine in the American public's persistent, nostalgic sympathy for the family farm.

Hamilton's Response to Smith and His Adaptation of Mercantilism

Alexander Hamilton (1755–1804) was intimately acquainted with the ideas of Smith and Quesnay, as evidenced by the pains he took to answer them. "If the system of perfect liberty to industry and commerce were the prevailing system of nations," he observed with a nod to Smith, "the arguments which dissuade a country, in the predicament of the United States, from the zealous pursuit of manufactures, would doubtless have great force." Those conditions did not apply in his day, when the United States was quite nearly "in the situation of a country precluded from foreign commerce." As for Physiocracy, this first US secretary of the treasury devoted the opening pages of his seminal *Report on Manufactures* (1791) to a politically obligatory recognition of agriculture's importance. While careful not to bruise rural sensitivities, Hamilton argued for a diversified economy that balanced farms with factories. For reasons of both power and wealth, he thought that the government ought to ensure self-sufficiency in "the means of subsistence, habitation, clothing, and defence."[14]

---

[12]   Irwin (1996), p. 66.
[13]   Jefferson (1784), p. 170.
[14]   Hamilton (1791), pp. 100, 101, and 135.

Hamilton's plan might be called "mercantilism with American characteristics," adapting older ideas to such local circumstances as steady immigration and an extensive hinterland. He was not the first to advance the doctrine of support to infant industries,[15] but here he might properly be compared to Columbus: Hamilton was the first to make the discovery stick. Arguing that it would be impracticable to "maintain, between the recent establishments of one country, and the long-matured establishments of another country, a competition upon equal terms," he also anticipated a terms-of-trade argument that would be revived in the mid-twentieth century by the proponents of import-substitution industrialization. He argued that an agricultural state is in a poor position vis-à-vis a manufacturing state because its own demand for finished goods is "constant and regular," whereas its partner's demands for products of the soil was "liable to very considerable fluctuations and interruptions." These asynchronous demands "must necessarily have a tendency to cause the general course of the exchange of commodities between the parties to turn to the disadvantage of the merely agricultural states."[16]

Hamilton's program to promote manufactures went well beyond erecting a high tariff wall, reserving a large role for the federal government. He foresaw a benevolent state fueled by tariff revenue that would provide credit through a central bank, offer bounties and prizes, encourage the transfer of technology, promote the immigration of skilled workmen, and otherwise intervene in favor of new industries. Nationalist policymakers would profess their fidelity to Hamilton's ideas for generations to come, but would typically strip his strategy down to its protectionist core. The First Congress set that pattern when it responded to the *Report on Manufactures* by raising tariffs modestly, then rejecting the proposed subsidies. Duties remained relatively low for the rest of Hamilton's unnaturally short life. The only important product of his industrial policy was the Society for Establishing Useful Manufactures in Paterson, New Jersey. Aptly immortalized as a town of "no ideas but in things,"[17] the Paterson experiment was neither chartered by the federal government nor replicated in other states.

When Economic Ideas Meet Political Pragmatism

The rejection of Hamilton's program reflects a broader theme in US public policy. Hartz called pragmatism "America's great contribution to the

---

[15]   See on this point Irwin (1996), chapter eight.
[16]   Hamilton (1791), p. 132.
[17]   William Carlos Williams, "Paterson," Book I (1946).

philosophic tradition,"[18] but pragmatism in actual practice might less charitably be considered intellectual rootlessness, opportunism, or even cynicism. Taking a "whatever works" approach to policymaking, and being beholden to an electorate with an even more practical turn of mind, politicians have rarely shown a firm inclination to adopt any one trade strategy explicitly, comprehensively, and permanently. While the received doctrines offered a menu of choices, policymakers have felt free to mix and match elements as circumstances (and constituents) may demand.

Each school had its supporters and detractors in a period of "ideology in transition" that reflected "an attempt to cling to the traditional republican spirit of classical antiquity without disregarding the new imperatives of a more modern commercial society."[19] Educated Americans knew their Smith: Colonel Hamilton kept *The Wealth of Nations* on his campaign desk, Benjamin Franklin ordered a copy from London while he represented his country in Paris, and the congressmen in Philadelphia knew that the book's closing pages advocated freedom for the colonies. As congenial as they found Smith's politics, many distrusted a division of labor that might perpetuate American economic subordination. Hamilton's contemporaries were likewise of two minds regarding mercantilism. This was the devil they knew, and its precepts offered "an arsenal of practices and policies that suited the needs of a new republic aspiring to commercial and industrial rank,"[20] yet a countervailing current of political thought rebelled against the mercantilist's major premise. Far from embracing power politics, many instead shared Jefferson's dream of an idyllic land that would be forever detached from Europe's decay and antagonism. And while they were eager to pile up silver and gold, in their ideal world this treasure would enable the pursuit not of power but of happiness. As for Hamilton's American variation on the theme, even the twenty-first-century lyricist who made him an improbable pop-culture icon stressed his frustrations in converting ideas to action.[21] Enacting Hamilton's full program would have required that legislators flout a widespread preference that government be small, both with respect to its functions and its financing. Many Americans then considered war, corruption, and government overreach to be all of a piece; many still do.

---

[18]   Hartz (1955), p. 10.
[19]   McCoy (1980), p. 10.
[20]   Bourgin (1989), p. 36.
[21]   Lyn-Manuel Miranda's "Cabinet Battle #1" neatly rendered in rap the Hamilton–Jefferson debate over the central bank, and even had Jefferson expressing Physiocratic sentiments, but not a single note in his *Hamilton: The Musical* (2015) covered *The Report on Manufactures*.

The basic facts of American life reinforced this pragmatic impulse. Partisanship and the imperatives of legislative compromise have always been the enemies of consistency in US foreign economic policy. That was true from the very start, when Hamilton and his Federalists frustrated the attempts of Jefferson and his partisans to pursue a credible reciprocity policy, and Hamilton's rivals returned the favor by blocking his neo-mercantilist program. Taussig's observation about these two parties could be repeated for later pairs: They were "influenced in their attitude to the question of protection most of all by its bearing on the other more prominent questions on which parties began to be divided."[22] In that era, partisan positions on trade were subordinated to foreign policy. In later periods, trade was tied to controversies over abolition and monetary policy. Pragmatism was also encouraged by a constitutional order that fragmented power vertically (between the states and the federal government) and horizontally (between the branches of government). The perennial regional conflict gave still more momentum to this centripetal spin. Even in its infancy the United States already was, by European standards, a sprawling and diverse country with multiple climate types, uneven resource endowments, and distinct social systems. These partisan, constitutional, and sectional divisions all militated against strategic coherence.

The Perennial Compromises: Selective Protection and Reciprocity

In place of a clear and consistent strategy, pragmatic policymakers will typically seek a functional compromise between contending or even contradictory options. Two hybrids bred from the purer strains have been perennially popular. Looking inward, policymakers have often sought to favor infant, rent-seeking, or declining industries through a policy of selective protectionism that is based on tariffs or quotas but is usually not supplemented by other government aid. Unlike subsidies, which are a drain on the treasury, protective tariffs have the added attractions of generating revenue without directly taxing Americans. Looking outward, policymakers often hope to aid exporters through an equally selective policy of reciprocity. As used in the United States, this term usually means a policy that aims to reduce foreign barriers through the threat of retaliation rather than the negotiated exchange of concessions. Selective protection and reciprocity are not mutually exclusive, and indeed are sometimes confused with one another – not least because each approach seeks to foist the costs onto foreigners – but the United States regularly practiced only the first of these options throughout the first century

---

[22] Taussig (1931), p. 13.

and a half of independence. The American capacity to pursue an active and effective reciprocity policy was constrained by its limited market size, and remained more a matter of theory than of practice until the late nineteenth and twentieth centuries.

From the Tariff Act of 1789 through the Hawley–Smoot Tariff Act of 1930, Congress pursued selective protectionism through periodic tariff revisions. Able writers from Taussig to Irwin[23] have related this history, and we need not replicate their accounts here. Suffice it to say that for much of this time the voices favoring protection at home and free-riding in the international system were stronger than the advocates of liberalization and negotiations, and that Congress took the lead. While political parties were often divided, they typically fought not over free trade versus protection, but instead over just how much protection to extend and which industries to favor. Tariffs were sometimes higher, as in the average 49% rate set in 1828 by the Tariff of Abominations, while enactments such as the Underwood Tariff of 1914 featured much lower average rates (9%).[24] What they all had in common was that Congress determined the rates autonomously. Apart from anomalies such as the Polk administration (1845–1849), in which Secretary of the Treasury Robert Walker actively promoted a more liberal policy, the executive remained a secondary player.

The Civil War was a watershed in this history. It was preceded by decades of conflict between one set of states that relied on slave labor to produce staple exports, favored open markets, and remained economically tied to England, and another section in which nascent industrialists hoped to reserve the domestic market for themselves. The greater Southern attachment to England dates to the colonial period. Just before the Revolution, fully 79% of the upper South's exports went to Great Britain, as did 71% of the lower South's, but the metropolis took in far smaller shares from the middle colonies (13%) and New England (18%).[25] Those ties survived independence, as did the Southern aversion to protectionism. "It was tariffs, not slavery," as Hofstadter observed, "that first made the South militant." Leaders resented these taxes as the most visible part of a seemingly exploitive "relationship between a capitalistic community and an agrarian one that did little of its own shipping,

---

[23]   Taussig's *Tariff History of the United States* went through eight editions from 1890 to 1930. Irwin's magisterial *Clashing over Commerce: A History of US Trade Policy* (2017) carries the story through the Obama administration.

[24]   For historic data on tariff rates see US Department of Commerce (1975), Volume 2.

[25]   Figures are for 1768–1772. Calculated from tables 5.2, 6.1, 8.2, and 9.3 of McCusker and Menard (1991).

banking, or manufacturing."[26] The original sectional crisis erupted over a Southern threat to nullify the highly protectionist tariff act of 1828. When the threat of abolition forced the final break, the South reiterated its implacable opposition to protection by drawing up an 1861 constitution specifying that no "duties or taxes on importations from foreign nations [shall] be laid to promote or foster any branch of industry."[27] Following the war, the victors in the more industrial, Republican, and protectionist states of the North had a freer hand to do just that.

The retaliation-based policy of reciprocity remained more aspirational than actual in the early years of independence. Its advocates could lay claim to an impressive pedigree, with Adam Smith having argued that "when some foreign nation restrains by high duties or prohibitions the importation of some of our manufactures" then retaliatory measures may be recommended "when there is a probability that they will procure the repeal" of the partner's restrictions.[28] That logic appealed to Jefferson, who inaugurated an American tradition in his 1793 *Report of the Secretary of State on the Privileges and Restrictions on the Commerce of the United States in Foreign Countries*. This great-granddaddy of the modern *National Trade Estimate* reports catalogued the barriers that trading partners imposed on US exports. Although Jefferson preferred to address these restrictions through "friendly arrangements" with partner countries, he laid out an alternative set of "principles, being founded in reciprocity, [that] appear perfectly just." The first was that, "Where a nation imposes high duties on our productions, or prohibits them altogether, it may be proper for us to do the same by theirs."[29] He repeated those same principles for shipping, the entry of merchants, and other areas where Americans might be subject to discrimination. Jefferson thus advocated a tit-for-tat strategy that would apply not just to trade in goods, but also to services and trading rights – two topics that would later be high US priorities.

Just as Jefferson and his fellows worked against Hamilton's program, so too did Hamilton balk theirs. The first secretary of the treasury objected to the reciprocity policy not out of passivity – aggressive initiatives often appealed to him – but instead from a more realistic assessment of the contending parties' relative powers. Hamilton had good cause to believe that the US economy then lacked the heft to intimidate London, and he outmaneuvered his

---

[26]   Hofstadter (1948), p. 78.
[27]   Article I, Section 8, Clause 1, at http://avalon.law.yale.edu/19th_century/csa_csa.asp.
[28]   Smith (1776), pp. 467–468.
[29]   Jefferson (1793), pp. 303–304.

opponents by promoting the Jay Treaty with Great Britain. This treaty under-mined the Jeffersonian approach by banning any commercial discrimination for ten years.[30]

BRITISH LEADERSHIP AND THE HEGEMONIC TRANSITION

The United States developed within a global system dominated by the British, forming a largely symbiotic relationship in which London cooperated with Washington more often than it clashed. Those occasional clashes could be quite severe, including renewed hostilities in 1812–1815, a threatened recogni-tion of the Confederate States of America in the US Civil War, and war scares involving such far-flung territories as Oregon (in the 1840s) and Venezuela (in the 1890s). Even so, the cousins would gradually find their shared interests more compelling than their differences. Just as London practiced benign neglect toward the colonies in the century that preceded its disastrous efforts to tax them, the independent states eventually enjoyed – after a few decades of confrontation and peril – the indulgence of English statesmen. Some British policymakers had the foresight to overlook the free-riding of their first former colony, playing a long game that would aid their descendants in the twentieth century.

The British Promotion of Global Trade

The British-led trade negotiations of the nineteenth century often receive more credit for global economic expansion than may be warranted. Three other processes that originated in England played a larger role: technological advances in manufacturing and shipping, autonomous liberalization, and the export of capital. Technology may have been the most significant of these factors, with O'Rourke and Williamson rather boldly stating that "*all* of the commodity market integration in the Atlantic economy after the 1860s was due to the fall in transport costs between markets, and *none* was due to more liberal trade policy."[31] London's autonomous liberalization may have accomplished more, and endured longer, than all of the treaties of the Pax Britannica. Historians usually identify the 1846 repeal of the protectionist Corn Laws as a monumental step, but it had important precursors. Two key reforms came in

---

[30]   One might suppose that the secretary of state would have controlled the content of this treaty, but lead negotiator John Jay was the chief justice of the Supreme Court and, more impor-tantly, a Hamilton ally.

[31]   O'Rourke and Williamson (1999), p. 30. Emphasis in the original.

1828, when London lifted the century-old restrictions that forbade skilled workers to emigrate and ended the national monopoly on the Caribbean carrying trade. Both of those actions benefitted the United States, as did the unilateral repeal of the Navigation Acts in 1849.

Britain turned to negotiated liberalization with the Cobden–Chevalier Treaty. This 1860 pact with France was the first node in an expanding network of formally bilateral, tariff-cutting agreements in Europe that collectively constituted the first multilateral trading system. Because the participating countries extended MFN treatment to one another, the concessions that any pair of them made were automatically spread to all their partners. These agreements stimulated trade, even if the effects were specific to the covered countries and products.[32]

The United States abstained from this treaty system, with presidents negotiating few tariff-cutting agreements prior to the 1930s and Congress approving even fewer (see Chapter 4). The reluctance to set tariffs by treaty was further reflected in the principle of conditional reciprocity. This made its first appearance in the 1778 Treaty of Amity and Commerce with France, in which both signatories stipulated that any future concessions to a third party would be extended to the other partner only "on allowing the same compensation." For example, if the United States were to cut tariffs in a new agreement with Spain those benefits would be available to France only if Paris "paid" the same concessions that Madrid had for these commitments. This principle was contrary to the unconditional MFN practice of European states and isolated the effects of the few tariff-cutting treaties that Congress approved.

Differences in the British and American Hegemonies

There used to be told an apocryphal tale that illustrated the exactness with which Japan copied England in the late nineteenth century. Japanese officials were so intent on emulating their fellow island nation that they salvaged a sunken Royal Navy cruiser out of Tokyo Bay, reproducing it in painstaking detail. Their replica promptly sank as well, taking on water through a gash that the shipwrights obediently duplicated. No such thing ever happened, of course, and neither did the architects of American hegemony slavishly replicate every aspect of their predecessors' actions. Before reviewing the events by which hegemony made the leap from London to Washington, it is useful to consider the different endowments and circumstances of the two hegemons, and how these affected their objectives and leadership styles.

[32]   Lampe (2009).

TABLE 2.1. *Comparison of the United Kingdom and the United States at Hegemonic Peaks*

	United Kingdom, 1870	United States, 1950
Population		
Total population (millions)	31.4	152.3
Share of global population	2.5%	6.0%
Net migration	Outward	Inward
Economy and Trade		
Share of global GDP	9.1%	27.3%
Share of global exports	29.5%	19.8%
Merchandise exports as share of GDP	12.2%	3.0%
Agricultural trade	Net importer	Net exporter
Military		
Military personnel (thousands)	257	1,460
Military personnel as share of population	0.8%	1.0%
Composite Index of National Capability	24.2%	28.4%

Note that data for the United Kingdom do not include the empire.
Composite Index of National Capability = An aggregate score for six components of national material capabilities, reflecting an average of a state's share of the system total of each element.
Sources: Some items are calculated by the author from more than one measure in the sources. Demographic and economic measures are from Maddison (2003). Military measures are from http://correlatesofwar.org/data-sets/national-material-capabilities.

Table 2.1 summarizes vital statistics for both countries at the peak of their respective hegemonies. The principal similarity was in their relative levels of military power. England and America each accounted for about one-fourth of global military strength, as measured by the Composite Index of National Capability. Just below 1% of the UK population served in the military as of 1870, and in 1950 the United States hit that mark precisely. The principal differences were in their overall size and economic leverage (higher for the United States) and in their economic vulnerability (higher for the United Kingdom). The United Kingdom held 27% of western Europe's GDP in 1870, but in 1950 the United States had that share of *global* GDP.[33] Looking more specifically at trade, the British controlled a greater share of the global market than would the United States. This also meant that London was more dependent on the trading system than Washington ever would be. Above all else, the United Kingdom was a net food importer. Its 1846 abolition of the Corn Laws

[33]   Calculated from Maddison (2003), p. 263.

was an epochal decision that not only reshaped global patterns of production and trade, but also made this hegemon's survival dependent on secure lines of supply to overseas breadbaskets. The United States is instead a land power of nearly continental dimensions that is beyond self-sufficient in food, and also in some other raw materials.

In a seeming contradiction, the United Kingdom managed at once to be an empire to its possessions and a hegemon to its peers. That was accomplished in part by extending little favoritism or restrictions to London's many overseas possessions, and by opening itself and its dominions to trade and investment. Gallagher and Robinson calculated that in the nineteenth century, countries outside the empire received more than 60% of British exports, almost 70% of British emigration, and more than 80% of British foreign investment.[34] No small share of those goods, people, and pounds went to the United States, where they helped to set in motion the Law of Uneven Growth. Whereas during 1820–1900 the British economy grew at a compound annual rate of 0.8%, the US growth rate was 2.5%.[35] It was only when the hegemon went into decline that the British reverted to the more restrictive policy of imperial preferences.

Several important implications spring from the United Kingdom's greater dependence on trade, and its smaller share of the global economy, at the peak of its hegemony. While trade per se was a vital national interest for British statesmen, their future American counterparts could instead treat trade more as an instrument with which to secure other ends than as an end itself. When conflicts arose between each hegemon's commercial and military interests, London was generally more prone than Washington to place wealth before power. We will see in Chapter 7 what that meant for the two hegemons' approaches toward international law and sea power. Another difference concerns the two leaders' faith in trade sanctions as a tool of foreign policy. This instrument has been less efficacious than US policymakers might hope, as is discussed in Chapter 10, but that would be doubly true for the United Kingdom. With Washington having greater leverage over other powers, and yet also being less vulnerable to the negative effects of trade restrictions, it has shown a greater willingness than London to threaten or impose sanctions on its adversaries, and to spurn its allies or run roughshod over them.

---

[34] Gallagher and Robinson (1953), p. 5, quoted in Kennedy (1976), p. 154. Note that the time periods in which these three expansions took place are not uniform (e.g., the emigration data cover 1812–1914).

[35] Calculated by the author from data in Maddison (2003).

US Policy during the Hegemonic Transition

The United States was quicker to acquire power than it was to exercise it. This period began with what Zakaria characterized as "imperial understretch," when the United States had yet "to develop interests commensurate with its power."[36] To the limited extent that American statesmen flexed their growing muscles in the latter half of the nineteenth century, they largely confined their adventures to the Caribbean and Pacific Basins. These included the forcible opening of Japan in the 1850s, the acquisition of Hawaii in a decades-long process in which trade treaties played a key role,[37] and an 1889 conflict with Germany over the Samoan islands. The country also mimicked British colonialism in the Spanish-American War of 1898, making a colony of Puerto Rico and protectorates of Cuba and the Philippines, and its construction of the Panama Canal imitated (and surpassed) the French feat in the Suez. These actions were complemented by a renewed interest in reciprocity, which one historian was to call "a new god" for that age's economic nationalists.[38] Those policymakers were actually dusting off an idol that is trotted out once every generation or two. Reciprocity proved to be just one more god that failed, however, primarily because Congress remained wary. Several laws in the late nineteenth and early twentieth centuries gave the president the power to impose retaliation on countries that restricted US imports, and also encouraged the negotiation of treaties to reduce tariffs. While the threat of retaliation did help to secure concessions from a handful of trading partners for a narrow range of goods, those reductions were only temporary and the Senate shelved the tariff-cutting treaties.

The persistent American preference for protectionism and free-riding would constrain policymakers until well into the twentieth century. Whereas the unweighted average tariff on manufactures in European countries was just over 9% in 1875, in the United States the average for all products was 42%. The gap closed only modestly by 1913, when the European tariffs averaged 15% versus 41% for the United States.[39] The composition of US production and trade gradually shifted in the meantime. The trade balance had chronically been in deficit before the Civil War, but in the mid-1870s it turned to a consistent surplus. It would stay that way for nearly a century, during which time the share of manufactures in US exports steadily rose.

---

[36]   Zakaria (1998), p. 44. That specific reference was to 1865–1889.
[37]   La Croix and Grandy (1997).
[38]   Wolman (1992), chapter 2.
[39]   Goldstein (1993), p. 95.

It was not until the First World War that Washington turned toward the more positive (if hubristic) aim of fighting the war to end all wars, and then to negotiate a peace in which cooperative economic relations were supposed to form the foundation for a new world order. Trade was a key component of President Woodrow Wilson's famous Fourteen Points for settling the war and establishing the peace. His second point called for freedom of navigation, and his third demanded the removal "of all economic barriers and the establishment of an equality of trade conditions among all the nations." The other allies did not share this newfound American enthusiasm for open markets, having already signaled in 1916 their plans for a Carthaginian peace that would restrict the enemy's postwar trade.[40] The Treaty of Versailles reflected the fact that England was on the way out, America was only part-way in, and neither the once nor the future hegemon let the better angels of their nature speak louder than the vindictive French. The treaty's only MFN provisions formed part of the punitive measures imposed on Germany, requiring that Berlin extend this treatment to the victors for three years without receiving anything like it in return. Yet if that covenant barely met Wilson's requirements, the Senate thought it went too far in overturning established American policies and in usurping legislative prerogatives. It became the most prominent item on the growing pile of rejected treaties.

One may only speculate on whether the League of Nations might have been more effective if the United States stayed inside the tent that it had erected. What is beyond debate is that this institution and its members showed little eagerness to deal with trade, or indeed with much else. Its only achievement in commercial diplomacy was to host ineffectual conferences on what we now call trade facilitation.[41] The league's authority diminished further with the departure of other major powers. Germany and Japan both withdrew in 1933, followed by Italy in 1937, and in 1939 the remaining members of the dwindling club expelled the Soviet Union.

Although the United States returned to its traditional isolationism and protectionism in the 1920s, it did take one step toward a more active commercial policy. In a classic study of the conditional MFN approach, the newly created US Tariff Commission argued in 1919 that while a cautious posture "was natural so long as the United States kept aloof from foreign complications,"[42] the country's new status demanded a more active approach

---

[40] The resolutions of the June, 1916 Paris Economic Conference of the Allies are in Hirschman (1945), Appendix B.
[41] See League of Nations (1942).
[42] US Tariff Commission (1919), p. 10.

to commercial diplomacy. The commission recommended that Washington replace this policy with "equality of treatment" for all US trading partners. Secretary of State Charles Evans Hughes accepted this recommendation in 1923, declaring that henceforth the United States would include an unconditional MFN clause in all bilateral commercial treaties.

From Hawley–Smoot to the Reciprocal Trade Agreements Act

The value of that shift in treaty practice was vastly outweighed by the Hawley–Smoot Tariff Act of 1930. Historians now generally concur that this last exercise in unhindered congressional tariff-making did not cause the Great Depression, but it did serve to spread and prolong the misery. Debate over the new tariff bill began when President Hoover proposed in 1929 an increase in agricultural tariffs to aid the dustbowl victims, who felt the effects of the Great Depression well before it hit Wall Street. The scramble for protection soon went beyond the rural economy, with the final package raising the average rate on dutiable products from 40% to 53%. Trading partners responded in kind, and trade quickly plummeted. Matters only worsened when the United States abandoned the gold standard in 1933. Many of its partners followed suit and devalued their own currencies; some also adopted clearing arrangements, barter requirements, currency restrictions, import licenses and quotas, and outright embargoes. Repeated efforts at multilateral diplomacy proved fruitless.

The New Deal inspired a profound change in American trade policy. At a time when both the White House and Capitol Hill were willing to experiment, Congress agreed to delegate tariff authority to the president. The Reciprocal Trade Agreements Act (RTAA) of 1934 gave President Roosevelt the power to reduce US tariff rates through executive agreements that did not require further action by Congress. From the first agreement with Cuba in 1934 through the 1946 pact with Paraguay, the United States concluded thirty-two agreements with twenty-eight partners. Each of these bilateral agreements included an unconditional MFN clause, making good on the 1923 decision to abandon a conditional MFN policy. The geographic concentration of the new agreements was quite tight, nearly all of them being with countries in the Western Hemisphere (17) or Europe (10). The sole exception was a 1943 agreement with Iran.

That Iranian agreement underlines how closely the new economic partnerships aligned with the emerging coalitions of the Second World War. None of the three Axis powers figured among the RTAA partners, although one early agreement was with a future Axis co-belligerent (i.e., Finland) and two others were with neutrals (i.e., Sweden and Switzerland). All of the other RTAA partners would eventually be at war with Nazi Germany, some on paper but many others in blood.[43] The most tragically mistimed of the agreements was with Czechoslovakia. That pact entered into effect in April, 1938, but was soon followed by another that would give appeasement – and all diplomacy – a bad name. In the Munich Agreement of September, 1938, Britain and France sought to placate Germany by betraying Czechoslovakia. President Roosevelt terminated the Czech trade agreement a week after Nazi troops overran that country the next March. Four other RTAA agreements would likewise be rendered moot by occupation.

TRADE POLICY IN AMERICAN HEGEMONY

If one had to put a definitive date-stamp on the role-reversals for London and Washington, the best candidate might be June 4, 1940. That was the day that Winston Churchill (1874–1965) spoke defiantly to a House of Commons that was still reeling from the near-death experience of the Dunkirk evacuation. Historians and filmmakers often repeat his call to arms, memorably declaring that "we shall fight on the beaches, we shall fight on the landing grounds, we shall fight in the fields and in the streets, we shall fight in the hills; we shall never surrender." This demonstration of anaphora is so stirring that one may easily miss the significance of Churchill's last twenty words: Britain would fight alone until "the New World, with all its power and might, steps forth to the rescue and the liberation of the old."[44] It was still eighteen months before the United States became a combatant, yet the prophetic prime minister rightly surmised that the Allied cause would be a joint Anglo-American operation in which London was necessarily the junior partner. Churchill and his successors would nevertheless make the most of a weak hand. The United Kingdom would act as a sort of hegemon emeritus long after the war ended, even when its own power became an object more of wistful remembrance than of envy.

The Anglo-American Group of Two

Washington began planning for the postwar economic and political order even before US entry into the hostilities,[45] and worked closely with the cousins

---

[43] All Latin American countries declared war against Germany, but only Mexico and Brazil committed troops.

[44] www.winstonchurchill.org/resources/speeches/1940-the-finest-hour/we-shall-fight-on-the-beaches/.

[45] For the history of these deliberations see U.S. Department of State (1949).

to devise the institutional bases of the new regime. The United Nations Charter of 1945 crowned a process that began with Anglo-American discussions in 1942. The same pattern followed for the Bretton Woods Agreement of 1944, which created the International Monetary Fund and the World Bank. The first major commitments on the future trading system came in two bilateral agreements, the Atlantic Charter of 1941 and the Master Lend-Lease Agreement of 1942. The Atlantic Charter stated that these two allies would "endeavor, with due respect for their existing obligations, to further the enjoyment by all States, great or small, victor or vanquished, of access, on equal terms, to the trade and to the raw materials of the world which are needed for their economic prosperity." Over the strong objections of Keynes and other imperial diehards, Article VII of the Lend-Lease Agreement more precisely called for "action by the United States of America and the United Kingdom, open to participation by all other countries of like mind" for "the elimination of all forms of discriminatory treatment in international commerce, and to the reduction of tariffs and other trade barriers."

Those broad principles were followed by the *Proposals for Consideration by an International Conference on Trade and Employment*. While this document bore a made-in-America label, being issued by the State Department in November, 1945, it had in fact been hammered out in "prolonged and difficult negotiations with the British."[46] It would take three more years of multilateral negotiations in England and then Cuba to transform this outline into the ill-fated Havana Charter of the International Trade Organization (ITO). While that 1948 charter covered a surprisingly wide range of issues (see Chapter 5), the 1947 negotiations over the modest GATT – which was intended to serve only as a stop-gap measure while the ITO Charter was being concluded and ratified – added little to the standard language of RTAA agreements.[47] The GATT would have to step in for the ITO after Congress refused to approve that organization's ambitious charter.

When many economic theorists and political practitioners had lost faith in free trade, and some toyed with statist options, the postwar US commitment to open markets was remarkable. Even the chief British negotiator in the first GATT round told his American counterpart that the United States then stood "virtually alone in the world in its belief that free enterprise can be a wise or

---

[46] Brown (1950), p. 54.
[47] As Jackson (2000) showed in a point-by-point comparison, "almost the entire range of GATT's substantive subject matter had been dealt with in one or more prior United States trade agreements" (pp. 209–210).

even a major rule for the conduct of economic affairs."[48] Some US negotiators shared these doubts. One veteran would observe decades later that he knew "of no one involved in working out the problems of international trade at the time who thought that free trade was a realistic goal or even a reasonable aspiration for a liberal economic system that had to be operated by sovereign states."[49]

The GATT initially recapitulated much of the wartime alliance. All but three of the 23 original contracting parties were among the signatories to the United Nations Declaration of 1942,[50] and the Soviet Union was the only major Allied combatant that did not join GATT. The Allied character of the GATT was to dissipate with the accessions of Italy (1950), West Germany (1951), and Japan (1955), by which time it had become associated with a new alliance. NATO and the multilateral trading system were both predominantly transatlantic institutions, and it is not happenstance that GATT and the Cold War had almost identical lifespans. Both Washington and Moscow established their respective economic alliances before they set up the parallel security structures. The creation of the GATT and the Marshall Plan preceded NATO by two years, when Washington still hoped that economic programs could be a substitute rather than a complement for an open-ended military commitment. The Soviet-led Council for Mutual Economic Assistance (1949) likewise came well before the Warsaw Pact (1955), the proximate cause for that latter development being West Germany's entry into NATO.

The GATT was born in the pivotal year of 1947, when the transition to the new global conflict had already reached the point of no return. The ideological bases of the Cold War had been laid out the year before in Moscow and Missouri, respectively, whence George Kennan (1904–2005) sent his "Long Telegram" in February and Churchill delivered his "Iron Curtain" speech in March. The most feverish period was the storied fifteen weeks that began on February 21, 1947, when London told the State Department that it could no longer maintain its commitments in Greece and Turkey, and ended when Secretary of State George Marshall (1880–1959) unveiled his eponymous plan for European reconstruction on June 5.[51] If any final proof were needed, these events confirmed that London had passed the torch to Washington.

---

[48] Memorandum of Conversation by Mr. William Adams Brown [with James R.C. Helmore, head of the British delegation in Geneva] (May 9, 1947), *FRUS 1947*, Volume I, p. 941.

[49] Diebold (1994), p. 336.

[50] The exceptions were Burma, Ceylon, and Rhodesia, each of which might be considered to have been covered by the British signature. Some of the countries that joined GATT had not signed the U.N. Declaration until 1943–1945.

[51] See Jones (1955).

The Domestic Diplomacy of Hegemony

Wary of the Versailles debacle, Roosevelt and Truman cultivated the support of the electorate and the opposition party. The American public was well-disposed toward the creation of new international organizations, at least as measured by the infant science of polling. Whereas only 33% of the respondents in a 1937 Gallup Poll believed that the United States ought to have joined the League of Nations, that figure rose to 50% in 1941 and 73% in 1942. Another 73% agreed in 1942 that the government should "take steps now, before the end of the war, to set up with our Allies a world organization to maintain the future peace of the world."[52] In 1943 FDR secured Republican backing for what was to become the United Nations system, just as Truman would win their support for the Marshall Plan and related initiatives. The instinctively isolationist opposition was willing to go only so far in abandoning its established orthodoxies, however, and Republican leaders felt compelled to draw the line somewhere. They stood their ground on trade, where the public remained leery. Whereas 79% of the respondents told *Fortune* in 1945 that an international organization should have the power to "[p]revent any member country from starting a war of its own against an outside country," only 45% thought that it should "[d]ecide what tariff rates should be charged by member nations."[53]

The constraints imposed by the domestic diplomacy of trade were already apparent in 1947, when the US negotiators in Geneva had to deal with a bill in Congress that threatened a 50% fee on imported wool. "Situation here serious as result failure to offer duty cut" on wool, the Geneva delegation warned Washington in the characteristically terse language of cable traffic. Given the high importance of wool to both the United Kingdom and Australia, the bill could "result complete suspension tariff negotiations with southern dominions and perhaps UK, and might endanger whole ITO project."[54] President Truman vetoed the offending bill, and Congress sustained him, but the episode underlined the limits of congressional forbearance. That same lesson would be driven home again in 1951, when Congress approved yet another bill to restrict agricultural imports, this time prompting US negotiators to pull that entire sector off the table. It would be decades before negotiators could reach a reasonably comprehensive multilateral agreement on agricultural trade, and those Uruguay Round commitments of 1994 would be better known for the

[52]   National Opinion Research Center (1945), p. 66.
[53]   *Fortune* (1945), pp. 68–69.
[54]   The Counsel in Geneva (Troutman) to the Secretary of State (April 28, 1947), *FRUS 1947*, Volume I, p. 918.

breadth of their exceptions than for the depth of their concessions. Physiocratic notions die hard.

Even more consequentially, Congress asserted its control over trade by blocking the Havana Charter. Republicans opposed it on grounds that hearkened back to the Versailles Treaty, complaining that negotiators had strayed too far beyond their mandate to negotiate on such arcane topics as intellectual property rights and competition policy. The Truman administration did not submit the charter to the Senate as a formal treaty, asking instead that Congress approve it via joint resolution. This procedure lowered the bar from two-thirds approval in the Senate to a simple majority in both chambers, but the Republican leaders – who had recaptured control over Congress in 1946, before losing it again in 1948 – did what Congress does best when they opted to do nothing at all. The administration had no power to force a vote, and in late 1950 Truman stopped trying to win congressional approval. The United States instead worked with its partners to make the bare-bones GATT stand in as the centerpiece of the trading system, a temporary expedient that would last for the entirety of the American half-century.

The Economics of Containment

The Truman administration placed just as high a priority on confronting the Soviet Union as it did on cooperating with Western Europe. The National Security Council determined in 1948 that "the overt foreign activities of the US Government must be supplemented by covert operations," and authorized the CIA to target the Soviet economy.[55] The specific instruments that planners identified at this early stage of the Cold War were oddly macro, such as "[c]ommodity operations (clandestine preclusive buying, market manipulation and black market operation)" and "[f]iscal operations (currency speculation, counterfeiting, etc.)."[56] Whether wholesale or retail, it is doubtful that US economic actions against the Soviet Union had much impact. The Kremlin's penchant for autarky, coupled with its abstention from the GATT and the US withdrawal of MFN treatment in 1951 (see Chapter 11),

---

[55] Note by the Executive Secretary (Souers) to the National Security Council, "NSC 10/1" (June 15, 1948), *FRUS 1945–1950*, pp. 706–707.

[56] Memorandum from the Assistant Director for Policy Coordination (Wisner) to Director of Central Intelligence Hillenkoetter, "OPC Projects" (October 29, 1948), *FRUS 1945–1950*, p. 729. The emphasis then placed on currency operations most likely stemmed from the high importance of that instrument in the immediate postwar struggle over control of Berlin and relations between the Soviet and Western occupation zones of Germany.

ensured that trade between the leaders of the two blocs would remain negligible for nearly all of the Cold War.

Washington had three strategic options. The most aggressive was rollback, which promised to confront Communism directly and to liberate the captive nations. The first Soviet test of an atomic bomb in 1949 rendered this option highly costly and improbable. Engagement was instead based on a policy of selective cooperation. Each of these options implied specific approaches for trade policy: Cooperative economic relations were the linchpin of engagement, just as economic warfare was an important component of rollback. In keeping with the established preference for pragmatism, Washington settled on a compromise. As initially formulated by Kennan and then inscribed in NSC-68, containment entailed the use of political, military, and economic instruments to prevent expansion of the Soviet empire. This sometimes reactive and improvisational strategy did not dictate any specific trade doctrine, and could be molded to accommodate whatever calibration might seem appropriate. The form of containment practiced by Presidents Truman, Nixon, Ford, and G. H. W. Bush all allowed for the maintenance or reestablishment of limited trade relations with the Soviet Union, while Presidents Eisenhower and Reagan each favored a harder line; Presidents Kennedy, Johnson, and Carter devoted more attention to relations with Soviet satellites and clients than to the empire itself.

GATT disciplines did not prevent the United States from prosecuting its containment policy. This was primarily a club of market economies, and the United States effectively denied full GATT treatment to five of the seven GATT contracting parties that were nonmarket economies for all or part of 1947–1994. It variously did so through GATT-authorized withdrawal of MFN treatment (Czechoslovakia in the 1950s), an embargo combined with the unilateral withdrawal of MFN treatment (Cuba in the 1960s), the invocation of GATT Article XXXV (the "non-application" clause) on a country's accession to the GATT (Hungary and Romania in the 1970s), or the imposition of a trade embargo combined with the invocation of GATT Article XXI (the national security clause) at a time of overt sanctions and covert operations (Nicaragua in the 1980s). The only departures from this rule were for Yugoslavia and Poland, two GATT countries that were granted special treatment for political reasons. Even these countries were later subject to trade sanctions during periods of martial law (Poland in the 1980s) or civil war (Serbia and Montenegro in the 1990s).

The Reversal in Partisan Polarities

The domestic diplomacy of US trade policy is primarily a struggle between the branches and the parties. Although the executive is almost always more favorably disposed toward open markets than the legislature,[57] the positions taken by the two parties are less firm or permanent. Protectionist Republicans fell into a predictable pattern of conflict with Democrats after the Civil War, and the lines changed little for the next century. It is nevertheless important not to exaggerate the degree of partisan differences. "Even the most liberal Democrats agreed with their Republican opponents that free trade was not in the national interest" during the late nineteenth century, according to Goldstein, with the parties concurring "that America had to be protected against cheap 'pauper labor,' that the idea of free trade was a manifestation of British imperialism, and that the notion of a home market was sound."[58] That did not change until the 1920s, when Democrats began to press harder for open markets.

Eisenhower was the first Republican president in twenty years, and when he took office in 1953 Ike opted not to roll back the Roosevelt and Truman trade policies. The parties slowly reversed the polarities they had held for nearly a century, so that by the end of the Cold War they were in precisely the opposite positions from where they had started. As early as the mid-1950s, one political scientist could report that "[p]arty cohesion on the tariff issue has given way to the bipartisan coalitions so familiar to the student of the American Congress." He presciently pointed to an economic transition in which the textile industry was migrating south, thus making the region's Democrats question their "time-honored reverence of free trade," while energy interests were "beginning to feel the competitive pinch of imported residual oil" and Republicans in Central and Eastern states responded "to the improving competitive position of the dominant economic interests of these regions."[59] Later analysts had similar takes on partisan political geography.[60] The reversal in polarities was well underway by the start of the first Nixon term in 1969, and was complete by Reagan's second inauguration in 1985.

By 1971 Washington's concerns over a dulled American economic edge, and its willingness to prop up the postwar economic order, approached

---

[57] The Trump administration is an obvious exception to this general rule, as is discussed in Chapters 3 and 16.

[58] Goldstein (1993), p. 128. See also Lake (1988), p. 98 and Shoch (2001), chapter 2 on the bipartisan concurrence over basic goals.

[59] Watson (1956), pp. 698–699.

[60] See, for example, Shoch (2001) and Irwin (2017).

a crisis. The first US trade deficit in living memory prompted President Nixon to suspend the convertibility of the dollar into gold and to impose a surcharge on imports. The administration still pushed for new GATT negotiations, leading in 1972 to the launch of the Tokyo Round. Here we see an example of the "two steps forward, one step back" approach that most American presidents have routinely practiced since the 1950s. Partisan politics now took on a new pattern. Democrats responded to Nixon's request for a new grant of negotiating authority by attaching restrictive positions to the bill in the House. Those were the opening shots in a five-year legislative skirmish that would not end until enactment of the Trade Act of 1974, an omnibus trade bill that mashed together liberal, protectionist, and reciprocity provisions.

Ronald Reagan finished the Republican transformation that Eisenhower and Nixon started, but not right away. Gauzy memories of a free-trading Gipper conveniently skip past his protectionist campaign promises of 1980 (apparel) and 1984 (steel), and his readiness to maneuver Japan into imposing "voluntary" restraints on automobile exports. By the end of his first term, however, Reagan and his party had moved toward free trade. The later patterns of partisanship were fairly simple. For nearly all initiatives between the 1984 and 2016 elections, most congressional Republicans took the pro-trade position in most policy debates. Almost the only important exceptions came when they felt an irresistible opportunity to cause electoral difficulties for Democrats. During the first Clinton term, for example, congressional Republicans soft-pedalled their support for NAFTA so as to exacerbate relations between the White House, congressional Democrats, and the unions, and in Clinton's second term their interest in denying him a win overcame an otherwise natural inclination to approve a new grant of negotiating authority. As for congressional Democrats, by the 1980s the majority could usually be expected to oppose market-opening initiatives unless at least one of the following conditions applied: (1) the negotiation was put forward by a Democratic president, (2) it was either multilateral or focused on a developed country partner (e.g., Australia or Canada), or (3) it was associated with either a favored diaspora (e.g., African Americans) or an important objective in foreign policy (e.g., Middle East peace).

WHERE WE GO FROM HERE

The US position in the world, and hence its approach to trade policy, traversed a grand arc from the dawn of independence through the closing days of the Cold War. The same country that was born to British colonialism, and whose first important trade strategist would adapt mercantilist ideas to American circumstances, eventually became the principal proponent of a doctrine that surfaced in the same year as US independence. Having grown up within a trading system dominated by British hegemony, the United States eventually took the former mother country's place.

This chapter has offered an overview of the obstacles that had to be cleared, leaving the details for later. One set of challenges concerns the domestic diplomacy of trade. In Chapter 4 we will examine the evolving relations between the executive and legislative branches in the making of trade policy, including the all-important issue of the legislature's grants of negotiating authority to the executive. It would have been all but impossible for the United States to act as a hegemon without congressional willingness to delegate authority to the president. We will also examine relations between the government and the private sector in Chapter 5, especially the widening range of issues that fall within the rubric of trade policy. That is one place where the domestic and international diplomacy of trade come together, with the hegemon taking the lead in the formation of the system's negotiating agenda. The history of US trade relations with Canada (Chapter 9) offers a detailed case study in the domestic diplomacy of trade and the conduct of North Atlantic relations.

A second set of challenges concerns the place of the United States in the trading system. While relations between the once and future hegemons were mostly peaceful, and the transfer of authority from London to Washington came when the cousins were allied against a common enemy, the Pax Britannica was sometimes more British than peaceful. In Chapter 7 we will examine the relationship between power and wealth over the course of nine world wars, and the different approaches that the United Kingdom and the United States took toward the development and execution of international law in this field. The historical evolution of hegemony and its challengers is also key to our reviews of US relations with Japan (Chapter 8), Russia (Chapter 11), and China (Chapter 12).

Before we consider those more detailed reviews, we must first bring the story up to the present day. The next chapter picks up the narrative around 1990, when the Cold War ends and new trials arise. The quarter-century that began during the presidency of George H. W. Bush was defined not only by the shift from one set of security threats to another but also by an acceleration of economic change. The Law of Uneven Growth and the process of Creative Destruction would be just as important in defining the trading system and US policy as was the radical revision in the security matrix. Both of those processes would put new strains on the international and domestic diplomacies of trade, and would play important roles in the radical redirection that the electorate approved in 2016.

3

After Hegemony:
Power, Wealth, and Trade Policy since
the Cold War

[S]ome think that all the answers to this year's problems can be found by spending what is called in Washington a peace dividend. It's like the next-of-kin who spent the inheritance before the will is read.

President George H. W. Bush, remarks to the Cincinnati Chamber
of Commerce (January 12, 1990)

INTRODUCTION

President Bush feared in 1990 that the chaos in the Soviet Union might take a bad turn, and believed that the United States should guard against a renewed flare-up of the Cold War. As wrong as this former CIA chief was in his specific diagnosis, at least in the short term, his broader prognosis was correct: It was too soon to conclude that conflict was obsolete and vigilance was redundant. The Air Force would be lobbing cruise missiles and smart bombs into Baghdad just 53 weeks after he spoke, and one decade later a new struggle would begin when jihadis flew hijacked airplanes into the nerve centers of American power (the Pentagon) and wealth (the World Trade Center). Neither the short nor the long war seemed imminent at the time, when some thought the end of history had arrived. Victory in the Cold War promised the integration of a truly global trading system, a pro-market Washington Consensus inspired developing countries to reevaluate state-led development strategies, and democracy was on the rise. The planets seemed to come into alignment, and while this global syzygy was short-lived it lasted long enough to produce the North American Free Trade Agreement (NAFTA) and the WTO.

Future historians may decide whether the quarter-century that began around 1990 is best characterized as the first phase of a post–Cold War and post-hegemonic era, or as the final phase of the pre-Trump era. That conclusion awaits the denouement of events that are still underway. We do know that all of the fillips that the trading system received in the early 1990s have long since disappeared: Bush's own son inherited and then squandered the peace dividend, the bifurcated challenges from the Soviet Union and Japan are now consolidated in US rivalry with China, and the developing world is once again divided between its trade enthusiasts and skeptics.

This chapter summarizes the economic and political trends that have characterized US trade policy, and its relationship to domestic welfare and international security, in the years since the end of the Cold War. Two themes dominate modern economic statesmanship. One is a diversified security matrix, which had been fixated on the Soviet Union and its clients but now features a disorienting array of nuclear, conventional, and low-intensity but high-profile challenges. The principal focus here is on a second and related theme: An accelerated economic transition that produced a doubly destabilizing process, with wealth being redistributed between countries even as its concentration within the largest country becomes more skewed. These twin trends in security and economics provoke an unresolved struggle over burden-sharing in the global order, and also bring a new level of complexity to the domestic diplomacy of foreign economic policy. This chapter reviews these developments in "big picture" fashion, laying out themes that are examined more fully in later sections that give equal time to the security issues.

THE ECONOMIC TRANSITION: UNEVEN GROWTH AND CREATIVE DESTRUCTION

Much of the dynamism in global relations can be traced to that process by which big and rich countries tend to grow slower than the small and poor. Scholars have variously called this phenomenon convergence,[1] the leader handicap, the advantages of backwardness,[2] or – as preferred here – the Law of Uneven Growth. And while analysts differ on what accounts for the disparity, the political consequences matter more than the economic causes. Just as Athens overtook Sparta, and Germany threatened to surpass the United Kingdom, the United States outgrew and then peacefully displaced its former colonial master. The question now is how Washington and the world will handle the relative decline of this hegemon and the rise of China.

Growth has been much more uneven since the start of the new millennium than it was in the closing decades of the past century. As can be seen in Figure 3.1,

[1] O'Rourke and Williamson (1999), pp. 6ff.
[2] Gerschenkron (1962).

Countries' and Regions' Share of Global GDP

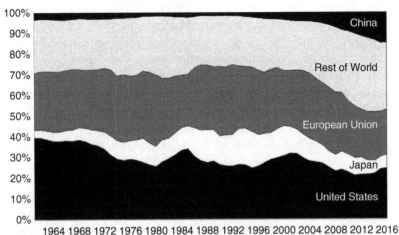

FIGURE 3.1 Shares of the global economy, 1961–2016.
Source: Calculated from World Bank data at https://data.worldbank.org/indicator/
NY.GDP.MKTP.CD. The EU share is based on membership as of 2016.

the three largest economies – the European Union,[3] Japan, and the United States – collectively held a large and fairly stable share of global GDP in the second half of the twentieth century. The division within this group shifted somewhat, with Japan's portion doubling from 1976 to 1994; that growth spurt caused no little anxiety for American voters and politicians, even though the challenge proved transitory. The pace of redistribution accelerated rapidly about a decade after the Cold War ended, with the share held by the largest developed economies falling from 68% in 2005 to 53% in 2016. The most consequential change came in the relative sizes of China and the United States. The US economy had been 9.1 times larger than that of China in 1960, and by 1987 the multiple had grown to 17.8, but then the gaps started to close. The US:China ratio fell to 9.6 in 1996, 5.0 in 2006, and 1.7 in 2016.

The Law of Uneven Growth finds its domestic complement in the notorious process of Creative Destruction, the results of which are even more divergent and disruptive: Some profit from its creativity, but others are destroyed. The shifts can readily be seen in the changing fortunes of specific industries and firms. Consider the companies that comprise the Dow Jones

---

[3] Note that for reasons of clarity and continuity, throughout this book the current title "European Union" will often be used even for periods in which that association had other structures and titles (e.g., European Community).

average, which began in 1896 with a dozen stocks. An era ended in 2018 when General Electric – the last survivor among the first twelve – was replaced in the index by Walgreens. Five of the others had already been absorbed into larger conglomerates, some of which are international, and the rest dissolved or went bankrupt. Half of the companies now in the Dow 30 were added in 1997–2010, and many did not even exist a generation ago. This is all good news for the owners and employees of Apple and Boeing, but not so much for stakeholders in the defunct American Cotton Oil or United States Rubber.

To switch the metaphor, how we perceive this continuous process of economic reinvention amounts to the great Rorschach test of American economic history. Each percipient's description of that great, black blob reveals whether their outlook is fundamentally optimistic or pessimistic. Those who see in it the happy butterfly of progress are the modern counterparts of John Adams (1735–1826), who put his own dark moods aside long enough to picture a bright future for his country and his progeny. "I must study Politicks and War," he wrote his wife from Paris,

> that my sons may have liberty to study Painting and Poetry Mathematicks and Philosophy. My sons ought to study Mathematicks and Philosophy, Geography, natural History, Naval Architecture, navigation, Commerce and Agriculture, in order to give their Children a right to study Painting, Poetry, Musick, Architecture, Statuary, Tapestry and Porcelaine.[4]

Americans who do not share this second president's educational and social advantages might not be as quick to embrace his optimistic vision of progress. They may mourn the loss of agriculture and manufactures more than they celebrate the birth of ever more refined arts and services, and hence see a menacing monster in that inscrutable smudge that is the US economic transition.

Few trends in American economic history are steadier than the move from manufacturing to services in the second half of the twentieth century. Services were already predominant in 1945, employing 1.7 persons for every one in manufacturing, and by 2016 the ratio was ten to one. This shift can be appreciated from a few comparisons: There are now two people working in motion pictures and sound-recording for every person in the motor vehicle industry, four people engaged in software publishing for every iron and steel job, and almost five offering legal services for every textile and apparel worker.[5] Those ratios would have seemed incomprehensible just a generation ago.

---

[4]   Letter of May 12, 1780, from John Adams to Abigail Adams, at www.masshist.org/digitaladams/archive/doc?id=L17800512jasecond.

[5]   Calculated from Bureau of Labor Statistics data at https://data.bls.gov/pdq/SurveyOutputServlet.

Employees in an Industry per 10,000 Nonfarm Jobs in the United States

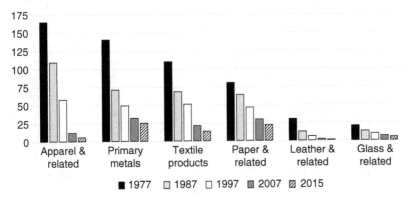

FIGURE 3.2 Employment in the principal protection-seeking industries, 1977–2015.
Note that the comparability of data for the periods before and after 1997 is complicated by the transition that year from the Standard Industrial Classification (SIC) to the North American Industry Classification (NAIC) nomenclature. While the categories appear to cover the same territory, it is possible that some SIC categories may be slightly broader or narrower than some of the corresponding NAIC categories. Data for apparel are based on SIC 23 and NAIC 315; data for primary metals are based on SIC 33 and NAIC 331; data for textiles are based on SIC 22 and NAIC 313 and 314; data for paper are based on SIC 26 and NAIC 322; data for leather are based on SIC 31 and NAIC 316; and data for glass are based on SIC 321–323 and NAIC 3272.
Source: Calculated from the Census of Manufactures (for employment by industry in 1977–2007), the Annual Survey of Manufactures (for employment by industry in 2015), and Bureau of Labor Statistics (total nonfarm jobs) data at www .bls.gov/ces/.

Creative Destruction has been especially disruptive for labor-intensive industries that face competitive challenges from lower-wage countries, most consequentially for the six shown in Figure 3.2. Back in 1977 they collectively employed nearly one out of every eighteen persons in the nonfarm sector; by 2015, these six industries provided fewer than one in 130 jobs.

At issue here is not just sector but class, with the owners of capital having more options than those who possess little more than the sweat of their brow. Competition killed some firms, but other manufacturers coped by outsourcing their inputs, moving operations off shore, or investing in labor-saving machinery. Whatever job-shedding strategy management might favor, every option other than bankruptcy will always be more disruptive for workers than for employers. Some displaced hands can find work in more competitive industries, but many others suffer either declining wages or permanent joblessness. The lost jobs may look to an outside observer like just another cost of doing business, yet for the working class they are more like the phantom limbs of an amputee. And while the rising trade deficit is not solely responsible for the secular decline in manufacturing, it is the cause most visible to the general public. Recent scholarship supports the contention that citizens are rational in their support or opposition to open markets, and confirms that those who are least likely to benefit from globalization are most likely to oppose it.[6]

THE NEGATIVE TOOLS: PROTECTIONISM, RECIPROCITY, AND SANCTIONS

Trade policy is subject to political laws of supply and demand. Elected officials and civil servants are in the business of supplying those policies, and they may take the initiative in new negotiations, but protectionism usually begins with demands from beleaguered industries. As one might expect, these demands stepped up in response to rising levels of import competition.

The US merchandise trade deficit has come to seem like a permanent feature of the global economic landscape, making it difficult to remember that the United States consistently ran a trade surplus for most of the twentieth century. It came as a shock when in 1971 the surplus turned to a $1.5 billion deficit, even if that imbalance was quite small by later standards. Whereas there were then just $1.03 in imports for every dollar's worth of exports, the discrepancy would rise to $1.61 in 1986 and peak at $1.86 in 2005.[7] Legislators began to introduce restrictive measures as soon as the ledger first edged toward red. Further waves of protectionist demands came in the 1980s, but over time both industry and government seemed to accommodate themselves to globalization. By the dawn of the twenty-first century, policymakers relegated trade to second-tier status. They would be forced to reconsider the downgrading of this issue after the 2016 presidential election (see Chapter 6).

---

[6] For example, the data presented by Ardanaz et al. (2013) show that a person's skill level is a central predictor of support for openness. Similarly, Owen and Johnston (2017) found that individuals in routine-task-intensive occupations will be negatively affected by trade, and thus more protectionist, and that this relationship will increase in the degree to which job tasks are offshorable.

[7] Calculated from US Census data at www.census.gov/foreign-trade/statistics/historical/gands.xls. As of 2017, there was $1.78 in imports for every dollar in exports.

The Barriers to Legislated Protection

The most obvious means of winning protection from Washington is also the oldest – seek help from Congress – but it is also far less certain. Presidents are now more powerful than Congress, and from Franklin Roosevelt to Barack Obama they all opposed most demands to impose restrictions on imports. That has not been a universal rule, as chief executives were ultimately responsible for nearly every high-profile act of protectionism in the modern era. Presidents typically made these concessions either while bargaining with Congress over a new grant of negotiating authority (see Chapter 4) or to fulfill a campaign pledge (see Chapter 6). Major examples include textile and apparel quotas first negotiated in the 1960s; the "voluntary" restraints on imports of Italian shoes in the 1970s and Japanese cars in the 1980s (see Chapter 8); and the restrictions slapped on imported steel in 1984, 1988, and 2002. Chief executives might not resist every temptation to promise protection, or oppose every demand that others make, but when they set their caps against it they almost always prevailed.

Demand for legislated protection spiked during the Reagan administration. This was a critical period in the economic transition: Many of the legacy industries from the glory days of American manufacturing were forced to decide between fighting and switching, with some of them demanding tariffs, quotas, or other barriers and others globalizing their operations. The textile and apparel industries, together with the allied sector of footwear, were especially adamant. Representative Newt Gingrich (Republican–Georgia), a future Speaker of the House who was then emerging from the back benches, led this campaign. The White House not only blocked their demands for tighter quotas, but in 1986 it launched a new round of multilateral negotiations that put this industry's existing protections on the table. That round was dominated by the US quest to secure new opportunities for its competitive, knowledge- and capital-intensive industries, and American negotiators were prepared to give up some of the protections still enjoyed by declining, labor-intensive sectors. In the round's clearest manifestation of this principle, the United States traded away the apparel quotas for stricter protection of intellectual property rights.

Seeing the writing on the wall, many of the remaining firms in the textile and apparel industry took up an implicit offer from President Reagan and his successors. Starting with the Caribbean Basin Initiative in 1986, and continuing through a series of other regional programs and free trade agreements (FTAs), the government used trade preferences to aid favored partner countries while also providing a "soft landing" for a struggling industry. The rules of origin in most of these programs and agreements conditioned duty- and quota-free treatment for imported apparel upon the incorporation of US fabric. This gave apparel producers an incentive to relocate their operations in the partner countries, and created a captive market for a struggling American textile industry. As discussed in Chapter 14, this admixture of liberalization and managed trade worked well for decades, but the partner countries have faced a stronger challenge from Asia since the final phase-out of global import quotas in 2005.

The system underwent a stress test in 2008–2009, when the Great Recession sparked widespread concerns that the United States and others might pull up the drawbridges. Fears of protectionist recidivism were high, with economists warning that the "political pressures ... are surfacing with increasing intensity around the world"[8] and that "the risk of a devastating resurgence of protectionism is real."[9] The panic was overblown, as neither Congress nor the White House said or did much to address trade policy at the end of the Bush administration or the start of the Obama administration. While protectionism was not a completely dead letter, few examples of US backsliding during and just after the crisis departed significantly from past practice.

The Obama administration opted not to make trade a priority during its first two years. Its overall approach might be deemed "passive free trade," in which the administration sought to restrain most protectionist impulses that arose in Congress. It was especially eager to ensure that any measures enacted were consistent with US legal obligations. That was demonstrated very early in the administration's tenure when it negotiated with Congress to ensure that the Buy American provisions in the 2009 economic stimulus package did not violate US obligations in either the WTO or the existing FTAs, and also that a "cash for clunkers" measure intended to stimulate sales of new cars was not discriminatory (see Chapter 8). The administration did not always restrain Congress, as shown by the enactment of a NAFTA-illegal restriction on Mexican trucks, and it also agreed to impose protection on Chinese tires. On the whole, however, it was as unwilling to acquiesce in new protection as it was to promote new market-opening initiatives. Activity did step up considerably in the second Obama term, which saw the initiation of one mega-regional negotiation (with Europe) and the conclusion of another (with the Pacific partners). These remained low-priority initiatives that the administration preferred to slow-walk, leaving it to the next president to conclude the

---

[8] Gamberoni and Newfarmer (2009).
[9] Dadush (2009), p. 1.

transatlantic talks and to move the Trans-Pacific Partnership (TPP) through Congress. That was not to be.

The Trade-Remedy Laws

While industries rarely win legislated protection, administered protection is readily available to any petitioner that can afford the legal bills. The trade-remedy laws allow industries to bypass the political process, and to cloak their demands for relief in such respectable garb as fairness, legality, and security. The four most significant laws are based on claims that imports are unfairly traded and should be penalized, or must be restrained because they are increasing at an injurious rate, or ought to be restricted because they threaten to impair the national security. The category also includes other, more arcane instruments that are rarely invoked.[10]

The antidumping (AD) law is the oldest and most frequently used of these statutes. Dumping is an unfair trade practice by which imported goods are sold at less than fair value, which may be below the cost of production, the price in the exporting country, or the price in third-country markets. A case typically begins when one or more firms file a petition, after which the Department of Commerce is responsible for determining the dumping margin (if any), and the US International Trade Commission (USITC) rules whether the imports cause (or threaten) material injury to the US industry. Both investigations are conducted in two stages. Provided that Commerce finds a final dumping margin above a *de minimis* level, and the USITC reaches a final affirmative injury determination, a duty equal to the dumping margin will be imposed.

The countervailing duty (CVD) law shares much in common with the AD statute, and cases under these twin laws are often prosecuted in conjunction with one another. The most important difference is that CVD cases are based on allegations of government subsidies rather than the pricing practices of firms. Petitioners used to resort less frequently to the CVD law than to its AD counterpart, but that was attributable primarily to a rule by which nonmarket economies such as China were legally immune from CVD cases. After the Department of Commerce did away with that rule in 2007, and Congress codified the reinterpretation in 2012, the pace of CVD petitioning began to catch up with the AD filings.

---

[10] These statutes include Section 406 of the Trade Act of 1974 (discussed later in this chapter) and Section 122 of that same law (allowing the president to impose restrictions against countries with large balance of payments surpluses). The Trading with the Enemy Act of 1917 and the International Emergency Economic Powers Act of 1977 might be classified either as trade-remedy laws or as instruments of economic warfare.

While the AD and CVD laws are treated as quasi-judicial statutes that are theoretically not subject to policymakers' whims, decisions to invoke the safeguards law are quite explicitly a matter of policy. Also known as the "escape clause," the global safeguards law[11] is a mechanism that allows domestic industries to petition for relief when import competition – fair or unfair – is alleged to cause serious injury. The safeguard first appeared in a bilateral agreement with Mexico in 1942, which allowed either government to withdraw any tariff concession if it found that "as a result of unforeseen developments" the product in question was "being imported in such increased quantities and under such conditions as to cause or threaten serious injury to domestic producers." This innovation was so popular in Congress that legislators demanded its replication in all future trade agreements, thus leading to the enshrinement of this mechanism in GATT Article XIX. The current safeguard law requires that the USITC determine whether increasing imports are a substantial cause of serious injury to the domestic industry. If its injury determination is positive, the commission will recommend a remedy (e.g., quotas or tariffs). The president then has wide discretion to accept, reject, or modify the commission's recommendations.

The national security statute is the most obscure of the principal trade-remedy laws. As discussed in Chapters 7 and 16, this law and its counterpart in multilateral trade law (GATT Article XXI) could pose a greater danger to the system than any of the other trade-remedy statutes. The origins of this law stretch back to the early 1950s, when American military planners (and the US coal industry) were worried by rising oil imports from the Middle East. This combination of security and protectionist concerns led in 1955 to the enactment of a law permitting the president to restrict imports for reasons of national security. President Eisenhower did just that the very next year, when the Suez Crisis – a Byzantine affair in which England, France, and Israel deceived the United States and invaded Egypt[12] – demonstrated that global energy markets were vulnerable to disruption. The 1955 law was later recast as Section 232 of the Trade Expansion Act of 1962, which gave the president broad authority to impose restrictions whenever goods are "being imported into the United States in such quantities or under such circumstances as to threaten to impair the national security." Investigations can be initiated either by petition from

[11] The discussion here concerns only the *global* safeguard under Section 201 of the Trade Act of 1974. Among the other safeguard mechanisms is one providing for rapid restrictions on perishable agricultural products.

[12] See Yergin (1991), chapter 24.

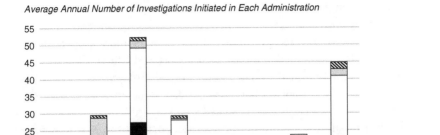

Average Annual Number of Investigations Initiated in Each Administration

FIGURE 3.3 Activity under the trade-remedy laws in presidential administrations, 1975–2017.

Note : Data are averages of full calendar years, including presidents' first year in office. Data for the Ford administration begin with the entry into force of the Trade Act of 1974 (January 3, 1975); data for the Trump administration are for calendar year 2017. AD and CVD cases are based on products rather than partners (e.g., if simultaneous petitions are filed against imports of a given product from three countries that is counted as one petition rather than three).

Sources: Compiled from US Department of Commerce at www.bis.doc.gov/index .php/forms-documents/section-232-investigations/86-section-232-booklet/file; US International Trade Commission at www.usitc.gov/trade_remedy/documents/his torical_case_stats.pdf, usitc.gov/trade_remedy/731_ad_701_cvd/investigations.htm, and www.usitc.gov/trade_remedy/documents/historical_case_stats.pdf; and World Bank at http://siteresources.worldbank.org/INTTRADERESEARCH/Resources/54 4824–1272916036631/7031714–1273097663359/7045138–1465854420750/GAD-USA.xls and http://siteresources.worldbank.org/INTTRADERESEARCH/Resources/54482 4–1272916036631/7031714–1273097858474/7045167–1465917411576/GCVD-USA.xls.

private interests, or by the administration on its own authority. The Department of Commerce conducts these investigations, receiving views from all other relevant government agencies (including the Pentagon).

Patterns in the Use of the Trade-Remedy Laws

The data in Figure 3.3 show the rise and fall, as well as an apparent revival, in the use of the trade-remedy laws since 1975. The trends generally confirm that resort to these laws peaked during the Reagan administration, when the average annual number of petitions was more than twice that of the Ford administration, but fell thereafter. It is unclear whether the later rise represents the start of a wholly new trend. The increase in petitioning under the Obama administration can be largely attributed to the aforementioned reinterpretation of CVD law, which led to a surge in filings against China. That rise was quite small compared to the sudden jump in the first year of the Trump administration. We do not yet have enough data to determine whether the stepped-up petitioning of 2017 represented a blip or a sustained trend.

The data also illustrate the shifting preferences that petitioners have for the distinct statutes. The modern era of US trade law began with enactment of the Trade Act of 1974, the first effect of which was to inspire nineteen industries to file safeguard petitions in just two years. The petitioners' expectations for ready relief were unwarranted. Six of these original nineteen cases were blocked by negative USITC determinations, and President Ford opted to provide protection for just three of the rest. That set a general pattern for Ford's successors, with either the commission or the president ruling out protection more often than not. Considering this low success rate, it is not surprising that petitioning fell in each succeeding administration (apart from a minor uptick in the Clinton administration) until it reached zero under Obama.

The second reason for the evaporation of safeguard petitions is that the WTO essentially outlawed this instrument. That was not the explicit intent of the Uruguay Round negotiators who drafted the Agreement on Safeguards, but dispute-settlement panels have interpreted that instrument in a way that makes it all but impossible for any country's safeguard measures to pass legal muster. From the time that the new agreement came into effect in 1995, nearly every country that has resorted to safeguard measures has seen them challenged, and every challenge thus far has led to a determination that the country violated the agreement. The United States conducted ten global safeguards investigations during 1995–2002, half of which led to the imposition of restrictions, but all of these actions were promptly challenged and then condemned in dispute-settlement cases. The last gasp seemed to come when George W. Bush fulfilled a campaign pledge by using this law to impose tariffs and tariff-rate quotas on steel imports in 2002. This offered only a temporary reprieve, with the United States lifting the restrictions after inevitably losing the WTO dispute-settlement case in 2003. The law then went into a deep freeze.[13] As discussed in Chapter 16, however, the Trump administration revived this statute in 2018 by granting protection to producers of washing machines and solar panels.

---

[13]   In 2016 the United Steelworkers filed, but almost immediately withdrew, a safeguard petition against aluminum.

The AD and CVD laws took up the slack for industries that were disappointed by safeguards. This fallback became even more prominent after enactment of the Trade Agreements Act of 1979, which some wit dubbed the Trade Lawyers Full Employment Act. Although the main purpose of this law was to approve the agreements reached in the Tokyo Round of GATT, this legislation also amended the AD law in ways that significantly aided petitioners. Congress frequently tweaked these laws in the decades that followed, with most amendments aimed at bending the laws toward the protectionist's definition of justice. Some of the changes were later undone in response to rulings by WTO dispute-settlement panels. These revisions have generally had the expected effect on the level of filing, rising with the enactment of laws that favor petitioners and then receding if those rules were reversed, but they may have had only a marginal impact on the general, downward trend that began around 1990. The data for 2017 suggest that this trend may have reversed in the Trump administration. That may be doubly true if the administration builds on a precedent it set that year, when for the first time in decades the Department of Commerce self-initiated a case without first awaiting a petition from the private sector.

Like the global safeguards law, the Section 232 national security statute demonstrates the trend by which the enactment of a law leads to an initial surge of filings, but activity drops off as petitioners discover how reluctant presidents are to invoke the statute. In actual practice most Section 232 cases have dealt with oil. Presidents used this and its predecessor statute to impose restrictions on oil imports five times, but prior to 2018 the law was used only twice on behalf of other industries. The most high-profile of these non-energy cases was a 1985–1986 episode concerning machine tools, in which President Reagan opted to negotiate voluntary restraint agreements with Germany, Japan, Switzerland, and Taiwan, and otherwise support the industry.[14] A 1981 ferroalloy case likewise led to an increase in Defense Department stockpiling. Other petitioners under Section 232 had to walk away disappointed, including producers of manganese and chromium, bearings, watches, circuit breakers, fasteners, and chemical equipment.

It appeared for years as if Section 232 had fallen into utter disuse, but one of the first acts of the Trump administration was to revive this mechanism. As is discussed in Chapter 16, the White House self-initiated investigations in 2017 against steel and aluminum, and these led in 2018 to the imposition of tariffs and a very high-profile round of tit-for-tat retaliation and counter-retaliation

---

[14] See National Security Decision Directive Number 226, "Machine Tools and National Security" (May 21, 1986).

with US trading partners. The Trump administration initiated a new Section 232 case in 2018, this time focused on the automotive sector. This indiscriminate use of the national security law, and the implied willingness to abuse the corresponding exceptions clause in the WTO,[15] posed what may be the greatest threat to the multilateral trading system by an administration that views trade relations through a mercantilist lens.

The Reciprocity Laws

As discussed in Chapter 2, the term *reciprocity* means a policy in which US objectives are pursued by threatening or imposing sanctions unilaterally rather than by offering to negotiate mutually beneficial agreements.[16] The Kennedy administration formalized the latest iteration of this policy in Section 252 of the Trade Expansion Act of 1962, which in turn morphed into Section 301 of the Trade Act of 1974. That law remains (as amended) the principal US reciprocity statute, supplemented by several others that are based on the same template.

The reciprocity laws were rarely invoked during the height of American hegemony. The principal exception to this rule was the Chicken War that the Johnson administration fought with the European Community, with the community's poultry-import restrictions leading in 1963 to a 25% retaliatory tariff on pick-up trucks. (That "chicken tax" was curiously imposed on a most-favored-nation rather than a targeted basis, and eventually had a greater impact on US-Japanese automotive trade and investment than on imports from Europe.) It was not until the 1980s that Section 301 became a major element in US trade policy, with the Reagan administration using the threat of retaliation in both a tactical and a strategic fashion. Beyond the immediate complaint that was at issue in any given case, the broader strategy of the White House was to threaten the aggressive use of unilateral enforcement if US partners did not agree to hold multilateral negotiations on the "new issues" of services, investment, and intellectual property rights. As discussed in Chapter 5, the law allowed US officials to characterize their objectives as legal rights that other countries were alleged to violate. These rights were more firmly established in domestic law than in the positive law of international agreements, leading analysts and partner countries to see matters in an entirely different light. Critics declared that these proposals were "thinly-disguised

---

[15] See Chapter 7 for a discussion of the legal and political significance of GATT Article XXI.
[16] That is to be distinguished from the common use of the term in the WTO, where "reciprocity" means the balance of concessions that are made by the participants in a negotiation.

protectionism" that would "risk trade wars through counter-retaliation"[17] and create "a poisoned atmosphere that conventional protectionists can hope to exploit for their own advantage."[18]

Section 301 was far more popular in Congress, which has always looked with greater favor on unilateral means of removing foreign barriers than it has on their mutual, negotiated reduction. This was a high priority for the omnibus trade bills of 1984 and 1988, each of which included provisions intended to force the administration's hand. For example, a new "Super 301" law required that the USTR identify specific foreign practices as targets for retaliatory trade cases. A similar statute known as "Special 301" provided for annual reviews of countries' intellectual property practices, and gave USTR the authority to threaten or impose sanctions. The omnibus trade bills of the 1980s also included several more specific reciprocity provisions dealing with such issues as government procurement, financial services, and telecommunications.

The reciprocity laws returned to their former obscurity after the Uruguay Round. This was the product of a grand bargain by which other countries made significant (if incomplete) concessions to the substance of Washington's demands on the new issues, producing agreements on services, intellectual property rights, and investment. In return, Washington agreed to a new institutional order that rested on two points. The first was replacement of the provisional GATT by the WTO, a bona fide international organization that represented a revival of the old American-sponsored (but congressionally rejected) International Trade Organization (ITO). The second institutional reform was the creation of an even stronger Dispute Settlement Understanding (DSU) that differed from its GATT predecessor in several respects. The new trade court does not allow any country to block a case by abusing the rule of consensus, it covers the full range of WTO agreements with a unified system, and is backed by an Appellate Body that provides greater consistency to the interpretation of the rules. In short, this compromise gave Washington recourse to international rules on the new issues, but required that disputes be adjudicated in the WTO rather than by national fiat. That change may also have improved the US chances for success in any given case. Pelc found that disputes in the WTO were more likely to produce the desired results than had unilateral cases. State threats that take multilateral form are typically seen as legitimate claims to which a country can bend without losing face, according to this logic, but unilateral threats may make the target state dig in its heels.[19]

---

[17] Cline (1982), p. 7.
[18] Bhagwati (1990), p. 36.
[19] Pelc (2010).

Article 23 of the DSU amounts to a tacit rebuke of the reciprocity policy, stating that when a member "seek[s] the redress of a violation" it "*shall* have recourse to, and abide by, the rules and procedures of this Understanding" (emphasis added). And if that were not explicit enough, the second paragraph specifies that WTO members shall not unilaterally "make any determination to the effect that a violation has occurred ... except through recourse to dispute settlement in accordance with the rules and procedures of this Understanding." Presumably feeling that this rule was sufficiently clear, the WTO membership took a collective pass when in 1999 it had an opportunity to hammer another nail into Section 301's coffin. The European Union had contended that the continued existence of this law was inconsistent with US obligations under the DSU, but the panel in *US – Section 301* adopted a diplomatic compromise. While the panel report conceded that the law appeared to violate Article 23, it also accepted US assurances that the law would be implemented only in accordance with WTO obligations.[20] In a turnabout, the European Union was later found in *EC – Commercial Vehicles* to have violated this DSU provision by taking unilateral action against Korea.[21]

This is yet another area where the Trump administration revisited what seemed to have been a settled matter of law and policy. The United States had discontinued its use of Section 301 in 1997, but exactly twenty years later the USTR initiated an investigation under this law into Chinese acts, policies, and practices related to technology transfer, intellectual property, and innovation. The announcement of this Section 301 case made no mention of the relevant WTO agreement or the rationale by which the USTR decided not to bring the matter to the multilateral system.[22] It instead implied that, in a throwback to pre-Uruguay Round practices, the United States would define and enforce its rights via domestic law rather than international institutions. The retaliatory measures announced in 2018 preceded, rather than followed, the initiation of a formal US complaint in the WTO. As discussed in Chapter 16, this development is second only to the aforementioned Section 232 cases in the existential threat that it poses to the multilateral trading system.

---

[20] The documents and details are posted at www.wto.org/english/tratop_e/dispu_e/cases_e/d s152_e.htm.

[21] See on this point Davey (2012), p. 47. Fittingly but improbably, this EU case happened to be numbered DS301. The documents and details of this case are posted at www.wto.org/english/ tratop_e/dispu_e/cases_e/ds301_e.htm.

[22] https://ustr.gov/about-us/policy-offices/press-office/press-releases/2017/august/ustr-announces-initiation-section.

The Shifting Composition of Sanctions

Trade sanctions are yet another instrument of US foreign economic policy that rose in importance toward the end of the Cold War, only to fade for a time after the West won that generational conflict. They have since been revived as a means of dealing with specific adversaries, especially Russia and "rogue" states in the developing world, but there are now at least as many American voices raised in opposition to sanctions as there are advocates for their use. For reasons that are more fully explored in Chapter 10, this is precisely what we would expect for a country that has seen its leverage diminish and its vulnerability rise.

The Soviet Union's autarkic economic strategy made Western economic sanctions ineffective in the short term, as it gave the Soviets a great buffer from Western pressure, and in the long term that same strategy made sanctions redundant. By attempting to isolate its economy from greed, class exploitation, and imperialism, Moscow also eschewed the benefits of competition and the positive side of Creative Destruction. The same command economy that could accomplish near-miracles in military and paramilitary sectors (e.g., the space race), with the native genius of Russian scientists being enhanced by espionage and German war booty, failed to deliver the more mundane goods that consumers demand. The Soviet stagnation confounded the forecasts of those US strategists who expected economic instruments to be key weapons in the Cold War. The CIA overestimated the resources that the Soviets would have at their disposal, warning in 1948 that Moscow might use "conventional business transactions for unconventional surprise attacks" such as raids on the stock and bond markets, forcing price disruptions through the preclusive buying or dumping of goods, etc.[23] Another CIA analyst predicted in 1956 that "the industrial production of the USSR will equal that of the United States by 1975."[24] That year would instead see a US economy 2.3 times larger than its Soviet counterpart.[25]

Similarly misplaced worries over the growth of the Soviet economy inspired Congress to enact Section 406 of the Trade Act of 1974, a narrowly focused trade-remedy law that allows the president to restrict imports from Communist countries. Just ten industries sought action under this law over the next three decades, only two of them targeting the Soviet Union. The anhydrous

---

[23] Central Intelligence Agency, "Possibility and Prevention of Unconventional Economic Warfare Attacks against the United States and Her Allies" (November 4, 1948), p. 1.

[24] Central Intelligence Agency, "Economic Warfare: Lecture to the Industrial College of the Armed Forces" [name of lecturer deleted] (March 26, 1956), p. 3.

[25] Calculated from Maddison (2003), pp. 274–275.

ammonia cases were almost comical. The USITC initially reached an affirmative injury finding in 1979, but President Carter decided that the recommended import restrictions were not in the national interest. The Soviet invasion of Afghanistan led him to reverse course in 1980, imposing a one-year emergency quota and requesting that the commission reinvestigate. Now it was the USITC's turn for second thoughts, voting 3–2 that the Soviet imports no longer injured the US industry. This decision terminated the president's temporary quota.[26] The only other Soviet case ended in 1983 when the USITC found that ferrosilicon imports caused no injury.

In a hint of future developments, China was targeted by seven of the remaining eight industries that filed petitions under Section 406 during 1977–1993.[27] Even in the waning days of the Cold War, however, one needed real foresight to believe that the Chinese economy would grow as fast as it did. In 1989, when the Chinese military put down the pro-democracy movement in Tiananmen Square, China still accounted for just 3% of US imports. There then followed nearly a decade of repeated debates in Washington, first real and then ritualized, over the renewal or withdrawal of MFN treatment from China. The United States would not fully normalize trade relations with China until 2000 (see Chapter 12).

In the dozen years that separate the fall of the Berlin Wall (1989) from the toppling of the twin towers (2001), Washington was more interested in sanctions reform than in the imposition of new restrictions. That trend was reinforced by three developments in 1990–1991 that seemed to obviate the need for these instruments, namely elections in Nicaragua and Russia and the end of South African *apartheid*. Even after the Long War began in 2001, the United States turned more often to preferences than to sanctions as a tool of foreign policy.

THE POSITIVE TOOLS: MULTILATERAL AND DISCRIMINATORY LIBERALIZATION

The end of the Cold War coincided with several important developments in trade negotiations. They included in 1994 the entry into force of NAFTA and the creation of the WTO, fulfilling aims that had been repeatedly frustrated in past generations. That same year also saw the emergence of mega-regional negotiations, with the Clinton administration launching ambitious talks with partners in both the Americas and the Pacific Basin. These initiatives were

---

[26] This case is recounted in Baker and Cunningham (1983), p. 380.

[27] For the full list of Section 406 cases see US International Trade Commission (2010).

followed by many smaller FTA negotiations in 2000 and beyond. Free traders had every reason to believe that the new millennium inaugurated an age in which a flurry of bilateral, regional, mega-regional, and multilateral negotiations would create an open world market and consign the tired, old North-South and East-West divisions to a distant past.

These hopes proved to be quixotic. Even as countries launched new trade negotiations, it became increasingly clear that the obsolete divisions of the Cold War were being replaced by new fractures. Negotiators repeatedly failed to carry trade talks all the way from conception to implementation. Some of the negotiations in which the United States engaged from 1994 through 2015 did succeed, but the progress was primarily limited to FTAs with smaller partners. The fiascoes included several bilateral and sub-regional negotiations, as well as three mega-regional initiatives and one multilateral round.

The Coalescence and Decay of the Multilateral System

The Uruguay Round may have created unrealistic expectations, having been negotiated in a period that appears more optimistic in retrospect than it seemed at the time. It came closer to achieving an ideal outcome than any of the previous GATT rounds, with ambitions actually growing from launch to conclusion. Three key elements that made it into the final package had not been contemplated at the start, chief among them being the WTO itself. This new institution represents an updated version of the failed ITO, having a wider jurisdiction and stricter dispute-settlement procedures than the GATT. This development was not even broached until Canadian and European officials floated the idea four years into the negotiations. And while the round had been launched on the basis of a "single undertaking," the meaning of that principle would undergo a fundamental change over the course of the round. Originally understood to be only a norm by which all issues on the table had equal standing – nothing was decided until everything was decided – it became instead a highly ambitious rule that bundled everything into a package deal. As finally implemented, the single undertaking obliged all WTO members to sign on to all of the agreements reached in that round, and even to adopt some older agreements that had previously been optional. The Uruguay Round negotiators also transformed a rather modest and technical mandate to review the functioning of the GATT system into a Trade Policy Review Mechanism that subjected all members to periodic examinations of their trade regimes.[28]

---

[28] See chapters 2 and 8 of VanGrasstek (2013).

Another important distinction is that Congress rejected the ITO Charter but approved the WTO, enacting the implementing legislation for the Uruguay Round in 1994. The significance of that point has diminished over time. American participation in the GATT received only tacit support in Congress, but this did not prevent the United States from engaging actively in that body for nearly half a century. By contrast, Washington's support for the WTO already looked wobbly when the institution was scarcely a decade old. That could first be seen in the redirection of US negotiating energy from multilateral to bilateral and regional undertakings, especially after the Doha Round took a bad turn in 2003, then in the round's living death after another disappointment in 2008, and finally in the Trump administration's denunciation of all things multilateral.

One consequence of the Law of Uneven Growth, combined with the broader WTO membership and its more democratic procedures, is a fundamental shift in global governance. The multilateral system had long been informally led by a Group of Two, with the original G-2 of the United States and the United Kingdom eventually giving way to an EU–US group. For decades these G-2 members reserved their commercial dealings with one another almost entirely to the multilateral system. Other countries frequently objected to a restricted, "green room" approach in which the major GATT decisions were made chiefly by the Quad (i.e., the G-2 plus Canada and Japan), a few other developed countries, and even fewer developing countries (principally Brazil and India), but the arrangement was undeniably productive. The G-2, and especially its Anglo-American component, made its last hurrah in the closing days of the Uruguay Round. The negotiations might never have been concluded if the US Trade Representative (Mickey Kantor) was not working with an EU trade commissioner from the United Kingdom (Leon Brittan) and a GATT director-general who was the type of Irishman whom Americans can readily mistake for an Englishman (Peter Sutherland). When this North Atlantic triumvirate cleared the main hurdles in 1993 it was the last time that the global community would entrust the outcome of a round to such an anachronistically narrow circle.

It took the system precisely a decade to confirm that this was the case. The WTO's Cancún ministerial meeting of 2003 was pivotal not just for the Doha Round but also for the trading system as a whole. In the run-up to that meeting, EU Trade Commissioner Pascal Lamy and US Trade Representative Robert Zoellick unveiled a deal to solve the Doha Round, and under the old rules they might well have succeeded. They instead epically failed to win over the rest of the WTO membership, with some developing countries protesting that the EU–US proposal did not go far enough and others claiming just the opposite. Until then, it had seemed that agreement between Washington and Brussels was both the necessary and sufficient condition for bringing any round to a successful conclusion. It has since been apparent that transatlantic concordance is no longer sufficient, and some wonder if it even remains necessary. Those doubts were prominent in 2008, when the largest members of the WTO tried once more to resolve the Doha Round in a mini-ministerial meeting. This time the collapse was chalked up to the inability of China and the United States to agree on Beijing's share of the burden, as well as India's unwillingness to shoulder even a token portion of it. The European Union had played a key part in setting the stage for this drama, and was in the green room for its final act, but by that time it was more a horrified spectator than a leading actor.

One reason for the decay of multilateralism is the diluted sense of a shared strategic purpose. WTO members are not divided by the old antagonisms of the Cold War, but neither are they united by them. The rising powers in the new institution include some original GATT contracting parties that had already been influential in the old order, especially Brazil and India, as well as others that did not accede until after the WTO was established. Chief among them are China and Russia, which respectively joined in 2001 and 2012; other new, large entrants included Taiwan (2002), Saudi Arabia (2005), and Vietnam (2007). Universality, diversity, and democracy come at a cost, as there is an inverse relationship between the number of decision-makers in a system and the efficiency with which it can act. No objective observer could say that the nearly universal WTO has executed its legislative function as effectively as did the smaller, more cohesive GATT club. It did produce some agreements during the post–Uruguay Round period of the "built-in agenda" (1995–2000), such as the Information Technology Agreement and several protocols on trade in services, but the launch of the Doha Round in 2001 marked the start of an especially unproductive run.

FTAs as Complements and Substitutes for Multilateral Agreements

The creation of the WTO, which culminated a half-century of progress toward a comprehensive and multilateral trade regime, came just when many of its most prominent members began negotiating discriminatory agreements in earnest. As an ideal, the trading system has long sought to achieve two seemingly complementary objectives: the reduction or elimination of trade barriers and an end to discrimination. The proliferation of FTAs implies that countries are willing to sacrifice nondiscrimination in pursuit of liberaliza- tion. The net results have been dubious: Each new failure in the WTO encourages countries to fall back on the Plan B of regionalism, and the political capital that they invest in FTAs comes at the WTO's expense.

Most of the FTA negotiations that the United States pursued before the WTO era complemented its multilateral initiatives. The Uruguay Round was quite deliberately bookended by the negotiations over the US–Canada FTA (begun in 1986 and concluded in 1988) and the North American FTA with Canada and Mexico (begun in 1991, concluded in 1992, and revised in 1993). The precedential nature of these FTAs, and where they fit in the larger US negotiating strategy, is reviewed in Chapter 5. The same may not be said for the much wider set of FTAs that the Clinton and Bush administrations launched between 2000 and 2005, when two successive administrations engaged in the trade policy equivalent of speed-dating. Many of these FTAs were discrete, transactional arrangements that they promoted more as rewards to favored political partners than for their commercial or precedential value. Negotiators also turned to the mega-regional option with the launch of the Trans-Pacific Partnership (TPP) in 2008 and Transatlantic Trade and Investment Partnership (TTIP) in 2013.

These initiatives often stumbled. Like Tolstoy's unhappy families, each of which are unhappy in their own way, every failed bilateral and regional initiative collapsed for reasons of its own. Some negotiations got bogged down by dealing with topics for which the US partner had more enthusiasm than capacity. "Thailand entered these talks with an almost total lack of preparation," the US embassy in Bangkok observed in early 2006, "and has fielded an FTA team inexperienced in negotiating anything remotely like the comprehensive trade and investment deal we are seeking."[29] That technical shortcoming might have been remedied with sufficient capacity-building, but the negotiations were suspended after the Royal Thai Army staged a coup later that year. Other negotiations failed as a result of negotiators' inability to wrap things up before the US grant of negotiating authority expired (Malaysia), a dispute over an unfriendly act of Congress (United Arab Emirates),[30] an election that brought a trade-skeptical government to power (Ecuador), or the partner's realization that it already got most of what it wanted from an existing preferential trade program (Southern African Customs Union).

This was a period when "competitive liberalization" was supposed to prod countries into negotiations at all levels of aggregation, such that bilaterals would impel regionals and even mega-regionals, and those negotiations would

---

[29] "Why Is This FTA Taking So Long?," cable of February 6, 2006, from the US embassy in Bangkok (06BANGKOK689_a).

[30] This case is recounted in Chapter 15.

in turn goose the multilateral talks. As it happened, mega-regional negotiations proved to be especially fragile. Prior to the TPP, the abortive Free Trade Area of the Americas (FTAA) and the free trade pact planned in the Asia Pacific Economic Cooperation (APEC) forum were the most important examples of failed mega-regionals. Both of these negotiations were launched in 1994 to establish free trade across wide geographic expanses, and both were undone by internal disputes. The APEC initiative began to crumble when countries demanded that their "sacred cows" (e.g., fish in Japan) be isolated from liberalization, with the exceptions soon growing so large as to make the rule seem unworthy of pursuit. The FTAA negotiations were plagued from the start by the perennial rivalry between the United States and Brazil, and matters only got worse with the emergence of a trade-skeptical bloc led by Cuba on the outside and by Venezuela on the inside. Each of these mega-regionals then fragmented into smaller initiatives, including numerous US FTAs reached during 2003–2006, several of which coalesced in the TPP. Every TPP country had previously been engaged in negotiating the FTAA, APEC, or both, and many of them reached bilateral agreements with one another between the collapse of those talks and the launch of the TPP.

In a pattern that may now sound monotonous, Donald Trump once more disowned the policies that he inherited. Just three days after he took the oath of office, the president directed the USTR "to permanently withdraw the United States from TPP negotiations, and to begin pursuing, wherever possible, bilateral trade negotiations to promote American industry, protect American workers, and raise American wages."[31] The only difference here is that one cannot assume that matters would otherwise have turned out differently. Hillary Clinton expressed doubts about the TPP during the 2016 presidential campaign, as had many congressional leaders. One can only speculate on whether a Clinton administration would ultimately have approved or rejected the TPP, or renegotiated it. The last of those options was probably the most likely, but that is now a matter of pure speculation.

FTAs as a Tool of Foreign Policy

If discriminatory agreements were so difficult to conclude and approve, why did Presidents Clinton, Bush, and Obama initiate so many of them? A few of these negotiations can be explained by traditional motives of export-promotion and job-creation, especially the mega-regionals and the FTA with

---

[31] www.whitehouse.gov/presidential-actions/presidential-memorandum-regarding-withdrawal-united-states-trans-pacific-partnership-negotiations-agreement/.

Korea. The great majority, however, can be seen more as inducements for the achievement of other aims. This association of trade preferences with foreign policy is an old story, as is the recognition that countries' perspectives on this issue are a function of their relative sizes. In his review of customs unions in the first half of the twentieth century, Viner observed an important distinction in talks between great and small powers. For a great power, "political objectives were the important ones, while the economic consequences of customs union were regarded without enthusiasm or even accepted only as a necessary price which had to be paid to promote a political end." The smaller partner would instead be attracted only by the economic opportunity, "while the political aspects were thought of as involving risks which might have to be accepted for the sake of the economic benefits with which they were unfortunately associated."[32] Those precise words could have been written six decades later.

Power figures prominently when Washington chooses its FTA partners, even if those partners focus instead on wealth. This is suggested by a single, revealing statistic: Out of eighteen countries in which the United States had major military bases in 2017, fourteen were actual or intended FTA partners (prior to Trump's election). These overlapping military and commercial circles encompass four countries with which FTAs were then in effect,[33] nine that would have been in the stalled TTIP,[34] and one TPP participant (Japan). The only friendly countries[35] with major bases that remain outside the FTA family are Norway, Qatar,[36] and Turkey. Another way to consider the security-trade nexus is to peruse the list of Major Non-NATO Allies (MNNAs), a formal designation that presidents have bestowed on seventeen countries. This group includes six countries with which the United States has FTAs,[37] four with which negotiations were conducted but not consummated,[38] and six with which FTAs were under consideration during George W. Bush's presidency.[39] Afghanistan is the only MNNA that never came close to negotiating

---

[32] Viner (1950), pp. 91–92.
[33] Australia, Bahrain, Korea, and Singapore.
[34] Belgium, Denmark (Greenland), Germany, Greece, Hungary, Italy, the Netherlands, Spain, and the United Kingdom.
[35] Cuba also hosts a US naval base, but does so under protest and cannot be considered a friendly partner.
[36] The United States and Qatar explored FTA negotiations during the Bush administration, but never launched them.
[37] Australia, Bahrain, Israel, Jordan, Korea, and Morocco.
[38] These include failed talks that were bilateral (Thailand), in the Free Trade Area of the Americas (Argentina), or the Trans-Pacific Partnership (Japan and New Zealand).
[39] Egypt, Kuwait, Pakistan, the Philippines, Taiwan, and Tunisia.

an FTA with the United States. The NATO allies include one FTA partner (Canada) and one group with which it engaged in abortive FTA negotiations (the European Union).

The links between foreign and trade policy were especially strong during George W. Bush's presidency, which was also the highpoint for FTA negotiations. Seventeen of the twenty actual FTA partners of the United States owe that status, in whole or in part, to actions taken during his tenure.[40] Nearly all of these talks, as well as a few FTA negotiations that the Bush administration initiated but was unable to complete, were associated with a narrow set of foreign policy goals. Ten of its FTA negotiations were with countries that joined the Coalition of the Willing, whether by providing troops or other support for the war in Iraq, and three other partners were members of regional groups in which one or more countries joined this alliance.[41] Six other FTA negotiating partners were moderate Arab or Muslim-majority states that cooperated in the Middle East peace process.[42] The only Bush-initiated FTA negotiation that did not fall into one of those three categories was with the Southern African Customs Union, which was largely inspired by domestic US political considerations; those talks eventually collapsed. This same set of objectives explains two of the three FTA negotiations that the Bush administration inherited from the Clinton administration, which included one future member of the Coalition of the Willing (i.e., Singapore) and one moderate Arab state (i.e., Jordan). Chile was the exception that proved the rule, but even its FTA got entangled in the run-up to the Second Gulf War by an unfortunate coincidence of timing (see Chapter 14).

The partners themselves had varying motivations for negotiating FTAs with the United States. Beyond an often exaggerated notion of just how great a boost they might expect from preferential access to a market that was already fairly open, regional jealousies and concerns over prestige were an important

[40] The Bush administration convinced Congress to approve one completed FTA that it inherited (Jordan); concluded and won approval for two FTAs that were actively under negotiation when it took office (Chile and Singapore); and initiated, concluded, and pushed through Congress another six FTAs that covered eleven trading partners. The administration also gifted three unapproved FTAs to the Obama administration, as well as the TPP negotiations.

[41] These included nine countries with which the administration concluded FTAs (i.e., Australia, Colombia, Costa Rica, El Salvador, the Dominican Republic, Honduras, Korea, Nicaragua, and Panama) and one with which negotiations were incomplete (i.e., Thailand). The countries associated with these FTA/Coalition partners were Ecuador (incomplete negotiations), Guatemala, and Peru.

[42] These included three countries with which the administration concluded FTAs (i.e., Bahrain, Morocco, and Oman) and three with which negotiations were incomplete (i.e., Kuwait, Malaysia, and the United Arab Emirates).

motivation. One reason why Kuwait and the United States actively explored an FTA in 2004–2005 was that Kuwaiti officials found it embarrassing that their neighbors in Oman and the United Arab Emirates were already in that queue.[43] Similarly, "Morocco beating Tunisia to the punch in achieving an FTA with the US has left the Tunisians consciously envious of Morocco's enhanced status and desiring to join the club."[44] This phenomenon was not limited to the Middle East. Prime Minister Helen Clark "as well as most of the politicians in New Zealand, seek the coveted FTA with US," according to a 2006 cable from the embassy in Wellington, "mainly because Australia got one."[45] Several other potential partners knocked on the door during the Bush administration, but did not get the answer that they wanted. To varying degrees of seriousness, FTA negotiations were preliminarily explored with Egypt, Kuwait, Mongolia, the Philippines, Qatar, Sri Lanka, Taiwan, Tunisia, and Uruguay. The failure to launch sometimes reflected no more than an inherent limitation on the number of FTA negotiations that the USTR could properly conduct at one time.

WHERE THE SYSTEM STOOD BEFORE THE RISE OF TRUMP

In a seeming contradiction, the aforementioned trend against protectionism coincided with unexpectedly high levels of internal and external opposition to new trade agreements. The end result is that trade policymaking from the presidencies of George H. W. Bush through Barack Obama became more difficult *in both directions* than it had once been. Economic and political elites seemed to have grown less interested in demanding or supplying protection not despite the rise in import penetration, but indeed because of it. Protectionism appears more threatening than enticing when a firm becomes more globalized in its investments, ownership, sources, and sales. At the same time, as is chronicled more fully in Chapter 4, legislators put up greater resistance to new trade agreements.

The apparent conundrum of "less protection *and* less liberalization" can be partly resolved by realizing that what has been at issue is not whether trade policy will move forward or backward, but that it instead shifted sideways. That movement is taken up in Chapter 5, which explains how the expanding scope

[43] See, for example, "Scenesetter for Secretary Rice's March 3–4, 2005 Visit to Kuwait," cable of February 22, 2005, from the US embassy in Kuwait City (05KUWAIT797_a).

[44] "Free Trade with the US: Are the Tunisians Ready?," cable of May 2, 2005, from the US embassy in Tunis (05TUNIS898_a).

[45] "Scenesetter for Visit of Adm[iral] Fallon and Gen[eral] Hester to New Zealand," cable of January 10, 2006, from the US embassy in Wellington (06WELLINGTON18_a).

of trade issues has produced a contagion of conflict in domestic politics. A field that was once treated as a subset of foreign and fiscal policy instead came to involve the conduct of social policy through other means, with trade agreements and disputes taking on such diverse and partisan topics as labor rights, the environment, and patent protection for pharmaceuticals. In contrast to the more traditional fights over free trade and protectionism, these newer issues could not as easily be resolved through accommodations and side payments.

This is not to say that those older, more traditionally commercial disputes had disappeared. While firms and professional politicians may have reconciled themselves to a more connected world, and old-school protectionism went out of style, they left behind a growing number of workers – or ex-workers – who did not share in the benefits of globalization. The neglect of this group created an underserved political market that Donald Trump was able to exploit, first by capturing the Republican Party nomination and then by winning an upset victory in the general election. Chapter 6 examines more precisely how these most traditional issues made a comeback in 2016, and what that might mean for the future.

4

The Domestic Diplomacy of Trade Agreements

Treaties formed by the Executive of the United States Are to be the Laws of the Land. To cloath the Executive with legislative authority, is setting aside our modern & much boasted distribution of Power into legislative, Judicial, and Executive – discoveries unknown to Locke & Montesquieu, and all the antient writers. It certainly contradicts all the Modern Theory of Government. And in practice must be Tyranny.

Senator William Maclay, diary entry (June 14, 1789)

INTRODUCTION

Scribbling in his diary exactly one month before a Parisian mob stormed the Bastille, Senator Maclay (1737–1804) fulminated against a less dramatic political revolution. Declaring that the executive's treaty power violated the checks and balances of the new constitutional system, this Pennsylvanian was the first in a long line of lawmakers to articulate a perennial anxiety: A president could transform his diplomatic authority into a virtual power to legislate. Those concerns are especially high for any international agreements dealing with matters that the Constitution reserves for domestic legislation. The tariff topped that list for the first century and a half of US independence.

For all else that has changed since 1789, the Constitution's provisions on foreign relations remain what Corwin famously deemed an "invitation to struggle."[1] The legislative branch typically wins that struggle when it comes to trade policy, either by exercising its constitutional prerogatives or by setting strict limits in delegations of authority to the executive. Congress experimented with such grants in the late nineteenth and early twentieth centuries, and has done so more thoroughly – but not permanently or freely – since the New Deal. This started in 1934 by giving the president the power to negotiate

---

[1] Corwin (1957), p. 171.

reciprocal tariff agreements, an authority that later gave way to a more expansive set of approval procedures for tariff and nontariff agreements. The "fast track," now known as trade promotion authority (TPA), did not constitute a comprehensive, permanent, or unconditional transfer of power. Every president from Franklin Roosevelt to Barack Obama had to bargain with Congress over the terms of his authority, and none of them could afford to take lawmakers' acquiescence for granted. The few who tried soon discovered how fiercely Maclay's successors defend the prerogatives of their institution.

Senator Maclay's fears over a power-hungry executive are mirrored in that same branch, where Congress is often seen as a meddlesome body that undermines presidential authority. Maclay and his fellows soon demonstrated their willingness to tread on diplomatic ground. President Washington had originally thought it proper for a chief executive not only to consult with the Senate after a treaty had been negotiated, but to do so prior to the negotiations – and in person. Actual experience quickly remedied his excessive solicitude toward a rival branch of government. Visiting the upper chamber in 1789 to discuss a treaty then slated for negotiation with the Southern Indians, Washington was appalled to discover just how seriously senators took their constitutional duty to provide not only their consent but their advice. After the lawmakers began proposing alterations in the administration's plans, according to the account passed down by John Quincy Adams (1767–1848), Washington grew so exasperated that when he "left the Senate Chamber he said he would be d–d if he ever went there again."[2]

This chapter reviews how the domestic diplomacy of trade agreements has evolved since the days of Washington and Maclay. The principal focus here is on how the two branches deal with one another in the development and pursuit of US trade objectives, and how domestic negotiations affect the external type. Two questions have always been pertinent. The simplest is whether lawmakers are willing to approve the agreements that presidents submit; the answer before 1934 was typically "no," but since then it has often been a negotiable "maybe." The second question concerns how lawmakers can leverage that conditional response, dickering with presidents who want to get to "yes." Will they make that approval contingent on changes to the executive's handiwork? Contrary to the common perception that under TPA rules Congress is now limited to simple, up-or-down votes, lawmakers still retain considerable power to shape agreements before, during, and even after the negotiations with trading partners. The bargaining can extend well beyond the agreement at hand, with legislators demanding – and often receiving –

---

[2] Quoted in Congressional Research Service (1984), p. 32.

presidential concessions on trade and other issues in exchange for the needed votes.

The US trade policymaking system is founded upon an unstable balance of power between the two branches, and the shifting postures of the two political parties can further exacerbate the disequilibrium. Considering the weakness with which the system is anchored, it is not surprising that it periodically slips its moorings and drifts aimlessly. Years may pass in which presidents may be denied new grants of authority, and when Congress either balks at agreements or sends them into legislative limbo. The greater surprise is that outright failures became rarer in the years after 1934 than they were in the preceding century. Not many pre–New Deal trade treaties won congressional approval, but since then Congress has rejected only a few. Even the setbacks can work to the advantage of American negotiators, allowing them to back up their frequent claims to foreign counterparts that a US demand must be met, or a foreign demand must be denied, if a proposed agreement is to have any chance of making it through Congress.

This analysis focuses on the system as it existed prior to the advent of Donald Trump. His election put in doubt two apparent constants in American trade diplomacy: Congress has ultimately approved every trade agreement negotiated since the first grant of fast-track authority in 1974, and the United States does not unilaterally abrogate any agreements once they are in force. In later chapters we will consider whether those points remain valid.

TREATY-MAKING BEFORE AND AFTER THE DELEGATION OF NEGOTIATING AUTHORITY

For all else that has changed over the past two centuries, trade is now and always has been subject to interbranch competition. This field of policy lies at the intersection of tax and foreign policy, with that first road being the one most traveled from 1789 to 1930, and policy taking a sharp turn after 1934. Congress remains much more than a backseat driver, however, and the two branches often fight over where policy ought to be headed and how it should get there.

The Constitutional Rules

Trade was no less an inspiration for the Constitution than it had been for the Declaration of Independence. James Madison (1751–1836) believed that the notoriously weak Articles of Confederation that preceded the Constitution had also prevented effective cooperation, deprived the government of tariff revenue, and left the states vulnerable to external exploitation and internal strife. He wrote in 1832 that if the Federal government had not developed the "power to regulate foreign commerce" the American people would "present the solitary and strange spectacle of a nation disarming itself of a power exercised by every nation as a shield against the effect of the power as used by other nations."[3]

While many of the Founders shared those concerns, they were also a cautious group who bore deep suspicions of executive authority. They therefore followed Madison's lead at the Constitutional Convention of 1787, devising a system of government that deliberately fragments power among competing institutions. Beyond such well-known checks and balances as the president's power to veto bills, and the countervailing power of Congress to override presidential vetoes, the drafters also posed a problem for future diplomats and lawmakers – not to mention US negotiating partners – by writing two contending provisions into the Constitution:

- **The Commerce Clause:** Article I, Section 8, Clause 3 gives Congress the power to "regulate Commerce with foreign Nations, and among the several States, and with the Indian Tribes."
- **The Treaty Power:** Article II, Section 2, Clause 2 states that the president "shall have Power, by and with the Advice and Consent of the Senate to make Treaties, provided two thirds of the Senators present concur."

Much of the history of US trade policymaking can be simplified as a clash between these two clauses, and a contest over whether policy will be made through the enactment of domestic or international law. For most of 1789–1933, Congress treated trade policy primarily as a branch of tax policy, and hence one in which it held the upper hand. Since that time, legislators have allowed the executive — on conditions — to treat trade as a topic for international negotiations.

The Treaty Power's two dozen words left it to the Senate to devise its own rules for the consideration of these instruments. The most unusual rule allows treaties to be amended as if they were ordinary bills. It was fittingly Senator Maclay who first proposed that a treaty be amended, moving in 1789 to strike a phrase from the same treaty that Washington had, to his regret, earlier come to discuss with the Senate. Maclay's amendment failed for want of a second, but no one objected in principle; his colleagues took it for granted that the motion was in order. It was not until the Jay Treaty of 1795 that the Senate

---

[3] James Madison to Professor Davis, available online at http://press-pubs.uchicago.edu/foun ders/documents/a1_8_3_commerces21.html. Also quoted in Bourgin (1989), pp. 40–41.

actually exercised this power. Even President Washington was disappointed with the trifling commercial concessions that John Jay brought back from London, and he accepted the treaty "only because he felt that its rejection meant war."[4] The Senate had no such compunction, and fixated on one especially irritating provision. Article 12 prohibited US carriers from transporting "any Molasses, Sugar, Coffee, Cocoa or Cotton in American vessels, either from His Majesty's [Caribbean] Islands or from the United States, to any part of the world, except the United States." The Senate gave its advice and consent solely "on condition that there be added to the said treaty an article" to suspend the offending language. President Washington or the Court of Saint James might well have blocked the Senate's aggrandizement of its authority if either of them summarily repulsed this as-yet unprecedented demand, but by ratifying the treaty and its additional article they explicitly consented not only to the specific revision but to the new senatorial power.[5]

Ever since then, senators have exercised and elaborated on their self-asserted right to revise treaties. They may do so by deleting articles, amending or even adding others, or otherwise shaping the meaning and interpretation of a treaty through reservations, understandings, and the like. The Gadsden Purchase Treaty of 1853, by which the United States bought a strip of land from Mexico for the transcontinental railroad, offers an extreme example. The Senate virtually rewrote the treaty, and even cut the price from $15 million to $10 million. The government of Mexico was then so impecunious that it accepted the treaty as amended.

The US treaty practice is also marked by lengthy delays, with the Senate's inaction often being a slightly less impolite form of rejection. While ordinary bills die if not acted on in the two-year congress in which they were introduced, treaties can remain live – or lead a zombie-like existence – for years or even decades. As of 2018, the most ancient instrument still moldering in the Senate Foreign Relations Committee's in-box was an International Labor Organization convention on the right to organize; it had been there ever since President Truman signed it in 1948. Another thirty-three treaties concluded during the twentieth century were also pending, and thirty others had been waiting for more than a decade.[6] The Senate's reputation as "the world's greatest deliberative body" may owe more to its pace than to its rhetorical excellence.

The Constitution is silent on the role of the House of Representatives in approving treaties, but most require the enactment of implementing

---

4   Beard (1915), p. 282.
5   See Bevans (1974), Volume 12, pp. 13–33 for the relevant texts.
6   Tabulated by the author from treaties listed at www.foreign.senate.gov/treaties/.

legislation. If a treaty cuts tariffs, for example, both chambers must approve a bill amending the tariff schedule. Here the House has an edge, with the Origination Clause of the Constitution (Article I, Section 7, Clause 1) providing that, "All Bills for raising Revenue shall originate in the House of Representatives; but the Senate may propose or concur with Amendments as on other Bills." One might suppose that the House would feel under a moral obligation to enact whatever implementing legislation may be needed to comply with any treaties that have won the requisite two-thirds approval in the Senate, but that view is not universally shared in the lower chamber. Lawmakers proved that in 1884, when the House refused to make the tariff changes necessary to implement a treaty with Mexico.[7]

How the Senate Handled Trade Treaties before 1934

Trade treaties faced several hurdles, not the least being congressional insistence that commerce is an exclusively legislative prerogative. Lawmakers drove that point home in 1844, when they refused to approve a treaty that the Tyler administration had negotiated with the German *Zollverein* (customs union). This was the first reciprocal trade agreement of the United States, but the Senate rejected it because legislators believed that the president had no constitutional authority to deal with commerce. Representatives reiterated that view in their aforementioned refusal to pass implementing legislation for the 1884 treaty with Mexico.

Table 4.1 summarizes the fate of trade treaties from Presidents Washington through Hoover. The Senate usually had no objection to treaties that merely granted MFN treatment (albeit in conditional form), but rejected almost all tariff-cutting agreements. Tariff treaties comprised the largest bloc of treaties that the Senate rejected.[8] Presidents submitted just twenty-seven such treaties to the Senate during 1789–1933, only five of which were ratified. Three of these treaties were defeated outright in a vote, with the requirement for a supermajority taking its toll (two of these three treaties would have been approved if a majority were sufficient). The main problem was that the rules made it easy for the opponents to block action altogether, as more than half of the twenty-seven tariff treaties never even got a vote.

The Senate's self-asserted power to amend treaties has long befuddled foreign statesmen whose own constitutional arrangements extend far less power to legislators, and who consider treaties to be inviolable deals.

---

[7] See Fisher (1985), p. 264.
[8] Fleming (1930), p. 72.

TABLE 4.1. *Senate Decisions on Trade Treaties, 1789–1933*
Raw numbers and percentages, for treaties submitted to the Senate for its advice and consent

	Not Brought to a Vote	Defeated by Amendment	Voted Down by Senate	Withdrawn by President	Approved by Senate	Total
US Tariff	15	1	3	3	5	27
Concessions	(55.6%)	(3.7%)	(11.1%)	(11.1%)	(18.5%)	(100.0%)
No US Tariff	3	8	0	0	131	142
Concessions	(2.1%)	(5.6%)	(0.0%)	(0.0%)	(92.3%)	(100.0%)
Total	18	9	3	3	136	169
	(10.7%)	(5.3%)	(1.8%)	(1.8%)	(80.5%)	(100.0%)

"Trade treaties" are defined here to include any treaties that make substantive commitments with respect to bilateral trade relations, typically including (but not always going beyond) the extension of MFN treatment.
Source: Calculated from Bevans (1968–1976) and Wiktor (1976–1994).

The Senate amended about one-fifth of all the treaties that it received before 1934.[9] Presidents have occasionally refused to complete the ratification process following the Senate's decision to amend a treaty. If the president is still willing to ratify it in altered form,[10] the other party to the agreement must either take it or leave it. They often left it, rejecting about one-third of the treaties that the Senate amended. This was sometimes just what a treaty's opponents intended, as they may find it easier to persuade other senators to kill a treaty by "improving" it, and thereby placing the onus on the other country.

For those few tariff-cutting treaties that the Senate approved in pre-hegemonic times, the partner was almost always an actual or potential candidate for annexation.[11] The sole exception to this rule was a minor agreement with France in 1832 that included a ten-year concession on wine; this was part

[9] According to Laski (1940), p. 189, the Senate amended 173 of 969 treaties submitted between 1789 and 1934. See also Wiktor (1976–1994), whose summary statistics (Volume 9, p. 358) show that 303 treaties submitted to the Senate during 1789–1976 were unperfected. The Senate was not responsible for the 67 that it approved without amendment, many of which failed to be ratified by the other part(ies). Of the 236 treaties that the Senate blocked, 132 (56%) were never acted on and 45 (19%) were defeated by amendment; only 16 (7%) were voted down.

[10] The power to ratify is often misunderstood. It is not the case that the Senate ratifies treaties; its power is limited to *consenting* to ratification. That power ultimately rests with the president, who may opt not to ratify a treaty even if the Senate gave its consent (e.g., if it approved an amendment that the president does not accept).

[11] This is not to suggest that territorial growth was always popular. Antebellum expansionist proposals were viewed through a sectional filter, such that Southern senators voted against new territories that were expected to vote with the free states and Northern senators voted against those aligned with slave states. Even after the Civil War, the failure to seize the opportunities

of an arbitration settlement rather than a bona fide trade agreement. All of the rest were either with an immediate neighbor, most notably a tariff agreement with Canada that lasted from 1854 to 1866 (see Chapter 9), or with island states whose destiny seemed manifest. Hawaii was the only one of these partners that eventually became a state, the annexation of 1898 having been preceded in 1875 by a reciprocal trade arrangement.[12] After the Spanish-American War of 1898 the United States reached a treaty that gave Cuba a 20% margin of preference in its access to the US market. The Senate also approved a tariff-reduction treaty with the independent country of Texas in 1843, but Texas did not accept it as amended by the Senate.

Changes in government can take their toll, as was exemplified by yet another commercial reciprocity treaty with Mexico. The negotiations began under the presidency of Franklin Pierce, and it was concluded between the 1856 presidential election and the swearing-in of President James Buchanan in 1857. Neither the outgoing nor the incoming president submitted this treaty to the Senate. This was not a matter of interparty rivalry; both men were Democrats, but Buchanan had wrested the party's presidential nomination from the incumbent Pierce (a common occurrence in the mid-nineteenth century). Something similar happened just after the 1884 election, when President Chester A. Arthur (a Republican) submitted to the Senate a set of treaties with the Dominican Republic and Spain (on behalf of Cuba and Puerto Rico), two of them extending MFN treatment to Cuba and Puerto Rico and three others providing reciprocal tariff concessions. The Senate approved the MFN treaties, but after Grover Cleveland (a Democrat) took office in 1885 he requested that the Senate return his predecessor's tariff-cutting treaties without further consideration. These episodes offer the only historical precedents for Donald Trump's decision in 2017 to erase the US signature on the Trans-Pacific Partnership.

Some other unperfected treaties are not shown in the table because they died either before or after the Senate got involved. Prior to the advent of modern communications, diplomats would sometimes negotiate pacts that exceeded their instructions. These were typically rejected by the president on arrival in Washington, as happened to a surprising number of mid-nineteenth-century MFN agreements with Mexico and Central American countries. There were also cases in which the United States approved a treaty, only to

---

for expansion can be attributed to what Zakaria (1998, p. 87) described as "a weak state structure that could not translate executive-branch schemes into government policy."

[12] Note, however, that the Senate had rejected in 1870 another tariff-reduction treaty with Hawaii.

be spurned by the other party. In one unique case, the Congress of the Dominican Republic turned the tables on the United States by amending an MFN treaty in 1854.[13] President Pierce withheld that treaty from the Senate.

One Adjustment to Standard Treaty Practice: Cafeteria Diplomacy

The difficulties in securing the Senate's consent inspired two responses from the executive. The most prominent was to develop alternative means for approving international agreements, as discussed in the next section. Another and subtler adaptation is what we might call "cafeteria diplomacy," a characteristically American practice by which policymakers select only those elements of a multilateral agreement that they wish to put into effect. Selectivity is not unique to US diplomacy, as other countries are free to lodge reservations to multilateral treaties, but no other country exercises this option so fully. American statesmen may participate in the negotiation of a treaty, ensure that it reflects their objectives, but still abstain from ratification of the full package.[14] That approach has the apparent attraction of allowing Washington to retain its own freedom of action while benefiting from the constraints imposed on other countries. This is an aspect of treaty practice that seems more worthy of the free-rider that the United States once was than the hegemon that it became, but traditions can die hard – especially when they carry such one-sided benefits.

The US decision to join the International Labor Organization, but no other body of the old League of Nations, offered an example of this practice. So too did the Senate's decision to reject two of the nontariff agreements reached in the Kennedy Round, as discussed later. The Vienna Convention on the Law of Treaties is another well-known case. The United States played a leading role in negotiating this instrument, which is mostly devoted to restating customary international law as already recognized by the United States. The Nixon administration signed the treaty in 1969, along with dozens of other countries, and sent it to the Senate in 1971. It has remained there ever since. The United States does abide by the terms of this treaty, but only in a voluntary and self-policed fashion.

The Law of the Sea Convention shows how cafeteria diplomacy can also extend to more substantive agreements. This instrument, which had been the subject of a nearly decade-long conference, sought to settle contentious issues

---

[13] This may be the only time that another country's legislature emulated the Senate by arrogating to itself the power to amend a treaty with the United States.

[14] See Bradley (2007) on the prevalence of signed but unratified treaties.

relating to commercial and military use of the seas. In 1981 the Joint Chiefs of Staff declared their support for the treaty because "it would preserve navigational freedoms that would probably otherwise be lost."[15] That did not overcome the Reagan administration's objections that the convention failed to meet US goals on deep seabed mining.[16] The White House settled on a compromise by which the United States would "accept and act in accordance with the balance of interests reflected in the Law of the Sea Convention relating to traditional uses of the oceans, such as navigation and overflight," per a classified directive that President Reagan signed in 1983, but make the rest of the treaty subject to case-by-case observance and enforcement. The United States would "recognize the rights of other states in the waters off their coasts, as reflected in the Law of the Sea Convention, so long as the rights and freedoms of the United States and others under international law are recognized by such coastal states."[17] This unilateral policy fragmented a de jure multilateral regime into discrete and negotiable de facto relationships. Even though he refrained from signing the treaty, President Reagan still declared in an unclassified paragraph of that same directive that the United States would – as permitted under the convention – establish an Exclusive Economic Zone that extended 200 miles off the coast. In 1994 President Clinton submitted the treaty to the Senate, which then honored its established traditions by neither approving nor rejecting the convention.

A related tactic is for the American negotiators to circumscribe the demands they make on other parties so as to avoid the necessity of securing congressional approval for the resulting treaty. It is a general principle of US treaty practice that the executive need not ask Congress to approve any agreement that is self-executing, including those for which domestic law is already in compliance. That was an important consideration during the post–Uruguay Round period of the built-in agenda (1995–2000), when WTO negotiators dealt with several items of unfinished business from the round. For example, they expanded on the General Agreement on Trade in Services by concluding protocols on telecommunications and financial services. The United States was a *demandeur* in both of those negotiations, and convinced many partners to make substantive commitments, but the American negotiators were careful not to take on any obligations that went beyond existing US law. Viewed from one perspective, this episode offered a good example of how negotiators can

---

[15] Memorandum from the Chairman of the Joint Chiefs of Staff (Jones) to Secretary of Defense Weinberger, "Law of the Sea Negotiations" (March 20, 1981), *FRUS 1981–1988*, Volume XLI, p. 359.

[16] See National Security Decision Directive Number 43 (July 9, 1982).

[17] National Security Decision Directive Number 83 (March 10, 1983), p. 1.

balance their simultaneous dealings at home and abroad so as to minimize interbranch conflict. From another perspective, it offers an equally good example of how to extract valuable concessions from trading partners without paying them anything in exchange.

Another Adjustment to Standard Treaty Practice: Alternative Negotiating Authority

The first major step that the United States took toward global leadership came in 1934, when Congress delegated tariff-cutting authority to the president. The Democratic majority approved the Reciprocal Trade Agreements Act (RTAA) six years before enacting the Selective Training and Service Act of 1940, the first peacetime conscription in US history. These two measures marked sharp breaks from the past, and together they foreshadowed the foundations of the postwar American hegemony.

At issue here is the delegation of negotiating authority from the legislative to the executive branch. The term is a misnomer, as it implies that the executive branch cannot engage in negotiations without the explicit approval of Congress; that is an inherent presidential authority. What is instead at issue is an alternative to formal treaty approval. Prior experience showed that some other mechanism would be needed if the United States were to negotiate rather than legislate its tariffs, and inspired some tentative efforts in the nineteenth and early twentieth centuries. Economists, political scientists, and historians have spilled much ink in their examinations of these early exercises in the negotiation or adjustment of the tariff, which variously provided for reciprocity, minimum and maximum tariffs, or the negotiation of international agreements.[18] We need not replicate that scholarship here for the simple reason that none of these earlier arrangements proved durable. A few experiments resulted in marginal and temporary changes, such as the reciprocity provisions in the 1880s, while others flopped altogether. For example, the Tariff Act of 1897 allowed the president to reduce US tariffs on a handful of enumerated commodities with any country that offered reciprocal concessions, but required that these treaties be approved by the Senate and that both chambers enact implementing legislation. President William McKinley concluded fourteen such conventions in 1899–1900, but the Senate never acted on any of them.

All of these special provisions can be seen as hesitant half-measures that were taken at a time when the United States had acquired the capacity, but not

---

[18] Lake's account (1988) offers the most detailed and enlightening discussion of these measures.

yet the will, to exercise serious and sustained leadership. Perhaps the most important functions performed by these pre–New Deal experiments were to (1) signal that the United States was slowly moving from the wholly autonomous conduct of trade policy toward a more active role; (2) set the precedent for a later, more lasting delegation of authority from Congress to the executive; and (3) test the constitutionality of such delegations.[19]

Another presidential option is to call a pact something other than a "treaty" and ask that Congress approve it through the enactment of ordinary bills or resolutions. This was the approach that the Taft administration successfully employed in its 1911 reciprocity treaty with Canada (which then came to nothing after the Canadian Parliament rejected the agreement), but the Truman administration could not convince Congress to do the same thing with the Havana Charter of the International Trade Organization in 1948. That last episode underlined the point that having recourse to special means for approving agreements does not obviate the need for the two branches to concur on the ends of those agreements.

The Reciprocal Trade Agreements Act Period (1934–1967)

The RTAA of 1934 marked the end of almost unbroken congressional dominance, and the start of executive ascendancy, in the making of trade policy. It allowed the president to treat a tariff-reduction deal as an executive agreement: Provided that an agreement fell within the limits prescribed by law, its approval and execution required only the president's signature. The RTAA facilitated thirty-two bilateral trade agreements that the Roosevelt and Truman administrations negotiated with twenty-eight countries, making substantial cuts in US and foreign tariffs, as well as US participation in the GATT negotiations from 1947 through 1967.

The new mechanism sat uneasily with the established US preference for protection, together with other elements of New Deal economic law that were more concerned about glut and competition than liberalization and trade. The National Industrial Recovery Act of 1933, for example, gave the president broad discretion to impose trade restrictions. The Export-Import Bank was created in 1934 to facilitate trade with the Soviet Union, but soon began to subsidize exports of manufactured goods to other trading partners.

[19]   Key decisions approving the right of Congress to delegate negotiating authority to the executive include the Supreme Court's decisions in *Field v. Clark* (1891) and *B. Altman & Co. v. United States* (1912). Those cases set the precedents by which the court later gave its blessing to the more lasting delegation of authority under the RTAA (see, for example, *Star-Kist Foods, Inc. v. United States* decided in 1959).

The Department of Agriculture turned to export subsidies in 1935, and saw the RTAA as just another means for disposing of surplus agricultural products. Section 22 of the Agricultural Adjustment Act of 1933 (as amended in 1935) provided for restrictions on imports that might interfere with the newly enacted price supports and production controls. This law would remain an important part of US agricultural trade policy for the next sixty years.[20] On the eve of the Second World War, nearly one-fourth of US dutiable imports were subject to quotas or tariff-rate quotas.[21]

Like their successors, the RTAA negotiators employed a variety of means to limit the concessions that they made. One approach was to allow only the principal foreign supplier of any good to bargain over reductions in the US tariff on that item. The rule gave the United States greater leverage over most of its partners, as America was more often the #1 supplier of any given item to the other party than vice versa. The principal-supplier rule was to become standard practice in the early GATT period, where it limited smaller countries' capacity to conduct tariff negotiations.[22] The US negotiators also narrowed their concessions to "more specialized classes of goods than those covered by the description in the Hawley-Smoot Act."[23] Such tariff reclassifications are the trade policy equivalent of gerrymandering: Just as politicians might try to manipulate the geographic boundaries of legislative districts in order to favor candidates of one party over another, so too can the nomenclature of the tariff schedule be gamed to restrict the benefits of a concession to a specific partner. For example, Congress might have originally set a single tariff for all manner of fruit, but negotiators could limit a concession by lowering duties only on apples. They might go further still by distinguishing green apples from red, or even resorting to "seasonal tariffs" for which the concession applies only to apples that are imported during the specific partner's growing season. More than two-fifths of the US concessions in the first eighteen RTAA agreements involved a new classification.[24]

Rules of origin offered another means of limiting the value of concessions. This instrument can easily be misused, with the rules being manipulated so as to encourage managed rather than free trade. This is

---

[20] Prior to the conclusion of the Uruguay Round, presidents employed Section 22 to restrict imports of sugar, cotton, tobacco, milk, peanuts, and other commodities. Most of those products are now subject instead to tariff-rate quotas.

[21] Diebold (1941), p. 37.

[22] This is one reason why multilateral tariff negotiations switched from the old request-offer approach to formula cuts (e.g., the Swiss formula) in the 1960s.

[23] Kreider (1943), p. 204.

[24] Ibid., p. 205. On the tendency for tariff schedules to become more detailed and complex, and the negotiators' mercantilist motivations for doing so, see also Haberler (1933), p. 339.

a practice that US negotiators learned from their hegemonic predecessors. Consider an especially blatant example in the 1933 agreement between the United Kingdom and Denmark: The price that Copenhagen paid to London for improved access to the British ham and bacon market was the stipulation that these products had to be wrapped in "jute cloth woven in the United Kingdom from yarns spun in the United Kingdom."[25] Rules of origin would likewise become an important instrument for the limitation or conditioning of trade benefits in US agreements, especially after the United States began in the 1980s to use preferences as a means of easing the economic transition for US textile and apparel producers (see Chapter 14).

Bargaining with Congress over Grants of Authority

As long as the president proposes and the Congress disposes, the greatest power of the legislative branch remains its prerogative to do nothing at all. Many are the initiatives that presidents have sent with high hopes to Capitol Hill, never to be heard from again. And even when presented with a yes-or-no decision, a cagey legislator will instinctively answer with a negotiable "maybe." Lawmakers have been rationally tight-fisted in their grants of authority ever since the first RTAA request, when they amended the proposal to allow only three initial years of power. By restricting each new extension of RTAA authority to short intervals, legislators ensured that the White House would be forced to bargain with them every few years.

Congress had intrinsic and extrinsic incentives to grant these presidential requests. The intrinsic value came from the large and diverse array of businesses that favor open markets, including export-dependent industries, shippers, and retailers. Many legislators' districts were so clearly competitive or noncompetitive as to make the choice obvious. Those with mixed constituencies could act as rational fence-straddlers, exploiting the extrinsic value of presidential proposals by pledging to exchange their tie-breaking votes for favors. Examples of such side-payments included import relief for declining industries, export subsidies for others, or the extension of trade adjustment-assistance to workers, firms, or communities that face import competition. The executive branch often pushed back, and usually managed to keep the price down, but almost invariably had to pay something for each renewal of its negotiating authority.

---

[25]   As quoted in Kreider (1943), p. 62.

Even when they did renew the RTAA authority, legislators used a variety of other devices to ensure that the executive did not make deeper or wider tariff cuts than they were willing to stomach. "Peril points" were the most contentious item in the 1940s and 1950s. This mechanism required that the Tariff Commission determine the minimum tariff necessary to protect domestic production and barred the executive from negotiating a lower rate without explaining its actions to Congress. The modern equivalent of this requirement is a rule by which the US Trade Representative (USTR) must seek the non-binding advice of the (rebranded) US International Trade Commission on the probable economic effects of any tariff-cutting agreements that are under negotiation. The commission's investigations and hearings are among the many mechanisms by which the private sector can influence trade negotiators.

The RTAA authority worked reasonably well from the mid-1930s through the 1950s, but began to run into greater difficulties in the 1960s. One problem was a growing concern in Congress that trade was being treated as "the hand-maiden of foreign policy." Legislators believed that as long as the State Department conducted commercial negotiations, diplomats would sacrifice American economic interests in exchange for political objectives. Congress therefore obliged President Kennedy to transfer authority to the Special Trade Representative in 1962, a new agency within the Executive Office of the President. This institution was later renamed the USTR in 1979. Despite its roles as the chief negotiator for the United States and principal trade advisor to the president, the USTR is often perceived to be more a creature of Capitol Hill than of the White House.

Another problem arose when negotiators turned to nontariff issues in the Kennedy Round (1962–1967) of GATT negotiations. Congress engaged in cafeteria diplomacy when it spurned two deals that required its explicit approval. The US negotiators had gone ahead with concessions on the highly protective American Selling Price (ASP) system of customs valuation even after legislators from twelve states wrote letters opposing the elimination of this system for benzenoid chemicals, and lawmakers representing another dozen states urged retention of the ASP system for rubber-soled shoes. The acting trade representative mistakenly believed that this opposition could be overcome, and that if the United States did not make a concession in Geneva "there is a serious risk that the negotiations will collapse."[26] Congress obliged the Johnson administration to shelve the ASP proposal, and its approval of the Antidumping Code specified that any conflicts between that agreement and

---

[26] Memorandum from the Acting Special Representative for Trade Negotiations (Roth) to President Johnson, "American Selling Price System of Customs Valuation" (February 15, 1967), *FRUS 1964–1968* Volume VIII, pp. 882 and 883.

US law would be resolved in favor of the latter – thus effectively nullifying the code. One story has it that members of the Senate Finance Committee held a post-hearing party at which the antidumping code's title was inscribed on a roll of toilet paper. An official later recalled "the humiliation of the Executive Branch explaining this to the foreign governments."[27] This unhappy experience convinced trade policymakers that they would need a new understanding with Congress before engaging in another GATT round.

The Fast Track Period (1974–Present)

The Nixon administration asked in 1969 that Congress grant a new form of negotiating authority to deal with nontariff matters, suggesting that the mechanism operate on the basis of a legislative veto. Congress instead wrote a law that more closely involves the legislative branch in the translation of an international agreement into domestic law. At a time when lawmakers debated the impeachment of the president and enacted the War Powers Resolution, reasserting authority over this most traditional congressional turf was a modest proposal.

The most important provision of the Trade Act of 1974 was this so-called fast track for ratifying new trade agreements. It would be rechristened as trade promotion authority in 2001, out of concern that the original nickname sounded too much like matters were being rushed. By whatever title, these rules handle trade treaties as congressional-executive agreements. This is a compromise between a treaty (where the Senate has the advantage) and an executive agreement (where the president has the advantage). In this approach, nontariff agreements are converted into implementing legislation that specifies the changes needed to bring US law into conformity with the commitments. That bill can then be approved by just a simple majority in both chambers of Congress (thus eliminating the need for two-thirds in the Senate), it cannot be amended (thus overcoming the Senate's self-made right to amend treaties), and is subject to strict deadlines (thus defeating the powers of a committee chairman or a determined minority to delay an initiative to death). That no-amendment rule is not quite as strong as it is often claimed to be, as we shall see shortly. With rare exceptions,[28] all significant trade agreements approved since the mid-1970s have come under these rules.

The fast track not only facilitated the approval of trade agreements, but also made it more difficult for Washington to practice cafeteria diplomacy.

---

[27] Malmgren (1983), p. 51.
[28] Congress approved the US–Jordan FTA in 2001 without the benefit of fast-track rules.

By bundling all of the items in a GATT round into a single package, as happened in 1979 and 1994, these new rules prevented Congress from setting aside any items that lawmakers found objectionable. The fast track amounted to a single undertaking for one country long before that became a multilateral norm in the Uruguay Round.

While the fast track was an innovation, the means by which it is extended changed little. Interbranch bargaining over new grants of negotiating authority continue to follow the patterns set in the RTAA period. Congress still places expiration dates on its grants of negotiating authority, presidents periodically request that Congress renew the mandate, and legislators use these opportunities to extract concessions. They usually do so by resorting to omnibus trade bills that bring numerous trade topics within a single bill. From the Trade Act of 1974 through the Bipartisan Congressional Trade Priorities and Accountability Act of 2015,[29] most of these legislative turduckens have been stuffed with at least four elements: a grant of negotiating authority that is accompanied by a declaration of the objectives for its use; amendments to the trade-remedy and reciprocity laws; authorization, renewal, or amendment of preferential trade programs for developing countries; and tariff suspensions for miscellaneous items. Some of the bills also dealt with trade adjustment assistance for displaced workers, firms, and communities, and the bargaining sometimes involved presidential concessions on other matters that were not formally a part of the bill. Still following that "two steps forward, one step back" dance that was first choreographed in the RTAA period, many of these concessions made outside the bill concerned protection for specific industries.

Bargaining over the Objectives of Trade Agreements

The same law that grants or renews the president's authority will always be accompanied by guidance for negotiators. The writing of these instructions became progressively more difficult when trade negotiations moved from tariff to nontariff issues, and then to other topics that have become politically tied to trade. As is discussed at greater length in Chapter 5, topics such as labor rights and environmental protection can provoke far more difficult partisan conflict than do the more traditional subjects of trade policy. Grants of authority can be held up for years while legislators try to reconcile their differences.

---

[29] Note that this latest (2015) package took a somewhat different approach by enacting the various elements not in one, omnibus bill, but in a bundle of related bills (i.e., the Bipartisan Congressional Trade Priorities and Accountability Act, the Trade Preferences Extension Act, and the Trade Facilitation and Trade Enforcement Act).

One of these droughts in negotiating authority started in the 103rd Congress (1993–1994), even though Democrats then enjoyed fully unified government. President Clinton appealed to his co-partisans by insisting that any new trade negotiations must deal with labor and environmental matters. Republicans refused to support this approach, and their opposition – in tacit cooperation with the growing protectionist wing in the Democratic Party – blocked a new grant of authority. The Sisyphean task faced an even steeper hill after Republicans took control of Congress in the 1994 elections. Clinton made only half-hearted efforts to win a new grant of authority in the 104th Congress (1995–1996), but revisited the issue in the 105th Congress (1997–1998). The two branches and the two parties spent months seeking to find some compromise between the demands that "non-trade" issues be treated either as mandatory or optional items in new agreements. A bill came close to being voted on in 1997, but the White House pulled it from consideration when it became clear that they did not have the votes. The Republicans decided to promote this issue in the run-up to the 1998 elections, more as a stunt than a serious undertaking. The White House did not support the bill, which failed in a late-September vote of 180–243. Only 15% of Democrats voted for it, versus 68% of Republicans.

The impasse was not broken until the electorate restored unified government in the 2000 elections, and even then by just a whisker. The Trade Act of 2002, which granted five years of authority, passed the House by just one vote in a late 2001 showdown. The G. W. Bush administration used that authority to approve several FTAs during its first six years in office, but both the TPA grant and unified government expired in 2007. Bush did not formally request renewed authority during his final two years in government, nor did Obama during his first term. The United States then went through yet another drought in negotiating authority, which was not to end until 2015. That latest grant extended TPA through mid-2018, allowing for a further, three-year extension if requested by the president and not rejected by Congress. Any grant after mid-2021 will require enactment of a new trade bill.

CONGRESSIONAL LEVERAGE UNDER TRADE PROMOTION AUTHORITY

The fast track gives Congress more opportunities to influence negotiations than had the RTAA. While that earlier mechanism gave legislators just one opportunity, allowing them to extract concessions whenever negotiating authority came up for renewal, the fast track offers three additional bites at the apple. Congress can attempt to influence the negotiations while they are underway by threatening to reject any agreement that does or does not contain some specific item. It can also exercise substantial authority in the translation of trade agreements into implementing legislation. Even after the implementing legislation has been drafted and introduced, members of Congress may threaten to reject the bill if the White House is not willing to cut deals. That bargaining might relate to the agreement in question, or some other issue in trade policy, or to some altogether different topic.

Influencing the Negotiation, Approval, and Implementation of Trade Agreements

Despite the almost universal belief that the fast-track rules prevent Congress from fiddling with the product of a trade negotiation, TPA does not actually reduce its role to a binary choice. Legislators have instead developed numerous ways to exert their authority even after they have delegated some of their constitutional authority, and have often forced substantive changes in agreements. The actual use of TPA has evolved in three phases.

The first period was from 1979 through 1994, which saw the negotiation of two multilateral trade agreements and the first three FTAs. It started[30] five years after enactment of the Trade Act of 1974, when Congress approved the Trade Agreements Act of 1979. This Tokyo Round implementing legislation hinted at the possibilities, as it included several provisions that departed from the letter of the GATT agreements. One reinterpreted a provision that set the terms by which developing countries were to be accorded the protection of an injury test in countervailing duty (CVD) cases. The injury test is an investigation to determine whether goods that are alleged to be subsidized injure the US industry; CVDs are imposed only if the US International Trade Commission finds injury or the threat of injury. The somewhat convoluted language agreed to in Geneva was intended to provide this defense to developing countries. The Senate exploited ambiguities in the text to ensure that developing countries would receive the injury test only if they agreed to reduce or eliminate their export subsidies. While this interpretation provoked a formal complaint by India[31] and protests from other countries, it was

---

[30] To be more precise, this is the first use of the fast-track authority to approve an ordinary trade agreement. That same authority is also available for agreements by which the United States extends MFN treatment to Communist (or transitional) countries that were denied this treatment as of 1974 (as discussed in Chapter 11). The first use of this authority came in 1975, when Congress approved an MFN agreement with Romania.

[31] The GATT panel hearing the Indian complaint was dissolved following an out of court settlement.

permitted to stand. In addition to this change, legislators tinkered with other trade-remedy provisions, won a commitment from the administration to reorganize the trade agencies, and inserted a provision calling for a North American FTA. The final package looked more like another omnibus trade bill than the implementing legislation for an agreement.

President Carter was not obliged to accept these changes when he sent the bill back to Congress for approval, but it would have been inadvisable to antagonize the lawmakers by ignoring their work and writing his own implementing legislation. Legislators sometimes consider themselves the unacknowledged poets of the world, and do not want their verse edited. So while it is literally true that Congress did not amend the bill after it was submitted, most observers failed to notice that it was the congressional trade committees that wrote this bill in the first place. The modest precedents set in 1979 were expanded on in 1986–1988, when lawmakers repeatedly intervened in the process of negotiating the US–Canada FTA and enacting its results (see Chapter 9).

The second phase in the use of TPA came in the first six years of the G. W. Bush administration (2001–2006), which is the only time that the no-amendment rule has been more or less faithfully followed. The sole exception concerned immigration-related items in the Chilean and Singaporean FTAs, which legislators forced the administration to revise before the implementing legislation proceeded. None of the other FTAs that the Bush administration submitted during these years were substantively altered in response to demands from Congress. Democrats who were unhappy with the agreements usually just voted against the agreements, thus leading to narrow and partisan margins of victory rather than to actual changes.

The 2006 congressional elections inaugurated the third period, forcing the Bush administration to take an entirely different approach toward FTAs and the Democrats who recaptured Congress. The agreements approved in the final years of the Bush administration, and in the first term of the Obama administration, offer the clearest example to date of how legislators can coerce the executive into revising an agreement. The Bush administration struck a deal with congressional Democrats in 2007 that required extensive renegotiation of the FTAs that were then pending with Colombia, Korea, Panama, and Peru.[32] Under this bargain, the administration pledged that it would not

---

[32]   The text of this agreement, which is no longer posted on any official websites, can be read at www.washingtontradereport.com/May10Agreement.htm. Note that the agreement did not

submit the implementing legislation for these pacts until they had been renegotiated to meet Democrats' demands on labor, environmental, and other issues, even though the Peruvian legislature had already approved the FTA as originally negotiated. While this bargain technically did not violate the ban against amendments to the implementing legislation, it produced the most substantial alteration of trade agreements in US history. The FTA with Peru was renegotiated and approved that same year, but the agreements with Colombia, Korea, and Panama were held up for four more years. In the end, those agreements were negotiated (or supplemented) three times: once as originally concluded, once by the Bush administration under the terms of the 2007 agreement with Democrats, and once more by the Obama administration in the months prior to final approval.

Congressional Votes on Trade Agreements

Trade agreements have become progressively more difficult to move through Congress. We can gauge the degree of resistance by marking the time elapsed between the president's notification to Congress of his intention to sign an agreement and his later signature of the agreement's implementing legislation. Between these two events comes the drafting of the implementing legislation, the debate over its passage, and any delays that may be forced by the executive or (more often) the legislative branch. If all parties act with deliberate speed, the interval should ideally not be much longer than about half a year.

The data illustrated in Figure 4.1 track the gradual elongation of the process, as well as the simultaneous widening in the partisan rift. The process lasted less than five months for the FTA with Israel in 1985, and took twice as long for the US-Canada FTA in 1987–1988. The elapsed time grew to fifteen months in the case of NAFTA in 1992–1993, which was stalled by the negotiation of side agreements by the new administration, and in 2004–2005 the maneuvers accompanying approval of the FTA with Central America and the Dominican Republic (CAFTA-DR) lasted eighteen months. Both the NAFTA and CAFTA-DR processes were also stalled by the political calendar; neither of the Bush administrations wanted to risk a loss by asking Congress to vote in the heat of the 1992 presidential election or the 2004 congressional elections. The two Bushes therefore held back their respective agreements until the danger of electoral consequences subsided. Matters were even worse

apply to Colombia, insofar as Democrats were so opposed to that FTA that they did not want to endorse it even in revised form.

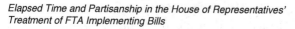

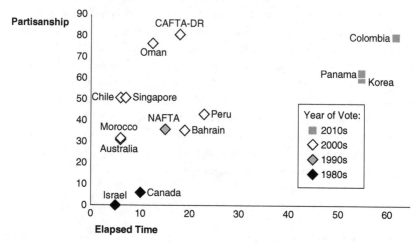

FIGURE 4.1 Rising difficulty in securing congressional approval for FTAs, 1985–2011.

Partisanship = Percentage of House Republicans voting for the implementing legislation minus the percentage of House Democrats voting for it.

Elapsed Time = Number of months between the president's notification to Congress of his intention to sign an agreement and his later signature of the agreement's implementing legislation.

Sources: Congressional Record and others.

for the FTA with Peru, when the interval lasted twenty-three months, but even that was short compared to the FTAs with Colombia, Panama, and Korea. The net result of the disputes, delays, and do-overs for these three agreements was that the domestic-approval process took about five years.

Chapter 5 examines how US trade politics have increasingly come to be dominated more by social than by commercial issues. That trend is matched here by congressional voting patterns in which the levels of partisanship and opposition may have little to do with the magnitude or import sensitivity of the trade involved. The degree of resistance that a given FTA must overcome is instead determined chiefly by other, less overtly commercial considerations, including the type of partner involved. As a general rule, Democrats in Congress have fewer objections to agreements with other developed countries than they do when the partner is a developing country. The FTAs with Canada and Australia were both approved fairly easily. The second exception concerns a distinction among developing countries. Members of Congress will sometimes show greater deference to the executive on those trade initiatives that are inspired by the imperatives of foreign policy, but that is not an absolute rule. While the FTAs with Bahrain, Israel, and Morocco were among the easier to approve, the agreement with Oman encountered the same sort of resistance as have FTAs with Latin American countries.

The Colombia FTA attracted more opposition than other contemporary agreements. This reflects a deliberate choice made by labor unions and their legislative allies, and was not based on the narrowest of sectoral, protectionist calculations. Unions and Democrats criticized Colombia's antilabor record, especially the murders of union organizers and officials. In 2006 Democrats refused even to negotiate with the Bush administration over the terms of the implementing legislation for that FTA, leading a frustrated White House to force matters in 2008 by sending its own version of the bill to Congress. This end-run around the congressional trade committees was unprecedented in the history of the fast-track rules, and the House responded with an equally unprecedented action: On the most partisan trade vote in the modern era, it removed the fast-track protections from the implementing legislation. That prevented the FTA from being acted on for the remainder of the Bush administration.

This case exemplifies how the practitioners of modern trade politics often place greater stress on principle than on protection. Colombia was only the #23 source of US imports in 2011, and even less of what it provided was import-sensitive. Nearly three-quarters of imports from Colombia in 2011 were energy products or copper, two commodities for which US industry's demand greatly outstrips domestic supply. Colombia had earlier been among the many second-tier suppliers of apparel to the United States, but by 2011 its share of the US apparel-import market had fallen to just 0.3%. By contrast, Korea supplied 2.5 times more imports than Colombia, and these were concentrated in such competitive sectors as electronics, automobiles, and steel. And while Korea was the target of seventeen antidumping petitions filed during 2000–2011, Colombia was subject to just one. In short, if unions and Democrats calibrated their opposition solely according to narrow calculations of protectionist interest they should have concentrated their fire on Korea. Throughout the maneuvering over these two agreements, it was widely expected in Washington that the Korean FTA would be passed as long as Seoul made a few more concessions to US demands on market access for automobiles and meat, but that Democrats would prefer to kill the Colombian agreement outright. The Korean agreement ultimately won support from only a minority among Democrats (31%), but that was nearly twice what the US-Colombia FTA received (16%).

HOW THE DOMESTIC DIPLOMACY OF TRADE AFFECTS
THE EXTERNAL KIND

These issues speak to the principal focus of this study – the role of trade in US foreign policy – only to the extent that they ultimately retard or enhance the ability of American negotiators to conclude meaningful agreements with their counterparts. It could be argued that from the negotiator's perspective there exists some optimal level of domestic opposition to the approval of trade agreements. Negotiators will not get far if Congress refuses altogether to make new grants of negotiating authority, or routinely rejects the agreements submitted for its approval. The positive side is subtler. The executive would suffer a reduction in leverage if Congress were perceived as a compliant rubber stamp. Negotiators can instead use the opposition that they face at home in order to pry otherwise difficult concessions from their foreign counterparts. The question then arises, how close does the existing system come to providing an optimal level of opposition?

The executive has learned how to use congressional recalcitrance to its advantage. Following a "good cop, bad cop" pattern that is familiar to fans of police dramas, legislators can play a usefully obstreperous role. While negotiators would usually prefer that Congress not kibitz, they would be remiss if they did not exploit these demands. As one veteran put it, "we can always threaten to turn Congress loose on another country, and that terrifies them."[33] The fact that the coordination between legislators and negotiators is imperfect is precisely what makes the tactic so effective. If foreign negotiators were to believe that Congress is really in the pocket of the executive, they would soon conclude that the good cop, bad cop act is nothing more than empty theatrics. That conclusion may often be warranted, but there have also been some notable episodes in which Congress made good on its threat to kill an agreement. For a modern negotiator with a sufficiently long time horizon, ancient debacles such as the Versailles Treaty and the Havana Charter serve a useful didactic purpose.

The principles and procedures discussed here are best understood by examining how they worked out in a specific episode. Chapter 9 offers a detailed case study in the domestic diplomacy of trade agreements, reviewing how Congress handled the FTAs that the United States reached with Canada in 1988 and then both of the North American neighbors in 1993. These twin examples illustrate how the executive and legislative branches of

---

[33] Malmgren (1983), p. 50.

the US government deal with one another in the launch, conduct, and conclusion of trade negotiations.

One pressing question is whether these well-established patterns are permanent features in the domestic diplomacy of trade, or if they will undergo significant and lasting changes in the age of Trump. From 1934 through 2016, every US president was – to varying degrees and in differing ways – committed to free trade and the negotiation of new agreements. In Chapters 6 and 16 we will examine how that pattern has now been broken. There is no doubt that Donald Trump takes an entirely different approach to trade agreements, and to his dealings with foreign governments and Capitol Hill. We have yet to see whether his departure from the norm represents a short-term detour, or is instead a new inflection point that separates the known past from an uncertain future.

5

The Expanding Scope of Trade and the Contagion of Conflict

The protective tariff is well established because large areas of adverse interests are too inert and sluggish to find political expression while an overwhelming proportion of the active interests have been given a stake in maintaining the system. One consequence of these circumstances is an amazing absence of conflicts arising from the legislation.

E. E. Schattschneider, *Politics, Pressures and the Tariff* (1935)

The central political fact in a free society is the tremendous contagiousness of conflict ... [T]he outcome of all conflict is determined by the *scope* of its contagion. The number of people involved in any conflict determines what happens; every change in the number of participants, every increase or reduction in the number of participants affects the result.

E. E. Schattschneider, *The Semi-Sovereign People* (1960)

INTRODUCTION

Schattschneider's evolving perception of conflict in the US political system neatly captures the differences between the trade politics of today and the not-so-distant past. His classic account of the Hawley–Smoot Tariff Act of 1930 described a closed loop in which the advocates of protection triumphed because their opponents were scarce, weak, and easily neutralized. That scene bore little resemblance to Schattschneider's later depiction of a crowded polity where conflict is contagious, and in which debates over public policy draw in persons whose own interests are not directly at stake. He was behind the times in 1935, failing to understand how the trade policy-making system had already changed. By 1960 he was well ahead of the curve, as it would be another few decades before trade politics ceased to be a game played only by narrowly focused economic groups. It has since become a free-for-all in which social and environmental activists are just as engaged as industries and unions. The new issues that are now associated with trade have profoundly altered the tone, conduct, and outcome of debates over trade initiatives. These issues have also affected not only the demands that US negotiators make on their foreign counterparts, but also their own ability to win approval for the agreements that they conclude.

Like Schattschneider, Adam Smith could be right even when he appeared to contradict himself. "It is not from the benevolence of the butcher, the brewer, or the baker that we expect our dinner," he observed in a celebrated passage of *The Wealth of Nations* (1776), "but from their regard to their own interest."[1] He was no less right when he noted in *The Theory of Moral Sentiments* (1790) that, "How selfish soever man may be supposed there are evidently some principles in his nature, which interest him in the fortunes of others, and render their happiness necessary to him, though he derives nothing from it, except the pleasure of seeing it."[2] Benevolence and altruism can be as strong a motivation for some people as greed and selfishness are for others. For newer participants in trade debates, "fair trade" has more to do with the conditions under which an imported product is made, and the impact of that production on foreign workers or the environment, than with the terms by which it is traded and its impact on US firms and workers.

The trade politics of a generation ago were conducted along lines that would look quite familiar to the Smith of 1776 or the Schattschneider of 1935, but today this issue attracts additional players whose motivations would be better understood by the Smith of 1790 or the Schattschneider of 1960. What we call trade was once conceived of almost exclusively as the movement of goods across borders; trade policy was confined to tariffs, quotas, and other instruments that directly regulate those transactions at the frontier; and the stakeholders in this field comprised a commensurately narrow set of interests and institutions. We have subsequently come to recognize that the scope of tradeables includes capital (i.e., investment), ideas (i.e., intellectual property), and even people (i.e., services), and that trade rules affect a greater array of policy instruments and regulatory authorities both at and behind the border. Trade policy has also gotten connected to many other issues, including some that are less directly related to the production, distribution, and use of goods (e.g., labor and environmental matters), and others that are linked only as a matter of political definition (e.g., the observance of human rights).

The newest divisions over trade bear a closer resemblance to social than to economic policy, and are consequently less susceptible to the difference-splitting bargains that had characterized policymaking in past generations.

---

[1] Smith (1776), pp. 26–27.
[2] Smith (1790), p. 1.

The most politically contentious and significant new issues tend to socialize political conflict by provoking people for whom jobs or profits are not the only things at stake. Some of them now define their interests to incorporate a wider range of topics affecting the quality of life. The more altruistic activists take the further step of concerning themselves with the welfare of others. They are like the members of the American League to Abolish Capital Punishment who, as Schattschneider noted, "obviously do not expect to be hanged."[3] This is not to say that the old divisions between free-traders and protectionists have disappeared altogether. We will see in Chapter 6 that the traditional topics came back with a vengeance in 2016, and the winner in that contest resurrected positions that serious candidates had not espoused in decades. The new trade politics add to, rather than replace, those older burdens in the domestic diplomacy of trade.

THE SCOPE OF ISSUES IN THE TRADING SYSTEM

The issues that fall within the jurisdiction of the trading system have increased over time, but that growth has not been constant, uniform, or irreversible. Table 5.1 tabulates the principal issues covered by some of the more important negotiations in which the United States was a participant from 1947 to 2015. Multilateral agreements went from covering four traditional topics in the immediate aftermath of the Second World War to a dozen in the Doha Round (three of which were later taken off the table), and discriminatory agreements such as NAFTA and TPP have gone still further.

This widening array of subject matter is the product of two distinct processes. The first is the deliberate result of affirmative choices that the United States and its trading partners have made to bring new issues to the table. Washington has been the most active and effective *demandeur* throughout the history of the present system, from the setting of the GATT template (which was taken from the Reciprocal Trade Agreements Act [RTAA] model) through the introduction of the "new issues" around which the Uruguay Round was built. Other would-be *demandeurs* have been less successful, as shown by the European Union's frustrations in the launch and early conduct of the Doha Round; Brussels failed to get labor rights and the environment on the table, and three of its four Singapore issues were removed a few years after the launch of those talks.

The issue base is also expanded through disputes that arise when countries impose trade-restricting measures in pursuit of noncommercial goals.

---

[3] Schattschneider (1960), p. 26.

The decision to challenge these measures in the dispute-settlement system is intentional on the part of the aggrieved country, but that is not the same as the community deciding to negotiate. The resulting litigation inserts new issues first through the actual cases, and then by inviting a backlash from those noncommercial interests that object to having their laws and policies made subject to trade rules.

Older Attempts at the New Issues

One of the oddities of the modern trading system is that it almost began in the late 1940s with an issue base that more closely resembled the expansive WTO than the modest GATT. The Havana Charter of the International Trade Organization (ITO) included provisions on some subjects that would not be taken up again by the international trading system for a few more decades (notably the interests of developing countries), others that were not on the agenda until the Uruguay Round (especially services, intellectual property rights, and investment), and still more that remain controversial to this day (namely labor and competition policy). The "temporary" GATT was instead designed to deal only with the traditional subject matter of trade. To the limited extent that it handled some of the other issues, they appeared only in the general exceptions list in GATT Article XX.

To put the later expansion of the trading system into proper perspective, it is useful to consider earlier, fruitless efforts to bring some of these same topics to the table. Issues that are advanced by a non-hegemonic *demandeur* face a difficult path, and even a hegemon may need to invest considerable political capital over an extended period to overcome other countries' resistance. Consider the case of trade in services, the most consequential expansion in the trading system. The United States successfully pushed this issue in the 1980s, but that came decades after developing countries tried and failed to reach enduring agreements on this topic. That was what happened in 1902, for example, when sixteen Latin American countries concluded the Convention on the Practice of Learned Professions in a hemispheric conference. This treaty allowed the citizens of each signatory to "freely exercise the profession for which they may be duly authorized by diploma or title granted by a competent national authority ... in any of the territories of the other nations." The United States signed this instrument, and President Theodore Roosevelt submitted it to the Senate, but it died there for want of action. While nine of the other signatories ratified the treaty, it had no lasting impact.[4]

---

[4] For the history and text of the treaty see Wiktor (1976–1994), Volume 3, pp. 411–416.

TABLE 5.1. *Issue Coverage of Selected Trade Agreements*
Years indicate date of signature

	GATT 1947	Havana Charter 1948	Tokyo Round 1979	US–Israel FTA 1985	NAFTA 1992–1993	Uruguay Round 1994	Doha Min. Declaration 2001	US–Korea FTA 2007	TPP 2015
Core Issues									
Tariffs	●	○	●	●	●	●	●	●	●
Antidump. & Countervail.	●	○	●	—	○	●	●	●	●
Safeguards	●	○	●	○	○	●	—	●	●
Uruguay Issues									
Intellectual Property	○	⊠	—	○	●	●	●	●	●
Agriculture	—	⊠	□	—	●	●	●	●	●
Services	—	⊠	—	○	●	●	●	●	●
Singapore Issues									
Competition Policy	○	⊠	—	—	●	—	⊠	●	●
Investment	—	⊠	—	●	●	●	⊠	●	●
Government Procure	—	—	□	●	●	□	⊠	●	●
Trade Facilitation	—	—	—	—	●	—	●	●	●
Other Issues									
State–Owned Enterprises	●	●	—	—	○	○	—	○	●
Labor Rights	○	⊠	—	—	●	—	—	●	●
Environment	○	—	—	—	●	●	●	●	●
Geographical Indications	—	⊠	—	—	○	○	●	○	●

Temporary Entry	—	—	—	◉	◉	•
Electronic Commerce	—	—	—	—	•	•
Anti-Corruption	—	—	—	—	◉	•
Regulatory Coherence	—	—	—	—	—	•

○ = An issue covered only as one of the general exceptions in GATT Article XX.

◉ = One or more full articles devoted to the issue. Does not include items in exceptions clauses (e.g., intellectual property). Data for NAFTA include the 1993 side agreements.

▣ = A GATT or World Trade Organization (WTO) agreement that is plurilateral (i.e., optional).

● = Full chapter, annex, appendix, or other section or side agreement devoted to the issue (or implied to be so by the terms of the Doha Ministerial Declaration).

⊠ = Issues that were either (a) in the failed Havana Charter but not in GATT or (b) covered by the Doha Ministerial Declaration but subsequently taken off the Doha Round table.

— = No explicit coverage.

Developing countries tried again to introduce services in the 1948 negotiations over the Havana Charter. Hoping to combat shipping cartels and other anticompetitive practices, India and Latin American countries pressed this issue in the ITO Preparatory Committee. The only satisfaction they received was a mechanism for complaints regarding "any restrictive business practices" in such activities as "transportation, telecommunications, insurance and the commercial services of banks." This compromise was rendered moot when Congress refused to approve the charter. Developing countries continued to press, and achieved some limited progress on shipping in the 1960s and 1970s.[5] The United Nations Conference on Trade and Development became a forum to negotiate over North–South trade in "invisibles" (i.e., services), and also took on other issues that would not be on the GATT agenda for decades (e.g., intellectual property rights) or are still outside the scope of the WTO (i.e., competition policy).[6] As long as the developing countries were *demandeurs* for a new international economic order, the United States was usually chief among the critics. Just the reverse would happen in the 1980s, when developing countries led the opposition to the new issues that the United States wanted in the GATT. Whether it opposed or championed an issue, Washington generally prevailed.

The United States did not succeed in promoting negotiations on services until it packaged this topic as a bundle of related sectors, and put its full power behind that campaign. Washington made a poor showing, for example, when it sought to advance talks in the single sector of motion pictures. Hollywood has been fighting protectionism in Europe since the 1920s, dealing with such barriers as screen quotas and discriminatory taxes.[7] The United States received only partial satisfaction when it negotiated bilateral pacts such as the Anglo-American film agreements of 1939 and 1948, and felt obliged to make a very unwelcome compromise in the original GATT negotiations. GATT Article IV explicitly permitted screen quotas, and the only concession it made to US demands was a vague suggestion that these restrictions be subject to a negotiated phase-out.[8] The GATT countries never made good on that

---

[5] See generally Cafruny (1987). See also Moss and Winton (1979) for the voluminous regional and international resolutions and other documents in which developing countries raised this issue over the ensuing decades.

[6] See the historical essays in UNCTAD (2004). Note that in the UNCTAD debates of the 1960s, as in the Havana Charter before it, the topic of competition policy went under the rubric of "restrictive business practices."

[7] On negotiations over trade in motion pictures see Jarvie (1992) and Puttnam and Watson (1998).

[8] The British rather than the French were the principal *demandeurs* for a screen quota carve-out in GATT. London's position would change in later years when the British film industry regained its competitiveness.

promise, and in the 1960s the Europeans dismissed a US proposal to negotiate on access for television programs on the grounds that the GATT did not deal with services. The Europeans would continue to treat what we now call audiovisual services as a "sacred cow," and their perennial antagonisms with Hollywood made for great drama in the final hours of the Uruguay Round, but the United States did succeed in bringing movies to the table – and winning concessions from some partners – precisely by redefining the scope of the system to include services.

The first important step in that direction came when representatives of the financial services industry realized that they were part of a much larger sector that could be organized into a potent powerful force. Led by American Express, these policy entrepreneurs began to proselytize an ever-growing circle of converts in Washington. Starting with other financial services providers, then their counterparts in other services, they formed the Coalition of Service Industries (CSI) in 1982.[9] CSI found a sympathetic ear in the Reagan administration, which was looking for precisely this kind of ally, but it took years for the United States to convince its partners that the topic belonged in trade negotiations.

The issue of intellectual property rights shows a similar progression in US priorities, and was likewise viewed quite differently by developing and developed countries. This subject had been folded into some pre-GATT trade agreements,[10] and was also included in the failed Havana Charter, but its only coverage in the GATT regime was via the exceptions clauses in GATT Article XX. It was instead the subject of numerous nineteenth- and twentieth-century multilateral agreements that came to be administered by the World Intellectual Property Organization (WIPO).[11] Developing countries pressed their own perspective on intellectual property in WIPO, demanding technology transfer and the compulsory licensing of patents, but the United States took just the opposite position. In place of negotiating for the wider distribution of protected knowledge through WIPO reforms, it sought to make the existing WIPO rules subject to the stricter dispute-settlement rules of the trading system. Together with services and investment, this topic was among the new issues that the United States advanced in the 1980s.

---

[9] See Marchetti and Mavroidis (2011) on the negotiating history of the GATS and the US origins of this concept.

[10] See Johnson et al. (1915), Volume II, p. 144.

[11] WIPO began its institutional life in 1893, when it was entitled the International Bureaux for the Protection of Intellectual Property. It acquired its present form and title in 1970.

Why the United States Advanced the New Issues

American advocacy of the new issues is one of many ways in which the economic transition, and especially the process of Creative Destruction, manifests itself in the international and domestic diplomacy of trade. Technology redefines what may be efficiently traded. Perishable agricultural products could not be transported over long distances until shipping and refrigeration were adequate to the task, for example, just as the creation of the Internet has opened up all manner of digital trade. Technology also accelerates shifts in competitiveness, and churns the composition of the pro-trade and trade-skeptical coalitions within countries. These manifestations of the economic transition determine how industries and workers define their trade interests, which then influence the government's negotiating positions. If US policymakers responded only to the industries that had favored open markets in the early days of hegemony, but later faced rising competition from imports, they would have reverted to protectionism no later than the early 1980s. They instead worked with the newer industries that were remaking the American economy so as to replace the legacy industries that had by then defected from the free-traders to the protectionists.

Industry may take the initiative, as in the case of trade in services, but so too can government. Policymakers sometimes devise their proposals with an eye towards maintaining or reshaping coalitions, as was demonstrated by the Kennedy administration's response when some charter members of the original RTAA coalition began to doubt the free-trade project. These included farmers and organized labor. The White House asked that Congress give it increased authority to negotiate tariff agreements with Europe on agricultural products, including a proposal that would allow for retaliation against any new European barriers to American farm exports. It also forestalled organized labor's defection by proposing a new program of Trade Adjustment Assistance (TAA) for workers whose jobs were displaced by imports. These maneuvers, coupled with a protectionist concession that bought off the textile and apparel industry, ensured that the Kennedy administration had a sufficiently large set of interests lined up in favor of its proposals. It won congressional approval for the Trade Expansion Act of 1962, granting the authority needed to participate in the Kennedy Round of GATT negotiations. The transatlantic agricultural negotiations ultimately failed, but TAA became a permanent feature of US trade policy and politics.

President Reagan faced a more serious challenge, and responded with a commensurately larger revision in US objectives. His administration's aim was not merely to prevent a few nervous supporters from wandering away, but to replace the departed with entirely new interest groups. The rising importance of trade had "increased the domestic economic impact of the industrial and regulatory policies of other governments," the USTR observed in a 1982 memorandum for the president, noting that the "United States needs to develop a new public consensus on how it can best deal with the changing realities of the world market place."[12] Reagan began by appeasing some protection interests, placating not just the usual suspects (e.g., apparel and sugar) but also apostates from the pro-trade coalition (i.e., automobiles and steel). Having isolated some of the opposition, his administration recruited new supporters among a large and well-heeled constituency. The formation of the Coalition of Services Industries that same year was quite timely, as it brought several new recruits that had heretofore played little or no role in trade debates. The same could be said for the promise to secure greater international enforcement of intellectual property rights, as well as stronger rules on foreign investment. The new issues won over such stalwarts as the Association of American Publishers, the American Bankers Association, the Pharmaceutical Manufacturers Association, the Recording Industry Association of America, and the Software Publishers Association. By the end of the Reagan administration, the composition of the pro-trade coalition – and the content of US trade agreements – was vastly different than what it had been at the start.

Domestic calculations explain why the Reagan administration wanted to appeal to the more competitive US industries, but to understand why it chose to do so via trade negotiations we need to consider what was unique about GATT. If intellectual property rights were a problem, why not address this issue in WIPO? The answer lay not in rules but in enforcement. While most international institutions monitor the members' compliance with their rules, none of them (apart from the United Nations Security Council) back that up with the same level of force. Even before the Uruguay Round, GATT provided for retaliation against a country that did not comply with a ruling. The proposal to bring intellectual property rights into GATT really meant taking the WIPO law-book to the GATT court. The substance of the WTO's Agreement on Trade-Related Aspects of Intellectual Property Rights (TRIPs) amounts to the incorporation of existing WIPO disciplines into a trade instrument, allowing retaliation-based complaints against countries that are alleged to violate these rights. The United States did just that in the years following the TRIPs agreement's entry into force, bringing intellectual property cases against several members. That same reasoning applied to services and investment, but there the negotiators could not rely solely on existing bodies of law.

[12] USTR William E. Brock, "Memorandum for the President" (November 10, 1982), p. 16.

This reinvigoration of the pro-trade constituency also meant weighing down trade debates with new political baggage, such as concerns over the impact of patent protection on the cost of pharmaceuticals. Together with the emergence of links between trade policy and the environment and labor rights, these concerns brought fresh recruits to the trade-skeptical coalition and recast the partisan politics of trade. We will return to that point shortly, and also address how the economic transition inspired subtler changes in the political preferences of the American public. Taken together, these two effects greatly complicated the domestic diplomacy of US trade policy.

How the United States Advanced the New Issues

The Reagan administration looked to the 1982 GATT ministerial conference as an opportunity to advance a more positive agenda, but its efforts to launch a round of negotiations built around the new issues were frustrated by questions from other developed countries and sharper objections from developing countries. Leaving that conference with nothing to show for it, the Reagan administration concluded that it needed to do a more effective job of salesmanship among both its richer partners (where appeals to their interests could be sufficient) and its poorer partners (where more coercive tactics might be in order).

Promoting negotiations over trade in services meant overcoming ingrained prejudices that dated back to the origins of modern economics. Although Adam Smith was himself a service provider, he considered practically anyone outside of agriculture and manufactures to be "unproductive labourers" whose work "perishes in the very instant of its production." That was how he characterized all manner of "frivolous professions" such as buffoons, musicians, and lawyers, as well as the court, the church, and the military.[13] The very concept of services as a tertiary sector that merits equal billing with the primary and secondary sectors seems not to have emerged until the 1930s,[14] and even after economists recognized this sector they still dismissed most services as "untraded" or "invisibles." The Reagan administration therefore invested time and money in sponsoring studies, conferences, and other activities aimed at enhancing awareness of just how widely traded services really are, and how liberalization in this area could affect competition in goods as well. The salesmanship helped to win over European leaders, and the Canadians

[13] Smith (1776), pp. 331 and 342.
[14] See the summary in Fisher (1939), the New Zealand economist who claimed that in Fisher (1933) he had coined the term.

were happy to negotiate an FTA that covered these issues as long as it insulated them from US protectionism in the primary and secondary sectors (see Chapter 9).

Resistance remained strong in the developing world. Leaders in such countries as Brazil and India doubted that they had service export interests of their own, and feared that national security was at stake in the communications and transportation sectors. They were also well aware of the costs implied by stricter enforcement of intellectual property rights, especially when their industries were predominantly imitators rather than innovators, and their governments were still just as likely to expropriate as to invite foreign investment. The Reagan administration responded to their resistance with a strategy of inducements and threats, letting partners know that the United States would act bilaterally or even unilaterally if they were unwilling to negotiate multilaterally.

The most immediate manifestation of the new strategy was a stepped-up use of the reciprocity laws. The Section 301 retaliatory law (see Chapter 3) had already been used to push the envelope of what "trade" is understood to encompass, with the very first case in 1975 involving a services dispute (Guatemalan cargo preferences). While most subsequent cases dealt with traditional goods-related issues, especially in agricultural trade, the new issues figured prominently in several of the more high-profile disputes in the 1980s. These included cases dealing with services (e.g., Argentina air couriers), intellectual property rights (e.g., Brazilian pharmaceutical patents), and investment (e.g., Indian restrictions on foreign investors). The policy was also bolstered by an increasingly aggressive use of the Generalized System of Preferences as an instrument of reciprocity, offering deeper preferences to countries that cooperated while curtailing them for countries that violated US standards (see Chapter 13).

The data in Table 5.2 show a remarkable similarity both in the absolute and relative numbers of cases that Washington pursued unilaterally in 1975–1997 and multilaterally in 1995–2017. A large share of cases in both periods concerned fairly run-of-the-mill issues involving goods, especially agricultural products. What is more revealing are the near-identical numbers and shares of Section 301 and WTO cases that were devoted to services and intellectual property rights. This observation strongly supports the contention that the United States achieved its larger objective of reshaping both the substance and the strength of the multilateral trading system, as the net effect of these reforms was to allow Washington to bring the same mix of complaints to the new, multilateral system as it had already pursued in unilateral demands.

TABLE 5.2. *Trade Complaints Brought by the United States, 1975–2017*

| | Brought to the Multilateral System | | Adjudicated by |
	US Complaints in the GATT (1975–1994)	US Complaints in the WTO (1995–2017)	USTR under Section 301 (1975–1997)
Primary Products	26 (62%)	43 (38%)	49 (42%)
Non-Primary Products	7 (17%)	25 (22%)	29 (25%)
Intellectual Property	0 (0%)	15 (13%)	15 (13%)
Services	0 (0%)	10 (9%)	13 (11%)
Multiple or Other	9 (21%)	19 (17%)	10 (8%)
Total	42 (100%)	112 (100%)	116 (100%)

Primary Products = Raw and processed agricultural products (WTO definition) plus fish and forestry products.
Multiple or Other = Cases involving taxation or investment, or multiple types of measures (e.g., market access and investment), or horizontal measures affecting both agricultural and manufactured products, or the use of Section 301 to implement the settlement of another dispute (in two cases involving Canadian softwood lumber).
Sources: GATT cases tabulated from data at www.worldtradelaw.net/databases/gattpanels.php. WTO cases tabulated from WTO data at www.wto.org/english/tratop_e/dispu_e/dispu_by_coun try_e.htm. Section 301 cases tabulated from USTR data at https://ustr.gov/archive/assets/Trade_ Agreements/Monitoring_Enforcement/asset_upload_file985_6885.pdf

When those complaints are brought within the terms of agreed international rules, however, the other country is more likely to concede the legitimacy of the process, and to focus its defense on the facts of the case rather than on the contention that Washington's actions are unilateral and extralegal.

FTAs as Precedent-Setting Exercises

Another means of advancing the new issues was to treat FTAs as multifunctional instruments. These agreements served simultaneously as an inducement to the immediate partner, a threat to third countries, and as laboratories for demonstrating how the new subject matter could be incorporated in trade agreements.[15] Each new initiative offered an opportunity not only to expand on the precedents set in the previous agreements, but to introduce entirely new issues. American negotiators threatened to "go bilateral" if the multilateral system did not adapt to the new US priorities.

[15] Note that while the direction of precedent-setting most typically went from FTAs to the multilateral system, the process was reciprocal (i.e., there were also ways in which the multilateral system set precedents for FTAs). See, for example, Marceau (1997).

The negotiation of the US–Canada FTA was a critical step in this direction. As articulated by Treasury Secretary James Baker in 1988, this agreement forced other countries to consider carefully the US proposals that were then on the table:

> If possible, we hope this follow-up liberalization will occur in the Uruguay Round. If not, we might be willing to explore a "market liberalization club" approach, through minilateral arrangements or a series of bilateral agreements ... Other nations are forced to recognize that the United States will devise ways to expand trade – with or without them.[16]

This approach, in which Baker called for "promoting liberalization on a number of fronts – multilateral, minilateral, and bilateral,"[17] came to be known as "competitive liberalization." It was to be a pillar of US policy for the next two decades. Successive administrations hoped that engaging simultaneously with numerous partners in a variety of negotiating configurations could force each one of them to make their best offers, and to build upon the rules governing the new issues.

This stepped progression can be seen for the rules governing trade in services. The US–Israel agreement (1985) was accompanied by a nonbinding Declaration on Trade in Services, and the US–Canada FTA (1988) included one full chapter on services in general and another devoted specifically to financial services. NAFTA (1992) topped that by deepening the commitments and adding a new chapter on telecommunications services. This FTA not only provided important precedents for the WTO's General Agreement on Trade in Services (GATS), but created an alternative model for future agreements. The NAFTA approach to services is so GATS-Plus that any FTAs that are based on this template are generally assumed to be more ambitious than agreements that adhere to the GATS model. A similar progression can be seen in these sequential agreements' provisions dealing with investment and intellectual property rights.

These precedents do not always have the intended demonstration effect on the multilateral system. Some topics found even in older FTAs are still not on the table in the WTO, and once an issue has made it onto the agenda there is no guarantee that it will remain there. When an issue is covered in successive trade agreements, however, the provisions tend to get more detailed. That can be seen in the sequence by which some items get promoted from the level of mere articles to entire chapters (Table 5.1). It can also result in legal verbosity.

---

[16]   Baker (1988), p. 41.
[17]   Idem.

For example, the TPP's intellectual property rights chapter runs to about 22,500 words, approaching the magnitude of the entire GATT 1947 (some 28,000 words, not counting the tariff schedules).

The issue coverage of FTAs often differs from what one finds in the WTO. Some developing countries – especially those outside of the Western Hemisphere – still negotiate "partial scope agreements" (i.e., FTAs from which many goods sectors may be excluded), or FTAs that do not include services, or that otherwise cover only part of the WTO issue base. By contrast, the FTAs negotiated by the United States and other developed countries are usually WTO-Plus (i.e., provide disciplines that go deeper than WTO rules) or WTO-Extra (i.e., include some issues that are not yet within the jurisdiction of the WTO). That sometimes reflects the desire of a *demandeur* to set a precedent for future multilateral negotiations; alternatively, that same *demandeur* may treat FTAs as an opportunity to build upon issues for which it was obliged to make compromises in an earlier multilateral negotiation. Either way, the scope of issues that fall within international rules may vary greatly from one agreement to another.

Trade Disputes as a Political Catalyst

Issues get brought to the trading system through disputes as well as negotiations, and this can exacerbate the contagion of conflict by dragooning new stakeholders into the debate. The process is nowhere more apparent than in the social issues of trade policy, especially those related to labor rights, environmental protection, and consumer rights. The GATT and WTO dispute-settlement systems have now spent decades dealing with the relationship between trade and social issues, with the system slowly coming around to the recognition that countries' measures should be judged with a view toward both trade law and other legitimate objectives in public policy. Even so, the letter and the spirit of GATT and WTO agreements usually carry greater weight in cases where trade collides with other issues. This can mean making short-term gains at the expense of the system's long-term prospects, as the cumulative effect of pro-trade decisions may be to push an ever-widening range of activists into the trade-skeptical coalition.

Part of the problem is generational. To the limited extent that the drafters of the GATT anticipated the "trade and" issues of the future, such as "trade and the environment," they did so in the exceptions clauses of GATT Article XX. Those exceptions were based primarily on topics that concerned the US negotiators and their RTAA partners in the late 1930s, especially the need to provide safe harbor for laws then on the books that might otherwise run afoul of market-opening rules. Some of the laws giving rise to those exceptions were already rather old by the 1930s, as exemplified by the protection that GATT Article XX(e) offers to any country's measures "relating to the products of prison labour." This clause was necessitated by a provision in US trade law that prohibits the importation of goods produced with convict or forced labor. That law has been on the books since 1894,[18] meaning that the only provision of WTO law that explicitly deals with trade and labor rights reflects the social conscience of US legislators precisely a century before the WTO drafters finished their work.

From the perspective of environmentalists and other social advocates, the ideal exceptions clause would mimic what GATT Article XXI provides on national security. As discussed in Chapter 7, that provision offers safe harbor whenever a country claims that some otherwise trade-restricting measure is necessary for its essential security interests.[19] The hurdles are higher for the issues related to GATT Article XX's general exceptions. A country may claim that a trade-related environmental law is justified by the need to "protect human, animal or plant life or health" or "conserve[e] exhaustible natural resources," for example, but that assertion is subject to scrutiny by panels and (since the advent of the WTO) the Appellate Body (AB). When panels and the AB pass judgment on laws that lie at the intersection of trade law and some other field of public policy, we should not be surprised if they frequently give the right of way to trade.

A series of cases in the 1990s had the effect of conscripting environmentalists – however unintentionally and involuntarily – as combatants in trade disputes. The Marine Mammal Protection Act was at issue in the tuna–dolphin case, for example, with Mexico contesting the dolphin-protection standards that this US law set for tuna fishing. Other challenges in the final days of the GATT and the early years of the WTO concerned US laws prohibiting the taking of endangered species by shrimp trawlers, the "gas-guzzler" tax on large automobiles, and standards on reformulated gasoline. While some panel decisions acknowledged the legitimacy of environmental objectives, the very fact that these laws were being challenged in a trade-centric forum led "greens" and other liberal groups to view the GATT and WTO dispute-settlement systems as a menace to the rules that they favored. This paradoxically encouraged

---

[18] This provision was originally enacted as Section 24 of the Tariff Act of 1894. The version now on the books is Section 307 of the Hawley–Smoot Tariff Act.

[19] That automaticity may now come under question. In Chapters 7 and 16 we examine the controversies surrounding the Trump administration's abuse of this provision in cases involving aluminum, steel, and the automotive sector.

consumer organizations – the ostensible representatives of those who should benefit from lower tariffs and prices – to join others who oppose an open market.

The Efforts to Reconcile Trade Liberalization with Social Goals

Negotiators treated these issues gingerly in the Uruguay Round, making modest accommodations to the post-1947 shift in the world's political center of gravity. In place of revising GATT Article XX, they reflected the new *Zeitgeist* in the language of the WTO preamble. The corresponding section of the GATT had reflected the priorities of policymakers who, in the aftermath of the Great Depression and the Second World War, associated mass consumption with happiness and peace. The drafters of the WTO were raised in a different era. Utilizing the standard orthographic codes of trade negotiators, who indicate the deletion of existing language with ~~strike-throughs~~ and the insertion of new language with underlines, we can see that transformation in the following mash-up of the GATT and WTO preambles:

> Recognizing that their relations in the field of trade and economic endeavour should be conducted with a view to raising standards of living, ensuring full employment and a large and steadily growing volume of real income and effective demand, ~~developing the full use of the resources of the world~~ and expanding the production and exchange of goods and services, while allowing for the optimal use of the world's resources in accordance with the objective of sustainable development, seeking both to protect and preserve the environment and to enhance the means for doing so in a manner consistent with their respective needs and concerns at different levels of economic development . . .

These preambular accommodations thus acknowledged the growing global concerns over sustainability, but the legal significance of this language remains a work in progress. The AB observed in 1998 that the preamble does offer "colour, texture and shading to the rights and obligations of Members,"[20] and further elaborated upon this point in three precedential cases that it decided in 2012. Each of these involved the relationship between WTO rules on technical barriers to trade (TBT) and US laws that had social aims. One ruling concerned US cigarette restrictions,[21] which were aimed at the social objective of reducing smoking by teenagers. From a trade perspective, the key issue was whether these restrictions violated the rule of national treatment:

[20] WTO Appellate Body (1998), p. 155.
[21] The other two cases concerned tuna and country-of-origin labeling.

Congress had generally banned the flavoring of tobacco, and hence prohibited clove cigarettes (all of which are imported), but also carved out an exception for menthol cigarettes (most of which are produced domestically). This case provided the opportunity for the AB to give guidance to panels on how to weigh social claims against trade rights. They "must carefully scrutinize the particular circumstances of the case" when determining "whether the detrimental impact on imports stems exclusively from a legitimate regulatory distinction rather than reflects discrimination against the group of imported products."[22]

The consequences of that ruling depend on one's perspective. On the one hand, it established a legal toehold for future cases, confirming that governments are entitled to make regulatory distinctions between products so long as they are based on legitimate objectives. Trade lawyers generally concur that these rulings from 2012 may, in future cases, ease the way for decisions in favor of social laws. On the other hand, the body found in this specific case that the US justification for banning clove cigarettes while exempting menthol did not rise to the level of a legitimate regulatory distinction. Critics of the WTO are not appeased by seemingly friendlier principles if in practice they still lose. The net effect on the domestic diplomacy of trade is to confirm what Schattschneider observed regarding the contagion of conflict, with antismoking activists forming yet another group of recruits to the trade-skeptical coalition.

LIBERAL IDEOLOGY AND THE DOMESTIC DIPLOMACY OF TRADE

One of the more intractable challenges that pro-trade advocates now face is growing opposition on the left-hand side of the political spectrum.[23] Free trade was once part of liberal orthodoxy because it was associated with cherished objectives such as international cooperation, peace, economic development, and consumer welfare. Today it is more common to hear trade agreements being criticized on the left as instruments that favor corporate interests over ordinary people in the United States and abroad,[24] and while free trade and globalization are anathema to the far right[25] they remain dogma in the less extreme segments on that end of that political spectrum.

---

[22] WTO Appellate Body (2012), p. 66.
[23] Issues on the right-hand side of this spectrum, including an antiestablishment wing of the Republican Party that objects to crony capitalism, are discussed in Chapter 6.
[24] See, for example, Brown (2004).
[25] See, for example, Buchanan (1998).

This challenge might be attributed in part to underlying changes in the economic foundation of society. One of the subtler consequences of the economic transition is a change in the policy preferences of the general public, and especially those persons who no longer feel a direct attachment to the industries that produce traded goods. The typical American has become ever more alienated from agriculture or manufactures, and few of the people in the large and growing services sector imagine that their jobs are tied to the global economy in the same way that producers of goods are. We may reasonably speculate that this is one reason why politically active citizens began to conceive of trade issues less in terms of how imports or exports might affect their own job prospects, and thought more about how globalization affected other topics that mattered to them.

Post-Materialist Values and Sociotropism

At issue here is the observed tendency of societies to place greater stress on "post-materialist" values as they develop economically. Abramson and Inglehart argued that countries undergo a "value shift" in which they move progressively from immediate concerns about such materialist values as economic and physical security "toward a greater emphasis on freedom, self-expression, and the quality of life."[26] Survey data show that post-materialist values are more prominent in developed than in developing countries, and that the value shift can be traced to economic progress and generational replacement. The same process affects the evolution of domestic trade politics. The shifting locus of trade debates from issues of jobs and economic security to social concerns over the quality of life – both at home and abroad – is thus one manifestation of a larger progression that has been underway for decades.

Post-materialist values can be seen in a society's rising propensity to protect the environment. The Kuznets environmental curve posits a U-shaped relationship between prosperity and environmentalism, such that a population's willingness to suffer environmental degradation may actually rise in the early stage of industrial development, but the mass of consumer/voters will eventually treat damage to the environment as an inferior good (i.e., one that they demand less as their incomes rise). Tolerance for pollution may be high in poor, growing economies, but the citizenry of a richer country may have a very different view. Trade might theoretically resolve this problem by allowing countries at all levels of economic development to situate themselves

---

[26]   Abramson and Inglehart (1995), p. 1.

wherever they wish on the ladder of economic opportunities and environmental costs, but that solution works only if environmental consciousness is delimited by national borders. To the extent that environmental problems cross frontiers (e.g., air pollution or global warming), or that environmentalists adopt a global perspective, activists may attack any proposals that are perceived to undermine environmental laws or encourage a "race to the bottom" among poorer countries that compete for environmentally risky investments. When environmentalists first got involved in trade debates, some of them were won over to the idea that liberalization might actually advance their agenda by kick-starting the adoption of post-materialist values in developing countries.[27] That did not last long, as the weight of opinion in environmental groups soon centered on concerns that the dispute-settlement provisions of trade agreements might be used to undo their laws.

This is one way in which sociotropism comes into play. Kinder and Kiewiet coined this term to mean a notion of fairness that transcends self-interest, such that a citizen who shares this orientation is motivated by concerns over the welfare of others.[28] While post-materialist values usually involve a redefinition of what people want *for themselves*, some activists take the next step by caring about the welfare of others. A sociotropically oriented person exemplifies the aforementioned phenomenon by which, according to Adam Smith, people derive pleasure from even a stranger's happiness. Or as John Donne would have it, "any man's death diminishes me/because I am involved in mankind."[29] Some scholars find evidence of sociotropic beliefs regarding trade. Mansfield and Mutz reported that the US public is guided less by the material self-interest of individuals than by perceptions of how trade affects the economy as a whole.[30] Davidson et al. concurred, finding "considerable evidence that, when citizens think about trade policy, unemployment plays a major role in their calculation and that this calculation contains a major sociotropic element."[31] Voters might think not only about how an initiative affects their own jobs, but also whether others might be put out of work.

There are two distinct ways that a sociotropic perspective might make a person less supportive of trade liberalization. One variant, which we might call domestic sociotropism, is based on the concern that opening the US market to foreign competition might cause other Americans to lose their

---

[27]   See, for example, Irwin (2017), p. 633 on the position of environmental groups in the 1993 debate over NAFTA.

[28]   Kinder and Kiewiet (1979).

[29]   John Donne, "No Man Is an Island" (1624).

[30]   Mansfield and Mutz (2009).

[31]   Davidson et al. (2010), p. 31.

jobs. By this line of reasoning, the knowledge that an open market in (for example) footwear might put cobblers in Maine out of business may matter more to a sociotropically inclined person in California than the expectation that her shoes might cost less. Alternatively, a globally sociotropic perspective might lead that same person to worry about the exploitation of workers in a Vietnamese shoe factory; those concerns may give rise to the growing calls for "fair trade." Either way, sociotropism may lead an otherwise apolitical person to view trade liberalization with suspicion.

Post-materialism, sociotropism, and internationalism come together in what Keck and Sikkink call transnational advocacy networks. These consist of "actors working internationally on an issue, who are bound together by shared values, a common discourse, and dense exchanges of information and services." Their purpose is to "mobilize information strategically to help create new issues and categories and to persuade, pressure, and gain leverage over much more powerful organizations and governments."[32] These networks are as old as the antislavery and women's suffrage movements, and their numbers have grown greatly since then. They were virtually unknown to the participants in the Havana Conference of 1948, but half a century later their successors at the WTO's Seattle Ministerial Conference of 1999 were painfully aware of just how many groups had turned against trade liberalization. It remains an open question as to how much of that meeting's failure can be laid to the demonstrators who surrounded the venue, as the negotiators on the inside had wide and deep divisions of their own. The street actions certainly did not help to launch a new WTO round, however, nor has the rising opposition to trade in left-leaning circles made life any easier for trade negotiators since the Doha Round began in 2001.

The Movement of Labor

Add to all of this the movement of US organized labor from the pro-trade to the trade-skeptical camp. The motivations here are murkier than in the case of other liberal groups, as there definitely exist solid economic reasons for unions to view globalization with suspicion. It would, however, be incorrect to characterize the changing position of labor as an exclusively sectoral matter. Ideological considerations have served at times either to delay or deepen the level of trade-skepticism among union leaders.

Modern observers may be surprised to learn that unions had been leading members of both the pro-trade and anti-Communist coalitions during the

---

[32]   Keck and Sikkink (1998), p. 2.

early decades of American hegemony. The labor movement's internal disputes over foreign policy in general, and on specific issues such as the Vietnam War and union ties to the CIA, have been the subject of scholarship that is as extensive as it is partisan.[33] Our more specific focus here is on labor's approach to trade. Unions representing a given industry tend to favor free or restricted trade according to their industry's competitiveness, but the strength of that commitment can be affected by other considerations. That is especially notable in the case of foreign policy. Anti-Communism served to delay the emergence of protectionism in the unions during the early decades of the Cold War. In recent years, solidarity with foreign unions has deepened labor's opposition to some specific initiatives such as the US–Colombia FTA.

Debates over the tariff have periodically caused rifts in the labor movement. Leaders in the American Federation of Labor (AFL) decided in the late nineteenth century to sidestep their disagreements and take no stand on trade, but one faction later bolted by forming the America's Wage Earners' Protective Conference in 1928. This trade-skeptical coalition remained a minority faction for decades. "In the late forties," as Frank observed, the only protectionist unions were "glass and pottery workers, watch workers, and a few fishermen's unions."[34] Within a decade they were joined by unions representing textile workers, coal miners, carpenters, bookbinders, hatmakers, and printers. At mid-century the main support for free trade came from the Congress of Industrial Organizations (CIO), a group that challenged the AFL for leadership of the labor movement. Its pro-trade position dates from the departure of John L. Lewis of the United Mine Workers as CIO president in 1940.[35] Thereafter the CIO was dominated by such export-oriented industries as automobiles, steel, and electrical machinery. The merger of the AFL and CIO in 1955, paired with the political imperatives of the Cold War, papered over the differences between the two groups.

The consolidated AFL-CIO still leaned more heavily toward the pro-trade than the trade-skeptical side during the Kennedy administration. It merely conditioned its support for open markets on the extension of trade adjustment assistance at home and the negotiation of international labor standards abroad.[36] Over the course of the next few decades, this federation's position would gradually move from one in which TAA was meant as a complement to liberalization, to another period in which it was desired as a substitute for

---

[33] See, for example, Gershman (1975), Hero and Starr (1970), and Radosh (1969).
[34] Frank (1999), p. 116. On the shifting positions of unions during the 1950s see Watson (1956), pp. 694–697.
[35] Hero and Starr (1970), pp. 48–49.
[36] See, for example, AFL-CIO (1961).

liberalization, and finally to one where it was treated as a complement to protection the form of tariffs, quotas, Buy American and local-content require-ments, or other interventionist options. The changing positions of the unions posed a problem for Democratic officeholders. Many of them moved in lockstep with this largest constituency group, and a very few set themselves in opposition to it, while a significant but declining number of them hoped to find some compromise.

The Shifting Positions of Religious and Consumer Groups

The original rationale behind left-leaning support for trade was the association between open markets and peace. This is a connection that dates at least as far back as Richard Cobden's campaigns against the British Corn Laws in the 1840s, when his allies included groups that favored free trade "not merely on account of the material advantages which it would bring to the community, but for the far loftier motive of securing permanent peace between nations."[37] Religious communities also linked free trade with abolition, although their views were not unanimous; the South's attachments to slavery, open markets, and religion made for an especially conflicted set of goals and trade-offs.[38]

In 1934, when the Roosevelt administration made its first request for tariff-cutting authority under the RTAA, nearly all of the witnesses who testified before the congressional trade committees were representatives of protection-ist industries. It would take years before most of the commercially motivated members of the pro-trade coalition came together to back this policy. The largest initial support instead came from noneconomic groups such as the Foreign Policy Association and the World Peace Foundation, each of which favored free trade for its supposed political consequences. The array of liberal groups that promoted open markets greatly expanded by the time that Congress took up the Trade Expansion Act of 1962. The religious community was especially prominent in those days, with pro-trade arguments coming from the Friends Committee on National Legislation, the United Church Women, the National Council of Jewish Women, the National Council of the Churches of Christ, and the General Board of Christian Social Concerns of the Methodist Church (more specifically its Division of Peace and World Order). Likeminded pro-RTAA groups included the American Association of University Women, International House, the League of Women Voters, and the United World Federalists. It is perhaps inevitable that free trade could not

---

[37] Cobden (1848).
[38] See Meardon (2008) on the antebellum debate in the United States. See also Palen (2015).

survive as a faith-based initiative, as only a few strands of the Judeo-Christian tradition are comfortable with the notion that greed might be good. By the late 1980s, some of these same groups – or their intellectual and political heirs – took a far more negative view of open markets. They generally based their concerns not on the impact of trade on relations between countries, but instead on how it affects the poor within countries.

Perhaps the oddest aspect of liberal trade skepticism is the evolving role of consumer organizations. There have been few critics of protectionism more acerbic than the muckraker Ida Tarbell, whose 1911 book *The Tariff in Our Times* portrayed these taxes as just one more trick by which the wealthy can deny fair wages to workers and quality goods to consumers. The intellectual tradition that associates protection with trusts and trust funds continued for at least another half-century. The switch came sometime between 1973 and 1993, a period bookended by two very different messages from consumer advocate Ralph Nader. In 1973 a Nader study group published a book (*The Monopoly Makers*)[39] describing trade protection in terms that parroted Tarbell. Two decades later, Nader contributed to *The Case against "Free Trade": GATT, NAFTA, and the Globalization of Corporate Power.*[40]

Today's consumer organizations tend to place a higher priority on product safety, environmentalism, and related issues than they do on prices, a point that exemplifies the middle- or upper-class orientation that seems to characterize many of these groups' outlooks. Instead of viewing the competitive firm as the consumer's tacit ally, and the tax-hungry state as their common enemy, they typically portray corporate greed as the central problem. If not restrained by the regulatory bodies of an interventionist state, they fear, corporations would cut corners at the expense of safety for consumers, workers, and the environment. To the limited extent that trade debates still consider the effect of open markets on consumer welfare (narrowly defined as prices and choice), that perspective is more often presented by market-oriented academics, think tanks, or journalists[41] than by formally constituted consumer organizations.

The end result is that trade liberalization went from being a topic that won support from otherwise disengaged groups because they saw it as an instrument of peace and shared prosperity to a subject that attracts opposition from very similar groups because of an entirely different set of externalities. It is uncertain just how much liberal groups contributed to the success of past pro-trade initiatives, but there is no doubt that the objections they raise today help

[39]   Green (1973).
[40]   Nader et al. (1993). See also Nader and Wallach (1996).
[41]   See, for example, Bovard (1991).

to shape a policymaking environment that is more hostile to new trade agreements.

Political Causes versus Economic Interests

The expanding scope of trade has changed not just the number of combatants on the field, but also how they fight and keep score. As recently as the 1980s, debates over trade were set-piece legislative battles between narrow ranks of contending economic interests. On one side were arrayed exporters, retailers, and industries that depend on imported inputs, and on the other were labor-intensive or inefficient industries and the unions associated with them. Those traditional, narrowly economic interests remain active, but over time they have been joined – and sometimes drowned out – by other voices that associate this issue with labor rights abroad, the global environment, domestic consumer safety, income inequality, and foreign policy. No longer just a question of whose ox is gored, trade has now become the focus of (among others) animal rights activists who are more concerned about the welfare of the ox than the livelihood of its owner.

These changes remade the tone and character of policy debates. While firms and labor unions act according to clearly identifiable economic *interests* in these matters, many of the new participants are ideologically inspired by political *causes* in which they have no financial stake. The newer entrants are interested in trade more for its political than its economic value, being less concerned by the effect of trade policy on sales and employment than on its utility to promote or retard some other end in domestic or foreign policy. These groups tend to put less faith in bargaining and compromise than do the traditional, typically more pragmatic interests. Both the tone and the outcome of a policy debate can be qualitatively different when participants are motivated by something other than narrow calculations of their own economic welfare. These new entrants are more likely to use the word "compromise" as a mark of opprobrium than approval, and cannot be easily bought off with exceptions or inducements.

One way to consider the difference between traditional and newer trade politics is to ask what has happened to the old norm of "reciprocal non-interference." This is the term that the youthful Schattschneider used to describe a practice in interest group tariff lobbying "under which it is proper for each to seek duties for himself but improper and unfair to oppose duties sought by others."[42] A producer of clothing would not try to block the

---

[42]   Schattschneider (1935), pp. 133–134.

producers of fabric when they demanded protection, for example, but would instead insist they be compensated for any tariffs on their suppliers by a protective tariff for their own finished goods. This same approach could be used by other groups whose objectives went beyond simple tariffs. In the 1970s through the 1990s, a president might buy votes for a market-opening initiative by (for example) granting export subsidies to wheat and imposing import quotas on steel. Neither wheat farmers nor steelmakers would object to the deal that the other group got, and both the ideologues and the industries that were devoted to freer trade were more interested in how these deals contributed to the larger objective – that is, whether the concession successfully bought off an opponent – than in how it might deviate from free-market principles.

The political dynamics of the new issues are entirely different, and encourage more direct confrontations between the contending parties. Some of the industries that are most supportive of trade liberalization are dogged by labor and environmental disputes, and are naturally hostile to proposals that provide aid and comfort to their adversaries. Conversely, the logic of trade-skeptics in the labor, environmental, and consumer movements seems to center on the contention that what is good for General Motors must be bad for America. In place of the reciprocal restraint that Schattschneider described, we instead see free-for-all fights in which the contending sides come from vastly different cultural and moral universes, and show no interest in coming to any accommodation with such alien antagonists. This is the application of *Schadenfreude* to trade politics: Ensuring that my opponent loses is equally important as – and indeed is identical to – ensuring that I win.

These divisions have greatly complicated the perennially difficult task of promoting cooperation between the executive and legislative branches, especially when government is divided. Partisan lines are much more deeply drawn on labor rights, the environment, and pharmaceutical patents than is the case for trade policy as it was traditionally defined. Effective trade policy-making has long depended on the ability of presidents and Congress to bargain with one another, such that (for example) a president who seeks a new grant of authority to negotiate trade agreements may be obliged to reach compromises with sheltered industries (which might be granted new protection or isolated from liberalization) and with unions that demand TAA for displaced workers. It is much harder to strike deals of that sort when there are fewer centrists in both parties, and when such deals are unacceptable to free-market purists among the Republicans and hardliners among the Democrats. The resulting disputes have become the leading flashpoint in US trade politics.

At a minimum, the new issues have complicated and elongated the debates that precede and follow the negotiation of new trade agreements.

FOREIGN ECONOMIC POLICY BEGINS AND ENDS AT HOME

If you should ask an economist about the causes and consequences of the expanding scope of trade policy you may well get a doubly optimistic answer. This expansion is the natural consequence of technological progress and the economic transition, with the trading system properly adapting its aims and rules to the changes in what is tradeable. It allows countries to engage in deeper integration, and to spread the benefits of liberalization and competition to an ever-wider range of activities. Negotiators may have a similarly positive take, appreciating the opportunities that arise for win–win trade-offs between issues. Grand bargains may be easier when negotiators do not have to deal with issues one-by-one, but can instead juggle numerous topics and sectors.

Ask that same question of a political scientist and you may get a very different answer, based on the complications that the economic transition may provoke in the private and public sectors. The economic transition can put the scare in business leaders who had once been at the forefront of the pro-trade movement. If their own competitiveness declines, it may not take long for their perception of borders to shift from obstacles to shields, and to demand the reimposition of barriers that they so recently disdained. Presidents may respond not just by cutting protectionist deals with some of them, but also replace others by bringing new issues and recruits to the table. Policymakers cannot invite new players to the game, however, without also attracting those groups' adversaries. Issue expansion can also be attributed to progressive changes in the political tastes of a postindustrial society; the laws that the new players promote may provoke a hostile response from other countries that read only the second word in the phrase "environmental protection." The net result may not be deeper integration, but mission creep. This contagion of conflict at home and abroad can erect new hurdles to the negotiation, approval, and implementation of trade agreements, making it ever more difficult for the trading system to function effectively. Even as presidents sought to negotiate more trade agreements with a wider range of countries, moving these pacts through Congress became more challenging.

The argument here runs counter to a theory of negotiations that one commonly heard in the immediate aftermath of the Uruguay Round (1986–1994), to the effect of "the more, the merrier." That round had seen a number of grand bargains made across issue areas, such as the elimination of textile and apparel quotas in exchange for the protection of intellectual property, and the US disavowal of unilateral retaliation in exchange for a broadening of the system's issue base and a strengthening of its dispute-settlement procedures. Those bargains were widely believed to be facilitated by a negotiating table that fairly groaned under the many and varied topics piled atop it. And in the optimistic environment of the time, marked by the end of the Cold War and the full flowering of the pro-market Washington Consensus, there was much to recommend that interpretation of events. The same could not be said for the present, more pessimistic environment in which countries devote more attention to their defensive than their offensive interests. One of the underlying reasons for that pessimism can be found in the domestic diplomacy of a shrunken hegemon. At a time when the US market accounts for a reduced share of the global economy, and when prospective partners have greater doubts that the agreements they reach might actually win approval from Congress, American negotiators have less sway over their foreign counterparts.

This is not to suggest that the new trade politics have entirely displaced the old. The 2016 presidential election confirmed that the traditional conflict between free trade and protection is alive and well and living in the Rust Belt. That is the focus of the next chapter, in which we chronicle the premature burial and sudden revival of protectionism. The new and the old politics of trade together suggest that Schattschneider may have been right in both 1935 and 1960. They also imply that the Smith of 1776 would be gloomy about the prospects for our own future.

6

Washington Slept Here:
How Trump Caught Politicians Napping on Trade

There always has been a recessive gene in the American character that has found protectionism appealing. But we've always been wise enough to reject it.

> Senator Phil Gramm, comments on withdrawal from
> the presidential race (1996)

We must protect our borders from the ravages of other countries making our products, stealing our companies, and destroying our jobs. Protection will lead to great prosperity and strength.

> President Donald Trump, Inaugural Address (2017)

INTRODUCTION

When Senator Gramm pulled out of the race for the Republican presidential nomination in 1996 he was especially bitter about the candidacy of Pat Buchanan. Espousing a doctrine of protectionism and nativism, Buchanan did unexpectedly well in the early stages of the race. Gramm was nonetheless confident that his party would ultimately choose a proponent of free trade as its standard-bearer. His confidence was well-placed that year, and the same would be true for each of the next four presidential races. Two decades later, however, Donald Trump proved that the protectionist gene was far from extinct. Running on a platform that echoed many of Buchanan's themes, he managed first to execute a hostile takeover of the Republican Party and then to win an upset victory in the general election.

How did Trump succeed where Buchanan failed? Genetic science teaches us that recessive genes will be expressed whenever they meet their match, which is precisely what appears to have propelled Trump. His position aligned with that of a substantial minority of the Republican electorate, together with sizeable numbers of independents, disgruntled Democrats, and people so estranged from the process that they had no prior party affiliations or voting records. In both phases of the election, this political neophyte put together winning coalitions by appealing to groups that had been economically and politically marginalized for decades. The most loyal core of Trump's base consists of women and (especially) men who consider themselves to be on the losing side of globalization. Their resentment is based not just on the economic consequences of open markets, but on the social distance that it creates between the winners and the losers. The very language by which Gramm spoke so dismissively to the economic vulnerability of the losers would, in time, contribute to the political vulnerability of the winners.

What is truly surprising is how the political professionals in both parties failed to perceive and exploit the growing resentment toward globalization. Trump disrupted what seemed to be a settled pattern in which protectionism was passé and policymakers were less interested in closing the US market than in opening foreign markets. Trade rose from a very low-profile issue to achieve top-tier status in the early 1990s, but receded thereafter as a focus of attention. The candidates who used to find protectionism rewarding abandoned this position when it came to yield fewer votes and campaign contributions. The veteran politician's trash can be the outsider's treasure, giving Trump an opportunity to exploit concerns over the trade deficit and lost jobs. Being unbound by the logic that had constrained previous Republican nominees, and not obliged to calculate how his positions might affect the inflow of campaign funds, he was free to appeal to a constituency that his rivals had left behind long ago.

The analysis that follows does not assume that trade policy was the decisive factor in the 2016 presidential election. It is all but impossible to assign specific values to the many different influences on the outcome, ranging from candidate characteristics, positions, and campaign funds to political cycles and the interventions – overt and covert – of other actors. The more significant point is the widespread perception among politicians that trade issues were indeed decisive, with protectionism having been one element in an unorthodox message that blended economic nationalism with xenophobia, racism, and class resentment. Above all else, Donald Trump's actions both on the campaign trail and in office suggest that he considered this issue to be critical to his strategy. He delivered quickly on several of the promises made in the campaign, most notably withdrawal from the pending Trans-Pacific Partnership and the launch of negotiations to revise NAFTA; the only significant promise that went by the wayside was the formal designation of China as a currency manipulator. The president even went beyond the pledges he made in the campaign, as demonstrated in 2018 by the tariffs he applied to aluminum and steel products under the national security law; those actions were consistent with the tone, but had never been specifically promised, by what he said on the campaign trail. As discussed in the concluding section of this chapter, the trade politics of the United States may long be affected by the perception among other Republicans that protectionism was a winning issue in 2016.

The trends reviewed here lay at the foundation of the US position in the trading system. For all else that has changed in the United States and the world over the past few generations, there had seemed to be two constants since the early 1930s: Every president from FDR through Obama was an internationalist, and all of them professed to be free-traders. While each chief executive felt compelled to make some compromises with protectionists, those have always been treated as the exception rather than the rule. By choosing a man who rejects the very underpinnings of US foreign economic policy, and treats protectionism as an objective rather than an epithet, the electorate sent the trading system into uncharted territory.

THE DECLINING SALIENCE OF TRADE FOR PROFESSIONAL POLITICIANS

The argument that follows is concerned as much with the political salience of trade policy as it is with the specific initiatives that elected officials choose to promote. *Salience* is the revealed preference of politicians to devote attention to an issue, as demonstrated by where they invest their political capital. A rational candidate will concentrate on topics that are electorally rewarding, but will take a pass on issues that do not contribute to the overarching objective of reelection. We can measure salience by examining the subject matter of the bills that members of Congress introduce, and by tallying the items on a president's agenda. The data show that while the salience of trade policy rose sharply in the twenty years that followed the emergence of a US trade deficit in 1971, it has since fallen from that peak. It is reasonable to suppose that these shifts spring from the same globalizing influences that led first to an increase in industry's demands for protection, but then tapered off as American firms accommodated themselves to globalization (see Chapter 3). As in the declining level of petitioning under the trade-remedy laws, disaffected workers were left behind in the process.

The Rise and Fall of Trade as Congressional and Presidential Priorities

The best way to measure politicians' interest in trade policy is to look at the bills that legislators introduce. Congress differs from some other legislatures in which the introduction of legislation may be the exclusive prerogative of the majority party or the executive, and hence indicates only what the leadership wants. It instead allows all members to sponsor any number of bills on any matter they wish. The result is that thousands of bills are introduced in each two-year congress, and while only a few become law they are all evidence.[1] The share of bills devoted to a topic tells us a lot about whether lawmakers think that a given subject is worth their while, even if they do not expect their bills to advance in the legislative process.

The data reported in Figure 6.1 quantify the salience of trade in both branches, based on a content analysis of all public bills. Between 1973–1974 and 1993–1994, the share of bills dealing with trade grew tenfold. The timing of that peak is unsurprising, considering all that was happening in the early 1990s: the conclusion and approval of both NAFTA and the Uruguay Round agreements, the launch of mega-regional negotiations in the Americas and the Asia-Pacific region (both of which ultimately failed), and continued concerns over US competitiveness and the trade deficit. Trade was also a hot topic in the 1992 presidential election, which was the first time that an unorthodox billionaire without prior political experience would run for the presidency on a protectionist platform. Third-party candidate H. Ross Perot captured 19% of the popular vote, and while that was not nearly enough to win it seems to have inspired emulation on Capitol Hill. Trade's Washington heyday passed as quickly as it came, even if congressional interest did not revert to the low levels of the early 1970s. Dealing with trade was less than one-third as attractive to the median legislator in the two years that Donald Trump ran as it had been in the first two years of Bill Clinton's presidency.

Presidents are no less rational on these matters than are members of Congress, even if their interests and powers are different. The data in Figure 6.1 also show the relative share of events and documents that every chief executive from Carter through Obama has generated on trade policy. This may not be quite as variable and revealing an indicator of salience as are bills, insofar as presidents do not fully control the flow of issues that reach the Oval Office. Some of the documents that a president routinely handles are mandated by existing law, or come to him because someone else enacted a bill, filed a petition, forced a crisis, or otherwise set in motion a process that stopped only when the buck reached his desk. Chief executives nonetheless have a great deal of discretion in deciding which

---

[1]   For example, in the 114th Congress (2015–2016) there were 6,536 bills introduced in the House of Representatives and 3,548 in the Senate. Only 329 of the bills made it all the way through the legislative process to become public laws, amounting to 5% of all House bills or 3% of the combined House and Senate bills. Calculated from data at https://congress.gov/browse/114th-congress.

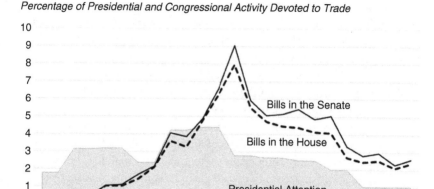

Percentage of Presidential and Congressional Activity Devoted to Trade

FIGURE 6.1 The salience of trade policy in the two branches of US government, 1969–2016.

"Presidential Attention" is the share of transcripts, press releases, executive orders, fact sheets, and other White House documents for which the title or description included (1) the word "trade" (excluding cases in which it had a meaning other than "international commerce," such as references to the Federal Trade Commission, the building trades, etc.) and/or (2) one or more of the words "import" (or "importation"), "export," "tariff," or "safeguard" (when used in a trade-related sense). The values represent averages for each four-year presidential term (with the Nixon and Ford presidencies of 1973–1976 counted as one).

"Bills in Congress" are the average for all public bills introduced in the House and Senate bills that included at least one of the following keywords and phrases in the text: "African Growth and Opportunity Act," "Andean trade," "antidumping," "Caribbean Basin Economic Recovery Act," "fair trade," "free trade agreement," "GATT," "General Agreement on Tariffs and Trade," "Generalized System of Preferences," "most favored nation," "NAFTA," "normal trade relations," "Omnibus Trade and Competitiveness Act," "Tariff Act of 1930," "trade act," "trade adjustment assistance," "Trade and Tariff Act," "Trade Expansion Act," "trade preferences," "unfair trade," or "World Trade Organization." These values are for each chamber in each two-year Congress.

Note that data on bills in Congress are not available in searchable form prior to 1973. Source: Calculated from data on the Library of Congress website at www.congress .gov/advanced-search/legislation (for the bills with trade content) and www .congress.gov/browse (for the total number of bills) and from documents posted by the American Presidency Project (www.presidency.ucsb.edu/ws/#axzz1JAjFyi1c).

topics they will emphasize, and control how much publicity they will accord to both the required and the elective subjects on their agendas. By determining which activities receive short shrift and which garner extra attention, we can get a good sense of just how highly a president values each issue.

The data again indicate that the salience of trade hit its peak with George H. W. Bush, when this issue accounted for more than 4% of the presidential paper trail. Trade's political profile dropped thereafter, and fell especially rapidly with the inauguration of Barack Obama. That was partly a function of decreased activity: Neither the executive nor Congress showed more than cursory interest in trade during Obama's first two years in office, and the only significant undertaking in his first term was to secure congressional approval in 2011 for the FTAs that he inherited. Trade activity accelerated in Obama's second term, but one could not tell that from the president's schedule. Even though the TPP negotiations now expanded in membership, and were complemented by a new grant of trade promotion authority and the equally ambitious Transatlantic Trade and Investment Partnership, trade accounted for just 1% of the documents and events in the first and second Obama terms. This observation speaks volumes about the low salience of trade at the very end of what future historians may label as the pre-Trump era of American trade politics.

Protection and Disputes in Presidential Election Years

It has long been a matter of folkloric belief that presidential election years are hazardous times for free-traders, and this contention finds support in the timing of safeguard cases during the last quarter of the twentieth century. As discussed in Chapter 3, the safeguards law provides for import restrictions even on fairly traded goods if they are imported in injurious quantities. Unlike technical statutes such as the antidumping law, safeguards require a presidential decision. Of the seventy-three safeguard petitions filed between enactment of the Trade Act of 1974 and the last pre-Trump case in 2001, twenty-six were scheduled so that an incumbent president seeking reelection would have to decide whether to grant protection during the twelve-month period preceding Election Day. The 1980 automotive case was also associated with a presidential reelection, even though the petition was filed too late for the US International Trade Commission (USITC) decision to come before the election (see Chapter 8), as was the steel case that the Bush administration self-initiated in 2001 to keep a campaign promise. Twenty-eight cases were thus associated with one of five presidential reelection years (i.e., 5.6 per year), compared to forty-five cases in the remaining twenty-one years (i.e., 2.1 per year). These patterns clearly confirm an association between protectionist demands and presidential elections before the WTO's Dispute Settlement Body seemed to outlaw safeguards.

Much the same pattern can be seen in the protectionist campaign promises that presidential candidates used to make. In four of the six presidential elections from 1980 through 2000 the Republican candidate promised major protection for import-challenged industries. Ronald Reagan pledged to protect the textile and apparel industry in 1980 (thus appealing to voters in the South)[2]; he made a similar promise to the steel industry in 1984 (thus appealing to voters in the industrial Midwest), and the two Bushes also offered protection to the steel industry in their respective 1988 and 2000 campaigns. No candidate in either party made similar promises for this type of "big ticket" protection in any election from 2004 through 2016. To the extent that presidential incumbents and aspirants still strike tough poses, they typically do so with respect to a specific country – China – rather than specific industries.

The disappearance of major, product-focused protectionism reflects three tectonic shifts in the political geography of presidential elections. The first is the declining level of employment in protectionist industries. Second, population growth has slowed in many of the states that host these industries, meaning that they have lost seats in the House of Representatives after each decennial census. Fewer House seats also mean fewer votes in the Electoral College, and thus less heft in presidential elections. For example, the industrial states of Michigan, Ohio, and Pennsylvania collectively controlled 73 electoral votes in the 1980 presidential election, so that a candidate who won all three states was 27% of the way toward racking up the 270 electoral votes needed to win the White House. They had been reduced to just 21% of that magic number in 2004, and 20% in 2012. The third change is in the contestability of states, with party lines becoming firmer over the decades. In 1980 there were 27 contested states controlling 336 electoral votes (62% of the available 538), but by 2008 there were just 18 states in play with 181 electoral votes (34% of the total). Several former "swing states" used to host troubled industries, and thus enticed protectionist appeals, but have lately turned so deeply Republican red or Democratic blue that neither party feels an incentive to contest them.

The data in Figure 6.2 illustrate the electoral stakes in four contests that featured protectionist promises, and one in which neither candidate went this way. The figure shows the total number of electoral votes associated with states that (a) were not firmly in either party's camp and (b) were home to significant

---

[2] That promise took the form of a September 3, 1980 letter to Senator Strom Thurmond (Republican–South Carolina) in which candidate Reagan promised to renew the Multi-Fiber Arrangement that was slated to expire in 1981 and to strengthen it "by relating import growth from all sources to domestic market growth." The text of the letter is in the *Congressional Record* of September 20, 1984 (pp. S11569–11570).

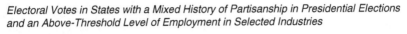

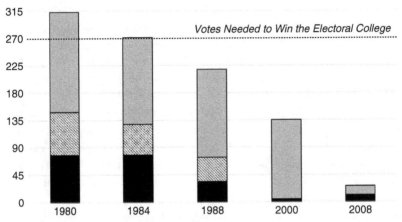

■ Iron & Steel States ⊠ States with Both Sectors ☐ Textiles & Apparel States

FIGURE 6.2 Electoral votes in protection-leaning swing states, 1980–2008.

A state is associated with an industry if employment in that industry accounted for at least 0.25% of the state's population in the election year.

Swing State = One that that split its vote in the four most recent elections, including the year in question. For example, a state was in play in 2008 if there was at least one election during 1996, 2000, 2004, and 2008 in which that state went Democratic and at least one election in that same period in which it went Republican, but was out of play if it went for either party all four times.

Note: Election years prior to 2008 in which the major-party candidates made no significant promises to protect major industries (i.e., 1992, 1996, and 2004) not shown.

Sources: Swing states determined on the basis of election results posted by the National Archives at www.archives.gov/federal-register/electoral-college/votes/vot es_by_state.html. Data for iron and steel are based on SIC 331 and 332 for 1977–1992 and on NAIC 331111 for 1997–2007; data for textiles and apparel are based on SIC 22 and 23 for 1977–1992 and on NAIC 313–315 for 1997–2008.

In each year the calculations of industry size for states are based on the Census of Manufactures that was conducted closest to that election.

numbers of steel and/or textile and apparel workers.[3] The aggregate data demonstrate how thoroughly the political economy of protection has changed.

---

[3] More precisely, this criterion requires that the industry employ at least 0.25% of the state's total population. That seemingly low threshold comports with the decision that the G. W. Bush campaign made to offer protection to the steel industry in the closing days of the 2000 campaign. The Bush pledge was reportedly made to sway voters in West Virginia, where jobs in the iron and steel industry accounted for just 0.27% of the state's population.

Reagan's 1980 promise to protect textiles and apparel targeted 19 swing states that then collectively controlled 235 electoral votes (87% of the needed 270). Four years later, when Reagan ran for reelection and promised to protect steel, that industry was associated with 9 of the states in play and 128 electoral votes (47% of 270). By 2008, however, the protectionist pool had all but emptied. Obama won both the sole remaining steel swing state (Indiana) and its counterpart among the textile and apparel states (North Carolina), doing so without resort to protectionism.[4] And while trade policy played a role in both presidential elections that followed, none of the four major-party nominees in 2012 and 2016 – not even Trump – made any sector-specific promises like those in the 1980–2000 races. Trump's later use of the national security law to impose tariffs on steel and aluminum was in keeping with the spirit of his campaign, but was not foreshadowed by any specific promises made in 2016.

Dispute-settlement cases have now taken the place of these most traditional forms of protectionism. Bill Clinton was the first president in the WTO era, and when he ran for reelection in 1996 his administration brought more cases to the WTO (17) than it averaged during 1995 and 1997–2000 (10.2). The total numbers dropped for George W. Bush, but the distribution remained comparable: He brought four complaints in 2004, versus an average of 2.7 per year in the rest of his presidency. The Obama administration approximately matched its predecessor's record, filing five complaints in 2012 and 2.3 per year in the rest of his term. For the full 1995–2016 period, the United States initiated almost twice as many cases in presidential reelection years (an average of 8.7) than in all others (4.5). The switch from protection to disputes implies not only that recent presidents have been more interested in enforcing access to foreign markets than in restricting foreign access to the US market, but also that they are content to employ low-profile policy tools. Promises to impose restrictions on a whole class of imports might make the first page of the newspaper in the states where that industry is a major employer, but stories about disputes in the WTO will usually be relegated to the business section (unless they result in high-profile confrontations). This switch is consistent with the general pattern by which trade policymaking seemed to have been transformed from an issue with mass appeal to a technical subject that is of principal interest to people who inhabit corporate boardrooms and academic offices.

---

[4] Those two states met the criteria for being considered swing states only because Obama won there in 2008; Republicans otherwise had an unbroken record in recent elections.

Campaign Contributions from Pro-Trade and Protectionist Interests

Campaign cash has also shifted away from protectionist interests. Trade-skeptical firms and unions still make contributions to politicians, but their purses have not grown as fat as those of the more pro-trade industries. The labor unions in particular now provide a smaller share of the money to candidates and parties than they once did.

One recurring theme in the literature of American trade policymaking holds that protection-seeking industries can use campaign contributions to expand their influence beyond the territorial limits of their operations. Or as Ferguson's Golden Rule has it, "To discover who rules, follow the gold."[5] Grossman and Helpman advanced a protection-for-sale model based on politicians' incentives to peddle influence, such that (for example) a legislator who represents a district in which there is no steel production might nonetheless be persuaded to favor protection for this industry.[6] Similarly, Gawande and Hoekman found a relationship between agricultural protection, subsidies, and campaign contributions.[7] One may certainly cite anecdotal examples of industries that have taken advantage of this legal form of graft. Consider sugar: Cane and beets are commercially grown in just ten, mostly small states, but the industry gives generously to legislators in the other forty. Those investments are widely reputed to account for this industry's continued protection from foreign competition. The data nevertheless suggest that the sugar money may be more of an exception than an exemplar.

Two caveats should be borne in mind when considering these numbers. The first is that the laws regulating campaign finance frequently shift through legislative revision and judicial rulings, resulting in a multiplicity of means by which interested parties can funnel money (directly or indirectly) to candidates. The reporting that follows is based on the most transparent of these instruments, the political action committee (PAC). PACs must file detailed information on their receipts and disbursements, but the industries and other interests that establish these committees may also resort to other, less transparent options such as independent expenditures and "soft money" contributions to political parties. The data may therefore be taken as broadly indicative of funding, but we might find somewhat different patterns if every form of campaign finance were equally transparent. Second, we may only guess how high a priority trade receives when PACs review candidates. The sugar industry may base its allocational decisions entirely on this issue, but the typical

---

[5] Ferguson (1995), p. 8.
[6] Grossman and Helpman (2002).
[7] Gawande and Hoekman (2006).

PAC probably considers a wider range of questions when deciding who will get its cash.

That said, the data reported in Table 6.1 strongly suggest that the rational, median candidate for the presidency or Congress will find it more rewarding to adopt positions favored by pro-trade sectors than to pander to protectionist interests. For every dollar that the protection-seeking PACs contributed to Federal candidates in 2016, the PACs associated with pro-trade industries made $2.22 in contributions. Moreover, the trends are moving in the direction of the pro-trade industries. The protectionist PACs provided 39% more money in 2016 than they did in 2000, but during the same period the pro-trade PACs very nearly doubled their contributions. It is especially important to note the decline of the protectionist unions, whose largesse fell 22% in absolute terms during 2000–2016. Simply stated, a politician who relies on PACs to fund a campaign might think twice before turning protectionist.

THE RISE OF DONALD TRUMP AND THE REBIRTH
OF PRESIDENTIAL PROTECTIONISM

And then came Trump. In his 2016 campaign he accorded trade policy, together with related topics such as illegal immigration, a higher profile than any other major-party nominee had in nearly a century. Trump repeatedly promised to withdraw from the as-yet unapproved TPP, to renegotiate NAFTA, and to impose tariffs on imports from China and elsewhere. How did a man running on an unapologetically protectionist platform manage to win the Republican nomination and then the general election?

At the risk of sounding glib, the simplest explanation is that Trump won precisely because he was so new to electoral politics that he did not know what could not be done – and so he did it anyway. This novice candidate may have had no inkling that a downtrodden and apathetic underclass did not vote, that protectionism was a loser of an issue, and that it was impossible for a Republican to capture the Democratic strongholds of Michigan, Pennsylvania, and Wisconsin. He paid no attention to that conventional wisdom, and doubled down on protectionism; many commentators, not least Trump himself, credit that position for his capture of all three states. Combined with his winnings in 27 other states, a victory in any one of these Midwestern states would have carried him past the 270-vote post. Taking these three states' 46 electoral votes left him with 36 to spare.

That explanation deserves greater elaboration. The Trump campaign reversed decades of apparently unbreakable patterns on three counts: He appealed to the protectionism of a truly "forgotten man," he more effectively

TABLE 6.1. *Campaign Contributions from Trade-Related PACs, Selected Campaign Cycles*
Total contributions to Federal candidates (presidential and congressional), in thousands of dollars

	2000 ($)	2008 ($)	2016 ($)	Change (%) 2000–2016
Protectionist PACs	11,204.4	16,862.3	15,527.0	+38.6
Agriculture	3,433.3	6,829.5	7,641.5	+122.6
Sugar	1,593.7	3,223.8	4,640.7	+191.2
Dairy	1,336.6	2,662.3	1,441.0	+7.8
Cotton	274.7	555.5	827.8	+201.3
Peanuts	228.2	387.8	732.0	+220.8
Industry	1,385.2	2,254.6	2,919.0	+110.7
Paper	469.3	609.9	1,157.5	+146.6
Iron and steel	423.0	988.0	823.6	+94.7
Cement	181.0	453.3	641.0	+254.1
Textiles and apparel	311.7	203.3	296.9	−4.7
Unions	6,385.7	7,778.1	4,966.5	−22.2
IBEW (electrical workers)	2,620.3	3,381.5	2,437.0	−7.0
United Auto Workers	2,150.0	2,010.4	1,066.9	−50.4
UNITE HERE (apparel)	388.0	1,067.1	761.9	+96.4
United Steelworkers	1,227.3	1,319.0	700.7	−42.9
Pro-Trade PACs	17,504.6	27,671.6	34,531.1	+97.3
Computers and Internet	2,507.2	5,584.8	10,129.5	+304.0
Retail (nonautomotive)	3,241.2	5,873.2	8,065.5	+148.8
Shipping (air and sea)	4,654.3	6,813.2	5,145.8	+10.6
Automobile dealers	3,418.2	3,611.7	4,345.5	+27.1
Food processors	2,720.2	3,755.4	3,733.7	+37.3
Boeing	706.9	1,413.8	2,086.0	+195.1
Caterpillar, Inc.	256.6	619.5	1,025.1	+299.5
Pro-Trade: Protectionist	1.6:1	1.6:1	2.2:1	

Note that columns may not add precisely due to rounding.
Sources: Calculated from data compiled by the Center for Responsive Politics' Open Secrets project (www.opensecrets.org/pacs/index.php), based in turn on Federal Election Commission data. Most categories shown here are the author's own, aggregating contributions from PACs associated with trade associations and individual firms.

exploited the challenge from China than any candidate had before, and he largely bypassed the established campaign-finance system.

The Reemergence of Protectionism and a Republican Underclass

Trump had to win the Republican nomination before he could contest the general election, and to that end he did two surprising things. One was to make an appeal to the underclass, which required that he poach on what is usually considered Democratic territory. He focused on lower-income whites, and especially white men without college degrees. His protectionist appeal might also look like an act of partisan plagiarism, but this is not an issue that Democrats have always owned. To the contrary, Trump brought the Republican Party back to the position that its congressional caucus (if not all of its presidents) held from the 1860s through the 1960s (see Chapter 2).

This novice candidate did not share the implicit assumption that workers' interest in protection will dissipate after their jobs are definitively lost. Today's steelworker who fears the competitive challenge of imports might represent a potentially powerful force, according to the usual logic, but the same cannot be said for the ex-steelworker who was pushed out of that industry many years ago. That is how things appear if we start from the premise that voters' preferences are rooted in their present sectoral affiliations, but what if something else is at work? What if the working class defines its interests precisely as a class, rather than in narrowly industrial terms, and what if this group's resentment against globalization and its beneficiaries – domestic and foreign – long outlasts its attachment to a dying industry? These are questions that only a few politicians, least of all the Republicans, seemed interested in addressing before Trump ran for office.

Both in the race for the nomination and in the general election, Trump tapped into one of the defining themes of the *Zeitgeist*. Income inequality has lately captivated the chattering classes, whether they choose to imbibe the topic by way of economics (e.g., Thomas Piketty's *Capital in the Twenty-First Century* [2014]) or biography (e.g., J. D. Vance's *Hillbilly Elegy: A Memoir of a Family and Culture in Crisis* [2016]). A paper by economists Pierce and Schott did not receive anything like that same level of attention, but did speak directly to the concerns of what became Trump's base. They found "higher rates of suicide and related causes of death, concentrated among whites, especially white males" in communities with greater exposure to the consequences of trade liberalization.[8] Their data suggested that the costs of the trade deficit can be counted not just in jobs and wages, but also in mental anguish, social isolation, addiction to drugs and alcohol, and self-destruction. Put another way, Trump engaged in severe hyperbole when he declared that "China is raping this country" via trade,[9] yet there was a more literal (if indirect) sense in which import competition was actually killing some Americans. Trump apparently knew what the professional politicians did

[8] Pierce and Schott (2016), p. 1.
[9] Quoted at www.cnn.com/2016/05/01/politics/donald-trump-china-rape/index.html.

not: A large pool of displaced workers, some of whom were so alienated that they had not voted in years,[10] could be rallied to support a man who spoke their language, acknowledged their pain, and promised to relieve it.

Scholarship confirms that Trump's intuitions aligned with public prejudices. Voters pay only limited attention to trade policy debates, even when relatively high-profile disputes erupt,[11] but research nonetheless shows that the general public is more open to the arguments made by the opponents than the proponents of trade liberalization.[12] Jensen et al. found that incumbent parties are particularly vulnerable to losing votes in swing states with many low-skilled manufacturing workers. This amounts to a sort of electoral mercantilism: Increasing imports are associated with decreasing presidential incumbent vote shares, while rising exports are associated with increasing presidential incumbent vote shares. They also found an Electoral College incentive for a candidate to protect the manufacturing sector, and to oppose trade agreements.[13]

China as an Economic and Security Challenge

Every good plot needs a villain, and China offered Trump an outstanding candidate. This is the one aspect of his campaign that involved the least innovation, as the 2012 candidates had already competed over who had the toughest and the smartest plan for countering the Chinese challenge. Republican nominee Mitt Romney repeatedly emphasized that he would declare China a currency manipulator and act against this subsidy, while President Obama touted the disputes he had brought to the WTO and the negotiation of the TPP as a regional counterweight. Trump appropriated Romney's message, and turned Obama's on its head.

---

[10] This point helps to explain the shortcomings of public opinion polls in 2016. The polls generally distinguish between registered and likely voters, with one of the major screens being the question of whether the respondent voted in the last election. To the extent that Trump brought to the polls some people who had not voted in 2012, and even some who had never voted at all, pollsters may have excluded an important group from their forecasts.

[11] See Guisinger (2009).

[12] Using survey data on American adults, Hiscox (2006) compared the views on trade by those who were variously read a statement with a pro-trade introduction (referring to job creation and consumer choice), those who were read an anti-trade introduction (referring to job loss and unfair competition), or were read both of these statements, or were give no introduction at all. Those subjects who were given the pro-trade introduction were no more likely to support trade liberalization than those who were given no introduction, but those who were read the anti-trade introduction (with or without the pro-trade introduction) were significantly more likely to oppose freer trade.

[13] Jensen, Quinn, and Weymouth (2017).

Considering the array of issues involved, there is nothing surprising about the role that the Sino-American rivalry played in the 2012 and 2016 elections. The rise of China directly addresses widespread anxieties over America's place in the world. While it may be a *post hoc ergo propter hoc* fallacy, many in the public – and some economic researchers as well[14] – attribute China's rapid rise with its accession to the WTO in 2001 and the consequent receipt of permanent normal trade relations from the United States. It did not help Hillary Clinton that it was her husband who shepherded this change in the US–China trade relationship through Congress, and that China's share of the US merchandise trade deficit rose steadily thereafter.

The Obama administration's timing and messaging on the TPP also provided two avenues of attack for Trump. China was not a party to the TPP, which US policymakers (if not all of their partners)[15] portrayed as a means of countering Chinese influence in the Pacific Rim, and yet Trump charged that this agreement "was designed for China to come in, as they always do, through the back door and totally take advantage of everyone."[16] While this was one of many Trump claims that earned a "pants on fire" rating from the fact-checking outfit PolitiFact,[17] such finger-wagging may matter little in the post-truth era. The Obama administration also gave Trump a gift by planning to postpone congressional debate over the TPP until a post-election "lame duck" session in which legislators would presumably feel less constrained by hostile public opinion. Reports of that intended maneuver merely contributed to the perception that the elites game the system to make end-runs around democracy.

The Marginalization of PACs by a Self-Financing Candidate

An unwritten law of presidential elections holds that victory goes to the candidate with the biggest war-chest. This was most recently demonstrated in 2012, when Obama vastly outspent Romney ($721.4 million to

---

[14]   See, for example, Pierce and Schott (2012), who demonstrated a close correlation between the rapid decline in US manufacturing employment and the extension of permanent normal trade relations to China in 2000.

[15]   As of 2016, nine of the twelve signatories to the TPP either already had or were negotiating FTAs with China. The three North American countries were then the only exceptions to this rule.

[16]   Trump comments at a Republican debate in Milwaukee, Wisconsin on November 11, 2015, as reported at http://theweek.com/speedreads/588181/rand-paul-embarrassed-donald-trump-over-china-tpp-during-gop-debate.

[17]   See www.politifact.com/truth-o-meter/statements/2015/nov/12/donald-trump/trump-says-china-will-take-advantage-trans-pacific/.

$449.5 million).[18] And as was discussed earlier, the weight of PAC money favors pro-trade over protectionist interests. Neither of those facts mattered to Trump. If the normal rules applied, he stood no chance: Clinton's campaign and associated committees spent $639.7 million, more than twice as much as those aligned with Trump ($302.4 million).[19] By that same logic, Trump should never have won the Republican nomination; the honor ought instead have gone to Governor Jeb Bush, whose $152.4 million bought four Republican National Convention delegates (1,233 shy of the number needed to win).[20]

Two factors allowed Trump to rewrite the rules by which campaigns are financed and elections are won. The first is that he could draw on his own considerable resources, which was especially important in the earliest stages of the race. There was little chance that Trump could have gotten much seed money from the usual sources of Republican campaign contributions, given the almost universal expectation that he could not possibly win the nomination (much less a general election). Even when he solicited contributions in the later stages of the campaign, Trump ran something akin to a guerrilla operation that lived off the land. His financial disadvantage was largely erased by all the unpaid coverage that he received from the 24-hour news channels, other traditional media, and the Internet's new media (both "fake news" and the legitimate variety).[21] Trump's reliance on rallies and free media, and thus his neutralization of PAC money, allowed him to reap with impunity the electoral benefits of a protectionist platform. His break from the campaign norm presaged an equally great break from the established patterns of US trade policy (and indeed from the presidency).

THE IMPACT OF TRUMP AND TRUMPISM ON PARTY POLITICS

With the benefit of hindsight, the triumph of protectionist demagoguery puts one in mind of what de Tocqueville said of the French Revolution: It was both unforeseeable and inevitable. No less than in the *ancien régime*, the build-up of resentment at the bottom, complemented by an almost smug complacency

---

[18]   Figures compiled by Open Secrets and posted at www.opensecrets.org/pres12/candidate.php?id=N00009638 (Obama) and www.opensecrets.org/pres12/candidate.php?id=N00000286 (Romney).

[19]   Figures compiled by Open Secrets and posted at www.opensecrets.org/pres16/candidate?id=N00000019 (Trump) and www.opensecrets.org/pres16/candidate?id=N00000019 (Clinton).

[20]   Open Secrets at www.opensecrets.org/pres16/candidate?id=N00037006.

[21]   It remains a matter of speculation, and formal investigation, just how much the Trump campaign also benefited from the intervention of Russian security services. That issue is addressed in Chapter 11.

at the top, made a cataclysmic eruption seem inescapable. The only mistake that Pat Buchanan made in 1996, and H. Ross Perot before him in 1992, was to push this issue too early. In presidential politics, as in comedy, timing is everything. It took a few decades of semibenign neglect for the postindustrial underclass to give up on the same politicians who seemed to have given up on them, and to follow a man who bluntly promised to kick over the tables on their behalf.

The advantages of retrospection are always great, but the future is now especially cloudy. Where will US trade policy be five or ten years after the 2016 election? It would be a great act of hubris to make confidential predictions on that point. We can nevertheless highlight a few patterns that help us to identify the range of possible scenarios, and make educated guesses as to their probability. The positions of the two political parties are the main focus for the remainder of this chapter; we will return to the larger picture of US policy during and after the Trump administration in Chapter 16.

Trumpism before Trump: Protectionist Recidivism and the Tea Party Movement

While Donald Trump's decision to stake out a protectionist position distinguished him from all other contenders for the Republican Party's 2016 nomination, he did not conjure this position out of the ether. The data illustrated in Figure 6.3 instead suggest that he benefited, whether through genius-level intuition or dumb luck, from a trend that his professional rivals either missed or did not believe: The bases of the two parties began changing places on trade during the Obama administration, the most immediate effect being the rightward gravitation of protectionist sentiment. Republican voters were still more favorably disposed toward trade than were Democrats prior to 2011, but the partisan positions flipped over the next several years. And while a bare majority of Republican voters still saw trade more as an opportunity than a threat in 2016, that left a very substantial minority whose anger could be leveraged.

The first sighting of this trend came in the 2010 congressional elections, when the insurgent movement then known as the Tea Party helped Republicans to recapture control of Congress. The candidates and office-holders who identify themselves with this faction take a dim view of the favors that the party's traditional, pro-business wing has extended to its cronies. To understand this division, it is important to recognize that trade liberalization is a subset of free-market economics, which envisions a larger role for the market than for the government. Some initiatives force lawmakers to choose which of these goals matters most, as they can come into conflict in several ways: Efforts to promote

Percentage of Respondents Who See Trade Mainly as an Opportunity
Rather than a Threat

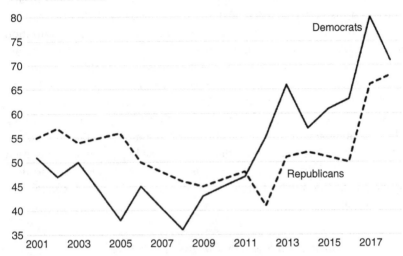

FIGURE 6.3 Popular support for trade by party, 2001–2018.
Note: No data are available for 2004, 2007, and 2010. Values for those years
interpolated from the prior and following years.
Source: Gallup poll at http://news.gallup.com/topic/trade.aspx.
Text of Question: "What do you think foreign trade means for America? Do you
see foreign trade more as an opportunity for economic growth through increased
US exports or a threat to the economy from foreign imports?"

exports may veer into subsidization, laws intended to combat other countries'
unfair trade practices may be exploited for protectionist purposes, programs that
aim to ease the adjustment costs of trade liberalization may blunt its positive
effects, and the process by which tariffs on specific imports are reduced or
waived may promote corrupt bargains between lawmakers and favored constituents or contributors. A traditional and pragmatic free-trader may be willing to
run those risks, rationalizing them as small prices to pay for a reasonably open
market, but the more zealous opponents of government involvement in the
economy take an entirely different view of a "pay to play" system in which the
state routinely intervenes. That is where the Tea Party wing distinguished itself
from the Republican Party establishment. Just as Democrats can become
incensed by the "trade and environment" and "trade and labor rights" issues
that we examined in Chapter 5, it is "trade and the state" that puts this group in
a high dudgeon. Paradoxical as it might appear, some of these legislators are
willing to see less trade if that also means less government.

When the Tea Party movement first arose there were signs that it might represent a return to the Republican Party's traditional isolationism and protectionism. Polls indicated that voters who identified themselves with this faction were, on average, even more skeptical of trade liberalization than Democratic voters.[22] An unsettled Republican leadership therefore made a concerted effort to win over the new congressmen affiliated with this group when three pending agreements came up for a vote in 2011, and in the end the Tea Party caucus in the House proved to be just as supportive of these pacts as were Republicans in general. Rather than voting against the pending FTAs, the members of this faction concentrated their ire on the trade adjustment assistance program and reauthorization of the Export-Import Bank; both programs had the backing of the establishment Republicans. This dissident faction nonetheless made clear that its votes could not be taken for granted on pro-trade initiatives.

Nomination Fights for Congress and the Presidency

The time seems already to have passed when presidents could take for granted the pro-trade leanings of either the Republican Party's base or its congressional caucus. At a minimum, the trade-skeptical wing of that party seems to be growing in size and influence. The most consequential struggles in the coming years may not be between Democrats and Republicans, but instead between the pro- and anti-Trump factions within the Republican Party; contests for the party's congressional and presidential nominations may be especially critical. Whether or not trade plays a prominent role in those internal fights, the results of these skirmishes may determine the future direction of US trade policy.

Democrats long had the reputation for engaging in "circular firing squads," and have by no means gotten past their penchant for internecine fighting, but in recent years it is the Republicans who seem most prone to ideological struggles. This poses a problem for incumbents who otherwise enjoy a great deal of job security. Reelection rates usually exceed 90% in the House of Representatives and 80% in the Senate.[23] When an incumbent is denied a new term, the chances may now be nearly as high that this defeat came in the renomination process as it did in the general election. That danger is

---

[22]   See, for example, the results of a 2010 poll conducted by NBC News and the *Wall Street Journal* posted at www.cnbc.com/id/39407846.

[23]   See the data reported at www.brookings.edu/wp-content/uploads/2017/01/vitalstats_ch2_full.xlsx.

significantly greater for Republicans than it is for Democrats, especially in the upper chamber. Of the nine Senate Republicans who failed to be reelected during 2010–2017, four had been denied renomination by their own party. (Another Republican who lost renomination won the general election in a write-in campaign.) The threat is somewhat lower for Republicans in the House, but even there nearly one-third (twelve out of thirty-seven) incumbents who were denied reelection during 2010–2016 could thank a fellow Republican for this involuntary retirement.[24]

At issue here is the transformation of the word "primary" from a noun to a verb. Ideologues in both parties can mount a challenge to the renomination of an incumbent who does not conform to their expectations, and even the threat of being primaried may make a risk-averse legislator reluctant to stand alone in the middle of the road. This is one reason why Republicans were less willing to work with the Obama administration than is usually the opposition party's wont. Pro-Trump activists likewise threaten to mount primary challenges to any incumbents whom they perceive to be insufficiently supportive of the president's agenda, a fact that could cow some otherwise pro-trade Republicans from interfering with White House plans to remake the trading system.

The internal struggles of the Republican Party may come to a head in the 2020 presidential election.[25] History offers some guidance here, with two rules governing the outcome of thirteen presidential races during 1948–2012 in which an incumbent president sought a new term.[26] The first rule was quite simple: The default result is an incumbent victory. The second rule is an equally simple exception: An incumbent president will nonetheless be defeated whenever he faces a credible challenger for his own party's nomination. Two of the presidents who suffered that fate – Truman in 1952 and Johnson in 1968 – were obliged to pull out of the nomination race after doing poorly in the New Hampshire primary. In both cases, the nominee of the opposition party went on to win the general election. Three other incumbents who faced strong challenges stayed in the race and won renomination, but were so weakened by the intraparty fight that they went down to defeat

[24] Numbers calculated by the author from multiple sources. The data for the House of Representatives do not include incumbents who lost their seats as a result of post-census redistricting in the 2012 election.

[25] This analysis assumes that President Trump completes his first term and seeks a second one. Both halves of that assumption may be more questionable for this president than for nearly all of his predecessors.

[26] Two of these presidents (Truman in 1948 and Johnson in 1964) originally took office on the death of a predecessor, and hence were able to run twice as incumbents.

in November; that is what happened to Ford in 1976, Carter in 1980, and Bush in 1992. Either way, there is an absolute and negative association between a credible renomination challenge and victory. All the presidents who evaded this challenge ultimately won, and all of those who faced it ultimately lost. The pattern holds equally true for both parties.

This history implies that Democrats' chances of denying a second term to Donald Trump may critically depend on the tacit assistance of insurgents in his own party. And while it might appear that challenges of this sort have gone out of fashion, having been a rarity since the nineteenth century,[27] intraparty antagonism is unusually severe in the Trump era. The chances for a nomination challenge may be higher for this president than for any of his predecessors in decades. Should that happen, it will be instructive to observe what role trade plays in the campaign mounted by Trump's challenger(s), and whether that issue is perceived as an advantage to the incumbent or the insurgent forces.

The Future of US Trade Politics

What comes next? Does the election of Donald Trump represent an exceptional and temporary deviation from the established patterns of policymaking and electoral politics, or does it instead portend a lasting shift in the political economy of US trade policy and the positions of the two major parties?

The key issue is whether Trump's reorientation of the Republican Party's posture proves durable. For most of US history there has been one party that could reliably be counted on to lean more toward open than to closed markets, but this distinction has not been stable. Republicans were rock-ribbed protectionists from the 1860s through the 1960s, followed by a transitional period; since the mid-1980s they have appeared just as firmly attached to open markets. The position of the Democratic Party moved in opposition to its Republican counterpart during those same periods. Will Trumpism bring about yet another change in partisan positions? Four potential scenarios suggest themselves, at varying levels of probability and consequence.

One scenario would see yet another reversal in partisan polarities, such that both parties return to the positions they held at the start of American hegemony. Were this to happen, the trade politics of the future would not be very different from those of the fairly recent past: Further progress on trade

---

[27] During 1844–1884 there were five incumbent presidents who were denied renomination by their parties.

liberalization would be limited principally to those periods in which the pro-trade party enjoys unified government. This scenario may be unlikely to emerge, however, as there is no evidence yet to suggest that elected officials in the Democratic Party are eager to reflect the higher levels of pro-trade sentiment that polls have recently captured in their electoral base. The reason for that sentiment may be found in the divide by which persons with higher education are more likely to identify as Democrats than as Republicans, and better educated persons are more likely (a) to have been exposed to the economic arguments in favor of liberalization and (b) work in services sectors that are less exposed to international competition. So far, however, trade appears to be one of the very few issues on which Democratic leaders in Congress seem more inclined than the Republicans to side with the Trump administration. While some future Democratic presidential candidate might do a "reverse Trump" and capture the party's presidential nomination on an unapologetically pro-trade platform, that character has yet to appear on the national scene.

The most extreme scenario envisions a thorough breakdown in the established two-party system, with the divisions between Republican Party's pro- and anti-Trump wings causing irreparable rifts and defections. Several variations on that scenario could emerge, with disgruntled Republican voters and officeholders having to decide whether their interests would be better served by switching their allegiance to the Democrats, or by forming a third party, or by washing their hands of politics altogether. The sorry history of third parties in the United States undercuts the likelihood that this scenario could reform the system. Any number of Republicans may make their own versions of the standard declaration that "I didn't leave the party, the party left me." Their departures may be less likely to undo the two-party system than they are either to undercut this one party or, in what may amount to the same thing, to purge its remaining centrists.

A related and more likely scenario entails a muddling of partisan lines, such that both parties will have significant pro-trade and trade-skeptical wings. In recent decades we have seen small pockets of iconoclasm in each party, with roughly 10% of the congressional Republicans demonstrating frequent or universal opposition to trade agreements, and a far more variable share of the Democrats taking the opposite position on a case-by-case basis. The Democrats' pro-trade wing might grow if a significant number of former Republican voters and even office-holders were to seek shelter in that party. That wing still constitutes a minority among Democratic office-holders, but they are among the party's more dynamic leaders. Prominent among them are the members of the New Democrat Coalition, a group "committed to pro-economic growth, pro-innovation, and fiscally responsible policies"[28] that represented over one-third of the House Democrats in the 115th Congress (2017–2018). It remains to be seen, however, whether this faction can effectively counterbalance the trade-skeptical views that are so prominent in the party's senior leadership in Congress as well as its rising ranks of progressive candidates.

As for the Republicans, this scenario of muddled partisan lines depends not on the personality, positions, or fate of one man, but on other candidates' interest in appealing to his base. No matter what Republican officials may actually think about Trump and his policies, and no matter what trajectory his presidency may take, they cannot unsee what they saw in 2016: Protectionism appealed to a considerable share of the electorate. It is therefore possible that the trade-skeptical wing of the congressional Republican caucus may experience a growth spurt, with some incumbent members of Congress being inspired to rethink the electoral consequences of their positions, and some entirely new legislators winning election. Unless that development were to be matched by a commensurately large increase in the pro-trade wing of the Democratic Party, it would bode very badly for trade liberalization in the United States.

A final possibility is that the Trump experiment will prove to be short-lived, as will his impact on the Republican Party's posture toward trade. While one could imagine Donald Trump being seen in the long run as a second Ronald Reagan who manages to redirect the policies of his party – albeit in precisely the opposite direction – it requires less effort and imagination to see him become a second Richard Nixon who departs in disgrace and repudiation. That scenario would appear especially likely in the event that his tenure were to end in a severe electoral drubbing, or be cut short by impeachment, resignation, or perhaps even a first-ever use of the cabinet's power of removal under the 25th Amendment of the Constitution. An early end to the Trump presidency would most likely mean a diminution of Republican power, but the experience of the 1970s suggests that the impact could be short-lived. Just as the Democratic beneficiary of Nixon's resignation served only a single term in the White House, it might take only one or two electoral cycles for partisan divisions to return to the pre-Trump status quo. One may only speculate on whether that would also mean a restoration of the Republican Party's pro-trade stance.

[28] https://newdemocratcoalition-himes.house.gov/.

While it is difficult to forecast which of these scenarios will prove most realistic, two points are eminently clear. One is that the hiatus in politicians' attention to trade policy has ended, and that it may be quite some time before this issue is moved again from the front to the back burner of American politics. The other is that this revival of trade as a political issue is virtually certain to complicate the already difficult task of reinvigorating US leadership in the trading system. Three of these four scenarios imply more chaos, more protectionism, or both, and the one that internationalists and free-traders should most favor – the restoration of the Democrats' traditional, pro-trade position – also appears the most quixotic.

The results of the 2018 midterm election were too preliminary and too ambiguous to tell us which scenario is most plausible. They may be read from one perspective as a sharp repudiation of Trump and his policies; the voters not only restored Democratic control of the House of Representatives for the first time since 2010, but did so by a healthy margin. That same electorate also kept Republicans in control of the Senate, and even expanded the size of their majority. The net effect may be greater polarization in Congress, with many Republican centrists in the House having retired (voluntarily or not) and several pro-Trump candidates ascending to the Senate. The consequences for future US policy are not self-evident. Trade remains the one issue on which this president's positions align more closely with the opposition than with the mainstream of the party that he hijacked. We should not be surprised if Democrats and Republicans were to settle in the short term for the least common denominator.

THE 2016 ELECTION AND AMERICAN HEGEMONY

Returning from the details of domestic politics to the broader issues of international economic relations, the events reviewed in this chapter should not surprise anyone who views the global system through the lens of hegemonic stability theory. The scholars in that tradition expect internal conflict to rise once the hegemon enters a period of decline, as Cafruny noted, when "the role of domestic structures looms larger in the regime."[29] If anything, the protectionist eruption that was over-predicted in the 1980s was overdue by the 2010s. The theorists of hegemonic stability thought they were seeing the start of it a generation ago, so the resurgence of pro-market liberalization in the 1990s was embarrassing to their argument. What they could never be expected to predict is just how sharp the reversal would be

---

[29]   Cafruny (1987), p. 35.

when it finally came, nor the party from which it would emerge, nor the idiosyncrasies of its messenger.

It may be years before we are far enough removed from the 2016 election to see that contest in its proper perspective, and know whether the rise of Donald Trump represented an utter and reversible fluke or was instead a true inflection point. Much will depend on when and how he leaves office, and whether other politicians imitate the substance (if not the style) of his positions. Trump's election does require that we attach an important qualifier to much of the analysis in the chapters that follow, as a president who knows little about history may make history matter even less. The analysis that follows must be read with a horizontal caveat: The trends presented here are based primarily on the world pre-Trump, and it is possible that seemingly well-established patterns have been disrupted either for years or for good. Where possible and appropriate, the examination identifies ways in which these points have already been modified. Trump's policies figure importantly in our review of trade relations with Russia (Chapter 11) and China (Chapter 12). In Chapter 16 we will return to the larger question of what Trump's presidency, and its aftermath, may mean for the United States, its partners, and the trading system.

PART III

TRADING WITH ALLIES

7

Defense versus Opulence:
Sea Power and Law in Anglo-American Hegemonies

As defence ... is of much more importance than opulence, the Act of Navigation is, perhaps, the wisest of all the commercial regulations of England.

Adam Smith, *An Inquiry into the Nature and Causes of the Wealth of Nations* (1776)

INTRODUCTION

Adam Smith was born into a tough world. War was slightly more common than peace in his day – the United Kingdom was at war for thirty-four of Smith's sixty-seven years – and while he lauded the economic advantages of trade he harbored no illusions about its supposed pacific power. "Being neighbours," he said of England and France, "they are *necessarily* enemies, and the wealth and power of each becomes, upon that account, more formidable to the other."[1] If Smith was wary of the French, he was doubly cautious about the fearsome Dutch. London and Amsterdam had already clashed repeatedly in their bids for naval supremacy, and in 1776 the fourth and final Anglo-Dutch War was just around the corner. The Navigation Acts, which aimed to displace the Dutch in the carrying trade, were both a cause and a consequence of those wars. In declaring his unqualified backing for these most protectionist and provocative English laws, Smith left no doubt that he put power before wealth.

The Navigation Acts did not survive England's hegemony, but they would live on in its largest ex-colony. Matters came full circle by the time of the failed Transatlantic Trade and Investment Partnership (TTIP) negotiations that Barack Obama started and Donald Trump suspended, where one of the chief objectives of Dutch and British negotiators was to convince their American counterparts to open the US shipping market to foreign

---

[1]   Smith (1776), p. 496. Emphasis added.

competition. Even before the TTIP negotiations collapsed, there appeared little chance that Washington would make meaningful concessions to this demand. American policymakers follow Smith in favoring defense over opulence, and place a high priority on preserving the coastal merchant fleet.

This chapter reviews relations between the hegemons, with special emphasis on sea power. In addition to wartime naval operations, this field encompasses control of trade, the use of ocean resources, and the deployment of marine economic power as an instrument of influence and deterrence.[2] Sea power is critically important to hegemony, and demonstrates how that status obliges a country to rethink the trade-offs between power and wealth. London found it expedient to revise its maritime doctrines at different stages of hegemony, and the positions that made sense to Washington during the British hegemony had to be reassessed when its own turn came. This did not mean changing positions in every area, as US policymakers sometimes show a strongly atavistic attachment to habit, but on some issues the turnabout could come jarringly fast.

This analysis also focuses on the drafting and enforcement of international law, especially where trade law intersects with security. From one perspective, international law may appear like a shield that protects the interests of smaller countries. It is founded upon the principles of sovereignty, the juridical equality of states, and nonintervention by external powers in internal affairs. The hegemon nevertheless plays a major role in devising that law, and in determining how it will be enforced.[3] The same body of law that is designed to keep markets open in peacetime can be so crafted as to maximize the hegemon's leverage in wartime, both by reducing the capacity of its adversaries to challenge it militarily and by constraining third parties that might resupply the enemy. The issues reviewed in this chapter test how far a hegemon will go to convince other powers that it treats its responsibilities as seriously as its privileges, and that its leadership is both beneficial and legitimate. The United Kingdom and the United States provided different answers to a series of questions about how a leader ought to balance its own wants with the needs of the system, to wit: Will the hegemon subordinate its own economic interests to security imperatives, and will it be bound by the same legal strictures that it wants other countries to honor? How much is it willing to

---

[2] See Tangredi (2002b), p. 3.

[3] In this chapter, as in the rest of the book, the term *hegemon* is used in the value-neutral sense commonly employed by political economists. This is to be distinguished from the usage in one school of legal studies, where Gramscian notions tend toward a negative appraisal of hegemonic aims and achievements. Examples include Buckel and Fischer-Lescano (2009) and Krisch (2005). For a broader view see Byers and Nolte (2003) and Mastanduno (2016).

invest, and what short-term gains might it forego, to foster an environment that is conducive to peaceful commerce, and in which all participants – even its challengers – enjoy the benefits of peace and prosperity? And when the hegemon declares that it is compelled to wage war in the name of peace, how will it balance the conduct of that war with its peacetime duty to promote an open trading system?

The subject matter of this chapter overlaps somewhat with that of Chapter 10, which examines the strategy and domestic diplomacy of sanctions. Some authors use the terms economic warfare and sanctions as synonyms, a practice that can produce great confusion. For the sake of simplicity, by economic warfare I strictly mean measures employed in wartime, and I treat sanctions as their peacetime counterpart. This chapter is devoted to the first of those topics, while most of Chapter 10 concerns peacetime sanctions. The only exception is the gray-area issue of what types of goods will be made subject to two related forms of trade restriction. In view of the close parallels to be drawn on this subject in economic warfare (i.e., the definition of contraband) and in sanctions (i.e., the scope of strategic export controls), they are handled together in Chapter 10.

BRITISH AND AMERICAN PERSPECTIVES ON TRADE, SEA POWER, AND THE LAW

Before we delve into the tangled history of Anglo-American disputes over trade, sea power, and the law, it is useful to start at a higher level of abstraction. Historians sometimes argue over the number of cases that might properly be classified as hegemonies. Beyond the Anglo-American pair on which this book is focused, good arguments can be made for the past hegemonies of the Netherlands and Venice. That debate need not detain us, apart from noting a critically important characteristic shared by all four powers: Each floated the dominant navy of its time. The association between naval power and British hegemony is indisputable, as is the model that inspired London. Writing exactly a century before the United States declared independence, Sir William Petty thought it feasible for England "to gain the Universal Trade of the whole Commercial World,"[4] and that the best way to achieve this end was to ape the Dutch. In the short term, that meant utilizing subsidies, monopoly rights, and other means to build the merchant and military fleets. In the longer term, it would also entail the provision of public goods.

---

[4] Petty (1676), pp. 114–115.

How Technology and Culture Shape Hegemony

There are solid reasons why the public good that we call maritime law developed earlier than did other topics in international law. Seagoing traders such as the Dutch and the English rely on rules to govern the rights and responsibilities of mariners, and the force to back them up, as precursors to an open global economy. While the hegemon is well situated to advance, interpret, and execute doctrines that bend the law to its own immediate purposes, it is well-advised to take the long view and not succumb to the ever-present temptation to manipulate the system solely for its own ends. Failure to exercise restraint may hasten the day when other members of the international community conclude that they ought not to trust too much in the hegemon's fairness and good intentions.

One important issue for each hegemon to decide is whether it will make public some goods that it might otherwise keep private. This can be illustrated with the example of navigational aids. Kennedy waxed poetic when he described London's "herculean task of charting the oceans" as an almost eleemosynary undertaking: By selling "superb charts ... at a minimal price to mariners of any nation in the belief that trade would benefit," the English reversed "the earlier selfish policy of keeping secret all cartographic knowledge."[5] The same may be said for the Internet and the Global Positioning System, a pair of related technologies that were originally devised to serve US security needs but became public goods that have profoundly transformed daily life. In both cases the hegemon opted to make broadly available a resource that it might have hoarded. Like London, Washington calculated that the strategic economic benefits of wide distribution outweighed the security costs of a foregone tactical advantage.

The maps/GPS example underlines the point that these hegemonies came in different technological eras. Multiple consequences stem from the fact that the English watch began in the age of sail and ended just as man took to the skies, while Americans presided over the rise of nuclear weapons, mass communications, and computers. These advances affect more than the conduct and outcome of wars. The rising costs and complexities of industrial-era warfare had just as great an effect on the course of history as did the wars themselves, and also scrambled the commercial and legal relationships among belligerents and neutrals.

Beyond the impact of technology, and the knock-on effects that these advances had on the finances and laws of war, we must also acknowledge

---

[5] Kennedy (1976), p. 164.

the importance of political culture. For all else that the cousins may hold in common, there are important differences in how they perceive the relationships between democracy and foreign policy, between the economy and national security, and their respective roles in the world. Those differences may be attributed in part to their distinct material and geographic endowments, as discussed in Chapter 2. The United Kingdom has always been more vulnerable to external shocks than the larger, more diverse, and economically self-sufficient United States. This may make British statesmen more cautious about adopting policies that leave their country vulnerable, and more attentive to the needs of their partners. Beyond those material differences, one also senses – hard as it may be to nail down precisely – a deeper British attachment to the notion that a country ought to cooperate with its neighbors. That observation might seem to be contradicted by the 2016 decision to exit from the European Union, but the very fact that Britain had once been willing to subordinate its national destiny to a regional body was evidence enough of the difference.

The Price of War and Peace

"In this world," Benjamin Franklin observed in his most oft-quoted aphorism, "nothing can be said to be certain, except death and taxes."[6] In Franklin's time, imperial wars were responsible for many of the deaths and most of the taxes. The United Kingdom was engaged in five world wars from 1688 through 1783, and four more after the United States became independent, even if only the last two conflicts bore titles that properly acknowledged their global magnitude (see Table 7.1). Franklin's countrymen were painfully aware that they could be dragooned into the mother country's wars, both as foot soldiers and financiers, as long as they remained a colony. The war fatigue brought on by frequent conflicts, most of them inspired by issues that meant nothing to North Americans, was the principal reason why the colonists broke away from the metropolis.

The events that connected the Fifth World War with the conflicts that immediately preceded and followed it offer an especially revealing example of the pull that war finance can exert on the great events of history. A young George Washington set off the French and Indian War – which metastasized into the Seven Years' War – when he led his Virginia militiamen in an intemperate attack on French forces in the Ohio valley. That Fourth World War produced not only a British victory and the transfer of Quebec to London,

---

[6]   Letter to Jean-Baptiste Leroy (1789).

TABLE 7.1. *North American Interests in the Nine World Wars*
Durations are for the war overall; North American involvement sometimes began or
ended in different years

Number	Duration	Title	Consequences for North America
First	1688–1697	War of the Grand Alliance (King William's War)	Local war aims focused on control of the fur trade. The war did not change the status quo.
Second	1701–1713	War of Spanish Succession (Queen Anne's War)	France ceded some North American territory to England in the postwar settlement.
Third	1740–1748	War of Austrian Succession (King George's War)	The British colonists captured Louisbourg (later returned to France in exchange for Madras).
Fourth	1756–1763	Seven Years' War (French and Indian War)	France ceded Louisiana to Spain, and most of New France (Canada) to the United Kingdom.
Fifth	1775–1783	Wars of the American Revolution	The United States won its independence, and France incurred a crippling debt.
Sixth	1793–1802	Wars of the French Revolution	An undeclared war with France in 1798–1800 put an end to the first US external alliance.
Seventh	1803–1815	Napoleonic Wars (War of 1812)	The inconclusive US–UK war was financed by the first US protectionist tariff.
Eighth	1914–1918	First World War	The British victory was Pyrrhic, but the United States shirked its hegemonic opportunity.
Ninth	1939–1945	Second World War	The war completed the transfer of hegemony from the United Kingdom to the United States.

Titles in parentheses indicate what the war was commonly called in North America.
Dates and titles adapted from Bailey (1980), p. 24.

but also a debt of £1.5 million. From the Revenue Act and the Townshend Acts of the 1760s through what the rebels called the Intolerable Acts of the 1770s, London insisted that the American colonists pay the costs of their past and present defense. The protests against these trade and excise taxes, followed by British and American attempts to coerce one another with commercial restrictions, eventually spawned yet another global conflict that would not end in North America until an older and wiser Washington allied with the French to win the Battle of Yorktown. The court at Versailles would learn to regret the investment that it made in freeing the American colonies from the English rival, as it incurred a war debt of its own that would, in time, generate a new cycle in which the demands for taxes sparked a revolution that plunged Europe into the Sixth World War.

The American rebels could not know that they left the empire a generation before its victory in the Seventh World War heralded the start of a prolonged period that offered a reasonably close facsimile of peace. In 114 of the 169 years that had separated the first British settlement in North America (1607) from the Declaration of Independence (1776), at least one of the five major European powers of the day – England, France, Russia, Spain, and the Netherlands – had been at war with one or more of the others.[7] The 169-year period from 1776 through 1945 was much less bloody. Substituting Germany for the Netherlands, the five major European powers fought one another for only 44 of these years. The new era was thus peaceful three-quarters of the time, versus the prior experience of being at war two-thirds of the time.

Fewer wars did not mean less military spending, but did concentrate the burden of that expense on one country. Total UK military expenditures during 1816–1860 were four times greater than those of the United States, and in the average year that country fielded 9.3 times as many men at arms. The ratios changed radically but temporarily during the US Civil War, followed by a slow and incomplete closing of the gap. Total British military expenditures were 1.5 times more than those of the United States during 1866–1913, and over that same period the average number of military personnel was 4.4 times greater. When one compares these burdens against relative capacities, however, the American taxpayers were getting off far cheaper than their British counterparts. Their economy was nearly as large as Britain's by 1866, and the US population was already 21% larger. By 1913, the United States had twice the population and 2.3 times the GDP of the United Kingdom. America would still not have as many men under arms as Britain until 1942, but by 1950 the US military was four times larger. It took only a decade or so for Washington to start complaining that London, Paris, Berlin, and Rome were not shouldering their fair share of the costs for collective security.[8]

---

[7] Author's calculations based on information in Langer (1972), passim. Only some of these were world wars.

[8] Comparisons in this paragraph calculated from the Correlates of War data at www .correlatesofwar.org/data-sets/national-material-capabilities, as well as GDP data from Maddison (2003). Note that the fiscal and demographic burdens on the United Kingdom in the latter period were arguably smaller than these comparisons might suggest, given its capacity to collect taxes and recruit soldiers in the empire.

Isolation, Neutrality, and Opportunism

Three related themes dominated American foreign policy during the years between Yorktown and Pearl Harbor. One was a sense of splendid isolation that made the country seem immune from the threat of foreign invasion. Abraham Lincoln eloquently expressed this view in 1838, declaring that the combined armies of Europe, Asia, and Africa "could not by force take a drink from the Ohio or make a track on the Blue Ridge in a trial of a thousand years."[9] This boast conveniently glossed over the War of 1812, but Lincoln was not the first politician who refused to let historical fact get in the way of a popular sentiment.

The second theme was the perennial role of neutrality in foreign policy. Contrary to the common practice of US statesmen from the Cold War to the present day, for whom another country's neutrality is often taken as prima facie evidence of anti-Americanism or complicity with rogues and totalitarians, their predecessors considered neutrality a high virtue. Neutrality should not be confused with isolationism or pacifism. "Unless your government is respectable, foreigners will invade your rights," Hamilton warned the Constitutional Convention, and "even to observe neutrality you must have a strong government."[10] While the phrase "armed neutrality" might sound like an oxymoron, it accurately describes the stance taken by the United States and other small-navy states that were prepared to fight for their economic and political rights. That led in the first generation of independence to an undeclared naval war with France, a failed attempt to use commercial coercion against the belligerents in the Anglo-French wars, and finally to the War of 1812. Washington would follow a comparable sequence a century later, when frictions with the belligerents in the (so-called) First World War initially provoked tensions with London and ultimately led to war with Berlin.

The third theme was a US desire to take commercial advantage of that neutrality. If the Europeans would not oblige them by becoming more virtuous, the next best thing for the pragmatic Americans was to profit from the ineradicable vices of the Old World. The most lucrative opportunities came in the carrying trade between the Caribbean and Europe. Much was at stake here, as the sugar-rich West Indies were economically more important to the United Kingdom than the lost colonies of North America.[11]

---

[9] Text at www.abrahamlincolnonline.org/lincoln/speeches/lyceum.htm.
[10] Elliot (1836), Volume 1, p. 463.
[11] In 1774, for example, North America accounted for 12.5% of British imports, versus 29.3% for the West Indies. See Maddison, op. cit., p. 93.

The restrictions that the French and British placed on trade in the Caribbean, and later in Europe itself, were felt throughout the US economy. In the judgment of Douglas North, the dean of American economic historians, during 1793–1814 "the commercial and military policies of England and France and the response of the American government to them were the source for every expansion and contraction"[12] in the United States. In Chapter 4 we already saw the importance that US policymakers placed on this issue, with the Senate stripping the Jay Treaty of a provision banning American traders from carrying Caribbean goods. That was only one incident in a perennial conflict that would not end until the British opened up their West Indian islands to foreign shippers in 1828.[13]

Hegemony and International Law

As important as these three themes have been in the development of US foreign economic policy, a fourth theme is conspicuous for its absence. While it would be going too far to suggest that the United States traditionally shows contempt for international law, no objective observer could fairly argue that this history has been marked by an excessive American zeal to comply with every dictate of that law.

The pragmatic instincts of American statesmen can be seen in a recurring habit of creating new, postwar international institutions, but then disparaging those same bodies when they fail to erase the differences in their members' interests. That pattern was compressed in the early twentieth century, when the Senate kept the United States out of the League of Nations. Significantly, the United Kingdom would remain (together with France) one of just two great powers that stuck with that institution to its bitter end. The debates of the British Parliament and the US Congress over the decision to go to war with Iraq in 2003 offer a more recent example of the Anglo-American differences. Many MPs saw the relevant United Nations resolutions as law, and pondered how those enactments empowered or bound them, but the same resolutions received only passing reference – and sometimes outright scorn – from their American counterparts. In that same vein, the United States "has never been willing to submit itself to the plenary authority" of the International Court of Justice, "and has typically reacted negatively to decisions by the Court that are adverse to U.S. interests."[14]

---

[12] North (1966), p. 36.
[13] Johnson et al. (1915), Volume I, p. 129.
[14] Murphy (2008), p. 1.

The United States is not the first hegemon to take a somewhat cynical approach to international law. The doctrines advanced by Huig de Groot (1583–1645), better known as Hugo Grotius, offer a good example of how power might seduce one toward the view that might makes right. While this great Dutch jurist is properly remembered for his role in creating international law, and for presenting a legal rationale for free trade well before the economists devised another set of arguments, that did not prevent him from promoting principles that elevated his own country's interests. In the *Commentary on the Law of Prize and Booty* (1603) Grotius defended a Dutch admiral who took a Portuguese merchantman as a prize even though the two countries were then at peace. The British did not follow this Dutchman in so nakedly asserting that a great power may control the trade of adversaries as well as neutrals in both war and peace. Their greater deftness began with the selection of Emmerich de Vattel (1714–1767) as London's principal legal muse. The Swiss jurist's *Law of Nations* followed Grotius in adapting Just War concepts to international law, yet he was more sympathetic to neutrals and more insistent on avoiding partiality.

The British in hegemony did not always consult the law books before they weighed their own interests. One may instead see how, when confronted with legally similar but politically distinct cases, they could find support in international law for what they intended to do in the first place. Consider how London approached two important rebellions. World history might have gone in a different direction if London had given in to the demands at home and abroad (especially Paris) for European intervention in the US Civil War. The British statesmen instead navigated that legal and political minefield with due caution. They merely acknowledged reality when they recognized the Confederate claim to belligerent status, and never took the far more consequential steps of extending diplomatic recognition to the South, providing other political or financial assistance, or even allying with Richmond.[15] Contrast that case with the decision a generation earlier not only to intervene on behalf of the Greeks in their war of independence from the Ottoman Empire, but also to devise a novel legal doctrine in service of that end. Naval interdiction is a coercive practice that London pioneered in 1827, taking joint action with France and Russia to bottle up the Turkish fleet in the seaport of Navarino. This unprecedented maneuver succeeded "without the blockading countries having formally declared a state of war with the Turks."[16] This British innovation set a precedent that the United States would later employ to

---

[15]   See, for example, the account in Hubbard (1998), passim.

[16]   Morabito (1991), p. 303.

good effect in the Cuban missile crisis of 1962 and in the lead-up to the First Gulf War in 1990–1991.[17]

It is difficult to discern a great legal distinction between the circumstances that led London to skirt the edge of war with Istanbul, but to exercise greater restraint with respect to Washington. While Prime Minister Palmerston and his colleagues seemed to treat the law as more than a mild suggestion in their approach to the US Civil War, the domestic and global politics of the matter – not to mention England's economic interests – also weighed more in favor of restraint than intervention.[18] The international law that Britain helped to form, and thus found it easier to obey, was sufficiently flexible to meet the hegemon's shifting policy needs in both circumstances.

The Law of War as a Barrier to Entry

The technology of war, coupled with the rule-making power of the hegemon, can be manipulated so as to create barriers to entry in the market for power. Adam Smith noted that while in the ancient world "the opulent and civilized found it difficult to defend themselves against the poor and barbarous nations," just the reverse was true in his own day. He attributed this historic shift to firearms, "an invention which at first sight appears to be so pernicious" but "is certainly favourable both to the permanency and to the extension of civilization."[19] This first step in the industrialization of warfare raised the entry fee to the great game. International law could likewise set standards for the legal conduct of capital-intensive combat that were beyond the means of smaller, poorer countries. That same point was doubly true for nonstate actors. One way of achieving this end is to outlaw cheaper, irregular expedients that even rebels can afford, such as unconventional formations on land (guerrillas, partisans, and terrorists) or at sea (pirates and privateers). The same is true for weapons that might disrupt the balance. That once meant prohibiting cross-bows, a cost-effective equalizer that allowed even a conscripted peasant to bring down an armored knight. In our own time, the nuclear powers are quicker to condemn the "dirty" bombs that terrorists might use to contaminate their cities than they are to negotiate reductions in their own arsenals.

The dispute over privateers illustrates the distinct paces at which the British and Americans have adapted their legal doctrines of sea power.

---

[17] See, for example, Robertson (1991).
[18] As is discussed in Chapter 10, those calculations were affected by the Union's superior conduct of economic warfare against the Confederacy, including the priority that it placed on ensuring the flow of cotton to England.
[19] Smith (1776), p. 708.

These semiformal, state-sponsored pirates were once synonymous with Britain. State-licensed raids on commercial vessels made for a flourishing business during 1689–1815, but the British banned the practice in hegemony. One can explain this shift either at the retail level of commercial interests, with the attraction of privateering declining after legitimate trade became more lucrative and the opportunity costs rose for merchants,[20] or by considering the wholesale security interests of the hegemon. By eliminating privateers, the British raised the cost of maintaining legal naval forces and thus reduced the capacity of smaller, poorer powers to put up effective resistance to the Royal Navy. American statesmen resisted that initiative, and clung to privateers much longer. The floating militia had served US interests well in the Revolutionary War, and again the War of 1812, and is legally fossilized in a constitutional provision (Article I, Section 8, Clause 11) that enumerates the congressional power to "grant Letters of Marque and Reprisal." It has now been ages since this anachronism was actively employed, but – as discussed later – its preservation remained a priority for American diplomats well into the nineteenth century.

   While the British turned against privateers long before the Americans did, it is instructive to consider the different approaches that London and Washington took toward actual pirates. In one of the more remarkable episodes of early American foreign policy, President Jefferson deployed the US Navy in 1801–1805 to quell the Barbary pirates that extorted tribute from ships plying the trade routes north of modern Morocco, Algeria, and Libya. This campaign acquired iconic status in the lore of the Marine Corps, which still celebrates its exploits on the shores of Tripoli. Historical pride should not distract us from asking why a newly independent republic felt compelled to dispatch its limited forces on a 5,000-mile expedition. Why had London not sent the Royal Navy out from its Gibraltar base to police this territory? "Perhaps the chief reason," in the insightful words of one diplomatic historian, "was that the commerce of the Mediterranean was thus reserved for those nations, like herself, wealthy enough to pay protection money."[21] Rather than acquiesce in the tacit British collusion with pirates, and allow this rent-seeking barrier to remain in place, the United States made its first military investment in open markets. This achievement was marred by the $60,000 ransom that Jefferson still paid the pirates to release American prisoners, but the episode nevertheless hinted at Britain's mixed commercial and security interests at the dawn of its hegemony, and the future proclivities of Americans in theirs.

---

[20]   See Hillmann and Gathmann (2011).
[21]   Bailey (1980), p. 65.

ANGLO-AMERICAN RELATIONS IN THE BRITISH HEGEMONY

Those broader distinctions between the English and American approaches to sea power and international law mattered only to the extent that they generated disputes over specific issues affecting war and trade. Three such topics were recurring sources of conflict between Washington and London during the British hegemony: the support and protection that they provided to their shipping sectors, the conflicting doctrines that they each advanced regarding the legal rights of neutrals in wartime, and the use of privateers as a naval auxiliary. The two North Atlantic powers confronted one another over these issues in war, in the negotiation of competing bilateral treaties, and in the multilateral diplomacy of international law.

British and American Support for Shipping

The origins of the Navigation Acts can be traced back to a 1381 law requiring that Englishmen use English ships. This law's 1651 successor, which offered the *casus belli* for the First Anglo-Dutch War (1652–1654), provided that no products of Asia, Africa, or America could be imported into England or its colonies except in ships owned and crewed by Englishmen or colonials. As illiberal as these laws were, they had an unexpected supporter. While Adam Smith was willing to risk England's future on its economic competitiveness, he also favored putting a ring-fence around those industries that he deemed "necessary for the defence of the country." He so valued a ready reserve of seamen that Smith thought a shipping monopoly was justified; similar logic led him to relax his general opposition to subsidies when it came to the herring and whale fisheries, and to producers of sailcloth and gunpowder.[22]

The Navigation Acts do not figure as prominently in the popular American imagination as the tax on tea, but they were among that array of mercantilist restrictions that ultimately provoked the colonists to revolt. Once the United States was independent, criticism gave way to imitation. Congress enacted sixty-nine laws between 1789 and 1913 that were intended to promote commerce, shipping, and shipbuilding, many of them inspired by their British forbears. These included the reservation of certain trades (especially coastwise traffic) to domestic providers, as well as subsidies, reciprocity laws, lower tariffs on cargoes carried in US vessels, and higher tonnage taxes on foreign vessels.[23] Some of these laws are still on the books.

---

[22]   Smith (1776), pp. 463, 518, and 523.
[23]   Enumerated in Johnson et al. (1915), Volume II, pp. 349–351.

James Madison was a strong advocate of reciprocity, arguing that American shipping would be excluded "altogether from foreign ports" if the country were "to leave her ports perfectly free, and make no discrimination between vessels owned by her citizens and those owned by foreigners, while other nations make this discrimination."[24] As on so many issues, Hamilton preferred to zig where Madison zagged. Fearing a trade war with Britain, he worked with senators to defeat several of the discriminatory and reciprocity provisions that Madison proposed in the country's first tariff bill.[25] One of the few reciprocity provisions that survived this legislative skirmish slapped escalating tonnage taxes on ships calling at US ports. The Tariff Act of 1789 set rates of 6¢ a ton on ships built and owned by Americans (whose cargoes also benefited from a 10% discount on tariffs), rising to 30¢ on US-built ships owned by foreigners and 50¢ on ships built and owned by foreigners. Congress periodically tightened or loosened these and related laws over the next two centuries, often in response to the treatment that US ships received in British ports.[26]

Wars, and the aftermaths of wars, were especially propitious times for shippers to seek increases in government support. The War of 1812 inspired an 1817 law that prohibited foreign participation in the US coastwise trade. The law also applied a rule of reciprocity to any country that imposed similar restrictions on American commerce,[27] by which products could be imported only in ships that were owned either by US citizens or citizens of the goods' country of origin. A similar pattern followed the First World War, when a post-bellum glut of ships – itself the product of overly generous shipyard subsidies during the war – inspired the Jones Act of 1920.[28] This descendant of the 1817 law requires to this day that any ships transporting cargo from one US port to another must be (1) constructed in the United States from US components, (2) owned at least 75% by US citizens, and (3) manned by US crews.

The British laws that had inspired these measures would be gone by the middle of the nineteenth century, sacrificed to the larger goals of hegemonic leadership and free markets. Parliament overcame the objections of a protectionist shipowners' lobby to repeal most of the Navigation Acts in 1847, followed in 1849 by the opening of English ports to all shipping on a reciprocal basis, and the repeal of cabotage laws in 1853. Here we find

---

[24] Remarks of April 9, 1789, in Rutland and Hobson (1977), p. 73.
[25] This episode took place before Hamilton became secretary of the treasury. See Irwin (2017), p. 90.
[26] See Marvin (1902), passim.
[27] According to Pitkin (1817), p. 302, this provision applied to imports from Great Britain, Finland, and Sweden.
[28] See Cafruny (1987), p. 66.

another example of how the United States has not fully replicated the British model of hegemony, and how when push came to shove the British generally privileged open markets over security.

The British Rule of 1756, the American Plan of 1776, and the War of 1812

One goal of preindustrial international law had been to devise rules that might isolate war to the immediate combatants. That meant drawing distinctions between the military and civilian spheres, and also between belligerent and neutral states. De Vattel addressed the question of how the belligerents ought to treat neutral states that continued to trade in wartime. He articulated the general principle that third countries would compromise their neutrality if they "affect to refuse selling me a single article, while at the same time they take pains to convey an abundant supply to my enemy, with an evident intention to favour him." Those same neutrals would be in the clear "if they only continue their *customary trade*"[29] with the belligerents. Thus the simple, core rules of international maritime law: Neutrals were free to trade with belligerents only if (a) they did so impartially, (b) restricted this trade to noncontraband goods,[30] and (c) allowed themselves to be searched. Those broad rules left considerable room for the development of contending British and American doctrines.

The key clash during the first century of US independence was between Britain's Rule of 1756 and the American Plan of 1776. The Rule of 1756 was a product of the Seven Years' War, and held that markets that are closed during peacetime cannot be lawfully opened to neutrals in wartime. This was a clever adaptation of de Vattel's principles to Britain's purposes, as it amounted to hoisting other empires by their own, protectionist petards: The French metropolis that ran a closed empire in peacetime would be obliged to live within those same limits in wartime, and the British asserted their legal right to make war on any putative neutrals that might dare to supply the enemy in defiance of this rule. This position was just as objectionable to France and the infant United States as it was favorable to the United Kingdom.

The US response was the Plan of 1776. As devised by the Continental Congress, this plan advanced the principle that "free ships make free goods" – that is, noncontraband goods destined for a belligerent are free from seizure when carried on neutral ships. This doctrine was recognized in the Treaty of Amity and Commerce that Benjamin Franklin negotiated in

[29] De Vattel (1758), p. 335. Emphasis in the original.
[30] See Chapter 10 on the tricky question of what is defined as contraband.

1778 with France, and subsequent US treaties expanded on that precedent. The 1799 treaty that a young John Quincy Adams concluded with Prussia broadcast the American intention to promote the free-ships doctrine. Washington and Berlin agreed in Article XII that when peace returned they would seek to establish "with the great maritime powers of Europe, such arrangements and such permanent principles as may serve to consolidate the liberty and the safety of the neutral navigation and commerce in future wars." American diplomats engaged in just such negotiations over the ensuing century, only to have second thoughts by the time that these goals appeared within reach.

These opposing Anglo-American principles were fought out in the Caribbean, where US shippers hoped to capture the wartime carrying trade of the English and French colonies. The Bourbon monarchy had reserved that trade to its own carriers, but military necessity forced the revolutionary leaders of the new France to throw their ports open to Yankee traders. The British predictably reasserted the Rule of 1756, and declared the United States to be at risk of losing its neutral status. There then came a long series of orders and counter-orders by which the British, the French, and the Americans each tried to get the upper hand. In 1793 London authorized the detention of all ships carrying goods to or from French colonies. American shippers employed a subterfuge by which they imported goods from the European powers' Caribbean and American colonies into the United States, then reexported them to Europe as US goods.

The belligerents did not long tolerate commercial opportunism under the flag of political neutrality. Both sides resented the American role in provisioning and enriching their enemy, and progressively stepped up the search and seizure of US ships. The Royal Navy further angered the United States by "impressing" (i.e., conscripting) any American seamen within their grasp whom they claimed to be British subjects. Tensions increased when the French Continental System and the British orders in council of 1807 moved from restraint on contraband to comprehensive blockades. The United States initially responded by imposing export embargoes on both belligerents, in hopes that cutting off US food and other staples (especially cotton for the English mills) would force them to lift their restrictions. The embargo had some limited success in winning concessions from the French, but not from the British. In an early demonstration of the domestic diplomacy of sanctions, this policy was also highly unpopular at home (see Chapter 10). The United States finally responded with the ultimate sanction. The War of 1812 left unsettled the underlying conflicts between the US and UK positions, with its only legacies being thousands of casualties, a burnt capital city, and a new national anthem.

The Multilateral Diplomacy of Sea Power

Great Britain's adherence to the Rule of 1756 lasted a century, with the Crimean War (1853–1856) providing the occasion for both London and Washington to revise their positions. In a sign that commerce now weighed just as heavily as security in London's calculations, it announced at the start of the war that it chose not to assert the right to search neutral vessels that traded with the Russian enemy. This switch overshadowed a minor American diplomatic coup. At a time when the czar was still fighting Britain, France, and the Ottoman Empire, his ministers concluded an 1854 treaty with the United States that explicitly enunciated the doctrine that "free ships make free goods." The American negotiators hoped to replicate this precedent with other partners, but the only takers in 1855–1856 were Nicaragua, Peru, and the Two Sicilies. Washington nonetheless treated the postwar Paris conference as an opportunity to win multilateral sanction for the principle. The American attendance was almost as significant as what the conference produced. This was not the first time that the country was active in multilateral negotiations, but it would have been the first such agreement of any real importance to which it adhered – had that happened. The United States would not be among the fifty-five countries that ratified the Paris Declaration Respecting Maritime Law (1856).

In another landmark decision, the British agreed to make permanent their wartime policy on the searching of neutrals. The Paris Declaration recognized that a neutral flag covers enemy goods (except for contraband of war), provided that neutral goods (other than contraband) are not liable to capture, and outlawed paper blockades (i.e., those that a navy lacked the wherewithal to enforce). Each of those provisions moved the law of war toward favored US positions, but another principle – the abolition of privateering – went the other way. Because the United States was still a maritime midget, and reserved the right to deploy this poor-man's navy, the balance of concessions was unacceptable to Washington. The US negotiators were also disappointed that the treaty left the definition of contraband up to the belligerents. They indicated that America could still sign if the powers agreed to abolish the right of belligerents to capture private property at sea, but Europeans did not relent on this point.

The Civil War would force American statesmen – or the Northern ones, anyway – to reconsider their position on privateers. Whereas the Union

Navy operated solely as a formal fleet, its weaker Confederate antagonist still relied on privateers. The effectiveness of this informal arm was limited by the Union blockade, and also by the cold reception that the rebel privateers received when they tried to bring their prizes to European ports. Even though the Confederacy was free to grant letters of marque to European ships, insofar as the rights and duties of the Paris Declaration applied only between signatories, foreign governments were not eager to encourage a practice that they had foresworn. No foreign captains raided for Richmond.

Washington participated in later international negotiations to revise the international law of war, neutrality, and trade, but received little satisfaction in those waning years of British hegemony. The US delegates to the Hague Conference of 1907 were disappointed once again in their efforts to secure immunity from seizure for private property. The London Naval Conference agreed two years later to a set of principles that was more favorable to neutral rights, but to no avail; in a sign that an increasingly challenged and declining hegemon had once more come to place security ahead of commerce, the House of Lords rejected the treaty in 1911. What little progress the diplomats had made toward the recognition of neutral rights would soon be completely undone by the First World War, when German raiders treated belligerent and neutral trade as fair game.

THE AMERICAN POSITION IN THE HEGEMONIC TRANSITION

The actual transfer of hegemony from the United Kingdom to the United States seemed to come rapidly in the middle of the twentieth century, with the relative positions of these two countries being radically different in 1946 than they had been in 1939. That sudden switch might best be compared to the overnight success that some musicians achieve only after decades on the road. The pecking order between London and Washington had persisted even when it was increasingly apparent that their respective political and military roles had not kept pace with changes in the economic and demographic foundations of power. A few episodes in the transitional period nevertheless prefigured the future.

Shifting US Perspectives in a Century of War

The United States might ideally have accomplished a smooth transition from the war with Mexico that began in 1846 through the fight against the Axis that ended in 1945, moving progressively from a position suitable for a generally disengaged free-rider to one more appropriate for an active hegemon. It was instead somewhat embarrassed by the conflicting positions it held at different times in this century of warfare. Naval operations in the Mexican War had given Americans a first view of how these issues appear from a belligerent's perspective, when the US Navy blockaded Veracruz and three other Mexican ports, and the inconveniences of the traditional doctrine were even more evident in the Civil War. This conflict gave both the United States and Britain the opportunity to experience belligerent/ neutral relations from the other side. While there were some important disputes over the extent of British impartiality, especially the sale of warships to the Confederacy, London generally fulfilled its obligations under international law; it also paid a postwar indemnity for those acts that crossed the line. The British restraint was not a matter of altruism, but stemmed from the interest in setting precedents that could be used to good advantage the next time that England was a belligerent and the United States a neutral. The more interesting consequence came in the newfound US appreciation for the need to enforce blockades strictly, including their application to neutrals.

This point can best be understood by juxtaposing the *Essex* and *Bermuda* decisions that were, respectively, rendered by the British High Court of Admiralty in 1804 and the US Supreme Court in 1865. The former case began when the Royal Navy captured the US merchant vessel *Essex* as it transported goods from the French West Indies. The *Essex* sought to evade the British ban on traffic between France and its colonies through the common ruse of a "broken voyage" (i.e., stopping at an American port before proceeding to the final destination). Citing the Rule of 1756, the British court declared this practice illegal. That decision (and the subsequent seizures of American merchantmen) enraged the American public, and was one of many steps that ultimately led to war, and yet it requires true subtlety of mind to distinguish the British decision from one rendered in Washington sixty-one years later. The *Bermuda* was a British ship that the US Navy seized while carrying contraband to the Confederacy. This ship took a route comparable to that of the *Essex*, only with a different transfer point (the British port of Nassau) and destination (Savannah, Georgia). Delivered on behalf of the court by Chief Justice Salmon P. Chase, who just a year earlier had a hand in enforcing these restrictions as Lincoln's secretary of the treasury, the Supreme Court's opinion observed that while the "interposition of a neutral port between the neutral departure and belligerent destination has always been a favorite resort of contraband carriers and blockade-runners . . . it never avails them when the ultimate destination is ascertained." The court concluded that "both vessel and cargo, even if both were neutral, were rightly condemned."[31]

The intellectual groundwork for the transfer of hegemony, and with it a major shift in naval doctrine, was being laid well before it became a fact. Alfred Thayer Mahan, the patron saint of the US Navy, believed at the turn of the century that the time had come for the United States to assert its sea power. Writing to President Theodore Roosevelt in 1904, Mahan warned that the policy of "free ships, free goods" had "lost the fitness it possibly once had to national conditions."[32] Roosevelt was no less a proponent than Mahan of military vigor, especially at sea, yet he was not ready to send more than a century of doctrine to Davey Jones' locker. TR and his successors would inch the United States toward a position that honored the exercise of power over the acquisition of wealth, a process that would not reach its logical conclusion until his cousin Franklin took office.

The United States reiterated its traditional position at the outbreak of the First World War. Britain and Germany employed embargoes and then blockades to weaken one another, and once again the United States acted in defense of its neutral rights. The main difference between 1803–1815 and 1914–1918 was in US economic and military strength; the belligerents in the Great War were acutely aware that this upstart manufacturing power could tip the balance in Europe. Like the Confederacy before it, Germany was a weaker naval power that could not defeat its opponent in a head-on battle at sea, and so it resorted to commerce destroyers. And just as Richmond had innovated the use of ironclads, Berlin took the next step by sending its raiders beneath the waves. By 1915 the German *Unterwasserboot* was the terror of the seas, and the British retaliated with a blockade on all German trade. The Allied powers also rationed shipments to neutral European countries in order to prevent transshipments to Germany, imposing hardships on these importers and their American suppliers.

This is when the patience that London had so long shown to Washington was first vindicated. Although there were some Americans who called for reprisals against Britain for its harassment of neutral shipping, not to mention opening the US mail, President Wilson was more tolerant of the cousins' violations of neutral rights than he was toward the German assaults. Perseverance paid off as their German antagonist became more desperate,

---

[31] "Opinion of the United States Supreme Court in the Case of 'The Bermuda,'" in Rappaport (1966), pp. 98 and 99. This was not the only episode in the Civil War that laid bare the gradual switch in the British and American positions. See, for example, Bailey (1980), pp. 327–331 on the *Trent* affair.

[32] Quoted in Moran (2002), p. 229.

resorting to unrestricted submarine warfare. That step, together with Berlin's proposal to Mexico City for joint action against the United States, pushed America into the war that would not end all wars.

The Anglo-American Alliance and the End of American Neutrality

The Second World War had a more profound and lasting impact on the foundations of US policy than had its predecessor. The American retreat into isolationism in the 1920s, as well as the return of protectionism in the tariff acts of 1922 and 1930, complemented the rebirth of neutrality. Inside of a few decades, all three of those doctrines would be jettisoned. In the process, the United States also switched the priorities that it assigned to power and wealth. As Dobson observed, after 1933 the United States dealt with "what it considered to be strategic threats to its survival from a succession of actual or potential aggressors," and did so through an economic statecraft that placed defense ahead of commercial gain.[33]

The first US steps toward the abandonment of neutrality were less an assertion of power by the future hegemon than an effort to keep its besieged predecessor in the fight. And just as the British had previously shown in their support of Greek independence, a great power can find ways to favor a warring party without becoming a belligerent. When London stood alone in its defiance of Berlin, and as long as domestic US politics made military intervention unthinkable, the Roosevelt administration became a material rather than a martial ally. That started with the 1939 amendments to the Jefferson-vintage Embargo Act, replacing the old ban on arms sales to belligerents with a cash-and-carry policy. The Royal Navy still commanded the surface, and so this amounted to a policy of selling arms only to the British. Washington further stretched the definition of neutrality in early 1941 with the Lend-Lease Act, which started nine months before the United States entered the war and was anything but impartial. Nazi Germany might have responded as Imperial Germany had a generation earlier, letting its U-boats loose on those American ships that then did a brisk transatlantic trade, but Hitler was not eager to give Roosevelt an excuse to switch from compromised neutral to active belligerent.

The German submariners came disturbingly close to winning the Battle of the North Atlantic, with Churchill later acknowledging that the "only thing that ever really frightened me during the war was the U-boat peril."[34] His appraisal was more realistic than that of Richard Cobden, who had claimed

---

[33] Dobson (2002), p. 306 and passim.
[34] Churchill (1949), p. 598.

a century before that Britain could complement its repeal of agricultural protection by scaling back the Royal Navy.[35] This leader of the Anti-Corn Law League reasoned that the opening of the British market to foreign grain proved London's good intentions, and that disarmament would allow all of Europe to enjoy the twin blessings of free trade and peace. A clear-eyed reading of history suggests that cashing in on Cobden's proposed peace dividend might have gravely imperiled the country. As advantageous as it was for England to export manufactures and import food, the resulting dependence made sea power all the more vital. By the mid-1930s, England imported most of its meat (53%), fruit (72%), sugar (75%), butter and cheese (83%), and wheat flour (84%).[36] Several factors contributed to Britain's victory at sea, including Alan Turing's cracking of the *Kriegsmarine*'s Enigma codes, the perfection of the convoy system, and innovations in antisubmarine warfare, but none were more important than two bits of foresight shown by some of Churchill's predecessors. The first was to ignore Cobden and ensure that the Royal Navy retained the wherewithal to keep the sea lanes open; the other was to cultivate friendly ties with their first former colony, fostering a relationship in which it was politically feasible for FDR to compromise American neutrality in Britain's favor.

Dean Acheson (1893–1971), who ran the State Department's economic warfare operations, later described just how vigorously he employed methods that would have driven his predecessors to apoplexy. The new techniques extended "far beyond the old blockade tactic used prior to 1914," he proudly wrote, to the point where "a ship could not move without allied permission" and "legal ideas about the rights of neutrals, neutral trade, and freedom of the seas became irrelevant to immovable ships."[37] The surest sign that the United States had cast aside time-honored principles came in its treatment of European neutrals. Germany posed an immediate threat to Sweden and Switzerland, but that did not prevent Washington from bringing to bear all possible pressure on Stockholm and Bern. In 1943 they agreed to curtail their trade with Germany, in response to a "combination of threats to restrict the two countries' overseas imports and the black-listing of their major firms, plus positive measures such as special permission to import certain highly demanded articles (petroleum products)."[38] One also supposes that the Swedes and the Swiss thought it prudent to position themselves for

---

[35]   Cobden (1848).
[36]   Mendershausen (1940), p. 38.
[37]   Acheson (1969), p. 48.
[38]   Wu (1952), p. 289. See also Dobson (2002), chapter 4.

a postwar world in which, as was increasingly apparent, the Germans would not be calling the shots.

Among the many casualties of the Second World War were a handful of words that once carried positive connotations, but henceforth had only pejorative meanings. These included not just *appeasement, propaganda,* and *protectionism,* but also *neutrality.* It went from a cardinal virtue practiced by fair-minded statesmen to a mortal sin committed by the fellow-travelers of America's enemies. Secretary of State John Foster Dulles (1888–1959) signaled the profound change in his 1956 declaration that "neutrality has increasingly become an obsolete" concept that was "immoral and shortsighted."[39] Many cold warriors concurred, and Dulles was unusual only in implicitly acknowledging the former American veneration for this principle. The composition and rhetoric of the Non-Aligned Movement, which was founded that same year in Yugoslavia, only served to harden US views. While some members of this putatively neutral group were democracies whose leaders genuinely hoped to avoid the taint of subordination to Moscow or Washington, the same cannot be said of the Soviet client states that would eventually dominate its meetings. Whatever nuance survived in the American view of neutrality would later be obliterated by President George W. Bush's 2001 pronouncement that "[e]ither you are with us or you are with the terrorists."[40]

SEA POWER AND SECURITY IN THE GATT/WTO SYSTEM

The GATT was among the earliest products of American hegemony, being established two years after the United Nations and two years before the North Atlantic Treaty Organization. As was described in previous chapters, the terms of this unique arrangement were largely based on the bilateral tariff agreements that the Roosevelt and Truman administrations negotiated under the Reciprocal Trade Agreements Act (RTAA). The GATT and its WTO successor made two perennial accommodations to US security demands, both of which stemmed from the new hegemon's efforts to reconcile the competing demands of wealth and power. One concerns the US insistence on a carve-out for the maritime transportation sector. The other is an exception for countries' national security policies that is far more permissive than the corresponding exceptions for other, more ordinary issues affecting trade. These exceptions

---

[39] The *New York Times* (1959).
[40] "Address Before a Joint Session of the Congress on the United States Response to the Terrorist Attacks of September 11" (September 20, 2001), *PPP 2001 Book II*, p. 1142.

have been the subject of episodic conflicts with trading partners, but successive American presidents have considered them to be politically inviolable.

Disputes over the Jones Act

Most WTO members have at least one "sacred cow" that they protect through monopolies, subsidies, or other interventions, and that they will fight hard to isolate from the same multilateral rules that liberalize trade in other sectors. Examples include the cultural exception that France and other members of the European Union insist on, especially with respect to the protection and promotion of audiovisual services (e.g., films, television, music, etc.), and the special treatment that countries such as Japan, Korea, Norway, and Switzerland demand for agriculture. The maritime services sector is the most sacred of all cows for the United States, and the most protected subsector is coastal shipping. No other industry in the United States has received such perpetual protection, dating to the early days of independence.

Preservation of this fleet is costly. One study found that coastal water transport would be about 60% cheaper, and consumer welfare would improve by $500 million annually, by relaxing or eliminating these restrictions,[41] while another put the consumer cost of the Jones Act at $1.8 billion per year.[42] While those concerns sometimes inspire the affected industries to seek reforms, they rarely make much headway in Congress. When combined with the support of the Navy and other security-minded segments of government and civil society, together with majorities on the relevant congressional committees, the interests supporting the Jones Act form an apparently unbeatable "iron triangle." Senator John McCain (Republican–Arizona) learned this when he attempted to enact reforms from his sequential perches as chairman of the Commerce Committee and the Armed Services Committee, arguing that the law imposes economic costs without enhancing national defense. He eventually concluded that "if he brought a reform bill to a Senate vote, he could not get 20 votes."[43]

If members of Congress are loath to reform this law autonomously, they are doubly opposed to allowing the executive to negotiate it away. The high importance that legislators attach to the shipping sector is shown by such widely separated episodes as the Senate's 1795 removal of an offending article from the Jay Treaty and the 1987 opposition to the Reagan administration's

[41] Lewis (2013).
[42] Grennes (2017).
[43] Ibid., p. 41.

partial concession to Canada on cargo-preference laws (see Chapters 4 and 9). Whatever inclination that the US Trade Representative (USTR) might otherwise have to entertain liberalization of the Jones Act would certainly have been restrained by a 1989 presidential directive. This document ordered the agency to "ensure that international agreements and federal policies governing use of foreign flag carriers protect our national security interests" and "promote . . . the readiness of the US merchant marine and supporting industries to respond to critical national security requirements."[44] That message was later reinforced by naming the USTR to the Maritime Security Policy Coordinating Committee.[45] Even in the Uruguay Round, which was built around US demands for the expansion of trade rules to cover services and issues of importance to capital- and technology-intensive sectors, Washington insisted on reservations for the cabotage laws.

The Apotheosis of Trade Law and Security: GATT Article XXI

The US negotiators who played so critical a role in shaping the rules of the GATT took a very different approach than earlier generations of American statesmen might have, were this body of law created in the eighteenth or nineteenth centuries. Their predecessors would have preferred a system that put the pursuit of wealth ahead of the exercise of power, and that immunized them from the pressures of belligerents. In hegemony, Washington has instead insisted that the system not interfere with trade-restricting measures that the United States might feel obliged to adopt in pursuit of national security.

The intentions of the GATT drafters can be seen in how they adapted the standard exceptions clauses of the RTAA bilaterals. Those earlier agreements bundled all exceptions clauses into a single article, and gave each signatory wide latitude to invoke them unilaterally. For example, Article XVII of the US–Mexico agreement (1942) provided that "[n]othing in this agreement shall be construed to prevent the adoption or enforcement of" eight types of measures, three of which related to security (i.e., arms sales, neutrality, or measures imposed "in time of war or other national emergency"); the rest concerned more standard economic fare (e.g., measures dealing with "human, animal or plant life or health"). Beyond dividing the exceptions into separate articles XX (general) and XXI (national security), and creating a dispute-settlement system to hear claims, the GATT negotiators made two

---

[44] "National Security Directive on Sealift" (October 5, 1989), p. 2.
[45] National Security Presidential Directive NSPD-41, "Maritime Security Policy" (December 21, 2004).

major changes. The first strengthened the pro-trade lean of GATT Article XX by inserting chapeau language that drastically limited countries' safe harbor for non-security measures. It specifies that trade-restricting measures are permitted only if they do not comprise "arbitrary or unjustifiable discrimination between countries," or amount to "a disguised restriction on international trade." The drafters also vitiated several of the specific incisions with necessity clauses, such that (for example) countries could claim an exception only for measures *"necessary* to protect human, animal or plant life or health." Dispute-settlement panels have further strengthened the system's trade-centric bias by reading the chapeau and necessity clauses to mean that restrictive measures violate GATT obligations if the country might have opted instead for some less trade-restrictive means of achieving the same end.

The GATT drafters took just the opposite approach to security issues, starting with their isolation in the separate Article XXI. This article is not conditioned upon any chapeau, and the decision as to what is necessary is left up to the invoking country. That is the clear implication of language providing that nothing in GATT shall be construed "to prevent any contracting party from taking any action which *it* considers necessary for the protection of *its* essential security interests." They also retained expansive language from the RTAA template, specifying that this exception applied to measures "taken in time of war or other emergency in international relations." By declining to provide a definition of what constitutes an "emergency," the drafters placed no limits on countries' claims. This deference carried over into the actual jurisprudence of Article XXI cases, where the invocation of national security became the trade law equivalent of those "Get Out of Jail Free" cards so familiar to anyone who ever played Monopoly. Thus far, no country invoking this GATT article has ever been obliged to justify its claim before a dispute-settlement panel. The mere suggestion that a country was prepared to invoke it – perhaps delivered in whispers over cocktail chatter, or in oblique but meaningful comments to the press – was often enough to deter a would-be complainant from initiating a formal process against measures for which an Article XXI defense might reasonably be anticipated. In the small number of cases in which a member proceeded to lodge a formal complaint, dispute-settlement panels have traditionally demurred from asserting their authority to pass judgment on another country's assertion of raison d'etat.

In short, the rules are far more deferential toward claims of national security than they are toward other types of concerns that might collide with trade. One class of issues is subject to intense scrutiny, and the other remains at the sole discretion of the invoking country. Although this approach may appear legally dubious, with Jackson characterizing Article XXI as "so broad, self-judging,

and ambiguous that it obviously can be abused,"[46] the near-automatic acceptance of invocations has heretofore been seen as a politically necessary norm.
It is founded upon recognition that countries might prefer to leave the system
altogether if the actions that they take in pursuit of national security were
subject to review not just by trade lawyers, but by foreign ones at that. Anyone
who doubts this point need only conduct a brief thought experiment, imagin-
ing what might happen if, in a moment of grave national peril, the trade
minister were to inform cabinet colleagues that some trade-restricting measure
the country had imposed in its confrontation with a prospective enemy was
found illegal by a panel in Geneva. It is easier to imagine the defense and
foreign ministers insisting that the country pull out of this multilateral trade
institution in protest of an outrage against its sovereign right of self-defense
than it is to see them meekly withdrawing the offending measures in obedi-
ence to the WTO's writ.

The Rarity of Article XXI Invocations

What is most remarkable about Article XXI is not the abuse that it might seem
to invite, but the infrequency with which countries have accepted that invitation. Even a cursory historical examination confirms that formal invocations
are very rare, and that fraud is even rarer. Prior to the advent of Donald Trump,
there were just three occasions in which the United States either explicitly
invoked Article XXI or publicly implied that it would do so. All three involved
countries that had affiliated with the Soviet Union only after joining the
GATT. The United States invoked Article XXI in 1949 in order to apply the
newly enacted embargo on exports of strategic goods against Czechoslovakia,
and did the same in 1985 when Nicaragua objected to an embargo imposed by
President Reagan. The Kennedy administration was prepared to cite this
article in defense of its embargo on Cuba, but that was rendered moot by
Cuba's failure to lodge a formal complaint.[47]

Only a handful of other GATT or WTO members have availed themselves of the security exception. The European Union did so twice, first in
a 1982 defense of the import restrictions that it (together with Australia and
Canada) imposed on Argentina during the Falklands/Malvinas war. It also
invoked Article XXI in 1991 to justify its withdrawal of preferential

---

[46] Jackson (1989), p. 204. For a detailed critique of GATT Article XXI and its use, see Hahn
(1991).
[47] Whitt (1987), pp. 603–631. See also the pseudo-invocation by the United States with respect to
the Helms–Burton law, as discussed in Chapter 10.

treatment from Yugoslavia; the breakup of that country made a panel moot. Developing countries took shelter in this article a few times. On the accession of Portugal in 1961, for example, Ghana stated that its boycott of Portuguese goods was justified under Article XXI because Angola posed a constant threat to the peace of the African continent. Honduras and Colombia settled a dispute in 1999 over their maritime boundaries, but Nicaragua objected and imposed a 35% tariff on all imports from Honduras and Colombia. Nicaragua then invoked Article XXI when those countries sought a panel. The parties eventually agreed to take the issue up in the International Court of Justice, and no WTO panel was formed. The article was also implicated in several cases that arose in 2017. Bahrain invoked it to justify actions that it took – together with Egypt, Saudi Arabia, and the United Arab Emirates – in a conflict with Qatar. Russia likewise invoked the article in one of a series of disputes with Ukraine. Perhaps the most notable aspect of that last case was not Moscow's decision to employ this legal loophole, but the full-throated support that it subsequently received from Washington.[48] That declaration was in keeping with established US positions, but also took on new urgency in light of the Trump administration's conflation of trade and security issues.

While critics might quibble over the specific policies that gave rise to each one of these invocations, the principal point is that such objections have traditionally been considered outside the proper jurisdiction of trade ministries or the WTO. Provided that the policy in question falls within the category of security policy, as all of the foregoing cases did, the larger purposes of the system are served by quarantining those topics that are above the pay grade of trade policymakers. That leaves just one pre-2018 case in which a country's invocation failed to pass the laugh test. This came in 1975, when Sweden imposed restrictions on footwear. Stockholm justified this measure by citing Article XXI, claiming that the country needed a viable industry to produce boots for its soldiers in the event of war. The trade community shamed Sweden into removing the offending measures within two years, but did so without formally obliging Stockholm to provide a legal justification for its invocation of Article XXI.

---

[48] See the submission entitled "Third Party Executive Summary of the United States of America" (February 27, 2018) in the case of *Russia – Measures Concerning Traffic in Transit* (DS512), as posted at https://ustr.gov/sites/default/files/enforcement/DS/US.3d.Pty.Exec.Summ.fin.%28public%29.pdf.

THE LINKS BETWEEN TRADE AND SECURITY

Leaders in the Anglo-American hegemonies found distinct ways to deal with the issues that lay at the intersection of trade and security. While both London and Washington had to strike balances, the choices they made often differed on two counts. One concerns the relative importance that they attached to power and wealth as objectives. As a very general rule, the more trade-dependent English showed a greater propensity to lean in favor of commercial goals. The other concerned the ways that they dealt with other partners in the global community. The two hegemons each approached their tasks as *primus inter pares*, but the Americans seemed a bit more prone than the English to put the interests of the *primus* ahead of the other *pares*.

The events reviewed above show how a country's view of an issue may change greatly as its own circumstances evolve. That general rule does not apply equally to all issues, however, as can be appreciated by comparing the different ways that the United States dealt with neutrality and support for shipping. Whereas the transition to hegemony had the effect one might expect on Washington's views toward neutrality, the same cannot be said for the US attachment to the cabotage laws. In contrast to the British, who did away with the Navigation Acts early in their own hegemony, American statesmen have not budged on this issue. That contrast seems all the more remarkable in light of the higher importance that the British might be expected to attach to all things maritime. One may only suppose that the answer lies not just in the greater British reliance on the Royal Navy for its security, but on the even greater degree to which Britain relies on trade for its prosperity.

The events reviewed in this chapter all predate the inauguration of Donald Trump, which may have started an entirely new phase in the relationship between trade and security. In Chapter 16 we will review how the Trump administration deals with this topic at two levels. From a strategic perspective, the principal theme in this administration's foreign economic policy is a throwback to a much earlier era. Far from accepting the premises of Anglo-American hegemony – that an open trading system serves both the commercial and security interests of the hegemon, and that this country has a special role in creating, leading, and maintaining that system – the administration strikes a stance that is transactional, nationalist, and mercantilist. One of the tactical manifestations of that strategic posture is the use of the Section 232 national security statute, which is the domestic counterpart to GATT Article XXI, as a means of imposing restrictions on imports. The administration initiated cases against steel and aluminum in 2017, imposing tariffs and quotas the next year, and in 2018 it also launched a new Section 232 case against the automotive sector. This policy, and its blatant abuse of the security exception, may pose a greater existential risk to the multilateral trading system than any other action taken by the Trump administration.

Returning to the historical perspective of this chapter, one may find precedents for these Trump administration attitudes and actions. They are consistent with views that were common when the United States was still a free-rider within the British hegemony, and that did not disappear altogether when it became America's turn to lead. The speed with which they have reoriented US policy has nevertheless been head-spinning, as is their capacity to accelerate Washington's retreat from leadership in the trading system.

8

The Sun Also Sets:
The Japanese Challenge to the US Auto Industry

The President and the Prime Minister ... expressed their concern about the rising pressure toward protectionism in many countries and affirmed that the United States and Japan are determined to continue their efforts to maintain and strengthen free and open trade principles embodied in the GATT framework. In this regard, the President expressed his appreciation for the voluntary action taken by the Government of Japan to restrain the export of automobiles to the United States at a time when the United States automobile industry is passing through a difficult adjustment period.

> Joint communiqué of President Ronald Reagan and Prime Minister
> Zenko Suzuki of May 8, 1981

Let's avoid steps that could result in protectionism, that would further contract global trade. Let's focus on how are we going to move our regulatory process forward in order that we do not see the kinds of systemic breakdowns that we've already seen.

> President Barack Obama, press conference of March 24, 2009

INTRODUCTION

Presidents Reagan and Obama each had to deal with uncertainty in the economy at large, and in the automotive sector in particular, upon taking office. Both administrations inherited automotive policy initiatives that were well underway during the postelection transition. Reagan pressed Japan to impose restrictive quotas on exports of its vehicles to the US market while also, in the Orwellian language of the foregoing communiqué, asserting that protection supported free trade. Twenty-eight years and four presidencies later, Obama spoke out against protectionism and negotiated with Congress to ensure that the pending automotive support package did not violate US obligations. This included a cash-for-clunkers program that was nondiscriminatory in principle, and in actual practice encouraged the scrapping of older, less efficient American cars for more fuel-efficient Japanese and Korean vehicles.

These two episodes in US–Japanese automotive trade underline key changes in political economy. At the domestic level, these incidents illustrate a fundamental transformation that has been underway since the early 1980s. That transformation entails the establishment of Japanese and other foreign transplants in the United States, greater dependence on global supply chains and strategic alliances for the Big Three US auto producers (Chrysler, Ford, and General Motors), a decline in the size of the automotive workforce (especially its unionized segment), and increasing numbers and influence for the auto dealers who sell Japanese cars. The result is a political landscape in which there are fewer players who perceive import protection to be in their interests; those few who still favor protection are now less powerful. These factors all ensure that the domestic diplomacy of automotive trade is quite different from what it once was.

The cases also speak to relations between hegemons and their challengers. The events of 1981 and 2009 demonstrate that while challenges may be inevitable, the hegemon's overthrow and its descent into protectionism are not. There was a time when Japan seemed like an unstoppable industrial juggernaut, and when the American public and policymakers feared that the country was in danger of irrevocably losing its edge – or that this had already happened. The case provides at least a broad analogy to the current rivalry between the United States and China, showing how in this instance the two sides were able to reach a *modus vivendi*.

One peculiarity of these twin case studies is that they might, in the near future, form not just a duo but part of a trio. As this book went to press, the Trump administration began an investigation of US automotive imports under the same national security law (Section 232 of the Trade Expansion Act of 1962) that it used earlier in 2018 to impose tariffs on aluminum and steel (see Chapter 16). What is most notable about this case is that it had not been requested by either the Big Three or the United Auto Workers (UAW), but was self-initiated at the direct orders of the president. Quite to the contrary, while the UAW expressed support[1] the manufacturers quickly dissociated

---

[1] The UAW statement declared that the investigation "should focus on imports from countries that have advanced their interests at the expense of U.S. industrial capacity, our work force and, in turn, our defense industrial base," specifically naming China, Germany, Japan, Korea, and Mexico, but said that Canada "should be exempted from any 232 actions on autos and auto parts." The UAW has members in both Canada and the United States. See www.prnewswire .com/news-releases/usw-supports-section-232-investigation-on-imports-of-autos-and-auto-parts-300655978.html.

themselves from the case. The Auto Alliance, which represents both domestic and transplant production, declared that "vehicle imports do not pose a national security risk to the U.S." and "urge[d] the Administration to support policies that remove barriers to free trade."[2] This case thus represents a sharp departure from the general pattern by which protectionist initiatives originate in the private sector, and succeed only if they overcome presidential resistance. The industry's response is instead entirely consistent with the trend-line discussed in this chapter. The pressures for automotive protection that had proved irresistible in 1981 were greatly diminished by 2009, and by 2018 the internationalized American industry stood foursquare against protection. If the investigation should result in meaningful restrictions on automotive imports, it will offer further evidence that the Trump administration is intent on turning back the clock – even if most segments of the relevant industry do not share that objective.

MACRO PERSPECTIVES ON THE US–JAPANESE COMPETITION

The protection that Reagan extended in 1981, and the actions that Obama sidestepped in 2009, cannot be properly understood without seeing where they fit in two much larger processes. One was the confluence of macro trends that began in the early 1970s and came to a head in the next decade, with global currencies fluctuating and the price of gasoline rising rapidly. As described later, those two trends conspired to make American consumers prefer fuel-efficient Japanese vehicles over the land-yachts that Detroit still thought that they wanted. The resulting trade deficit with Japan fed into the second major trend, which concerned the public reaction to globalization in general and the relationship with this challenger in particular. The 1981 episode came at a time when the United States mattered far more to the global economy than vice versa, and the sudden drop in the share of American-made vehicles on the roads offered inescapable evidence that something had gone seriously out of kilter. By 2009, Americans had grown more accustomed to globalization and were better able to take its blows in stride.

The Rise of OPEC and the Fall of the Yen

Two verities that had shaped US foreign policy since the late 1940s came under serious challenge in the 1970s. One held that the sole threat to American

---

2 https://autoalliance.org/2018/05/24/auto-alliance-statement-response-trump-administration-sec tion-232-investigation/.

security came from the Soviet Union and its satellites, with the United States having already fought one Asian land war to a stalemate and being engaged in the last throes of another. Washington had also seen a succession of conflicts in the Middle East through that same Cold War lens. From the crises in the Suez (1956) and Lebanon (1958) through the Six-Day War (1967) and the Yom Kippur War (1973), American leaders thought more in terms of superpowers, client states, and proxy wars than they did about local grievances among the immediate warring parties. Washington was forced to reassess its perspective when in 1973 the Arab members of the Organization of Petroleum Exporting Countries (OPEC) responded to US support of Israel by imposing an oil export embargo. The resulting price shock was outdone at the end of that decade when the Iranian Revolution and the Iran–Iraq War produced even greater supply disruptions. We can now see in those oil shocks, and their associated conflicts, an augury of the issues that would cast a long shadow in the post–Cold War period.

The first oil shock came not long after another verity of the old order was shattered. From the creation of the Bretton Woods monetary system in 1944, the US dollar had played the same, stabilizing role for the global economy that gold had in the Pax Britannica. That bedrock of the trading system could last only so long as Washington and its partners had the political will to tolerate economic imbalances, and by the 1970s that resolve was seriously tested. Currencies floated freely after Nixon suspended the convertibility of the dollar into gold in 1971. The trends were initially favorable to the United States. A dollar bought ¥358 in 1971, but by 1979 it bought just ¥195. That trend sharply reversed in 1980, however, with a 22% spike in the value of the dollar coming just in time to exacerbate the rising price-competitiveness of Japanese cars.[3]

Taken together, the oil shocks and floating currencies of the 1970s eroded another foundation of US foreign economic policy. Even before Washington took on hegemonic responsibilities in the Second World War, the automotive industry and its workers were the strongest supporters of the trade agreements program. Presidents from FDR to JFK could consistently depend on the Big Three and the UAW to support their priorities in trade and to help manage relations with Congress. There was no irony intended when a classic study of mid-century trade politics entitled a chapter "Detroit: Hotbed of Free Trade."[4] The currency and oil shocks forced both the unions and (after a lag) the firms to reassess their positions. A lower yen made Japanese cars less expensive, while rising gasoline prices made those same, fuel-efficient cars more attractive. The

---

[3] For more detailed considerations of the effect of exchange rates on actual US automotive trade with Japan see Aizcorbe (2007) and Crandall (1987).

[4] Bauer, Pool, and Dexter (1963).

Yen per Dollar and 2015 Cents per Gallon of Gasoline

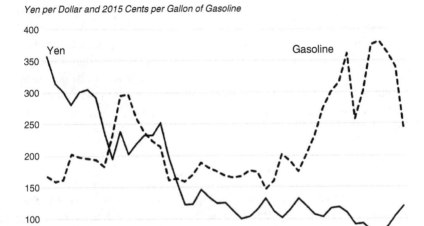

FIGURE 8.1 Prices for the yen and gasoline, 1971–2015.
Sources: Yen per dollar are for the first day of each year, as reported by the Federal Reserve Bank of St. Louis at https://fred.stlouisfed.org/series/DEXJPUS. Gasoline prices are the average historical annual gasoline pump price (expressed in 2015 dollars) as reported by the Department of Energy at www.energy.gov/eere/vehicles/fact-915-march-7–2016-average-historical-annual-gasoline-pump-price-1929–2015.

major trends can be seen in Figure 8.1. American consumers were especially sensitive toward changes in the price of gasoline, which had been gradually declining for decades. Expressed in 2015 dollars, it had dropped from $2.62 per gallon in 1935 to $1.72 in 1970. The effects of the first oil shock were more psychological than economic, with the novelty of gas lines being greater than the relatively modest rise to $2.03 in 1974, but the second oil shock sent prices to $2.95 in 1980.[5] Imports from Japan rose rapidly, and the Big Three took a big, collective hit. American automobile production dropped from an annual rate of 9.1 million units assembled in January, 1979 to 6.2 million in January, 1980, and tumbled further to 5.7 million in January, 1981.[6] These challenges produced political demands that elected officials could not ignore.

The data shown in Figure 8.1 fairly beg a question: If Washington imposed import restrictions at the start of the Reagan administration, when the yen was

[5] The nominal prices for the four years cited in the paragraph were 19¢, 36¢, 53¢, and $1.19, respectively. See https://energy.gov/eere/vehicles/fact-915-march-7–2016-average-historical-annual-gasoline-pump-price-1929–2015.

[6] Federal Reserve data at www.federalreserve.gov/releases/G17/iphist/autohist_sa.txt.

cheap and gas was expensive, why did the same thing not happen during the Obama administration? Currency pressures were not a factor this time, with a dollar buying 17% fewer yen in 2009 than in 2008, but gas prices were critical once more. A gallon cost $1.47 in 1998, but $3.61 in 2008. Even after slipping to $2.58, the 2009 price remained in oil-shock territory. The renewed demand for fuel-efficient vehicles might have made the Big Three just as nervous in 2009 as it had in 1980. We will soon see why they did not make new demands for protection.

The Perception of "Japan as #1"

Understanding these two episodes also requires that we consider an important shift in public perceptions. American society in the early 1980s was caught up in a widespread concern that Japan was overtaking the United States as the technological and economic leader. Much of the concern in the Reagan years had to do with the specific industrial sector at issue. Cars are special, both commercially and socially. Their economic significance can be seen in the first and second places that automobiles and oil take in the list of the world's most traded commodities, with the precise order shifting according to the price of crude. A car is typically the largest or second-largest purchase for any consumer, depending on whether that person is also a homeowner. It is not surprising that the automotive sector became the highest-profile segment of the US–Japanese economic competition. Throughout the 1980s, when American concerns over losing out to Japan hit their peak, the ubiquitous visual cliché for this struggle was television news footage of Japanese vehicles rolling off cargo ships onto American ports.

Automotive production is also an iconic industrial sector that hosted two revolutions in the twentieth century. One came after the First World War, when Ford and General Motors tossed aside craft production for the new science of mass production; the next came after the Second World War, when Toyota developed lean production based on "teams of multiskilled workers at all levels of the organization [using] highly flexible, increasingly automated machines to produce volumes of products in enormous variety."[7] The advantages of lean over mass production spread to other industries, and are credited in some circles for Japan's rapid rise to industrial preeminence. Womack et al. dated the turning point to 1955, when American automotive production first exceeded 7 million vehicles per year, North America produced nearly three-quarters of the world's cars, and imports were a great rarity on the US roads.

---

[7]   Womack et al. (1990), p. 13.

Thereafter the share of production outside the United States rose rapidly, and imports gradually took a larger slice of the American car market.

To all this must be added the cultural factor. The rivalry with Japan carried overtones not of a friendly competition with an ally, but of a revanchist struggle with a once and future enemy. Americans viewed Japan in the 1980s in much the same way that the prior hegemon saw its challenger a century earlier. Just as the 1890s spawned a growing English literature on the dangers of Germany's economic and military expansion, whether through alarmist works of nonfiction[8] or in penny dreadfuls that gave lurid accounts of future German invasions,[9] so too did the Japanese challenge inspire a wave of literary hysteria. Authors in both periods likened commercial competition to warfare. Former Commerce Department official Clyde Prestowitz exemplified the tone, asserting that "the Japanese government views industrial performance as akin to national security and pours enormous energy into ensuring that its industry is the world leader."[10] A related subtheme focused on the allegedly treasonous practices of those former US elected officials and civil servants who prostituted themselves as lobbyists and advisors. Pat Choate claimed that by "spending at least $100 million each year to hire hundreds" of these lobbyists Japan was "running an ongoing political campaign in America as if it were a third political party."[11] (Choate himself would later do precisely that, joining fellow protectionist Ross Perot on the Reform Party's 1996 presidential ticket.)

Art imitated life in both countries. In Japan, this took the form of a dark literary genre known as the "business novel."[12] In the United States, novels and especially movies expressed rising anxieties over lost competitiveness, whether the theatrical mask was laughing (e.g., the 1986 film *Gung Ho*) or crying (e.g., the 1989 film *Black Rain*). These works of fiction often hearkened back to the Second World War, implicitly asserting that Americans now faced either an unrepentant Japan that was intent on an economic Pearl Harbor or a vengeful Japan that longed to pay the United States back for Hiroshima and Nagasaki. Perhaps the most widely read among these offerings was the 1992 novel (later the 1993 film) *Rising Sun*. Writing as much like a political pamphleteer as a storyteller, Michael Crichton larded that novel with cautionary vignettes about Japanese predatory practices and world-weary characters who repeatedly

---

[8] See, for example, the popular *Made in Germany* (1896) by Ernest Edwin Williams, as well as the summary of this and similar works in Hirschman (1945), pp. 54–55.

[9] See, for example, the collections of Clarke (1995) and Moorcock (1976).

[10] Prestowitz (1988), p. 13.

[11] Choate (1990), p. xv.

[12] The genre is alternatively known as the "industry novel." See, for example, Prindle (1989) and Shimizu (1996).

issued dire warnings about where the United States was headed. Unusual for a novel, it included a bibliography listing dozens of books and articles support-ing Crichton's view of an economic life-or-death struggle.

Those cultural expressions of an economic and political death-match helped to shape the environment in which US trade policy was made from the late 1970s through the 1980s. While one may only speculate on just how great an impact they ultimately had on policymakers' decisions, it is note-worthy that this theme in fiction and film seemed to recede around the same time that the Japanese economy began to stagnate.

THE REAGAN ADMINISTRATION AND THE VOLUNTARY EXPORT RESTRAINTS

Those later decades of Japanese decline were nowhere in sight when Ronald Reagan took the oath of office in 1981. He instead inherited a policy debate that was already well advanced, with a bipartisan consensus favoring the imposi-tion of restrictions on Japanese cars. The only real surprise was that this had not yet happened; the only real question was precisely how it would now be done.

The Carter Administration's Reticence

Democrats are usually perceived as protectionists and Republicans as free-traders. While that view is frequently vindicated at the congressional level, the picture is quite different in the White House. A few Democratic executives have made concessions to protectionist industries, typically through the "two steps forward, one step back" approach that presidents often take to secure support for market-opening initiatives, but most significant protectionist con-cessions over the past few generations have come from Republicans. The case of automotive restrictions in 1980–1981 exemplifies this phenomenon. President Carter was under great pressure to aid the auto industry, but the market was not restricted until he was replaced by a man whose protectionist actions often belied his free-trade pronouncements.

The Carter administration's first policy response to the industry's woes was to provide aid to the Chrysler Corporation, which sought a loan guarantee in 1979 to forestall bankruptcy. The administration and Congress agreed that this firm was, in terms often repeated in the 2008–2009 financial crisis, "too big to fail." It was not until the next year that another of the Big Three producers proposed import protection. This took the form of Ford's support for a petition that the UAW filed in June, 1980 for relief under the safeguards law.[13] This law allows a president to impose temporary tariffs, quotas, or other restrictions on imports (see Chapter 3). That can be done only on the recommendation of the US International Trade Commission (USITC), which can propose restrictions if it finds that rising imports are a substantial cause of serious injury to the domestic industry.

This case presented an opportunity for Carter's reelection campaign, as Secretary of the Treasury G. William Miller made clear in a July 1, 1980 memo to the president. Without actually mentioning the obvious fact that Election Day was coming in November, and that this contest threatened to put an elephant in the room, he implied that Carter had the opportunity to unleash an October surprise. The USITC's "injury determination could be made in early October" if the president requested expedited action (which he did), and even "before USITC's recommendations for relief are submitted" it was within the US Trade Representative (USTR)'s "authority to initiate discussions with the Japanese" on voluntary export restraints.[14] Carter had repeatedly rejected that option, however, and even the looming prospect of an electoral defeat did not persuade him to take any precipitous action. Not that a switch in time would have saved him; even if a protectionist gesture swung Michigan back to Carter, the only effect would be to boost his paltry stock of electoral votes from 49 to a slightly less embarrassing 60. That would still be 210 votes shy of the 270 that he needed for reelection.

Although the Carter administration had given the impression that it was eager to invoke safeguards, this path was blocked by the USITC's negative injury determination. Congress then seized the initiative during the transition between the Carter and Reagan administrations. Meeting in a "lame duck" session, legislators promoted a resolution that would authorize the president to negotiate import quotas. On December 2, 1980, the House of Representatives approved by 317–57 a measure authorizing the president to negotiate an "orderly marketing agreement" to limit car and truck imports. The Senate Finance Committee approved a similar measure the next day on a vote of 11–2. Although that resolution was not enacted, and would not have had the force of

13   The precise timing of the petition was curious, as it would have been more logical for the UAW to file a few months earlier so as in increase its leverage. Had the union done so, and had the USITC reached an affirmative injury determination, President Carter would have been required to consider the matter in the final weeks of the campaign.

14   Memorandum from Secretary of the Treasury Miller to President Carter, "Automobile Industry" (July 1, 1980), *FRUS 1977–1980*, Volume III, pp. 722–723. The memo called for an "orderly marketing agreement" rather than a VER, which amounts to the same thing.

law, it underlined the strong, bipartisan congressional interest in limiting automotive imports from Japan.

The Reagan Administration's Options

The incoming Reagan administration had many options that it might have pursued in response to these pressures. The first would be to allow the market to decide whether and what kind of automotive industry would survive. That was the course of action most consistent with the new president's pro-trade rhetoric, and voices in his cabinet advocated this position. Secretary of the Treasury Don Regan was outweighed, however, and the question soon became not whether but how to restrict the market. Some options would have been difficult or impossible to pursue without violating US obligations under the GATT. Automotive tariffs have long been relatively low in the United States. Even the notoriously protectionist Hawley–Smoot Tariff Act of 1930 imposed only a 10% tariff on automobiles. The rate was cut in successive tariff negotiations to 7.5% by 1960, 5.5% by 1968, and 3% by 1973.[15] The Tokyo Round negotiations brought the rate down to 2.5%, where it remains to this day. Light trucks comprise the one segment of the automotive sector that is still subject to high tariffs (25%). Concerns over GATT-legality also militated against domestic-content legislation and US-imposed quotas.

"Voluntary" export restraints (VERs) emerged as the least objectionable option. It was also a familiar fallback. The UAW had been advocating a Japanese VER since 1974,[16] and the union was far from the first US interest to happen on this solution. Japan's willingness to agree to such restrictions went at least as far back as a 1935 agreement to limit its textile exports to the United States,[17] and the country's export-led, postwar recovery inspired American industry and policymakers to demand the same thing many times over. In 1973 a frustrated Ministry of International Trade and Industry supplied the US Embassy with a list of nearly two dozen items that were already under some form of voluntary export restraint.[18] These had variously resulted from

[15]   Toder et al. (1978), p. 19.
[16]   See U.S. Mission in Tokyo, "UAW Proposal for Voluntary Restraints on Auto Exports to US Rejected by Toyota and Japan Automobile Manufacturers Association: Press Reports," cable of April 5, 1974 (1974TOKYO04568_b).
[17]   Tumlir (1985), p. 39. The "Gentleman's Agreement" of 1907, by which Japan agreed to restrict the movement of workers to the United States, might arguably be the very first of these semiformal arrangements for the voluntary (if coerced) restriction of economic activity.
[18]   The list included some big-ticket items, such as textiles, steel, television sets, calculators, and bicycles, as well as many more specific goods such as spectacles, baseball gloves, and polyvinyl alcohol.

pressures delivered directly by a US industry to its Japanese counterpart, or in response to demands from Washington acting on behalf of industry, or to avoid antidumping action. "The MITI official who supplied information," according to a cable to Washington, "asked that it be kept within US government, pointing out that Japan was at present being pressed by EC to provide same type of information and was reluctant to do so."[19] This was all part of a larger pattern in which Japan resented being treated as something less than a full GATT contracting party. In the 1970s there were still nine countries whose invocations of the non-application clause (GATT Article XXXV) with respect to Japan remained in effect,[20] and removing this discrimination was a perennial priority for Tokyo.

One attraction of VERs, from the Reagan administration's perspective, was that they bore no US fingerprints. That legal fiction allowed a putatively free-trading administration to reconcile its policies with its rhetoric. The supposedly voluntary and unilateral nature of the VERs, however, did not prevent US legislators who were opposed to Japanese imports from treating the policy as if it were a legal obligation, including claims that Japan had "violated" its terms by shipping vehicles in excess of the stated limits.

The VERs in Practice

On May 1, 1981, the Japanese Ministry of International Trade and Industry conceded to Washington's pressure when it announced that producers would limit their shipments to the United States to 1.68 million units annually. Although the United States decided in 1985 not to request a further extension of the agreement, Japan maintained the restrictions until they were terminated in 1994. The quotas did not prevent growth in the total value (as opposed to unit numbers) of automobile imports from Japan, apart from plateauing in the first year of the program. The reason was simple: Being restricted in the number of vehicles but not total value, Japanese exporters made the most of the limitations by switching to

[19]   U.S. Mission in Tokyo, "Japanese Voluntary Restraint Agreements," cable of December 21, 1973 (1973TOKYO16469_b). There is no reliable inventory of all the VERs to which Japan agreed. A former Department of Commerce official told the author that when he took office in the early 1980s the Department of State sent him a box full of such commitments affecting a range of products, most of which had never been made public.

[20]   These countries were Austria, Cyprus, Haiti, Ireland, Kenya, Mauritania, Nigeria, Senegal, and South Africa. As enumerated in U.S. Mission in Geneva, "Meeting GATT Council October 21," cable of October 7, 1974 (1974GENEVA06257_b). The mission observed that "as in past ... U.S. may wish support Japan" on this issue.

higher-value units.[21] Bilateral trade tensions increased once again in the early 1990s, prompting Japanese officials to reduce the VER from 2.3 to 1.65 million units in 1992. The VER was formally terminated two years later, as part of Japan's implementation of the Uruguay Round results.

The VER had multiple consequences for the United States, Japan, and third countries. It was costly for US consumers, with one study finding that they had to pay an average of about $1,200 more (in 1983 dollars) per Japanese car, and suffered a combined welfare loss of some $13 billion; the loss to the US economy as a whole totaled some $3 billion.[22] According to another study,[23] the VER reduction in 1992 saved 1,234 jobs in the United States but also imposed a $1.7 billion cost on consumers and a quota rent loss of $1.2 billion. The VERs created opportunities for other producers. Imports from Canada, most of which were supplied by the Big Three, began to recapture lost market share. European producers enjoyed higher prices in the restricted US market. Korean producers benefited significantly from this opportunity, which fortuitously coincided with their entry into the North American market. In the long term, the VERs paused – but did not halt or reverse – the relative decline of the Big Three. While the US producers did improve quality, they continued to lose ground to Japanese makes (both transplants and imports) and to other foreign firms.

Another consequence of the VERs was to accelerate the establishment of Japanese transplant factories in the United States. As is discussed at greater length below, this development would, over time, carry profound consequences for the domestic diplomacy of US automotive trade policy.

THE OBAMA ADMINISTRATION AND THE AUTOMOTIVE SUPPORT PACKAGE

As in 1980–1981, the Obama administration inherited a policy debate that was already mature before the election and ripened during the transition. The proximate cause of the financial crisis that erupted in late 2008 was the bursting of the housing bubble, but the resulting economic turmoil affected all segments of the economy. The auto industry was hit especially hard, with

---

[21] According to at least one participant in these events (in correspondence with the author), that upgrading was part of the US strategy. By encouraging Japanese producers to compete at the higher end of the market, the VERs would also give more breathing room for the smaller cars that Chrysler and Ford were then bringing onto the market.

[22] Berry, Levinsohn, and Pakes (1999). For a much lower estimate of the cost to consumers see Dardis and Decker (2005).

[23] Hufbauer and Elliott (1994), p. 100.

consumers postponing purchases of "big ticket" items. Automobiles had been assembled in the United States at an annual rate of 4.0 million units in January, 2008, but one year later this fell to just 1.3 million.[24] Imports dropped as well, but the shares of the US import market held by major foreign suppliers were remarkably steady both before and after the outbreak of the crisis.

The US Response to the Financial Crisis

In a series of steps taken during late 2008 through 2009, the US government provided massive aid to both the financial and automotive industries (among others). This bailout included billions of dollars in loans and other forms of support to domestic automotive producers, though not in equal degrees; whereas the relationship between the government and GM grew especially tight,[25] Ford declined direct government aid. The question of whether this aid discriminated against foreign automotive producers is complex. There were no elements of the support packages that explicitly provided for trade-distorting measures such as tariffs or other border barriers, domestic content requirements, or export subsidies. Government aid to industry may nevertheless distort markets by erecting barriers to exit and favoring some producers over others. That is especially true for those kinds of support that are made available only to domestic firms and not to the transplant operations of foreign firms. It is also possible that the state may acquire control or influence over the decisions of the firm, and seek to exercise this power in ways that are intended to favor investment and production in the domestic market.

These measures were nonetheless quite innocuous when compared to the blatant protectionism of 1981. At no time did the Obama administration or Congress approve new tariffs or quotas on imports of automobiles. To the contrary, there were two notable episodes in which some members of Congress advocated discriminatory initiatives that were either defeated or significantly modified. In one instance Congress considered but rejected a Buy-American provision affecting purchases by government agencies. The House of Representatives had approved an appropriations bill (H.R.3183) stating that, "None of the funds made available in this Act may be used to purchase passenger motor vehicles other than those manufactured by Ford,

---

[24] Federal Reserve data at www.federalreserve.gov/releases/G17/ipdisk/auto_sa.txt.

[25] The Obama administration and GM reached an arrangement on March 30, 2009, by which, in exchange for funds already committed by the US Treasury and a new injection of $30.1 billion, the US government received approximately $8.8 billion in debt and preferred stock in "New GM" and approximately 60% of the equity.

General Motors, or Chrysler." This item would not even permit the procurement of vehicles made in the United States by transplant factories. There was no such language in the Senate version of the bill, however, and the Buy-American requirement did not appear in the compromise version produced by a House–Senate conference committee in September, 2009.

The other measure was the cash-for-clunkers program. The Consumer Assistance to Recycle and Save (CARS) Act of 2009 provided credits to consumers who traded in old, fuel-inefficient vehicles when buying or leasing new, more fuel-efficient vehicles. Congress explicitly chose the nondiscriminatory route by opting between two very different versions of the program. One was the Accelerated Retirement of Inefficient Vehicles Act of 2009 (H.R.520), as introduced in the House in mid-January, 2009. This bill did not discriminate between domestic and imported vehicles. Another measure would have provided credits only for North American vehicles. Sponsored principally by legislators from automobile-producing states in the Midwest, the original version of the CARS Act (H.R.1550) would have limited credits to the purchase of vehicles assembled in the United States or, for some classes of vehicle, in North America (i.e., Canadian or Mexican vehicles would qualify). Although this bill gave the program its name, the discriminatory provisions did not survive negotiations with the Obama administration. The White House made clear to Congress that the president did not want to take any actions that violated US obligations under existing trade agreements.

On May 19, 2009, the House Committee on Energy and Commerce passed the compromise bill by a bipartisan vote of 50–4. In the June debate over this measure on the floor of the House of Representatives the sponsors introduced letters of support from a wide range of interested parties, including US and foreign-owned automobile manufacturers as well as labor unions and business organizations. The House voted for the bill by 298–119, with Democrats favoring it overwhelmingly (239–9) and even some Republicans giving their support (59–110). The measure was later attached to an appropriations bill that both houses of Congress then approved in mid-June.[26] President Obama signed the bill into law on June 24, 2009. The program proved to be much more popular than its sponsors or critics had originally expected, burning through the initial $1 billion in a week. Congress approved additional funding, but that money too was soon exhausted and the program ended in August, 2009.

---

[26] The Senate did not vote on this measure as a separate initiative so no partisan breakdown is available.

The Least Protective Option

The most pertinent aspect of the cash-for-clunkers program, for our present purposes, is that this was a post-materialist measure that privileged the general objectives of economic stimulus and environmentalism over the sectoral, nationalist interests of auto workers and producers. The program's designers and administrators were well aware that many of the most fuel-efficient vehicles sold in the US market were either imported or made in the United States by Japanese and Korean firms,[27] and that the law was likely to be more beneficial to them than to the Big Three. The data on actual usage confirm the tilt: Of the 401,274 passenger cars, 274,602 light trucks, and 1,966 heavy trucks that were purchased using the program's incentives, just 49% were manufactured domestically.[28] The net change was a further internationalization of the American fleet. Toyotas accounted for only 3% of the trade-in vehicles, for example, but for 18% of the new vehicles; 29% of the trade-ins were Fords, compared to 13% of the new vehicles.[29]

This program's Japanese counterpart did raise questions over discrimination. Japan introduced in 2009 an Eco-friendly Vehicle Purchase program that provided credits to consumers who scrapped older vehicles for new, more efficient cars. The program excluded vehicles certified under the Preferential Handling Procedure (PHP) regulations. Significantly, all vehicles exported to Japan by US manufacturers enter Japan under the PHP regulatory protocol for certification, meaning that American cars were not eligible for the Japanese version of cash-for-clunkers. There then followed a series of protests and threats from the Big Three, members of Congress, and the USTR. On January 19, 2010, the Trade Ministry announced that its car-scrappage program was being altered to allow the incentives to be offered to suitable cars imported under the PHP.

The United States thus took a more liberal approach to its program than did Japan and, more significantly, US policy was decidedly more pro-trade in 2009 than it was in 1981. Far from imposing unilateral import restrictions or encouraging Japan to restrict its exports, this time the rescue packages for the auto industry were remarkably free from the kinds of economic nationalism that Detroit demanded, and that Washington supplied, a generation earlier.

---

[27]   See the data posted at www.fueleconomy.gov/feg/bestworst.shtml.
[28]   U.S. Department of Transportation, National Highway Traffic Safety Administration (2009), p. 36. Note that the report did not identify how many of these US-produced vehicles were Big Three versus transplants.
[29]   Ibid., pp. 22 and 24.

EXPLAINING THE DIFFERENT OUTCOMES FOR THE TWO ADMINISTRATIONS

What accounts for the differences between these two episodes? If one were to hazard a prediction based on the oral traditions of US trade politics, the likelihood for a protectionist outcome would seem to be higher in the more recent case (a very deep, lengthy recession and a Democratic president) than in the older one (a brief recovery between successive recessions and a Republican president). The gasoline prices reported earlier would also seem to provide as much impetus for protection in 2009 as they had in 1981. Why did just the reverse happen?

The differing outcomes of these two episodes can best be understood as the consequence of long-term shifts in the US industry. Those shifts are emblematic of the larger economic transition in which services have overtaken manufacturing and activity is increasingly international. The industry has undergone four major changes: (1) greater globalization through outsourcing and strategic partnerships; (2) the rise of "transplants" in US parts and vehicle manufacturing; (3) reduced influence of the unions; and (4) the increasing political strength of automobile dealers, especially those who sell imported vehicles. The net result has been a decrease in the number and influence of those interests that favor import protection, and a concomitant rise in the size and power of those interests that favor an open market.

The Consequences of Globalization

The first change that separates 2008–2009 from 1980 to 1981 is the greater globalization of the Big Three. In that earlier incident the firms' global operations were limited primarily to the sourcing of some parts overseas and the practice of "captive imports" (i.e., imports of vehicles purchased from foreign partners). All three producers then imported pickup trucks made by partners in Japan, and Chrysler also imported Japanese-made passenger cars.[30] Apart from their own investments in Canada, most of the Big Three production in foreign plants was restricted to sales in the host countries or the surrounding region. Moreover, the Big Three's captive imports were dropping: Whereas these transactions accounted for 41% of all vehicle imports in 1975, by the first half of 1980 they had fallen to 27%.[31] So while the outsourcing of parts

---

[30] GM's partner was Isuzu, Ford's was Toyo Kogyo, and Chrysler's was Mitsubishi. See USITC (1980), p. A-17.
[31] Ibid., p. A-25.

had reached a sufficiently high level in 1980 for the Big Three to prefer VERs over domestic-content legislation as the chief form of import protection, the industry's overall level of globalization was still low enough that the firms favored a closed US market for finished automobiles. Since that time their dependence on global supply chains has grown considerably, and made traditional protectionism more costly.

The second major change is the domestication of Japanese automotive firms, including transplant assembly operations as well as investments in the US auto parts sector. The decision to invest was not taken by the Japanese firms, nor by Volkswagen before them, solely on the basis of economic considerations.[32] The Askew-Yasukawa Agreement of 1980, in which the two governments agreed to promote Japanese firms' investment in US parts and vehicle production, was intended to defuse tensions. Honda was the first Japanese company to announce its plans to establish a production facility in the United States, with its first US-made vehicles entering the market in 1982 (i.e., the first full year in which the VERs were in effect). Most other companies soon followed, including Nissan (1982), Mitsubishi (1985), Toyota (1985), and Mazda (1987). The relationship between the Japanese producers and their US rivals also grew closer with the forging of strategic alliances. Each one of the Big Three paired up with a partner for activities ranging from collaborative research and development to joint production: Chrysler with Mitsubishi, Ford with Mazda, and General Motors with Toyota. Chrysler was even more globalized during 1998–2007, when it was the junior partner in the DaimlerChrysler venture.[33] These alliances have all served to restore, at least in part, the US firms' support for more open trade in automobiles. The US industry now prefers FTAs over multilateral liberalization, as their terms are more easily manipulated, but it no longer pursues outright protectionism.

These trends have not affected Japan alone. European firms actually preceded their Japanese competitors in establishing US plants, and Korean producers later joined the gang. All of these foreign investments have further globalized the US industry, and diminished the range of local actors and decision-makers who may be prone to demand or supply protection. The industry reached a tipping point in 2018, when an automotive monitor

---

[32] Volkswagen began production in the United States of the subcompact Rabbit in 1978, having purchased a plant that Chrysler owned but never used. Some observers believe it is no coincidence that this investment came at a time when protectionist initiatives threatened Volkswagen both through legislation and the trade-remedy laws.

[33] Following Chrysler's bankruptcy in 2009, it was owned until 2011 by Fiat, the UAW, and the governments of the United States and Canada. After the government divestments in 2011, it has been a subsidiary of Fiat.

projected that foreign makers in the United States would likely equal the output of their American rivals for the first time.[34]

The Consequences of the Economic Transition

Viewed at a high level of abstraction, this case offers an illustration of the political consequences of the economic transition. The principal theme in that transition is the movement from goods to services, which in this specific sector means the relative decline of automotive production and the rise of auto-related services. For every person employed in the manufacture of auto parts or finished automobiles in 2009, there were 0.6 persons working in motor vehicle and parts wholesale trade, 0.9 in auto parts and accessories stores, 1.5 in automotive repair and maintenance, and – most important of all – 1.7 in new car dealerships.[35] In sum, by the time that Obama took office the services segments of the automotive sector employed 4.7 times more people than the manufacturing segment, and we should not be surprised by a corresponding reshuffle in their relative capacities to influence policy. It also meant an increase in the power of multinational firms (both US and foreign), and a corresponding decline in the political power of the unions.

Three trends stand out here: Automobile production now employs fewer people than in the past, more of those workers are employed by foreign firms, and fewer of them are UAW members. As recently as 1995 there were 251,300 persons employed in the manufacture of automobiles and light trucks in the United States, but this figure fell to 119,500 in 2009. During the same period the number of persons employed in the manufacture of motor vehicle parts fell from 786,900 to 418,700. The traditional Midwestern core of the industry now accounts for a smaller share of the total, and forms just one part of the region known as Auto Alley. This North–South corridor starts in the Midwest but extends far south into states where the workforce is less unionized. Automotive parts are also increasingly made outside the United States, or are domestically produced by foreign-owned companies.

Perhaps the most important difference between 1980–1981 and 2008–2009 is the diminished size of the UAW. Several factors have contributed to this decline, including some that are economic (downsizing and automation) and others that are at least partly political (the migration of production from pro-

---

[34]   Roberts and Stoll (2018), citing WardsAuto data.
[35]   All figures from the Bureau of Labor Statistics (BLS). Note that comparable data are not available for 1980–1981 in most sectors (other than new car dealerships) because of changes in the nomenclature that the BLS employs.

union to right-to-work states). The net result is that membership in the union, which broke the million-member level in 1950 and peaked at 1,527,858 in 1979, declined to 468,096 members in 2008 and 392,166 in 2009.[36] Membership in the UAW is not a precise measurement of unionization in the automotive industry, insofar as there are many auto workers that are not members of the union (especially those who work in transplant operations and/or in factories located in the Southern states) and also many UAW members who are not part of this industry.[37] The membership numbers nevertheless offer a rough gauge not of the size of the automotive labor force per se but of its more organized and politically influential members. Those numbers are unambiguously down.

The relative power of auto workers and dealers is particularly revealing. Whereas in 1981 there were 1.8 UAW members for every person employed in new car dealerships, by 2009 those dealerships employed 2.4 persons for every UAW member.[38] When one further considers that auto dealerships are widely distributed, and that there are probably very few congressional districts outside of the most densely populated urban centers without at least one of them, it is obvious that this group is in a better position than the UAW to exercise influence over members of Congress. As of 1981, the dealers who sold Japanese cars were the only local actors who still favored an open market. Their numbers, however, were limited. In 1980 there were 23,379 dealerships in the United States that sold vehicles made in the United States and Canada, and 16,967 that sold imported vehicles, but only 4,407 dealerships that sold Japanese cars.[39] That number grew by more than 50% over the next few decades, such that by 2008 there were 6,811 dealer franchises selling Japanese brand vehicles in the United States, employing 310,575 people.[40] That amounted to one-third of all new automobile dealerships in the United States.[41]

Dealers of imported automobiles did have a voice in 1980, a year that marked the tenth anniversary of the founding of the American International Automobile Dealers Association (AIADA), but in those days it was still somewhat muted.

---

[36]   Data for UAW membership supplied to the author by the UAW Research Library, based on average annual dues-paying members.

[37]   The union also represents workers in some closely related industries (e.g., aerospace and defense, heavy trucks, and farm equipment) as well as others that bear little or no apparent relationship to automobiles or parts. These include workers in other manufacturing industries (e.g., household appliances, brewing, lawn and garden equipment, etc.), as well as technical, office, and professional workers (e.g., draftsmen, industrial designers, engineers, etc.).

[38]   Calculated by the author from U.S. Bureau of Labor Statistics data for new car dealerships, and UAW membership data supplied by the UAW Research Library.

[39]   USITC (1980), p. A-22.

[40]   Figure provided to the author by the Japan Automobile Manufacturers Association.

[41]   Author's calculation, based on the fact that (according to the National Automobile Dealers Association) there were 20,770 new car dealerships in the United States in 2008.

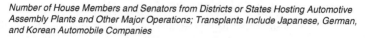

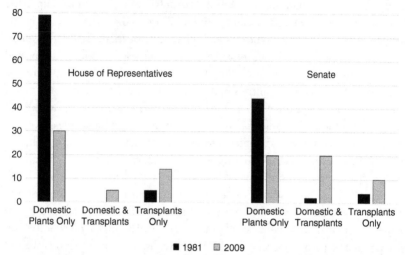

FIGURE 8.2 Representation of automotive districts and states in Congress, 1981 and 2009.

Sources: Company websites, Congressional Quarterly *Congressional Districts in the 1980s* (1983) and *Congressional Districts in the 2000s* (2003), and other sources.

AIADA originally formed to fight proposals in 1970 that would have established quotas on cars and other imported products. Volkswagen was then the leading source of imported cars, and US Volkswagen dealers were distressed that the National Auto Dealers Association refused to take a stand against protectionism. AIADA's numbers were nevertheless too small in 1980–1981 to form an effective counterweight to the combined position of the Big Three and the UAW.

Changes in Congressional Districts and Campaign Contributions

A great deal of scholarship has focused on the social and economic issues surrounding the transplant of Japanese production, managerial styles, and even culture to US communities. Less attention has been paid to the impact that these transplants have had on the political interests and activities of people in those communities and on the politicians who represent them in Congress. As can be seen in Figure 8.2, however, the raw numbers suggest that the landscape in Congress was fundamentally different in the two periods. As of 1981, there were overwhelmingly more House and Senate seats held by

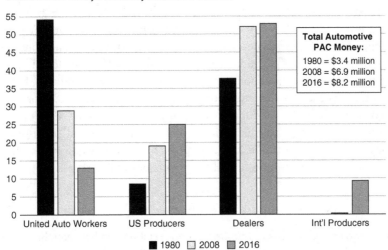

Shares of PAC Money Provided by Automotive Interests

FIGURE 8.3 Automotive PAC money in the 1980, 2008, and 2016 election cycles. Note : 1980 data are for total PAC expenditures; 2008 and 2016 data are PAC contributions to Federal candidates.

Sources: 1980 data from Federal Election Commission at www.fec.gov/data/com mittees/ as compiled by the author. 2008 and 2016 numbers from Federal Election Commission data as compiled by the Center for Responsive Politics' Open Secrets project (www.opensecrets.org/pacs/index.php).

legislators whose constituents included workers in Big Three plants, balanced against a very small number of lawmakers whose districts hosted transplants. By 2009, the states hosting transplants (with or without Big Three facilities) outnumbered the few states in which the Big Three were still the only producers, and the relative strength of the domestic and foreign plants was on the same order of magnitude for representation in the House.

These changes are complemented by shifts in the campaign contributions that different segments of the industry make to presidential and congressional candidates. The data in Figure 8.3 show the contributions made by political action committees (PACs) associated with segments of the automotive industry in 1980, 2000, and 2016. The automotive firms themselves actually provide only a small share of the industry's total campaign contributions, and they lack a consistent message on trade. It is instead more revealing to contrast the campaign contributions that come from the most reliably protectionist segment of the industry (unions) with those made by the most pro-trade segments (dealers and international producers). The UAW's share of total automotive

PAC money fell from 54% in 1980 to 29% in 2008. By contrast, the combined shares of the two most pro-trade segments rose from 38% to 52%. That disparity had grown wider still by 2016, when the shares fell to 13% for the UAW and climbed to 62% for the dealers and international producers. Put another way, as of 1980 every $1 in PAC money provided by the UAW was matched by just 70¢ from the dealers (and nothing from the international producers), but by 2008 the dealers plus the international producers provided $1.80 for every UAW dollar. By 2016, that disparity had grown to $4.79. In short, the numbers reported here offer a specific example of that broader trend discussed in Chapter 6 whereby the PAC money of pro-trade groups has grown larger and faster than the contributions of the protectionist interests.

WHAT CAN THE US–JAPANESE RIVALRY TELL US ABOUT CHINA?

These two episodes speak not just to the trade relationship between the United States and Japan, and especially the sector with the highest profile in that relationship, but also to the broader question of how challengers and hegemons relate to one another. Had this chapter been written a generation ago, and had it conformed to the conventional wisdom of that time, it might have started from the premise that Japan was well on its way toward displacing the United States as an industrial powerhouse. It might then have examined whether the pressures that gave rise to the VERs would be replicated for other industries, and what the long-term prospects might be for a declining leader and its rising challenger. If so, it would have unintentionally offered an object lesson in why historians are best advised to focus more on the distant, known past than to speculate on the future trajectory of current events.

We instead know now that the Japanese challenge proved to be surprisingly ephemeral, and that the rise that had seemed so impressive in the 1960s and 1970s would be followed by an equally unanticipated stagnation in the 1990s and 2000s. Or to attach numbers to that claim, the Japanese economy rose from 20% the size of its US counterpart in 1970 to 38% in 1980, and then 53% in 1990, but fell thereafter to 48% in 2000 and 27% in 2016. Making an even sharper comparison, Japan was almost five times larger than China in 1980 (economically if not demographically), but by 2016 the Chinese economy was more than twice as big as Japan's.[42]

The most facile conclusion suggested by these developments concerns the perils of blindly projecting any established trend into a speculative future.

---

[42] Calculated from World Bank data at https://data.worldbank.org/indicator/NY.GDP.MKTP .CD.

Mark Twain once showed the absurdity of assuming the unbroken continuity of current tendencies when he noted that the natural straightening of the Mississippi was shortening that river by "an average of a trifle over one mile and a third per year." This meant that "seven hundred and forty-two years from now the Lower Mississippi will be only a mile and three quarters long."[43] Established trends have a pesky habit of giving way to new ones. We should not casually assume that the impressive growth rates that China has achieved over the past few decades will continue ad infinitum. Quite to the contrary, there is already evidence of a slowdown in that country's expansion, and the demographic challenges will loom ever larger as time passes. The case reviewed here does not tell us either that China will experience a reversal comparable to Japan's, nor that it will escape that trap, but should instead remind analysts and policymakers that expectations for the future must always be made with humility and with due regard for the wide degree of uncertainty.

A more sophisticated reading of these events suggests that there are ways that challengers and hegemons might move from conflict to cooperation. The globalization of the US automotive industry has changed the perspectives of most stakeholders: The Big Three are now more tightly integrated into global value chains, Japanese and other foreign producers of parts and cars have substantial investments in the United States, dealers want to maintain access to imported as well as domestically produced vehicles, and elected officials have greater incentives to keep markets open than they do to close them. The UAW is the only major player that still has an unambiguous interest in protection, and its political power today is a fraction of what it was in Reagan's day. Looking backward, all of these developments explain why Obama did not go the way of Reagan. Looking forward, we may ask whether the relationship between the United States and China might go the way of the relationship with Japan on at least some issues. The Sino-American rivalry covers a wider range of topics than does the US relationship with Japan, including competition for military supremacy in the Pacific Basin, but that has not precluded the deepening of trade and investment ties. Might that eventually lead to a less confrontational posture on the economic side of the relationship?

It is possible to imagine a future in which Chinese investment in the United States reaches a level comparable to that of Japan. Department of Commerce data suggest that we may be headed in that direction, showing that in 2015 there were already 44,000 Americans employed in such operations. That was still only about one-twentieth the magnitude of US employment in Japanese

---

[43] Twain (1883), chapter 17.

investments, which accounted for 856,000 jobs, but it was not so long ago that there were close to zero Americans employed in Japanese-owned plants.[44] For the time being, however, one hears far more often about the Chinese investment in Treasury securities than in brick-and-mortar operations. Both types of investments imply the potential for Chinese influence over American policymakers, but in very different ways; the threat to dump securities carries a much harder edge than a reminder to a legislator that Chinese firms provide jobs to constituents. It may be years or decades – if ever – before the Sino-American relationship follows the trail that Japan blazed, in which cooperation is more common than confrontation. As explored in Chapter 12, there are many pitfalls into which the relationship with Beijing might tumble before that happens.

[44]   Data posted at www.bea.gov/international/factsheet/.

9

Canada and the Domestic Diplomacy of US
Trade Policy

As of this moment, Canada will become part of the United States of America ...
To ensure that this transfer of power takes place smoothly and without incident,
transport aircraft and helicopters of the United States Air Force carrying troops and
equipment are now landing at airports in all major Canadian cities and at all Canadian
Armed Forces bases.

Address by the fictitious US president in Richard Rohmer, *Ultimatum* (1973)

Every Canadian has a complicated relationship with the United States, whereas
Americans think of Canada as the place where the weather comes from.

Margaret Atwood, interview in *The Paris Review* (1990)

INTRODUCTION

General Richard Rohmer of the Royal Canadian Air Force is one of several
authors to imagine a US invasion of his homeland. The principal difference
among them is in the natural resources that they expect the perfidious
Americans to covet: Whereas the invaders in Rohmer's fantasy were after
Canada's oil and gas, another subgenre of this "Yanks are coming" literature
fears for the safety of the country's water.[1] Nor is fiction stranger than truth.
The year after Rohmer's novel went to print, the United States declassified
a 1935 plan for the US invasion of Canada. Not to be outdone by the release of
War Plan Red, the Canadians dusted off an even older blueprint of their own.
Defence Scheme No. 1 was a 1921 contingency plan by which Canada would,
under British leadership – and perhaps with Mexican and Japanese conni-
vance – act on the principle that offense is the best defense.[2] Today these real
and imagined wars would strike most Americans as bizarre fantasies. To the

---

[1] See, for example, the graphic novel *We Stand on Guard* by Vaughan et al. (2016). See also
   Danson (2012).
[2] For excerpts from both plans see Lippert (2015).

limited extent that they think about Canada at all, they might more readily recognize themselves in Margaret Atwood's characterization of the relationship.

The very different perspectives that these two Canadian novelists bring to North American relations are each reflected in the analysis that follows. This chapter starts with a brief review of the history of US–Canadian trade relations, featuring some events that make General Rohmer's perspective seem less delusional. In the nineteenth century those relations were tied to existential questions for Canada, with commercial reciprocity and annexation – whether forceful or voluntary – being commonly portrayed in both countries as inter-changeable options. Even today, trade negotiators are among the few Americans who would not be surprised to see how frequently their northern neighbors cast them as the villain in their histories and literature. One of the dirty little secrets of the North American trade policymaking community is just how well the two countries' negotiators exemplify the old saw about familiarity breeding contempt. The origins of this contempt are lost to history,[3] but the two sides engage one another often enough to ensure that the mutual scorn is self-perpetuating. Over the past generation the represen-tatives of Washington and Ottawa have concluded the bilateral US–Canada FTA (CFTA), followed by the trilateral North American FTA (NAFTA), and met thereafter in a series of bungled initiatives that were variously hemispheric (the Free Trade Area of the Americas), mega-regional (the Trans-Pacific Partnership), and multilateral (the Doha Round of the WTO). Even though the US and Canadian objectives in these negotiations were more congruent than conflicting, participants from other countries are often surprised by just how hostile and even petty the two countries' negotiators can habitually be to one another.

The remainder of this chapter conforms to Atwood's expectations, as it presents a decidedly and deliberately Washington-centric perspective on North American trade relations since the mid-1980s. The principal aim is to use the CFTA and NAFTA experiences as case studies in the domestic diplomacy of US trade policy. More specifically, the episodes offer detailed examples of how the executive and legislative branches of the US government deal with one another, illustrating the points made in earlier chapters. And just

---

[3] There is nonetheless a certain concordance in the stories that one hears. American trade negotiators often complain that their Canadian counterparts engage in games that veer into outright cheating, such as altering negotiating documents to suggest that matters that are still under discussion have been settled. (To use the language of negotiators, this means "removing brackets" from text that ought still to remain in brackets.) Rather than deny these charges. Canadian negotiators will typically disparage the Americans for their whining.

as Atwood might expect, US policymakers treated Canada almost as an after-thought both times. The principal utility of the CFTA, as far as members of Congress were concerned, came in the leverage that it gave them in their dealings with the Reagan administration. Canada was even less of a factor in the domestic diplomacy of NAFTA, where America's southern neighbor figured far more prominently – and participated much more actively – in the interbranch negotiations.

A CAPSULE HISTORY OF US–CANADIAN TRADE RELATIONS

There have always been policymakers on both sides of the border who agreed with Robert Frost that "Something there is that doesn't love a wall."[4] They tried numerous times to knock down the barriers that inhibited commerce between Canada and the United States, and employed many different means of negotiating and approving these pacts. Some of the negotiations conducted prior to US hegemony made it partway through the process, and one produced an agreement that was in force for just over a decade, but none of the pre-1936 deals were deep or permanent. The two countries were not able to achieve much until the United States displaced Britain as Canada's principal political and economic partner.

War and Trade under British Hegemony

The Canadians who fantasize about an American invasion are not fabricating these stories out of whole cloth. While the acquisition of Canada disappeared ages ago as a subject of serious consideration in the United States, it was a recurring topic during the century that followed the futile invasion that Benedict Arnold and Ethan Allen led in 1775. The Articles of Confederation (1781) took a friendlier approach, inviting Canada to accede and be "entitled to all the advantages of this union." This was an exceptional offer, insofar as no other candidate could receive that same treatment "unless such admission be agreed to by nine states," but Canada declined this opportunity to become the fourteenth state. It instead gave refuge to thousands of distraught Loyalists, and their anti-US sentiments would color North American relations for genera-tions to come.

Well into the twentieth century, Washington's rapport with Ottawa was largely defined by the state of its relations with London. The border was an ever-present source of conflict, but also offered the opportunity for

---

4   Robert Frost, "Mending Wall" (1914).

cooperation. The special Anglo-American relationship that was to reach full flower in the Second World War had antecedents stretching back more than a century, beginning with three agreements to resolve US-Canadian tensions: the Treaty of Ghent (ending the War of 1812), the 1817 Rush-Bagot Treaty (reducing armaments on the Great Lakes), and the Convention of 1818 (setting the boundary).[5] From time to time, North Atlantic statesmen contemplated grander designs. In 1949, for example, the Truman administration's Policy Planning Staff suggested that the United States "be prepared, in the event that the British ask for this, to join with them in setting up a committee to study problems of economic union or closer political association." Such an arrangement might include "the U.K., or the U.K. and Canada."[6]

Conflict was nevertheless more prominent than cooperation in the first half of the nineteenth century, which was peppered by repeated episodes of actual or threatened war. Americans remember the War of 1812 as a failed attempt to enforce the rights of US seamen, and still resent the British decision to torch Washington. Canadians know that it was also a sordid attempt to drag them into the union, and that the war's first act of state-sponsored arson was the American burning of their Legislative Assembly in York. Americans were not scrupulously impartial when a failed Canadian rebellion broke out in 1837; frictions over that conflict brought Washington and London close to war. Another war scare came in the 1840s, when Britain and the United States sorted out competing claims in the Pacific Northwest. James K. Polk is surely the only man ever to win the presidency with a slogan based on latitudinal coordinates – "Fifty-Four Forty or Fight" – but not the only one to take advantage of London's general inclination to remain on good terms with its former colony. Polk resolved this boundary dispute through peaceful negotiations and compromise, and had to redirect his expansionist demands to what became the Mexican War of 1846–1848.

A mid-century dispute over fishing rights produced yet another alarm, but this time the two parties took a new approach. They sweetened the treaty that resolved the fisheries dispute by adding reciprocal tariff reductions. That 1854 bargain was principally restricted to agricultural products and other raw materials, and American manufactures continued to face high Canadian tariffs. It was nevertheless the most substantive and enduring commercial

---

[5] Drake (2010).
[6] Position Paper for the Discussions With the British and Canadians on Pound-Dollar Problems, Prepared by the Policy Planning Staff, "PPS 621" (September 3, 1949), *FRUS 1949*, Volume IV, p. 828.

arrangement between these countries prior to the 1930s, lasting for just over a decade.

There are numerous respects in which the reciprocity treaty of 1854 was tied up with the impending sectional crisis in the United States. One concerns what the treaty was *not*: It came at a time when the British League in Canada declared its support for annexation by the United States. That was a political nonstarter, being opposed both by London and by those American Southerners who knew that the proposed new states would outvote them in the Senate. Free trade was nevertheless an acceptable alternative to annexation, and one that appealed to the South's traditional pro-trade sentiments. What no one in Canada, the United States, or the United Kingdom could anticipate in the 1850s was how the later demise of this treaty would also be linked to the Civil War. The United States abrogated it in part out of Union frustration over the Confederacy's use of Canada as a staging area for raids and intrigues, and anger toward the British position in several wartime spats. Protectionism also played a role, with Northern coal, fish, and lumber interests favoring abrogation. The absence of the Southern free-traders made for a one-sided debate in Congress when in 1865 the Senate approved a resolution of abrogation by 33–8, and the House passed it on a voice vote.[7] In 1869 Senator Charles Sumner (Republican–Massachusetts) calculated that England owed a $2.1 billion indemnity to the United States for its actions in the war, a sum that – he broadly implied – London might just cover by turning over the deed to Canada. (They settled three years later for $15.5 million in cash.)

There then followed several exercises in frustration, with the two sides repeatedly failing to replace the old treaty with a new pact. The 1874 treaty was among the deepest yet shortest-lived of these failed efforts. It went well beyond the model of its 1854 predecessor, covering not just agriculture but manufactures. That did not matter, because the Senate withheld approval. Canada responded by adopting the National Policy, an essentially mercantilist mix of high tariffs on manufactures, lower tariffs on raw materials and intermediates, and state investment in a coast-to-coast rail system. Obeying the law of unintended consequences, the new tariffs "served principally to inundate Canada in a wave of American investment."[8]

The two countries negotiated another tariff agreement in 1910, and Congress approved the implementing legislation by 268–89 in the House and

---

[7] Nineteenth-century trade relations between Canada and the United States are best summarized in Robinson (1911).

[8] McNaught (1988), p. 295.

53–27 in the Senate.[9] The Canadian Parliament then turned the tables on Congress, voting down its own implementing bill in 1911. The Liberals who negotiated the treaty would have happily approved it, had the electorate allowed them, but the party was forced to call an election and lost its majority. Canadian historians attribute this defeat to the Conservative Party's portrayal of the agreement as a threat to the country's sovereignty, promising the voters "No Truck or Trade with the Yankees."[10]

Persistent Themes in the Failed Negotiations

These relations were strongly affected by the evolving position of Canada within the British Empire. Canadian economic and political interests have always placed a premium on preferential access to the hegemon's market, but that target shifted with the transatlantic transfer of hegemony. The United States did not displace the United Kingdom as Canada's leading trade partner until the 1920s. North American trade then resembled the flows that once typified exchanges between developing and developed countries: Canada exchanged its food, fish, lumber, and newsprint for US manufactures. The political rhetoric of trade also resembled its North–South counterpart, albeit with a reversal of these cardinal directions. Canadians craved American capital, much of it in the form of the branch plants set up by US multinationals, but reserved the right to decry the resulting foreign domination of their economy.

The British adoption of free trade came at some cost to Canada, as the repeal of the Corn Laws in 1846 meant losing preferential access to its major export market. That prompted the Canadian Parliament to approve resolutions calling on London to open trade negotiations on their behalf with the United States. The British government was favorably disposed, but Washington demurred. Canada then acted unilaterally in 1847 to eliminate the discrimination in its tariffs; they had been set at 12.5% on US manufactures and 5.5% on British, but were now equalized at 7.5% each. As a final entreaty to its neighbor, in 1849 Canada approved a bill that amounted to a conditional and tacit negotiation between the national legislatures. It would provide for the free admission into Canada of certain US goods (primarily agricultural and other raw materials) if the United States reciprocated by removing its own tariffs on the same products imported from Canada. Some voices in Washington were prepared to respond favorably to this initiative, but nothing came of it.

---

[9]   Ellis (1939), p. 78.
[10]   Stairs and Winham (1985).

Canadians sometimes responded in kind to US protectionism. That was what happened in 1897, when Parliament sharply raised duties just months after Congress approved the Dingley Tariff Act. Sometimes a spike in US rates had just the opposite effect, encouraging Canadians to propose the negotiation of preferential treatment. Here we see a corollary to the paradox of preferences: If a large country's trade barriers rise, its partners will have a greater incentive to secure access to that market. Thus the enactment of the protectionist Payne–Aldrich Tariff Act of 1909 was a catalyst for the failed reciprocity agreement of 1911, just as approval of the Hawley–Smoot Tariff Act of 1930 initially inspired retaliation,[11] but then led to new tariff agreements in 1935 and again in 1938.

Canadian policymakers also have an unfortunate habit of setting examples for their American counterparts that they later come to regret. Antidumping laws exemplify this practice, with Ottawa having pioneered them in a 1904 statute that was originally aimed at restricting imports of US steel. That innovation inspired copycats in Washington, and the American steel industry – much to the annoyance of its Canadian competitors – would become the most frequent petitioner under this law. The Auto Pact of 1965 offers another example, being a response to Canada's unilateral adoption of local-content rules. In later years, the Buy-American rules would be second only to the trade-remedy laws as an irritant for both the federal and provincial governments in Canada.

The two sides often tried to work around the inconveniences of formal treaty ratification, and Congress sometimes acquiesced. The aforementioned Canadian overture of 1849 offers just such an example. A similar episode played out in 1888, when Secretary of State Thomas Bayard proposed that the countries negotiate tacitly through the approval of complementary legislation. A joint commission approved a plan whereby Canada would reciprocate if Congress were to remove duties on certain products, and legislation to that end began to advance in both countries' legislatures. The initiative collapsed when the House of Commons balked. The two sides then fell back on a modest Plan B, negotiating yet another fisheries treaty; even that scaled-down initiative failed in the US Senate. Unorthodox legislative procedures were more successful a generation later, but only to a point. When Congress approved the 1911 reciprocity agreement it did so simply by passing the implementing legislation, never taking up the agreement as a formal treaty. That was a wise choice, insofar as the Senate vote on the reciprocity bill fell one short of the two-thirds that would have been needed to approve a treaty.

[11] See McDonald, O'Brien, and Callahan (1997).

When the Canadian electorate revolted, however, it made this a procedural distinction without a practical difference.

Most of these episodes involved at least the suggestion that annexation was a suitable substitute for commercial integration. That possibility was sometimes advanced by Canadians who were eager for closer ties, and who saw in the German *Zollverein* a model in which commercial reciprocity was a first step toward political union. Canadian nationalists would raise that same flag, but with the contrary aim of arousing popular indignation; they were often tacitly (if unintentionally) aided by those American proponents of commercial integration who made no secret of their grander designs. That point is illustrated by the 1888 fisheries treaty. Credit for the Senate's lopsided vote against that treaty (27–30) can be laid to the machinations of Chairman John Sherman (Republican–Ohio) of the Senate Foreign Relations Committee, an expansionist who was too clever by half. Sherman hoped that rejecting the treaty would worsen an already parlous Canadian economy, leading the people to demand their own annexation. They instead responded by strengthening commercial bonds with England. History repeated itself during congressional debate over the 1911 reciprocity agreement, when Representative "Champ" Clark (Democrat–Missouri) declared on the House floor that he looked forward to the day "when the American flag will float over every square foot of the British North American possessions clear to the North Pole."[12] The Canadian nationalists whom Clark offended could not have been mollified when he was elected Speaker of the House just two months later.

Trade Agreements in American Hegemony

Canada responded to the enactment of the Hawley–Smoot tariffs in 1930 by stepping up its own protection and discrimination. Two years later, the United Kingdom imposed stricter limits on non-empire goods under the Ottawa Agreements, and provided deeper preferences for Commonwealth countries. Canada and the other dominions followed suit with trade preferences for British products and protection for their own infant industries. That preferential scheme was anathema to Washington, which for decades to come would see discrimination as worse than protectionism. High tariff walls were bad enough, in the view of US policymakers who were now intent on negotiating away their own barriers, but it was much worse when other countries were allowed to tunnel under that wall.

---

[12] Quoted in Tansill (1943), p. 463.

Canadian legislators and statesmen soon reconsidered, and began exploring the prospects for a reciprocal trade agreement with the United States. Writing to Secretary of State Hull precisely one year before Congress approved the Reciprocal Trade Agreements Act (RTAA) in 1934, the US chargé reported that Ottawa was eager to parlay.[13] Canada was to be the sixth RTAA partner of the United States, with the agreement taking effect on the first day of 1936. The British were initially less open to negotiations than was Canada, but their caution declined as the prospects for a new war loomed larger. The US–UK agreement that entered into force on January 1, 1939, was a watershed event in the reformation of economic and political ties between the two countries; a second US–Canada agreement took effect on the same day. The immediate, economic impact of these agreements was limited by the war that started for both Britain and Canada on September 3, 1939, but they were important steps in creating the North Atlantic alliance. The United States and Canada achieved heretofore unprecedented levels of cooperation during the war, especially in the coordinated output of their defense industries. The war even saw the formation of the 1st Special Service Force, better known as the "Devil's Brigade," an elite American-Canadian commando unit that fought with distinction in Italy and France. It was the forerunner of the closer military cooperation that was to come in the Cold War and after 9/11.

Even hegemony could not wholly reverse the well-established pattern of failure, as Washington and Ottawa discovered early in the postwar period. Precisely one day before the GATT was signed in Geneva, Canadian officials proposed in Washington that the two countries reach a more comprehensive trade treaty. This proposal initially met with a skeptical response from the United States, but the two governments then spent five months exploring the possibility in greater depth. By March, 1948 the Truman administration was ready with a plan for the "[i]mmediate removal of all duties by both countries," and noted that the "Canadians consider the proposal, if implemented, to be one of the most momentous decisions in their history."[14] The topic remained on the agenda in bilateral discussions through 1949, and also arose a few times in the internal deliberations of the Eisenhower administration, but these were all false starts. Prime Minister Lester Pearson – who had been the Secretary of State for External Affairs during the 1947–1949 episode – would later tell senior US officials that the initiative failed "because the government would not face

---

[13] The Chargé in Canada (Boal) to the Secretary of State (March 29, 1933), *FRUS 1933*, Volume II, p. 39.

[14] Memorandum by the Assistant Secretary of State for Economic Affairs (Thorp) to the Under Secretary of State (Lovett), "Proposed Elimination of Trade Barriers between the United States and Canada" (March 8, 1948), *FRUS 1948*, Volume IX, p. 406.

the repercussions during the six to nine years of painful adjustment which secondary industries in Canada would have to make."[5] The episode none- theless had an important impact on the concurrent multilateral negotiations, leading the United States to moderate its traditional opposition to the forma- tion of regional arrangements (see Chapter 13).

The most lasting experiment came in 1965, when Canada and the United States negotiated an agreement eliminating tariffs on automotive products. The Auto Pact was devoted to managed trade rather than liberalization, being principally aimed at containing the Canadian local-content rules. The Johnson administration negotiated this agreement as an alternative to waging a potentially ruinous trade war just when bilateral relations were warming, and was willing not merely to tolerate but even to encourage – within limits – higher mandated levels of Canadian content in the transplant operations. This was also the last significant market-opening initiative that would win the support of the United Auto Workers, a union with members in both countries. President Johnson convinced Congress to enact the imple- menting legislation for the agreement as an ordinary bill. The Auto Pact became the first in a series of North American integration agreements, and the sector that it covered became a recurring preoccupation in the later CFTA and NAFTA negotiations; it was also a high priority in the Trump adminis- tration's demands on NAFTA renegotiation. The agreement also had a major impact on the world's most traded manufactured product, with Canada being the #2 supplier of automobiles to the United States in 2017 (after Mexico and before Japan), and this sector being second only to oil in the total US–Canada trade relationship.

The US–Canada FTA

Canada became the second FTA partner of the United States, but could have been the first. In 1973 a National Intelligence Estimate observed that Canada's relationship with the United States had matured, with Canada "sloughing off . . . the national inferiority complex" and developing "a reservoir of genuine respect and friendship for the US."[16] In 1974 – the same year that the United States declined an Israeli invitation to negotiate an FTA (see Chapter 15) – Washington held out an offer to Ottawa (as well as Mexico City), with

[15] Memorandum of Conversation with Prime Minister of Canada Lester Pearson, "Canadian Internal, Trade and Defense Affairs" (May 23, 1963), *FRUS 1961–1963*, Volume XIII, p. 1207.
[16] National Intelligence Estimate NIE 1-1-73, "The World Oil Crisis: Economic and Political Ramifications for Producers and Consumers" (December 5, 1973), *FRUS 1969–1976*, Volume XXXVI, p. 750.

a provision in the Trade Act of 1974 proposing the negotiation of a North American FTA. Four years passed before a committee of the Canadian Senate recommended that Ottawa take up this offer,[17] and it took longer still for the initiative to work its way through both capitols. In the meantime, the United States would negotiate an FTA with Israel precisely a decade after that idea was first broached.

The proximate cause for the CFTA, like some of its predecessor agreements, was Canadian alarm over US protectionism. Canadian officials frequently noted that the country could be "sideswiped" by Washington's responses to other countries' misdeeds, and that Ottawa needed to lock in its access while it still could. Those concerns were also prominent in the Reagan administration's internal calculations, with an interagency group acknowledging that while relations had greatly improved any "protectionist measures taken by the US could affect Canada so adversely that public support for closer ties could evaporate."[18] Prime Minister Pierre Trudeau appointed a Royal Commission on the Economic Union and Development Prospects for Canada in 1982, and in 1985 his successor would take up the commission's recommendations that Canada pursue free trade with the United States. The Reagan administration had already asked that Congress include Canada in the section of the 1984 trade bill that granted fast-track treatment for the US–Israel negotiations. Legislators were about to do just that when Canadian elections once more intervened, replacing the Liberal Trudeau with Prime Minister Brian Mulroney (Conservative). Anxious not to prejudge the new government's aims, Congress pulled that provision from the pending bill. This meant that when the Reagan administration later renewed its request to Congress it would have to go through the usual procedure of laying its proposal before the trade committees and giving them an opportunity to raise any objections.

THE DOMESTIC DIPLOMACY OF THE US–CANADA FTA

By the time of the CFTA negotiations, the American view of Canada more closely conformed to Margaret Atwood's sense of not-so-benign neglect than it did to General Rohmer's fears of manifest destiny. That can be seen in a journalistic kerfuffle that erupted just as the talks were launched. Flora

---

[17]   See the discussion of this report in "Canadian Senate Advocates Free Trade with US," cable of August 10, 1978, from the US embassy in Ottawa (1978OTTAWA03967_d).

[18]   Interagency Group Number 52, "Post-Quebec NSSD on US Policy Toward Canada" (June 25, 1985), p. 2.

Lewis wrote a laudatory column for the *New York Times* under the title "Worthwhile Canadian Initiative," which struck the *New Republic* "as possibly the most boring headline ever written." The editors observed that each "word taken alone is sleep-inducing"; strung together, they were "virtually lethal."[19] As unkind as that characterization may sound, it quite accurately captured the remarkably low political profile held by a profoundly significant economic agreement.[20] It also gave a foretaste of how the negotiations would be handled in Congress. Despite the fact that the world's largest bilateral trade relationship was at stake, lawmakers were far more interested in the extrinsic value of the deal – that is, what they could make the president pay for it – than in its own, intrinsic value.

The CFTA is one of the few, significant trade agreements of the United States that was launched, concluded, and approved entirely in one presidential administration. Most of the other major agreements have stretched over two or even three presidencies, such that NAFTA better exemplified the general rule than did its bilateral predecessor. Even within that compressed timeframe, members of Congress took full advantage of three opportunities they had to kibitz in the bilateral negotiations. The first of these came when Congress was asked to approve the initiation of negotiations. The second opportunity came between the release of an initial text in October, 1987, and the formal signing of the final agreement in January, 1988; this legally mandated "layover" period gave legislators the opportunity to review the text and demand changes. The third opportunity came in the process of translating this agreement into domestic implementing legislation. The maneuvers that lawmakers executed in all three of these phases offer detailed examples in the domestic diplomacy of trade, and in how Congress dickers with the president over the price he must pay for approval of his initiatives.

The US–Canada Launch and Revisions to Trade-Remedy Laws

The negotiations were proposed when officials in both branches of the US government were considering broader changes in trade law. The most recent omnibus bill had been the Trade and Tariff Act of 1984, a hasty

---

[19]   See the *New Republic* Staff (1986). The editors ran a contest to see if any other real-world article could top the soporific quality of that column's title. For the record, the winner was "Debate Goes on Over the Nature of Reality."

[20]   The author bases this assertion on his own experience as an advisor to the government of Quebec during the CFTA and NAFTA negotiations, part of which entailed gauging the attention that US policymakers, interest groups, and opinion leaders devoted to these initiatives.

compromise that left no one fully satisfied. Chief among the unfinished business, from the White House perspective, was the failure to give a green light for new multilateral negotiations. Without a new grant of negotiating authority, the US negotiators would not have a clear mandate for the coming Uruguay Round (1986–1994). Congressional leaders were also disappointed that the 1984 law addressed only some of their proposals, and hoped for another opportunity to amend the trade-remedy laws and promote a more aggressive reciprocity policy. Here was a formula for confrontation that would affect the entirety of the CFTA process: While the Reagan and especially the Mulroney administrations viewed bilateral negotiations as the best means of avoiding an assertive new trade bill, legislators saw it as their best means of achieving one.

The first hurdle that the administration had to clear was congressional approval for the launch of negotiations. The 1984 trade law specified that the executive would enjoy fast-track treatment for an FTA with Israel, and also for any other country if (1) it informed the congressional trade committees of its plans and (2) neither of these committees explicitly voted to deny fast-track treatment for those talks. The Reagan administration duly notified the trade committees in December, 1985 that it intended to initiate these bilateral negotiations with Canada. The House Ways and Means Committee offered no objections, but the initiative encountered unexpected resistance in the Senate.

Members of the Senate Finance Committee had no real objections to a Canadian trade agreement, but saw the president's request as the only available means to express their dissatisfaction with the administration's conduct of trade policy. Led by Chairman John Danforth (Republican–Missouri) of the International Trade Subcommittee, the dissidents believed that the executive took an insufficiently aggressive approach to reversing the trade deficit, and did not consult adequately with Congress in setting policy. Danforth focused on the export side of the ledger, advocating the stepped-up use of reciprocity statutes to reduce foreign barriers to US goods and services. Other committee members proposed further amendments to the trade-remedy laws as a means of restricting imports. Both the export- and import-oriented legislators needed a new omnibus trade bill to advance their respective causes. The Reagan administration was reluctant to revisit this territory, and declared much of the legislation then pending in Congress to be protectionist. It would not even send witnesses to testify before the congressional committees that held hearings on the bills.

One of the issues under debate was of special importance to US–Canadian trade. American loggers claimed in a 1983 countervailing duty (CVD) petition that the low stumpage fees charged by provincial governments amounted to a hidden subsidy. This claim did not pass muster with the Department of Commerce, so the industry backed legislation that would redefine the law. Senators had already linked this issue to the proposed FTA in October, 1985, when half the members of the Finance Committee signed a letter. "[A]n early resolution of the softwood lumber trade issue," they wrote President Reagan, "would facilitate Finance Committee consideration of any Administration proposals relating to the negotiation of a free trade agreement with Canada." The warning should have set off alarm bells for anyone familiar with the history of North American trade relations, where lumber has often been (together with pork and steel) atop the list of problem sectors, but the Reagan administration hoped that it could handle this issue as part of the CFTA negotiations.

These hopes were dashed at an April 11, 1986, hearing of the Finance Committee, where US Trade Representative Clayton Yeutter walked into an ambush. He heard a litany of complaints over lumber and other sectors, as well as broader dissatisfaction with the administration's inattention to congressional concerns on trade. Several senators explicitly threatened to reject the request for fast-track treatment. Recognizing that the Finance Committee was holding the CFTA hostage, the White House resolved to pay the least possible ransom. They calculated that it would be better to yield on the limited issue of lumber subsidies, and to pledge closer consultations during the coming negotiations, than to negotiate a new trade bill under duress. The administration therefore promised the lumber industry and its allies in the Finance Committee that the Department of Commerce would employ a more favorable methodology in any future CVD case. The lumber deal convinced a splinter faction to back off from the threat to withhold fast-track authority. At an April 23 meeting the Finance Committee declined on the narrowest possible vote (10–10) to disapprove the request. The negotiations could go forward, but Danforth and his allies had gotten their pound of flesh.

The Maritime Industry and the End-Game of the CFTA Negotiations

The stratagems of the maritime industry demonstrate both the ability of Congress to force changes in a trade agreement and the potential vulnerability of the fast-track rules. This mechanism is so highly prized by US negotiators that it can itself become the target of legislative hostage-taking. The fast track's special ratification procedures are a legal fiction, with the deadlines and ban on amendments being nothing more than a gentlemen's agreement between the two branches of government. Congress cannot actually deny itself the exercise of its constitutional authority to make laws, and the fast-track statute explicitly states that the no-amendment pledge and the time limits are established "with full recognition of the constitutional right of either House to change the rules (so far as relating to the procedures of that House) at any time, in the same manner, and to the same extent as any other rule of that House." Congress could hypothetically vote to scuttle the fast-track rules whenever it pleased, and this possibility almost left the realm of the hypothetical during the final weeks of CFTA negotiations.[21]

The maritime industry protested the terms of a draft CFTA text released in October, 1987. This incomplete agreement presented in broad outline all of the bargains that the negotiators had struck, but had not yet put into formal language. One chapter would have altered the cargo-preference laws, which set minimum percentages for various classes of government-financed shipments that must be carried in American vessels. An obscurely worded section of the draft provided that any future extensions in the scope of these laws would be open for bidding by Canadian shippers. For example, if the percentage of cargo reserved for domestic carriers in a certain class of shipments were to rise from 50% to 75%, Canadians could compete for the newly protected 25%. Even this partial and conditional concession, which amounted to a targeted stand-still pledge rather than true liberalization, was unacceptable to American shippers. A broad coalition of maritime firms, unions, and associations had already worked with its friends in Congress during 1986–1987 to warn the negotiators not to touch the shipping laws, and the Department of Transportation carried their water in interagency meetings. The shippers looked beyond the immediate issue of competition with Canada to the precedent that the CFTA might set for a multilateral deal in the Uruguay Round, fearing that the Reagan administration might sacrifice shipping interests in its eagerness to reach a broader agreement on trade in services.

These warnings had been only partially successful, so the industry worked with the rules committees in both chambers of Congress to finish the job. The Senate Rules Committee approved a resolution in September, 1987, that would permit amendments to the maritime provisions of a CFTA implementing bill. Twelve of the thirteen members of the House Rules Committee signed a letter to the president in which they threatened to take similar action. Both moves were meant as shots across the bow, warning that the integrity of the fast track was imperiled. The Reagan administration took these threats seriously, and set out to change the offending section. The negotiators first

---

[21] Congress would do just that in a 2006 dispute over the US–Colombia FTA; see Chapter 4.

tried to finesse the issue by refining the language in the CFTA's transportation annex. These efforts failed, leading the negotiators to deep-six the entire annex. This was a total victory for the shippers, and an embarrassing setback for both the American and Canadian negotiators.

Drafting the US–Canada Implementing Legislation

The preceding discussion has centered on tactics that rely on brute force, in which lawmakers build bargaining power by assembling coalitions and confronting the executive. Another approach owes more to blue pencils than to purple rhetoric. The most intense bargaining between the branches comes in the period between the negotiation of a trade agreement and the formal introduction of the implementing legislation. Contrary to the common view of the fast track, the implementing legislation for a trade agreement does not come directly from the executive, but is developed in congressional committees much like any other bill and is subject to similar give-and-take. The trade committees held what were then called "non-markup" sessions, so named because they were designed to produce a "non-bill"[22] to be sent to the president before he sent it back to them. Legislators could propose interpretations of the agreement that differ from what the negotiators may have intended, seek to have items appended to the draft bill that were not contemplated in the pact, or request commitments from the president in its implementation (as recorded the "statement of administrative action"). The language emerging from this process was not legally binding upon the president, who could submit an implementing bill that differed substantially from the non-bill that the trade committees produced. This would be inadvisable, however, as the support of the committee members is crucial for enactment.

Lawmakers sought to enhance their leverage by issuing tacit and explicit threats to reject the agreement if it were not interpreted and enhanced in the ways that they demanded. Many of them employed the time-honored tactic of signing hostile letters to the president and other officials, expressing objections to specific aspects of the pact. Several such letters circulated on Capitol Hill during late 1987 and early 1988, and garnered so many signatures that even long-time supporters of the initiative publicly speculated that the agreement might be in serious trouble. The Reagan administration faced the same

---

[22]   This was at least was the rather confusing terminology used in 1979 (see Jerome [1990]) and 1988. By the time that the NAFTA implementing legislation was written in 1993, the terms "mock markup" and "mock bill" were used.

problem that it had in the 1986 showdown, but soon opted to bargain with Congress. Once again, the objective was to make the minimal number of concessions in order to ensure final approval. Representatives of the executive branch therefore attended the trade committees' non-markup sessions, presenting arguments against some of the more troublesome proposals while yielding when necessary.

The most unusual part of this process concerned the additional items that legislators appended to the bill, even though they appeared nowhere in the agreement itself. Among the ornaments that the House Ways and Means Committee hung on its version of this Christmas tree were one that allowed for (but did not require) the negotiation of import restraints on Canadian steel, and another that called for further talks to eliminate Canadian grain transportation subsidies. The Senate Finance Committee's version provided a special retaliatory mechanism against Canadian subsidies; clarified that any trade-remedy amendments made prior to the CFTA's entry into force would apply to Canada; defined the relationship between the agreement and state laws; authorized renegotiation of the automotive provisions; and included other language relating to ethyl alcohol, Cuban trade sanctions, and inspection of Canadian meat.

One example may suffice to illustrate the tinkering. Senator Max Baucus (Democrat–Montana) was disappointed that the CFTA would phase out US tariffs on Canadian copper, lead, and zinc, without requiring that Canada eliminate its subsidies to these nonferrous metals. The executive opposed a Baucus proposal that would allow the United States to reimpose pre-CFTA tariffs on these metals if Canada did not agree to reduce or eliminate its subsidies, but then reluctantly accepted a more complicated mechanism that senators Baucus and Danforth sponsored. Their amendment allowed firms to file petitions with the US Trade Representative (USTR) if they face increased competition under the CFTA from subsidized Canadian industries. The USTR then had the authority to pursue a reciprocity investigation, under threat of retaliation. The senators also obliged the administration to monitor imports of zinc alloys from Canada. These provisions became the basis for a later series of US–Canadian trade disputes.[23]

Not every maneuver succeeded, as exemplified by a failed attempt to secure subsidies for uranium. A bill then under consideration in Congress would have imposed an escalating fee on nuclear power plants that used more than

---

[23] These provisions were also amended by the NAFTA implementing bill to provide that the USTR had additional authority to order the monitoring of a NAFTA country's subsidy practices.

37.5% imported uranium, and in March, 1988, the Senate approved this proposal as an amendment to another bill. Senators who opposed these fees repeatedly warned that the proposal threatened to undo the CFTA, but that threat – and the leverage it created – was precisely the point. While the amendment passed narrowly (47–45), the two-vote margin was sufficient to melt down the Reagan administration's opposition to a bailout for the uranium industry. The White House agreed to a support package that included $1 billion for environmental cleanups and $750 million for government purchases of uranium, and was even willing to write the deal into the CFTA implementing bill. The bargain began to fall apart, however, after one uranium company that sought to defeat the CFTA altogether publicized the deal. The White House eventually got the best of both worlds. Opposition in the House gave it an excuse to keep the support package out of the CFTA implementing legislation, putting it instead in the pending Nuclear Regulatory Commission Authorization Act. The Senate approved that bill on August 8, 1988, but the House failed to take the measure up before adjourning. The White House had bought off an opponent without actually paying the bribe.

The CFTA and the Omnibus Trade Bill

The Omnibus Trade and Competitiveness Act of 1988 (OTCA) owed its existence to the Reagan administration's twin need for ratification of the CFTA and a new grant of negotiating authority for the Uruguay Round. These two initiatives had been politically linked since 1986, and there was a serious danger that either or both of the administration's priorities might fail if the White House did not give Congress what it wanted. The trade legislation under consideration in the House was widely viewed more as an exercise in partisan posturing than as a serious effort at lawmaking. The more protectionist faction among the House Democrats hoped to score points in that year's congressional elections; the group's leader, Representative Richard Gephardt (Democrat–Missouri), also had an eye on the 1988 presidential election. Gephardt sat on the Ways and Means Committee, which developed a trade bill in 1986 that would place tight limits on the president's negotiating authority and make major changes to the trade-remedy laws.

The Reagan administration unveiled its own draft bill in February, 1987. This bare-bones proposal would do little more than extend fast-track negotiating authority for the Uruguay Round and make some modest changes in the trade-remedy and reciprocity laws, but it did signal a willingness to bargain. It was soon shunted aside in favor of the proposals advanced by House

Democrats and a bipartisan group in the Senate. The House and Senate passed their versions of the bill in April and July of 1987, respectively, which were then sent to an extraordinarily large and slow-moving conference committee.

Congress renewed the tacit linkage between the CFTA and the OTCA in early December, 1987, when the chairmen of the two trade committees sent a joint letter to the administration. They proposed a schedule under which the president would not submit the CFTA implementing legislation to Congress before June 1, 1988. The unstated purposes behind this request were to see where the Democratic presidential nominating race was headed, and also to prevent the administration from forcing an early vote on the Canadian agreement before Congress completed its deliberations over the OTCA. The White House initially resisted, but then relented in a mid-February agreement. The pledge ensured that Congress could hold off a final vote on the CFTA implementing legislation until after they reconciled the two versions of the bill, and the president had either signed or vetoed the result.

President Reagan ultimately did both. He vetoed the OTCA when it was first presented to him in May, 1988, primarily due to an issue that was only politically linked to trade. A controversial provision in the bill would require employers to give advance notice to their workers before closing a plant. This proposal was one of the chief partisan disputes of 1988, and was caught up with that year's presidential campaign. After failing in June to override the veto, Democrats removed the offending sections from the trade bill. The Senate passed the revised OTCA by a vote of 85–11 on August 3. Like several of his predecessors, Reagan felt obliged to accept a trade bill with which he was not entirely happy in order to obtain the coveted negotiating authority; he was unusual only in the lengths to which he went in actually vetoing the first version of the bill. The president also allowed the plant-closing bill to pass into law without his signature, after Congress approved it as a stand-alone measure by a veto-proof margin.[24]

The second, successful OTCA contained all the standard fare of omnibus trade bills. Its liberal elements renewed presidential negotiating authority, while the restrictive parts were mostly aimed at amending the trade-remedy laws. Some of these provisions were particularly ironic in the light of the original Canadian motivation for the CFTA, as they redefined US antisubsidy law in ways that were specifically intended to deal with Canadian pork and lumber. Canada was not only denied an outright exemption from these laws, but the CFTA implementing legislation specified that any amendments

---

[24] For a more detailed discussion of this incident see Shoch (2001), pp. 130–134.

enacted prior to the agreement's entry into force – such as those made by the OTCA – would apply to Canada. Other provisions in the bill were intended to transform the safeguard law into a tool of industrial policy, and to bolster the reciprocity policy by creating the so-called Super 301 law.

Once all of the bargaining over the CFTA and the OTCA provisions was completed, Congress approved the two packages in short order. The House and Senate passed the final version of the OTCA by overwhelming votes in July and August, respectively, and President Reagan signed it into law on August 23. The House had already approved the "United States-Canada Free-Trade Agreement Implementation Act of 1988" by a vote of 366–40 on August 9. The Senate then approved the bill by 83–9 on September 19, which President Reagan signed into law nine days later. The experience put the lie to the common belief that it is impossible to achieve trade liberalization in an election year, but also reiterated the general rule that Congress makes presidents pay for any liberalization that they request.

The CFTA and the Twin Elections of 1988

The Canadian parliamentary election of 1988 became, like its 1911 predecessor, a popular referendum on the trade agreement. There were two major differences: This time it was the Liberal Party that took the trade-skeptical position (even though the FTA was originally Trudeau's idea), and while the Conservative Party won both times the 1988 results allowed the agreement to be ratified. The flavor of the campaign can be appreciated from a television ad that the Liberal Party aired that year, dramatizing an imaginary negotiating session. "Since we're talking about this free trade agreement," said the American negotiator who pulled a pencil from his pocket, "there's one line I'd like to change." After his Canadian counterpart innocently asked what line he meant, the American leaned over a map. "Well, this one here," he said as he commenced erasing the border. "It's just getting in the way." The unseen narrator asked voters to consider, "Just how much are we giving away in the Mulroney free trade deal? Our water? Our healthcare? Our culture?"[25] The Canadian electorate was evidently concerned enough to reduce the Conservative majority from 211 to 169 out of 295 seats in Parliament, but not so worried as to turn out either Mulroney or his agreement.

The United States also had an election that year. The FTA might have gotten caught up in those electoral politics, had the parties chosen different standard-bearers, but this was not to be. In a contest between Reagan's vice

---

[25]   The ad entitled "Border" is posted at www.youtube.com/watch?v=jKQPw9vmGo4.

president (George H. W. Bush) and the governor of a state that is slightly closer to Ottawa than it is to Washington, DC. (Michael Dukakis of Massachusetts), the political profile of the CFTA dwindled to Atwoodian levels of insignificance. The votes in Congress to approve this agreement, which were cast just weeks before Election Day, were deceptively large and bipartisan. They also attracted close to zero public attention. The agreement entered into effect on January 1, 1989.

THE DOMESTIC DIPLOMACY OF NAFTA

It had been Washington's plan all along to pursue an agreement with both of the neighbors, as was shown in the invitation that Congress extended in 1974. Those plans were temporarily shelved while the CFTA negotiations were underway. In response to President Reagan's request for options on Mexico, the USTR argued in early 1988 that the time had not come for the negotiation of a bilateral FTA. The agency was concerned that Congress and the private sector were not yet ready for that option, and that "any mention of a possible FTA with Mexico at this time could jeopardize congressional approval of the U.S.-Canada FTA."[26] Soon after that matter was squared away, however, the American and Mexican governments proceeded to explore the possibilities. It did not take long for those plans to move from exploration to a serious reconnaissance. Policymakers in Ottawa far preferred to retain uniquely open access to the world's largest market, but nonetheless felt compelled to protect their interests when they learned of these bilateral discussions in early 1990. By the time that President Bush gave Congress formal notification later that year of his intention to enter into these negotiations, all three countries were at the table.

The fight over the negotiation and approval of NAFTA would require a greater investment of political capital than had the CFTA. Prior to November 17, 1993, when the House of Representatives approved the NAFTA implementing legislation by a vote of 234–200, there were several points at which the initiative seemed in danger of failing. The Bush and then the Clinton administration had to overcome a great many obstacles: changes of government in both the United States and Canada, extended negotiations over the terms of side agreements on environmental and labor issues, a bumpy first year for the new president, a resurgence of congressional assertiveness in all areas of public policy, continued criticism from former presidential candidate Ross Perot, and sharp divisions within the Democratic Party.

---

[26] Memo from the Trade Policy Staff Committee Subcommittee on Mexico to the Trade Policy Review Group, "U.S.-Mexico Trade Relations" (January 28, 1988), p. 4.

Much of the domestic diplomacy of NAFTA was comparable to what had happened in the CFTA case, and so in the interests of analytical economy the presentation that follows offers a compressed version of events. It highlights a few ways in which this process deviated from the path set by its predecessor, as well as those aspects of the internal US bargaining that focused more on Canada than on Mexico.

The Politics of NAFTA

The domestic diplomacy of an FTA with a developing country requires a heavier political lift from Congress than one with a country that seems "just like us," especially for Democrats, and this time lawmakers had greater concerns over the intrinsic importance of the agreement itself. This also became the first instance in which Congress got deeply involved in the demands that trade negotiators deal directly with labor and environmental issues. The Bush administration addressed these demands in a May, 1991 Action Plan that detailed its NAFTA objectives, and also concluded a memorandum of understanding with Mexico on workers' health and safety. These steps helped to secure congressional approval for fast-track authority, but the partisan divide was ominous. Whereas 87% of Republicans in the House approved this grant, only 35% of the Democrats did. Neither the action plan nor the negotiations were to resolve the Democratic demands on these newest issues, which would get caught up in the 1992 presidential campaign, in the debate over approval of the agreement, and in nearly every other important US trade negotiation thereafter.

The NAFTA negotiations began in early 1991, at a time when it was widely believed that President Bush – still savoring a quick victory in the First Gulf War – would easily win reelection the next year. By mid-1992, when the NAFTA negotiations were reaching their conclusion, his popularity had declined precipitously. There was real cause for concern that then-Governor Clinton might make a campaign issue out of the NAFTA. Independent candidate Ross Perot had already done so, portraying this agreement as a betrayal of US economic sovereignty and a threat to jobs. Clinton instead struck a compromise, declaring that he would seek NAFTA ratification only if it were accompanied by side agreements on the environment, labor issues, and import surges. This was Clinton's first opportunity to "triangulate" between two extremes, which would become his signature style. Despite concerns from the governments of Mexico and Canada, negotiations over these side agreements began shortly after President Clinton was inaugurated in January, 1993.

The talks went on for months, and did not produce final agreements until mid-August. This gave NAFTA's opponents time to organize.

The domestic Canadian politics of this initiative were quite different from what they had been in the CFTA. The final weeks of the ratification debate in Washington coincided with another national election in Canada, bringing the Liberal Party back into power. The declared intentions of Prime Minister-elect Jean Chrétien to renegotiate portions of the agreement added yet another complication to the US political equation. The United States and Canada never did agree to a renegotiation, but Chrétien's ambivalence gave his government more leverage than its predecessor had in 1988. The Clinton administration would probably have felt free to press Ottawa even harder if the pro-NAFTA Conservatives remained in power.

The NAFTA Side Agreements and Side Letters

The debates over congressional approval of the Tokyo Round agreements in 1979, and then the CFTA in 1988, had already demonstrated just how legislators could use the fast-track rules to their advantage. The NAFTA debate in 1993 took this process to the point where Canada and especially Mexico were obliged to negotiate three times: first with the Bush administration over the agreement, second with the Clinton administration over the side agreements, and third with Congress over the terms of the implementing legislation and a great many ancillary deals. NAFTA as implemented differed in many respects from NAFTA as negotiated, but officials in all three countries believed that they had to choose between an altered NAFTA or none at all.

The government of Mexico was an actual or virtual participant in much of the congressional approval process, bargaining hard for every available vote. There were some arrangements between the Clinton administration and Congress that could take effect only with the active concurrence of Mexico City, and many of the deals that appeared to have been struck solely between the executive and legislative branches of the US government needed at least tacit approval from Mexican authorities. Some of these bargains took the form of "side letters" exchanged between Secretary of Commerce and Industrial Development Jaime Serra Puche and US Trade Representative Mickey Kantor.[27] Their practice was thus quite different from what Canada had done in 1988, when the Mulroney government neither participated in the bargaining nor raised serious, public objections to the changes that Congress was making in the CFTA.

---

[27] For further NAFTA examples see MacArthur (2000).

Several of these bargains concerned further restrictions on US imports from the NAFTA partners. Most of these deals affected Mexico, including side letters and/or language in the implementing legislation and statement of administrative action on such issues as the graduation of Mexico from the Generalized System of Preferences; import restrictions on sugar, frozen concentrated orange juice, and peanuts and peanut products; and provisions allowing for "snapback" of tariffs on numerous items imported from Mexico (e.g., fresh fruits, vegetables, flowers, brooms, etc.). A few of these bargains dealt with both Mexico and Canada, such as a provision in the statement of administrative action by which the Clinton administration pledged that it "will give special priority to negotiating the acceleration of tariff reductions for [Mexican and Canadian tariffs on] ... dry beans, bedding components, cream cheese, flat glass, major household appliances, potatoes and wine."[28]

The Clinton administration struck some classic pork-barrel deals. A few of them were related to the NAFTA, such as authorizations for a $3 billion North American Development Bank, a Southwest Regional Animal Health Biocontainment Facility, and a Center for the Study of Western Hemispheric Trade. Others went much farther afield. One legislator is rumored to have secured White House support for a new order of the C-17 military transportation aircraft produced in her district, for example, and other particularistic bargains involved a highway project in California, a plutonium research laboratory in Texas, $1.2 billion in subsidies to the US shipbuilding industry, a manufacturing technology center in Virginia, and a Small Business Administration urban lending program.

The NAFTA-approval process gave members of Congress an opportunity to revisit some issues that dated back to the CFTA. One sore point concerned the operation of Extraordinary Challenge Committees (ECCs) that could be appointed to review the findings of binational panels that had considered complaints arising from trade-remedy cases. The original purpose behind ECCs was to review truly extraordinary instances of (for example) allegations of conflicts of interest on the part of a CFTA binational panel's members. Members of Congress wanted it easier to make such challenges, and obliged the administration to amend the rules for their formation and operation. The end result was to bring back an old issue, when in 1994 the Clinton administration used these new standards to establish an ECC in yet another Canadian softwood

---

[28]   For more details on these deals see VanGrasstek (1997).

lumber case.[29] *"Plus ça change,"* as they would say in Quebec, *"plus c'est la même chose."*[30] Other items in the NAFTA implementing bill that related to the northern neighbor concerned retaliatory trade provisions against Canadian restrictions on cultural industries, trade in wheat and barley, and the temporary "snapback" of pre-CFTA tariffs on fruits and vegetables whenever certain price and quantity triggers were met.

There was just one issue on which Mexico City and Washington were unable to reach a deal that satisfied both sides. The NAFTA negotiators had agreed to allow Mexican trucks onto US roads, a concession that was viewed quite differently by economic analysts (for whom this seemed like a necessary complement to the liberalization of trade in goods) and to members of Congress (with even some free-traders fearing how this concession might appear to their constituents). The Clinton administration did not comply with the liberalization schedule set in the agreement, and the dispute was to continue for well over a decade. It ultimately led to retaliation by Mexico in 2009. That pressure produced a new deal between the countries in 2011, but its implementation remains a source of friction to this day.[31]

WHERE WASHINGTON AND OTTAWA HEADED AFTER NAFTA

In keeping with Margaret Atwood's characterization of what Americans think of Canadians, this chapter has focused on what bilateral trade relations tell us about US trade politics. The history reviewed here suggests that while there have been times when Washington devoted just as much attention to the high politics of war and peace in this relationship as the low politics of trade and investment, the latter set of issues have come to dominate. More than that, Americans now take Canadians so thoroughly for granted that even when they were redefining the terms of the world's largest bilateral trade relationship, members of Congress were more focused on the extrinsic than the intrinsic value of that initiative. They saw the bilateral agreement more as an opportunity to extract concessions from the administration on new trade laws, and to warn it against making multilateral concessions on maritime services, than as a means of regulating commerce with the country's leading partner. The CFTA and NAFTA episodes amply illustrate how the two branches deal with one another in the making of trade policy, and how foreign partners

---

[29] It should be noted that in this case there were allegations of bias and conflicts of interest on the part of members of the binational panel. The original standards for seeking an ECC therefore appear to have been met in this instance.

[30] The more things change, the more they stay the same.

[31] See Carbaugh (2011) and www.tecma.com/us-mexico-cross-border-trucking-dispute/.

can be relegated to the sidelines. This self-regard is all rather reminiscent of the old lines, "Enough about me, let's talk about you. What do you think of me?"

A few observations are in order on the place of these sequential North American trade agreements in the trading system. Many Canadian policymakers thought that by entering into FTA negotiations with Washington they would fight the trade war to end all trade wars, putting an end to trade-remedy cases and other disputes, but they were in for a Wilsonian-level disappointment. The CFTA and NAFTA instead had precisely the effect that one would expect of a successful agreement: Trade between the partners grew at a healthy pace, and that growth generated ever more disputes. The two partners brought twenty-nine cases against one another under the CFTA and NAFTA between 1994 and 2017, and did not confine their disputes to this forum. From 1995 through 2017, Canada brought eighteen complaints against the United States in the WTO's Dispute Settlement Body; these accounted for nearly half of all Canadian complaints in the WTO. The United States brought seven complaints against Canada.[32]

The partners' differing approaches towards the simultaneous CFTA/ NAFTA and Uruguay Round negotiations is quite revealing. For the United States, the North American negotiations offered excellent opportunities to advance broader objectives in the multilateral system by setting precedents on the new issues (see Chapter 5). Canada took a more ambivalent view toward its growing dependence on the United States, and saw the Uruguay Round as an opportunity to resurrect plans for a bona fide global institution. Initially inspired by US trade lawyer John Jackson, in 1990 Canadian officials formally proposed "a new world trade organization ... to cope with the rapidly changing international trading environment."[33] They encountered serious skepticism from American officials, who doubted that Congress would be willing to accept in the 1990s the same type of deal that it rejected in the 1940s, but in both periods the scope of issues ultimately made the difference. Congress refused to take up the Havana Charter because it dealt with a wider range of subjects than they were then willing to place in multilateral hands, but was then convinced to approve the WTO in 1994 precisely because it incorporated all of the new issues that the United States was then promoting. However

---

[32] These cases are catalogued at www.nafta-sec-alena.org/Home/Dispute-Settlement/Decisions-and-Reports and www.wto.org/english/tratop_e/dispu_e/dispu_by_country_e.htm.

[33] Letter of April 9, 1990, from Minister of Trade John Crosbie to his counterparts in the Quad and GATT Director General Arthur Dunkel, as quoted in VanGrasstek (2013), p. 58. See chapter 2 of that book for more on the genesis of the Canadian proposal, the US response, and the ensuing talks among the Uruguay Round participants.

unwittingly, Canada thus played critical roles in advancing the US agenda at three stages: by agreeing to set the first important precedents on these issues in the CFTA, then greatly elaborating upon those precedents in NAFTA, and finally by proposing institutional reforms that would bring the multilateral rules on these topics under the same roof.

The story did not end there, as Canada became one of the most promiscuous of all trade negotiators. As a general rule, each of the subsequent initiatives in which both Canada and the United States were engaged ended up failing; these included the Free Trade Area of the Americas, the Asia Pacific Economic Cooperation talks, the Doha Round, and the Trans-Pacific Partnership (TPP). By contrast, the negotiations in which Canada engaged without the United States have succeeded. Its FTA with the European Free Trade Association[34] entered into force in 2009, and was a prelude to the much larger Comprehensive Economic and Trade Agreement with the European Union that took effect in 2017. Canadian FTA partners also include numerous countries in the Americas, Asia, the Middle East, and – in recognition of an important Canadian diaspora community – Ukraine. If one were to add to this list the Canada-China FTA negotiations that seemed imminent in 2018, Canada might soon enjoy free trade with virtually every country in the world that (a) accounts for large or even modest shares of the global economy and (b) is not averse to the negotiation of discriminatory agreements.

Matters came full circle at the end of 2016, when Ottawa agreed immediately after the US presidential election to enter into negotiations for the revision of NAFTA. The Canadian side would be led, fittingly enough, by a new Trudeau government. Its efforts to appease the Trump administration did not dissuade Washington from playing hardball, with the president repeatedly threatening to abrogate NAFTA unilaterally or to conclude his trade war by reaching a separate peace with Mexico. Trump went so far as to slap restrictions on Canadian steel and aluminum in 2018, and to threaten the same fate for Canadian-made cars, on the grounds that these imports threatened US national security. That claim might strike even General Rohmer as improbable, and inspire nostalgia for the days when – per Margaret Atwood – Canadians fell below the American radar. These talks produced an agreement in principle at the end of September, 2018, which Donald Trump dubbed the United States Mexico Canada Agreement (USMCA) so as to distinguish it from its NAFTA predecessor. That change was far more than rhetorical, for while there are many respects in which the new agreements resembles the old there are numerous points at which it incorporates principles that are founded

---

[34] The members of this group are Iceland, Liechtenstein, Norway, and Switzerland.

more upon managed trade than free trade. The more restrictive rules of origin for automotive trade, for example, amount to a reversion of Auto Pact-era principles, and seem at least as dedicated to achieving state-directed outcomes as they are to creating market-driven opportunities. The Trump administration's emphasis on outcomes over opportunities – not to mention its efforts to reward favored Midwestern constituencies – can likewise be seen in the concessions it wrung from Canada on dairy products.

Like the TPP before it, the USMCA reflects Washington's concerns over competition with Beijing. The TPP was founded upon two successive presidents' goal of strengthening ties with partners in the Pacific Basin so as to compete effectively with China, even while recognizing that most of those same partners would also cut deals with Beijing. By the time that those regional talks ended in 2015, the three North American countries were the only TPP signatories that did not either (a) already have FTAs with China or (b) were in the last stages of negotiating or approving them. In a major concession to the Trump administration, Canada and Mexico agreed to include a provision in the USMCA that freezes the status quo. Article 32.10 of the draft agreement requires that any party (read: Canada or Mexico) must inform the others (read: the United States) at least three months before commencing negotiations for an FTA with a nonmarket country (read: China). It further provides that if any party were to enter into such an agreement, that step would "allow the other Parties to terminate this Agreement on six-month notice and replace this Agreement with an agreement as between them (bilateral agreement)."[35]

The US negotiators thus obliged their Canadian and Mexican counterparts to acquiesce to a new principle by which Washington's partners must choose sides in an emerging bloc system. That principle bears a disquieting resemblance to the logic by which Vladimir Putin saw the Ukraine's trade agreement with the European Union as a provocation, and compelled this former Soviet republic to renew its fealty to Moscow; that demand ultimately precipitated not just rejection of the EU agreement but turmoil inside Ukraine and Russia's annexation of Crimea (see Chapter 11). This analogy should not be drawn too far; it would out-Rohmer Rohmer to spin a scenario in which Canada's refusal to make a pledge of commercial monogamy led to American occupation of Canadian territory. This provision nonetheless underlines the profound changes that the Trump administration may bring to the global trading system, even while the United States continues to treat relations with Canada as a means of dealing with altogether different issues.

---

[35] Note that the precise terms of this provision, together with all other language in the September, 2018 draft, is subject to a legal review for accuracy, clarity, and consistency.

PART IV

TRADING WITH ADVERSARIES

10

The Strategy and Domestic Diplomacy of Sanctions

[W]e will not send or import from Great Britain this fall, either on our own account, or on commission, any other goods than what are already ordered for the fall supply.
[W]e will not send for or import any kind of goods or merchandise from Great Britain, either on our own account, or on commissions, or any otherwise, from January 1, 1769, to January 1, 1770, except salt, coals, fish-hooks and lines, hemp, duck, bar lead and shot, wool-cards, and card-wire.

Boston Non-Importation Agreement (1768)

INTRODUCTION

Americans got in the habit of employing commercial sanctions for political purposes even before they ceased being Englishmen. John Hancock (1737–1793) and other Boston merchants who backed the Non-Importation Agreement, together with their counterparts in other ports, used boycotts to pressure London into repealing the Stamp Act (1765) and Townshend Acts (1767). They minimized the impact of the sanctions on their own commercial operations by grandfathering the exports and imports they had already contracted, and by enumerating a list of exemptions. The signatories also kept at the backs of their minds, and in their back pockets, a resort to smuggling. The ploy worked. The British merchants howled so loudly that Parliament undid the offending taxes.

The paradox of sanctions ensures that not all campaigns produce similarly impressive results. A successful measure has to strike a difficult balance: The trade that it puts at risk must be valuable enough to inflict real pain on the target, and yet not so great for the sender as to prevent it from carrying out the threat. Hancock and company managed to find that sweet spot. That worked well once, but the round of sanctions that followed in the next decade led first to counter-sanctions and then to war. The experience of the 1770s is more representative than that of the 1760s, with most analysts agreeing that sanctions tend to fail more often than they succeed (although few such failures presage the outbreak of war). The earlier episode was also unusual insofar as the private sector was the instigator. Businesses today prefer to block sanctions altogether; failing that, they will try to outdo their colonial-era predecessors in proposing exceptions. The incentives to lobby against sanctions are even greater now that they involve an array of measures that extends well beyond boycotts, including controls over exports of strategic goods and even complete bans on economic ties.

Much of the existing literature on sanctions is focused on the eminently practical question of whether this instrument is effective, and most verdicts are fairly negative. "It would be difficult," Baldwin wrote a generation ago, "to find any proposition in the international relations literature more widely accepted than those belittling the utility of economic techniques of statecraft."[1] One summary of Realist studies found that "while most cases of international economic sanctions ... sustained over a sufficiently long period of time did produce at least some economic hardship in the target countries, in no instance were the economic sanctions themselves primarily responsible for inducing changes in the political behavior of the target regimes."[2] The same authors found that economists typically reached the same conclusion, albeit for slightly different reasons. In the most widely read of these analyses, Hufbauer et al. reported mixed results in their comparative study of 116 sanctions cases. They found that only 35% of the cases reached a successful result.[3]

In place of plowing any more furrows in heavily tilled soil, we may start instead by stipulating that sanctions may indeed achieve their aims something like one-third of the time. We should also recognize that the significance of that proportion is a matter of opinion. A fan whose baseball team loses two-thirds of its games will quite justifiably be disheartened, but may still prize the one slugger on the franchise who puts up an impressive .333 batting average. We can only wonder what sort of averages might be calculated for other instruments of foreign policy, from jawboning, soft power, and foreign aid to saber-rattling, covert operations, and war. In place of reaching some overarching conclusions about the general utility of sanctions, and how they might stack up against the available complements and substitutes, this chapter instead has two simpler tasks.

[1]   Baldwin (1985), p. 57.
[2]   Kaempfer and Lowenberg (1990), p. 176.
[3]   Hufbauer et al. (1990).

The first task is to place this subject in context by providing an historical overview of US sanctions and the approaches that the British and American hegemons took to trade and security. The principal differences are that the latest measures are typically imposed during peacetime, and the United States is less dependent on trade than was the United Kingdom in hegemony. Combined with important distinctions in US and European perspectives, those factors define the challenges to devising and implementing an effective regime. Our examination at the domestic level highlights the roles played by private interests and the legislative branch, both of which may complicate the coherent pursuit of sanctions.

The second task is to consider how the economic transition has affected the American capacity to deploy sanctions effectively. While Washington is better situated than other players to use this instrument, given the large US market size and low level of trade dependence, the trends are eroding that advantage. The degree of American leverage over other countries, as measured by the shares of their economies that are tied up in bilateral trade, has been dropping for years. That trend is matched by concurrent increases in US vulnerability to the negative effects of sanctions, globally if not bilaterally. While trade sanctions remain an important tool of foreign policy, the threat to employ them may now carry less weight with target states than in past decades, and Washington may find it more costly to make good on these threats. The net result may be either a further reduction in that batting average, or a subtler change by which policymakers risk fewer at-bats.

This chapter's principal focus is on sanctions that are imposed on exports and imports of goods and services, whether broadly or narrowly defined, without respect to the specific firms or individuals that are involved in these transactions. These are to be distinguished from the asset freezes, travel restrictions, or other "smart" sanctions that are more precisely targeted against persons or entities that are alleged to engage in drug trafficking, terrorist financing, arms smuggling, human rights violations, or other proscribed activities. That variety of sanction, which has become increasingly common in recent decades, often bears a closer resemblance to law enforcement than to the more traditional trade restrictions that are imposed for reasons of foreign policy. We will take up "smart" sanctions in Chapter 11, including the sharp reaction that they have inspired on the part of oligarchs and officials in Russia.

SANCTIONS IN TWO HEGEMONIES

Sanctions have long been on the menu of US options, as illustrated by the non-importation agreements of the 1760s. Policymakers of the early republic continued to demonstrate great faith in their capacity to leverage America's limited economic resources into political influence. The actual results were rather dubious, especially in the lead-up to the War of 1812 and in the South's failed strategy during the Civil War, but as the United States rose in power and wealth so too did its propensity and capacity to use this tool.

An Anomaly: Agricultural Export Embargoes in the Nineteenth Century

The differences in US foreign economic policy before and during hegemony are often easy to spot, with ambitions being notably less expansive in the earlier period. Washington's position on the rights of neutrals versus the powers of belligerents evolved as one might expect when the United States moved from free-rider to challenger, and from there to hegemony, for example, as did policy toward colonies and newly independent states. Conversely, there are a few areas in which the ambitions of policymakers outpaced the country's capacity to make good on their demands. Agricultural export sanctions fall in that latter category.

The anomalies described here are all the more remarkable for the region and the sector from which they emerged. The United States has always been a net agricultural exporter, and the Constitution ensures that rural voters enjoy an outsized electoral influence. Representatives of the agricultural community usually prize wealth over power, preferring to remain aloof from global affairs while making the most of export opportunities. Tom Paine (1737–1809), for example, saw a bright future for an independent and neutral America that "will always have a market while eating is the custom in Europe."[4] That rural propensity to combine economic engagement with political isolation is periodically challenged by policymakers who see food and fiber exports as a tool of leverage. The original exponents of this latter view were Southern statesmen who flouted not just their region's traditional position, but also their own avowed priorities. James Madison's evolving stance is especially instructive. Although he was a lifelong devotee of reciprocity (i.e., the threat of trade restrictions to extract *commercial* concessions), he spoke out in 1787 against embargoes (i.e., the threat of trade restrictions to extract *political* concessions). When Madison proposed to the Constitutional Convention that the latter measures be banned, characterizing them as unnecessary, impolitic, and unjust, only three states backed him.[5] Winning that fight might have saved him

---

[4]   Paine (1776), p. 20.
[5]   Madison (1787), p. 629.

a quarter-century later from a war that was avoidable and inadvisable, and that produced consequences he neither anticipated nor desired.

The War of 1812, better known to contemporaries as Mr. Madison's War, was partly caused by the failure of trade sanctions. The American aims in that war were as varied at the start as they were frustrated at the end, including a lifting of the European belligerents' restrictions on trade, an end to the British impressment of American seamen, and the conquest of Canada. It followed a half-decade of frustrated efforts to coerce England and France into respecting America's neutral rights. Congress approved the Embargo Act of 1807 when Madison served as Jefferson's secretary of state, shutting down all foreign trade, and when Madison ascended to the presidency he promoted a Non-Intercourse Act of 1809 that banned trade only with England and France. The Macon Bill of 1810 took a still more discriminating tack, cutting off trade with the enemy of whichever belligerent lifted its restrictions on the United States. The resulting ban on imports of English goods lasted from March, 1811 through the outbreak of war in June, 1812. It could be argued that these pressures actually had the desired effect, with Parliament suspending the contested order in council in mid-1812, but news of that concession did not reach the United States until after the shooting started. The incident thus foreshadowed another, better-known communications failure at the end of the war, when in 1815 the lopsided US victory in the Battle of New Orleans came three weeks after the Treaty of Ghent made peace.

The one constant during 1807–1815 was the antagonism between the Southerners who pursued a hard line against England and the Northerners who resented them for it. The New Englanders who detested Napoleon were not much better disposed toward Madison. One historian described the economic consequences of his policies in language that anticipated the grievances of some Trump supporters in 2016: "Ships rotted at their moorings; forests of bare masts sprang up in many harbors; grass grew on once bustling wharves; soup kitchens opened their doors; bankruptcies, suicides, and crimes increased."[6] The domestic opposition to the embargo, which its detractors anagrammatically disparaged as the "ograbme," grew so bitter in New England that the commanding general of the Federal forces "was ordered to be ready to put down insurrection [and the] coast was patrolled by men-of-war and revenue cutters."[7] Madison ultimately got just the opposite of what he and Jefferson wanted. The economic isolation brought on by sanctions and war incubated not only domestic manufactures, but also a new lobby to demand

---

[6] Bailey (1980), p. 125.
[7] Marvin (1902), p. 115.

post-war import protection. Rarely has a policy so scrupulously obeyed the law of unintended consequences. By bringing about a war that Jefferson and Madison professed to abhor just as much as Alexander Hamilton had, albeit for different reasons, these third and fourth presidents also created a political environment that favored Hamiltonian economic policies.

A later generation of Southern statesmen would have a similarly overblown notion of King Cotton's ability to coerce London. The Confederacy did appear well positioned to deploy sanctions at the start of the Civil War: One-fifth of the British population was directly or indirectly employed by the cotton textiles industry, and 80% of their raw material came from the South.[8] Richmond hoped that a cotton embargo would force England to back its rebellion, but did not grasp the paradox of sanctions. "The Confederacy was more dependent on cotton than any of the industrialized nations it sought to coerce," as one historian concluded, and its leaders "failed to recall the domestic hardships" that the trade restrictions of 1807–1815 had produced.[9] Cotton production continued, war and policy notwithstanding, and just enough fiber made its way to England. Maintaining that flow was a Union priority, and was greatly facilitated by the US Navy's capture of Port Royal, South Carolina in late 1861. This victory was doubly valuable, strengthening the blockade while also safeguarding cotton exports. The South may have out-generaled the North on the battlefield, but Washington proved more adept than Richmond at economic warfare. It also benefitted from a bumper crop in 1860 that left the English mills with sufficient stocks to weather initial disruptions, and from the emerging production in Egypt and India. The English textile manufacturers remained in business throughout the Civil War, reducing one potential source of pressure that might have pushed London into diplomatic or even military intervention in favor of the Confederacy.

Controversies over the Scope of Trade Controls

Those two nineteenth-century episodes were exceptional. For most of the British hegemony the United States was neither a target nor a sender of sanctions, but a neutral that resented the restrictions imposed by European belligerents. In Chapter 7 we already explored the legal rights of neutrals to trade in contraband and noncontraband goods, holding in abeyance just what distinguishes one class of goods from another. That topic is handled here because it so closely parallels the scope of peacetime sanctions. Two questions

---

[8]   Hubbard (1998), p. 22.
[9]   Ibid., p. 27.

are pertinent with respect to both contraband in war and sanctions in peace. The first concerns the specific types of goods that may be targeted for restrictions, which can be arrayed along a spectrum that ranges from very specific instruments of warfare (e.g., arms and ammunition) to all economic activity. The second question concerns the range of targeted entities, which might mean imposing restrictions narrowly on the sender's own nationals, or pursuing them in conjunction with allies, or applying them in an extraterritorial manner against third-country persons. We will take up that discussion later in this chapter.

Negotiators in the eighteenth and nineteenth centuries repeatedly tried to reach a consensus on where to draw the line between the hardware of war and peace and thus to isolate contraband from ordinary trade. This project was complicated by steady advances in mankind's capacity to commit state-sanctioned murder. The Industrial Revolution, which coincided with the start of British hegemony, made it progressively more difficult to distinguish between military and nonmilitary goods. What would later be called "dual-use" items – that is, goods that are equally useful to soldiers and civilians – became increasingly pervasive. The problem grew knottier still with each new stand-off weapon that allowed warring parties not only to slaughter one another at great distances, but to cause mayhem in the enemy's population and production centers. This march towards total war can be seen first in the development of long-range artillery, then air power, and finally in nuclear weapons and intercontinental missiles.

Matters were further complicated by the different motivations of richer, more powerful states as against their smaller, poorer, and less technologically advanced antagonists. A country that expects to be at war fairly often, and has the means to rule the seas, will favor a wide definition of contraband that allows it to cut off its adversaries from resupply. Weaker belligerents will instead want to define contraband strictly as military goods, while neutrals would prefer that there be no restrictions at all. The United States moved from one status to another as it ascended the ladder of international power, and the preferred composition of its contraband lists kept pace with the country's rising ambitions and authority.

The narrow contraband lists in the Franco-American treaty of 1778 offer a useful comparison with the 1794 Jay Treaty between the United States and the United Kingdom. Article 26 of the 1778 treaty, which was based on the Plan of 1776 (see Chapter 7), took two approaches to limiting the scope of contraband. The first was to draw up what today's trade negotiators would call a positive list of goods that are clearly contraband, with the Americans and French confining that list to bona fide weapons such as "Arms, great Guns,

Bombs with the fuzes," etc. The treaty also provided an explicit, negative list of items that "shall not be reckoned among Contraband or prohibited Goods." These included a range of enumerated raw materials, food, and manufactures, as well as "all other Goods whatever, which have not been worked into the form of any Instrument or thing prepared for war by Land or by Sea." Article 18 of the Jay Treaty instead reflected the expansive British demands. It identified as contraband some items that had appeared on the negative list of the Franco-American treaty, and it had no negative list at all. The Jay Treaty explicitly conceded "the difficulty of agreeing on the precise Cases in which alone Provisions and other articles not generally contraband may be regarded as such," and allowed either party (read: London) to place additional items on the list of prohibited goods. The only sop that this treaty threw to US sensitivities was the promise of indemnification for any seizures of goods that went beyond the agreed list.

Washington's position evolved in the latter half of the nineteenth century, when the contraband lists that it drew up in the Civil War and in the Spanish-American War of 1898 illustrated the expanding range of goods that one belligerent might deny to another. In 1862 the Treasury aimed not just at arms, munitions, and naval stores, but also enumerated goods (e.g., metals, paddle-wheels, etc.) that "can or may become applicable for the manufacture of marine machinery, or for the armor of vessels."[10] A generation later, the United States announced lists of both absolute and conditional contraband. While the former was limited to arms, munitions, war supplies, and horses, the latter included coal and "materials for the construction of railways or tele-graphs, and money, when such materials or money are destined for the enemy's forces," and an undefined category of "provisions" when those mate-rials were "destined for an enemy's ship or ships, or for a place that is besieged."[11] That last point did not have much practical significance for a war in which the first and last shots were separated by just ten weeks, but it foreshadowed the more ambitious contraband lists that were to come.

While nineteenth-century statesmen tried to carry on their predecessors' project of insulating civilians from war, their successors were either less humanitarian or less hypocritical. In 1911 the House of Lords rejected the Declaration of London, a multilateral agreement that would have established an elaborate typology of contraband, conditional contraband, and

---

[10] The Secretary of the Treasury (Chase) to Collectors of Customs (May 23, 1862), in Department of State (1934), p. 447.

[11] The Secretary of the Navy (Long) to Blockading Vessels and Cruisers, General Orders No. 492 (June 20, 1898), in Department of State (1934), pp. 489–490.

noncontraband goods. Even if the declaration acquired the force of law, it would likely have fallen victim to the First World War. That conflict saw the dawn of strategic bombing, a practice that would be perfected in the next contest. By the dawn of the atomic age, Wu would dismiss what he called the "strategic materials fallacy." He argued that in a modern economy it is no longer "possible to distinguish between military needs and civilian needs and to segregate the corresponding import requirements accordingly."[12] In addition to blurring these lines, planners now associated the enemy's will to resist with civilian morale. Beyond calculating how long it might take an active belligerent to wear out its tanks and deplete its stockpile of ammunition, strategists also pondered how long the populace would tolerate a regime that failed to feed, clothe, house, and protect them.

These shifts led to two huge expansions in how strategic trade controls are conceived and imposed. The first was to scratch out the formerly bright line that separated war from peace, with Washington advocating Cold War restrictions even on countries with which it had never been at war. The second accommodation was to downplay the distinctions between weapons and other goods, and to consider potentially all items as fair game. This sometimes meant drawing up peacetime contraband lists that went much farther than the British ever did in war, and sometimes meant taking the final step of forbidding virtually all economic ties to an adversary. Balanced against these expanded controls was the necessity of coordination with the allies. The United States in hegemony was capable of conducting a war on its own, even if it desired the material and moral support of the allies, but collaboration was indispensable for the execution of sanctions and strategic export controls. Just as England in the 1860s found alternative sources of supply for cotton, so too could the Warsaw Pact of the 1950s and beyond find ways to skirt any economic controls that the United States might unilaterally impose. American diplomats did win allied support, but only to a point. While the partners agreed in principle that some classes of goods had to be denied to the East, they frequently clashed over the details.

US and European Perspectives in the American Hegemony

The paradox of sanctions rests on the fact that trade with any given adversary might fall into either of two problematic categories. At one extreme are those countries with which trade is so small as to make sanctions economically tolerable but politically ineffective; at the other extreme are those with which

---

[12] Wu (1952), p. 11.

trade is so large as to make sanctions economically formidable but not politically credible. One recurring problem of Cold War diplomacy was that the Soviet Union and its allies fell into the first category for the United States, but they were closer to the second category for the European allies. The domestic side of the problem was quite manageable for American policy-makers, insofar as US firms that might otherwise speak out against sanctions perceived little commercial incentive to do so (trade with the Communists being quite small) and a potentially high political cost (they did not want the stigma of appearing unpatriotic). The calculus was quite different on the other side of the Atlantic.

The European allies differed from the United States in several key respects. Some distinctions heightened the economic sensitivity of trade with the East, including Western Europe's greater proximity to that market, higher overall dependence on trade, and paucity of natural resources (especially hydrocarbons). Other differences made war more worrisome, starting again with greater proximity to the potential aggressor, the Europeans' more scarring experience in two world wars, and a political culture that saw warfare as an anachronism that enlightened statesmen had banished from the Old World. Many Europeans also believed that any rational interlocutor wished to avoid bloodshed just as fervently as they did, and were quick to ascribe harmless or even benevolent aims to countries that Washington instead considered actual or potential adversaries. While the allies worked to align their positions, Western Europeans were generally more reluctant to confront Moscow directly, and were always aware that the burdens of adjustment to any changes in policy (positive or negative) would usually fall more heavily on them than on their American partners.

The severity of these transatlantic distinctions differed from one partner to another. As in so many other areas, the British position could be conflicted. The United Kingdom often aligned itself with the European partners, and in opposition to its hegemonic successor, but London remained capable of reasserting its own authority when circumstances demanded. Thus while the British were usually "critics of U.S. assertions of extraterritorial jurisdiction," when war broke out in the South Atlantic in 1982 they "applied their freeze on Argentine assets broadly."[13]

One manifestation of the transatlantic division came in the distinct American and European approaches to "differentiation" in the treatment of Warsaw Pact countries. This policy aimed "to encourage diversity among the

---

[13]   Wallace (1983), p. 1103.

Eastern European countries in order to reduce Soviet influence," using economic or diplomatic concessions to induce a widening space between these countries and Moscow.[14] Both the United States and its partners encouraged differentiation, but perceived the costs and benefits in distinct ways. The first major example came in response to Poland's partial estrangement from the Soviet Union. Washington encouraged these independent impulses through loans, a loosening of US export restrictions, and (after 1960) the extension of MFN treatment to imports of Polish products. The economic impact of this policy was greater for the European partners, including much higher levels of imports that they would need to absorb from Poland. Similar issues would arise once again after Poland acceded to the European Union in 2004, a costly expansion that obliged Brussels to make deeper reforms in the community's farm policies. Differentiation was also important in the West's relations with Hungary and Romania.

The frictions were especially severe during the Reagan administration, when a series of incidents laid bare the widening differences between the United States, its allies, and third parties. These included episodes in which Japanese firms were sanctioned for having sold submarine-related technology to the Soviets, and when the United States urged Argentina, Australia, and Canada to join a grain embargo following the invasion of Afghanistan. A central goal of US policy was "to minimize the potential for Soviet exercise of reverse leverage on Western economies based on trade, energy supply, and financial relationships."[15] That policy provoked an especially intractable dispute in 1981, when the United States imposed restrictions on the exportation of oil and gas equipment to the Soviet Union so as to limit European dependence on Soviet energy. The next year, Washington expanded these restrictions "to include equipment produced by subsidiaries of U.S. companies abroad as well as equipment produced abroad under licenses issued by U.S. companies."[16] The United States threatened (but ultimately abandoned) extraterritorial sanctions against European firms that collaborated with the Soviet Union in the development of its energy exports.[17] Echoes of that dispute can be heard today, with energy trade still being among the levers that Moscow can pull to influence Europe (see Chapter 11).

---

[14] Haus (1992), p. 15.
[15] National Security Decision Directive Number 75, "U.S. Relations with the USSR" (January 17, 1983), p. 2.
[16] National Security Decision Directive Number 41, "December 30, 1981 Sanctions on Oil and Gas Equipment Exports to the Soviet Union" (June 22, 1982), p. 1.
[17] See Marcus (1983) and Zaucha (1983).

The Cold War and the Coordinating Committee

The Coordinating Committee (CoCom) was the principal forum in which the United States and its European allies hashed out their differences over strategic trade controls during the Cold War. Initially created in 1949 as an arrangement between the United States and six Western European countries,[18] the membership of this body grew to include other North Atlantic Treaty Organization (NATO) countries plus Japan and Australia. CoCom had some characteristics in common with the early GATT: It was a primarily transatlantic and informal institution that operated largely upon a sometimes fractious consensus. Stating the problem in classic legal terms, a CIA analyst succinctly characterized CoCom in 1956 as "a league of like minded neutrals applying agreed economic sanctions in which no one of the participating countries has the rights of a belligerent," and where the "effectiveness of the economic sanctions depend entirely on the willingness of the members to apply their national controls in the overall economic defense system."[19]

The key dispute was in the scope of CoCom ambitions. Whereas Europeans preferred the narrow goal of a purely strategic embargo that would prohibit "only the trade that makes a direct and significant contribution to an adversary's military capabilities," the more ambitious US objective was "to weaken the military capabilities of a target state by weakening that state's economy."[20] The split was especially gaping during the periods of 1949–1958 and 1980–1984. Mastanduno found that the United States was generally unsuccessful in its efforts to win collective support for wide-ranging controls on East–West trade. In one respect this failure relates to the paradox of preferences, insofar as Washington was not prepared to make its allies whole for the economic losses that they would suffer from the proposed restrictions. "In neither the 1950s nor the 1980s," he concluded, "was the United States willing to open home markets sufficiently to compensate Western Europe for the economic costs of comprehensive economic denial in East-West trade."[21] He further argued that while the Truman, Eisenhower, and Reagan administrations all had the option of coercing the allies, such as threatening to end military cooperation

---

[18]   The founding members included Belgium, France, Italy, Luxembourg, the Netherlands, and the United Kingdom.

[19]   Central Intelligence Agency, "Economic Warfare: Lecture to the Industrial College of the Armed Forces" [name of lecturer deleted] (March 26, 1956), p. 5.

[20]   Mastanduno (1992), p. 13. Note that he rather broadly defined that latter policy as "economic warfare."

[21]   Ibid., p. 14. For alternative views on the European response to American pressure, see Adler-Karlsson (1967) and Førland (1990).

or economic engagement, each of them believed that the costs of a hard line exceeded the benefits.

Even when the allies agreed in principle that the restrictions on East–West trade ought to cover only strategic goods, considerable room remained for disagreement over what items met that description. As already implied by the contraband lists of the nineteenth century, many goods are equally useful for civilians and soldiers. Transportation equipment has always figured prominently on the dual-use roster, which also encompasses (among other areas) computers and communications equipment. The United States was generally more prone than the allies to classify a given item as strategic, but was also given to internal disputes; the departments of Commerce, Defense, and State each placed different emphases on the economic, security, and political consequences of classification decisions. The main way that the allies handled these issues was to adapt the older principle of conditional contraband, meaning that certain types of goods might be permitted or banned on a case-by-case basis according to the nature of the end-user and its plans. Goods that fell within the negotiable middle ground could be exported only if licensed. The licensing system thus offered a means to balance the competing interests of power and wealth, even if different countries and departments had distinct levels of zeal in their scrutiny and denial of licenses.

CoCom formally dissolved in 1994, giving way to the Wassenaar Arrangement. This new order, together with the Missile Technology Control Regime and the Nuclear Suppliers Group, is intended to limit the spread of advanced weapons and technologies. The principal differences between these new arrangements and CoCom are that Russia is now inside the tent, and there is no single target of the controls. The degree of coordination is nonetheless imperfect, as demonstrated by such controversies as Russian support to the Iranian missile industry.

Controversies over Extraterritoriality

A sender must also decide what persons will be bound by its restrictions. The least ambitious approach, but the simplest to implement, is to impose these obligations solely on the sender's own nationals. That may mean prohibiting individuals from traveling to the target state, banning companies from exporting to or investing in that country, or otherwise restricting direct economic ties. The obvious disadvantage is that this approach may impose losses on the sender's private sector while having only limited impact on the target country, except in those rare cases where the sender is the sole international provider of some essential good or service. The principal advantage is that this approach is least likely to antagonize third countries, apart from the sometimes tricky question of how the sender state will treat the foreign affiliates of its own firms (or vice versa).[22] A more effective but complicated approach, as already discussed in the CoCom case, is to work in a coalition. The third and most problematic option is for the sender to define the sanctions unilaterally, but to enforce them in an extraterritorial fashion. This typically means making involuntary coalition partners out of third-country persons, and threatening to penalize them if they do not comply with the sanctions regime.

Issues of extraterritoriality involve an entirely different level of intra-alliance conflict than do coalition efforts such as CoCom, and comprise one of the most difficult sources of friction in the transatlantic relationship. "In the U.S. jurisprudence of economic sanctions," according to one legal scholar, "there are no meaningful legal limits to [their] extraterritorial application."[23] The problem is especially acute in cases where diaspora communities in the United States have great sway in Congress, and may force the enactment of restrictions that favor aggressive confrontations with the target country over the maintenance of good relations with allies. Nowhere is that more prominent than in US relations with Cuba, where even presidents may subordinate their foreign policy goals to electoral imperatives.

Third countries have long been subject to periodic swings in policy toward Cuba. The Cuban Assets Control Regulations (CACRs) originally applied only to US firms. They were amended in 1975 to bring foreign-based affiliates of American companies within the scope of the prohibitions, but 1988 amendments allowed the licensing of transactions between Cuba and US-owned or controlled foreign-based firms when the laws of the host country require (or local policy favors) trade with Cuba.[24] The Cuban Democracy Act of 1992 closed the latter loophole, and also prohibited any ship that had recently visited a Cuban port from entering a US port. The Cuban Liberty and Democratic Solidarity Act of 1996, more commonly called the Helms–Burton Act, brought transatlantic disputes to an altogether new level. In this case the extraterritorial nature of the sanctions was the very point, with the sponsors hoping to dissuade new investments and encourage divestment. The State Department vigorously opposed the draft law in 1995 as "an unprecedented extraterritorial application of United States law" that it found "very

---

[22] At issue here is how "US persons" are defined. The sanctions against Cuba and Asian Communist countries have generally applied to a broader range of US persons than have the sanctions against other countries. See Malloy (1990), pp. 590–592.

[23] Malloy (1990), pp. 579–580.

[24] Ibid., pp. 358–363, for the evolution of US law and policy on this point.

difficult to defend under international law."[25] The resulting conflict between Washington and Brussels was one of the most serious rifts in the history of the alliance, and soon spilled over into transatlantic commercial diplomacy. It also contributed to the defeat of an important post–Uruguay Round initiative.

The Helms–Burton law was the subject of the very first formal complaint that the European Union brought against the United States in the WTO's Dispute Settlement Body, claiming in 1996 that the law was inconsistent with ten articles of the GATT and GATS agreements. The United States refused to participate in the panel, but also hoped to avoid invoking the national security exception so early in the WTO's institutional life. In place of formally citing GATT Article XXI,[26] the US delegates merely implied that possibility by declaring that the WTO "is not an appropriate forum for resolving differences over what is essentially a disagreement over foreign policy" and gravely warned that pursuing this case "may well jeopardize what we and others have worked so hard to achieve."[27] The stakes only rose when the extraterritorial aspects of the Iran and Libya Sanction Act of 1996 got thrown into the mix.

After a year of rancor, maneuvering, and stalemate the two sides pledged in 1997 to resolve their differences amicably. They hoped "to develop agreed disciplines and principles for the strengthening of investment protection, bilaterally and in the context of the Multilateral Agreement on Investment (MAI) or other appropriate international fora."[28] Those MAI negotiations had been launched in the OECD after the Uruguay Round, when both the United States and the European Union were disappointed by the shortcomings of the WTO's Agreement on Trade-Related Investment Measures. Instead of the MAI solving the Helms–Burton problem, however, it was Helms–Burton that helped to sink the MAI. The failure to bridge transatlantic differences over this issue was not the sole reason for the collapse of those negotiations in 1998, but it was high on the list of divisive topics.

Extraterritoriality continues to be a sensitive subject in transatlantic relations. US and EU diplomats are acutely aware that Congress is looking over their shoulders whenever sanctions are proposed against a third country, and that legislators may be tempted to adopt measures that aim to force reluctant

---

[25] Analysis of the Department of State, as reproduced in the *Congressional Record* Volume 141 (October 12, 1995), p. S.15106.

[26] See Chapter 7 on the purpose and use of GATT Article XXI.

[27] "Statement by the Department of Commerce and Office of the United States Trade Representative Concerning the EU's WTO Challenge to the LIBERTAD Act" (February 20, 1997).

[28] "Understanding between the United States and the European Union" (April 11, 1997).

allies into aligning their policies with those of the United States. The recent campaigns involving sanctions against Iran, Russia, and Syria were not initially as challenging as the earlier conflicts arising over Cuba, Iran, and Libya, due largely to a closer convergence in the goals of US and EU policy, but European negotiators remain wary over the prospects for new disputes on old grounds.

That transatlantic comity came under stress as soon as Donald Trump was elected. In addition to showing great disdain for the European Union, and condemning the NATO partners for their failure to match US levels of defense spending, the new administration made clear that it did not feel bound by the commitments that its predecessors had made to contain the Iranian nuclear program. While that case was in the minority of sanctions campaigns that yielded positive results, with Tehran being compelled to come to terms in order to win relief from comprehensive, global restrictions, it was one of many areas where the new administration seemed eager to disassociate itself from both its predecessor and the European Union. Its decision in 2018 to decertify the Iran deal not only meant the reimposition of US sanctions on Iran, but renewed threats of extraterritorial sanctions on the transatlantic allies. Two factors may make this new US–EU conflict more complicated than its 1990s-era predecessor: The relative capacity of the United States to bring pressure on real adversaries and putative allies has deteriorated (see later), and it comes at a time when Washington and Brussels no longer share a commitment to open markets and the multilateral system (see Chapter 16). The end result could be even more divisive than the Helms–Burton dispute of a generation ago.

AFTER HEGEMONY: DECLINING LEVERAGE AND RISING VULNERABILITY

Sanctions and strategic trade controls have always been an option for Washington, stretching back to the days when that name signified a man rather than a place, but they have not been equally important in every period of American history. The data illustrated in Table 10.1 offer one clue as to why the final years of the Cold War were something of a golden age for the study of sanctions, as this is when the targets peaked with respect both to number and diversity. It is equally significant that the number decreased thereafter, with fewer countries still subject to sanctions in the 2010s than a generation earlier. What accounts for that reduction? There are both demand-side and supply-side perspectives on that question. The decline in demand is probably the most important factor, with several of the former targets having abandoned Communism, overthrown dictators, abolished *apartheid*, or otherwise

TABLE 10.1. *Duration and Type of the Principal US Import Sanctions, 1950–2018*

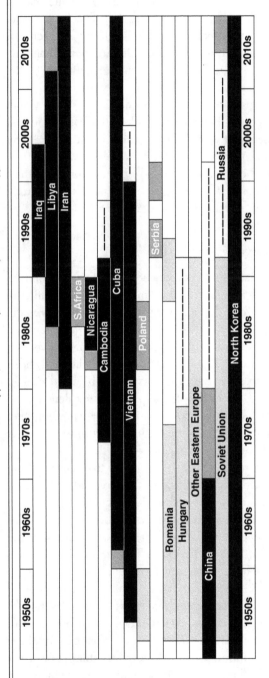

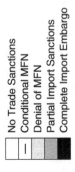

Note: The data here relate solely to import sanctions. They do not cover sanctions related to US exports, aid, investment, financial transactions, immigration, etc. Some sanctions not covered here were very limited in scope or duration. Note that there were some variations among the countries included in "Other Eastern Europe." For some countries subject to "Complete Import Embargo" there are certain, narrow exceptions.
Sources: Adapted from data in many and varied sources.

evolving so as to render sanctions moot. At the same time, US policymakers may now be less eager to go down this route because they perceive a weaker ability to wield this weapon effectively. This declining capacity is a consequence of an economic transition in which the American economic footprint has shrunk even as trade has become more significant to the US economy.

These calculations are all the more critical if the United States takes a go-it-alone approach to trade sanctions. The obvious work-around for diminished American clout is to act in concert with coalition partners, but – for reasons discussed earlier – that often proves difficult. The challenges of coalition diplomacy are greater still when Washington, Brussels, and other partners do not share a consensus view on how to manage their relations with common adversaries, or even what countries should be so designated.

US Leverage and Vulnerability

The capacity of the United States to deploy sanctions effectively depends as much on its tolerance for pain as it does on the American ability to inflict it. At issue here are *leverage* (the trade that a country controls) and *vulnerability* (the share of trade in the country's GDP). Both metrics can be calculated either with respect to a country's relationship to the world at large, or vis-à-vis specific partners. Measured this way, the United States has traditionally been in a uniquely strong position to utilize sanctions. Its status as the world's largest market gives it greater leverage, even while its comparatively low dependence on trade makes it less vulnerable to blowback from its own sanctions or other countries' counter-sanctions. In short, Washington has historically been better able than any other capital to manage the paradox of sanctions.

The data illustrated in Figure 10.1 nevertheless suggest that the trends are not favorable, and that the American advantages are lower today than they were a few decades ago. The early 1990s offer a useful point of comparison on three grounds: That is approximately when the use of sanctions peaked (see Table 10.1), it marked the end of the Cold War, and also witnessed the transition from the GATT to the WTO systems. The level of US leverage today is about half what it had been in the early 1990s, but US vulnerability is now about half again what it was in that earlier time. We should not be surprised if the median target is commensurately less awed today than it would have been by that same threat a generation ago, nor if the costs of sanctions are more apparent today to US businesses and policymakers. The challenges for sanctions enthusiasts are made greater still by the rising capacity of other parties to fill the gaps in trade and investment, which now

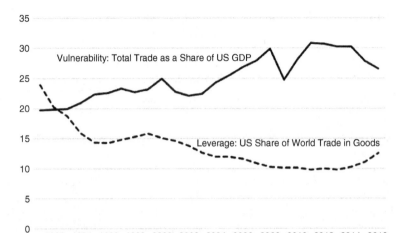

FIGURE 10.1 Changes in US leverage and vulnerability for sanctions, 1991–2016.
Note that WITS data for the United States are not available prior to 1991.
WITS data (leverage) are for goods only; total trade based on goods and services.
Source: US shares calculated from World Integrated Trade Solution (WITS) data
at https://wits.worldbank.org/CountryProfile/en/Country/WLD/Year/LTST/Trad
eFlow/Export/Partner/all/. Share of US GDP from World Bank data at https://data
.worldbank.org/indicator/NE.TRD.GNFS.ZS

include not just America's allies but also China, Russia, and even "rogue" states in the developing world.

Table 10.2 provides more specific data on bilateral relationships between the United States and likely targets for sanctions. The table shows the relative levels of trade with an eclectic list of thirty countries that (for various reasons) either are now or might at some time be targeted for pressure. One factor has not changed since the dawn of American hegemony: In any bilateral relationship involving the world's largest economy, that country's vulnerability will always be lower than its leverage because (by definition) its GDP is larger than that of its adversary. In most cases, that gap is extremely wide. With the sole exception of China, as discussed later, bilateral trade with these potential targets never accounts for more than one-third of 1% of US GDP; in most cases it is considerably below that level. The more relevant metric is instead the declining US leverage. Washington's leverage in any given relationship is typically one or two orders of magnitude higher than its vulnerability, and yet that advantage fell during 1995–2016 for two-thirds of the relationships shown in the table. In some cases the drop was quite dramatic, with four of these potential targets having had at least 10% more of their economies tied up in

TABLE 10.2. *Changes in the US Capacity to Impose Sanctions on Selected Countries, 1995 and 2016*

	US Leverage: Bilateral Trade as Share of the Partner's GDP			US Vulnerability: Bilateral Trade as Share of US GDP		
	1995	2016	Change	1995	2016	Change
US Leverage Decreased						
Algeria	5.82	3.27	−2.55	0.03	0.03	0.00
Bolivia	6.90	4.53	−2.37	0.01	0.01	0.00
China	7.76	5.08	−2.68	0.74	3.05	2.31
Dem. Rep. of the Congo	6.10	0.72	−5.38	<0.01	<0.01	0.00
Ecuador	13.87	9.89	−3.98	0.04	0.05	0.01
Egypt	5.95	1.45	−4.51	0.05	0.03	−0.02
Ethiopia	2.34	1.42	−0.92	<0.01	0.01	0.00
Indonesia	4.95	2.68	−2.27	0.14	0.13	−0.01
Liberia	38.04	9.75	−28.29	<0.01	<0.01	0.00
Nigeria	19.16	1.49	−17.67	0.07	0.03	−0.04
Pakistan	3.49	1.97	−1.53	0.03	0.03	0.00
Philippines	16.27	5.82	−10.46	0.16	0.10	−0.06
Russia	1.71	1.53	−0.18	0.09	0.11	0.02
Saudi Arabia	9.86	5.17	−4.69	0.18	0.18	0.00
Sudan	0.47	0.07	−0.40	<0.01	<0.01	0.00
Thailand	10.34	9.46	−0.88	0.23	0.21	−0.02
Turkey	2.55	1.97	−0.59	0.06	0.09	0.03
Uganda	0.61	0.46	−0.15	<0.01	<0.01	0.00
Venezuela	18.28	2.95	−15.33	0.18	0.08	−0.10
Zimbabwe	3.05	0.30	−2.75	<0.01	<0.01	0.00
US Leverage Increased						
Belarus	0.66	0.68	0.02	<0.01	<0.01	0.00
Cambodia	0.90	15.60	14.70	<0.01	0.02	0.02
Haiti	23.87	24.06	0.19	0.01	0.01	0.00
India	2.49	2.73	0.24	0.12	0.33	0.21
Nicaragua	11.55	34.78	23.22	0.01	0.02	0.02
Qatar	3.75	4.28	0.53	<0.01	0.04	0.03
South Africa	3.16	3.75	0.59	0.06	0.06	0.00
Ukraine	1.30	1.72	0.42	0.01	0.01	0.00
United Arab Emirates	3.64	6.35	2.71	0.03	0.12	0.09
Vietnam	2.19	24.78	22.59	0.01	0.27	0.26

Recent Venezuelan GDP data are for 2014. Data not shown for countries (a) with which the United States has little or no trade (e.g., Cuba, Iran, and North Korea) or (b) recent GDP data are not available (e.g., Libya and Syria).

Sources: Calculated from US International Trade Commission DataWeb data at https://dataweb .usitc.gov/ and World Bank GDP data at http://data.worldbank.org/indicator/NY.GDP.MKTP .CD.

trade with the United States in 1995 than they did in 2016. For most of the others, the drop was equal to at least 2% of their economies.

The ten exceptional cases merit additional attention, especially the three countries for which US leverage increased by more than ten percentage points. In all three cases, the partner's export success can be traced to the post-1995 liberalization of the US apparel market. Apparel accounted for 40% of Vietnam's 2016 exports to the United States, and the share was higher still for Nicaragua (50%) and Cambodia (85%). If Washington were of a mind to sanction any or all of these three countries, the concentration of their exports in a single sector would make it quite easy to devise a package of coercive measures. They nonetheless remain the exceptions that prove the rule. Most of the other countries for which US leverage increased from 1995 to 2016 saw only small rises in the relative levels of their trade with the United States.

The Special Case of China

It may be taken as a general law of modern trade policy discussions that one can speak for no more than a few minutes, nor write for more than a few pages, before using some variation on the words "especially China" or "except for China." That is as true for the political economy of US sanctions policy as it is for most other areas. In one sense, the Chinese case is not exceptional: The declining US leverage over this one partner was on the same order of magnitude as the average for all countries shown in Table 10.2. The exception relates instead to the unusually high US vulnerability. Sino-American trade in 2016 was equal to 3.1% of the American economy, or about half again as much as the combined US trade with all twenty-nine of the other countries shown in the table. China is thus the only one of these potential sanctions targets for which the US vulnerability is significant. Beijing still has more at risk in this relationship than does Washington, and yet the gap is much smaller than for any other potential target.

Nor is this merely a question of what damage the United States is willing to self-inflict via the imposition of sanctions on China. Beijing is fully capable of retaliation, and was prepared to employ counter-measures even when the magnitude of the trade relationship was just a tiny fraction of what it would one day become. That was clear as far back as 1983, when the CIA observed that Beijing "responded to US textile trade restraints with a clearly orchestrated 'retaliation,' cutting imports of product lines – wheat, soybeans and textile fibers – sales of which were important to US producers and exporters but which China could reduce temporarily without hurting its domestic economy." Chinese officials also showed a reasonably sophisticated understanding of US trade politics. In 1985 Langley expected China to target timber exports in the next round of tit-for-tat measures, should Congress enact a protectionist bill that was then under consideration. "Beijing realizes the importance of its purchases to timber producers in the Pacific Northwest," the CIA advised, "and would expect those firms to lobby against protectionist legislation."[29] Over the ensuing three decades the Chinese capacity to counterpunch grew tremendously.

This is the context in which we must see the Trump administration's targeting of China in disputes over trade and security, as well as the speed with which China replied in kind. President Trump has on many occasions stated that the problems in US trade relations with China can be traced back to the stupidity of his predecessors and their advisors, and implied that the imbalance could be easily resolved by making clear to Beijing that the United States was prepared to close its market.[30] The numbers reported here suggest that Trump is in an even less advantageous position than Bill Clinton was at the start of his presidency. Clinton had promised on the 1992 campaign trail that he would be tougher with China than was George H. W. Bush, and yet after just over a year in office he felt obliged to make a humiliating climb down by delinking China's trade status from its human rights practices (see Chapter 12). Consider the differences in leverage and vulnerability in 1995 versus 2016. If Washington were to impose across-the-board sanctions today, the pain inflicted on China would be about one-third less than that same action would have achieved in 1995, but the price imposed on the US economy would be more than four times greater. At press time, the United States and China were caught up in a blistering sequence of sanctions and counter-sanctions in what might become a widening trade war. While it is uncertain what the final result of the conflict will be, and how far Washington and Beijing will go in their hostilities or in an eventual truce, there is no doubt that China is better positioned now to trade blows with Washington than it was a generation ago.

THE DOMESTIC DIPLOMACY OF SANCTIONS

Drawing a line between the domestic and international politics of sanctions means making something of an artificial distinction. Whether we are

---

[29] Central Intelligence Agency, Directorate of Intelligence, "China: Prospects for Retaliation Against US Protectionist Legislation [Deleted]" (October 2, 1985), pp. 2–3.

[30] See, for example, www.pbs.org/newshour/politics/trump-complains-about-stupid-trade-with-china.

considering New England's revolt against the sanctions that preceded the War of 1812, the differing perspectives that distinct US government agencies took toward strategic export controls in the Cold War, or the effects that domestic interests might feel today from a round of sanctions and counter-sanctions with China, these issues are always as much about domestic diplomacy as they are about the international kind. One peculiarity of managing the paradox of sanctions is that this instrument is typically wielded by a democracy against an autocracy. The target government may thus be better positioned to ignore or suppress whatever dissent may arise at home, should the sanctions take an economic bite, while the sender's political system can make it more difficult to pursue sanctions consistently and coherently in the face of domestic opposition.

Legitimate and Illegitimate Campaigns to Undermine Sanctions

One constant in the modern political economy of sanctions is their unpopularity with the business community. Few modern cases may be cited in which protectionist industries or their allies in Congress have promoted sanctions for cynical, commercial purposes. Although the Cold War did offer some isolated episodes in manipulation,[31] they represent the exception rather than the rule. To the extent that greed motivates business interests to be involved, they have more frequently organized in opposition to sanctions than in favor of them. Speaking to the paradox of sanctions, Hirschman observed that if the losses from a stoppage of trade "fall with special weight upon certain groups within the country, these groups are likely to form a sort of 'commercial fifth column.'" The most serious of these potential vested interests, he thought, would "consist of the producers for export and of the industries using imported raw materials," and he expected these industries to "exert a powerful influence in favor of a 'friendly' attitude toward the state to the imports of which they owe their existence.[32]

Large and law-abiding firms will typically oppose sanctions through legal means, lobbying against their adoption or in favor of exceptions and reforms.

---

[31] Among the industries that supported restrictions on trade with Communist countries during the Cold War were glass makers who competed with Czechoslovakia, and glove producers who argued that soldiers could not fight a literally cold war without wool gloves. The most successful advocates were the fur producers who convinced Congress to include in the 1951 trade bill a provision banning fur imports from the Soviet Union and China. Senator Joseph McCarthy (Republican–Wisconsin) was one of the cosponsors of this measure, which appealed both to his ideological leanings (opportunistic though they were) and the economic interests of his mink-farming constituents.

[32] Hirschman (1945), p. 29.

Groups such as the National Foreign Trade Council (founded in 1914) and the closely associated USA*Engage (a coalition formed in 1997) devote much of their energies to this issue. That battle also plays out in the perennial struggles between the economic and national security agencies of the US government. The commercial attractions of high-technology exports pit the Department of Commerce and its clients against the security community, especially the Pentagon and the Department of State. The compromise is to advocate reforms in the export-licensing process that are intended to make licensing decisions quicker and more predictable; presidents have opted for that route at least as far back as 1988.[33] The advocates of a more liberal policy took full advantage of the opportunities presented by the breakup of Communism, and successive administrations have sponsored a series of initiatives aimed at reducing the bureaucratic barriers to exports of dual-use items. This started in January, 1990, when President George H. W. Bush ordered a review of CoCom policy; it led four months later to "a comprehensive proposal for modernizing the multilateral export control system."[34] Similarly, the next President Bush approved directives to shift the balance more toward export promotion,[35] and President Obama signed a presidential policy directive on conventional arms transfer policy that called for US government support to exporters.[36]

Less reputable businesses may undermine sanctions through such illicit means as smuggling and sanctions-busting.[37] The central rule of the domestic diplomacy of sanctions is simple: The level of political resistance to any given sanction will rise with the local economic pain that the measure imposes. A corollary to that rule holds that the more unpopular a sanction is, and the greater the unmet demand (and thus the inflation of prices) for the item being restricted, the more likely that the rules will be flouted. That was true in the

---

[33]   See, for example, National Security Decision Directive Number 320, "National Policy on Strategic Trade Controls" (November 20, 1988).

[34]   National Security Directive 39, "COCOM Policy towards Eastern Europe and the Soviet Union" (May 1, 1990), p. 1.

[35]   National Security Presidential Directive/NSPD-55 "Dual-Use Trade Reform" (January 22, 2008), and National Security Presidential Directive/NSPD-56 "Defense Trade Reform" (January 22, 2008).

[36]   Presidential Policy Directive/PPD-27 (January 15, 2014).

[37]   Recent scholarship has focused on the capacity of private firms in the sender state, as well as its allies, to undermine the effectiveness of sanctions. Biglaiser and Lektzian (2011) found that US investors pull out of countries targeted for sanctions prior to their imposition, but that the disinvestment is not permanent and that capital tends to return after the sanctions are imposed. Barry and Kleinberg (2015) found that firms will respond to coercive measures against a trading partner by looking for alternative sources of profit, and will shift investments to states that can provide indirect access to the sanctioned economy (i.e., sanctions-busters).

years preceding the Revolution, when patriotic merchants had mixed motivations. "For men like John Hancock," according to one account, "a concerted 'Buy American' campaign could serve as a useful nationalist smoke screen through which to increase one's profit rate, as prices rose in response to shortages." Those profits rose still further when the patriots resorted to smuggling to restock their shelves. This case was special, yet not unique. Frank provided numerous historical examples of "exceedingly wealthy men who speak forcefully about nationalism in public but who, in private, use economic nationalism to feather their own economic nests, while privately violating the very economic boycotts they so vehemently pronounce."[38]

The lines that separate legal from illegal anti-sanctions activity depend in the first instance on how fully Congress empowers the agency that is charged with enforcement. That point is illustrated by one of the classic examples of a failed sanctions campaign, when in the 1930s both the League of Nations and the United States aimed to halt Italy's aggression against Abyssinia (modern Ethiopia). The State Department backed the league's oil sanctions, but while it could ask companies to comply it had no authority to compel them. Larger companies with greater concerns over their public image did as asked, but that only enhanced the rent-seeking opportunities for smaller companies that "hired tankers, bought gasoline, delivered it to the Italian armies, and made sizeable profits."[39] Texaco offers a contemporary and comparable example, even if its public penance was only retroactive. In the 1930s this firm was headed not by a Texan but a Norwegian, and Torkild Rieber's admiration for Adolf Hitler eventually became an embarrassment. The firm's 1940 decision to sponsor the New York Metropolitan Opera's weekly live broadcast was intended as "a way of establishing itself as an upright corporate citizen."[40] That act of philanthropic atonement lasted until 2004, with the final Texaco-sponsored broadcast aptly being Wagner's *Götterdämmerung*.[41]

Partisanship and Constituent Interests in Favor of Sanctions

Sanctions policy in a democracy faces two problems. As we have already seen, economic interests will often organize to oppose the imposition or effective implementation of those measures; the paradox of sanctions makes this instrument difficult to use effectively. Conversely, there are times when political

---

[38] Frank (1999), p. 21.
[39] Kindleberger (1970), p. 97.
[40] www.trilliuminvest.com/chevron-texaco-axes-metropolitan-opera-sponsorship-figuring-that-63-years-of-atonement-is-enougha/.
[41] www.nytimes.com/2003/05/21/arts/chevrontexaco-to-stop-sponsoring-met-s-broadcasts.html.

interests may pressure the state to use sanctions more vigorously than a cold calculation of net national interests might counsel. Just as business interests typically form the core of the anti-sanctions lobby, diasporas or other political groups usually take the lead in promoting sanctions. And while businesses may find their most natural ally in the Department of Commerce, the proponents of sanctions will typically focus their lobbying on elected officials.

When members of Congress vote on sanctions they may have to weigh economic against ideological pressures. The choices can be especially difficult in cases where the legislator's partisan inclinations point in contradictory directions. A modern Republican's pro-trade instincts might normally lean toward opposition to new sanctions (or removal of existing sanctions), but what if the target country in question is a left-leaning regime that the same legislator might normally oppose on ideological grounds? The dilemma also arises, albeit in reverse, for a modern Democrat.

The data summarized in Table 10.3, which cover three countries for which the United States normalized trade relations, imply that the answer depends on the actual level of trade with the country in question. At issue in all three cases was the other country's status under the Jackson–Vanik law. As explained in Chapter 11, this provision in the Trade Act of 1974 provides a roadmap for the extension of MFN treatment to Communist countries. That treatment can be extended provisionally if the country (a) concludes an MFN agreement with the United States and (b) does not restrict its citizens' freedom of emigration. The law further allows for the permanent extension of MFN relations if Congress removes the country altogether from the Jackson–Vanik law. China, Russia, and Vietnam each initially received MFN on a conditional basis and then, after the passage of a decade or two, were graduated from the law. In all three cases, trade between the United States and the partner in question was quite low when the first vote was cast, but the partner's share of US imports grew substantially by the time that Congress was asked to approve permanent normalization. All three cases show the same pattern: Democrats and Republicans voted according to their respective party's political leanings the first time, but were more likely to fall in line with their party's trade policy positions after trade flows increased. That meant rising support from Republicans, and declining support from Democrats. The higher the economic stakes, the greater the chances that legislators will view an initiative as trade policy rather than foreign policy.

The data suggest that it does not take much actual trade to prompt legislators to switch over from political to economic calculations. It may depend as much on the import-sensitivity of the products involved as it does on the overall magnitude of trade. Consider the case of Vietnam, which in 2006

TABLE 10.3. *Degrees of Partisanship in Votes on Normalizing Trade Relations,*
1980–2012
Average percentages in the House of Representatives voting in favor of extending
MFN/NTR treatment; cases listed in order of most recent vote on permanent NTR

	Republicans (A)	Democrats (B)	Partisan Difference (A – B)	Share of US Imports in Year of Vote
China				
1980: Approve MFN agreement	54.4	89.4	−35.0	0.4%
2000: Approve permanent NTR	74.2	34.6	+39.6	8.3%
Change from 1980 to 2000:	+19.8	−54.8		+7.9%
Vietnam				
1994: Lift the embargo	4.2	84.8	−80.6	<0.1%
2006: Approve permanent NTR	67.6	48.9	+18.7	0.4%
Change from 1994 to 2006:	+63.4	−35.9		+0.4%
Russia				
1991: Approve MFN agreement	68.1	90.4	−22.3	0.2%
2012: Approve permanent NTR	97.4	78.9	+18.5	1.3%
Change from 1991 to 2012:	+29.3	−11.5		+1.1%

Note that "most favored nation" (MFN) was the terminology employed prior to 1998, the year that Congress decreed that it would henceforth be called "normal trade relations" (NTR). There is no substantive difference between MFN and NTR.
Data for US imports from Russia in 1991 are for all of the Soviet Union.
Source: Calculated from roll-call vote data at www.congress.gov/roll-call-votes. Votes prior to 1989 are from the *Congressional Quarterly Almanac.*

provided just 0.4% of total US imports. Apparel accounted for 38% of US imports from Vietnam that year, and the country had quickly advanced to fifth place among foreign suppliers; by 2008 it would be second only to China. That was evidently a strong enough performance to make Democrats much warier in 2006 than they had been in 1994.

The Cuban case underlines the point that presidents can be just as subject to electoral pressures as are members of Congress. The enactment of both the Cuban Democracy Act and Helms–Burton can be attributed in part to election-year pressures, being approved in the years that Bush (1992) and Clinton (1996) sought reelection. One consideration that undoubtedly weighed in these two incumbents' minds was the Cuban-American vote in New Jersey (which had fifteen electoral votes in the 1990s) and especially Florida (twenty-five votes). Taken together, these two states offered almost one in seven of the 270 votes needed to capture the Electoral College. Those pressures were especially strong for the Clinton administration, which had originally opposed Helms–Burton but then changed its position following a February, 1996 incident in which Cuba shot down two airplanes piloted by Cuban-Americans.

THE PARADOX, AND CONTINUED ATTRACTION, OF SANCTIONS

The events reviewed in this chapter speak to why sanctions fail more often than they succeed. Some of the reasons for that low batting average relate to obstacles that the sender must overcome, especially the opportunities that a democracy provides for disadvantaged sectors to lobby against a policy for which they are expected to bear the costs. Conversely, the autocracies against which these sanctions are directed may be better able to suppress domestic opposition. The data also show that the capacity of the United States to pursue an effective sanctions policy may diminish as a consequence of the reduced American ability to inflict pain on a target state, the rising US vulnerability to the effects of its own sanctions or the other side's counter-sanctions, and the renewed prospects for intra-allied conflict.

Despite these inherent problems and frequent failures, sanctions have a persistent appeal for policymakers in the United States. We ought to expect this to continue three reasons. The first reason is that the world is not becoming a friendlier place. The data reviewed above in Table 10.1 showed, as we might expect, that the number of major sanctions declined in the immediate aftermath of the Cold War. That period saw not only the end of a long-term, global struggle, but also coincided with the abolition of *apartheid* and a hiatus in conflicts with Soviet client states. It did not take long for old frictions to take new form, however, and for still others to emerge in new corners. The number of targets has not yet returned to the levels achieved a generation ago, but may be moving in that direction.

Another reason why we might expect sanctions to remain a popular menu item is a simple function of psychology. Partial reinforcement is based on the principle of "accelerated resistance to extinction after occasional reinforcement,"[42] meaning that sporadic rewards may more effectively

---

[42]   https://psychologydictionary.org/partial-reinforcement-effect/.

encourage a given behavior than do continuous rewards. Policymakers might favor sanctions in more or less the same way that amateur gamblers are drawn to slot machines, where the occasional thrill of a win – with all of its gongs and flashing lights – may be so exhilarating as to make them forget that the machine swallows more silver than it disgorges. The minority of sanctions campaigns that produce favorable results may carry greater weight with statesmen and elected officials than do the larger number that flop, and on net the total perceived rewards may exceed the total actual costs.

A final reason why we might expect sanctions to remain an important tool in US foreign policy is not because they are effective, but because they solve the more immediate problem of being seen to "do something" in response to intractable problems. The cynic's rejoinder to the question of whether sanctions are effective is not a simple yes or no, but another question: Effective at what? Foreign economic policy begins and ends at home, and the policymaker who opts for this approach may be more focused on an immediate domestic problem than on long-term prospects for relations with the target state. As between doing nothing and letting slip the dogs of war, sanctions might well offer a happy medium. Or to quote a lyric that made its own contribution to the great debates of the 1980s, "It's what happens when your choices/Are narrowed to fashion or violence."[43] There may be times when sanctions amount to little more than a foreign policy fashion statement, but that symbolism may be less costly to the sender than the all too real violence of war.

That last point may be especially important for policymakers who deal with nuclear states such as China and Russia. The former country is far more rich and powerful now than it was a generation ago, and the decline of the latter has been just as spectacular, and yet each of them remains fully capable of responding in kind to any military action that the United States might employ against them. That simple fact makes policymakers' minds naturally turn to other, less lethal means by which they might seek to coerce Moscow or Beijing – or at least be seen trying to do so. In Chapter 11 we will consider how this has been a persistent theme in US relations with Russia, but also how the paradox of sanctions has frustrated the repeated American efforts at economic coercion. We will observe just the opposite side of the problem in Chapter 12, which shows how the revival of close economic ties between the United States and China makes it very costly for American presidents to carry through with their threats.

---

[43]   The Waitresses, "Jimmy Tomorrow," on the album *Wasn't Tomorrow Wonderful?* (1982).

11

Russo-American Relations and the Paradox of Sanctions

I have no business in the U.S. or with Americans. It doesn't bother me. Except now I'll
stop going to McDonald's.

Evgeny Prigozhin's response to sanctions imposed by the U.S. Treasury
(March 15, 2018)

INTRODUCTION

Sometimes called "Putin's chef," and more pointedly known for his coordinating role in Russia's 2016 election meddling, Evgeny Prigozhin embodies
the established pattern and current status of sanctions in Russo-American
relations. For well over a century, the United States has periodically sanctioned Russia on either a wholesale, country-wide basis, or – as has now
become the fashion – focused on a retail basis against individuals such as
Prigozhin. The nonchalance with which this oligarch received the news that
he had been named and shamed also followed a well-established pattern.
Sanctions on Russia have been just as ineffective as they are frequent, owing to
the low level of economic relations between the two countries. This simple
truth transcended the rise and fall of Communism. Politics came before
economics during the final years of the Romanov dynasty, remained in that
order for the eight decades that followed Lenin's victory, and have not changed position in the post–Cold War world. Low economic stakes make it
politically easy for Washington to impose sanctions, but also ensure that
these measures are equally painless for Moscow to endure.

This chapter presents a series of cases that collectively form
a multifunctional study that speaks not just to the paradox of sanctions, but
also to the movement of people and the conduct of diaspora diplomacy.
Migration was central to each of these episodes, being either the cause of
the dispute or the lever used in retaliation. While trade can affect the preferences of the American public, immigration will help to determine who

comprises that public in the first place. The first significant confrontation in the nineteenth century was sparked by the treatment that Russian officials meted out to Jewish Americans who wished to visit their relatives, and Soviet restrictions on Jewish emigration were a leading source of friction in the twentieth century. Disputes over official anti-Semitism have now receded, but both the United States and Russia still fall back on travel restrictions in their mutual exchanges of twenty-first century sanctions.

The episodes chronicled in this chapter show a great deal of continuity in their causes and their conduct, but the story takes a new twist in the age of Trump. The latest incident started when the United States replaced 1970s-vintage trade sanctions with a new set of travel and financial restrictions on specific persons, and Russia's first response to these "smart" sanctions came in kind: It banned the adoption of orphans by American foster parents. Moscow also mounted a sub rosa influence operation, supporting the US presidential candidate who seemed more favorably disposed toward their interests. The Kremlin's original aim seems to have been limited to weakening the victor in that election, and it may ultimately do just that – only the president whom they undermined was not the one they expected to win.

US–RUSSIAN TRADE RELATIONS BEFORE THE REVOLUTION

The Russo-American political relationship was cordial, though low key, in the first century of American independence. The two countries' common interests were based on shared antipathies toward third parties. Both chafed at British domination of the seas, with Catherine the Great having formed the Armed Neutrality of 1780–1783 in tacit alliance with the Americans during the Revolutionary War, and in 1854 they reached a precedential treaty built around the cherished American principle of "free ships make free goods" (see Chapter 7).[1] They also felt a mutual animosity toward France, which invaded Russia in 1812 and threatened to recognize the Confederacy half a century later. Just as American merchantmen won the gratitude of Czar Alexander I by defying Napoleon I's blockade,[2] Czar Alexander II repaid the debt by opposing Napoleon III's proposals to favor the rebellious South.

These somewhat parallel political interests were not matched by close commercial ties. The data in Figure 11.1 show just how small Russo-American trade was

---

[1] Remarkably, this treaty survived all of the subsequent changes in government and is still in force with respect to the United States, the Russian Federation, Ukraine, and Nicaragua (which acceded in 1855).

[2] See Marvin (1902), pp. 119–121.

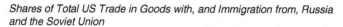

Shares of Total US Trade in Goods with, and Immigration from, Russia
and the Soviet Union

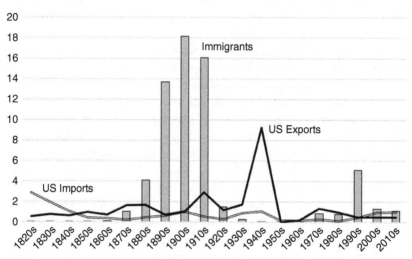

FIGURE 11.1 US trade and immigration from Russia and the Soviet Union, 1821–2016.

Note: Latest trade data are for 2016; latest immigration data are for 2013. Decades are 1821–1830, 1831–1840, etc.

Source: Trade data for 1821–1850 are from Homans (1857). Trade data from 1851 to 1890 are from US Bureau of Statistics (1896a and 1896b). Trade data from 1891 to 1990 are from the Statistical Abstract of the United States (various issues). Trade data from 1991 to 2016 are from the US International Trade Commission's DataWeb at https://dataweb.usitc.gov/. Immigration data for 1821–2000 are calculated from figures in US Department of Justice (2001), Table 2, for 2001–2010 from US Immigration and Customs Enforcement data at www.dhs.gov/xlibrary/assets/statistics/yearbook/2010/table21d.xls, and for 2011–2013 for that same source at www.dhs.gov/publication/yearbook-immigration-statistics-2013-naturalizations.

in the nineteenth century. The most significant exchanges at that time concerned land and people. Russia could have been a territorial rival of the United States, with its North American outposts stretching from the Aleutian Islands to northern California, but this prospect ended when Washington bought Alaska in 1867. For less than two cents an acre, the United States acquired a vast territory that yielded great wealth from the Gold Rush to the Alaska oil pipeline. The conduct of the Cold War, and perhaps even its outcome, may have been very different if the Soviet Union held a huge swath of North American real estate.

    The United States also attracted a mass migration of Russian Jews, especially after the 1881 assassination of Czar Alexander II sparked a new round of repression. In 1880 there were only 35,722 Americans who had been born in Russia (not all of them Jews), representing just 0.1% of the population. New waves of immigrants boosted this share to 0.6% in 1890, 1.1% in 1900, and 2.5% in 1910.[3] By the turn of the century, many American Jews had risen to positions of prominence in business, politics, and the law. This diaspora lost no love on either the czars or (after a time) their Communist successors. Beginning in the 1860s, tensions arose over Russian pogroms and mistreatment of American Jews. Some of these incidents led to representations at the highest level, offering an early example of human rights as an object of US foreign policy. The most persistent problem was the "passport question," with Russian officials refusing entry to foreign Jews and denying visas to naturalized American citizens who hoped to visit their Russian relatives. Russian law also forbade subjects from becoming citizens of a foreign country without permission. This law, which anticipated the future Soviet emigration policy, sent some visiting US citizens to prison.

Trade and politics became entangled when American diplomats and Jewish leaders contended that the Russian refusal to honor US passports violated the terms of the 1832 Treaty of Commerce and Navigation. Article I provided for the reciprocal liberty of persons "to sojourn and reside in all parts whatsoever of said territories," and guaranteed that they would "enjoy ... the same security and protection as natives of the country wherein they reside." Russian officials took the position that they fulfilled this obligation by treating American Jews just as shabbily as Russian Jews. Refusing to recognize US passports was, by this reasoning, no different than denying free internal transit to the czar's subjects. This interpretation of the treaty became a cause célèbre in the Jewish community. Americans of other faiths joined this struggle, in part because the Russian government also restricted the entry of Baptist missionaries, Catholic priests, and other religious travelers.

The issue divided the legislative and executive branches of the US government. The House of Representatives first passed a resolution on this topic in 1879, calling for renegotiation of the treaty. The House approved several similar resolutions in later years, but it would be decades before the Senate would also favor abrogation or renegotiation of the treaty. Political support grew after the turn of the century, with the Democratic and Republican party platforms of 1904 and 1908 condemning Russian policy. In 1911 the House approved a resolution of abrogation by a vote of 301–1. The Taft administration felt obliged to act when the Senate seemed certain to pass the same resolution. Secretary of State Philander Knox told the Russian ambassador that "the easiest way to avoid the embarrassments likely to be

---

[3] Calculated from U.S. Department of Commerce (1975), pp. 14 and 116.

produced by a discussion of the pending question in Congress would be" to terminate the old treaty and negotiate a new one.[4] The Russian foreign minister took up the first half of this proposal, and thus the mutual denial of MFN treatment, even though he thought it "incomprehensible that the United States should deliberately consider the sacrifice of a present and prospective market of hundreds of millions of dollars." The parties did not pursue his suggested "arrangement by which the United States might cooperate for the transfer of all Jews from Russia to the United States."[5]

The abrogation of the treaty did not cause a major downturn in commerce, which was soon stimulated by the outbreak of the First World War. American exports to Russia peaked in 1917 at $407 million (7% of the US total), which was fifteen times higher than the level achieved in 1913. What went up soon went down, with 1918 exports to revolution-torn Russia plummeting to a mere $18 million. This boom-and-bust pattern would be repeated a generation later.

US–SOVIET TRADE RELATIONS

World history entered a new era in October, 1917, when the Bolsheviks ousted a provisional government that had deposed the czar. America was just then on a temporary detour from its traditional isolation, and joined with England and France in a futile intervention to overthrow the new Soviet government. The Communists' calls for world revolution also deeply worried American industries and policymakers, prompting the first in a series of "red scares." While the United States and its allies failed to topple the revolutionary government, Washington's withdrawal of diplomatic recognition – then still a novelty in American diplomacy – would live on for sixteen years.

Restoration and Removal of MFN Treatment

President Roosevelt recognized the Soviet Union through an exchange of notes in 1933. Washington's principal objective was to suppress interference in the US political system, but American officials also hoped to expand exports. They were not interested in standard trade negotiations, arguing that MFN access to the Russian market was meaningless as long as the state controlled foreign trade. The US side insisted that Moscow make a quantified

---

[4]   Letter cited in a December 15, 1911 cable from the secretary of state to the US ambassador in Russia, in US House of Representatives (1918), p. 695.

[5]   Cable of the American ambassador to the secretary of state dated December 16, 1911, in ibid., pp. 696–697. See Chapter 12 for a comparable declaration made by Chinese leader Deng Xiaoping.

commitment to increase purchases of American products. In exchange for the renewal of MFN treatment, Soviet officials reluctantly pledged in a 1935 side letter to purchase $35 million of American goods. Trade actually grew beyond that level, and also beat the $40 million goal set in a 1937 agreement, before soaring in the Second World War. Vastly outdoing their czarist predecessors in the last war, and taking full advantage of the Lend-Lease Act, this embattled ally took in about one-fifth of US exports during 1942–1945.

The new struggle began almost as soon as the guns fell silent in Central Europe. All of the opening moves had been made within two years of the armistice: Pro-Moscow governments took control in Eastern and Central Europe, Winston Churchill gave a name to the "iron curtain" that bisected Europe, President Truman committed the United States to defeating Communist insurgencies in Greece and Turkey, and the Marshall Plan was born. Trade quickly reverted to the established pattern, especially after Foreign Minister Molotov rejected American aid (an offer that was not made in earnest). It declined still further in 1949 with the imposition of Western export controls on strategically significant goods.

The Cold War took a dangerous turn when war broke out between the two Koreas in 1950, provoking congressional demands for economic sanctions. In its own internal deliberations, the Truman administration concluded that control of strategic exports to the Soviet Union was more important than restrictions on imports, and that the West otherwise benefited from continued trade with the East – including imports of strategic minerals. The White House thus preferred to leave MFN treatment in place. Republicans were still the party of protection, and were also highly critical of how Democratic presidents Roosevelt and Truman had dealt with the Soviet Union and "lost" China. Given the political climate of the time, government officials were understandably sensitive to charges that the State Department was employing the trade agreements program to benefit Communist countries.

The Republican Congress used its leverage over trade policy to force a withdrawal of MFN from Communist countries. The president's tariff-negotiating authority was due to expire, and Congress wrote an MFN-denial provision into the Trade Agreements Extension Act of 1951. It required that "as soon as practicable" the president must "take such action as is necessary to suspend, withdraw or prevent" the extension of concessions to imports from the Soviet Union and "any nation or area dominated or controlled by the foreign government or organization controlling the world Communist move-ment." If Truman vetoed the bill he would have denied himself the ability to conduct further tariff negotiations in the GATT. The United States formally withdrew MFN treatment from the Soviet Union through a diplomatic note that took effect on January 5, 1952. Similar orders were issued with respect to nearly all Communist countries.[6]

The removal of MFN treatment was only one of many steps that the US government took to restrict trade with the Soviet Union, and not among the most consequential. A later CIA analysis concluded that the subsequent decline in imports could not be attributed solely to higher tariffs. The "only item of significance which was apparently affected by the withdrawal of MFN treatment was tobacco," and many goods for which US imports from the Soviet Union "declined or disappeared by 1952 were either duty-free, or the differential between the 1930 and the MFN rates was negligible or nonexistent."[7] Put another way, these sanctions came early enough in the US hegemony that trade negotiations had not yet produced a significant gap between the MFN and non-MFN rates.

The Soviet Union and the GATT

At three points in the Cold War there was some prospect that the Soviet Union might join the multilateral trading system. It had participated in the Bretton Woods conference of 1944, which created the World Bank and the International Monetary Fund, but even after the Soviets secured favorable terms (with the active assistance of a compromised American official)[8] it still opted not to join either of those financial institutions. Four years later, Moscow decided at the last minute not to attend the Havana conference that produced the International Trade Organization charter. Five of the other six invitees that declined to attend were either neighbors or satellites of the Soviet Union.[9] The rifts between the former allies had already grown wide.

The 1951 law and its successor statutes would govern US policy toward the accession of Communist countries to the GATT and then the WTO. Because these laws placed conditions on the extension of MFN treatment, they prevented full US adherence to the core obligations of GATT Article I (i.e., universal and unconditional MFN treatment). It therefore became a firm

---

[6] Yugoslavia received an exemption for reasons of international politics, and Poland would be exempted a few years later primarily for reasons of US diaspora politics.

[7] Central Intelligence Agency, Directorate of Intelligence, "Probable Effects of Most Favored Nation Treatment on Soviet Exports to the United States" (May, 1970), p. 2.

[8] Historians still dispute the nature of the Soviet relationship with Harry Dexter White, the senior American official at the Bretton Woods conference. The weight of evidence suggests that White was at least unusually sympathetic to the Soviet position, but opinions differ on whether he was formally an agent of influence. See Schlesinger (2004), Skidelsky (2000), and Steil (2013).

[9] Brown (1950), p. 135.

principle of US policy to invoke the non-application clause (GATT Article XXXV, now WTO Article XIII) upon the GATT or WTO accession of any country that is subject to this law or its successors. That special, political provision of GATT law allows any country to act as if another country were not a GATT contracting party or a WTO member. The practical consequences of non-application are that (a) each party may deny MFN treatment to the other, and (b) neither of them may bring complaints over this or other discriminatory acts to the multilateral dispute-settlement system. The United States could fully recognize a country's GATT or WTO status only if Congress enacted legislation that "graduated" it from the list of partners subject to these conditions. This is why Congress had the final say in the WTO accessions of China and Russia.

Soviet participation in GATT was also on the table in 1972, when Washington proposed this as a natural complement to détente. Secretary of Commerce Peter Peterson reportedly sent a letter to Minister of Foreign Trade Nikolai Patolichev, inviting the Soviet Union to take part in the Tokyo Round; this is one reason why the Tokyo Ministerial Declaration of 1973 was open to participation by countries that were not yet GATT contracting parties. The Soviets never responded to the invitation. The Politburo instead reached a determination in 1972 that "at present, it is not practical for the USSR to participate in the GATT in any form, be it observer or full member."[10]

The Soviet Union showed renewed interest in the multilateral system during the waning years of the Cold War, but this time it was Washington's turn to reject the initiative. Moscow had hinted at its desire to join the Uruguay Round negotiations in late 1985, and made an official request a month before the round was launched in 1986. This was barred by a provision in the ministerial declaration that, in contrast to the Tokyo Round declaration, was "written specifically to block Soviet and Bulgarian participation."[11] The Soviets later applied for GATT observer status in 1990, which is typically a prelude to formal accession negotiations. The United States and Japan initially opposed this request, but soon relented in the face of near-unanimous support from other countries. They nonetheless stressed that the favorable "decision on observer status should in no way prejudge a possible future application for accession."[12] No more came of this before the collapse of the Soviet Union.

---

[10] The author is grateful to Victor Ognivtsev for these facts and quotes, based on documents that are not as yet publicly available.

[11] Haus (1992), p. 92.

[12] Ibid., p. 96.

Détente and the Jackson–Vanik Amendment

The Soviet preference for autarky suited both Washington and Moscow for most of the Cold War, and reinforced the deceptive appearance of a clean separation between economic and security issues in the struggle. While the Eisenhower administration was publicly committed to the rollback of Communism, as opposed to Truman's less ambitious containment policy, its security and economic policies were not much different. Presidents Kennedy and Johnson were more occupied by conflicts at the periphery of superpower relations than by economic relations between them, although both authorized wheat sales to the Soviets. And while President Johnson proposed in 1966 that Congress allow him to renegotiate MFN treatment with the Soviet Union and Eastern Europe, it took Congress two years even to hold hearings on the proposal.

Richard Nixon tried to break this pattern when he pursued détente with the Soviet Union, using the normalization of trade relations as a sweetener. In 1971 he removed wheat from the list of products that required an export license, and the next year the two countries signed a $750 million, three-year wheat deal. Washington and Moscow also negotiated a much broader agreement in October, 1972 that would restore MFN treatment and pay off Soviet Lend-Lease debts. Because the congressionally mandated denial of MFN treatment was still law, the agreement required the approval of Congress. The Nixon administration therefore proposed that the 1951 legislation, which had been redrafted in 1962 and 1963, be redefined once more. The administration's proposal would provide that MFN treatment be extended to a nonmarket economy either upon its accession to the GATT or whenever Congress approved a bilateral agreement providing this benefit.

Politics again intruded, echoing the same anti-Semitic themes that had dominated relations before the Russian Revolution. The trade agreement came several weeks after the Soviet Union imposed an exit fee on emigrants. The unstated purpose of the fee, which rose according to the emigrant's education, was to restrict Jewish emigration to Israel and the United States. Whereas in 1911 Congress demanded that the United States deny MFN treatment to Russia because that country would not allow American Jews into the country, it now refused to grant MFN until the Soviets let Russian Jews out of the country. Democrats adopted the same tactics that Republicans had employed in 1951. President Nixon had been hoping since 1969 to launch a new GATT round, but had yet to secure the necessary grant of negotiating authority. Senator Henry Jackson (Democrat–Washington) and Representative Charles Vanik (Democrat–Ohio) linked this request to their insistence on a stricter policy toward the Soviet Union, introducing proposals in their respective chambers that would have denied MFN treatment to any nonmarket economy that impeded free emigration. Although the administration strongly opposed this initiative, Jackson and Vanik won bipartisan support. Their proposal became part of the already lengthy maneuvering over what would become the Trade Act of 1974. It got a further boost in October, 1973 when Egypt and Syria launched a surprise attack on Israel, and the Soviet Union supported its client states.[13]

The votes on the Jackson–Vanik amendment offer a test of the influence that economic and diaspora groups have on members of Congress. On December 11, 1973, the House rejected by 106–298 a motion to strike this provision from the bill. The margin of opposition to the motion, and thus support for Jackson–Vanik, was notably but not overwhelmingly greater among Democrats (82%) than Republicans (63%). The more interesting pattern concerned the ethnic composition of legislators' constituencies. Only 5 of the 106 votes against the Jackson–Vanik amendment were cast by congressmen from districts in which the Jewish population was greater than the national mean (13,814). Representatives who voted against the amendment had, on average, just 3,045 Jews in their districts; among those who voted to retain the amendment, the average was 17,623.[14] American farmers had profited from wheat exports under détente, but did not provide much countervailing pressure in this debate. Even in the country's most agricultural districts, there was less than a 50–50 chance that the legislator would vote against the sanctions. Other economic groups expressed only muted opposition to the proposal. Exporters valued the extension of new negotiating authority more highly than the political price that Congress demanded, and could not credibly threaten to withhold their support for the pending trade bill as a whole.[15] Business groups were not about to jeopardize the global gains they expected from a new GATT round for the sake of as-yet unrealized trade opportunities with the Soviet Union.

American and Soviet negotiators sought to salvage the agreement, and Secretary of State Kissinger received informal assurances that Soviet emigration policies would be liberalized. This formed the basis of a deal between

---

[13] See Bard (1987), p. 50.

[14] These calculations are from the author's estimations of the numbers of Jews in each congressional district as of 1972, based on data in Bureau of the Census (1973) and Fine and Himmelfarb (1973), pp. 308–315.

[15] For a list of the firms and groups that expressed reservations over Jackson–Vanik, and yet did not place a high priority on defeating this initiative, see U.S. House of Representatives (1973), pp. 5267–5276.

Senator Jackson and the Ford administration in October, 1974 by which the bill would allow a president to waive the freedom-of-emigration requirements for a country that made significant progress. The bill passed, but the deal fell apart when Moscow denied in 1975 that it had agreed to change its policies under threat of sanctions. The Kremlin also retaliated by letting out fewer Jews, and by taking in less American wheat. In the end, none of the parties involved – Soviet or American, economic or political, urban or rural – were satisfied with the outcome. This episode remains Exhibit A for critics who argue that sanctions are either ineffective or counterproductive.

The End-Game of the Cold War

The Cold War went into a higher gear when Ronald Reagan took office in 1981, and for a time it appeared that the two superpowers might be accelerating to an armed confrontation. In retrospect, this was the moment when the predictions made in NSC-68 – the 1950 paper laying out the National Security Council's vision of economic and military containment – finally began to be realized. The economic and human costs of the Soviet Union's decade-long war in Afghanistan, coupled with the burden of a stepped-up arms race and stagnation in Eastern Europe, pushed its economy to the breaking point.

Mikhail Gorbachev took power in 1985, hoping to restore vitality through *glasnost* (openness), *perestroika* (economic restructuring), and closer engagement with the West. His reforms proved to be too little, too late. The dissidents grew bolder, ordinary people lost faith in the Communist system, and the republics sought independence. By the time that George H. W. Bush became president in 1989, the Soviet Union was on the brink of dissolution. Some of its better-heeled citizens were already heading for the exits, and Moscow was either unwilling or unable to enforce its former restrictions. In place of the old *refusenik* problem, there were now "enormous backlogs of applicants for admission as refugees to the United States."[16] The Bush administration sent extra staff to Moscow to process the applications, and promoted legislation "to establish a special immigration category that would allow 30,000 people of special foreign policy interest to enter the United States each year for five years."[17]

Détente revived in the final months of the Soviet Union's existence, one product of which was a new US–Soviet trade agreement. It provided for

---

[16] National Security Directive 27, "Soviet Emigration Policy" (October 2, 1989), p. 1.
[17] Ibid., p. 2.

reciprocal MFN tariff treatment within the conditional terms of the Jackson–Vanik law. Bush submitted the agreement to Congress in August, 1991, just days before Communist hard-liners launched a failed coup against Gorbachev. Congress approved the agreement in November, and Bush signed it into law on December 9. It came too late to affect trade with the collapsing empire, as the Soviet Union ceased to exist before the end of the month. This agreement was nevertheless put into effect for Russia and several other successor states. The newly independent Russian Federation gained MFN access to the US market on June 17, 1992, more than forty years after the Soviet Union lost this status.

TRADE RELATIONS WITH THE RUSSIAN FEDERATION

The United States and Russia enjoyed a brief honeymoon of sorts, but concern remained over the treatment of Russian Jews. This was the principal obstacle to the full normalization of trade relations, which could not legally be accomplished without the graduation of Russia from Jackson–Vanik. While it might be argued that Washington's refusal to take this step had no practical significance, the continued imposition of political conditions looked like a vote of no confidence in the permanence of post-Soviet reforms. This issue also made for a more complicated path toward Russian entry into the trading system. Moscow began negotiating for GATT accession in 1993, but Washington could not extend full GATT or WTO treatment to Moscow until Russia was graduated.

Early Attempts at a Reset

Russian statesmen placed a high priority on eliminating this obstacle. At the Vancouver Summit in 1993, President Boris Yeltsin asked that the United States graduate Russia from Jackson–Vanik and remove the other legal discriminations. That would have complemented other steps that Washington and Moscow took in the 1990s to normalize economic and political relations. In addition to supporting Russian membership in the WTO, the United States favored its participation in the Wassenaar Arrangement arms-control group in 1996 and the Group of Eight (formerly seven) leading economies in 1998. But while the Clinton administration might have wanted to comply, it encountered sharp opposition from an American Jewish community that still feared a resurgence of official anti-Semitism. The business and agricultural groups that supported Russia's graduation were as outgunned in this episode as they had been in 1911, 1951, and 1972. The 1993 act "For Reform In Emerging New

Democracies and Support and Help for Improved Partnership (FRIENDSHIP) with Russia, Ukraine, and Other New Independent States" struck several of the less consequential Cold War laws from the books, but left Jackson–Vanik untouched. President Clinton also designated Russia for benefits under the Generalized System of Preferences, meaning that Russia now received treatment that was even better than MFN.

The outbreak of the new War on Terror temporarily pushed Washington and Moscow closer together, prompting the George W. Bush administration to propose in late 2001 that Russia and six other former Soviet republics be granted permanent NTR (PNTR)[18] through graduation from Jackson–Vanik. American Jewish organizations now had a decade of positive experience, and the successor organizations of the National Conference on Soviet Jewry and the Union of Councils for Soviet Jews both favored graduation.[19] Their switch was almost certainly a necessary condition for graduation, but it was not sufficient. Graduation would also require support from economic interests, and here too the landscape had changed.

The slow rise in bilateral trade came with some sharp growing pains. The output of Russia's steel, aluminum, and uranium industries was no longer channeled to the production of arms and ammunition, but was instead causing disruption in Western markets. This led to a flurry of antidumping cases, the negotiation of an agreement curtailing Russian aluminum production in 1994, and another to restrain steel exports in 1999. Later complaints centered on Russian agricultural import restrictions. The US poultry industry should have been part of a new "Russia Lobby," insofar as this country briefly became the industry's largest export market, but Russian poultry protection instead alienated the whole US agribusiness complex. Groups such as the American Farm Bureau Federation took the position that Russia's graduation from Jackson–Vanik should be withheld until the terms of Russian accession to the WTO were settled, including resolution of the chicken dispute.[20]

The policy debate in 2001–2002 thus represented the mirror image of 1972–1974, with Jewish groups now acquiescing to graduation and agricultural groups insisting upon conditions. Of all the Russo-American diplomatic

---

[18] Since 1998 it has been US law and policy to use the term "normal trade relations" (NTR) in place of the more traditional MFN, and to designate unconditional MFN as permanent NTR (PNTR). The terms NTR and PNTR are used hereafter in this chapter, and in the corresponding sections of the chapter on US relations with China (Chapter 12), insofar as this is the proper US legal terminology. In deference to global practice, and to avoid confusion, elsewhere in this book the more traditional term MFN is used when discussing such issues as the non-preferential tariff rates of the United States (both before and after 1998).

[19] See U.S. House of Representatives (2002).

[20] See the group's testimony in the April 11, 2002 hearing, op. cit., pp. 58–61.

episodes recounted here, this is the only time that economic concerns seemed to outweigh political considerations. Once more, a pending trade bill offered leverage to Congress. The Senate appended to the Trade Act of 2002 a "sense of the Senate" resolution stating that it supported "terminating the application of [the Jackson–Vanik law] to Russia in an appropriate and timely manner."[21] Senate Finance Committee Chairman Max Baucus (Democrat–Montana) clarified that this meant "we should extend PNTR when we have a clear picture of the terms on which Russia will join the WTO."[22]

WTO Accession, Graduation from Jackson–Vanik, and the Magnitsky Law

The negotiations over Russian accession to the WTO were unusually long, lasting eighteen years, but were finally concluded in late 2011. Rather than waiting for Congress to act on the Jackson–Vanik problem, Moscow and Washington agreed on a unique approach that accelerated Russian accession. In all prior cases the non-application clause had been invoked by just one country, more often an incumbent than an acceding member. This time the invocation was mutual. In a face-saving measure for Russia, both countries filed notifications to the WTO in December, 2011 that they were invoking WTO Article XIII. Each of them understood that they would mutually disinvoke non-application as soon as Congress acted to grant PNTR to Russia, as indeed they did almost precisely one year later.

That latter part of the formula became trickier than either the US or Russian policymakers professed to expect, although even a cursory reading of history should have acquainted them with the well-established pattern by which apparently technical economic matters can quickly get enmeshed in the politics of Russo-American relations. The latest critics focused not on anti-Semitism or Communism, but instead on broader concerns over human rights, democracy, corruption, and the rule of law in Russia. A remarkably bipartisan group of legislators, including liberal Democrats as well as veteran Republican cold warriors, coalesced around the case of Russian lawyer and whistleblower Sergei Magnitsky.

While Magnitsky offered the symbolic focus for this incident, playing a role comparable to that of Aleksandr Solzhenitsyn a generation before, the real moving force was William Browder. This former client of Magnitsky embodies the multiple ironies of Russo-American relations over the past two

---

[21] Section 4204 of H.R.3009, as approved by the Senate on May 23, 2002.
[22] *Congressional Record* Volume 148 Number 67 (May 22, 2002), p. S4679.

decades. He is the grandson of Earl Browder, who served during 1930–1945 as general secretary of the Communist Party USA, but – in an act of generational rebellion once-removed – the younger Browder became an investment banker and was among the first Western capitalists to deal with post-Soviet Russia. In the view of Russian officials and oligarchs, who tend to conceive of economic transactions in starkly zero-sum terms, Browder invested not wisely but too well. They conspired to deprive him of his gains, which they saw as Russian losses, and Browder responded by defending his rights in court and becoming a vocal critic of the regime's political repression. The Russian government pursued a range of retaliatory measures against him, to the point where Browder had a well-founded fear for his own safety. It was Magnitsky who paid the ultimate price, being arrested after he began working with Browder on an anticorruption case. This Russian lawyer died while in custody in 2009, and the forensic evidence pointed to severe maltreatment.[23]

Outrage over the Magnitsky case, as well as other evidence of Russia's reversion to old habits, coincided with the end-game of the WTO-accession negotiations. It thus set up yet another iteration in the now-familiar game by which economic relations serve as leverage in a political dispute. Moscow's American critics knew they would never have a better opportunity to push the Sergei Magnitsky Rule of Law Accountability Act through Congress. The "smart sanctions" in this law targeted specific officials implicated in Magnitsky's death or certain other offenses. In addition to freezing any assets that these persons held in the United States, the bill would also deny visas for travel to the United States. None of the advocates of these sanctions seemed to be aware of the irony involved in that latter point, with the United States now imposing politically motivated restrictions on the movement of people. And far from viewing the matter with any sense of historical or philosophical detachment, the individuals targeted by this law took the rebuke just as personally as its authors had intended. The tone coming from Moscow suggests that the response was not proportional to the injury that the law did to its national economic interests, which remained as small as ever, but instead by the magnitude of the insult to a small circle of oligarchs and *apparatchiks*. "Who steals my Purse steals Trash," as Othello had it, "But he that filches from me my good Name/Robs me of that which not enriches him/And makes me poor indeed."[24]

It required months of confrontation and maneuvering for the White House and Congress to reach the obvious compromise that would satisfy everyone

---

[23]   See Browder's memoir (2015) for full details.
[24]   Othello, *Othello* Act III, scene III.

except the Russians: The PNTR and Magnitsky bills would be combined into one, thus exchanging one set of sanctions for another. From the narrow perspective of trade law, the key difference was in the implications for Russia's WTO membership. Whereas the Jackson–Vanik sanctions took a form that legally obligated the United States to invoke non-application on Russia's accession to the WTO, the Magnitsky sanctions did not. The switch met the minimum needs of all interested parties in the United States, and so the bill passed by an unusually wide and bipartisan margin. The House approved it 365–43 in November, 2012, and the Senate followed the next month with a 92–4 vote. This allowed both the United States and Russia to disinvoke non-application, and thus to recognize one another's status as WTO members.

Policymakers in Russia did not celebrate the end of this policy debate. They instead took great offense at the Magnitsky penalties and sought a suitable counterattack. The form of retaliation that they initially chose hearkened back to the earlier disputes over emigration: The Kremlin decreed that Americans could no longer adopt Russian orphans. This was not a popular move in Russia, where it was widely seen as harmful to children. Many of those denied the opportunity to emigrate to the United States suffered from medical conditions for which much better treatment was available in their prospective new home country. Russian officials also took their revenge by mounting another, less overt campaign. It would not be apparent until years later just how great an impact their resentment, and their retaliation, might have on the domestic politics of the United States and on relations between the two countries.

THE DETERIORATION IN US–RUSSIAN RELATIONS

The events that took place in and around 2012 normalized US relations with Russia in two senses of the term. In the narrow, commercial meaning, trade relations between Washington and Moscow were restored to normal for the first time since 1951. With the benefit of a few years of hindsight, we can also see that this was just about the time that policymakers in both countries culminated a decade of backsliding into the "old normal" of mistrust, rivalry, and confrontation. The unusually good rapport that coincided with the overlapping presidencies of Clinton (1993–2000) and Yeltsin (1991–1999) ended with the political ascension of Vladimir Putin. He took power on the final day of the twentieth century, and over the ensuing years Moscow's level of xenophobia and authoritarianism rose steadily, as did its willingness to confront the United States. The graduation of Russia from Jackson–Vanik represented the last of several attempts to put US-Russian relations on a more cooperative footing.

Understanding the renewal of Russo-American conflict, and its relationship to trade, requires that one consider how Putin seems to conceive of these issues. As was already alluded to with respect to the Browder/Magnitsky affair, this former KGB officer and his confederates appear to take a mercantilist outlook in the fullest sense of that term, including a zero-sum view of commercial exchanges and a close association between economics and security. It is not surprising that this perspective, together with a multiplicity of foreign policy disputes and Russian reentry into the global economy, has led both Moscow and its Western adversaries to unsheathe old economic weapons. The only innovation is that Russia now sends sanctions as frequently as it receives them. In another reversion to the old normal, Western pressure has not yet resulted in significant changes to Russian policy. In the event that sanctions work, that result will undoubtedly be due more to the economic pressures brought by the European Union than by the concurrent US measures.

The economic confrontations moved in parallel with the stepwise adoption of more aggressive security postures in both Washington and Moscow. The first serious sign of trouble came in 2002, when Russia strongly objected to US withdrawal from the Anti-Ballistic Missile Treaty. Then came accusations that the Bush administration encouraged anti-Russian revolts in Georgia and Ukraine in 2003 and 2004, respectively. Russia also protested an American plan to build an antiballistic missile defense system in Poland in 2007. Secretary of State Hillary Clinton's attempted reset of relations was soon thwarted. Putin accused her of inciting the protests that followed Russian legislative elections in 2011, an incident that would later be cited as an inspiration for Moscow's meddling in the US presidential election. These episodes, as well as the East–West frictions in the former Yugoslavia, the Middle East, and Asia, began to resemble the Cold War. The most serious rupture, however, was rooted in controversies where economic and political conflict blended seamlessly. First in Georgia and then in Ukraine, the two sides quarreled over the extent to which the states of the former Soviet Union may be permitted to look to both East and West in their commercial and security arrangements.

East–West Competition in the "Near Abroad"

The principal provocation, from Moscow's point of view, was the eastward march of two Western alliances. Numerous former Warsaw Pact members, including a few ex-Soviet republics, have joined both NATO and the European Union since the end of the Cold War. As summarized in Table 11.1, those twin processes proceeded at similar paces. East Germany started it all in 1990, when its reunification with West Germany brought it automatically into both bodies. By the end of that decade other Eastern European or ex-Soviet republics would complete their own accessions. Viewed from the Volga, the parallel movement of the NATO and EU frontiers looked like an offensive trek across what Moscow considers the "near abroad."

The character of this East–West rivalry took a more ominous turn in 2008, when the Russian government applied economic and then military pressures against Georgia. It eventually sent troops into that sovereign state, then recognized "independent" enclaves that were inconveniently located within the borders of this former Soviet republic. After Western countries objected, Russia threatened to expand the import restrictions that it had imposed on Georgia by extending them to the United States, the European Union, Turkey, and Ukraine. The Kremlin pressed ahead despite the consequences for its own WTO accession. "It seems increasingly clear," the US embassy in Moscow opined in a 2008 cable, "that Russia has written off any chance of a near-term WTO accession and is intent on registering its displeasure by increasing protection for domestic producers – and if those countries supported Georgia, so much the better."[25] The Georgia crisis eventually proved to be just a speed-bump in Russia's WTO accession, but also offered a glimpse of what was to come.

Putin drew the line at Ukraine, perhaps fearing that the proposed EU–Ukraine association agreement of 2012 was a first step toward incorporating one of the largest former Soviet republics into NATO. When the European Union and Ukraine launched their FTA negotiations in 2008, the US embassy in Kyiv reported that many European officials saw these talks "as a way to bring Ukraine as close to Europe as possible without EU membership, which is not on the EU agenda at the moment because of 'enlargement fatigue.'" The embassy nonetheless stated that "an EU-Ukraine FTA is strongly in the U.S. national interest, as it is a further step anchoring Ukraine in Euro-Atlantic institutions," and recommended that the United States "support the EU-Ukraine negotiations in every appropriate manner."[26] Putin took a similarly strategic view of the matter,

---

[25] "Russia-Ukraine Trade Relations Strained," cable of September 10, 2008 from the US embassy in Moscow (08MOSCOW2720_a).

[26] "Ukraine's Next Step toward the EU: A 'Deep' Free Trade Agreement," cable of September 22, 2008 from the US embassy in Kyiv (08KYIV1875_a).

TABLE 11.1.   *Eastern European Countries' Status in the European Union and NATO*
Dates show the year in which an agreement entered into force

	Agreement with EU	Joined NATO	Joined EU
Reunification			
East Germany[a]	—	1990	1990
Joined NATO before EU			
Bulgaria[a]	1995	2004	2007
Croatia	2005	2009	2013
Czech Republic[a]	1995	1999	2004
Hungary[a]	1994	1999	2004
Poland[a]	1994	1999	2004
Romania[a]	1995	2004	2007
Joined EU and NATO in the Same Year			
Estonia[b]	1998	2004	2004
Latvia[b]	1998	2004	2004
Lithuania[b]	1998	2004	2004
Slovakia[a]	1995	2004	2004
Slovenia	1999	2004	2004
Status in Flux			
Albania	2009	2009	Candidate
Armenia[b]	—[c]	—	—
Bosnia and Herzegovina	2015	Aspiring	Potential
Georgia[b]	2016	Aspiring	—
Kosovo	2016	—	Potential
Macedonia	2004	Aspiring	Candidate
Moldova[b]	2016	—	—
Montenegro	2010	2017	Candidate
Serbia	2013	—	Candidate
Ukraine[b]	2017	—[d]	—

Potential: Potential candidate.
Note: "Agreement with EU" includes association agreements, Europe agreements, or other agreements with similar titles, which are often (but not always) treated as precursors to EU accession.
[a]   Member of the Warsaw Pact at the time of its dissolution in 1991.
[b]   Former Soviet republic.
[c]   Negotiations completed in 2013 but agreement not signed.
[d]   Ukraine began the process of NATO accession in 2008, but has not actively pursued accession since 2010.
Sources: European Union at https://europa.eu/european-union/about-eu/countries_en; NATO at www.nato.int/cps/en/natohq/topics_52044.htm and www.nato.int/cps/en/natolive/topics_37750.htm.

and insisted that Ukraine could not be economically allied with both Moscow and Brussels.

Moscow had already threatened trade sanctions against Ukraine when that country acceded to the WTO in 2008, employing "increasingly belligerent trade policies" that included threats to impose a "reduction in the number of Ukrainian goods subject to duty-free entry in Russia, the possible imposition of new tariffs, and a delay in lifting the import quotas on Ukrainian sugar and spirits for up to five years."[27] The EU–Ukraine agreement brought matters to a head, with Putin demanding that President Viktor Yanukovych choose sides. Yanukovych triggered a popular uprising, and was forced to flee Ukraine, when in 2013 he chose Moscow over Brussels by denouncing the EU agreement. Russian forces invaded Crimea almost immediately after Yanukovych left, and annexed that territory in 2014. Moscow also provided support and direction to paramilitary forces fighting the Ukrainian government, evidently seeking to acquire still more Ukrainian territory.

The West responded more vigorously than it had to Russia's invasion of Georgia in 2008, but only up to a point. The United States and the European Union were not about to risk a potentially catastrophic confrontation with a nuclear power, limiting their military support for Ukraine to providing "defensive" weapons. Their economic sanctions were similarly restrained, bearing a closer resemblance to the Magnitsky law than its Jackson–Vanik predecessor. These US and EU sanctions single out individuals and entities responsible for violating the sovereignty and territorial integrity of Ukraine, including members of Putin's inner circle, targeting them for travel and financial restrictions. The Obama administration also suspended export credits and financing for development projects, and prohibited goods and services destined for certain energy projects. In response to such escalations as the downing of a Malaysian airplane, the United States and the European Union added more individuals, entities, and activities to the list.[28]

The Limited Effectiveness of Trade Sanctions

Would these measures be powerful enough to deter further Russian aggression, and perhaps force Moscow to relinquish Crimea? Or would we simply see a repetition of the established pattern whereby Washington finds it easy to impose sanctions, but it is equally easy for Moscow to ignore them? The Ukrainian crisis remains a live issue as of this writing, but the available facts warn against expectations of a break from the past. The US leverage is still quite limited. Even though American imports from Russia did increase from

---

[27] "Russia-Ukraine Trade Relations Strained," cable of September 10, 2008 from the US embassy in Moscow (08MOSCOW2720_a).

[28] See www.state.gov/e/eb/tfs/spi/ukrainerussia/ for the US measures. The corresponding measures of the European Union are enumerated at http://europa.eu/newsroom/highlights/special-coverage/eu_sanctions_en.

1996 through 2011, and Russia enjoyed an ever-larger bilateral trade surplus, the trend is less important than the magnitude. While the sanctions have been galling enough to provoke a harsh political response from Russia, the actual trade involved remains too small to force Moscow into reassessing its policies.

Bilateral trade declined after 2011, but the data suggest that sanctions are not responsible for this drop. It predated the Ukraine crisis by two years, and can primarily be traced to the falling price of energy products. About half of the decline in US imports during 2011–2017 was in just one product (fuel oil), and most of that was caused by a reduction in the average annual unit price (which fell from $99.81/barrel to $40.38/barrel) rather than the reduced level of imports (which fell only 17% by volume). The removal of Russia from the Generalized System of Preferences (GSP), which President Obama announced in October, 2014, was even less significant. The program had extended duty-free treatment to a range of Russian products since 1994, but its actual benefits were slim. Imports under this program had peaked at $738 million in 2005, accounting for just 5% of all US imports from Russia. More than one-quarter of those imports were in one product (copper wire), and without the GSP that item would have been subject to an MFN (NTR) tariff of just 3%. In short, here we see a case in which the paradox of preferences overlaps with the paradox of sanctions. The benefits of the GSP were too small to serve either as an inducement or a threat in Washington's dealings with Moscow.

With US–Russian trade thus sticking stubbornly to the historical script, the effectiveness of the sanctions depends instead on the European Union. This bloc is Russia's top trading partner, even with sanctions in place, supplying 38% of its imports in 2017 and taking in 45% of its exports. Put another way, the European Union was 6.8 times more important than the United States as a supplier of Russian imports, and 14.5 times greater as a destination for Russian exports.[29] Viewed in the abstract, the European Union should have considerable leverage over Russia. One analysis observed that it is "roughly five times more important to Russia than vice versa," with its imports being "equivalent to almost 10 per cent of Russia's economic output," yet EU exports to Russia amounted to just 1% of the European Union's GDP.[30]

The European Union nevertheless operated under some notable handi-caps. Sanctions could still be costly to the sender, with the European

[29] Calculated from EU data posted at http://trade.ec.europa.eu/doclib/docs/2006/september/tra doc_113440.pdf.

[30] Bond et al. (2015), p. 4.

Commission estimating that they could knock 0.3 percentage points off EU economic growth in 2014, and 0.4 in 2015.[31] That is considerably less than they cost Russia – the International Monetary Fund estimated that the sanctions and counter-sanctions reduced Russian output by as much as 1.5%[32] – but risk-averse European democracies may have less leeway on this issue than does a determined and autocratic neighbor. Even in pre-Putin days, Drezner found that "Russia was willing to incur greater costs" than were its adversaries in showdowns over sanctions.[33] The EU members that rely on Russian oil, gas, or nuclear fuel may not be as ready to take a hit. "The longer sanctions go on without achieving the hoped-for improvement in the situation in Ukraine," according to one analysis, "the deeper the divisions within the West will become" and the "more likely it will then be that some EU countries will block renewal of sanctions."[34] Even if these concerns did not lead to the outright collapse of the sanctions, they inspired some potentially crippling loopholes. Gas is an important exception, for example, and the subsidiaries of blacklisted Russian banks operating in at least seven EU member states were exempted from the financial measures. In short, even when the European Union and the United States act in concert they may not have sufficient leverage to force a change in Russian policy. Brussels is at least as susceptible as Washington to the paradox of sanctions.

Moscow retaliated with counter-sanctions of its own. In August, 2014 it banned imports of meat, fish, milk, cheese, fruits, and vegetables from the United States and the European Union, as well as Australia, Canada, and Norway. This counterattack meant higher prices for Russia, but that apparent cost can actually be spun as a gain. Drezner argued that in some cases "target governments may, for domestic reasons, *prefer* to be sanctioned" insofar as "an embargo strengthens import-substitution sectors by giving them rent-seeking opportunities." He thought this was "particularly true if the target regime is authoritarian," where foreign economic pressure may "permit target regimes to strengthen state control over the economy and readjust the impact of sanctions policies away from its most powerful supporters."[35] By 2014 Russia was already meeting its own needs for grains, potatoes, vegetable oils, sugar, and poultry. The country still depended on imports of dairy products, beef, pork, vegetables, and fruit, but the sanctions had the effect of stimulating

---

[31] See Pop (2014).
[32] International Monetary Fund (2016). Another study (Kholodilin and Netsunajev [2016]) estimated that the sanctions cost Russia 1.97% of its GDP.
[33] Drezner (1999), p. 308.
[34] Bond et al. (2015), p. i.
[35] Drezner (1999), p. 13.

domestic production.[36] Just as the US action against Russia seems to have had no discernible impact, so too has Moscow's response had little effect on Washington. The United States had sold just $1.7 billion worth of agricultural products to Russia in 2013, amounting to less than 1% of total US agricultural exports. By 2017 these shipments had fallen to $192 million, but an 88% cut from very little only makes for something even less significant. In short, both sides found it relatively painless to engage in the now-familiar game in which commercial sanctions provide the appearance of activity, but their capacity to accomplish change is bounded by the limited magnitude of existing trade flows.

US–RUSSIAN RELATIONS UNDER THE TRUMP ADMINISTRATION

It is evident to even the most casual observer that relations between the United States and Russia under the Trump administration offer a new example of what Churchill famously called "a riddle wrapped in a mystery inside an enigma."[37] In this instance the relevant events in Washington and New York are (as of this writing) just as obscure as those in Moscow, and one may only speculate as to whether or when at length the truth will out – much less what that truth might reveal. One certainty is that this latest episode deviates in a crucial respect from the established historical patterns in Russo-American sanctions. Whereas all previous incidents have been marked by the low level of economic relations between the two countries, we find in this instance a very small but key group of persons for whom the economic stakes are quite high.

The Psychological Operations of 1917 and 2016

Allen Dulles (1893–1969) exemplified the point that hindsight is easier than foresight, even if one happens to be a spy. Hoping that a new generation might learn from his mistakes, this lifelong operative shared an experience from his early career in a 1958 talk to the CIA Office of Training. Dulles related an episode from his posting to Bern during the First World War, when he was told one day that "a funny, long-haired man" wanted to meet with him. Dulles opted instead to keep a tennis date.

> The man I didn't see was Lenin, and Lenin, a few weeks after that, was put in the sealed train, one of the cleverest psychological operations that was ever pulled off by an intelligence service … and sent through Germany up to

---

[36] See Shagaida et al. (2014).
[37] Churchill (1939).

Finland and from Finland into Moscow and he was there in time to lead the November revolution.[38]

Dulles was not the only one to underestimate Lenin's potential. The Imperial German authorities who sponsored his return from Swiss exile to revolutionary Russia never dreamed just how successful this strangest and most temporary of bedfellows would be, nor how much blowback their country would suffer in the decades to follow. Neither the young American spook nor his German counterparts knew that this pivotal event in 1917 would turn out to be the most consequential covert operation of the twentieth century. A future historian might well conclude that a comparable exploit that came ninety-nine years later held the same, dubious distinction for the twenty-first century. And while there are respects in which this latest psy-op was the reverse of the earlier one – the Russians were now the instigators rather than the target, and they backed a billionaire instead of a Bolshevik – the missions shared two critical characteristics. The original intent in both 1917 and 2016 was merely to disrupt the adversary, backing a provocateur in order to exacerbate the enemy's internal divisions. Both cases also demonstrate the law of unintended consequences, having impacts far in excess of what the operators expected.

Any self-respecting historian is naturally cautious about using loaded terms such as "unique" or "unprecedented." Domestic US politics offer some loose historical parallels to the Russian intervention in the 2016 election, such as the Citizen Genêt Affair of 1793–1794, the British machinations aimed at bringing the United States into the First World War, and the propaganda campaigns of Britain and Germany that inspired enactment of the Foreign Agents Registration Act of 1938. There are also examples of presidential candidates who are alleged to have colluded with foreign adversaries so as to undermine the party in power, including Richard Nixon in 1968 and (with less supporting evidence) Ronald Reagan in 1980.[39] History also offers exceptions to the diplomatic norm by which foreign governments refrain from openly expressing a preference. In 1984, for example, "Chinese officials startled visiting Americans by indicating their clear preference for the reelection of Ronald Reagan" because his "commitment to free trade seemed more advantageous to Beijing," and four years later Deng Xiaoping "announced publicly his hope that Vice President Bush would prevail over his Democratic opponent."[40]

---

[38] Untitled and undated transcript of remarks made by Dulles at a 1958 holiday party of the CIA Office of Training.

[39] On Nixon, see Gibbs and Duffy (2013); on Reagan see Sick (1991).

[40] Cohen (1990), p. 207.

Some US allies in Europe and the Middle East have likewise gotten into the habit of making their preferences known. One nonetheless looks in vain to find historical parallels to the active measures that Moscow deployed in 2016.[41] Closer comparisons can instead be found in fiction, from Sax Rohmer's *President Fu Manchu* (1936) to Richard Condon's *The Manchurian Candidate* (1959, adapted to film in 1962 and 2004). Yet some of the more salacious allegations surrounding the *kompromat* that Moscow is widely rumored to have on Trump are stranger than fiction.

The truth remains elusive. We do not yet have the luxury of Dulles' forty-one years of hindsight, and a great deal has yet to be revealed as to just what happened between Trump, Putin, and their intermediaries. The most significant of the known-unknowns concern (a) whether and to what extent the Trump campaign may have knowingly and actively colluded with the Russian interests that wished to promote this dark-horse candidate and undermine the expected victor, and (b) the actual extent to which that meddling affected the outcome of the election. Point (a) is still the subject of active investigation by a special counsel, and its findings may produce either clarity or (perhaps more likely) the same sort of controversy that followed the Warren Commission's 1964 report on the Kennedy assassination. No matter what information that investigation may unearth, it may be all but impossible to reach any definitive conclusions regarding point (b). Something has gone seriously wrong, however, when wild-eyed conspiracy theorists are not the only ones asking whether the decisive factor in a US presidential election was a lengthy intervention of the Russian intelligence agency, or an eleventh-hour announcement from the American counterintelligence agency. Things are worse still when the prima facie evidence for answering "both" is at least as strong as the case for "neither."

Economic Ties and Political Interests

In place of making one more contribution to the endless speculation on these points, which extend well beyond the subject matter of the present study, we may instead bring the analysis back to this chapter's main focus. In two respects this latest episode of Russo-American sanctions shows continuity with the past, but another goes in just the opposite direction. One point of

---

[41]   To be more objective, one looks in vain for evidence of a comparable campaign by a *foreign* intelligence service to influence an election *in the United States*. The CIA's operations in the Italian election of 1948 and the Chilean election of 1970, and quite probably in numerous other contests, may offer the closest historical parallels.

continuity concerns the sequence of events that appears to have inspired Moscow to undertake this operation. Disputes involving the movement of persons are a recurring theme in the relations between these countries, as most recently exemplified by the Magnitsky Act's sanctions on travel by Russian persons, and the Kremlin's counter-sanctions on adoptions. The latter half of that pairing offered the pretext for the infamous Trump Tower meeting of June 9, 2016, in which senior campaign officials met with Russians who dangled the promise of "dirt" on Hillary Clinton five weeks before the Republican National Convention. The White House would later claim that the meeting focused on Russian adoptions, but even that seemingly innocent subject meant a plea for the removal of sanctions for which the Russian adoption ban was a countermeasure.

The other point of continuity is in the greater interest that the legislative branch shows in imposing sanctions on Russia than does the executive. Congress approved the Countering America's Adversaries Through Sanctions Act by huge and bipartisan margins in 2017, but the Trump administration showed great reluctance to enact or implement this law. Even on this point, there is a great difference between past presidents' reluctance to take steps that they considered inadvisable for reasons of policy, and the possibility that this president's stance is influenced by concerns over how it might affect his own economic interests or legal jeopardy.

This case departs from the historical norm in a more significant way. Economic ties between the United States and Russia still weigh lightly on the scale of national accounts, yet there are specific individuals for whom these links are extraordinarily significant. One such person is retired Lieutenant General Michael Flynn, a Trump campaign advisor and (for twenty-four days) the administration's first national security advisor. While the full extent of Flynn's relationship with Moscow remains under investigation, it is common knowledge that Russian interests – including the Kremlin-financed RT television network – were prominent clients of his consulting firm.[42] These connections were even tighter for Paul Manafort, who had multiple interests in Russia and Ukraine before becoming chairman of the Trump campaign. Other characters in the president's orbit with economic or other connections to Russia include campaign advisors Carter Page and George Papadopoulos, and personal lawyer Michael Cohen.

The most intriguing and pertinent questions surround the candidate's own economic ties. Here the available evidence suggests that Trump may resemble such notable past exceptions as Armand Hammer (the American industrialist

---

[42]   Mazzetti and Rosenberg (2017).

whose dealings with the Kremlin spanned nearly all of Soviet history) or Pepsi Cola (the firm that struck a celebrated barter deal in 1972 to exchange American soft drinks for Soviet vodka). Those two cases illustrate how a specific fortune might be hitched to Moscow even when the overall level of bilateral economic interactions remains minuscule. As of this writing, both the magnitude and the provenance of economic dealings between Russia and the Trump Organization, as well as affiliated persons, remain the subject of intense scrutiny. Where that inquiry might ultimately lead lies beyond the scope of our present inquiry. It is possible that every Russia-related interest of Donald Trump and his entourage has been entirely above board, with one school of thought suggesting that any corruption in that relationship was only prospective. The candidate's frequent and fulsome statements of admiration for Russia's authoritarian leader, according to this theory, can best be understood as part of a post-election plan to cash in after his anticipated loss. By that logic, the electoral upset was just as great a surprise to the candidate as it was to everyone else. But perhaps it would not be so great a surprise to Allen Dulles, who might well chide his careless countrymen for having gone on a collective tennis date in 2016.

12

Trading with the NME:
The Chinese Challenge to US Hegemony

All nations, big or small, should be equal; big nations should not bully the small and strong nations should not bully the weak. China will never be a superpower and it opposes hegemony and power politics of any kind.

> Chinese statement in the Shanghai Communiqué (February 27, 1972)

Realistically, however, we must recognize that where you have a Communist country dealing with a capitalist country, or non-Communist country, the possibilities of trade are seriously limited[.]

> President Richard Nixon, responding to a question at a dinner party
> in Texas (April 30, 1972)

INTRODUCTION

The tea leaves seem to have been poor prognosticators in 1972. The Chinese had far too modest an impression of their own potential power, and President Nixon badly lowballed the future magnitude of East–West trade. Viewed in the rear-view mirror of history, one may only wonder whether the inaccuracy of their respective predictions might be attributed to a lack of imagination or to willful blindness. Today it is difficult to fathom how anyone might think that the home to nearly a quarter of the world's population would remain perpetually impotent and impoverished. Yet we can fault neither Nixon nor his hosts for failing to anticipate the speed of the turnabout. Who would have thought that one could go from self-crippled giant to contender for hegemony in just half a century? Certainly not Nixon, who confessed to second thoughts near the end of his life. "We may have created a Frankenstein," he told his former speechwriter.[1]

The rapid rise of China makes US economic statesmanship more challenging than it was in Nixon's time. Cold warriors could treat trade and foreign

---

[1] Safire (2000).

policy as separate topics because the military and commercial antagonists were distinct. The Soviet Union was an inefficient and largely autarkic empire that accounted for a trivial share of global trade, whereas Japan was a close ally that had forsworn military force and was still living off its own peace dividend. Power and wealth were linked at the top level of grand strategy, but high politics and low politics rarely met at the tactical level. The prospects for collisions are far greater now that China has become the principal challenger to the United States in both spheres.

This chapter reviews the historical evolution and current status of trade relations between Washington and Beijing. The first half of the story focuses on direct ties between the principals, and especially the role of trade in defining political relations. Once these relations were normalized, it did not take long for conflicts to emerge at the bilateral level, and then to be complemented by rivalry in trade relations with third parties. That comprises the second half of this analysis, giving a new twist to the familiar Cold War theme of competition at the periphery. FTAs might not look much like proxy wars, and yet their role is somewhat comparable to the military adventures of the Cold War. The principal difference, beyond the fact that they are ostensibly about wealth rather than power, is that FTAs give third parties more options: It would not have been possible to be a joint member of NATO and the Warsaw Pact, but a country can now have FTAs with both of the world's largest economies. Only a handful have done this so far, but the number will grow. Although the smaller countries that negotiate multiple FTAs will typically disavow any noncommercial intention behind those agreements, neither Beijing nor Washington treats these economic alliances as purely commercial undertakings. And despite their claims that discriminatory trade agreements are complements rather than substitutes for the multilateral system, these declarations wear thin as the global commitment to multilateralism attenuates, and as the level of Sino-American confrontation rises across a spectrum of issues.

THE DIVERSE ROOTS OF A SPECIAL RELATIONSHIP

Before examining the history and status of Sino-American trade relations, it is useful to identify two special aspects of this relationship. One concerns the unique place that China has always held in the Western imagination, owing primarily to its extraordinary size. The other is the growing importance of the Chinese diaspora in the United States, which had long been kept small through discrimination but shows signs of reaching a politically significant magnitude.

The Three US Objectives in China

When Americans have looked to China they have traditionally seen the same three things that Marco Polo did in the thirteenth century: a rich market; a potentially dangerous rival; and an object of religious, social, or political evangelization. The relative weight placed on these goals has shifted with the perceived opportunities and risks. Commercial and evangelical desires dominated US policy in the nineteenth century, when Washington left power politics to the British and other Europeans, but conflict took first place in the twentieth century. All three goals have competed for primacy since the late Cold War. The advocates of normalizing trade relations with China argued that this would serve each of these objectives, as it would provide opportunities for mutual gains, build a counterweight to the Soviet Union, and promote positive change in China. Critics see just the opposite, with China threatening to displace the United States commercially, use its economic strength as the foundation for political and military power, and provide an unwelcome object lesson for other developing countries that might distrust the uncertainties of democracy and the market.

Viewed in context, China's recent economic growth looks like the restoration of a long-lost status quo. Adam Smith had good cause to observe in 1776 that while "China has long been one of the richest ... and most populous countries in the world," it was "stationary" in his own time.[2] Figure 12.1 shows that as of 1820, when Britain's hegemony was in its infancy, that leader was not quite one-sixth of the way toward overtaking the Chinese economy. Beijing's relative decline over the next century was just as spectacular as its recent resurgence has been. The European and Japanese predations produced less turbulence than did such domestic scourges as the Tai Ping rebellion, a succession of war lords, and civil war. The bloodshed and stagnation continued well after the Communist victory in 1949. The Cultural Revolution of 1966–1976 plunged the country into another decade of chaos, costing millions of lives. China's portion of global GDP had plummeted from one-third in 1820 to one-twentieth in 1950, and still held that same share in 1973 – even if 23% of the world lived there.[3]

It is little wonder that Richard Nixon saw so little prospect for trade between the United States and what was then the world's largest basket case. He was instead motivated primarily by the interests that Washington and Beijing shared in confronting Moscow. That focus on power was understandable, but also short-sighted. Washington analysts were then so caught up in a debate

---

[2]   Smith (1776), p. 89.
[3]   Calculated from Maddison (2003), p. 261.

GDP of the United Kingdom = 1

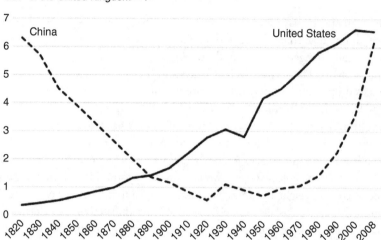

FIGURE 12.1 Relative sizes of the Chinese and US economies, 1820–2008.
Note: Chinese data are missing for several decades. Values have been interpolated based on the available data, assuming steady rates of growth or decline between one known value and another.
Source: Calculated from the Maddison Historical GDP Data available at www .worldeconomics.com/Data/MadisonHistoricalGDP/Madison%20Historical%20 GDP%20Data.efp.

over whether China's relations with the Soviet Union more closely resembled those of the compliant Bulgaria, the schismatic Yugoslavia, or the overly adventurous Cuba, that they failed to consider the possibility that Beijing might displace Moscow altogether.

The stakes here are systemic. The relative ease of the transition from UK to US hegemony was deceptive. The transfer of hegemony from one power to another, or even the attempt to bring it about, is more typically accompanied by great violence. "As its relative power increases," according to Gilpin,

> a rising state attempts to change the rules governing the international system, the division of the spheres of interest, and, most important of all, the international distribution of territory. In response, the dominant power counters this challenge through changes in its policies that attempt to restore equilibrium in the system. The historical record reveals that if it fails in this attempt, the disequilibrium will be resolved by war.[4]

---

[4] Gilpin (1981), p. 187.

Today this is commonly called the Thucydides Trap. As summarized by Allison, there are always "dangers when a rising power rivals a ruling power," as happened in the Athenian challenge to Sparta that Thucydides chronicled in history's first history. This phenomenon extended well beyond the ancient world: In twelve out of sixteen "cases over the past 500 years, the result was war." Even when the parties avoided war, keeping the peace "required huge, painful adjustments in attitudes and actions on the part not just of the challenger but also the challenged."[5] If we take that as a universal law, and further assume that the recent surge of Chinese power and wealth will not give way to the same sort of stagnation that eventually befell Japan (see Chapter 8), the implications are unsettling. The American electorate is not noted for its eagerness to make huge, painful adjustments in peacetime, leading to speculation about which of two other alternatives might ensue. One possibility is war; another is that Beijing might have more to say than Washington about adjustments in the global system.

It would be reassuring, but naive, to assume away the possibility of a Sino-American war. The most likely *casus belli* would be a dispute involving Washington's allies, with the Asia-Pacific region offering an unfortunately large pool of candidates. Chief among these is the perennial threat of a forced reunification with Taiwan; Beijing's claims in the South China Sea run a close second. Recent events have proven that the forceful acquisition of territory has not gone out of style, and armed conflict may be just as possible in this theater as it was in Iraq's capture of Kuwait and in the Russian predations on Georgia and Ukraine. As for the widespread and comforting belief that nuclear weapons make superpower conflict unthinkable, Chinese leaders did not share that opinion in 1950. They went beyond mere contemplation soon after the Chinese Revolution, making good on their threat to intervene in the Korean War. And even if the United States and China do not stumble into a shooting war, the Cold War offers numerous examples of how their respective allies might set upon one another; the Korean peninsula presents a perennial danger.

We may nevertheless confine our examination to other, more peaceful means of confrontation. One reason to move along is that while the probability of direct war is above zero, taking all in all the chances seem well below 50–50. Another reason is that the analysis here would be rendered moot if war were to erupt. Putting aside that most direct and destructive form of confrontation, we can see how Sino-American competition for wealth, prestige, and influence is one of the defining elements of the twenty-first century.

---

[5] Allison (2015). See also Allison (2018).

The China Hands and the Diaspora

Beyond commerce and war, there are two social factors that help to define the Sino-American relationship. One is the aforementioned matter of evangelization, which once took literal form in religious campaigns and has since been supplemented by broader efforts to encourage political and social change in China. The other is the Chinese diaspora in the United States, which for many years mattered only as a source of friction between the countries but may eventually become a more significant factor in American policymaking.

The first American missionaries went to China in 1807, and over the next century and a half they would be among the primary carriers of culture between the two countries. This evangelizing impulse had a reciprocal quality to it, with many of the missionaries (or their children) joining the corps of "old China hands" who were to play so important a role in twentieth-century foreign policymaking. They also included soldiers, journalists, historians, novelists, and captains of industry. While there was great diversity among these old hands, most of them were committed to the ideas that both the United States and China represent great cultures, there exists a special relationship between them, and yet China has more to learn from the United States than the other way around. This attitude was exemplified by the businessman-hero of the 1933 novel *Oil for the Lamps of China*, whose "brain held tenaciously the image of the ancient civilization, into which for five years he had been trying to fit himself, in order that he might change it."[6] One could still hear echoes of those expectations in the 1990s, when Congress repeatedly – and heatedly – debated renewal of China's MFN status. Whether cynically or sincerely, the advocates of closer trade with China often insisted that trade has the ancillary benefit of promoting positive evolution in Chinese politics and society.

One reason why the old China hands were so influential in US policy is that they filled a vacuum that might otherwise have been occupied by a substantial diaspora. That lacuna was no accident, but rather the product of state and Federal policies to exclude Chinese immigrants. This issue was one of the principal sources of conflict between the United States and China in the nineteenth century, and it would return in ironic form late in the twentieth century.

The Burlingame Treaty of 1868, so named for the freelancing American diplomat who represented China, granted MFN treatment to Chinese

---

[6] Hobart (1933), p. 170. Or to put it in terms of a Broadway musical, "I Love You, You're Perfect, Now Change."

immigrants. This promise put the Federal government at odds with the state of California, where Chinese migrants were subject to official and unofficial discrimination. At the very time that US diplomats were pressing their complaints to the czars on the treatment meted out to Russian Jews and their American relatives (see Chapter 11), the Chinese emperor could have raised substantially similar concerns with the United States. The pressures to restrict Chinese immigration grew so strong that both political parties demanded revisions to the treaty, leading to a new pact in 1880 that allowed restrictions so long as they did not amount to a permanent prohibition. Congress then enacted the Chinese Exclusion Act of 1882, in which the only apparent concession to the new treaty was (in response to a presidential veto) a ban for ten years rather than twenty. Immigration declined sharply, and prevented China from joining Ireland, Israel, Italy, and other countries whose own burgeoning diasporas have been so influential in shaping US policy toward the kin state.

Another century would pass before the Chinese diaspora in the United States would start to reach a politically appreciable size. The immigration reforms of 1965, followed by the renewal of Sino-American relations a decade later, facilitated a new influx. There were just 99,735 Chinese-born persons in the United States in 1960, and still only 286,120 in 1980, but by 2016 the number had ballooned to 2.1 million. If we include people born in Hong Kong and Taiwan, as of 2016 there were 2.7 million US residents who had been born in China (0.7% of the total population), 3.4 million who spoke Chinese at home (1.0%), and 4.2 million persons of solely Chinese ancestry (1.3%).[7] They comprised the tenth-largest diaspora in the United States.[8]

The evidence for this diaspora's influence over trade policy has thus far been limited to a single, surprising case. Although some Chinese-Americans were active in the recurring debates over MFN status from 1989 to the mid-1990s, the voting data in Congress suggests that the diaspora did not exert much pull until the 2000 debate over full normalization. The most identifiable impact came from the American citizens of Taiwanese origin, who attached high importance to the normalization of relations with China because this was a prerequisite for Taiwan's WTO accession. The terms of that accession had actually been settled long before the deal was struck with China, but diplomats in Geneva had decided in 1992 that Taiwan would not be permitted to accede until China had completed the process; that in turn

---

[7] Calculated from Census data at www.census.gov/population/www/documentation/twpsoo29/tabo3.html and https://factfinder.census.gov/faces/nav/jsf/p.s/index.xhtml.
[8] www.diasporaalliance.org/americas-largest-diaspora-populations/.

could not happen until trade relations with China were fully normalized, allowing the United States to avoid the invocation of the WTO non-application clause (Article XIII). The pro-Taiwan segment of the Chinese diaspora is small but highly organized, and many of its members are pragmatic businesspeople for whom the prolonged battle over China's trade status had become an unwelcome impediment to further trade and investment. They put their weight behind the Clinton administration's initiative, and while it is doubtful that they made the difference between the campaign's success or failure they do seem to have swayed some votes.

It is not clear whether that one case was a unique exception or a harbinger for the future. There certainly is precedent for a rising Asian country to move from antagonist to partner. As discussed in Chapter 8, the growth of Japanese investment in the United States helped to transform the domestic diplomacy of trade relations between Washington and Tokyo. It is possible that rising levels of Chinese investment in the United States, coupled with immigration and a complex supply chain, might exert a similar pull on relations with Beijing. For those demographic and economic factors to produce political results, however, they will have to overcome a difficult history.

A CAPSULE HISTORY OF SINO-AMERICAN TRADE RELATIONS

As in so many other areas of foreign economic policy, the pattern of US relations with China changed greatly on the American achievement of hegemony. In this instance the shock was multiplied by a coincidence of timing, with the victory of the Communist Revolution following hard on the heels of Washington's ascent to leadership. These two giants were estranged from one another in the first half of the Cold War, and spent the second half slowly restoring their economic and political ties. The events of prior generations nevertheless continue to color relations between Washington and Beijing, providing a rich source of Chinese resentment for past discrimination and humiliation.

From US Independence to the Dawn of Hegemony

The earliest trade between the United States and China predated American independence, even if it came by a circuitous route: It was Chinese tea that the patriots dumped into Boston Harbor.[9] Direct trade began shortly after Yankee traders were free from the English blockade. The ship *Empress of China* set

[9]   This according to Cohen (1990), p. 2.

sail from Boston in 1784, returning the next year from Canton. Trade in the early years followed a triangular pattern, with American manufactures being exchanged for furs on the Pacific coast, and these furs were then traded for Chinese tea, silk, and ginseng. This trade grew without any government intervention. The United States had no diplomatic representation in China for the first seven decades of American independence, other than the semi-official appointment of a merchant to serve as consul.

The "unequal treaties" of the nineteenth century relegated China to second-class status by ensuring that the country did not enjoy autonomy in its trade policy. The 1843 treaty that Great Britain imposed on China was the insult that London added to the injury of the First Opium War. It was soon followed by similar accords with the United States and other Western countries. These instruments all required that China accept the tariff rates imposed upon it by outside powers, and to do so on an MFN basis (i.e., any concession extracted by one power was immediately claimed by the rest). Those same powers eventually took up tariff collection as well. China was not to regain control over the setting and execution of its tariff for nearly a century. The United States participated in the formation and exploitation of this treaty system, but did so in its own way. While the Europeans and (later) the Japanese established quasi-colonial spheres of influence in Hong Kong, Macao, and other treaty ports, the United States was content to engage in trade without territory. The concerns of American merchants and diplomats over exclusion from the spheres of the other powers gave rise in 1899 to the Open Door policy, in which the United States sought to ensure that other power did not prevent access to the territories that they controlled or claimed.

A closer look at Chinese diplomatic tradition suggests that it is not inequality per se that was so objectionable to scholars and statesmen, but that China was now getting the shorter end of the stick. That reversed centuries of practice in which other Asian states were obliged to acknowledge their fealty to China. Worse yet, from Beijing's point of view, was that those traditional tributary states were now being brought under European and Japanese control. While this treaty system imposed humiliating conditions, they were not unique. Several other countries that evaded outright colonization were forced to accept similarly asymmetrical treaties in the nineteenth century. Japan was the largest one to retain a semblance of sovereignty, and eventually set an enviable example of parity with the West. (That was not fully achieved until Japan defeated Russia in the war of 1905.) Others that were consigned to this murky space between subordination and independence included the Congo, Egypt, Iran, Morocco, Tunis, and Turkey. There was also ample precedent to demand that Westerners accused of offenses in China be tried only in Western courts; Americans and Europeans learned to expect this extraterritorial treatment in the Ottoman Empire.

This system of unequal treaties came under increasing challenge in the first half of the twentieth century, with Chinese nationalists demanding the restoration of tariff autonomy. The United States and other parties to the Nine Power Treaty (1922) made very modest concessions to China, providing for slight increases in its tariff rates, but still constrained the country's exercise of commercial sovereignty. It was not until 1928 that the United States supported China's right to control the tariff. Even then, the qualifying language in the bilateral Treaty Regulating Tariff Relations mitigated the practical value of the US concession. The importance of this development was soon overshadowed by war, civil war, and revolution, followed again by war. These events rendered moot whatever benefits that China might otherwise have derived from its new status in trade relations with the United States.

Wartime Allies and Cold War Adversaries

The Sino-American relationship seemed set to mature after the Second World War. Walter Lippmann gave voice to a common American attitude when he observed in 1943 that "with independence, unity, and the industrialization of their country, the vast numbers of the Chinese nation should in the course of time organize themselves as a great power."[10] That sentiment took concrete form at the San Francisco Conference of 1945, which paid this notion forward by granting China one of the five permanent seats on the United Nations Security Council. China was among the founders of the GATT, and participated in the Havana Conference of 1948. The United States and China also negotiated a new Treaty of Friendship, Commerce, and Navigation in 1946. The bilateral agreement provided for reciprocal and unconditional MFN treatment, and thus undid over a century of discrimination – just in time to see it come back with a vengeance.

These bilateral and multilateral economic negotiations coincided with the final stages of the Chinese Revolution. That event alone might not have produced an irreparable rift. The Truman administration's principal objective was to prevent China from becoming a Soviet satellite. In hopes of "contribut[ing] to such centripetal forces as may develop" between Beijing and Moscow, Washington favored "restoration under appropriate security restrictions of ordinary economic relations with China."[11]

---

[10]	Lippmann (1943), pp. 113–114.
[11]	"Note by the Executive Secretary of the National Security Council (Souers) on United States Policy Regarding Trade with China" (February 28, 1949), *FRUS 1949*, Volume IX, p. 830.

The administration maintained this posture even after the advancing Maoist forces denounced GATT obligations in the ports they captured. "As matter policy," Secretary of State Dean Acheson cabled to US posts in China, the United States "would prefer convince Commies if possible GATT provides equal benefits Chinese exports."[12] The deposed Kuomintang government declared China's withdrawal from GATT in March, 1950, after that government withdrew from the Chinese mainland, and the new China did not refute this claim. The pullout may be the only issue on which the two Chinese governments agreed, as the revolutionaries-turned-statesmen viewed GATT as an instrument of capitalist exploitation and the latest manifestation of the discredited treaty system.

Any chance for normal relations disappeared with the outbreak of the Korean War. This conflict brought a distinction to China that the Soviet Union never shared during the Cold War, when direct fighting between US and Chinese forces broke out in November, 1950. One may only speculate on how many of the 33,739 American battle deaths in the Korean War were directly attributable to the People's Liberation Army,[13] but there is little doubt that the Chinese intervention meant the difference between an imminent US victory and a protracted stalemate. The resulting economic sanctions went even farther for China than for the Soviet Union, with the United States imposing an almost total embargo.

The Normalization of Trade Relations: From Ping-Pong to Conditional MFN

The normalization of relations with China, as pursued from the Nixon through the Clinton administrations, was based on the recognition that containment had run its course. Chief among the benefits from rapprochement was Sino-American defense cooperation, capitalizing on roughly parallel interests vis-à-vis the Soviet Union. The potential for bilateral trade was a distant second for Washington, which treated commerce more as a means than as an end. Prior to the Soviet collapse in 1991, American policymakers typically viewed relations with China through a Cold War lens. When considering the regional implications of Chinese growth, for example, the CIA opined in 1986 that while "an economically stronger China could appear more menacing, both militarily and economically, to some South East Asian

---

[12]   Cable of May 17, 1949, in ibid., p. 940.
[13]   U.S. Department of Veteran's Affairs (2017), p. 1.

countries, we suspect these countries would turn to the United States for support, not to the Soviet Union."[14]

The first moves toward formal relations actually started two years before the celebrated and semiofficial visit of American ping-pong players in Beijing, when in 1969 the Nixon administration signaled its aims by easing trade controls on China. It approved modifications so as "to permit general licenses for exports of food, agricultural equipment, chemical fertilizer and pharmaceuticals," and foresaw further tweaks to "import and export controls in non-strategic goods to permit a gradual development of balanced trade."[15] The White House followed up in 1972 by moving China to a less restricted category on the Commodity Control List, and lifting the "requirement that subsidiaries of U.S. firms in COCOM countries obtain a Treasury license in addition to a host country license for the export of strategic goods" to China.[16] Nixon nevertheless drew the line at China's interest in MFN treatment, which remained "a subject for later discussion."[17]

It took the better part of a decade for Washington and Beijing to normalize their political relations, and even then China's trade status was still marked with an asterisk. The United States transferred its diplomatic recognition from Taipei to Beijing in 1979, and concluded that same year an Agreement on Trade Relations between the United States of America and the People's Republic of China. This agreement was negotiated and approved under the Jackson–Vanik terms, meaning that China's MFN status was conditional on the freedom-of-emigration requirement set by that US law. The unintentional humor of the requirement was not lost on the Chinese, who (for good or for ill) are not as susceptible to historical blindness as their American counterparts. Deng Xiaoping treated the issue whimsically when he reportedly offered "to provide the United States with as many as 10 million Chinese, if necessary, to demonstrate his commitment to freedom of emigration."[18]

President Carter wished to be even-handed in his treatment of China and the Soviet Union, and "personally preferred to grant most-favored-nation status to both countries."[19] When Deputy Secretary of State Warren

---

[14] Central Intelligence Agency, Directorate of Intelligence, "The Global Consequences of China's Trade Expansion: A Look at the Future [deleted]" (October 30, 1986), p. 45.

[15] National Security Decision Memorandum 17, "Relaxation of Economic Controls Against China" (June 26, 1969), p. 1.

[16] National Security Decision Memorandum 155, "Relaxation of Restrictions on Trade with People's Republic of China" (February 17, 1972), p. 1.

[17] National Security Decision Memorandum 170, "US-PRC Trade" (June 8, 1972), p. 1.

[18] Harding (1992), p. 96.

[19] Carter (1982), p. 202.

Christopher testified before Congress in support of the China agreement he noted that the administration hoped to resubmit the 1972 US–Soviet agreement "soon."[20] But just as the Soviets managed to sabotage that MFN agreement by an untimely eruption of anti-Semitism, their invasion of Afghanistan in December, 1979 – a month after Christopher's testimony – intervened to block any attempt to revive that instrument. Full normalization of Russo-American trade relations would not come until two decades after the collapse of Communism. With Congress now encouraged to "play the China card," the agreement with Beijing won wide approval in both the House (294–88) and the Senate (74–8). Some legislators still opposed the agreement on political grounds, while others warned that failure to complement MFN with stricter antidumping rules "could result in thousands of lost jobs in industries such as textiles, steel, clockmaking, nonrubber footwear, leather, [and] mushrooms."[21] Those objections came chiefly from Republicans, who were still in transition from the party of protection and Cold War confrontation to the party of free trade and engagement.

MFN treatment stimulated a rapid increase in US imports. With the average tariffs on Chinese products falling from 30% in 1979 to 11% in 1981,[22] imports rose from a cumulative $2 billion in 1971–1980 to $60 billion during 1981–1990.[23] Exports to China also climbed, but not nearly as rapidly. The CIA was eerily accurate in a 1986 "estimate that by the year 2000 China is likely to double its share of world exports to become a trading power equaling Canada or Italy." It would in fact be the seventh-largest exporter that year, sandwiched precisely between Canada (#6) and Italy (#8). That same report nonetheless missed the mark by predicting that "China's trade expansion will help improve the US trade balance,"[24] as that account was already turning negative. Labor unions and Democratic policymakers became increasingly uneasy with the economic consequences of this relationship, even as growing numbers of businesses and Republican officeholders accommodated themselves to it.

[20]   U.S. House of Representatives (1979), p. 101.
[21]   U.S. Congress, House of Representatives, Committee on Ways and Means (1980), p. 13.
[22]   Calculated from U.S. Department of Commerce, *Highlights of U.S. Export and Import Trade* (FT-990).
[23]   Calculated from U.S. Department of Commerce data and the U.S. International Trade Commission's DataWeb.
[24]   Central Intelligence Agency, Directorate of Intelligence, "The Global Consequences of China's Trade Expansion: A Look at the Future [deleted]" (October 30, 1986), p. 1.

The Normalization of Trade Relations: From Tiananmen to WTO Accession

Trade relations between the United States and China would not be fully normal until MFN treatment was transformed from a conditional concession to a solid legal right. This was one of Beijing's goals when it began the process of GATT accession in 1986.[25] That move predated the Tiananmen incident by three years. The crushing of a pro-democracy movement shocked US public opinion, and produced a decade of fights between the parties and the branches in the United States. The first serious confrontation came in 1990, when the House passed a bill that would have made further extension conditional upon human rights criteria, and also approved a resolution to undo MFN treatment. Both of these initiatives died for want of action in the Senate. Legislators tried repeatedly thereafter to overturn President Bush's annual decisions to renew MFN treatment, or impose conditions on China's access to the US market. Several of these proposals were approved in either or both houses of Congress, and while each of the ensuing presidential vetoes was sustained the votes in the Senate were sometimes very close.

There then followed a lengthy process by which two successive presidents redefined the links between trade and human rights in US relations with China. The Bush administration sought to disaggregate the various disputes in the bilateral relationship and to deal with them under separate laws and procedures. The US Trade Representative (USTR) threatened China with retaliation if it did not remove barriers to US goods and enforce intellectual property rights more strictly, and reached agreements with China on both matters in 1992. The United States and China also signed a memorandum of understanding on prison labor exports.

Candidate Bill Clinton pledged in 1992 that he would take a harder line with Beijing, but moved toward accommodation in three phases. The first was in 1993, when he signed an executive order that extended MFN for one more year while threatening revocation if China did not comply with the Jackson–Vanik freedom-of-emigration requirements and the agreement on prison labor. He gave the secretary of state a year to recommend whether to renew MFN. The White House warned that the administration would "continue to press for full and faithful implementation of bilateral agreements with

---

[25]   China initially notified the GATT of its intention to "resume" its status as a contracting party, but the United States and others insisted that the country had to negotiate its accession de novo.

China on market access, intellectual property rights, and prison labor" under US trade laws.[26]

The second step followed in 1994, when the Clinton administration was forced to admit that it could not carry through with the threat to curtail China's MFN treatment. Here the paradox of sanctions was in full view. While it is difficult to locate the precise tipping point at which the economic magnitude of a relationship makes comprehensive sanctions politically infeasible, that boundary had evidently been passed sometime before Clinton's second year in office. China then took in just 2% of US exports, but already provided 6% of US imports. At a time when ever more American manufacturers outsourced production to China, and a retailer (Wal-Mart) was the largest employer in the United States, the political power of those importers could not be ignored. Even though Clinton agreed with Secretary of State Warren Christopher's conclusion "that the Chinese did not achieve overall significant progress in all the areas outlined in the Executive order relating to human rights," he decided that continued MFN treatment "offers us the best opportunity to lay the basis for long-term sustainable progress in human rights and for the advancement of our other interests with China." The president therefore announced that he was moving "to delink human rights from the annual extension of most-favored-nation trading status for China [and] . . . to place our relationship into a larger and more productive framework."[27] The policy differences between the Clinton administration and its predecessor had been narrowed to semantics and nuances.

China remained subject to the annual reviews of its MFN status, and the opponents' annual efforts to overturn the president's decision became a repetitive and futile ritual. The outcome of these later contests was never in real doubt, owing to solid and consistent Republican support. The only lasting consequence was yet another semantic shift, when in 1998 Congress decreed that the age-old term "most favored nation" would henceforth be replaced with the anodyne "normal trade relations" (NTR). The change in nomenclature stems from the frustration of lawmakers who grew weary of explaining to irate constituents that China was not actually the "most favored" nation in US trade policy, but was instead receiving the same, normal treatment extended to nearly all other countries.

The Clinton administration then took the third and final step, completing the process of normalizing Sino-American trade relations. It concluded the

---

[26] "Report to Congress Concerning Extension of Waiver Authority for the People's Republic of China" (May 28, 1993), in *PPP 1994*, pp. 775–776.

[27] "The President's News Conference" (May 26, 1994), in *PPP 1994*, p. 991.

WTO-accession negotiations with China in late 1999, and convinced Congress to approve it the next year.[28] This was accomplished by enacting a bill that gave the president the authority to graduate China from Jackson–Vanik on its accession. The bill also included some provisions reflecting bargains to which China had agreed, as well as others that were outside the terms of the accession deal (e.g., an annual review of US relations with China). It passed primarily with Republican votes; 74% of the House Republicans favored it, but just 35% of the House Democrats. China's accession to the WTO was made official on December 11, 2001, and the country was granted permanent NTR on January 1, 2002.

COMPETITION AND RIVALRY IN SINO-AMERICAN TRADE

It could be argued that Sino-American trade has never been normal, and may never be so, if we understand that to mean a degree of politicization no greater than that in the typical bilateral relationship. Commercial ties between these two countries have always been clouded by political considerations, which variously meant the near-absence of diplomatic relations during the first half of the nineteenth century, the juridical inequality that the Western powers imposed on China for the better part of a century, and the complete or partial estrangements in the latter half of the twentieth century. The trade relationship has been nominally normal since the dawn of the twenty-first century, but NTR status and WTO membership are dwarfed by an overwhelming political fact: China is the only viable challenger for hegemony. It has fully replaced Japan as the main US rival in the economic sphere, even if matters are more complicated in the military sphere. By contrast with Russia, which has not let its greatly diminished capacity dampen its risk-taking, the rising levels of Chinese power and ambition seem to be tempered with an admirably long time horizon.

The Concentration of US Trade Instruments on China

Over a very short period, China went from being entirely off the radar in US trade policy to being its principal target. The United States now has a two-speed approach to the conduct of trade disputes, reserving the higher gear for

---

[28]　Congressional approval is not ordinarily required for the terms of a country's accession to the WTO. The fact that China was subject to the Jackson–Vanik law required the graduation of China, however, and the bill by which that was accomplished became the functional equivalent of implementing legislation for the accession agreement.

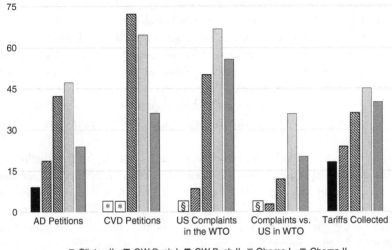

FIGURE 12.2 The weight of China in the instruments of US trade policy, 1997–2016.
*Countervailing duty (CVD) petitions against China were not legally possible prior to a revised interpretation of the law in 2007.
§Dispute-settlement complaints in either direction were not legally possible prior to China's WTO accession in 2001.
Shares of antidumping (AD) and CVD petitions calculated on the basis of total countries and products named in petitions. For example, if in a given year there is one AD petition filed against imports of Product X from China and one other country, plus another AD petition filed against imports of Product Y from only one other country, China accounts for 33.3% of all AD petitions.
Sources: AD and CVD petitions calculated from World Bank data at http://data.w orldbank.org/data-catalog/temporary-trade-barriers-database and US International Trade Commission data at www.usitc.gov/trade_remedy/731_ad_701_cvd/investiga tions/completed/index.htm. WTO complaints calculated from WTO data at www .wto.org/english/tratop_e/dispu_e/dispu_by_country_e.htm. Tariff data calculated from USITC DataWeb data at http://dataweb.usitc.gov/scripts/INTRO.asp.

China. This can be appreciated from the data in Figure 12.2, which summarize the shares of the main policy instruments that are directed at China. If one gives equal weight to each to these five measures, China's total share of US trade frictions and disputes rose from just 5% in the second Clinton term to 52% in the first Obama term. This composite score did ease back to 35% in the second Obama term, but there is good reason to expect that this may have been only a temporary respite. The trend might well have continued, had the US electorate chosen a normal president in 2016, but its choice instead shattered the old norms and expectations.

The surge in antidumping (AD) cases can be attributed not just to the rising share of US imports originating in China, but to special rules. China is subject to the unique methodology employed for nonmarket economies (NMEs), in which price comparisons are made not against the exporting country but instead against a market-oriented "surrogate" country (typically India). This makes it much easier for petitioners to show high rates of dumping.[29] It is thus more attractive for petitioners to bring cases against China and Vietnam than any other country.

The concentration of trade-remedy laws on China was further abetted by a decision in which the country lost its earlier exemption from countervailing duty (CVD) investigations. The Department of Commerce had previously read the law to mean that NMEs were immune from CVD investigations, based on the theory that it is impossible to isolate and assess the impact of subsidies in an economy that amounts to one big subsidy. The department reversed this doctrine in a 2007 case involving imports of Chinese paper, after which China rapidly went from being wholly exempt from this law to being its principal target. The law briefly took a new turn in late 2011, when the Court of Appeals for the Federal Circuit struck down the application of CVDs to imports from China, but yet another about-face quickly followed: In 2012 Congress approved legislation restoring Commerce's interpretation. This bill received not only the unanimous backing of House Democrats, but also got nearly as much support (83%) from House Republicans.

As for the WTO disputes, the cases involving the United States and China are now many and varied. Will the future pattern of Sino-American cases follow the same trajectory as transatlantic disputes? During the first ten years of the WTO (1995–2004), the United States and the European Union (or its members) brought a total of sixty-two complaints against one another, collectively accounting for about one-fifth of all WTO disputes. The numbers then fell to the point where the United States did not bring a single complaint against the European Union from 2010 through 2017, and was subject to just two EU complaints during that period.[30] One explanation for this rapid drop was that Washington and Brussels had come to see the drawbacks of playing tit-for-tat, with each one responding to any new filing with a retaliatory case against the other. The initial effect of that game was probably to multiply the

---

[29] See Morkre, Spinanger, and Tran (2008).
[30] Calculated from WTO data at www.wto.org/english/tratop_e/dispu_e/dispu_by_country_e .htm and www.wto.org/english/tratop_e/dispu_e/dispu_status_e.htm.

total level of litigation, but over the longer term the associated costs and ill will may have convinced the two players that there were better ways to manage their disagreements. Their decision to launch the Transatlantic Trade and Investment Partnership negotiations in 2013 implied that they preferred nego-tiation over litigation.

Could we see that same sequence in the US–China relationship? The data in Figure 12.2 suggest that the first half of that process – a reduction in the relative number of WTO disputes – might already have been underway in the second term of the Obama administration. Compared to the first term, the years 2013–2016 saw a small but appreciable drop in China's share of the US complaints, and a greater decline in the share of complaints against the United States that came from China. Those trends were then over-whelmed by a surge in complaints from China and many other WTO mem-bers. They collectively gave the United States a pass in the first several months of the Trump administration, notwithstanding the new government's provoca-tions, but then the floodgates opened. From November, 2017 through August, 2018 they brought twenty-one complaints against the United States; that was nearly as many as all the complaints brought against the United States in the eight years of the Obama administration (twenty-four). China brought five of these latest twenty-one cases. The United States responded in kind during that same ten-month period, though not on the same scale, bringing two com-plaints against China and five against other WTO members. [31]

One apparent anomaly in the data is the slight decline in China's recent portion of total tariffs, despite its rising share of total US imports. That is a product of the shifting composition of US imports, which are gradually moving out of low-tech, high-tariff goods such as apparel into higher-tech, lower-tariff items such as computers. That trend says more about the upgrad-ing of China's industrial base than it does about US policy choices.

Four other instruments not shown in Figure 12.2 have also been a part of the Sino-American frictions, two of which now seem moot. One is the selective safeguard instrument that was available during 2001–2013. Negotiated as part of its WTO accession, this instrument was also incorporated in the law extending PNTR to China. President Bush declined to take action on any of the six petitions that were filed under this law in his term, but President Obama did grant protection to the tire industry in a 2009 case. That law has since expired. Another possibility concerns the formal designation of China as a currency manipulator. At issue here is the Exchange Rates and International Economic Policy Coordination Act of 1988. The law requires that the

[31]   Calculated from WTO data at www.wto.org/english/tratop_e/dispu_e/dispu_status_e.htm.

Treasury annually "consider whether countries manipulate the rate of exchange . . . for purposes of preventing effective balance of payments adjustments or gaining unfair competitive advantage in international trade." Countries may be subject to negotiations "for the purpose of ensuring that such countries regularly and promptly adjust the rate of exchange between their currencies and the United States dollar to permit effective balance of payments adjustments and to eliminate the unfair advantage." President Trump frequently claimed on the campaign trail that he would name China under this law, as did Mitt Romney before him in the 2012 election. Romney could not, and Trump has not.

The Trump administration also elevated two other long-neglected laws in its conflicts with China, namely sections 232 (national security) and 301 (reciprocity). Neither of them are included in the tabulations of Figure 12.2 because each of these statutes lay dormant for decades, only to be revived by the Trump administration in 2017 (see Chapter 3). We will return to these laws in Chapter 16, examining more closely what their return means both for Sino-American relations and the larger issues of US trade strategy.

Sino-American Negotiations over Trade and Investment

Over the long term, how the United States and China engage one another in negotiations may be more consequential than how they confront one another via unilateral actions or WTO dispute-settlement. The available options include deals that are reached inside the WTO, a bilateral or regional FTA negotiation, and a bilateral investment treaty (BIT).

China's WTO membership necessarily alters the US perception of that institution and any concessions made there. This situation is similar in one respect to how Congress approached MFN treatment early in the Cold War, when any tariff reductions might (however implausibly) be portrayed as favors to Moscow, but with an important difference. That earlier problem was easily solved in 1951 by removing MFN treatment from the Soviets and their satellites, which affected very little trade and was uncomplicated by GATT status (apart from the special case of Czechoslovakia). By making that concession to Republican demands, the Truman administration safeguarded its own authority to continue negotiating in the GATT (see Chapter 11). That distinction cannot be so easily drawn now that China is a WTO member. The only ways to ensure that China does not benefit from any agreements reached in the WTO are to negotiate them only on a plurilateral basis (which China opposes), or to abstain from multilateral negotiations altogether. The United States appears to have pursued that second option, however informally, in the decade following 2008.[32] Modest accomplishments such as the Trade Facilitation Agreement of 2013 fall far short of completing the Doha Round, raising serious questions about whether the WTO members are willing to let this institution execute its legislative function. As we will take up in Chapter 16, a Trump administration withdrawal of the United States from the WTO is not out of the question.

Is it possible that the United States and China might negotiate an FTA, either in bilateral form or in some other regional configuration? That seems even more fanciful today than a US–Japan FTA would have sounded in the 1980s, but the fact that Washington and Tokyo eventually entered the TPP negotiations suggests that there is wisdom in never saying never. The prospects for such a deal might also be advanced by the apparently chaotic and impulsive approach that President Trump takes even toward larger strategic questions. It is nonetheless quite difficult to imagine a bona fide FTA – that is, one that meets the WTO requirement of eliminating tariffs on substantially all of the trade between its parties – being negotiated with China any time soon. Even if the White House were to favor that approach, it would be a hard sell in Congress.

The prospects for a BIT are much better, even if progress toward that end has been excruciatingly slow. BITs are generally devoted more to the protection of investors' rights, and the settlement of any disputes that might arise between an investor and the host government, than they are to liberalization. They have played only a minor role in US foreign economic policy, with just forty such instruments in effect as of 2018; most of them were reached with relatively small developing countries or transition economies in the 1990s.[33] Beijing and Washington first entered into BIT negotiations in the last year of the George W. Bush administration, followed by on-again, off-again talks during the Obama administration. The Trump administration showed some interest in reviving this process on taking office. While a BIT between the United States and China appears to be low on both countries' priority lists, one could well imagine either or both sides favoring its advancement at some point – if for no other reason than to give the appearance of doing something productive.

Sino-American Rivalry in Trade with Third Parties

For want of significant, direct trade negotiations between Beijing and Washington, the most important role for trade agreements in this relationship

---

[32] See VanGrasstek (2013), especially pp. 447–456, for the US and Chinese roles in the failed 2008 effort to solve the Doha Round in a mini-ministerial meeting.

[33] See the list at www.state.gov/e/eb/ifd/bit/117402.htm.

TABLE 12.1. *The FTA Networks of the United States and China*
Status of partners as of October, 2018; GDP data for 2016

FTA Partners of the United States Only

In Effect:		Negotiating with United States:
Bahrain	Jordan	European Union
Dominican Rep.	Mexico	United Kingdom
El Salvador	Morocco	*21.7% of Global GDP*
Guatemala	Nicaragua	
Honduras	Oman	
2.0% of Global GDP		

FTA Partners of the United States and China

In Effect with United States and China:	Negotiating with United States and China:	Negotiating with China:	Under Study with China:
Australia	Japan	Israel	Canada
Chile	*6.0% of Global GDP*	*0.4% of Global GDP*	Colombia
Costa Rica			Panama
Korea			*2.5% of Global GDP*
Peru			
Singapore			
4.5% of Global GDP			

FTA Partners of China Only

In Effect:		Negotiating with China:	Under Study with China:
Brunei[a]	Maldives	India	Bengal
Cambodia	Myanmar	Mauritius	Fiji
Georgia	New Zealand[a]	Moldova	Mongolia
Hong Kong	Pakistan	Norway	Nepal
Iceland	Philippines	Sri Lanka	Palestine
Indonesia	Switzerland	*4.1% of Global GDP*	Papua New Guinea
Laos	Taiwan		*0.1% of Global GDP*
Macao	Thailand		
Malaysia[a]	Vietnam[a]		
5.0% of Global GDP			

[a] TPP participants that do not have bilateral FTAs with the United States.
The table includes all FTAs, whether in the form of bilateral, sub-regional, or regional agreements. GDP data are not available for Bengal, Palestine, or Taiwan, and hence are not included in the Chinese totals.
Except for the proposed FTA with Japan, all agreements shown for "FTA Partners of the United States and China" are already in effect for the United States.
Sources: China's FTAs at http://fta.mofcom.gov.cn/english/fta_qianshu.shtml. USFTAs at https://ustr.gov/trade-agreements/free-trade-agreements. *GDP data at* https://data.worldbank.org/indicator/NY.GDP.MKTP.CD.

is indirect. As can be seen from the data in Table 12.1, some fifty-one countries or regional groups are actual or potential FTA partners for either or both of these economic giants. Washington paused when Trump arrived, but then launched new talks with European Union, Japan, and the United Kingdom in 2018.

Like the United States, China is well-positioned to treat trade agreements as an instrument of power. That point rests on two characteristics that distinguish these countries from all others: Each typically accounts for high shares of any given partner's total trade, and yet each of them is less dependent on that trade – globally and bilaterally – than are their partners. Beijing and Washington are equally capable of exploiting these asymmetrical relationships, even if there are a few differences at the margins. The United States is even less trade-dependent than China, with exports of goods and services being equal to just 12% of US GDP in 2016; exports then accounted for 20% of Chinese GDP. Both were still below the world average of 29%.[34] As for their relative weight in other countries' economies, China has been overtaking the United States in much of the world. Even among the many countries for which China has moved into the top spot, however, the United States often remains the second largest partner.

Compared to the United States, which concluded its first FTA in 1985 and had three partners by the turn of the century, China is a relative latecomer to this game. Beijing started with the special cases of Hong Kong and Macao in 2003. Next came an agreement with the Association of Southeast Asian Nations (ASEAN) in 2004,[35] and Chile became China's first extra-regional FTA partner in 2005. By 2013 its negotiations had reached Europe, concluding agreements with Iceland and Switzerland. China had FTAs in effect with twenty-four countries by 2018, most of them in Asia and the Pacific Rim; that was four more than the United States. It was also actively negotiating FTAs with seven other partners, and exploring the prospects for nine more. These included the Regional Comprehensive Economic Partnership, which covered several existing FTA partners plus India and Japan.

The potential utility of FTAs as a tool of diplomacy can be seen in the competition between China and Taiwan for diplomatic recognition. There had been a time when more countries recognized Taipei than Beijing, and when Taiwan filled the permanent Chinese seat on the United Nations

---

[34] According to World Bank data at https://data.worldbank.org/indicator/NE.EXP.GNFS.ZS, as of 2016 the only countries for which exports were relatively less important than they are for the United States were Egypt, Pakistan, and seven least-developed countries (i.e., Afghanistan, Burundi, Ethiopia, Kiribati, Nepal, Sudan, and Yemen).

[35] The ASEAN members are Brunei, Cambodia, Indonesia, Laos, Malaysia, Myanmar, the Philippines, Singapore, Thailand, and Vietnam.

Security Council. That began to change when the General Assembly voted 76–35 in 1971 to seat Beijing, and accelerated after the United States transferred its recognition in 1979, to the point where in 2018 only seventeen countries still recognized Taiwan.[36] All of these holdouts are fairly small; several are micro-states such as Kiribati and Swaziland. Both Chinas have long used such incentives as the building of sports stadiums to induce countries either to retain or switch their recognition, and they have lately employed FTAs for that same purpose. Taiwan concluded FTAs with four Central American countries and Panama between 2003 and 2007, for example, prompting China to persuade Costa Rica to switch diplomatic allegiances in 2007 and then negotiate an FTA in 2008. The cross-straits competition eased somewhat in 2010, with the conclusion of the Economic Cooperation Framework Agreement between Beijing and Taipei. In addition to being an FTA, this initiative offers a framework through which China no longer objects to Taiwan's negotiations of FTAs with third countries. Taiwan still has little to show for it, with its only new FTAs between 2010 and 2017 being reached with New Zealand and Singapore. Both of those countries instead recognize China as China (and also as an FTA partner). By that time, Beijing had far outstripped Taiwan in the negotiation of FTAs.

The more consequential race is between the United States and China. Prior to the 2016 election, the United States was unambiguously ahead on the FTA scoreboard. Its edge came not in the sheer number of partners, but in their collective economic size. At the time that Trump took office, the combined values of the US economy and those of its 20 FTA partners amounted to 34% of the global economy. Adding the TPP and TTIP agreements would have brought that up to 63%, but Trump shredded the first agreement and suspended negotiations for the second. That decision could have allowed Beijing's FTA network to take first place, with the combined value of China, its actual FTA partners, and the agreements under negotiation or study comprising 37% of world GDP. Calculations of this sort may well have been decisive in prompting the course correction that the Trump administration announced in October, 2018, when it followed up the renegotiation of NAFTA by launching separate FTA talks with the European Union, Japan, and the United Kingdom.

Developing countries that negotiate FTAs with both Beijing and Washington may find that the import profiles of these two countries carry different implications for partners. The Chinese pattern of trade more closely

---

[36] Panama switched recognition to Beijing in 2017, and the Dominican Republic and El Salvador did so in 2018. See www.mofa.gov.tw/en/AlliesIndex.aspx?n=DF6F8F246049F8 D6&sms=A76B7230ADF29736.

conforms to the mercantilist ideal of importing inputs and exporting finished goods. Raw materials or intermediate products consistently account for a larger share of China's imports (44% in 2016) than do consumer goods (13%); just the reverse is true in the United States, where the lower-processed materials accounted for 24% of imports in 2016, and 38% were consumer goods. The difference is even wider when it comes to developing countries. Whereas these two categories of goods each accounted for 28% of US imports from Latin American and Caribbean countries, just 3% of Chinese imports from that region were consumer goods; most of the rest (89%) was raw materials or intermediate products. The disparity was wider still for sub-Saharan Africa, for which only 1% of Chinese imports were consumer goods, versus 21% for the United States.[37] A developing country that looks to an FTA with Washington may hope to become an alternative source of supply for goods that the United States might otherwise import from China. When that same country seeks an FTA with China, it might be negotiating over the terms by which China imports raw materials that will be incorporated in its exports to the United States.

The Trans-Pacific Partnership

The TPP had been, prior to the election of Donald Trump, the most economically and politically significant of all mega-regional trade agreements. Its economic importance was defined by who was inside, with the dozen TPP signatories collectively accounting for 39% of the world economy, while its political significance was defined by who was left outside. The Bush and Obama administrations both treated the TPP primarily as an American-led answer to the rise of China. Not all of the TPP countries view the agreement in that same light; Mexico is the only one among them that, as of 2018, was not at some stage of pondering, negotiating, or implementing an FTA with China. A closer examination of the diplomatic history of this initiative nevertheless reveals that some of those same Chinese partners are disquieted by Beijing's growing role in the region, and hoped to shore up their relationship with the United States.

The conclusion of the TPP negotiations in late 2015 marked the culmination of a decades-long process of proposals and negotiations. Discussions aiming at some form of Pacific trade agreement have been underway since at least the mid-1960s, and the first solid plans came in the

---

[37] Calculated from World Integrated Trade Solution (WITS) data at https://wits.worldbank.org/Default.aspx?lang=en.

next decade.[38] This more specific negotiation began in 2005 as a modest initiative known as Plan Four (P-4) covering four small countries (Brunei, Chile, New Zealand, and Singapore) that collectively accounted for just under 1% of global GDP that year. The largest TPP expansions came when the United States joined in 2008, followed by Japan in 2013. Others that came to the table during 2008–2013 include two additional developed countries (Australia and Canada) and four developing countries in Latin America (Mexico and Peru) and Asia (Malaysia and Vietnam). Prior to the Trump administration's withdrawal from this agreement, it was widely expected that many more countries might accede. The most frequently mentioned candidates included four countries with which the United States already has FTAs (i.e., Colombia, Costa Rica, Korea, and Panama) as well as two other partners that would be wholly new (i.e., the Philippines and Taiwan).

China figured prominently in the Bush administration's decision to accept the invitation from the P-4 countries, and in the Obama adminis- tration's resolve to expand it. Singapore's original pitch to Washington stressed the Chinese boogeyman, with Trade Minister Lim Hng Kiang telling his American interlocutors in 2008 "that without U.S. engagement in a regional agreement, the architecture would follow China's 'model,' based on an overtly political agenda." Echoing views that Adam Smith expressed almost a quarter of a millennium earlier, Lim said that, "We can't just be rich and not safe." Negotiating with these four countries was not very enticing to the US officials, as two of them were already among Washington's FTA partners, but they told their Singaporean collea- gue that the game would be more attractive if Tokyo were to join. "[I]f the U.S. commits to the P4 process soon," a USTR official said to Lim, "it would expect Japan to be ready to 'jump in the pool' within six to nine months."[39] It took Tokyo longer than that to take the plunge, but strategic issues were prominent in Tokyo's calculations. Japanese officials had already stressed in 2006 a concern that China viewed FTAs "as more of a political than an economic exercise and were not interested in the creation of a serious, advanced regional free trade agreement," but were instead using the "lure of the vast Chinese domestic market" in order to "entic[e] the ASEAN countries into their orbit."[40]

---

[38] For a summary, see Drysdale and Garnaut (1989).

[39] "Singapore Encourages U.S. Involvement in P4, Hopes for P8 Negotiations in 2009," cable of September 8, 2008 from the US embassy in Singapore (08SINGAPORE961_a).

[40] "METI Says ASEAN Plus 3 FTA 'Inevitable,'" cable of June 8, 2006 from the US Embassy in Tokyo (06TOKYO3164_a).

The TPP negotiations involved some tricky bilateral relationships, as exemplified by the case of New Zealand. The United States pointedly excluded New Zealand from its FTA negotiations with Australia in 2002, despite the fact that Australia and New Zealand have one of the world's most comprehensive economic integration agreements. Political issues are more important to the US calculations. Formerly strong security relations between the United States and New Zealand began to deteriorate after the 1984 election brought to power a Labour government committed to barring nuclear-armed and -powered warships. This put it on a collision course with the US Navy, which will neither confirm nor deny the presence of nuclear weapons on board its vessels. President Reagan directed in 1985 that New Zealand should no longer be treated to "the 'special relationship' of a very close ally" if it is not "complying with the necessary responsibilities."[41] Trade and security issues got further knotted when later Labour governments placed a high priority on the negotiation of an FTA, but also expressed misgivings over Washington's prosecution of the Long War. While New Zealand kept out of Iraq because "it lacked UN sanction," it thought that its subsequent deployment of "troops to Afghanistan in support of Operation Enduring Freedom (OEF) warrants [an FTA] on strategic grounds."[42] It was not until 2007 – the year that Wellington began negotiating its own FTA with China – that the Bush administration began to soften its line. The USTR then agreed to develop "a cooperative work plan to address specific trade issues, including the possibility of expanding P-4 (NZ, Singapore, Brunei, Chile) FTA as the basis for US-NZ free trade."[43]

The work of years can be undone in just days, as Donald Trump proved almost immediately after assuming the presidency. As already noted, he signed on January 23, 2018 a memorandum directing the USTR to withdraw the United States from the TPP and to negotiate bilateral agreements instead. The eleven other TPP countries eventually decided to implement this agreement without its largest signatory. The only continuity with its predecessors came in the primacy that the Trump administration accorded to Japan, announcing in September, 2018 that this would be its first FTA negotiating partner. It added the European Union and the United Kingdom in October.

---

[41] National Security Decision Directive Number 193 (October 21, 1985), p. 1.

[42] "Scenesetter for Visit of Adm[iral] Fallon and Gen[eral] Hester to New Zealand," cable of January 10, 2006 from the US embassy in Wellington (06WELLINGTON18_a). Wellington attached the same significance to its contribution of engineers to Iraq; see "GNZ Aims to Cool Expectations for U.S. FTA," cable of March 24, 2006 from the US Embassy in Wellington (06WELLINGTON230_a).

[43] "Your Visit and Expanding US-NZ Cooperation," cable of August 30, 2007 from the US embassy in Wellington (07WELLINGTON646_a).

THE FUTURE OF SINO-AMERICAN TRADE RELATIONS – AND THE WORLD

We may reasonably expect the state of relations between the United States and China to be the most significant influence on the future development of the global trading system. Size alone makes this obvious: These two countries jointly account for 21% of world exports, 23% of its imports, 23% of the population, and 39% of the global economy.[44] More to the point, they also comprise 100% of the contenders for hegemony. Even though it cannot be taken for granted that China will continue to grow at the levels it has achieved in recent decades, nor that the relative position of the United States will fall behind China, the trends are undeniable. They prompt leaders in these two countries, and in all others, to anticipate a changing global environment in which Beijing's influence will rival – and in some ways surpass – that of Washington. Even if this does not entail recognition of a leadership role for China that is comparable to that exercised by the United States, it will undoubtedly require significant accommodations.

Much more is at stake here than the odd tariff, antidumping order, or free trade agreement. The last transfer of global leadership was deceptively easy. It was fortunate for the outgoing and incoming hegemons, and for the world, that London and Washington were on the same side in the most destructive war in history. The cousins worked closely to design the postwar global system, and devoted especially close attention to the trade component of that regime. It would be particularly ironic if it were the United States, and not China, that were to take the lead in either dismantling the remnants of that system or, at the least, requiring it to get on without Washington. That is what happened to both the League of Nations and the International Trade Organization, and Trump's withdrawal from the TPP implies that he may be prepared to repeat that move in the WTO. That is an issue to which we will return in Chapter 16.

---

[44] Calculated from World Bank data at https://data.worldbank.org/indicator/BX.GSR.GNFS .CD, https://data.worldbank.org/indicator/BM.GSR.GNFS.CD, https://data.worldbank.org/i ndicator/SP.POP.TOTL, and https://data.worldbank.org/indicator/NY.GDP.MKTP.CD.

PART V

TRADING WITH DEVELOPING COUNTRIES

13

The Strategy and Domestic Diplomacy of Trade Preferences

[O]ur commercial policy should hold an equal and impartial hand; neither seeking nor granting exclusive favors or preferences; consulting the natural course of things; diffusing and diversifying by gentle means the streams of commerce, but forcing nothing ... constantly keeping in view that it is folly in one nation to look for disinterested favors from another; that it must pay with a portion of its independence for whatever it may accept under that character[.]

President George Washington, Farewell Address (1796)

INTRODUCTION

George Washington hoped that trade would allow the infant United States to benefit from membership in the community of nations without exposing itself to the machinations of Europe. Aiming for splendid isolation from foreign intrigues, coupled with a mercenary interest in the economic benefits of political neutrality, US policymakers favored equality of treatment over the preferential schemes of the United Kingdom and its European rivals. Nondiscrimination in trade and neutrality in war were, for these early states-men, two sides of the same coin. Generations would pass before the United States began to engage in discriminatory arrangements of its own, and a century more until the exceptions outweighed the rule.

The first of those exceptions coincided with the earlier US forays into power politics, extending preferences to Cuba and the Philippines after the Spanish-American War of 1898. Nondiscrimination otherwise remained a key princi-ple in the first half of American hegemony, with the only new and significant exceptions to that rule being the sanctions imposed on most Communist countries after 1951 and the Auto Pact negotiated with Canada in 1965. The principal shift in American policy in early hegemony did not concern US discrimination per se, but rather Washington's tolerance for – and indeed its own advocacy of – its allies' regional integration initiatives. The United

States saw the elimination of intra-European trade barriers as a prerequisite to the restoration of prosperity and collective security.

The United States did not move decisively toward the adoption of its own discriminatory measures until it implemented the Generalized System of Preferences (GSP) in 1976, the first of several programs extending preferential treatment to developing countries. Discrimination deepened in the mid-1980s, and moved from merely autonomous programs to reciprocal agreements. Washington first got into the FTA game with Israel in 1984 and then, more consequentially, with Canada in 1986. The number of FTA partners grew tenfold over the next three decades, as FTAs became a key element in the alliance structure. Yet while the political importance of preferences has risen, their relative economic importance has dwindled. Although the United States now extends either one-way or reciprocal preferences to 144 of its trading partners, versus another 85 countries and territories that receive no preferences, the partners that get this advantage account for a diminishing share of total imports.

This chapter examines the paradox of preferences, a phenomenon in which the hegemon deploys discrimination as a tool of economic statesmanship just when this instrument begins to lose its utility. Average US tariff rates were quite high, and related instruments such as quotas were quite restrictive, when the United States first began to negotiate nondiscriminatory trade agreements that were initially bilateral (1934–1946) and then multilateral (from 1947). Its market was far more open in 1976 than it had been in 1946, meaning that the potential benefits of discrimination were greatly diminished. The margins of preference were lower still after the Tokyo and Uruguay rounds ended in 1979 and 1994. It was only then that the United States began to offer many of its partners a means of evading tariffs altogether.

Understanding the full dynamics of this process requires that we consider the *political* economy of discrimination. A narrower focus on the bare economics of preferences would mean rehashing the perennial and unresolved debates over whether discrimination creates new trade or merely diverts existing flows, and the extent to which these options may be second-best to multilateral liberalization. The key political issues center on discrimination as a tool of persuasion, pressure, or patronage. Preferences can be a reward for past favors, an inducement for new ones, or support for faltering economies. Any subsequent threat to remove these benefits can be considered a low-grade form of sanction. As Wu put it, "in the absence of a complete unity of political purpose, every act of conditional aid given by one country to another can be interpreted as coercion."[1] At issue here is what Hirschman called the influence effect, which arises whenever a large country extends preferences to a small partner. These favors produce "relationships of dependence and influence between nations."[2] He asserted that in a "world of many sovereign states it [is] an elementary principle of the power policy of a state to *direct its trade away from the large to the smaller trading state*."[3] The smaller country's dependence on the larger market is not merely a mundane commercial matter, in this view, but something that the bigger state will seek to magnify economically in order to exploit politically.

But just how successful are preferences in achieving that end? How highly do the actual or prospective beneficiaries prize open access to the US market? The attraction of preferential market access ought to be lower for foreign leaders now than it would have been in the past. The potential value of preferences has been undercut by the general reduction of tariff barriers (preference erosion) and by the proliferation of preferential programs and agreements (preference dilution), as well as by the limitations that Congress and other actors have imposed on these instruments. Even so, some foreign leaders retain an unrealistically high expectation of the benefits that they might derive from striking such a bargain. This may allow US negotiators to take advantage of the influence effect longer than the facts might warrant.

US POLICY THROUGH EARLY HEGEMONY: OPPOSITION TO PREFERENCES IN PRINCIPLE

The United States went through two periods in which it opposed the discriminatory trade practices of the United Kingdom and other European powers. When Washington was itself devoted to the practice of protectionism, but nonetheless hoped that its exporters could take a free ride on the liberal impulses of its partners, it saw discrimination as a means by which the Europeans unfairly excluded American goods from their markets. That resentment only grew when the US turn came to provide leadership, and the colonial preferences provided by the Europeans – and especially the English – were equated with the very protectionism that the United States had learned to abhor.

---

[1] Wu (1952), p. 187. Note that the full quote was in italics in the original.
[2] Hirschman (1945), p. 15.
[3] Ibid., p. 31. Emphasis in the original.

The US Position in the British Hegemony

Having preferential access to the US market in pre-hegemonic times might have been highly advantageous, had the United States engaged in discrimination. This was not to be. Apart from a few short-lived experiments in the late nineteenth and early twentieth centuries, the typical American practice from independence until the New Deal was to apply the same, usually high tariffs to all partners on a nondiscriminatory basis. The First Congress set the precedent in its deliberations over the original tariff bill, with the Senate reversing the House by striking from the bill a provision that would apply lower rates on imports from countries that reached commercial treaties with the United States. James Madison had promoted this idea, but Alexander Hamilton convinced the upper chamber to reject it.[4]

The US approach to discrimination, as in so many other areas, would follow in hegemony the path set by the United Kingdom. The only major difference is that London employed preferences long before it achieved hegemony, then decided that it had to disavow these anachronisms early in its leadership. "The colonial policy of the period of [British] mercantilism was definitively abandoned in 1855," by Kreider's estimation, as that was the year that "the United Kingdom had ceased to demand preferential treatment in her colonial markets."[5] It was followed in 1860 by the removal of preferences for colonial products in the UK market. The golden age of British nondicrimination was to last for nearly two-thirds of a century. It began to fade during the First World War, starting with the introduction of more favorable licensing treatment for the colonies, and then disappeared with the rebirth of tariff preferences in 1919. The Ottawa Agreements of 1932 would complete that process, bringing the United Kingdom and its dominions back to the naked discrimination that London had practiced before hegemony.

The experience of the next hegemon would be remarkably similar to the middle and late stages of that UK progression. The United States took the first important step to replace its long-standing policy of nondiscriminatory protectionism with nondiscriminatory liberalization when it did away with the conditional MFN principle in 1923, then adopted a discriminatory policy when it concluded its first FTA in 1985. The interval separating those two events (sixty-two years) is nearly identical to the sixty-four years separating Britain's abandonment (1855) and return (1919) of colonial preferences. To carry the comparison further, both hegemons took a little over a decade

---

[4] See Rutland et al. (1977), p. 55.
[5] Kreider (1943), p. 12.

to make the transition from cautious to eager discrimination. Thirteen years separated Britain's initial move toward the reimposition of discrimination and the negotiation of the Ottawa Agreements, and fifteen years passed between the first US FTA (1985) and the first time that it took on more than one FTA negotiation at a time (2000).

Frictions in the Hegemonic Transition

Previous chapters have noted the relative ease with which hegemony passed from London to Washington, and the efforts of British statesmen to remain on good terms with the United States from the mid-nineteenth to the mid-twentieth centuries. That is what one sees when looking down from a high historical altitude, but the closer that one gets to the granular level of policy the more apparent are the frictions in that Anglo-American relationship. Those irritants were especially prominent in the years between the first and second world wars, when disputes were worsened by the contradictory directions then being taken by the incumbent and incoming hegemon. The imperial preferences that London adopted almost precisely when Washington turned towards negotiated liberalization were maddening to American officials, who considered discrimination to be worse than protectionism, but they could only complain and cajole as long as their negotiations with the English were strictly bilateral and confined to tariffs. In just a few years, the outbreak of war would accelerate the consummation of their relationship.

This wartime alliance transformed Anglo-American relations, and yet the cousins remained far apart on trade discrimination. More was at stake here than trade between the immediate parties. From Washington's perspective, there was not much difference between London's imperial preferences, Germany's controls on trade with the smaller states of Europe, and the Japanese attempt to establish a Greater East Asia Co-Prosperity Sphere; each bloc was incompatible with the US vision of a world in which states were sovereign and markets were open and nondiscriminatory. Churchill was a true believer in England's civilizing mission, and frequently stated that he had not become prime minister just to preside over the dismantling of the empire. Washington would never place as high a priority on ending the imperial system as London did on preserving it. These issues would continue to plague the transatlantic trade relationship long after the war, although the level of British discrimination would gradually dissipate. The average margin of preference on English imports from the Commonwealth had been 17–20% in 1937, but fell to 11–13% in 1949 and

9% in 1957.[6] In later decades these preferences would be folded into the ones that the European Community extended to former colonies, which gave rise to a new but familiar transatlantic dispute.

Washington made a down-payment on its new status in 1942 when the Roosevelt administration extended unconditional MFN treatment to all countries with which the United States was not then at war. This wartime decision was initially more important for its symbolism than for its substance. By this time there were only a handful of commercially significant countries that had not yet obtained MFN treatment through existing treaties or new Reciprocal Trade Agreements Act (RTAA) agreements. The United States also moved to eliminate the few discriminatory elements that remained in its own trade regime. The State Department proposed in 1945 that preferences for Cuba and the Philippines be eliminated, along with similar practices by the United Kingdom and other powers, in the negotiations for an International Trade Organization (ITO).[7] The United States concluded just such a postwar agreement with Manila, phasing out the Philippine preferences over three decades. The Cuban authorities successfully resisted a similar initiative, but that reprieve was short-lived. Washington's relationship with Havana would move quickly from positive discrimination to negative discrimination after 1959.

Preferences in the Multilateral System

Washington's position on preferences has evolved over the span of its hegemony, based on the interplay of four contending interests. On the negative side, the traditional US uneasiness over discrimination was now exacerbated by a concern over the "leveling" demands of developing countries. By the logic of the poorer countries, the emergence of a more democratic global system permitted the creation of what would eventually be called a new international economic order; from Washington's perspective, this seemed more like demagoguery and an effort to soak the rich. Those arguments against discriminatory schemes had to be weighed against two political considerations that pointed in the opposite direction. One was the need to shore up allies, especially in Western Europe, and the perception that this would be more rapidly achieved if those partners eliminated the barriers to trade with their neighbors.

---

[6] Patterson (1966), p. 232.

[7] See Memorandum by the Acting Secretary of State to President Truman, "Proposal to Establish an International Trade Organization" (September 7, 1945), *FRUS 1945*, Volume VI, pp. 118–119.

American policymakers also hoped to avoid the diplomatic isolation that would come from being the sole holdout against developing country demands, creating an opportunity that friend and foe alike might exploit. For the first half of the Cold War, the arguments for discrimination lost more often than they won; just the reverse was true in the second half and beyond.

Before any such programs or agreements could be put in place, their legality in the multilateral system first had to be settled. American planners originally hoped that the postwar trading system would treat discrimination and protectionism as equally valid targets for elimination. As finally crafted, both the GATT and the ITO explicitly grandfathered existing preferences and allowed for the negotiation of FTAs and customs unions, and implicitly established means to waive MFN rules in favor of other discriminatory arrangements. Commentators have long been puzzled as to why the US position eased on this point. Some attributed the switch to an American desire to promote European integration, or an effort to placate London's imperial interests, or to curry favor with developing countries. Later scholarship established yet another motive, with these rules being the permanent consequence of a brief flirtation with the neighbor. As discussed in Chapter 9, the United States and Canada considered an FTA in the immediate postwar period. The archival evidence supports the contention that the prospect of a comprehensive agreement with Ottawa inspired Washington to push "behind the scenes to amend the Havana Charter to allow free trade areas" so as "to shape global trade rules to accommodate the US-Canada trade treaty – which, fate would have it, was never signed or ratified."[8]

A preferential trading regime to benefit developing countries has been on the table at least as far back as the ill-starred ITO project. It has also traditionally been more easily advanced in UN-based negotiations in which the developing countries can outvote the United States than it has in the GATT and WTO, which came to operate on the more restrictive basis of consensus decision-making. While the ITO's Havana Charter provided for preferences in the interests of economic development, the supposedly temporary GATT did not. The notion of special treatment languished until the early 1960s, eventually coalescing around the plans for a UN Conference on Trade and Development (UNCTAD) in 1964. This then became a permanent organization that sponsored a new conference every four years. For a time, UNCTAD challenged GATT as the principal North–South trade forum. It would eventually evolve into an institution whose functions (if not always its tone) is more complementary

---

[8] Chase (2006), p. 3.

than competitive with the WTO, but only after a few decades of sometimes impassioned clashes.

Generations of American statesmen have distrusted the involvement of UN agencies in trade negotiations. Under Secretary of State George Ball did not hold back in a late 1963 memo to President Kennedy, characterizing UNCTAD as an expression of "the discontent of the less developed countries with the GATT, which they regard as an institution run by and for the benefit of the great trading nations; and the tactical interest of the Soviet Union in undermining the GATT primarily for political purposes."[9] American officials were also leery of "another effort to establish a world trade organization,"[10] which by the early 1960s meant to them a radical break from the preferred GATT practice of reducing barriers and letting the market find its own level. The Reagan administration's later decision not to sign the Law of the Sea Convention reflected this perennial concern, with CIA Director William Casey warning "that acceptance of Third World ideological principles in a seabed mining treaty would establish a negative precedent for other future global negotiations on matters such as outer space, the radio spectrum and Antarctica."[11] Similar concerns would inform the American approach to UN negotiations over the Millennium Development Goals of 2000, and then the Sustainable Development Goals of 2015. Both sets of objectives, including such trade components as comprehensive preferences for the least-developed countries, are viewed in many developing countries as binding obligations. Washington instead treats them as aspirational statements of soft law.

US POLICY IN AND AFTER HEGEMONY: SUPPORT FOR PREFERENCES IN PRACTICE

Over the course of its hegemony, the United States made three key shifts in its policy on discrimination. The first move came in the early postwar decision to support discrimination as a tool of European integration. The second shift came in the 1960s, when the United States reluctantly agreed to the creation of global preferences for developing countries. The third step came in the 1980s, when the United States became a far more active practitioner of trade discrimination.

---

[9] Memorandum from the Under Secretary of State (Ball) to President Kennedy, "United Nations Conference on Trade and Development" (November 12, 1963), *FRUS 1961–1963*, Volume IX, pp. 623–625.

[10] Central Intelligence Agency, Office of Current Intelligence, "United Nations Conference on Trade and Development" (March 20, 1964).

[11] Memo from the Director of Central Intelligence to the Chief of the Geography Division (January 21, 1982), p. 2.

The rationale for each new program was usually more political than economic, variously aiming to counter Soviet influence, encourage alternatives to drug crops, or promote stability through the alleviation of extreme poverty. Once the United States began negotiating FTAs in 1985, the political objectives became even more precise and diverse. Discriminatory programs and agreements proliferated to the point where the exceptions overwhelmed the rule.

The instruments summarized in Table 13.1 show that most US trading partners already received preferential treatment by 1990, and that the numbers grew larger still by 2017. The deepest (and reciprocal) preferences come via FTAs, which typically phase out tariffs on nearly all products over ten to fifteen years. Regional programs offer the second-highest level of preferential treatment, starting in 1985 with the Caribbean Basin Initiative (CBI). Most of the Spanish-speaking CBI beneficiaries eventually negotiated FTAs with the United States, leaving this program primarily to the Anglophone Caribbean islands. The CBI extends duty-free treatment to the great majority of US imports, as does the African Growth and Opportunities Act (AGOA). The United States also offered special treatment to four partners under the Andean Trade Preferences Act (ATPA) of 1991; it has since expired. The least generous of these preferential programs is the GSP, which excludes a great many products of interest to developing countries (although least-developed countries are now eligible for GSP treatment on a more extensive list of products). Taken together, these various programs and agreements allow about one-fifth of all US imports to enter preferentially.

Support for European Integration

The first crack in the US opposition to discrimination came in the immediate postwar period, when Washington placed a higher priority on European economic and political recovery than on the preservation of its traditional position. American policymakers saw regional integration as a means of overcoming the perennial rivalries between France and Germany while also bolstering the Western alliance against the Soviet Union. This is a notion that had been developing for the better part of a decade. American planners were already considering the shape of a post-war settlement when the Nazi invasion of France was just beginning, with an internal State Department memo touting the "obvious economic advantages to be gained by the establishment in Europe of various blocs or free trade groups of states."[12]

---

[12] "Memorandum [by Hugh R. Wilson] Arising from Conversations in Mr. Welles' Office, April 19 and 26" (May 1, 1940), in U.S. Department of State (1949), p. 458.

Trade Preferences

TABLE 13.1. *US Preferential Trade Agreements and Programs, 1990–2017*

	Countries		Imports Entering Preferentially (%)		Average US Tariffs (%)	
	1990	2017	1990	2017	1990	2017
Preferential	**138**	**144**	**33.9**	**41.7**	**2.1**	**0.7**
Free Trade Agreements	2	20	56.9	48.8	0.7	0.1
Developed countries	1	2	57.4	43.4	0.7	0.1
Developing countries	1	18	44.4	52.3	0.2	0.2
Autonomous Preferences	136	124	11.8	16.2	3.4	2.6
Ordinary GSP	114	57	11.0	11.0	3.2	2.7
GSP for least developed countries	—	13	—	15.2	—	12.6
Caribbean Basin Initiative	22	16	23.5	16.7	6.9	0.9
African Growth & Opp. Act	—	38	—	55.4	—	0.1
Nonpreferential	**56**	**85**	—	—	**4.1**	**2.0**
Developed countries	31	40	—	—	3.3	1.3
Developing and transitional	25	45	—	—	6.0	2.6
China	1	1	—	—	8.3	2.7
All other	24	44	—	—	5.5	2.3
Denied MFN/Other Sanctions	**11**	**3**	—	—	**3.5**	**0.3**
World	**205**	**232**	**14.4**	**18.8**	**3.3**	**1.4**

Data for the GSP exclude those countries that are additionally designated for either of the regional programs.

Imports Entering Preferentially = Share of imports entering either under this program or other programs that would cover the same items (e.g., any imports from a CBI, ATPA, or AGOA country that are imported under the GSP are included in this figure).

Source: Calculated from U.S. International Trade Commission DataWeb data available at https://dataweb.usitc.gov/.

Policymakers placed so high a priority on a future European economic integration that they were debating the advisability of a plan "to link France and western Germany with the proposed Netherlands-Belgium economic union"[13] even while the Normandy invasion was still underway in June, 1944.

The momentum toward European integration slowed just after the war, when American officials recoiled at the enormity of the Nazi crimes. As wary as Washington was of Stalinism, Soviet totalitarianism seemed to pale in comparison to the form that Germany had practiced with such chilling

[13] Whidden (1945), p. 8.

efficiency. Secretary of the Treasury Henry Morgenthau proposed that Germany be denuded of its heavy industries and its people sent to toil in the fields. The immediate postwar diplomacy of Europe also intervened, with the Soviet Union and France also favoring German pastoralization and demanding reparations. It took a few years of confrontation, and a final divorce in the US–USSR marriage of convenience, before *realpolitik* overtook retribution and American strategists opted not to make a desert and call it peace.

It was the Marshall Plan rather than the Morgenthau Plan that defined US policy toward European integration. "Some form of political, military and economic union in Western Europe will be necessary if the free nations of Europe are to hold their own against the people of the east united under Moscow rule," the Policy Planning Staff concluded in 1948.[14] Congress gave its blessing by approving language in the Mutual Security Act that "encourage[d] the economic unification and the political federation of Europe." Europeans rightly remember Jean Monnet and Robert Schuman as the fathers of the European Union, but a fair appraisal of diplomatic history would credit American pressure as much as European inspiration. It might never have gotten off the ground without the advocacy of Secretary Marshall, his deputy Will Clayton, and other statesmen who had to overcome strong resistance from their European counterparts.[15]

American support for European integration went only as far as the borderlands dividing West from East. In a diplomatic corollary to the dictum that generals are always fighting the last war, postwar statesmen on both sides wanted to prevent the unification of German lands. American policymakers devoted considerable effort, and ran great risks, to prevent the incorporation of West Germany or its capital into the Soviet bloc. This was also a major theme of the Austrian State Treaty (1955), including an anti-Anschluss provision by which the United States, the Soviet Union, and their respective allies obliged Austria not to "enter into political or economic union with Germany in any form whatsoever." That provision apparently posed no bar to Austria's accession to the European Union in 1994.

Independence and Postcolonial Preferences

European and American statesmen had distinct approaches to trade with the emerging countries of Africa, the Caribbean, and the Asia-Pacific region.

---

[14] Report by the Policy Planning Staff, "PPS/23: Review of Current Trends" (February 24, 1948), *FRUS 1948*, Volume I, Part 2, p. 510.

[15] See on this point Steil (2018). See also Healey (2011) and Rappaport (1981).

Some four dozen former European colonies gained their independence in the two decades that followed 1945, and more were to come. While the United States preferred that all developing countries be treated equally, and on a nonpreferential basis, Europeans favored preferences in general and wanted to go farther still with their newest ex-colonies.

Here again Washington's perceptions and priorities broke sharply from pre-hegemonic positions. The United States had been the original postcolonial, developing country, and in its early years it shared most weaknesses of newly independent states. These included not just low levels of income and dependence on a narrow range of commodity exports, but fragile domestic institutions, political instability, and military insecurity.[16] Empathy toward other European colonies inspired generations of American policymakers to support their independence, in word if not always in deed, but now the hard facts of the Cold War forced a reassessment. While this did not mean halting the withdrawal of colonial forces, Washington felt compelled to fill voids left by departing Europeans. The positive experience with the Marshall Plan encouraged the optimistic belief that a similar program for the developing countries, named "Point Four" for its place in Truman's 1949 inaugural address,[17] could achieve comparable economic and political results. Foreign aid and Peace Corps volunteers were to become one side of the coin; mutual security treaties and Green Beret missions would form the other.

The debate over North–South trade has been conducted within a "trade, not aid" paradigm at least as far back as the early 1950s,[18] even if those options are not mutually exclusive. The very first years of the post-war era were the only time that aid outweighed trade. In 1947 the US government made $6.1 billion in grants and loans, more than two-thirds of which went to Western Europe. This total was slightly higher than the $5.8 billion in US merchandise imports from all sources that year. That would never happen again; imports from all sources would be twice the level of aid in 1950, more than three-to-one in 1960, and seven times larger in 1970. The pattern nevertheless varied widely for specific regions. Trade was far more important than aid in US relations with Latin America and the Caribbean throughout the American hegemony, with

---

[16] For a perceptive examination of this issue, see Lipset (1979).

[17] Truman proposed a four-point "program for peace and freedom," the fourth being "a bold new program for making the benefits of our scientific advances and industrial progress available for the improvement and growth of underdeveloped areas." See www.trumanlibrary.org/whistle stop/50yr_archive/inagural20jan1949.htm.

[18] The expression "trade, not aid" appears to have been coined in a 1953 proposal of the British Commonwealth. See Memorandum by the Secretary of State to the President, "British Proposals on 'Trade, Not Aid'" (February 18, 1953), *FRUS 1952–1954*, Volume VI, pp. 889–890.

the value of grants and loans to that region being equal to just 5% of US merchandise imports from there in 1960. The pattern was quite different for Asian developing countries, where aid was equal to 128% of imports in 1960. Africa fell between these two cases, with aid reaching as high as 43% of imports in 1965.[19] Subsequent decades saw trade rise and aid fall, to the point where in 2017 the value of US imports from developing countries was thirty-seven times larger than the total foreign aid budget.[20]

The only surprise is how long it took for US policymakers to complement aid and related initiatives with trade preferences for developing countries. Apart from preferential distribution of import quotas for such products as coffee and sugar, the United States generally did not discriminate among its partners in the developing world until the mid-1970s.

Reverse Preferences and Generalized Preferences

With independence came demands for a new international order. Those demands were primarily expressed in regional conferences during the 1950s, and came together in the first UNCTAD conference (1964). The report of UNCTAD Secretary General Raúl Prebisch, *Towards a New Trade Policy for Development*, blended free-market and planned-economy ideas. Parts of it read like a scheme that a reincarnated Alexander Hamilton might craft if he had been commissioned to devise a strategy not just for one emerging, post-colonial economy but for a whole class of them. In addition to providing for import substitution industrialization (a.k.a. protectionism), a greater role for national and global government in managing the economy, commodity agreements, and increased foreign assistance, the proposal favored nonreciprocal preferences for developing countries. It suggested that "the industrial countries could establish a quota for admitting manufactured goods from the developing countries free of duty," and proposed that developing countries be eligible for preferential treatment up to the value of the quota.[21] This was the kernel of what would become the GSP.

Representing the United States at UNCTAD's inaugural meeting, George Ball stressed reciprocal negotiations as the best means for reducing the barriers to developing country exports.[22] This was to be the principal theme of

[19]   Calculated from data in U.S. Department of Commerce (1975), pp. 872–875 and 905.
[20]   Budget data from www.state.gov/r/pa/prs/ps/2017/05/271052.htm.
[21]   UNCTAD (1964), p. 118.
[22]   See Memorandum from the Under Secretary of State (Ball) to President Johnson, "United Nations Trade and Development Conference" (March 30, 1964), *FRUS 1964–1968*, Volume XXXIII, pp. 628–629.

US policy toward trade and development for the decades to come, but that stance would be moderated in two ways. Washington would sometimes relent to international pressure that favored preferences, largely out of concern that it could not stand alone in its advocacy of non-discrimination. The US negotiators reluctantly agreed at the second UNCTAD conference (1968) to join in a system of generalized, non-reciprocal, and non-discriminatory preferences. The second modification was that US policy would respond to specific problems in favored regions, offering to create new, more targeted preferential programs as part of a larger support package.

The first US step toward preferences came in response to concerns over European discrimination. Presidents Johnson and Nixon treated the GSP as a remedy for the "reverse preferences" by which the former mother countries not only extended preferential treatment to imports from newly independent countries, but required that these favors be partially reciprocated by preferential access for European goods. That form of latter-day colonialism worked to the disadvantage of all those countries that had won their independence in the eighteenth and nineteenth centuries, namely the United States and Latin America. The US solution was to replace these doubly discriminatory preferences with a generalized North–South system. Johnson came out in favor of the GSP at the 1967 summit of Western Hemisphere leaders, declaring that the United States was "ready to explore with other industrialized countries — and our own people — the possibility of temporary preferential tariff advantages for all developing countries."[23] As leery as Washington had been of global preferences, it was prepared to back a program that supported other American republics.

Putting the GSP into effect required that the United States conclude three negotiations. The program could be made legal only if the GATT countries granted unanimous consent to waive Article I's MFN rule. They approved a ten-year waiver in 1971, and later made it permanent in a 1979 declaration that is commonly known as the Enabling Clause. This Tokyo Round agreement allowed countries to "accord differential and more favorable treatment to developing countries, without according such treatment to other contracting parties."[24] Another negotiation engaged Brussels, with American officials proposing a bargain in 1973: In exchange for European assurances that they would "not require or seek reverse preferences as part of its trade arrangements with specified less developed countries," the United States "will not challenge in GATT the agreements in question on the grounds that they are inconsistent

---

[23] Quoted in U.S. Department of Agriculture (1968), p. 22.
[24] For the text of the enabling clause, see Jackson et al. (1995), pp. 1115–1118.

with Article XXIV."[25] The third negotiation was domestic. As described in the next section, the GSP could not go into effect without congressional approval. While that was secured as part of the Trade Act of 1974, Congress modified the proposal that the Nixon administration submitted. Those modifications weakened the value of the GSP preferences, and their potential use as an instrument of reciprocity, primarily by taking entire sectors off the table.

The Turn to Regional Preferences and FTAs

The controversy over reverse preferences illustrates a perennial problem in US policy toward trade and development: Any move to favor one set of developing countries will be seen as a slight to other, less favored regions. The proposal to aid Latin countries by obliging Europe to adopt a more generalized system provoked a warning from the State Department's Africa desk that "[s]erious problems for U.S. relations with most African countries would result if we set as conditions for a generalized scheme the elimination of special preferences and reverse preferences."[26] These concerns did not deter the Nixon administration from choosing the option that best aligned with traditional US regional priorities.

This problem of robbing Peter to pay Paul reemerged decades later in Washington's resistance to a new UN proposal by which duty-free, quota-free (DFQF) treatment would be extended to all imports from all least developed countries (LDCs). The United States is rhetorically committed to DFQF, having signed on to the UN's Millennium Development Goals in 2000 and the WTO's Doha ministerial declaration in 2001, but no such program has ever been seriously promoted in Congress. The principal obstacle is a concern on the part of African LDCs and their supporters in the Congressional Black Caucus that the DFQF principle would undermine the special preferences for sub-Saharan Africa. The only LDCs that are denied more or less open access to the US market are Asian countries such as Bangladesh and Cambodia. African countries fear that duty-free treatment for those countries' apparel products would come at their expense.

The next step in the evolving US position was to negotiate FTAs, starting in 1984 with Israel. Washington chose that first partner for political rather than economic reasons (see Chapter 15), but when it turned to Canada in 1986 it

---

[25] U.S. Mission to European Union, "US-EC Consultations: Follow-Up Talks on Preferences" (cable of April 11, 1973), 1973ECBRU01993_b.

[26] Action Memorandum from the Assistant Secretary of State for African Affairs (Newsom) to the Deputy Under Secretary of State for Economic Affairs (Samuels), "Tariff Preferences for Less Developed Countries" (September 20, 1969), FRUS 1969–1976, Volume IV, p. 541.

took on what was then the world's largest bilateral trade relationship (see Chapter 9). As was already discussed in Chapter 5, those first FTA negotiations were also inspired by a demonstration effect. The Reagan administration was eager to bring services, investment, and intellectual property rights to the negotiating table, and also to issue the subtle threat that it was prepared to negotiate on these issues bilaterally if its partners were not willing to take them up in the GATT. The US–Canada agreement then gave way to the trilateral NAFTA, which came into effect in 1994, and between 2000 and 2006 the pace of FTA negotiations stepped up considerably. By 2012 the United States had FTAs in effect with twenty countries.

All but two of these twenty FTA partners are developing countries, and there is a sense in which this final step toward discrimination was just a stronger version of the established US position on trade and development. Washington has long contended that developing countries would be better off negotiating reciprocal agreements than by maintaining high tariffs at home and seeking preferential access abroad. FTAs simply took that proposal to the next level, offering virtually complete and free access to the US market in exchange for countries' agreement to provide that same access to their own markets. The great majority of the countries that accepted the bargain already received preferential access under one of the existing programs. The only three FTA partners that did not enjoy preferential access at the time of the negotiations were Australia and two developing countries (Korea and Singapore) that had been graduated from the GSP in 1989. The rest benefited from the comprehensive Andean or Caribbean programs (nine countries), or from the partially preferential access of the GSP (seven countries), or the special case of the US–Canada Auto Pact. Why were all of these countries willing to pay what appears, by mercantilist calculations, to be the high price of free access to their own markets in exchange for a marginal expansion of existing preferences?

The FTA partners had three different takes on this problem. A few of them approached the question in the way that free-traders would hope, seeing the negotiation of an FTA as a means of backstopping national reforms in order to encourage foreign investment. Mexico and Chile each enacted significant economic reforms in the years leading up to their FTA negotiations, but leaders in both countries worried that international capital might doubt the permanence of autonomous programs. They aimed to reassure these prospective foreign partners by anchoring the reforms in enforceable treaties. At the other extreme, some partners focused very narrowly on how an FTA might offer preferential access in those high-tariff sectors that were not covered by their existing preferences. Calculations of this sort were especially important to those Middle Eastern countries that depended on apparel exports, as is discussed in Chapter 15.

Nearly half of the FTA partners seem to have been influenced by a US negotiating tactic that dates back to the prior hegemon. This involved the threat that a partner's existing market access could be at risk if it did not negotiate a permanent and reciprocal agreement. When Britain negotiated a series of agreements in the late 1930s, "A promise from the United Kingdom to cease *raising* the tariff proved to be a sufficient inducement to other nations to reduce their tariffs."[27] This variation on the old tactic of the "negotiating tariff" (i.e., imposing higher rates just before a negotiation) allowed London to extract some very asymmetrical concessions. Several of the US FTA partners were similarly concerned that their existing access might be at risk. Canadian policymakers worried that Washington could give in to the growing demands from protectionist industries for more aggressive use of the trade-remedy laws (see Chapter 9). Developing countries in the Western Hemisphere were often motivated by fear that the special, preferential trade programs from which they benefited might not be renewed when the latest authorizations expired. American negotiators exploited these fears, possibly exaggerating the degree of congressional opposition to the reauthorization of autonomous, time-limited programs.[28]

Only two countries ultimately lost their special, preferential access to the US market due to failure to convert existing preferences into FTAs. Bolivia and Ecuador were beneficiaries of the Andean program, and both were covered by the US offer in 2004 to negotiate an FTA with the group. Bolivia never joined the talks, and Ecuador withdrew on the election of a nationalist government in 2006. They also became members of the Venezuelan-led Bolivarian Alliance, a trade-skeptical and anti-US group. By then the Andean initiative had already fragmented into separate Colombian and Peruvian talks. President Bush removed Bolivia from the program in 2008 because of that country's failure to cooperate in counter-narcotics efforts, and Ecuador's benefits lapsed in mid-2013 when the last authorization of the

---

[27] Kreider (1943), p. 58. Emphasis in the original. His data showed that for 14 trade agreements negotiated in the late 1930s the other party made on average 92.0 concessions to London, compared to just 5.3 UK concessions.

[28] This is the author's opinion, based on numerous discussions with policymakers in Washington, Central America, and Andean countries during 2003–2010. Viewed from my vantage point, it seemed unlikely that Congress would allow the various components of the CBI program to lapse, nor would it permit the ATPA to disappear as long as Colombia was a beneficiary. Policymakers in the beneficiary countries nevertheless held a different view, and their US counterparts seem to have been energetic in encouraging them toward that conclusion.

program expired. Both of them then reverted to GSP status. The experience was quite different in the abortive FTA negotiations with the Southern African Customs Union, as those partners withdrew from the talks after they concluded that Congress would not allow their preferences to lapse under AGOA. Their assessment proved correct.

THE DOMESTIC DIPLOMACY OF PREFERENCES

The domestic diplomacy of preferences affects the potential use of these programs and agreements as instruments of foreign policy. On the economic side, domestic industries and their allies in Congress may demand limitations on the scope of products that are eligible for preferential treatment, or otherwise act to restrict the benefits. On the political side, groups or legislators that are focused on relations with specific countries might act either to promote or retard enactment of these programs. Both economic and political interests may appreciate the potential leverage of these programs, and seek to influence the specific, tactical uses to which they are put in dealings with the beneficiary countries.

Product Exclusions

The sometimes conflicting needs of trade and foreign policy influence the evolving US approach to product coverage in preferential programs and FTAs. Foreign policy objectives would be best served by comprehensive product coverage for any programs that extend preferences to friendly countries, thus making the inducement as attractive as possible, but domestic industries might balk. They may demand that the terms of a program or agreement be devised to limit their own exposure to import competition, sometimes through outright exclusions (especially for the GSP) and sometimes via restrictive rules of origin (especially for regional preferences and FTAs).

Product exceptions are crippling for the GSP. When President Nixon first declared his support for this program in 1969 he proposed broad product coverage without any limits. Congress nonetheless wrote a number of constraints into the program. In addition to limiting its coverage to about half of all products that are subject to duty, making such key sectors as apparel and steel ineligible for designation, the rules also provide various means to remove products or countries from GSP privileges (e.g., through the "competitive-need" limits on countries' benefits for specific products). Many US industries have used the GSP annual review process to petition for the removal of products from the program, either on a global or a country-specific basis. The annual reviews also allow the beneficiary countries to petition for better treatment, whether through the designation of new products, the redesignation of products that had been removed, or the granting of waivers from the competitive-need limits.

The aggregate data show just how limited the GSP preferences are. In 2017 only 11.0% of the imports from the beneficiaries of the ordinary GSP program, and 15.2% of imports from LDCs, entered duty-free under this program (see Table 13.1). The average tariff paid on imports from the beneficiaries of the regular GSP program was, at 2.7%, slightly higher than the average 2.6% tariff paid on imports from developing and transitional economies that are not designated for this program (see Table 13.1). Average tariffs are actually far higher on imports from those LDCs whose GSP benefits nominally cover a considerably wider array of products;[29] their average 12.6% tariffs are explained by this group's dependence on exports of apparel, products that even they cannot ship duty-free under this program. The data also show that the average tariff imposed on imports from developing countries (with or without preferential treatment) is about twice that charged on imports from developed countries (1.3%). That disparity is the consequence of choices that each group made decades ago. During the years that developing countries demanded special and differential treatment in the trading system, and largely abstained from tariff negotiations in the GATT, the United States and its developed-country partners were busily cutting deals that reduced or removed the tariffs imposed on the products that they trade with one another. The results suggest that developing countries might have done well to follow the advice that George Ball gave them in 1964.

The Actual Coverage of Preferential Programs and Agreements

Table 13.2 summarizes just how thoroughly the GSP was undercut, showing tariff treatment for the top 25 US imports from the median developing country in 2017. The unweighted, average applied MFN tariff on these items was 4.1%. Receiving GSP treatment would bring this average down to 3.8%, meaning that the program's benefits amounted to little more than a rounding error. The reason for the GSP's almost negligible value is that only two of these top twenty-five items were both dutiable on an MFN basis and eligible for duty-free treatment under this program. Nearly half of the remaining items were

---

[29] The special GSP benefits for LDCs were first authorized in 2000. Many of the non-apparel items that are denied GSP treatment when imported from other developing countries are GSP-eligible when imported from the LDCs that are designated for this special treatment.

TABLE 13.2. *Tariff Treatment of the Top 25 US Imports from Developing Countries,*
1934–2017
Applied MFN tariff rates, in percentages

	Pre-RTAA (1934)	Pre-Uruguay Round (1994)	2017
Dutiable and GSP-Eligible in 2017			
4011.10.10 New rubber pneumatic radial tires	10.0	4.0	4.0
7113.19.50 Precious metal jewelry and parts	80.0	6.5	5.5
Dutiable but Not GSP-Eligible in 2017			
2709.00.10 Crude oil testing <25° A.P.I.	5.0	0.4	0.1
2709.00.20 Crude oil testing ≥25° A.P.I.	10.0	0.8	0.2
2710.19.06 Fuel oil <25° A.P.I.	10.0	0.4	0.1
2710.19.11 Fuel oil ≥25° A.P.I.	20.0	0.8	0.2
2710.12.45 Light oil mixtures	20.0	0.8	0.2
6110.20.20 Sweaters etc. of cotton	50.0	20.7	16.5
6110.30.30 Sweaters etc. of manmade fibers	90.0	34.2	32.0
6203.42.45 Men's/boys' cotton trousers etc.	90.0	17.7	16.6
6204.62.80 Women's/girls' cotton trousers etc.	90.0	17.7	16.6
6302.60.00 Toilet linen and kitchen linen	40.0	10.3	9.1
8703.23.01 Motor vehicles	10.0	2.5	2.5
Duty-Free as of 2017			
3004.90.92 Medicaments packed for retail	30.0	6.3	Free
7102.39.00 Nonindustrial diamonds, worked	10.0	Free	Free
8471.70.40 Magnetic disk drive storage units	35.0	3.9	Free
8473.30.11 Printed circuit assemblies	35.0	3.9	Free
8517.62.00 Switching and routing apparatus	35.0	8.5	Free
8542.39.00 Electronic integrated circuits	35.0	4.2	Free
8802.40.00 Airplanes and other powered aircraft	30.0	Free	Free
Duty-Free as of 1934			
0306.17.00 Other shrimps and prawns, frozen	Free	Free	Free
0901.11.00 Coffee, not roasted	Free	Free	Free
1801.00.00 Cocoa beans	Free	Free	Free
2713.11.00 Coke, petroleum, not calcined	Free	Free	Free
4001.22.00 Technically specified natural rubber	Free	Free	Free
Unweighted average without GSP treatment:	29.4	5.7	4.1
Unweighted average with GSP treatment:	25.8	5.3	3.8

Based on the top twenty-five items among total US imports from GSP beneficiary countries in 2017. Item descriptions are greatly shortened here. Note that some of these items (e.g., disk drives and integrated circuits) did not exist in 1934; the rates shown for that year are those that applied to the category into which those items fell. Rates shown for oil and derivatives are ad valorem equivalents calculated on the basis of average prices for MFN imports in 2017, with 1934 and 1994 rates estimated by the author from historical price data.
Source: Calculated from U.S. International Trade Commission DataWeb data at https://dataweb .usitc.gov/.

duty-free on an MFN basis, thus rendering preferences moot, and nine other dutiable items were not eligible for the GSP. Five of those items were oil products that are subject only to nuisance-level tariffs, but five others faced tariffs that approached or exceeded 10%.

The exclusion of apparel from the GSP was especially damaging to the program. Average US tariffs on total nonpreferential imports were just 1.7% in 2017, but apparel was – with an average tariff of 15.6% – at the top of the very short list of sectors that are still subject to high MFN barriers. Although apparel accounts for just 3.8% of all imports, tariffs on this sector make up 34.2% of total tariff revenue. The only other important sectors that come close to the tariffs on apparel were those on yarns and fabrics (average MFN tariffs of 6.2%), dairy products (6.5%), footwear (11.7%), and luggage (12.9%); there are also some specific agricultural products that remain subject to high tariffs or restrictive tariff-rate quotas. Most of those goods are ineligible for GSP treatment.

The data in Table 13.2 do suggest that programs with near-universal product coverage, such as AGOA and the CBI, might have been very effective – had they been available in 1934. A program with universal coverage would have given the median developing country a nearly 30% average margin of pre-ference. By 2017, however, that margin had been knocked down to just 4%. For most developing countries, that is much less significant than such structural constraints as higher shipping costs. And while these programs do offer vastly more generous product coverage than the GSP, they are not universal. The most significant restraint that Congress has imposed are the rules of origin for apparel, which are stricter for some programs than others (see Chapter 14). There are also some specific items that lawmakers have either carved out of these programs or made subject to special conditions. Over half of all imports from the AGOA beneficiaries entered under these preferences in 2017 (much of it oil), but just 16.7% of imports from the CBI countries (Table 13.1).

And what of FTAs? These agreements are subject to the requirement in GATT Article XXIV that they cover "substantially all of the trade" between the parties, a vague and elastic standard that allows for a negotiable range of exceptions. The scope of products covered by their duty-free treatment is wider than in the regional programs, with just under half of all imports from FTA partners entering preferentially in 2017 (and most of the rest being duty-free on an MFN basis), but even for these countries the coverage is not absolute. Some of the more notable exclusions have been the dairy sector in the two FTAs with Canada, and sugar in the agreement with Australia. While the outright product exclusions from US FTAs are usually kept to a very short list, some of the other ways in which tariff concessions are limited can be tantamount to exclusions. Among these alternative means of restricting concessions are elongated phase-out periods, tariff-rate quotas, safeguards, and a snap-back mechanism that provides for a reimposition of duties if imports from the partner country exceed certain "trigger" levels. The US negotiators prefer to employ these alternative means of limiting concessions over outright exclusions, presumably because this approach has at least the appearance of being more compliant with WTO rules.

Preferences as Reciprocity: The Tactical Level

Policymakers who favor discriminatory programs and agreements sometimes place different emphases on their strategic versus their tactical purposes. As was already discussed in Chapter 3, considerations of foreign policy play a critical role in the selection of FTA partners. That has been equally true for the creation for special, regional programs. But what of the actual execution of these programs? Should they be considered in much the same way as ordinary trade agreements, with the government creating opportunities by removing barriers but then getting out of the way, or should they instead be leveraged to extract concessions from the beneficiaries? For both legal and political reasons, these programs more readily lend themselves to tactical use than do FTAs or multilateral liberalization.

The most significant legal difference between preferential programs and trade agreements comes down to the distinction between a negotiable privilege and an enforceable right. The tariff concessions that countries make in trade agreements, whether multilateral or discriminatory, are treaty commitments that they cannot breach without cost to their reputations; violations risk dispute-settlement proceedings or outright retaliation. The legal standing of the GSP and other preferential schemes is far shakier. These programs are authorized at the multilateral level only through waivers, and their real terms are instead set by the authorizations that Congress enacts. This leaves wide scope for lawmakers and negotiators to treat these preferences as negotiable benefits that can be expanded or contracted in response to the beneficiary country's policies. Using preferences as an instrument of reciprocity is inconsistent with the spirit of the original GSP proposal, but developing countries have never mounted a legally effective challenge to the uses to which American policymakers have put these preferential programs.[30]

---

[30]   There was one instance in which India successfully challenged similar aspects of the European Union's GSP program; see www.wto.org/english/tratop_e/dispu_e/cases_e/1p.sum _e/ds246sum_e.pdf.

Reciprocity has always been an element in the GSP. Washington used countries' original designation for benefits in 1975 as opportunities to raise concerns with several of them over pending disputes on expropriations and other issues,[31] and the utility of the program was even higher a decade later. The Trade and Tariff Act of 1984 provided that beneficiary countries could lose some or all of their GSP privileges if they did not respect labor rights, protect intellectual property, resolve investment disputes, and meet other stipulations. The process further empowered the US Trade Representative (USTR) to offer countries more secure benefits on some products if they made concessions to US demands. The 1985–1987 GSP general review afforded US negotiators an opportunity to raise issues with their counterparts in several beneficiary countries in 1986, with the results of these consultations leading to continued privileges for some countries and reduced preferences for others. The annual reviews of the program can be used in the same way.

Two recent examples illustrate how the USTR may try to use the GSP as leverage, sometimes leading to concessions by the partner and sometimes to the low-grade sanction of partial or total suspension of privileges. The agency had removed Argentina from the program altogether in 2012 in an investment dispute, but in 2017 it reinstated some of these privileges "following resolution of certain arbitral disputes with U.S. companies, new commitments by the Argentine government to improve market access for U.S. agricultural products, and improved protection and enforcement" of intellectual property rights. The USTR announced that same day that it was partially suspending Ukraine's GSP benefits in another intellectual property dispute; Kyiv had not been as cooperative as Buenos Aires in accommodating US demands.[32] Other preferential trade programs offer similar leverage to US negotiators. The USTR used the enticement of CBI benefits in 1983–1984 to obtain commitments from Central American and Caribbean countries (e.g., on piracy of satellite transmissions), for example, and in 1992–1993 declined to designate Ecuador and Peru for benefits under the Andean Trade Preferences Act until they resolved expropriation disputes with US firms.

[31] See, for example, the Jamaican bauxite investment dispute discussed in Action Memorandum from the Assistant Secretary of State for Inter-American Affairs (Rogers) and the Assistant Secretary of State for Economic and Business Affairs (Enders) to Secretary of State Kissinger, "Jamaica: AID Loan for Rural Education" (June 11, 1975), *FRUS 1969–1976* Volume E-11, Part 1, pp. 1155–1161.

[32] https://ustr.gov/about-us/policy-offices/press-office/press-releases/2017/december/trump-administration-enforces.

Country Coverage and Diaspora Politics

As was implied in the earlier discussion of reverse preferences, presidents and the foreign policy establishment have traditionally taken the lead in deciding which regions may be favored by preferential programs. As in so many other areas, however, presidents propose and Congress disposes. The legislative branch does not always share the same priorities as the executive, and the chances that a given proposal will emerge from Congress more or less unscathed – or even make it out at all – will depend significantly on the positions adopted by the business community, labor unions, diasporas, and other members of civil society.

The country coverage of the GSP illustrates this point. As originally proposed by President Nixon, the program was to apply to all developing countries other than China, Cuba, North Korea, and North Vietnam. The debate over congressional approval coincided with the first oil crisis, and the Senate responded by denying GSP benefits to any countries that participated in the OPEC oil embargo. This restriction was largely symbolic, considering the low level of tariffs applied to the oil and derivatives that dominate in the exports of OPEC members (see Chapter 15). Congress also wrote graduation provisions into the program, which evolved into the current rule that a country will be removed whenever the World Bank designates it as a high-income country. Between the graduation of some countries on this criterion, the removal of others for policy reasons, and the upgrading of some relationships from GSP to regional preferences or FTAs,[33] this program has come to encompass a shrinking number of partners. The number of eligible products also dwindled when the Uruguay Round moved more items to the free list. The net result is that from 1984 to 2017, the share of total US imports that entered duty-free under the GSP fell from 4.1%[34] to 0.9%.

The nexus between foreign economic policy and domestic politics is even tighter whenever discriminatory trade initiatives involve diasporas. Democrats are generally more prone than Republicans to distinguish between partners on these grounds, seeking to promote positions favored by constituent groups that are tied to what researchers call the kin state.[35] Those ties sometimes militate in favor of preferences, as in the case of the CBI or the AGOA. The possibilities are demonstrated by two votes cast during the 98th Congress (1983–1984). More than half (56%) of Democrats voted in 1983 to

---

[33] Note that countries that are designated for the CBI or AGOA will retain their GSP status, but countries that negotiate FTAs with the United States will be removed from the GSP.
[34] Lande and VanGrasstek (1986), p. 70.
[35] See, for example, Shain and Barth (2003).

approve the Caribbean Basin Economic Recovery Act, but the next year 64% of Democrats voted to remove the Asian newly industrialized economies from the GSP. The differing levels of support for these two regions can be readily understood as the joint product of diaspora considerations and rising Democratic concerns over the contributions of the "Asian tigers" to the US trade deficit. By contrast, Republicans appeared to see no differences between preferences for the Caribbean (90% voting for the bill) and Asia (91% opposing the removal of GSP).

Even astute politicians can miscalculate the political power of these attachments, as President Clinton did in the late 1990s. He mistakenly believed that he could win support for a new grant of fast-track authority from the members of the Congressional Black Caucus (CBC) by linking this request to the proposed AGOA. While some CBC members passionately supported AGOA's preferential treatment for African goods, others saw it as a threat to their constituents' jobs in textiles and other labor-intensive industries. Only twenty-one of the thirty-six members of the caucus voted for AGOA, meaning that the level of support for the proposal among CBC members (58%) was not much higher than among all other Democrats (48%) and was somewhat lower than it was among Republicans (68%). In the end, both the pro- and anti-AGOA factions in the CBC resented the implication that their votes on fast track could be bought in this way.

THE ACTUAL IMPACT OF PREFERENCES ON IMPORTS

We have seen several reasons to doubt that preferences may have a major impact on US imports from the beneficiary countries. The most significant of these, as predicted by the paradox of preferences, is the erosion in margins of preference. To the extent that the hegemon was successful in its earlier efforts to promote nondiscriminatory liberalization, and to reduce tariffs on an MFN basis, there will be less scope for preferential treatment when it later opts to deploy preferential programs and agreements. The average US tariff rate on dutiable goods was relatively high in the first year after the Second World War (26%), but it was less than half that level (12%) when Prebisch first called for preferences in 1964, and GATT negotiations made further cuts by the time that the program came on line. The benefits of these programs and agreements may also be undercut by the exclusions of countries or products, restrictive rules of origin, and the threat or actual removal or preferences in disputes with the beneficiary.

Preference dilution can be just as significant as preference erosion. This occurs when the proliferation of discriminatory instruments serves to diminish the benefits that any given country enjoys in its preferential access to the US market. Erosion and dilution can be illustrated using the case of windshield wipers imported from Mexico, which supplied 81% of wiper imports during NAFTA's first year of operation (1994). Mexico's preferences were partly undercut in the ensuing years by preference erosion, with the MFN tariff being cut in the Uruguay Round from 3.1% to 2.5%, and also by the preference dilution brought on by the US–Korea FTA. Mexico was still the #1 provider of these wipers in 2017, but its market share had fallen to 42%. Preference erosion contributed to the rise of imports from China, which now held 21% of the import market, and preference dilution helped Korea capture another 11%.

These limitations undercut the capacity of preferences to stimulate US imports from the beneficiary countries, as confirmed by the data reported in Table 13.3. Whether we look at shares of total US imports or compound annual rates of growth, these aggregate data show the same results. The market share held in 2017 by the countries that receive preferential access was virtually unchanged from their share in 1990. Imports from these countries did enjoy a slightly higher than average rate of growth during 1990–2007, but this was followed by a slightly lower than average rate in 2007–2017. The results for FTA partners were especially disappointing: Their growth rate in the first period was just 0.1% better than the world at large, and in the latter period these countries precisely matched the global average. We may only assume that these same countries would have had even lower growth rates if they did not enjoy FTA access, but saying "it could have been worse" may be cold comfort to partner countries that presumably expected to achieve much more by bargaining over preferential entry into the US market.

One observation that fairly leaps off the page is the above-average growth rate that China achieved in both periods, even though it received no preferences. Quite to the contrary, the average tariffs on Chinese products were five percentage points above the global average in 1990, and were still almost twice the average level in 2017. The performance of this one country offers further support for the general contention that the level of tariff protection in the US trade regime today is too low to provide much of a benefit to those countries that are exonerated from the payment of these taxes.

THE POLITICAL UTILITY OF PREFERENCES

The paradox of preferences is based on an anomaly in time. While a newly minted hegemon may couple high tariffs with an equally high commitment to nondiscrimination, both of those factors may diminish over time.

TABLE 13.3. *US Imports by Partner's Tariff Treatment, 1990–2017*
Shares of total US imports and compound annual rates of growth

	Entered into Force	Share of US Imports (%)			Compound Annual Growth (%)	
		1990	2007	2017	1990–2007	2007–2017
Preferential	—	**43.5**	**45.4**	**43.3**	**8.7**	1.4
FTA Partners		33.9	34.1	34.1	8.5	1.8
Canada	1989	18.6	16.1	12.8	7.5	−0.4
Mexico	1994	6.0	10.8	13.4	12.2	4.1
Asia-Pacific	2004–2012	6.6	3.8	4.3	4.9	3.2
Other Latin	2004–2012	1.1	1.2	1.4	9.3	2.9
Middle Eastern	1985–2006	0.8	1.3	1.2	11.5	1.1
CAFTA-DR	2006–2009	0.9	1.0	1.0	9.1	2.3
Autonomous Preferences		9.6	11.3	9.2	9.5	−0.2
GSP Beneficiaries	1976	6.5	7.2	7.9	9.1	2.7
AGOA Beneficiaries	2001	2.5	3.3	1.1	10.4	−9.1
CBI Beneficiaries	1985	0.6	0.7	0.3	9.5	−8.4
Nonpreferential	—	**56.5**	**54.6**	**56.7**	**8.2**	2.2
China	—	3.1	16.6	21.6	19.7	4.6
European Union	—	20.2	18.1	18.5	7.7	2.1
Japan	—	18.2	7.5	5.8	2.9	−0.7
All other	—	15.0	12.4	10.7	7.2	0.4
World	—	**100.0**	**100.0**	**100.0**	**8.4**	1.8

Data for all countries shown in 1990 and 2007 according to their status in 2017, whether or not they held that same status in those earlier years.
Other Latin Partners = Chile, Colombia, Panama, and Peru.
Middle Eastern Partners = Bahrain, Israel, Jordan, Morocco, and Oman.
Asia-Pacific Partners = Australia, Korea, and Singapore.
GSP Beneficiaries = Excludes all beneficiaries of the CBI and AGOA programs.
Source: Calculated from the U.S. International Trade Commission's DataWeb at https://dataweb .usitc.gov/.

The hegemon will eventually reach the point where it sees real value in discrimination as a tool of economic and foreign policy, but by that time it will have cut most of its own MFN rates to a level that renders preferences less useful.

To this paradox we may add yet another and related one, this time focused on the differences between the economic and political utility of preferences. Simply stated, foreign leaders often place a higher premium on winning preferential access to the US market than might seem warranted by the actual capacity of this advantage to stimulate trade. Executives, diplomats, and legislators who are not well-schooled in the details of trade policy will generally attach a far higher value to preferential market access than may be warranted, owing to greatly exaggerated notions of both the size of the US market and the height of the barriers to it. That may lead them to overestimate the benefits to be had by obtaining preferential access. Their US counterparts may well take advantage of the opportunities when the political utility of preferential access is greater than their economic utility. That gap may not last long, however, and policymakers in the partner country may acquire a more realistic sense of the commercial stakes if they task their subordinates with careful analysis of the barriers and the issues. This is one reason why a fair number of the FTA negotiations that were launched after the Uruguay Round ultimately failed. What sounds irresistible to a president or prime minister may lose its luster when lower-level officials make an objective assessment of the actual costs and benefits.

The next two chapters offer greater detail on what preferences have meant for US foreign policy. In Chapter 14 we consider the repeated attempts that have been made over the centuries to promote economic integration in the Americas, which has been a recurring objective for Washington ever since Latin American countries wrested their independence from Spain and Portugal. Chapter 15 takes up another history that is shorter, but no less eventful, looking into the role of trade discrimination as a tool of US policy in the Middle East. Both analyses show why there are at least as many examples of failure as there are of success in FTA negotiations between the United States and its developing country partners.

14

The Elusive Integration of the Americas

PANCHITO PISTOLES: We're three happy chappies
                      With snappy serapes
                      You'll find us beneath our
                          sombreros.
                      We're brave and we'll stay so
                      We're bright as a peso —

DONALD DUCK: Who says so?

JOSÉ CARIOCA AND   We say so!
PANCHITO PISTOLES: The three caballeros!

Lyrics to the title song in *The Three Caballeros* (1945)

INTRODUCTION

In a demonstration of what would later be called soft power, Nelson Rockefeller treated Donald Duck as a wartime asset. Working as a dollar-a-year man running the Office of Inter-American Affairs, this multimillionaire was tasked with winning goodwill in Latin America and ensuring the smooth flow of its raw materials to US defense plants. Rockefeller deployed Walt Disney on a friendship tour of the region and subsidized his films, the most memorable being *The Three Caballeros*. This was a ground-breaking mix of animation and live action in which Disney's famous duck cavorted with a samba-loving parrot and a trigger-happy rooster. The film struck one contemporary reviewer as "a firecracker show which dazzles and numbs the senses without making any tangible sense,"[1] thus joining a long string of US overtures to Latin America that produced more flash than substance.

---

[1]   Crowther (1945). See also Kalat (ND).

That Disney cartoon came toward the end of one of those rare periods in which the United States and its Latin American neighbors enjoyed something close to political and economic alignment. Franklin Roosevelt's Good Neighbor Policy undid much of the bad will that other American presidents, from James Monroe to FDR's cousin Teddy and beyond, had engendered in the region. It was soon followed by the divisions of the Cold War and all that it entailed, setting up a decades-long competition with the Soviet Union and (eventually) its regional clients. Later presidents inaugurated programs that helped to restore something of the comity that surrounded the Good Neighbor Policy, including Kennedy's Alliance for Progress at the height of the Cold War and George H. W. Bush's Enterprise for the Americas Initiative just as that lengthy struggle was ending. Bill Clinton tried once more in 1994, launching negotiations that aimed to produce a Free Trade Area of the Americas that was supposed to incorporate every country other than Cuba. None of these initiatives proved to last any longer than FDR's program.

The history of inter-American economic relations is dominated by a boom-and-bust cycle in the attention that Washington attaches to this region. It is virtually an historical constant that the approach taken by the United States toward its Latin American partners is determined by the imperatives of the US relationship with some other, extra-hemispheric rival or adversary. That role has most prominently been played by France, Germany, the Soviet Union, and now China; Washington's approach to the region has also been indirectly influenced by the members of the Organization of Petroleum Exporting Countries, Islamic fundamentalists, and other threats to American power and wealth. The Americas can become a secondary theater in the US conflict with the adversary of the day, leading Washington to develop emergency measures in order to deal with the threat, but this has always been followed by a reversion to the mean after the danger has passed.

This chapter takes a two-step approach to reviewing this cyclical pattern in US relations with Latin America. The first step is to examine the overall pattern in somewhat greater detail, summarizing the more important periods and episodes in the evolution of these relations. The second step is to scrutinize two sectoral initiatives more closely. Apart from the automotive industry, where two-way trade is uniquely important in US relations with Mexico, the two most important sectors in trade with the region are energy and apparel. In both cases, Washington saw in Latin America a possible solution to problems that first emerged in late hegemony: the Middle Eastern challenge to energy security, and the Asian challenge to the textile and apparel industry. In both cases, the United States has used trade agreements and other instruments to promote closer relations with the region. Each of those sectoral initiatives were rewarded with initial success, but the latest trends suggest that much of their potential has now played out.

Two elements dominate the history of economic integration in the Americas. The first is that the United States is often the most vocal proponent of regional commercial initiatives, with this position usually being based on a confluence of economic and security goals. The second is that while there will often be at least a few Latin countries that are willing to take up the proposal, another group will harbor deep suspicions of Washington's motives. Whether those doubts are grounded in economic or political concerns, they lead either to the collapse of the initiative or to its fragmentation into distinct, bilateral undertakings.

The Failed Conferences and Agreements of the Nineteenth Century

The tensions between US unilateralism and regional cooperation were evident from the start, and generated distinct responses to the renewed threat of European colonialism. Most of Latin America won its independence from Spain between 1810 and 1825. In the final years of those struggles there were alarming reports that France – once again a reactionary power under a restored Bourbon dynasty – was conspiring to help Spain reconquer the lost republics. The leaders of the United States and the newly independent countries were both opposed to that menace, but handled it differently.

John Quincy Adams dealt with this threat first as secretary of state under President James Monroe, and then as president. In 1823 he drafted Monroe's warning that the United States "could not view any interposition ... by any European power in any other light than as the manifestation of an unfriendly disposition toward the United States." This principle was to be a mainstay of US foreign policy for well over a century, but never produced the regional gratitude that American statesmen thought that it deserved. The traditional Latin view of the Monroe Doctrine is that it was not backed up by sufficient power when it was most needed, and then received altogether too much when Washington adopted quasi-colonial aspirations of its own.

Simón Bolívar (1783–1830) proposed in 1825 that a Pan-American Congress meet at Panama to discuss the impending threat. His original aim was to establish a defensive military alliance that might also liberate Cuba and Puerto Rico. While Bolívar did not invite the United States, the governments of Colombia and Mexico extended their own invitations. Secretary of State

Henry Clay (1777–1852) readily accepted, being a passionate supporter of Latin American independence. He prepared instructions for the US delegates to deal with peace, commerce, maritime law, and neutral and belligerent rights, and prophetically suggested that the delegates discuss the possibility of a Panama canal.[2] President Adams was decidedly less enthusiastic. He had far more international experience than the bumptious Clay, but lacked Clay's feel for domestic diplomacy. By seeking congressional approval for the mission, Adams inadvertently inaugurated the recurring practice by which Congress acts to temper the executive's integrationist aims. Nearly five months passed between Adams' request and the final vote, a delay that proved quite literally fatal. One of the US delegates died of fever in Cartagena while braving the heat of a journey to Panama. The other wisely chose not to travel during an unhealthy season, but did not arrive until the conference ended.

The United States later went from conflicted invitee to reluctant host. Secretary of State James Blaine (1830–1893), who had been trying for the better part of a decade to call another inter-American meeting, presided over the Washington conference of 1889–1890. Blaine's original aims related at least as much to power as to wealth – he offered to mediate struggles then underway in Central and South America – but he also hoped that regional peace would "stimulate the demand for articles which American manufacturers can furnish with profit."[3] Inspired by the German *Zollverein*, Blaine proposed a hemispheric customs union. This plan faltered in both its international and domestic diplomacy. While a skeptical Congress gave its blessing to the gathering, it left considerable doubts that it would approve any ambitious results. Those doubts were purely hypothetical, as Blaine's plans did not clear the first hurdle. Instead of agreeing to a customs union, the conference declared that liberalization "should be approached by gradual steps." These would begin with "the negotiation of partial reciprocity treaties among the American nations."[4] Secretary Blaine followed up with a series of bilateral talks. More than a century would pass before the United States once again sought an ambitious, hemispheric trade agreement, and that proposal for a Free Trade Area of the Americas would likewise fragment into numerous distinct negotiations.

Blaine's treaties did no better than the other trade agreements that the United States negotiated before hegemony. As summarized in Table 14.1, Congress rejected nearly all of the tariff-cutting treaties that the United

---

[2] Burton (1958), p. 151.
[3] Letter of Blaine to President Arthur (February 3, 1882), in Rappaport (1966), p. 124.
[4] International American Conference (1890a), p. 105.

TABLE 14.1. *Status of Past and Present US Trade Agreements with Latin American Countries*
FTA *partners listed in order of agreement's entry into force; other countries listed in rough order of distance from the United States; years indicate an agreement's entry into force*

	Bilateral MFN Treaties	Tariff-Cutting Treaties	RTAA Agreement	GATT/WTO Accession	Free Trade Agreement
Current FTA Partners					
Mexico	1832, 1848	~~1857, 1860, 1884~~	1942	1986	1994
Chile	1834, 1931, 1940	—	—	1949	2004
El Salvador	1850, 1874, 1926	—	1937	1991	2006
Guatemala	1852, 1924	—	1936	1991	2006
Honduras	1865, 1928	—	1936	1994	2006
Nicaragua	1868, 1924	~~1899~~	1936	1950	2006
Dominican Rep.	1867, 1924	~~1884, 1900~~	—	1950	2007
Costa Rica	1852	—	1936	1990	2009
Peru	1852, 1874, 1888	—	1942	1951	2009
Colombia	1825, 1848	—	1935	1981	2012
Panama	1939	—	—	1997	2012
Other Partners					
Cuba		1902	1934	1948	—
Haiti	1865, 1926	—	1935	1950	—
Venezuela	1836, 1861, 1938	—	1939	1990	—
Ecuador	1840, 1936	~~1900~~	1938	1996	—[a]
Brazil	1829, 1923	—	1935	1948	—
Bolivia	1862	—	—	1990	—[a]
Paraguay	1860	—	1947	1994	—
Argentina	1854	~~1899~~	1941	1967	—
Uruguay	—	—	1942	1953	—

Note: The bilateral MFN agreements with the Central American countries were preceded in 1826–1847 by a treaty with the Central American Federation. Similarly, an MFN agreement with the Peru-Bolivian Confederation was in force 1838–1858.
Italics = Agreements that entered into force but were subsequently abrogated or superseded.
~~Strikethrough~~ = Agreements not approved by the Senate or (where applicable) the House of Representatives.
Includes only countries that were independent prior to 1945.
Note that the 1884 treaty with Mexico technically was approved by the Senate, but is shown here as rejected insofar as the House subsequently failed to approve any changes in the US tariff schedule.
Agreements that were negotiated but not submitted for congressional approval are not shown here.
[a]Ecuador was originally a party to the negotiations that were intended to create a US-Andean FTA, but exited the talks after a change of government in 2006. Bolivia was an observer to these negotiations, but never became a formal participant.
Sources: Department of State, Treaties in Force (at www.state.gov/documents/organization/2734 94.pdf); Office of the U.S. Trade Representative at https://ustr.gov/trade-agreements/free-trade-agreements; Bevans (1968–1976); and Wiktor (1976–1994).

States reached with Latin American countries prior to the Reciprocal Trade Agreements Act (RTAA) of 1934. In addition to four of Blaine's agreements, Congress defeated one treaty with the Dominican Republic and three with Mexico. The US–Cuban treaty on commercial relations, which established a 20% margin of preference for Cuban products, was the exception that proved the rule.

The Good Neighbor Policy and the Early GATT Period

FDR's Good Neighbor Policy marked the highpoint in inter-American political and economic relations. United by a common enemy – although there were some Nazi sympathizers in the Southern Cone – the American republics achieved an unprecedented degree of diplomatic and economic collaboration. Brazil and Mexico took the further step of committing troops to the war. Trade negotiations were a key component of hemispheric cooperation, and the United States reached RTAA agreements with all but four Latin American countries.

The eagerness of Latin countries to negotiate trade agreements can be seen in the greater number of RTAA agreements reached from 1934 through 1946, as compared with the FTAs concluded in a period of similar length (1993 through 2006). Bolivia was the only country in the region to be entirely isolated from the benefits of the RTAA agreements, at least until the Roosevelt administration extended MFN status to all remaining countries in 1942. Chile and the Dominican Republic did not need to negotiate RTAA agreements because they already enjoyed unconditional MFN access to the US market under pre-1934 treaties, and hence could free-ride on other countries' agreements without making any concessions of their own.[5] Panama acquired that same status through a separate agreement in 1939 that did not include tariff concessions. The difference might also be attributed to the greater ease with which RTAA agreements could be approved, and the level of benefits. The opportunity cost of not reaching an agreement was greater when the tariff wall was still high, but by 2017 the average tariff imposed on all US imports from the nine non-FTA partners in South America was just 0.8%.

While Latin American countries were almost universally attracted to the RTAA opportunity, they later took very diverse approaches to the GATT.

---

[5] About half of the Latin countries that did negotiate RTAA agreements also enjoyed unconditional MFN access to the US market, and thus might likewise have opted to be free-riders. They may have concluded that it was still advisable to negotiate with the United States so as to make requests on products of interest to their own exporters.

Brazil and Cuba were the only ones in GATT from its inception,[6] and while half a dozen other countries joined in the first decade there were others who held out until the 1990s (see Table 14.1). One reason for this reluctance was a concern that GATT was unfriendly to developing country demands for what was later called special and differential (S&D) treatment. Already at the Havana conference of 1948 the "Latin American countries generally argued that raising tariffs and imposing new preferences for economic development purposes would be good for the trade of all countries."[7] That position would be a part of regional economic orthodoxy for three decades, leading most Latin countries to view trade liberalization with suspicion.

Import Substitution Industrialization and Regional Integration

Argentine economist Raúl Prebisch, whose ideas acquired greater currency when he headed up a sequence of international organizations, helped to transform temporary expedients into full-fledged development strategies. The protectionist measures that most Latin American countries had adopted during the Great Depression and the Second World War were "the accidental byproduct of government efforts to save foreign exchange," according to Harris, rather than "a deliberate policy of industrialization."[8] Prebisch's more comprehensive arguments for import-substitution industrialization (ISI) were nearly identical in premise and conclusion to what Alexander Hamilton had called for in his *Report on Manufactures*, down to the matter of the declining terms of trade. Like Hamilton, he believed that a country with a diversified array of industries was less susceptible to fluctuations in demand, prices, and other exogenous shocks. And while Prebisch conceded that free trade was beneficial in the Pax Britannica, he saw a different relationship in the Pax Americana. Whereas Britain had imported raw materials from the region, the more self-sufficient United States had less need for them. Prebisch argued that the developing countries now had to rely more on the national and regional market than on the new hegemon. In short, just when the United States had most fully repudiated Hamilton, his thesis came back to refute the new American appeals for liberalization.

The ISI-led development strategies that so many Latin American countries followed over the ensuing decades stand in contrast to the export-led

---

[6] Chile is a special case. Owing to a delay in its completion of the ratification process, it may be considered either the last of the original GATT contracting parties or the first of the acceding countries.

[7] Brown (1950), p. 157.

[8] Harris (1986), p. 17.

approaches of Asian economies, which variously took a liberal form (as in Hong Kong and Singapore) or was more mercantilist (as in Japan and Korea). The protectionist policies so prevalent in Latin America instead had heavy anti-export biases. Subregional integration schemes such as the Central American Common Market (founded in 1960) and the Andean Pact (1969) could expand the internal market, and thus reduce the inherent inefficiencies of the ISI model, but their effectiveness was constrained by imperfect product coverage and perennial squabbles over which country would host the more prestigious industries (e.g., steel and automobiles). Those internal frictions can be seen to this day in the Southern Market (Mercosur) of Argentina, Brazil, Paraguay, and Uruguay.

The long-term consequences of import-restricting versus export-friendly strategies can be understood by making rough comparisons between the larger economies of Latin America and Asia. As of 1960, the average per capita income in Brazil, Chile, Colombia, Mexico, and Peru was $317, equal to 11% of US per capita income. That figure was also a little below the $339 achieved in Hong Kong, Korea, and Singapore. By 1980, however, it was apparent how much better those Asian economies' interests had been served. Their average income had risen to $4,111 (33% of the US level), as compared to just $1,751 (14%) for the five Latin American countries. Trade policy was not the sole determinant, with the Latin countries continuing to lose ground even after they turned to a more market-friendly approach. As of 2016 the relative value of their average income ($6,261) was precisely what it had been in 1960 (11% of the US level), but income in the Asian economies was up to $41,394 (72%).[9]

Comparisons of this sort, coupled with the outbreak of the Latin American debt crisis in the early 1980s, would lead many of the region's leaders to reconsider their position. The most immediate effect of the resulting Washington Consensus – so named for the broad agreement among the World Bank, the US Treasury, and market-oriented think tanks – was to force a reconsideration of earlier decisions to stay outside the multilateral trading system. Only half of the Latin American countries were contracting parties to the GATT as of 1980, but all of the rest began or completed their accessions in the ensuing decade. Even more consequentially, many countries in the region began to negotiate FTAs with major, extraregional economies. Mexico was the first Latin American country to enter into such negotiations with the United States, and over the next two decades another dozen would

[9]   Calculated by the author from World Bank data at https://data.worldbank.org/indicator/NY.GDP.MKTP.CD.

start down that same path (two of which would stumble along the way). Latin countries would ultimately account for eleven of the twenty US FTA partners.

Shifting Regional Priorities in US Foreign Policy

The pattern of US policy in the Cold War was cyclical. Whenever a crisis led Washington to conclude that it had accorded insufficient attention and resources to Latin America, it would develop a program and announce it with great fanfare; once the perceived danger receded, attention and support shifted elsewhere. Thus the perspectives, conclusions, and recommendations emanating from Milton Eisenhower's study trips to the region in 1953 and 1959 were repeated in the 1961 report of President Kennedy's Latin American Task Force, and later reappeared in the Kissinger Commission's 1984 report on Central America. All three administrations viewed unrest in Latin America as a twin product of social inequality and Soviet interference, and recommended that the United States respond by devoting increased economic and military resources to the region. Eisenhower's Social Progress Trust Fund, Kennedy's Alliance for Progress, and Reagan's Caribbean Basin Initiative (CBI) all stemmed from the same theory of containment through economic development, and each was accompanied by expanded foreign assistance and security operations.

The rise and fall of the Kennedy administration's Alliance for Progress illustrates this progression, as well as the short attention span of Congress. This policy was the US response to the Cuban Revolution, and Congress was willing to grant what President Kennedy requested: increased appropriations of foreign assistance, creation of the Peace Corps, and US adherence to the International Coffee Agreement. When the locus of Cold War attention shifted to Southeast Asia, so did the bulk of foreign assistance. President Johnson found it increasingly difficult to pry new funding out of Congress, and President Nixon officially declared the termination of the Alliance for Progress in 1969.

The Bush administration's Enterprise for the Americas Initiative suffered from a similar lack of urgency. Unlike the earlier programs, it was divorced from the Cold War. President Bush proposed in 1990 a bundle of measures intended to encourage the democratic and market-oriented reforms then being undertaken throughout the region, including debt relief, trade liberalization, and new funding for the Inter-American Development Bank (IDB). The absence of a real crisis made members of Congress question the need for action. Coupled with a recession at home and the collapse of the Soviet Union, this apathy proved hard to overcome. Congress never appropriated all of the funds that the administration sought for the IDB, and restricted the administration's debt-relief plans. The only Bush initiative in the region to which Congress gave its full support was the preference program for the Andean countries.

The Caribbean and Andean Preferences

Two regional trade programs that fit within that general pattern merit closer attention. Both of them illustrate the political motivations that lead Washington to propose tighter economic ties, but also demonstrate the paradox of preferences. The effectiveness of both of these late-hegemony initiatives was constrained by the limited margins of preference available in a market for which most goods faced only modest tariff barriers.

The CBI is a nonreciprocal preferential arrangement through which the United States provides duty-free access to its market for many products. The initiative encompasses a range of public- and private-sector programs that aim to promote increased foreign and domestic investment in nontraditional sectors of the Caribbean Basin countries. As originally proposed in 1982, the program would have offered duty-free treatment to all products except for textiles and apparel. More than a year passed before Congress enacted the original CBI bill, and the legislature made several amendments that reduced its effectiveness. The most important of these amendments cut the duty-free benefits by subtracting canned tuna, petroleum and derivatives, footwear, watches and watch parts, and transshipped Cuban sugar.

American imports from the Caribbean Basin actually declined in the first few years of the program's existence, leading to critical examination in congressional hearings and a series of proposals to enhance the CBI preferences. The most successful of these proposals was put into effect by executive order in 1986, when the Reagan administration extended special quota treatment to Caribbean Basin apparel. From then on, the administration or Congress tinkered with the program every few years. Laws such as the Caribbean Basin Economic Recovery Expansion Act of 1990 aimed to enhance the benefits by extending the CBI preferences in perpetuity, making more goods eligible, or otherwise providing for further benefits at the margins (e.g., by increasing the duty-free allowance for US tourists returning from the region).

The Andean Trade Preferences Act (ATPA), which was in effect from 1991 to mid-2013, was similar in several respects to the CBI. It too was intended to provide special trade incentives to a specific area of interest to the United States, in this instance on the theory that enhanced opportunities in legitimate trade would encourage the beneficiary countries not to sell illicit narcotics. These benefits were extended to Bolivia, Colombia, Ecuador, and Peru.

How well did these programs do? Their economic results, being constrained by low margins of preference, were generally consistent with the modest patterns discussed in Chapter 13. As for the broader US goals that gave rise to these programs, it is virtually impossible to quantify the extent to which they helped to achieve the intended results. Security issues remain an important concern in the Caribbean Basin, and especially in Central America, but are now of a different character; whereas the main US concern in the early 1980s centered on the Cold War and Soviet influence, it is today focused on gang violence and illegal migration. Andean drug trafficking is no less prevalent today than it was a generation ago, although the center of gravity for cartel violence shifted from the Andean countries to Mexico. With both problems having thus moved more sideways than either forward or back, there is little point in trying to assign either credit or blame to the preference programs. Both the Caribbean and the Andean programs gave way to the next phase in US policy toward the region, with the beneficiaries of those two programs forming the largest blocs among the new FTA partners of the United States.

From NAFTA to the TPP

NAFTA marked a major shift from autonomous to reciprocal preferences. As was already described in Chapters 5 and 9, this initiative came shortly after the US–Canada FTA entered into effect, and was intended to set important precedents for new trade agreements. In addition to providing a WTO-Plus template on such issues as trade in services (GATS-Plus) and intellectual property rights (TRIPs-Plus), NAFTA reordered the relationship between the United States and what was still its major developing-country trading partner. The agreement implicitly rejected the contention that developing countries have a legal or moral right to S&D treatment, and that preferences ought to be extended on a one-way basis. The US negotiators insisted that Mexico make reciprocal concessions on tariffs and other matters, and not be granted substantial exceptions from NAFTA disciplines. Mexican negotiators did not initially accept that position, and their proposals for asymmetrical treatment ranged from elongated periods for the removal of tariffs to less onerous rules for sanitary and phytosanitary regulations. The US negotiators did freeze Mexico's existing preferences, such that all of the products for which it enjoyed duty-free treatment under Generalized System of Preferences (GSP) retained that status from the first day of implementation, but resisted most other S&D demands.

Washington quickly began treating NAFTA as a template for a new relationship with the rest of the Americas. The agreement entered into effect at the start of 1994, and at the end of that year the Clinton administration hosted the Summit of the Americas in Miami. Still flush with the end of the Cold War, the Washington Consensus, and the conclusion of the Uruguay Round, the assembled leaders pledged to conclude a Free Trade Area of the Americas by 2005. That year eventually proved to be the turning point, but not as originally planned. By the time that the IV Summit was held in Argentina the rifts had proven irreconcilable, with some Latin American countries returning to the traditional emphasis on intra-Latin integration (as exemplified by Mercosur) and others taking a more overtly anti-US stand (as led by Cuba and Venezuela).

In a repetition of the 1890s experience, the FTAA process fragmented into a series of bilateral and sub-regional talks. One of those initiatives split again, with the planned US–Andean FTA instead yielding bilateral FTAs with two of the partners (Colombia and Peru) while two others (Bolivia and Ecuador) aligned themselves with the Venezuelan bloc. That fragmentation seemed to reverse course for a time, with five of the twelve countries in the Trans-Pacific Partnership being American republics (i.e., Canada, Chile, Mexico, Peru, and the United States), but that initiative proved to be just one more disappointment in the long and frustrating history of inter-American integration.

The Foreign Policy of FTAs

The US motivations in selecting its FTA partners often had more to do with foreign policy than with commercial aspirations, although in some cases it is difficult to say where one set of objectives ends and the other begins. That is certainly true for the US rivalry with Brazil, which carries over into a general antipathy toward Mercosur. Some Washington policymakers see twin economic and political benefits in undermining that trade bloc, and to that end they have periodically dangled an FTA before Uruguay – an offer that would likely oblige this partner to leave the regional group. In 2006 that prospect had the further attraction of antagonizing Venezuela, with the US embassy in Montevideo observing that "an FTA with Uruguay would hand a defeat to [Hugo] Chavez, at a time when Venezuela is formally being inducted into Mercosur."[10]

The links between trade policy and security initiatives were quite close during the presidency of George W. Bush, and FTAs were the biggest prize

---

[10]   "Scenesetter for Upcoming Trade Talks in Washington," cable of June 6, 2006 from the US embassy in Montevideo (06MONTEVIDEO555_a).

that the administration could bestow on an ally. Just as his father had instituted the Andean trade preferences as an antinarcotics program, the second President Bush treated comprehensive FTAs as a weapon against the twin threat of narcoterrorism. Colombian Foreign Minister Fernando Araujo concurred, characterizing the FTA as "the 'economic arm of Plan Colombia,' whose ratification was essential for Colombia to promote long term economic stability and help resolve long-standing social problems."[11] The relationship between FTAs and the war in Iraq is especially notable in Latin America. The only countries in this region that joined the Coalition of the Willing in 2003 were also FTA candidates, and the only FTA candidates that did not join the coalition were members of regional groups in which at least one other member joined the coalition.

FTAs do not always support Hirschman's expectation about preferences producing dependence and political influence (see Chapter 13). Two contrary cases offer evidence that even an FTA partner may still show independence in its relations with Washington. Consider the case of Chile in the run-up to the 2003 invasion of Iraq. The FTA negotiations with Santiago had started in the final weeks of the Clinton administration, and carried on into that third year of the Bush administration. In contrast to Central American and Dominican Republic FTA (CAFTA-DR) countries, four of which not only joined the Coalition of the Willing but actually sent troops to Iraq,[12] the government of Chile was internally divided over the legality and advisability of the proposed military campaign. That debate acquired special significance because, as fate would have it, Chile held one of the rotating seats on the United Nations Security Council just when (a) the council was deliberating the resolution authorizing the use of force and (b) Congress was considering the implementing legislation for the US–Chile FTA. The Bush administration let Santiago know that it linked these two issues, and matters came to a head when the Chilean UN representative – acting in defiance of instructions – voted against the US position. In the end the episode did not prevent the approval of the agreement, making it appear that the US threat to tank the FTA was only a bluff, but this confrontation did make for some anxious moments.[13]

The case of Nicaragua is also exceptional. The Sandinista Revolution offered the original inspiration for the CBI, ousting long-time US ally Anastasio Somoza in 1979. The economic support that the Reagan

[11] "Foreign Minister Araujo Meeting with WHA PDAS Shapiro," cable of April 27, 2007 from the US embassy in Bogotá (07BOGOTA2835_a).

[12] The Dominican Republic, El Salvador, Honduras, and Nicaragua all contributed troops to the Spanish Brigade in Iraq.

[13] This episode is chronicled in *El País* (2007), Muñoz (2008), and Weintraub (2004), p. 91.

administration extended to the rest of Central America, including aid and trade, complemented the economic sanctions and covert operations that it directed against Managua. Washington's bête noire at this time was Daniel Ortega, the Sandinista who led Nicaragua first as coordinator of the junta (1979–1985) and then as the elected president (1985–1990). Relations improved greatly after the 1990 elections brought Violeta Chamorro to power. In quick succession, Washington lifted the sanctions and extended CBI treatment; a decade later, it negotiated CAFTA-DR with Managua and its neighbors. That FTA entered into force for Nicaragua in 2006, but seven months later the country decided on a narrow vote to send Ortega back to the presidency. He was reelected by much more impressive margins in 2011 and 2016. These contradictory events brought Managua the odd distinction of being both an FTA partner of the United States and a member in good standing of the Venezuelan-led Bolivarian Alliance. The fact that Nicaragua's preferential access to the US market is provided by a treaty rather than a law makes it more difficult, but by no means impossible, for Washington to threaten the removal of these benefits in the event that relations with Managua take a new turn for the worse.

The Impact of FTAs on Imports

How much of a boost do FTAs provide? We saw in Chapter 13 that preferences generally extend modest assistance – if any at all – to their recipients. Beneficiaries outperformed the world average during 1990–2007, but typically underperformed it in 2007–2017. One reason for the difference may be the lower MFN tariffs (and lower margins of preference) that reigned after the final phase-in of the Uruguay Round results in 2005. That same description generally applies to the regional preferences for the Andean and Caribbean countries.

Are those points equally valid for FTAs? Figure 14.1 offers one take on that question, providing data on the performance of imports from all twenty FTA partners. The figure does so by situating each of these partners along two dimensions. One is the constructed average tariff on the products imported from that partner, which is the author's estimate of the average tariff that would be applied to a country's imports in 2017 if those same goods were subject to MFN rates. This tells us the margin of preference enjoyed by the partner. We should normally expect that the higher this margin, the greater the boost that the FTA extends to this country. That expectation can be measured by examining the difference between the compound annual rate of growth in total US imports, and imports from a specific partner, in the years since that

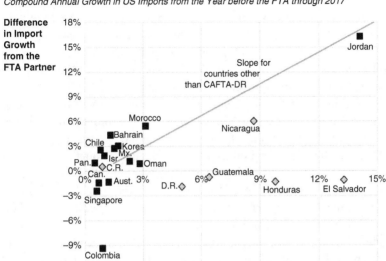

FIGURE 14.1 Relationship between pre-FTA tariffs and growth in US imports.
Difference in Import Growth from the FTA Partner = Difference between the
compound annual rates of growth in (a) imports from this partner from the year
before the FTA entered into force through 2017, and (b) imports from all
US partners during that same period.
Margin of Preference = Author's calculation of the average tariff that would be
paid on US imports from the FTA partner in 2017 if those imports paid MFN rates.
Source: Calculated from the US International Trade Commission's DataWeb at
https://dataweb.usitc.gov/.

partner's FTA entered into force. The data generally confirm that the performance of imports from FTA partners is indeed a function of the margins of
preference that they enjoy – provided that we ignore the CAFTA-DR partners.
Apart from four of those six countries (to whom we will turn shortly), there is
a fairly clear slope by which higher margins of preference translate into higher
rates of growth. Colombia is also an outlier; its case is taken up below in the
analysis of US energy trade.

The average applied US tariff on imports from those FTA partners for
whom full data are available[14] was 2.2% in the year preceding an agreement's
entry into force, or about the same as the average tariff applied to imports from

---

[14] Note that all calculations in this paragraph are based on FTA partners other than Canada and
Israel, as data are not available on average pre-FTA tariffs applied on imports from those first
two partners.

all partners. The constructed average tariff for these countries was 4.1% in 2017. The implication is obvious and simple: Imports from the FTA partners grew faster in sectors that would otherwise be subject to above-average tariffs. The constructed average tariff in 2017 was higher than the average pre-FTA tariff for fourteen partners, and less than or equal to the pre-FTA rate in four other cases. Textile and apparel products do not figure as prominently here as one might think. Preferences notwithstanding, most FTA partners have lost market share to more efficient Asian producers, to the point where this sector's share of US imports from the FTA partners as a group fell from 4.5% in 2004 to 2.0% in 2017. It is instead a product of rising US imports from these partners in other sectors where tariffs are higher than average, but still below the 15–20% range that is typical for apparel. The best rates of increase are typically in such otherwise high-tariff sectors as shoes and other leather goods, processed fruit and vegetable products, plastics, chemicals, and furniture.

This observation is consistent with the principal message of the paradox of preferences. If imports increase at a higher rate for those items that would otherwise be subject to relatively high tariffs, it stands to reason that FTAs would be even more beneficial if the average US rates were still high for most goods. With these agreements instead being negotiated at a time when many of those tariffs have already been removed, and all of the rest have been reduced, the impact on imports is understandably limited.

And what accounts for the anomalous CAFTA-DR results? While the results for Costa Rica and Nicaragua approximate those of other FTA partners, imports from the four other countries in this agreement greatly underperformed. The deviations from the general pattern stem from two facts: Much of what the United States imports from these countries is apparel, and while these partners do benefit from exoneration of the high tariffs in this sector they are also subject to onerous rules of origin. The importance of those points is discussed at greater length in the next section, together with the special case of Nicaragua (for which rules of origin were more forgiving). In all goods *other than* apparel, the growth in US imports from the CAFTA-DR countries from 2005 to 2017 was much greater (75%) than was the corresponding rate of increase in non-apparel imports from all sources (41%). Costa Rica did better than its peers because it has been the most successful in transitioning out of the apparel business.

THE DECLINING UTILITY OF TEXTILE AND APPAREL PREFERENCES

As the foregoing discussion suggests, apparel is an exceptionally important product not just in total US trade but more specifically with this region. That is no accident. Over the course of the last generation, Washington used trade programs and agreements to promote apparel coproduction arrangements to serve the twin purposes of shoring up regional allies and providing a soft landing for a US industry caught on the wrong side of Creative Destruction. That strategy was quite successful for decades, but it cannot indefinitely evade the logic that underlays the paradox of preferences.

Where Apparel Fits in the US FTA Strategy

From the 1960s through the end of the Uruguay Round, the Multi-Fibre Arrangement (MFA) and its predecessor arrangements established strict limits on US apparel imports. Originally created to restrict imports from Japan and other Asian exporters, the MFA eventually imposed quotas on almost all significant apparel suppliers in the developing world.[15] The sources of these imports changed as specific partners moved up the ladder of industrial sophistication, leaving behind this labor-intensive sector as they ascended into more capital-intensive industries. As of 1970, nearly two-thirds of US apparel imports came from Hong Kong, Japan, Korea, and Taiwan.[16] Their collective share was down to 17% in 2000, and less than 1% in 2017.[17] Latin American countries took up much of that slack, a trend that the market started and that the government eventually promoted.

The US textile and apparel industries demanded import protection for generations, but over time the costs of this protection became ever more apparent. De Melo and Tarr calculated in 1992 that the number of jobs that would be lost to workers in this field (247,000) by eliminating the MFA quotas would be largely made up by new jobs in other, generally higher-income and higher-technology sectors (202,700).[18] Policymakers believed that the broader interests of the United States would be better served by just such an upgrading. That meant reordering national policy and the trading system so as to hasten – yet also soften – the economic transition and its movement from labor-intensive, low-technology industries to other sectors with just the opposite profile. That was one of the grand bargains of the Uruguay Round, in which developing countries agreed to phase in stricter protection of intellectual property rights on the same, ten-year schedule by which the United States and other developed countries agreed to phase out the MFA. That bargain was

[15] On the origins of the quota system, see Friman (1990), especially chapter four.
[16] Arpan et al. (1982), p. 57.
[17] Author's calculations.
[18] De Melo and Tarr (1992), pp. 89–90.

complemented by preferential programs and agreements through which the United States encouraged the creation of captive markets for US textile producers in Latin America and other favored regions.

Competitors, Partners, and Clients

The US approach to apparel trade preferences is part of a broader strategy to balance the needs of domestic and foreign policy. Although not explicitly declared, these initiatives were based on the principle that it is better to encourage coproduction with favored partners in Latin America than to lose out altogether to Asian imports. Policymakers recognized that the United States could not efficiently maintain an apparel industry behind protective barriers, given the high US wage rates, but also realized that they could provide a soft landing for this sector while creating new markets for textile producers. In the short to medium term, they would offer preferential market access to selected partners, taking in their apparel on a duty-free, quota-free basis – provided that the partners made these garments from US fabric. The quotas would be phased out over the long term, so that the preferences for these partners would eventually be limited to tariff treatment, but that phase-out had the additional virtue of creating leverage in the Uruguay Round. This strategy had a win-win-win appeal for two decades.

The inspiration for these programs came from what was originally known as the 807 program, after the item in the tariff schedule that covered this special category of imports.[19] Under 807, US materials would be assembled in off-shore facilities that were usually called *maquiladoras*. On the reentry of finished products into the United States, duty would be paid only on the foreign value-added. The arrangement thus favored the more capital-intensive textile sector over the more labor-intensive apparel sector. The 807 program accounted for just 3% of US apparel imports in 1970, but rose to 10% in 1974.[20] As of 1976, Mexico provided nearly half of the imports under 807, with most of the rest coming from other countries in the Caribbean Basin.[21] The principles that underlay the 807 program were then expanded upon to create a larger strategy in which the United States imported apparel from three classes of countries:[22]

---

[19]   Note that item 807 was the number found in the older Tariff Schedule of the United States. That nomenclature was replaced in 1988 by the Harmonized Tariff System, in which the 807 program was instead classified as 9802.

[20]   Arpan et al. (1982), p. 73.

[21]   Ibid., p. 74.

[22]   These categories are the author's terminology, and do not represent any official designations.

- *Partners* in coproduction enjoy special access via preferential agreements and programs that is conditional on meeting strict rules of origin.
- *Clients* benefit from a hybrid of foreign aid and managed trade through which they enjoy the same market access as the partners without having to meet those rules of origin.
- *Competitors* in Asia and other regions do not enjoy preferential access to the US market, and imports from these countries are obliged to pay high MFN tariffs.

The United States typically insists on a yarn-forward rule of origin when negotiating an FTA with a partner. This is the second-most restrictive of all possible rules, being less demanding than fiber-forward but stricter than fabric-forward. While it permits a producer to use material made from fibers that might come from anywhere in the world, all subsequent processes must generally be performed in one or more of the FTA member countries. Some flexibilities can be built into an FTA, providing several means by which certain types or amounts of otherwise nonoriginating materials such as fabrics or buttons can be incorporated into a finished garment that still qualifies for FTA treatment.

Membership in these groups is not fixed. Some of the countries that were most competitive a generation ago produce very little apparel today, with their wage scales and industrial sophistication both having moved higher up the ladder. Those countries are shown in Table 14.2 as post-competitive. There are also some middle cases, such as Nicaragua, which might be classified as either a partner or a client. It is a partner by way of CAFTA-DR, but is the only country in this group that benefited from generous rules of origin. Those special rules explain why Nicaragua did much better than its neighbors in post-MFA apparel exports to the United States. Being less constrained in its fabric sourcing, Nicaragua managed to increase its share of the US apparel-import market from 0.7% in 2004 to 1.4% in 2014. Its preferential rules of origin expired in that latter year, and while Nicaragua maintained about the same market share in the years that followed it is unclear how long that might last.

The Results

These arrangements worked well for a time, achieving the desired results for both the United States and its partners, but the walls began to close in after 2005. That year marked the end of the MFA quotas that had protected the US industry and, as the partner countries later came to realize, also provided

TABLE 14.2. *US Trade in Textiles and Apparel with Selected Countries, 1994 and 2017*

	Share of US Textile and Apparel Imports (%)		Average US Textile and Apparel Tariffs (%)		US Textile and Apparel Exports as % of Imports	
	1994	2017	1994	2017	1994	2017
Competitors	30.9	70.1	14.2	14.7	10.9	6.7
China	14.2	35.5	11.9	13.5	13.1	4.4
Other Asians	16.7	34.7	16.1	15.9	9.1	8.9
Partners	20.6	15.4	7.7	1.5	84.3	67.9
Latin FTA partners	16.0	13.4	8.0	1.4	53.6	54.4
Other FTA partners	4.6	2.0	6.5	1.7	129.4	158.2
Clients	2.5	4.1	11.1	1.1	27.0	8.3
Middle Eastern	1.5	2.3	7.0	0.2	20.8	6.5
Haiti and Africa	1.0	1.8	17.2	2.3	36.6	6.5
Post-Competitive	34.2	7.4	16.0	8.3	29.9	38.3
Asian	24.4	2.6	17.2	6.2	23.9	45.2
European Union	9.8	4.8	12.9	9.4	44.9	34.6
Rest of World	11.8	3.0	15.6	11.0	31.6	57.5
US Total	100.0	100.0	13.5	11.5	35.4	13.9

Textiles and Apparel = All items in chapters 50–63 of the Harmonized Tariff Schedule.
Other Asian competitors = Bangladesh, Cambodia, India, Indonesia, Malaysia, Pakistan, Sri Lanka, Thailand, and Vietnam.
Latin FTA partners = Chile, Colombia, Costa Rica, Dominican Republic, El Salvador, Guatemala, Honduras, Mexico, Nicaragua, Panama, and Peru.
Other FTA partners = Australia, Canada, Bahrain, Oman, and Morocco.
Middle Eastern Clients = Egypt, Israel, and Jordan.
Haiti and Africa = Haiti and the beneficiaries of the African Growth and Opportunities Act.
Asian Post-Competitive = Hong Kong, Japan, Korea, and Taiwan.
Source: Calculated from the U.S. International Trade Commission's DataWeb at https://dataweb .usitc.gov/.

guaranteed market shares to many otherwise uncompetitive producers in the developing world.

The data in Table 14.2 show that the market share held by the Asian competitors more than doubled from 1994 to 2017, and that the clients also experienced modest increases over the same period, but that all other countries lost ground. The most that Latin America partners could hope for was to maintain a more or less steady share over this period; nearly all of them fell behind. The tariffs applied on imports from these countries decreased substantially, at a time when the tariffs on the competitors held steady, but the

Latin partners are constrained both by their own higher labor costs and by restrictive US rules of origin. The bottom line for those rules can be appreciated by comparing the differences in US export:import ratios. Whereas in 2017 the United States exported 68¢ worth of fabric or other textile and apparel goods to the partner countries for every $1 in imports from them, it exported just 7¢ to the competitors. The clients get the best of both worlds, facing tariffs that are comparable to those imposed on the partners while incorporating US inputs at about the same rate as the competitors.

This strategy made a valuable contribution to several domestic and international goals. It helped to bring the Uruguay Round to a successful conclusion, including the grand bargain of intellectual property protection for the elimination of apparel quotas – even if many developing countries later felt buyer's remorse on both sides of that deal. It also eased the transition for US apparel producers (for whom production off-shore was preferable to bankruptcy) and textile producers (who benefited from a captive market), while reducing the costs of apparel for American consumers. It persuaded several partners to convert one-way preferences to reciprocal agreements, which further entailed a number of pro-market reforms in those countries, and strengthened their economic and political ties with the United States. For all that it achieved, however, this strategy may now be reaching the end of its useful life. There is good reason to expect that the share of the US apparel-import market that is held by low-wage Asian countries will continue to increase, the shares held by the FTA partners in the Americas will experience a commensurate decline, and that much of the capital and labor that those countries devoted to this industry will need to be reallocated to other sectors. That last point is precisely what has happened in so many other countries that initially got into manufactures by way of this sector, but then moved on to other, more sophisticated lines as their wages and skill levels rose.

ENERGY SECURITY AND THE AMERICAS

Energy security has been especially important to the United States since the 1970s, and was one of the chief motivations for the sequential FTAs in the Americas generally and with the North American neighbors in particular. Oil imports are perceived to pose a threat to national security whenever (a) they reach a level that makes the United States vulnerable to disruptions in supply, or (b) they originate in countries that are actively or potentially hostile to US interests. Both of these conditions were present in the aftermath of Middle Eastern crises from the mid-1950s through the 1970s, and periodically led to the imposition of import restrictions. It was only later that trade preferences were added to the toolkit of energy trade policymakers, with Washington using preferences to encourage energy imports from the Western Hemisphere.

Energy Security through Trade Restrictions and Trade Liberalization

All other things being equal, energy planners prefer to import from countries that are closer – geographically and politically – than from those that are distant. In 1969 the National Security Council advised the president that it was best to give "preference to imports from Canada over imports from Venezuela, to imports from Venezuela over Iran, to imports from Iran over the balance of the Middle East."[23] While that last point would change a decade later, the principle remains: Oil may be physically fungible, but its suppliers and the intervening sea lanes do not present identical risk profiles and should not be treated equally.

The US oil-import market was strictly controlled from the late 1950s to the early 1970s, and has been subject to a variety of restrictions ever since then. The main objective in the earlier years was to avoid dependence on the Middle East and promote imports from Canada, and the resulting price distortions had some perverse consequences. The US oil-import regime of the early 1970s was so favorable to Canada – still a net importer – that Canadians shipped their own product south and relied on imports from the Caribbean and South America to fill domestic needs.[24] President Nixon removed the Eisenhower-era restrictions, but they soon returned. In 1975 President Ford placed a $3/barrel fee on imported crude oil and a $1.20 fee on imported petroleum products; he lifted these fees the next year. Congress balked in 1979 and again in 1980 when President Carter sought to impose an oil-import fee. These were the last efforts by a US president to impose general restrictions on oil imports.[25] From that time forward, restrictions have instead been more precisely targeted at radical regimes. The Carter administration imposed an embargo on trade with Iran during the 1979–1981 hostage crisis; despite some fluctuations in the coverage and enforcement of these restrictions over the ensuing decades, they continue to block imports of Iranian oil. Libya has been under embargo since 1982 (which was only partially lifted after

[23] Memorandum from the President's Assistant for International Economic Affairs (Flanigan) to the President's Assistant for National Security Affairs (Kissinger), "National Security Aspects of the Oil Import Quota Problem" (December 4, 1969), *FRUS 1969–1976*, Volume XXXVI, p. 67.
[24] Central Intelligence Agency, Directorate of Intelligence, "Canada's Changing Economic Relations with the United States" (June, 1971), p. 23.
[25] The Reagan administration turned down a Section 232 petition in its final weeks, as did the Clinton administration in 1994 and 2000.

the 2011 overthrow of Qaddafi), and Iraq was subject to sanctions between 1990 and 2003 (as modified by the oil-for-food program beginning in 1996). Both the Iranian and the Libyan sanctions were imposed under the Section 232 national security law (see Chapter 3).

Trade liberalization was a latecomer to US deliberations over energy security. This option merited no mention at all, for example, in the Reagan administration's National Security Decision Directive Number 134. This 1984 energy strategy focused instead on such topics as freedom of navigation in the Persian Gulf and the need for adequate stockpiling; the only role that it saw for diplomacy was to coordinate with other oil-importing countries in the event of an emergency.[26] The neglect of trade liberalization as a tool of energy statecraft may be understandable, given the low level of US tariffs on energy products. Crude oil is subject to a tariff of just 5¼¢ or 10½¢ per barrel, depending on the grade, which amounts to nothing but a nuisance for a product that typically sells in the $50–100/barrel range.[27] The main attractions that oil-exporters might perceive in an FTA with the United States are apparent only when those countries are seeking to diversify their economies and escape the "resource curse."

NAFTA may owe its existence to a coincidence in timing, with the Iranian Revolution coming just when substantial new oil reserves were discovered in Mexico. While President Carter failed to persuade Mexico to negotiate an energy trade agreement with the United States, and Canadian statesmen were equally skeptical when the Reagan administration proposed a similarly narrow deal, both neighbors eventually opted to seek more comprehensive agreements with the United States. NAFTA is now one of many preferential arrangements for favored suppliers. Duty-free privileges were also offered to Caribbean Basin and sub-Saharan Africa partners in the Trade and Development Act of 2000.[28]

The place of oil in NAFTA is somewhat ambiguous. Article 2102 is a nearly verbatim repetition of the GATT national security clause (Article XXI), but it is modified by another provision (Article 607) providing that a country cannot use Article 2102 to justify "a measure restricting imports of an energy or basic petrochemical good from, or exports of" such goods to another NAFTA

---

[26] See National Security Decision Directive Number 134 (March 27, 1984).
[27] Note that prior to the Uruguay Round this tariff was unbound, meaning that Washington could theoretically have increased it to any level it wished, but the United States agreed to bind (though not reduce) the tariff in that round.
[28] That law is the authorizing legislation for both the African Growth and Opportunity Act and the Caribbean Basin Trade Partnership Act.

country except in certain cases.[29] These provisions have not been tested by the efforts of either the neighbors to impose export restrictions, nor by any US effort to restrict oil imports. American energy planners nevertheless work from the assumption that North American supplies should be considered secure in any future emergency.

The Shifting Sources of US Energy

The development of new oil fields throughout North America, including increased production in the United States, has led to a much greater security of supply. For a time that meant a rising share of imports from Latin American countries, but the mix later shifted to Canada and the United States itself. Domestic production reached a watershed in September, 2013, when it exceeded imports for the first time since 1995.[30] As important as energy security was in encouraging the negotiation of trade agreements with oil suppliers in the Americas, those partners are smaller suppliers now than they were before the advent of FTAs.

The trends can be seen in Figure 14.2, which show that the share of oil coming from outside the Americas is far smaller today than it was just a decade ago. Over that same period, however, the share coming from Mexico and other Latin suppliers has also fallen. At the time that the US-Canada FTA entered into effect, Canada supplied only about one-third as much oil to the United States as did Latin America. Canada surpassed the region as a supplier in 2012, and by 2017 it shipped just over twice as much product to the United States as did all of Latin America. The importance of Latin America as a provider of crude oil to the United States peaked in 2002, when the region provided 30% of imports and 18% of total supply. By 2017, the region's share had declined to 25% of imports and 10% of total supply. The United States was now an oil exporter to numerous Latin America countries, and a net exporter to some of them. These trends reiterate the point that oil trade is determined more by actual production than by the very marginal influence that can be exerted by trade preferences. From 2006 to 2016, the compound annual rate of growth in oil production was 6.1% in the United States and 3.4% in Canada, but it was –4.0% in Mexico and –3.2% in Venezuela; those latter declines could not

---

[29] These cases are drawn more narrowly than those in GATT Article XXI, applying to measures necessary to "supply a military establishment of a Party or enable fulfillment of a critical defense contract of a Party," "respond to a situation of armed conflict involving the Party taking the measure," or relating to nuclear weapons (thus involving uranium and other fissionable materials).

[30] https://energy.gov/maps/us-crude-oil-production-surpasses-net-imports.

Millions of Barrels per Day

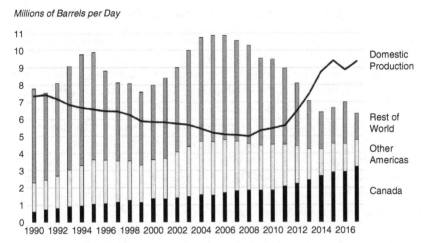

FIGURE 14.2 US production and imports of crude oil, 1990–2017.
Note: Imports are not net of US exports. "Other Americas" includes both Latin America and the Caribbean.
Source: Domestic production from Department of Energy at www.eia.gov/dnav/pet/pet_crd_crpdn_adc_mbblpd_a.htm. Imports Calculated from the US International Trade Commission's DataWeb at https://dataweb.usitc.gov/, based on HTS 2709.

be compensated for by the 2.0% growth rate in the rest of the Latin America and the Caribbean.[31]

The case of the US–Colombian FTA exemplifies the point that trade agreements are not always successful in promoting energy imports from a partner. As was seen earlier in Figure 14.1, US imports from Colombia fell sharply in the years following that FTA's entry into force. Much of that poor performance can be attributed to sharp reductions in energy prices. Imports of oil, gas, and coal from Colombia had peaked at $16.8 billion in 2012 (the year that the agreement entered into effect), but plummeted to $7.1 billion in 2017; that decline was largely a function of falling oil prices, with the actual quantities of imports not changing much from 2012 to 2017. Even if one excludes these energy goods from the calculation, however, US imports from Colombia still fell from $7.8 billion in 2012 to $6.4 billion in 2017.

---

[31] Calculated by the author from data posted at www.bp.com/content/dam/bp/en/corporate/pdf/energy-economics/statistical-review-2017/bp-statistical-review-of-world-energy-2017-full-report.pdf.

When Post-Materialist Values Clash with Energy Security

The case of US policy towards oil trade in the Americas, and especially with Canada, offers another example of the conflicts that can arise over post-materialist values. Energy security had once been a leading goal in foreign policy, but the priority attached to this objective has diminished with increasing levels of domestic production and rising concerns over the environment. As was discussed in Chapter 5, the domestic diplomacy of trade policy has been altered by changing political tastes in the American public, including a greater propensity to favor environmental protection. The oil spills of the *Exxon Valdez* (1989) and the *Deepwater Horizon* (2010) are much fresher memories than the first (1973) or second (1979) oil crises, with the latter events occurring before many Americans were even born, and the clashing priorities of energy security versus environmental protection play out in partisan politics and in US trade relations with the neighbors.

The two political parties generally agree on the need to reduce dependence on foreign oil, albeit for somewhat different reasons. Environmentalists and Democrats prefer that energy consumption in general be reduced, and that there be greater reliance on sustainable sources. Most of those sources are domestic by definition, such as solar, wind, and hydropower. The Republican perspective is based both on concerns over national security and by ties to oil companies. The members of the two parties may each take some satisfaction from recent trends in the sourcing of US oil and gas imports, but Democrats are more troubled by the underlying cause for these trends. Production of oil and gas in the United States has risen greatly in recent years, due largely to the increasing use of hydraulic fracturing (more commonly called "fracking"). Vast domestic reserves of hydrocarbons that had once been beyond economic reach are now being exploited, thus allowing the United States to reduce its imports of oil and increase its exports of natural gas and refined products. The clashing partisan perspectives on fracking are reflected in legislative battles at the Federal, state, and local levels.

This contagion of conflict has also spread to trade policy, especially in the Americas. Of all the energy-related disputes between the Obama administration and the Republicans in Congress, none was as severe as the fight over the permitting of a new pipeline that would bring Canadian oil to the United States for refining. Environmentalists objected strongly to the proposed Keystone XL pipeline, as the extraction of petroleum from oil sands is considered to be especially damaging. They also raised concerns over the oil spills that could occur along the pipeline. Their opponents charged that the environmentalists were being short-sighted and self-defeating, as the oil will be transported anyway and that the alternative routes – including rail and trucks – would be more prone to spills than a pipeline. That conflict carried on throughout the Obama administration, and was not resolved until President Trump took office. One of his first acts was to undo his predecessor's position.[32] This order is not likely to be the last word on the issue, nor on the multifaceted issues surrounding energy security, trade, and the environment.

THE PERENNIALLY ELUSIVE GOAL

The commercial integration of the Western Hemisphere has been a recurring theme of US foreign policy, sporadically pursued by American statesmen for nearly two centuries, but they have repeatedly failed to annihilate distance as thoroughly as they wish. That has been just as true over the past few decades as it was in prior generations. The latest trends can be reduced to a single sentence: After a few decades of initiatives aimed at promoting closer inter-American economic relations, which met with widely varying degrees of success, the United States is now drifting away from its southern partners. This can be seen in the reversal of policy initiatives and in actual levels of trade and investment.

The sudden downgrading of the region as a focus of US commercial diplomacy is striking. During 1991-2006 the United States negotiated FTAs with eleven countries in the region, and also attempted to conclude a Free Trade Area of the Americas. There have been no new bilateral or sub-regional FTAs reached since then, and the Trump administration reversed course first by pulling out of the TPP and then recasting NAFTA more as an instrument of managed than of free trade. Its actions in other areas, such as demands for a wall on the US-Mexican border and proposed cuts in foreign assistance, reinforce this trend towards economic disengagement from the neighbors.

The raw numbers reinforce these points, showing that trade and capital have not followed the flag as faithfully as statesmen hoped. Trade did for a time: Total US merchandise trade with Latin American and Caribbean countries rose from $228 billion 1996 to $782 billion in 2012, growing at a compound annual rate of 8% per year. That total then dropped to $747 billion in 2017, a 4% decrease from 2012. Capital flows have been more disappointing. Latin America's share of US foreign direct investment actually began to decline at about the same time that the United States started to negotiate FTAs in the region. As of 1995, Mexico and Central America hosted

---

[32] www.whitehouse.gov/presidential-actions/presidential-memorandum-regarding-construction
-keystone-xl-pipeline/.

4.8% of US international capital; by 2017, their share fell to 2.0%. The South American share peaked at 8.0% in 1997, several years before US FTA negotiations reached that continent, but in 2017 they held just 2.2% of US foreign direct investment.[33]

Several causes may be cited for this continental drift. They include the decline in apparel and oil trade, as chronicled in this chapter, as well as the crowding-out effect from China's growing footprint. The most important point, for our present purposes, is that these economic trends are not beholden solely to the intentions of trade negotiators. Even when they liberalize markets on a reciprocal and preferential basis, the paradox of preferences acts to limit the actual impact of their initiatives. That point is just as true for the Middle East as it is for Latin America, as is explored in the next chapter.

---

[33]   Calculated from Bureau of Economic Analysis data at https://www.bea.gov/itable/index.cfm.

15

War, Peace, and Trade in the Middle East

Across the globe, free markets and trade have helped defeat poverty and taught men and women the habits of liberty. So I propose the establishment of a U.S.-Middle East free trade area within a decade, to bring the Middle East into an expanding circle of opportunity, to provide hope for the people who live in that region.

President George W. Bush, University of South Carolina
commencement address (2003)

INTRODUCTION

Having unleashed shock and awe on what had been the fourth-largest army in the world, but was now downgraded to the second-largest army in Iraq, President George W. Bush hoped to complement his military campaign with a more peaceful path to change in the Middle East. His decision to promote an FTA between the United States and the region was something akin to the practice of American air commanders who accompanied every briefing on their bombing of Iraq by detailing the humanitarian daily rations they had airdropped to civilians. And like that repackaged army chow, which was reportedly discarded by all but the hungriest recipients, Bush's offer got few takers. Only three small countries reached FTAs with the United States, representing just 9% of the economies, and 14% of the population, among the potential partners to whom Bush had made his appeal.

These results were entirely predictable, as the initiative offered little and demanded much. The region's major oil exporters already enjoyed something close to duty-free access for their principal exports, and even the countries that exported high-tariff apparel knew that the window was closing for viable competition in the US market. Bush made his pitch just two years before the last remnants of 1960s-vintage apparel quotas were to disappear, after which even duty-free treatment might not allow the Arab producers to compete with the scale economies and low wages enjoyed by their Asian rivals. Little else that these countries exported was still subject to high US tariff barriers, and the limited commercial attractions of Bush's offer were further undercut by the political strings that he attached. The deal was implicitly conditioned on an end to the Arab League boycott of Israel, and might also demand that the potential US partners forswear oil embargoes as a political weapon. It would thus amount to a permanent cease-fire in the half-century of economic warfare among the Arab countries, Israel, and the United States. A few countries were willing to pay the price, but most concluded that the costs were not matched by the meagre advantages that Washington offered.

The events discussed in this chapter offer an extended case study in the paradox of preferences. The proposed US–Middle East FTA might have been attractive, were the offer made when US trade barriers were still high, but by 2003 those barriers were low and falling. This episode also illustrates two recurring themes in the political economy of the Middle East. On the economic side, discrimination remains rampant. From the stick of the Arab League boycott to the carrot of American FTAs, all parties have an entrenched predilection to politicize and discriminate. As for the region's diplomacy, there is no novelty in this initiative's failure. That goes with the territory.

REGIONAL SANCTIONS AND MULTILATERAL RULES

The many and varied departures from MFN treatment in the Middle East ensure that trade in this troubled region is neither politically neutral nor governed solely by market forces. Much of that discrimination dates to the Second World War and its immediate aftermath, when all the key elements that define American relations with this region emerged: the creation of the state of Israel, independence for a critical mass of Arab countries, the founding of the Arab League, and the beginning of large-scale US oil imports. That same period also witnessed the establishment of the GATT as an instrument of nondiscriminatory trade liberalization, including disciplines that permit exceptions to this general rule for reasons of security or regional integration. Taken together, these disparate elements produced discrimination on the part of both exporters and importers of oil, a boycott on Israel (followed later by US countermeasures), Arab reluctance to join the GATT and be subject to its rules, and the gradual spread of regional and extra-regional trade arrangements that are inspired more by political than commercial aspirations.

US Policy toward the Arab League Boycott of Israel

The Arab League boycott of Israel is the original and politically most significant instrument of discriminatory trade in the Middle East. It first arose in
1944 – four years before the Jewish state came into existence – when the newly
formed league adopted a resolution recommending that all Arab states establish national boycott offices to block trade with Jewish-owned businesses in
Palestine.[1] A decade later the Arab League banned trade with third-country
companies that have economic or political ties to Israel (the secondary
embargo) and with third-country companies that have ties to companies
found to violate the secondary embargo (the tertiary embargo). This meant
expanding the scope of economic conflict to otherwise neutral countries,
a group that then included the United States. In 1967 the CIA reported that
among the US firms blacklisted were Ford, Sears Roebuck, Kaiser Industries,
RCA, and Coca Cola, but also observed that in no instance "has any Arab
country cut itself off from the only major supplier of essential or especially
desirable commodities for any extended period of time."[2]

The US response to the boycott has gone through three phases. The first
phase lasted from the inception of these restrictions until the mid-1970s, when
Washington did little more than express rhetorical opposition. In 1953 a State
Department position paper opined that the cost of the Arab boycott to Israel
"is, in effect, paid for by grant aid funds authorized by the United States
Congress."[3] The National Security Council nevertheless approved a policy
by which the United States would "[w]ork for eventual elimination of the Arab
economic boycott of Israel," together with related steps such as "resist[ing]
Arab efforts to impose a secondary boycott on U.S. trade with Israel" and
"help[ing] to restore normal commercial intercourse ... between Israel and
the Arab states."[4] That policy was classified Top Secret, however, and was
accorded a correspondingly low profile for another two decades. Washington
did not penalize either the Arab League countries or the domestic and third-
country firms that cooperated. The US reticence can be chalked up to two
points: American officials did not wish to set any precedents that might
impinge on their own ability to employ sanctions against other adversaries,
and it would take another quarter of a century before US relations with Israel

[1] For a capsule history of the boycott, see chapter 2 of Feiler (1998).
[2] Central Intelligence Agency, Directorate of Intelligence, "The Arab Boycott – A Study in
     Gamesmanship" (August 1, 1967), p. 1.
[3] Department of State Position Paper, "Israel" (May 5, 1953), *FRUS 1952–1954*, Volume IX,
     Part 1, p. 1198.
[4] Statement of Policy by the National Security Council 1, "United States Objectives and Policies
     with Respect to the Near East" (July 23, 1954), ibid., p. 535.

achieved that closeness that would later seem to have been present since the creation.

The second phase lasted from the late 1970s until the early 1990s. During this period the United States took a stronger stand against the boycott's secondary and tertiary aspects, based on the prejudicial effect on American multinational enterprises. President Jimmy Carter made this a campaign issue in 1976, when he criticized the weakness of the Ford administration's anti-boycott policy. After the inauguration, however, he emphasized that the US goals were not aimed at the core of the sanctions. "A primary boycott is perfectly acceptable in international affairs," he declared, acknowledging that the United States engaged in similar policies.[5] The Carter administration's principal innovation was the 1977 revision of the Export Administration Act, an anti-boycott law that prohibits such activities as refusing to do business with Israel or furnishing information about a firm's business relationships. Carter also succeeded in bringing Israel and Egypt together at the Camp David meetings of 1979, where Anwar Sadat agreed to open economic relations with Israel. He was rewarded by a US pledge to provide parity in foreign assistance, but the other Arab countries retaliated by suspending ties to Cairo. The net result may have cautioned other countries against following suit, insofar as "U.S. aid could hardly compensate for the abrupt cessation of all Arab aid, trade, and capital flows" to Egypt.[6]

The Reagan and G. H. W. Bush administrations generally followed the Carter precedents. They combated the nonprimary aspects of the boycott by enforcing the anti-boycott laws, and called upon Arab countries to renounce the policy, but neither administration made strenuous efforts to end the primary boycott. The negotiation of the US–Israel FTA in 1984 marked two innovations: It was the first FTA that the United States ever reached, and was the first use of a bilateral trade agreement as a tool of US diplomacy in the Middle East. This set the precedent for the Clinton administration to launch FTA negotiations with Jordan in late 2000, followed by the G. W. Bush administration's region-wide proposal in 2003. President Reagan also signed a 1986 law requiring that the Treasury maintain a list of countries that require cooperation with the boycott.

Both the boycott and Washington's response entered a third phase in the 1990s, a decade that began with hopeful signs for Middle East peace. Several of the Arab League states contributed to this atmosphere by relaxing or even

[5] "Remarks and a Question-and-Answer Session with Department [of Commerce] Employees" (February 9, 1977), in *PPP 1977*.
[6] Handoussa and Shafik (1993), p. 25.

ending their enforcement of the boycott. The Clinton administration pressed the advantage, attacking not only the costs imposed on US firms[7] but also the primary boycott. This policy achieved some success. Several Arab countries were willing to suspend or even terminate the boycott after signing of the Israeli-Palestinian Declaration of Principles in 1993: Kuwait announced that it would no longer participate in the secondary and tertiary boycotts, Israel and Jordan signed a declaration that called for an end to all economic boycotts, and the members of the Gulf Cooperation Council (GCC) – Saudi Arabia included – announced that they would end their participation in the boycott's nonprimary levels. The process slowed with the assassination of Israeli Prime Minister Yitzhak Rabin in 1995, and halted with the outbreak of the second *intifada* (i.e., Palestinian uprising) in 2000. It nevertheless lasted long enough for US statesmen to link the boycott to foreign economic policy, and for Congress to codify the connections (e.g., in a 1994 law preventing the State Department from entering into contracts with anyone engaging in the boycott at any level).[8]

The Impact of GATT and WTO Rules on the Boycott

This third period also saw several Arab countries begin the process of accession to the GATT and then the WTO, opening a new avenue for US leverage. Prior to this time, only a handful of Middle Eastern countries had formally joined the multilateral trading system. Israel was the first country in the region to do so permanently.[9] Its GATT accession in 1962 may have dissuaded other countries from following suit, as that would have given Israel the right to pose probing questions to them in an open diplomatic forum.

The boycott and the GATT were roughly contemporaneous, and it was at least theoretically possible that the new regime might ban unilateral sanctions. The topic arose in the negotiations over the proposed Havana Charter of the International Trade Organization, but "issues were raised that proved insurmountable" and "all reference to boycotts was eliminated"[10] from that ill-fated treaty. No such language was adopted in the less expansive GATT. Some

---

[7] A study requested by the Clinton administration concluded that in 1993, "U.S. businesses experienced total lost sales because of the boycott of approximately $410 million." U.S. International Trade Commission (1994).

[8] Title 22, Section 2679 of the U.S. Code.

[9] Lebanon and Syria were among the original GATT contracting parties, but they had joined on the basis of a bilateral customs union. They dissolved that agreement in 1951, leading both countries to withdraw from the GATT. Lebanon thus had to start from scratch when it began WTO-accession negotiations in 1999, as did Syria in 2010.

[10] Brown (1950), p. 106.

claimed that the boycott violated the letter or the spirit of GATT, and there is a hint that these concerns contributed to Syria's 1951 withdrawal from the GATT.[11] The United States did not press the matter in those early days, partly for want of opportunities (only three Arab countries acceded before the 1990s) and partly out of concerns over the appearance of hypocrisy (it being difficult to miss the similarities between the boycott and US sanctions on Cuba). This inaction might also be attributed to the somewhat ambivalent nature of relations between the United States and Israel in the first decades of that state's existence.

Israel took the initiative, with its 1962 GATT accession coinciding with Egypt's first and failed attempt to join GATT. The documentary history is unclear on the extent to which Cairo's failure to conclude those talks can be laid to its adherence to the boycott.[12] The issue arose again in 1970, when Egypt completed the process. The Israeli representative challenged the validity of the boycott under GATT Article XI, which generally bans quotas. The other contracting parties nevertheless approved Egyptian accession, and Israel opted not to block it. That was a power that all contracting parties held in principle, owing to the GATT norm of decision-making by consensus, but in practice the United States was almost alone in exercising a unilateral veto in accessions.[13] Egypt protected the integrity of the boycott by invoking the "non-application" clause (GATT Article XXXV) upon its accession, thus allowing it to pretend as if Israel were not in the GATT.[14] Egypt's invocation of this clause set the pattern for Morocco in 1987 and Tunisia in 1990.

The only other Arab countries that entered GATT before the 1990s were former colonies that did so through a process of succession rather than accession, and thus were legally barred from invoking non-application. GATT Article XXVI:5(c) allowed countries that had been colonies of other

[11] A World Bank mission to Syria in 1955 observed in its report that "Syria has left GATT because it preferred to be free in its commercial policy," and also declared that "membership in GATT could not readily be reconciled with embargoes." See International Bank for Reconstruction and Development (1955), p. 236.

[12] The later working party on Egyptian accession reported a statement by the Israeli representative that "the boycott had been considered by the 1962 Working Party and because of it, full accession had not been recommended at that time." The Egyptian representative disputed that characterization. See GATT Contracting Parties (1970), p. 40. A contemporary analyst instead attributed Egypt's failure to concerns over the state-centric nature of its economy; see Curzon (1965), pp. 305–306.

[13] Washington exercised this prerogative by withholding consensus for the attempted GATT accessions of Bulgaria and the Soviet Union, and for a time also blocked the WTO-accession plans of Libya, Iran, and Syria.

[14] See Chapter 11 for a fuller explanation of the origins and use of the GATT and WTO non-application clauses.

GATT contracting parties to acquire de facto status upon independence, and become a full contracting party via succession. This process involved much less stringent scrutiny and fewer commitments than ordinary accession. Countries that succeeded to GATT could invoke non-application with respect to existing GATT contracting parties only if their mother countries had made such an invocation. Neither Britain nor France had done so with respect to Israel, and thus foreclosed any chance for Bahrain or Kuwait (former British colonies) or Mauritania (a former French colony) to fall back on this option. The only way that they could have invoked non-application would be to undergo the more stringent process of accession under GATT Article XXXIII (as Tunisia and Morocco opted to do). Qatar and the United Arab Emirates were special cases that did have the option of invoking WTO Article XIII, but they both acceded during a hopeful period in the Arab–Israeli peace process and opted against non-application.

The legality of the Arab League's boycott has been a frequent and growing irritant in the WTO, and has been caught up with the league's demands for observer status. That is a courtesy that used to be extended on a more or less automatic basis, with the GATT and then WTO inviting representatives of sister organizations to participate in the meetings of some of its bodies. The dispute over extension of that same courtesy to the Arab League and the Islamic Conference stretches at least as far back as the 1970s,[15] and grew more intense as more Arab states joined. Israel and the United States repeatedly withheld consensus for the extension of this status to the Arab League, much to the annoyance of that group's members. They made several attempts to undo this blockage, including demands that the issue be put to a vote, but the WTO's informal norm against voting proved stronger than the sympathy other members felt for the Arab predicament. The Arabs announced in 2005 that they would routinely block all other organizations' requests for WTO observer status unless and until their own group was granted this treatment.[16]

US Linkage of the Boycott and Accessions

One characteristic of GATT diplomacy that carried over unchanged into the WTO period was the asymmetrical nature of accessions. Multilateral negotiations are generally based on reciprocal exchanges of concessions in which all

---

[15] See, for example, the US mission in Geneva's March 23, 1978 cable entitled "GATT and the Islamic Conference" (1978GENEVA04524_d). "In our estimation," the mission rather testily observed, "continued agitation of the question by the Israelis [on this issue] is counterproductive and could lead to the politicization in the GATT that all of us should seek to avoid."

[16] For a fuller discussion, see VanGrasstek (2013), pp. 164–166.

parties are expected to get at least as well as they give, but not so for accessions. These are one-way bargains in which the applicant "pays" for its membership, and for past liberalization, by making concessions that are not reciprocated by anything more than the ordinary benefits of membership. And while the demands made by the incumbent members are usually confined to commercial matters, nothing prevents those countries from raising more overtly political issues.[17] We have already seen that Israel did so with respect to Egypt in that country's two GATT-accession attempts. The United States began to do the same thing, and with greater effect, in the very last days of the GATT system.

The near-universal scope of WTO membership, and the surge in accessions, facilitated the stronger US demands for an end to the boycott. The number of Arab countries in the system rose from just three prior to the Uruguay Round to nine upon the WTO's entry into effect, and thirteen as of 2017. With the United States having agreed to lift its objections to the formation of working parties on the accessions of Libya (in 2004), Iran (in 2005), and Syria (in 2010), all remaining Middle Eastern countries are now at some stage of WTO accession. During the late 1980s, this was a process that the United States supported principally for its salutary effects on the acceding countries' domestic economic and political reforms. Beginning in the early 1990s, the US negotiators have been more explicit in linking these negotiations to the end of the boycott.

Saudi Arabia's decision to seek GATT accession in 1993 was an important milestone, and prompted US policymakers to step up their demands. US Trade Representative Mickey Kantor made the first public declaration of linkage between the boycott and accession in a 1994 congressional hearing, where he promised that "GATT accession will not be supported by the United States until the *secondary and tertiary* boycotts are ended."[18] Congress then codified the policy by writing it into the Uruguay Round Agreements Act of 1994. Section 133 states the "sense of the Congress" that the US Trade Representative (USTR) "should vigorously oppose the admission into the World Trade Organization of any country which, through its laws, regulations, official policies, or governmental practices, fosters, imposes, complies with, furthers, or supports any boycott." Such resolutions are generally taken to be nonbinding, but the USTR interpreted this provision to require its opposition

---

[17]   For further details on the special nature of WTO-accession negotiations, see VanGrasstek (2013), chapter 4.
[18]   U.S. Congress, House of Representatives, Committee on Foreign Affairs (1994), p. 37. Emphasis added.

to the accession of any country that participates in *any* aspect of the Arab League boycott. This point was further defined in a 1996 exchange of correspondence in which Kantor's successor, Ambassador Charlene Barshefsky, stated that the USTR had informed Saudi Arabia "that the issue would have to be resolved prior to approval of Saudi Arabia's WTO accession, or Saudi Arabia's admission would be opposed by the United States."[19]

The new policy coincided with a thaw in Arab–Israeli relations. Egypt had already disinvoked non-application when it reached a separate peace with Israel in 1979, and both Morocco and Tunisia allowed their own invocations to expire on the WTO's 1995 entry into effect. Jordan and Oman both acceded in 2000, and neither of them invoked non-application. Their accessions came six years after Jordan and Israel reached a peace and trade agreement, and four years after Oman exchanged trade missions with Israel. The successes were not universal. Saudi Arabia completed its accession in 2005, followed nine years later by Yemen, and yet each of them remains on the Treasury's list of countries that require cooperation with the Arab League boycott. How that might be reconciled with the assurances that USTR gave to Congress remains something of a mystery.[20]

POLITICAL ISSUES IN FTA NEGOTIATIONS

Trade relations can be more readily linked to political topics in bilateral FTAs, which are by definition more political than is membership in a multilateral body devoted to nondiscriminatory trade. As discussed in Chapter 4, political considerations have often outweighed purely commercial calculations in the selection of US FTA partners. That is nowhere more evident than in the Middle East, where disentangling power from wealth is a fool's errand.

The data in Table 15.1 suggest a fairly tight relationship between the trade treatment that the United States extends to Middle Eastern countries and

---

[19] Letter of Representative Robert Matsui to US Trade Representative Charlene Barshefsky (August 2, 1996), and letter of Ambassador Barshefsky to Representative Matsui (October 25, 1996).

[20] Saudi Arabia specified in its WTO-accession commitments that it would not impose the secondary or tertiary embargoes, but reserved the right to maintain the primary embargo. In 2005 the author posed a question about this to a USTR official engaged in the Saudi accession negotiations. That official said that the United States had received satisfactory assurances, leading the USTR to conclude that it had complied with congressional requirements. When the author pointed out that Saudi Arabia nonetheless remained on the Treasury list, that official responded by disavowing any knowledge of the existence of this legally mandated roster. It is impossible to say whether that admission of ignorance was genuine, or instead reflected an institutional choice on USTR's part.

TABLE 15.1. *Trade Relationship of Middle Eastern Countries with the United States*

	FTA Partners	GSP	Nonpreferential	Sanctions
Neither an OPEC Member nor an Arab League Boycott Participant	Bahrain[a,c] Israel Jordan Morocco Oman[a,c]	Djibouti[b] Egypt Mauritania[b] Somalia Tunisia	—	Sudan
Boycott (not OPEC)	—	Lebanon Yemen	—	Syria
OPEC (not Boycott)	—	—	Algeria	Iran[b]
Both OPEC and Boycott	—	Iraq	Kuwait[c] Qatar[c] Saudi Arabia[c] United Arab Emirates[c]	Libya

[a] These countries had participated in the Arab League boycott as of 2003, but later changed their policies.
[b] These countries are also designated for benefits under the African Growth and Opportunities Act.
[c] Member of the Gulf Cooperation Council.
[d] Iran is not a member of the Arab League and thus does not participate in its boycott, but neither does it trade with Israel.
Sources: GATT/WTO status from WTO. Boycott status from Department of the Treasury, "List of Countries Requiring Cooperation with an International Boycott" *Federal Register* Volume 83, Number 145 (January 8, 2018), p. 966.

their participation in two other regional initiatives. As a general rule, countries that are neither OPEC members nor participants in the Arab League boycott of Israel receive preferential access to the US market on either a comprehensive and reciprocal basis (i.e., the five FTA partners) or on a partial but one-way basis (i.e., six countries designated for the Generalized System of Preferences [GSP] or African Growth and Opportunities Act [AGOA] benefits). The only exception to this general rule is Sudan, which is subject to sanctions on other grounds. Conversely, most of the countries that participate in the boycott and/or OPEC are either limited to MFN treatment or made subject to sanctions. This rule is not quite as strong, there being three exceptions to it (i.e., Iraq, Lebanon, and Yemen). Even with these exceptions, the treatment extended to 17 of the 21 Arab countries exemplifies the inverse correlation between the positive discrimination that the United States offers and the two forms of negative discrimination that Washington seeks to combat.

Preferential Trade Arrangements as a Tool of Influence

The United States could not start playing the FTA game until Washington stopped thinking of trade agreements as strategic, global instruments and began considering their more tactical potential at the bilateral and regional levels. America had been the system's principal advocate of nondiscrimination and multilateralism for decades. Its original antagonist on this issue was Middle Eastern, as was the partner in the first major US departure from multilateralism.

Lebanon played a key role in the talks that produced the Havana Charter and the GATT, where the United States argued in favor of a strict MFN provision. Lebanon acted "as spokesman for the Arab League," according to a contemporary analyst, and "pressed throughout for regional preferences that would allow the Arab countries to co-ordinate their economic policies."[21] The Lebanese proposal was incorporated both in the failed Havana Charter and in GATT Article XXIV. Despite the US misgivings, these provisions allow countries to conclude FTAs and customs unions as long as they meet certain criteria that are neither precisely defined (e.g., the vague requirement that these agreements cover "substantially all of the trade" between the parties) nor strictly policed. By the time that the WTO came into being, regional agreements had gone from being exceptional to nearly ubiquitous.

The use of trade liberalization to promote regional peace dates back to the English hegemony. During the Second World War London proposed that a Middle East Economic Council be formed to deal with (among other things) "schemes for removing economic barriers between particular groups of countries in the region, including the establishment of customs and currency unions."[22] The council was never established, but that did not deter the Eisenhower administration from making a regional proposal of its own in 1953–1954. The United States was then prepared to offer substantial increases in economic assistance to Lebanon, Israel, Jordan, and Syria, provided that these countries agreed to the cooperative use of water in the Jordan River basin. All four of them expressed some support in principle for this proposed Jordan River Authority, but in actual

---

[21] Brown (1950), p. 72.
[22] Gomaa (1977), p. 120.

practice this body never progressed beyond a twinkle in the eyes of American diplomats.

US FTAs in the Middle East

Israel took the initiative in 1974 by proposing FTA negotiations with the United States, just when the US role in the region was starting to transition from attempted honest broker to explicit Israeli ally. American officials "expressed considerable doubt that kind of bilateral trade projects in Israeli paper would be feasible" because "bilateralism in trade had long been contrary to policy" and the "implications of undertaking bilateral arrangements with one country would be worldwide."[23] The United States still saw discriminatory proposals more in terms of their deleterious effect on the system than on whatever contribution they might make toward attaining regional goals. That changed over the next decade, and by 1984 it was the United States that promoted an FTA with Israel. The Jewish state was still a very small trading partner, and this initiative was more important for its political than for its commercial effects.

Although the US–Israel FTA began as a purely bilateral undertaking, Washington has periodically treated it as the potential nucleus of a broader arrangement. One manifestation of that aim is the 1995 Agreement on Reciprocal Duty Free Treatment to the West Bank and Gaza Strip, which extended the terms of the US–Israel FTA to the lands that could form the basis for a future Palestinian state. The FTA might thus form part of the famed "two-state solution" to the Israeli–Palestinian conflict, were that ever to come to fruition. The benefits of this FTA have also been extended to two of Israel's neighbors. Jordan first established trade relations with Israel in 1995, and three years later these two partners joined with the United States to establish Qualifying Industrial Zones (QIZs) in Jordan. The QIZs allow goods that meet certain rules of origin, including at least 8% Israeli content, to enter the United States duty- and quota-free. The agreement thus lets Jordan "piggyback" on the US-Israel FTA. Egypt concluded a similar arrangement in 2004, which was meant "to reward Egypt for its support for the Middle East Peace Process and to encourage Egyptian-Israeli trade ties."[24] The QIZs grew to cover large shares of trade. The US–Jordan FTA took effect in 2001, but it was

---

[23] "Simon Visit: Meeting with Minister of Commerce and Industry Bar-Lev," cable of July 14, 1974 from the US embassy in Tel Aviv (1974TELAV04055_b).

[24] "Scenesetter for U/S Hormats Meeting with Minister Rachid," cable of November 19, 2009 from the US embassy in Cairo (09CAIRO2172_a).

not until 2009 that Jordan shipped more to the United States under its own FTA than it did under the QIZ program. As for Egypt, the QIZs still accounted for just under half of all exports to the United States in 2017.

It was against this backdrop, as well as the outbreak of the Second Gulf War, that the Bush administration proposed an FTA with the entire Middle Eastern region in 2003. That proposal had a triple political intention. It was aimed simultaneously at proving that the United States could also use peaceful instruments in its dealings with Muslim countries; at promoting the positive political and social changes that are supposed to be the natural consequence of open markets; and at striking a commercial armistice between Israel and its neighbors. But would the Arab countries respond positively to this invitation?

There were some early signs that they might. At least eight countries in the region took preliminary steps toward accepting the US invitation, and the GCC gave its conditional blessing when in 2005 the group's secretary general confirmed that each member state had the right to sign an FTA. The GCC members include two countries that would eventually conclude FTAs with the United States (i.e., Bahrain and Oman), and three others that headed in that direction but never completed the journey (i.e., Kuwait, Qatar, and the United Arab Emirates). Egyptian and American officials were also actively discussing an FTA by 2005, and Cairo was still interested as late as 2012.[25] In the end, however, neither Egypt nor any of the other large countries in the region – most notably Saudi Arabia – signed on to the initiative. That failure may be attributed both to the political price that the United States demanded of its prospective partners, as well as the limited economic benefits that it could offer in exchange.

Linkage to the Arab League Boycott

While political issues figured more prominently than commercial interests in inspiring this Bush administration proposal, US officials were careful to remain diplomatically silent on the precise level of their ambitions. They never explicitly said whether their true objective was limited to removing the negative discrimination against Israel that had been in place since the founding of the Jewish state, or if they sought the more ambitious goal of replacing negative with positive discrimination by making Israel a full participant in the proposed arrangement. The one point on which US statesmen were clear was

---

[25] See for example "Progress with Customs and Trade Reform in Egypt," cable of November 29, 2005 from the US embassy in Cairo (05CAIRO8937_a), and "Report on meetings in Egypt," cable of August 30, 2012 from Robert Hormats (C05792113).

opposition to the boycott of Israel. When the president first made his proposal an official noted that FTA partners must meet WTO standards, and responded to a reporter that "for a country to be … compliant with its obligations in the WTO, it cannot engage in such government boycotts."[26] The overall impression was that US negotiators intended to make renunciation of the boycott a prerequisite for the conclusion of an FTA, but not necessarily for the initiation of negotiations. They also appeared reluctant to state this condition too bluntly in public.

This policy achieved a partial success. At the time that President Bush made his proposal there were eleven countries on the Treasury's list of those requiring cooperation with the boycott, but as of 2018 the number had been reduced to nine (see Table 15.1). Significantly, the two countries that renounced the boycott were among the three that reached FTAs. This objective was moot for Morocco, which did not require boycott compliance as of 2003.[27]

Bahrain was one of two success stories, even if it was already moving in that direction before the FTA negotiations. The USTR observed in 2003 that "Bahrain is officially committed to enforcing the primary aspect of the Arab League Boycott of Israel,"[28] but also that "enforcement is inconsistent," and that when "outdated tender documents require enforcement of the Arab League Boycott … such instances are usually quickly remedied upon request." The USTR could later report that "Bahrain abolished its boycott law and enforcement office in September 2005 while preparing to sign its Free Trade Agreement with the United States,"[29] and there was no doubt that these two developments were linked. The US embassy in Manama characterized the closure of the Israel boycott office "in connection with [FTA] ratification" as a congressional "requiremen[t] for U.S. ratification." It also acknowledged that the US demand "generated some blowback in Bahrain."[30]

Removing Bahrain and Oman from the list of boycotting countries was clearly a gain, but the magnitude should not be exaggerated. As can be seen from the data in Table 15.2, their combined population was just 5.9 million and their combined GDP was less than one-sixth that of Saudi Arabia. Even if these countries no longer participate formally in the boycott, there is no

---

[26] "Transcript of Background Press Conference Call to Discuss Proposed Mideast Free Trade Area Announced by President Bush" (May 9, 2003), p. 4.

[27] Libya is the only Maghreb country that requires compliance with the boycott, a distinction that it held both in 2003 and in 2017. None of the other four Maghreb countries (i.e., Algeria, Mauritania, Morocco, and Tunisia) do so.

[28] USTR (2003).

[29] Office of the U.S. Trade Representative (2016), p. 20.

[30] "Scenesetter for Commerce Secretary Gutierrez's February 26–28 Visit to Bahrain," cable of February 19, 2006 from the US embassy in Manama, Bahrain (06MANAMA238_a).

evidence to suggest that they actually trade with Israel.[31] Data posted by Israel's Central Bureau of Statistics indicate that Egypt and Jordan are the only Arab countries with which the country had significant trade in 2016, and even then it was quite low. Egypt accounted for 0.1% each of Israeli imports and exports, and Jordan for 0.1% of Israeli exports and 0.5% of imports. The data also show very low levels of trade with Algeria, Djibouti, Mauritania, Morocco, Somalia, and Tunisia.[32] Bahrain and Oman appeared nowhere in the Israeli trade data.

The Rising Level of Congressional Scrutiny

Congress took an active interest in the negotiation of these FTAs. Here we see two important aspects of congressional involvement in trade negotiations. One is the well-known game of "good cop, bad cop," in which American statesmen can point their foreign counterparts to Congress whenever they want to underline the political necessity of making some unpalatable concession. Bahraini officials clearly would have preferred not to make any commitments on the boycott, but the US negotiators found it quite useful to argue that Congress would never approve the FTA without this concession.

The FTA negotiations also demonstrate that the congressional bad cop really can be bad, from the perspective of the executive good cop, insofar as legislators may make some demands that go beyond what the US negotiators think is feasible or helpful. Democrats in Congress have become increasingly insistent that FTAs transcend purely commercial matters, setting higher standards on social issues such as labor rights and environmental protection. This has produced a contagion of conflict in domestic trade politics, as reviewed in Chapter 5, with partisan disagreements over these issues proving more intractable than were older disputes over free trade versus protectionism. There was a time when Democrats were willing to give a pass on these issues when it came to the Middle East, where they were initially more interested in an FTA's foreign policy benefits than in its social implications. Thus the US–Israel FTA won unanimous support in 1985, the US–Jordan FTA passed the House on a voice vote in 2001, and well over half the Democrats voted for the FTAs with Morocco (2004) and Bahrain (2005). By the time that the FTA with Oman came up for approval in 2006, however, Democrats insisted that the G. W. Bush administration address their demands on the social issues.

---

[31] Rumor has it that Israel may trade with a wider range of Arab states, but the unofficial character of this alleged trade provides further evidence of the political impediments to Arab–Israeli economic exchanges.

[32] Data at www.cbs.gov.il/fortr12/impexp/mesukam_e.html?SortBy=1.

TABLE 15.2. *Economic Characteristics of Middle Eastern Countries*

	Average Applied US Tariff (%)		Apparel (% of US Imports)		Petroleum (% of US Imports)		2016 Population (Millions)	2016 GDP ($Billions)
	2003	2017	2003	2017	2003	2017		
Existing FTAs as of 2003							**15.9**	**334.9**
Israel	0.1	0.1	3.1	0.3	0.1	0.0	8.4	299.4
Jordan	0.4	0.1	86.4	80.6	0.0	0.0	7.6	35.5
Unweighted average	0.3	0.1	44.8	40.5	0.1	0.0		
New FTA Negotiated after 2003							**40.3**	**201.5**
Bahrain	7.9	1.6	43.3	0.2	1.3	11.6	1.4	31.1
Morocco	3.7	2.1	19.2	10.7	4.5	0.0	34.4	100.6
Oman	3.7	0.1	21.7	7.7	47.8	20.4	4.5	69.8
Unweighted average	5.1	1.3	28.1	6.2	17.9	10.7		
Incomplete FTA Talks							**117.9**	**1,022.7**
Egypt[a]	6.7	0.3	33.8	45.0	12.9	6.6	91.5	330.8
Kuwait	0.5	0.1	1.6	<0.1	69.1	76.3	3.9	114.0
Qatar	4.8	0.4	25.8	<0.1	4.8	24.8	2.2	164.6
Tunisia[a]	6.5	3.0	34.4	14.1	16.7	17.2	11.1	43.0
UAE	4.4	0.3	23.1	0.2	19.3	15.5	9.2	370.3
Unweighted average	4.6	0.8	23.7	11.9	24.6	28.1		
No FTA							**129.3**	**1,053.0**
Algeria[a]	0.1	0.1	0.0	<0.1	53.1	93.6	39.7	166.8
Djibouti[b]	2.0	0.1	0.0	0.0	0.0	0.0	0.9	1.7

Iraq[a]	0.2	0.1	0.0	<0.1	76.3	82.0	36.4	180.1
Lebanon[a]	0.9	0.8	3.8	4.9	0.0	0.0	5.9	47.1
Mauritania[b]	1.6	<0.1	9.6	<0.1	0.0	89.3	4.1	5.4
Saudi Arabia	0.4	0.2	<0.1	<0.1	73.2	75.8	31.5	646.0
Somalia[a]	0.0	0.8	<0.1	0.0	0.0	0.0	10.8	5.9
Unweighted average	0.7	0.3	1.9	0.7	28.9	48.7		
						Total:	303.4	2,612.3

[a] GSP beneficiary.

[b] AGOA (and GSP) beneficiary.

Note: Table excludes Middle Eastern countries that were subject to sanctions as of late 2003 (i.e., Iran, Libya, Sudan, Syria, and Yemen) and hence presumably ineligible for the proposed FTA negotiations.

Source: Calculated from U.S. International Trade Commission DataWeb at https://dataweb.usitc.gov/, and World Bank population and GDP data at http://data.worldbank.org/indicator/SP.POP.TOTL and http://data.worldbank.org/indicator/NY.GDP.MKTP.CD.

Apparel is category 84 in the Standard International Trade Classification (SITC), and petroleum is SITC category 33.

Disappointed with the administration's response, they gave this agreement only slightly more support than they had to the Central American FTA in 2005 (see Chapter 4). In this one respect, the Middle East was no longer so special.

While the Bush administration managed to secure approval for the Oman FTA over the opposition of congressional Democrats, its concurrent negotiations with the United Arab Emirates were scuttled by a more serious problem. Members of both parties objected strongly when the UAE-based firm Dubai Ports World sought the management contract for several seaports in the United States. Memories of the 9/11 attacks were still fresh, and 2006 was also a congressional election year, thus bringing unusually great scrutiny to this controversial proposal. It was soon blocked by a bill in Congress. The Bush administration argued strenuously against the legislation, but without effect: The House approved the bill with nearly as much support from Republicans (87%) as from Democrats (96%). The vote was so galling to the emirates that they suspended the FTA negotiations. No other Arab country has entered into FTA talks with the United States since that time, although it is difficult to say how much of that reluctance may be attributed to the sour taste left by this one episode.

ECONOMIC ISSUES IN FTA NEGOTIATIONS

The region-wide FTA that President Bush proposed would have been quite large, had it come to be. As of 2003 there were fifteen Arab countries with which the United States (a) did not yet have an FTA and (b) were not then subject to sanctions. The vital statistics on these countries, plus Israel and Jordan, are reported in Table 15.2. Taken together, the fifteen countries that might have become new FTA partners had a population of 287.5 million persons – almost precisely equal to the population of the United States that year. The three countries that ultimately concluded FTAs with the United States were instead home to 40.3 million persons. That is not a negligible number, being somewhat larger than the population of California, but it represented just 14% of the total for these fifteen countries. These partners controlled an even smaller share (9%) of the fifteen countries' combined GDP. By any reasonable economic standard, the proposed Middle Eastern FTA must be counted as a failure. Why were Arab countries unenthusiastic?

The simple answer is that President Bush's invitation fell short in two respects. As reviewed above, it made heavy demands on the political side. We now conclude by examining the light economic benefits that were offered in return. And while it is difficult to quantify the weight that Arab countries placed on the economic benefits versus the political costs, we can certainly specify with some precision just how limited the potential commercial benefits were.

The Low Level of Pre-FTA Barriers to the US Market

This initiative exemplifies the paradox of preferences: The hegemon turns to preferential trade programs only after it has pursued multilateral liberalization on a nondiscriminatory basis, and the success that it achieved early in its hegemony will inevitably undercut its later ability to use preferences as leverage. The proposal for a regional FTA might have been more attractive when Arab–Israeli disputes first broke out in the mid-1940s, and US border barriers were still high. By the time that the United States got around to playing the FTA game, its MFN tariffs had been reduced to the point where exoneration from these import taxes could provide little inducement to most trading partners. The attraction of the offer nevertheless varied from one partner to another, depending on the composition of its exports and the corresponding tariff rates of the United States.

We can appreciate that point by looking to US imports in 2003 from three categories of prospective Arab FTA partners. As can be seen from the data in Table 15.3, average tariffs were nearly 5% for the three countries that carried this process to conclusion, and far lower for the seven countries that passed on the opportunity altogether; the five countries that engaged in incomplete FTA negotiations (to various stages) fell between these extremes. The reasons for these bottom-line differences are readily apparent from the sectoral break-downs: Oil predominates in the exports of the countries that opted against FTAs, while textiles and apparel figures much more prominently in the exports of the countries that took up this offer. Here again, the countries that almost negotiated FTAs fall in the middle. Both the oil and apparel sectors are special cases that are explored in greater depth in the text that follows, each of which required that trade policymakers consider the larger implications of concluding an FTA with the United States. At the highest stage of abstraction, however, the data clearly support what the paradox of preferences would lead us to expect: The lower the tariff wall that any country already faced in its access to the US market, the less attractive this FTA offer appeared.

That conclusion is reinforced by the country-specific data already shown in Table 15.2. Two generalizations can be made about all of the countries that took up the US offer, and about all but one of the countries that went partway down that path: (1) average applied tariffs were relatively high, and (2) apparel accounted for a major share of the country's exports to the United States. The reverse is true for all of the countries that turned down the offer. As for oil,

TABLE 15.3. *US Imports from Potential Arab FTA Partners, 2003*

	Share of Total US Imports from Subgroup			
	Concluded FTAs (3 Countries)	Incomplete FTA Talks (5 Countries)	Did Not Pursue FTA (7 Countries)	Average Applied MFN Tariff for Region (%)
Hydrocarbons and Chemicals	**28.8**	**53.1**	**96.6**	**0.3**
Mineral fuels	26.2	46.4	86.2	0.3
Inorganic chemicals	0.2	0.6	0.3	<0.1
Organic chemicals	2.4	6.1	10.1	1.0
Textiles and Apparel	**28.6**	**18.8**	**0.2**	**15.3**
Cotton yarns and fabrics	1.0	1.4	<0.1	5.7
Apparel and clothing, knitted	4.0	5.4	0.1	17.3
Apparel and clothing, not knitted	22.9	11.1	0.1	15.9
Other made-up textile articles	0.7	0.9	<0.1	7.9
Food and Agriculture	**10.4**	**0.3**	**0.2**	**2.6**
Fruits and nuts	2.2	<0.1	<0.1	0.8
Meat and fish preparations	1.6	0.1	0.0	2.5
Processed vegetables, fruits, etc.	1.5	0.1	<0.1	5.9
Beverages, spirits, and vinegar	0.0	0.1	0.2	2.4
Other	**32.2**	**27.8**	**3.0**	
Salt, sulfur, stone, cement, etc.	5.1	1.2	1.6	0.0
Jewels, jewelry, etc.	2.9	1.0	0.2	0.2
Aluminum and articles	2.7	1.8	<0.1	0.1

Electrical machinery, televisions, etc.	7.8	0.5	<0.1	0.2
All other	18.8	23.3	0.2	—
Total	**100.0**	**100.0**	**100.0**	—
Weighted average tariff on all imports	**4.9**	**3.3**	**0.3**	—

Based on total US imports in 2003 from three countries that concluded FTAs with the United States (i.e., Bahrain, Morocco, and Oman), five countries that took steps toward FTA negotiations but did not complete the process (i.e., Egypt, Kuwait, Qatar, Tunisia, and the United Arab Emirates), and seven other countries that were eligible for such negotiations but did not pursue them (i.e., Algeria, Djibouti, Iraq, Lebanon, Mauritania, Saudi Arabia, and Somalia).

Average Applied MFN Tariff for the Region = The average tariff applied by the United States in 2003 on imports from all fifteen countries. Preferential imports under the GSP and AGOA are excluded from this calculation.

Source: Calculated from U.S. International Trade Commission DataWeb data at https://dataweb.usitc.gov/.

it comprised a comparatively small share of the exports for two of the three eventual FTA partners, and for four of the five that held incomplete talks, but was the principal product for three of the countries that turned down the offer. The data offer only one anomaly, with Kuwait showing greater interest in an FTA than purely commercial considerations might suggest. This exceptional case can be quite easily explained by the special relationship that Kuwait acquired as a result of the First Gulf War, although that relationship was evidently not quite special enough to carry the talks all the way through to completion.

The attractiveness of the US proposal may also have been undercut by the existing preferential programs from which some of these countries benefited. In contrast to Latin America, where several countries were induced to negotiate FTAs so as to preserve their existing preferences (see Chapter 14), the Arab countries that already enjoyed preferential access seem to have taken those programs for granted. None of the three countries that took the United States up on the FTA offer were beneficiaries of those programs, but all eight of the countries that declined the invitation enjoyed duty-free access for some products under the GSP. Two of them were also eligible for the more generous preferences of the AGOA. They may well have decided that there was little benefit in exchanging their existing preferences for the deeper, more certain, but costlier access that an FTA provides. Mauritania was the one country for which this calculation may have been difficult, given its somewhat high level of apparel exports, but this country could more easily achieve duty-free access for those products by taking fuller advantage of its AGOA preferences. One of the principal differences between AGOA and the GSP is that the former program does cover apparel, provided that the country reaches an agreement with the United States to avoid diversion in this sector. And while Mauritania has never obtained that special designation, it would presumably find it much easier to reach that agreement than to negotiate an FTA.

The Special Case of Apparel

The data confirm a close correlation between countries' dependence on apparel exports and their receptiveness to the FTA offer, but that is not the whole story. Two other factors affected cost–benefit analyses of this opportunity. The costs of concluding an FTA with the United States include the stricter rules of origin that the United States traditionally demands in this sector, which generally condition duty-free imports of a partner's apparel on the incorporation of US fabric (see Chapter 14).

The benefits of the deal also had to be gauged against the imminent demise of the quota system that controlled US apparel imports from the early 1960s through 2005. Developing countries had made the elimination of those quotas one of their principal objectives in the Uruguay Round, and this became part of a grand bargain: The developed countries would phase out those quotas over ten years, and the developing countries would phase in greater protection for intellectual property rights at the same pace. By the time that President Bush proposed the US–Middle Eastern FTA in 2003, however, many developing countries were feeling buyer's remorse for both sides of that deal. They came too late to the realization that while the apparel quotas were costly and restrictive from a global perspective, the system also amounted to a market-sharing agreement that offered guaranteed access at inflated prices to many countries whose apparent competitiveness was artificial and transitory. The apparel quota phase-outs had been underway for eight years when President Bush made his FTA offer. By then it was painfully apparent to producers in the Middle East – and most of the developing world – that the lion's share of the new opportunities was being captured by such efficient, low-wage producers as China, India, and Pakistan.

The Arab countries thus knew that if it took two years to negotiate and approve an FTA with the United States, the agreements would be taking effect just when the last of the quotas were eliminated. They might then enjoy duty-free access to the US market, or at least see those duties phased out over time, but might also be encumbered with costly rules of origin. A rational trade policymaker would do well to ask whether it was logical to strike an agreement with permanent implications for the entire economy in order to acquire advantages for a single sector, especially when those advantages might prove to be ineffective or have a decidedly brief shelf-life. This is a point on which Bahrain decided to try its chances. That country's minister of industry and commerce stressed to US officials the importance that he attached to the textile sector, and while he recognized that Bahrain's "textile industry will not be able to compete with China or India ... with the FTA, it can be competitive if it upgrades its production."[33] Morocco and Oman similarly concluded that the benefits exceeded the costs. Did the actual results vindicate that judgment?

The data Figure 15.1 imply that the countries accepting this deal did better with FTAs than they would have done without them, but that the net effect was marginal. The agreements with Bahrain and Morocco entered into effect

[33] "Secretary Discusses FTA with Minister of Industry and Commerce Fakhro," cable of March 1, 2006 from the US embassy in Manama (06MANAMA305_a).

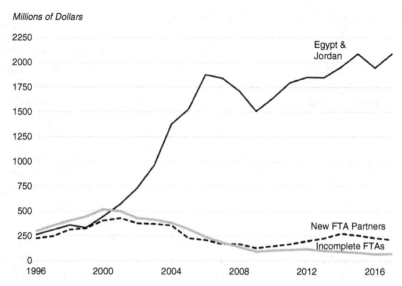

FIGURE 15.1 US imports of apparel from selected Middle Eastern FTA partners, 1996–2017.

Apparel is category 84 in the Standard International Trade Classification.

New FTA Partners = Bahrain, Morocco, and Oman.

Incomplete FTAs = Kuwait, Qatar, Tunisia, and the United Arab Emirates.

Source: Calculated from U.S. International Trade Commission DataWeb at https://dataweb.usitc.gov/.

in 2006, followed by Oman in 2009. The share of US apparel imports originating in those three countries rose modestly between 2009 and 2014, declining a bit thereafter, but they never returned to the levels that they had achieved when the MFA phase-out was still in its early stages. These three countries definitely did better than did the four other Middle Eastern countries that showed initial interest in negotiating FTAs, but never completed the process. The collective shipments to the US import market by these four hold-outs had been higher than those of the FTA partners when the MFA was still in force, but fell faster thereafter before plateauing in 2009–2017.

The most revealing comparison is not between these actual and would-be FTA partners, but between all seven of those countries and the two that receive even better treatment under the QIZ program. Imports grew dramatically after the United States extended this special status to Jordan in 2001 and then to Egypt in 2004, then remained fairly steady in the post-MFA period. Returning to the terminology employed in Chapter 14, we see here the difference between being a partner that is obliged to source its fabric in the United

States, and a client that can (within limits) source its fabric freely. Whereas all three sets of Middle Eastern apparel exporters had roughly similar shares of the US import market in the last decade of the twentieth century, the gap in their export performance is now quite wide. Readers will recall a similar pattern in US imports from its CAFTA-DR partners, with Nicaragua – the sole country in that group to receive truly preferential treatment under that agreement's rules of origin – being the only one whose apparel shipments have grown since the FTA entered into force (see Chapter 14). Both the Middle Eastern and the Central American cases underline a corollary to the paradox of preferences: Now that even apparel tariffs are a fraction of what they once were, preferential rules of origin matter more than does preferential tariff treatment.

The Special Case of Oil

The Bush administration's FTA proposal was not aimed at promoting further US imports of oil, gas, and derivatives from the Middle East, as that would have contradicted the larger American objective of reducing dependence on insecure sources of supply. As was already discussed in Chapter 14, FTAs have been one instrument in a decades-long efforts to promote energy production and trade in the Western Hemisphere. Rather than reversing that policy, and promoting more imports from the Arab countries, the larger US aim in its dealing with Arab oil exporters was to reduce the prospects for future restrictions on these countries' oil shipments to the world at large. That would ideally be accomplished both by lowering the tensions that might lead to a repeat of the politically motivated export restrictions of the 1970s, and also by making these countries' trade, investment, and regulatory policies more market-friendly. Neither of those objectives was very appealing to these prospective FTA partners, for whom even the weak disciplines of the WTO were a hard sell.

These points explain why the biggest oil-exporters did not take the United States up on the offer. While all the Arab countries that either began or concluded FTA negotiations with the United States exported at least some oil to the United States in 2003, only two of them – Kuwait and the United Arab Emirates – were OPEC members. Significantly, neither of these countries went all the way in their talks.

Had an OPEC country concluded an FTA with the United States, Washington might have had the opportunity to replicate with these countries the same deal that Canada and Mexico made in NAFTA. The duty-free access that the United States extends to North American oil is nearly insignificant, given the very low level of the MFN rates. These countries' pledge to forego any use of import and export embargoes in this sector was far more important. It is difficult to imagine such a deal being very attractive to an OPEC country. OPEC has not always been able to enforce discipline on its members, and is further undercut by rising oil production among non-members, but it has undoubtedly managed to inflate prices well above what a free market would yield.

Washington's second-best option has been to negotiate on these issues in WTO accessions. The trade-off there has been delicate, and the results limited. While it may be argued that OPEC's practices are fundamentally at odds with the WTO, certainly in spirit and quite probably in law, the United States and the European Union have calculated that it is better to have these countries inside the system and subject to a weak interpretation of its rules than to remain outside the system and subject to no disciplines at all. That has meant turning a blind eye to those aspects of OPEC that most blatantly violate such WTO rules as the general prohibition of quantitative restrictions. The United States and other developed countries acquiesce in the rather creative argument that a country may comply with its WTO obligations if it merely restricts the *extraction* of oil, provided that it does not restrict the *exportation* of that product after it has been siphoned from the ground. The US and EU negotiators nevertheless sought marginal concessions in the WTO-accession negotiations. In the case of Saudi Arabia, for example, this Byzantine distinction inspired the negotiation of somewhat hazy rules that are intended to limit the extent to which it may engage in the "two-tier pricing" of its hydrocarbons (i.e., provide these raw materials to domestic refiners at a lower cost than their foreign rivals pay). It is entirely possible that Riyadh would have been obliged to make firmer and more substantial commitments affecting its oil, were it to negotiate an FTA with the United States, but that is just one of several reasons why the FTA proposal was a nonstarter.

THE LIMITED SCOPE FOR FTAS IN THE MIDDLE EAST

The foregoing events show why discrimination remains a major element of trade in the Middle East, but also why one specific form of discrimination – FTAs with the United States – provides only a small part of the larger picture. The proposed agreement's benefits exceeded the perceived costs for a few countries, but they form a decided minority. This is in large part a consequence of the paradox of preferences. When coupled with the demand that a partner country not boycott trade with Israel, and that the oil exporters renounce the weaponization of their commodity, the proposed regional FTA would amount to a peace treaty that ended generations of economic warfare.

The only scenarios in which these countries would be willing to make such a bargain would have to be based on political rather than economic calculations. It is possible to conceive of a regional peace settlement that is complemented by the negotiation of a trade arrangement, but it is highly doubtful that the chain of causation would move in the reverse order. The perceived economic benefits of open access to the US market are just too small to induce radical shifts in these countries' foreign policies.

PART VI

TRADE, TRUMP, AND THE FUTURE

16

Power and Wealth in the Trump Administration and Beyond

To expect ... that the freedom of trade should ever be entirely restored in Great Britain, is as absurd as to expect that an Oceana or Utopia should ever be established in it. Not only the prejudices of the publick, but what is much more unconquerable, the private interests of many individuals, irresistibly oppose it.

Adam Smith, *An Inquiry into the Nature and Causes of the Wealth of Nations* (1776)

By means of the protective system governments stimulate the growth of industries dependent on this legislation for their existence, and these industries form the fighting legions behind that policy.

E. E. Schattschneider, *Politics, Pressures, and the Tariff* (1935)

INTRODUCTION

Adam Smith may have been both pleased and chagrined if he knew how poorly he forecast the future of British trade policy. The American political scientist E. E. Schattschneider did no better when he predicted that the protectionist US system would last forever, arguing that the "very tendencies that have made the legislation bad have ... made it politically invincible."[1] These pessimists differed only in the amount of time it took for each of them to be contradicted. Smith has the better excuse, going to his reward long before London adopted the policies that he proposed. Schattschneider could not make the same plea, as Washington took the first major step toward leadership the year before his book saw print.

We may derive two lessons from these experiences. The first is that social scientists of all stripes would be well-advised to couch any prognostications in cautious language. The second is that we should all consider how changes in a country's status might alter its perspectives and goals. What neither Smith

---

[1] Schattschneider (1935), p. 288.

nor Schattschneider understood was that they each described a country on the verge of hegemony. That status fundamentally transformed the objects and options for Anglo-American statesmen, and the two countries' responses profoundly revised the systems in which these two dons found so much fault.

Even scholars who focus on the causes and effects of hegemony may misjudge the system's direction. They first recognized the importance of American leadership just when doubts emerged regarding its trajectory in the 1970s, and the reservations surrounding the future of US power and wealth only grew in the 1980s. The end-game and the aftermath of the Cold War inspired a sprawling literature devoted to the question of whether that victory would give Washington its second wind. Some political scientists believed that the United States would advance from strength to strength. Economists and historians, as well as a few political scientists who supped at the same table, were more prone to consider decline an inevitable consequence of external challenges or internal decay.[2] They all proved to be right, each in their own time. The optimists could feel vindicated in the 1990s, when the US economy experienced the longest expansion in modern history. This was also a peaceful interval that was punctuated by only a few disturbances of manageable proportions. The United States was in a stronger position at the end of that decade than it was at the start, but that was not to last. The words "peace" and "prosperity" would not figure prominently in any objective description of this new millennium's opening decades, which have instead been marked by unusually sharp shocks to both spheres. Those jolts coincide with a relative decline in the power and wealth of the United States, as well as Washington's diminished willingness to provide leadership.

Heilbroner was onto something when he observed that "the foresight of even the greatest economists has been bounded because they were unable to see around the corners of history and espy changes in the institutional or technical framework" of economic activity.[3] The same goes for political scientists, historians, and other analysts, not to mention business persons, diplomats, elected officials, and voters. In place of courting hubris by attempting to forecast the future, this concluding chapter instead has two modest objectives. First, it picks up from earlier chapters by placing our current predicament in context, summarizing how thoroughly the Trump administration has undone what appeared to be settled. The second step is to consider where the world might be headed once this latest experiment in policymaking

---

[2] For examples of these various strands of scholarship, see Gilpin (1987), Nau (1990), Nye (1990), Olson (1982), and Rosencrance (1990).

[3] Heilbroner (1986), p. 317.

is only a memory. The aim is not to make predictions or prescriptions, but to highlight the most pertinent questions that the United States and the world face with respect to wealth, power, and the trading system.

US TRADE POLICY IN THE TRUMP ADMINISTRATION

Much of this book has highlighted the many ways that Donald Trump flouts seemingly well-established conventions of domestic and international governance. In assessing what his presidency may mean for the future of the trading system, we need to avoid the common pitfall of focusing solely on the quirks of one individual. Beyond running afoul of the general norm against ad hominem attacks, even if the target does not feel constrained by that rule of civility, that would mean missing the larger picture. Trumpism may well outlast Trump, and the pervasive challenges that gave rise to it will remain no matter what fate has in mind for the man. The political wave that he rode into office was a natural (though not inevitable) consequence of the economic transition, including both the Law of Uneven Growth and the process of Creative Destruction, and transcends the tenure of any one administration.

Much of what the Trump administration proposes is a throwback to older positions of the United States. These include the reawakening of some dormant statutes that had been active up until the advent of the WTO, and the revival of other policies that the United States outgrew long ago. The most important of these anachronisms is based on beliefs that predate American independence, and that have periodically resurfaced ever since.

The Shirking of Hegemony and the Reversion to Mercantilism

Policymaking in the Trump administration might appear at first blush to represent an extreme example of American pragmatism, given the multiplicity of perspectives among top advisors and the sometimes wild swings from one position to another, but its approach to trade policy is somewhat more consistent. It takes negative form in the abdication of hegemonic responsibilities (which these critics prefer to call "globalism"), and is more affirmatively expressed as a plan to "make American great again." Those four revealing words quite economically highlight the nationalism and nostalgia at the core of this administration's policies. The same ideas can most efficiently be reduced to a single word.

Mercantilism is the defining principle of this administration's approach to foreign policy, conflating economic and security objectives in precisely the same way the classical mercantilists did. As discussed in Chapter 2, mercantilism starts from the major premise that all political and economic relations are hierarchical dealings, and the minor premise that power and wealth are interchangeable and zero-sum. Mercantilists see trade as an essential component in power relations between states, believe that any country's gain is necessarily another's loss, and argue that the state should intervene to promote a positive trade balance. According to that logic, only a chump would follow the policies that Washington did in hegemony. In place of considering the United States the leading member in a community of like-minded states, and working with its partners to achieve mutual gains, the Trump administration instead defines commercial aims in terms that are at once narrowly nationalist yet broadly aggrandizing.

Here it is quite appropriate to focus on the man himself. Trump exemplifies the point that real-world economic practitioners typically have a greater affinity for zero-sum thinking than for the positive-sum inclinations of economic theory. It is no mere coincidence that the only two businessmen to make credible runs for the presidency in all of American history[4] – H. Ross Perot in 1992 and Donald Trump in 2016 – were also the most protectionist candidates since Herbert Hoover left office in 1933. Men who have lived in the rough-and-tumble world of economic competition may be naturally inclined to see these relations in transactional terms, and to count each exchange as either a win or a loss. It should not surprise us when they take a similar approach to the goals of foreign policy (economic and otherwise).

This turnabout in America's international position is complemented by a topsy-turvy approach to the domestic diplomacy of trade. One perennial feature of US trade relations is the uncertainty that foreigners feel in interpreting the mixed messages that they receive from a diverse and cacophonous set of officeholders. This is all quite deliberate, both by constitutional design and for reasons of strategy. Leaders in the executive and legislative branches know that they can jointly squeeze more concessions from their foreign counterparts if they play an effective game of "good cop, bad cop," and that game may be all the more successful if even the good cop is not always sure when the bad cop is merely play-

---

[4] In all the presidential elections from 1788 through 2016, Perot and Trump were the only two serious contenders who never held any other elective office, a cabinet position, or major military appointment. There have been others who spent more time in business than in politics, such as the Republican nominees in 1928 (Herbert Hoover) and 2012 (Mitt Romney), but they were not entirely new to government. The closest historical analogy is publisher Horace Greeley, the Democrat who lost to Ulysses Grant in 1872, yet even he had served one term in Congress. In keeping with the general pattern, however, Greeley was also a protectionist (putting him at odds with most Democrats in his day).

acting. What is new about the Trump administration is that the roles have been reversed, such that it is now Congress that feels compelled to be the voice of reason. Or to use a slightly different image, Donald Trump has never made any secret of his belief in the "madman theory" of negotiations. According to this notion, playing the madman can work to one's advantage by keeping adversaries guessing and encouraging them to settle quickly. It does not make for a well-ordered policymaking system.

The surprise comes in the low value that this businessman-president attaches to goodwill, defined as the "primary intangible asset of a company, generally comprised of reputation, contact networks, intellectual property, and branding."[5] Just as the firm's goodwill is indispensable to maintaining the loyalty of its customers and the confidence of its creditors and partners, so too do experienced statesmen prize their country's reputation for bargaining in good faith and keeping its commitments. Trump instead taps into that part of the national character that is untroubled by the suggestion that it is acting in contravention of international law, and that sees multilateral organizations as cabals in which unscrupulous foreigners conspire to cheat Americans. Viewing with suspicion any configuration in which there are two or more other countries present, the Trump administration strongly prefers to conduct all diplomacy on a bilateral basis.

Even while Trump is not the first politician to reiterate some variation on Will Rogers' outdated observation that the United States has never lost a war or won a negotiation, none of his predecessors placed so little stress on the principle of *pacta sunt servanda* ("agreements must be kept"). The Trump administration instead seems to treat any commitments made by prior presidents as corrupt bargains or one-sided deals that it is free to violate, abrogate, or renegotiate. Or to put his practices in terms discussed in Chapter 4, Trump feels free not only to engage in cafeteria diplomacy, but to do so retroactively. Of all the areas where he leaves his mark, this may have the most lasting impact on the US position in the world. A future president could reverse almost any specific action that the current chief executive might take, but that would merely reinforce the message that whatever the United States promises (or threatens) today may hold only until the next change of government. A bell cannot be unrung.

---

[5]   https://thelawdictionary.org/goodwill/.

Trump's Policies toward Allies and Adversaries

The Trump administration's transatlantic dealings are deeply affected by its high contempt for the European Union, sometimes considered the ultimate expression of antinationalist globalism. This sense of scorn, coupled with a disinclination to recognize Russian aims for what they are, casts doubt on principles that thirteen prior administrations held as sacrosanct. They all agreed that America and its partners share an interest in democracy, open markets, and collective security, and should stand up with the allies to confront any countries that challenge these values. The questions that Trump raises over burden-sharing in the alliance extend well beyond his own frequent complaints regarding the relative levels of US and EU defense spending – a point on which he is not factually incorrect[6] – or equally narrow questions such as which specific goods might be subject to strategic export controls, or whether US sanctions on Iran will also apply to European firms. With memories of past conflicts growing ever hazier, and the relationship between Moscow and Washington in a dangerous state of flux, the underpinnings of the transatlantic relationship seem to be at stake. Trump puts at risk not just the WTO but NATO as well and the very concept of collective security. That same disregard for traditional friends carries over to other allies such as Japan, Korea, Canada (also a NATO member), and especially to Mexico.

If the Trump administration's approach toward allies and neighbors is surprising, its policies toward Russia are downright baffling. Some specific aspects of that relationship raise questions that are beyond troubling. Even if the current investigations produce evidence to support the less damning theories of what happened in 2016, and exonerate Trump from the deepest suspicions regarding his motivations and actions, there remains the disturbing question of why this president seems to view autocrats not just with tolerance but with admiration and envy.

This puzzling attitude toward other countries' internal politics is another relapse into the past. Nearly every president from Washington through Taft took an essentially agnostic view of both the means by which another government came to power and its record on democracy and human rights. Provided that the other country was not openly hostile to the United States, and respected the rights of American citizens, presidents did not pass judgment on that government's legitimacy. Theodore Roosevelt hinted at the coming change when in 1904 he attached his own corollary to the Monroe Doctrine,

---

[6] According to World Bank data at https://data.worldbank.org/indicator/MS.MIL.XPND.GD .ZS, in 2016 military expenditures were equal to 3.3% of GDP in the United States and 1.5% in the European Union.

rather baldly asserting the right to teach the neighbors that they ought to elect good leaders, and Woodrow Wilson gave this new position a global scope. In the century that followed the end of the First World War, presidents were prepared to use a variety of instruments to encourage other countries to change not just their policies but their leaders, or even their forms of government. The forms that encouragement took ranged from words and money to subversion and troops, with trade policy being an important part of the toolkit. Whether in the "nice" form of preferences or the more aggressive form of sanctions, every president from FDR through Obama leveraged access to the US market in the pursuit of political aims. The renewed American indifference under Trump might be spun positively as a remedy for past excesses and an expression of humility, but that is a virtue not normally associated with this administration. It instead appears to be of a piece with the current team's disregard for the values that previous presidents espoused, even if they did not always embody those same tenets or pursue them consistently.

The most important relationship is with China, and here the Trump administration is obliged to deal with the coincidence of its most pressing challenges in trade and security. China is the main contributor to the US trade deficit, and is close to overtaking the United States in sheer economic size. Arresting that process, and ensuring the continued primacy of the United States, would appear to be the principal economic objective of this administration. The pursuit of that goal is vastly complicated by China's prominent role in other foreign policy challenges. The most immediate of these is North Korea, where finding a peaceful solution to the problem of nuclear weapons on the peninsula requires collaboration between Washington and Beijing. The Trump administration has tried to pursue that objective even while it confronts China on trade, but it may be increasingly difficult to isolate one set of issues from the other. That may prove more challenging if the two countries take up other security issues for which their positions are even further apart, such as the status of Taiwan and territorial claims in the South China Sea.

One peculiarity of the US relationship with China is the virtual nullification of two important tools of foreign economic policy. Trade preferences for China are off the table; we will return shortly to the question of how preferences for third countries affect relations with Beijing. Third-country relations are also important when it comes to sanctions, given the Chinese capacity to reinforce or undermine any campaign that the United States might propose for other countries, but the time passed long ago when Washington could credibly threaten to impose and indefinitely sustain economy-wide sanctions on Beijing. Even when the Trump administration imposed sanctions on China in 2018, it was initially at pains to target these at products and sectors that were least likely to provoke opposition from consumers or industrial users. As discussed in Chapters 10 and 12, the economic ties between these two countries were already too tight in the early 1990s for the United States to make good on its threats to withdraw MFN treatment, and the inexorable logic of the paradox of sanctions has further circumscribed the American options since then. China's stunning economic growth, and the rising levels of US GDP that are tied up in that relationship, put one in mind of some memorable dialogue from the film *Giant* (1956). After an upstart Texan struck oil, one of the local grandees chided the man's cattle baron antagonist. "Bick," he advised, "you shoulda shot that fella a long time ago. Now he's too rich to kill."[7]

The Revival of Dormant Trade Laws

The United States may no longer be in a position to deploy full-scale sanctions against China in political disputes, but the Trump administration has been eager to show its willingness to use narrower restrictions in its pursuit of commercial aims. Here it salvaged a statutory wreck: From Jefferson to Clinton, American presidents periodically employed the reciprocity laws to threaten retaliation against countries that violate US trade rights. The chief reciprocity law (Section 301 of the Trade Act of 1974) sank into obscurity after the Uruguay Round, but the president ordered it up from the deep when in 2017 he directed the US Trade Representative (USTR) to investigate Chinese intellectual property practices. That investigation led in 2018 to the imposition of retaliatory tariffs on a wide range of Chinese products. Predictably, this was quickly followed by Chinese counter-retaliation against US exports. While the conflict remains a live issue at press time, early results suggest that Beijing is just as capable as Washington of engaging in trade warfare and sustaining its economic costs. The most consequential outcome of the dispute may not be which side is ultimately deemed the winner or the loser, or how much short-term damage they do to one another and to third parties in the interim, but the extent to which they each succumb to the temptation to reach a settlement that amounts to managed trade. That would not portend well for the trading system.

The restoration of Section 301 is one of several steps that not only entail a resurgence of unilateralism, but also imply the possibility that US membership in the WTO may be at risk. In addition to the Chinese intellectual property case, in which the administration brought a formal complaint to the WTO's Dispute Settlement Body (DSB) only after

---

[7] www.tcm.com/tcmdb/title/76242/Giant/quotes.html.

announcing its own conclusions and plans to retaliate, it resurrected two other trade laws that had fallen into disuse and are legally problematic in the WTO. One is the global safeguards statute (Section 201 of the Trade Act of 1974), and the other, more dangerous provision is the national security law (Section 232 of the Trade Expansion Act of 1962).

The safeguards law had seemed to be undone by an unbroken series of DSB cases in which the countries that impose restrictions have invariably been found to violate their obligations under the WTO Agreement on Safeguards. Ever since the Bush administration was required in 2003 to reverse the steel restrictions that it had imposed in 2002, Washington treated Section 201 as a dead letter. That all changed when producers of washing machines and solar panels filed safeguard petitions in 2017, leading the Trump administration to impose import restrictions in 2018. We may reliably anticipate that these safeguard actions will be found to violate WTO obligations, which will then set up a potentially hazardous confrontation. Past administrations have felt legally obliged to lift the restrictions they imposed under the safeguards law, but Trump seems far less intent on trimming his policies to meet the terms of international agreements and the rulings of dispute-settlement panels. His administration may put up greater resistance in a safeguards case than (for example) an antidumping matter, considering the president's personal involvement in the decision. That defensiveness may only be multiplied by the credit that Trump has claimed for protecting these two industries.

It is by that same logic that the Section 232 cases may be even more dangerous to the trading system than the safeguard measures, insofar as they began and ended in presidential decisions. At issue here are a pair of cases that President Trump initiated in 2017, when he directed the secretary of commerce to investigate the threat that steel and aluminum imports allegedly pose to national security. The inquiry was to focus on such factors as "the domestic production . . . needed for projected national defense requirements" and "the existing and anticipated availabilities of the human resources, products, raw materials, and other supplies and services essential to the national defense."[8] There is no indication that these same issues raised any alarm in the Pentagon. To the contrary, the Department of Defense filed a formal comment expressing concerns about "the negative impact on our key allies" that would result from unilateral protectionism.[9] That did not prevent the Department of

---

[8] See www.whitehouse.gov/the-press-office/2017/04/20/presidential-memorandum-secretary-commerce.

[9] Department of Defense, "Response to Steel and Aluminum Policy Recommendations," posted at www.commerce.gov/sites/commerce.gov/files/department_of_defense_memo_response_to_steel_and_aluminum_policy_recommendations.pdf.

Commerce from second-guessing the military, and finding in 2018 that these imports do impair the national security. The president then followed the department's recommendation that he impose tariffs. Shortly thereafter the Trump administration doubled down on this strategy when, in defiance not just of law but common sense, it initiated a new Section 232 case against the automotive sector. That represented a huge escalation, with imports of auto-mobiles and parts being more than six times greater than steel and aluminum imports.

The National Security Cases and a Potential WTO Withdrawal

These national security cases pose a far graver danger to the trading system than the administration's revival of the safeguard and reciprocity laws. Beyond the direct presidential imprimatur that these Section 232 cases bear, and the presumably greater implied resistance to an unfavorable ruling, the products involved are inherently important. Steel, aluminum, and the automotive sector collectively accounted for 16% of US imports in 2017. The share of imports and domestic production that may be affected is greater still when one counts the many items that incorporate these metals. And despite the Trump administration's frequently declared intention of taking on China, that coun-try accounted for just 5% of US imports in the three affected sectors. The great majority came instead from Japan (15%), the European Union (17%), Canada (19%), and especially Mexico (28%).

What makes these natural security cases especially hazardous, from a regime perspective, is the unique legal and political character of the US statute and its WTO counterpart. Unlike the actions taken under other trade laws, which are all explicitly commercial instruments that are undeni-ably within the WTO's jurisdiction, claims of national security occupy a realm where the multilateral system has thus far feared to tread. As discussed in Chapter 7, the United States and other countries have heretofore operated on the basis of an implicit bargain by which all countries pledged to be sparing in their invocation of the national security clause (GATT Article XXI), repairing to it only in cases of true necessity; in return, the rest of the membership would refrain from challenging any action based on this extraordinary provision. By deliberately flouting the first half of this deal, the Trump administration seems to be daring its adversaries to challenge it on the second half.

We may only speculate on the depth of the administration's motives or the extent to which it thought through the likely consequences of its actions. Its decision to pursue the metals cases under Section 232, and the implied readiness to invoke Article XXI, may have been only a cynical attempt to game the multilateral trading system by taking advantage of the twin loopholes in domestic law (Section 232 being the most discretionary of the trade-remedy laws) and the WTO (Article XXI being the most discretionary of the exceptions clauses). It may alternatively have been intended as a deliberate incitement. Whether or not this is what the White House wanted, the decision to bypass the ordinary trade laws forced the rest of the WTO membership into choosing among four undesirable outcomes.

- The administration's original aim may have been to pressure other steel- and aluminum-producing countries into negotiating market-sharing arrangements. Similarly, the aim of the automotive 232 case may be to revive the voluntary export restraints (VERs) solution of the 1980s. These would be great retrogressions, bringing back the "gray area" measures that were the source of such anxiety prior to the Uruguay Round. The difference is that the area is gray no more, with WTO rules now quite explicitly prohibiting "voluntary export restraints, orderly market-ing arrangements or any other similar measures on the export or the import side."[10]
- The United States might hope to get away with unilateral restrictions simply by invoking GATT Article XXI, slapping this rule down like a trump card. One obvious danger is that this would invite other coun-tries to follow suit, imposing new restrictions on any other goods or services for which they might claim a connection to national security; these could range from food and high-technology items to communica-tions and transportation services.
- In the alternative, a DSB panel and/or the Appellate Body could toss aside the tradition of deference and decide that it had the authority to pass judgment on a prima facie abuse of GATT Article XXI. Trump might well opt to feign indignation at the provocation he induced, and treat it as an excuse to withdraw from a body that had disrespected not just the economic interests but the national security of the United States.
- WTO members might forego the usual process and impose retaliatory restrictions without first seeking leave via a DSB ruling.

Perhaps with an eye to the dangers inherent in each of the first three options, major WTO countries proved quite ready to move on that fourth option and challenge the assertion in Trump's notorious tweet, "Trade wars are good, and easy to win."[11] They carried out their counter-retaliatory threats in mid-2018,

---

[10] Article 11.1(b) of the WTO Agreement Safeguards.
[11] www.cnbc.com/2018/03/02/trump-trade-wars-are-good-and-easy-to-win.html.

plunging the United States into a full-fledged conflict not just with China, but also Canada, the European Union, and others. Some of these partners advanced the creative argument that the US action was a safeguard, even though Washington made no such claim, and hence one for which the relevant agreement permitted a retaliatory response. Canada made no such pretense, implying that its action was based not so much on WTO law as on the *lex talionis* (i.e., an eye for an eye). Smaller countries such as Argentina and Indonesia preferred to bargain for exemptions by agreeing to impose WTO-illegal export restrictions. The more disheartening sign, from a regime perspective, was the willingness of the Chinese to contemplate that same route and to seek a settlement based more on managed than free trade.

The fact that the United States was willing to accept any of these options, singly or in some combination, fairly begged an uncomfortable question: Should countries remain nominally in the organization while they dishonor its rules and norms, or would it be more honest to abandon the WTO project altogether and go back to a self-help system? The question is not merely rhetorical. Whether the crisis is brought on by the Section 232 cases, or through some other avenue, there is a better-than-even chance that sometime in the Trump tenure the United States will explicitly threaten to leave the WTO. Whether or not it actually follows through would be a tactical matter affected by any number of unforeseeable factors, but no one should doubt the willingness of the Trump administration to make good on such a threat. Skeptics need look no farther than the president's disavowal of the TPP, followed in 2017–2018 by withdrawals from other agreements (notably the Paris Agreement on climate change and the Iran nuclear deal) and institutions (especially the Human Rights Council and the United Nations Educational, Scientific, and Cultural Organization). All of these moves signaled that this administration is prepared – perhaps even eager – to pull out of groups that it considers inimical to American interests.

The Renegotiation of Existing Trade Agreements

As an alternative to withdrawal from an agreement or an institution, the United States may instead renegotiate its terms. It took first aim at NAFTA, and spent the better part of 2017 and 2018 negotiating with its Canadian and Mexican partners; it repeatedly threatened unilateral abrogation. As intrinsically important as North America trade is, both to the partners and to the world, the extrinsic implications of the renegotiation are even wider. There is a well-established practice by which the precedents set in US talks in the immediate neighborhood spread to the rest of the system. That can be seen not just in the original NAFTA agreement (Chapter 5), but also in such innovations as the safeguard provisions in the 1942 agreement between the United States and Mexico (Chapter 3).

The NAFTA renegotiation dragged on well past the administration's first year in office, and got caught up in the trade war that it declared in 2018. The tariffs that the Trump administration imposed on steel and aluminum in mid-2018, together with the threat of similar measures in the automotive sector, fell more heavily on Canada and Mexico than on any other partners. That may well have been the point, with the White House hoping to coerce the neighbors into accepting the new NAFTA terms that it proposed. The imposition of tariffs on selected sectors was a somewhat more targeted variation on the administration's oft-repeated threat to abrogate the agreement altogether. Both Canada and Mexico responded with retaliatory tariffs on steel, aluminum, and an array of other products.

The Trump administration viewed NAFTA renegotiation from an entirely different perspective than either its neighbors or its predecessors. Its approach represented a fundamental change in the purpose of trade agreements, with the aim having shifted from the creation of opportunities to the management of outcomes. Instead of setting the terms by which countries will reduce barriers to trade and investment, then allow the market to sort it all out, the administration explicitly adopted the mercantilist goal of seeking to run up a trade surplus. The Trump administration hoped to achieve that end through such means as the manipulation of the agreement's automotive rules of origin. It also obliged its partners to forswear the negotiation of FTAs with China (see Chapter 9).

Beyond the revision of existing FTAs, the Trump administration also aims to reach new, bilateral agreements that conform more closely to its illiberal pre-dilections. The first clean sheets of paper with which it will start are agreements with the European Union, Japan, and the United Kingdom, the plans for which were announced in late 2018. The model that emerges from those talks might form a new template that can then be applied to deals with other partners, perhaps forming the kernel of a new – and possibly post-WTO – system of agreements.

TRADE AFTER TRUMP

While we cannot know when or under what circumstances it will come to pass, the day will arrive when the world may join Othello in bidding, "Farewell the neighing Steed, and the shrill Trump."[12] No matter when or

---

[12] Othello, *Othello* Act III, scene III.

how it happens, it would be a mistake to assume that the departure of one man means the disappearance of an endemic problem. The economic challenges that contributed to his electoral victory will still be with us, and policymakers in the United States and the wider world will still need to deal with those underlying issues.

Managing the Decline of Hegemony

Just as it is difficult to assign a precise date to the start of American hegemony, so too are there problems in deciding when it ended – or even if we have already reached that juncture. That determination is best left to future historians. We should not be surprised, however, if they mark January 20, 2017 as a turning point. That was the first time since 1909 that an inaugural address lauded protectionism as a legitimate object of public policy. We may only guess whether the next person to take the oath of office will carry on with that same set of priorities, or will instead call for a return to policies favored by every president from FDR through Obama. It is equally unclear whether that restoration might be complemented by an explicit bid to renew American leadership, or how the rest of the community might respond. That may depend on how far Trump will have gone in his threatened disruptions to the established order.

Even if we start from the proposition that the United States is already a post-hegemonic power, it does not follow that American influence has come to an end. Here it is useful once more to consider the differences between the UK and US hegemonies, and the significance of their distinct geographic and demographic endowments. British hegemony was one of several historical anomalies, comparable to the fortunes of Venice and the Netherlands, in which a determined and efficient naval state acquired greater influence than its size might suggest was possible. That power departed as quickly as it arrived. Even if it took two world wars to topple London, in the greater scheme of history the span from 1913 to 1945 was just a blink of Clio's eye. By contrast, the United States accounts for much larger shares of global population, territory, and resources than the United Kingdom ever did, and is not nearly as susceptible to so rapid a reversal of fortune. Provided that none of the coming conflicts pass the nuclear threshold, it would require great imagination to see the United States occupying a position comparable to that of modern Britain any time soon – no matter how rapidly its principal rival might grow, and notwithstanding any second- or even third-place rankings it might achieve on some metrics of power and wealth.

While Washington may be better able to handle relative decline than was London, there are two reasons why the diminution of US power may have larger consequences for the trading system. The first is that the openness of the system today may owe more to rules and leadership than to technology and economic efficiency. O'Rourke and Williamson attributed the expansion of trade during the Pax Britannica more to economic advances than to British political leadership.[13] That is to be distinguished from the latter half of the twentieth century, when (they argue) most of the integration could be traced to negotiated liberalization rather than to technology. Innovations such as jet aircraft, containerization, and the Internet are important, by this view, but not nearly as much as the application of US power in trade negotiations. If this assessment is correct, it implies that declining hegemony will be more consequential now than it was the last time.

Managing the Sino-American Rivalry

The second reason why Washington's decline may be more disruptive than London's stems from serious questions concerning the next country in line. Even if China were willing to exercise leadership, and to give as much weight to the community as it does to itself, the hand-off might not be smooth. It is highly unlikely that relations between China and the United States could achieve anything approaching the level of Anglo-American comity in the 1940s, meaning that the world may be in for some exceptionally chaotic times in the years to come. Even if China and the United States do not engage in direct conflicts while passing one another on the escalator of history, it is not certain that Chinese officials will offer the same type of leadership if and when they get to the top.

Two important caveats bear repeating. The first is that, notwithstanding the Law of Uneven Growth, one cannot assume that China will inevitably overtake the United States. History offers numerous examples of failed challengers. The more skittish American policymakers and opinion leaders at the start of the Cold War thought that the US stage directions would eventually read "exit, pursued by a bear"; a generation later, the Japanese juggernaut seemed equally unstoppable. Neither Moscow nor Tokyo was able to sustain the momentum of their growth, and we should not assume that Beijing will necessarily succeed where those earlier challengers stumbled. There are any number of factors – political, demographic, and social – that could serve to slow or even reverse the fevered pace of Chinese growth. History's second cautionary note

---

[13]   O'Rourke and Williamson (1999).

suggests that a hegemon and a challenger need not remain in perpetual struggle. It is possible that here, too, the evolving relationship between Washington and Tokyo could offer an object lesson for relations with Beijing.

That said, odds are that the Sino-American rivalry will get more intense before it gets better, if indeed that ever happens. There can be no doubt that China is increasingly confident in challenging the United States. Beijing announced two major programs in 2013 – the Belt and Road Initiative and the Asian Infrastructure Investment Bank – that signaled a new level of ambition, and that demonstrated its willingness to provide public goods. The bank is especially notable from a hegemonic perspective, due to the widespread perception that it is deliberately designed as an alternative to the US-sponsored, Washington-based World Bank. The Obama administration had actively discouraged its allies from joining this new bank, but Japan and Mexico are the only major economic partners that took this advice.[14] China has also been increasingly active in trade negotiations, including bilateral, regional, and multilateral initiatives.

The nature of the relationships that Beijing hopes to have with other countries remains an issue of real concern. The UK and US versions of hegemony were at least rhetorically committed to the concept of a first among equals, and while each of them were known to throw their weight around they typically favored persuasion over coercion. Future Chinese leaders may find inspiration in other, less cooperative archetypes. The models in China's own past, whether one looks to the imperial period or the second half of the twentieth century, suggest a preference for hierarchical relations and a readiness to exert authority. Consider as well what Gilpin concluded when he examined the Soviet bloc in the waning days of the Cold War. Power alone "is not sufficient to ensure the development of a liberal international economy," he observed. "Hegemony without a liberal commitment to the market economy is more likely to lead to imperial systems and the imposition of political and economic restrictions on lesser powers."[15] This then begs the question of whether China has that requisite commitment. One may find plenty of evidence either to support or refute that contention when examining a country that is at once home to the world's largest Communist system and the world's second-largest market.

Over the medium term, much may depend on what use the United States and China wish to make of the WTO. In the ideal, this multilateral institution

---

[14]   The European Union per se is not a member, but the largest EU members are. Taiwan is not a member, but not for want of trying.

[15]   Gilpin (1987), p. 72.

offers a forum in which both powers could work out their bilateral differences while also encouraging further liberalization by the rest of the membership. Those prospects would of course disappear if the United States were to leave the WTO, at which point the remaining members would have to choose between treating the rump body as the new League of Nations (an organization that tried to get on without the United States) or the new International Trade Organization (where the other members decided it was not worth the effort). One suspects that the former option is more likely to be tried than the latter; that is certainly what happened with the TPP, which now has eleven members rather than twelve. It is easy to imagine the members of the WTO, and perhaps those of the TPP as well, keeping the US seat warm in case the next president should be of a mind to return. In the meantime, however, China may show more initiative than the United States in regional and global trade talks.

Managing the Challenges of Global Governance

Whether or not the United States stays in the WTO, and even after Trump leaves office, there may be considerable reluctance in Washington to negotiate new, multilateral liberalization. Here we could see the MFN principle play precisely the opposite role that it did in the nineteenth century, when Western powers used it to force China to extend to all of them whatever concessions it had given to any one of them. In the twenty-first century, US policymakers may not want to make MFN concessions to any partners so as to avoid extending them to China. If Washington makes a fetish of withholding any new concessions from China, there are only two circumstances in which it might be willing to negotiate in the WTO. One is to aim for agreements that are not based on an MFN principle, but instead plurilateral undertakings that return to the "code reciprocity" principles that were common before the Uruguay Round. Countries might alternatively negotiate zero-for-zero agreements in which a critical mass of the WTO membership, including China, agree to the elimination of all tariffs on some sectors or products, focusing on industries in which China is a net importer rather than a net exporter. Each of those options might have some natural appeal to policymakers in the United States, but China can easily use the WTO rule of consensus decision-making to delay or block any initiatives to which it objects.

Unless the United States and China settle on some formula that permits them to move ahead together in the WTO, they may allow that institution to go slack while they each concentrate instead on FTAs or other bilateral approaches. To the extent that the United States freezes its current levels of MFN treatment, and liberalizes its tariffs and other trade barriers only on a discriminatory basis, it will treat any countries outside its FTA circle – China above all – as the least-favored nations. China would almost certainly reciprocate. Here we could see American policymakers caught between the twin paradoxes of preferences and sanctions. Just as the scope for preferential treatment is now quite circumscribed by the generally low levels of MFN tariffs, so too does that discrimination affect China very little. One could well imagine policymakers contemplating new barriers so as to widen the difference between how China and other countries are treated, but here is where the paradox of sanctions arises. The already close economic ties between the US and Chinese economies raise the price that the United States would pay for imposing any new restrictions, as well as any counter-sanctions that might follow.

The potential departure of the United States from the WTO matters only if we assume that the organization might otherwise escape the doldrums in which it has now been for years. The subtler risk is that Washington might remain a nominal member of the WTO but restrict its Geneva activities to rhetoric and dispute-settlement cases. That may not be sustainable. Analysts sometimes liken the problem of domestic trade politics to riding a bicycle: If you don't move forward you fall over.[16] In applying that bicycle theory to the trading system, we might think of the twin wheels of negotiations and disputes. The vehicle does indeed need forward momentum, but it can actually remain upright for extended periods with only minimal effort. If we take away one of those wheels, however, and rely solely on the dispute-settlement system, things suddenly get quite wobbly. Even a skilled practitioner has to expend great energy to keep a unicycle upright, and this unwieldy conveyance may lurch backward just as often as it moves forward. With the passage of each unproductive year, the WTO bears an ever closer resemblance to a unicycle; that appearance may grow all the more striking if the unlucky cyclist is required to juggle an ever-growing number of disputes.

A related issue that cries out for solution, but will likely remain a source of perennial conflict, is just what range of issues should be defined to fall within the trading system. A field that was once confined to border instruments that directly affected the movement of goods has come to encompass a far wider range of topics at and behind the border, some of which are more commonly considered matters of social rather than foreign economic policy. Those

---

[16] For the etymology of the metaphor (as first enunciated by Bergsten), see Destler and Noland (2006).

expansions were often made at the behest of the United States, which was responding to the shifting interests of its industries and the post-materialist tastes of the electorate, but the accommodations did not ensure domestic tranquility. To the contrary, these efforts to retain or replace nervous members of the pro-trade coalition resulted in a contagion of conflict and a deepening of partisan divisions. At the international level, it has required that US trading partners – and especially developing countries – take on deeper commitments in a wider set of issues than ever before. Even some economists have doubts regarding the advisability of this development. Rodrik, for example, has proposed a norm by which countries should be allowed to uphold national rules on such matters as taxes, labor policy, and consumer health and safety, even "by raising barriers at the border if necessary, *when trade demonstrably threatens domestic practices enjoying broad popular support.*"[17] While reserving comment on whether such a pull-back is advisable, we may focus instead on the critical question of how it might be accomplished. It would be one thing for the United States and the rest of the community to reach a negotiated consensus by which some issues were taken off the negotiating table. It would be something else altogether if the downgrading of post-materialist issues were to come about as a consequence of China's ascent, and a reshaping of the system to conform to Beijing's eminently materialist priorities.

Managing the Domestic Diplomacy of Trade

Applying Occam's Razor to the present predicament, the challenges to the trading system can be cut down to three progressively smaller slices. If we accept the premises of hegemonic stability theory, the maintenance of an open trading system depends above all on the presence of a willing and able hegemon. The hegemon's disposition, in turn, depends on a favorable correlation of domestic economic and political forces. And at the very core of the problem is the apparent abdication of responsibilities by the presidency and the Republican Party.

This is not to say that the problem is unique to the United States, or to one electoral cycle. Trump's surprise victory was just one of several shocks that voters dealt to the liberal order in 2016. It was complemented by an equally unexpected victory for the Brexit forces in the United Kingdom, as well as votes against economic integration elsewhere in the European Union, and was preceded by the European Parliament's 2012 vote against the Anti-Counterfeiting Trade Agreement. Domestic

---

[17] Rodrik (2018), p. 224. Emphasis in the original.

US politics should thus be understood to form one arena in a larger set of struggles. That said, Washington remains ground zero. Even if the United States no longer chooses to behave like a responsible hegemon, and even if other countries grant it less deference than before, its domestic politics will continue to exert tremendous influence on the trading system.

Prior to the arrival of Donald Trump, the growing partisan rifts over trade already rendered policymaking dependent on two rare elements. One was the declining propensity of the electorate to choose unified government, and the other was the equally diminishing propensity of elected officials to engage in the give-and-take that divided government requires. It was not very long ago that presidents and members of Congress found it possible to make trade policy even when they were from different parties. Trade politics in the 1980s were difficult but ultimately productive, with policymakers managing to enact significant laws and negotiate important agreements. That was also a time when the word "compromised" was more often used affirmatively as a verb in the past tense (as in "we compromised") than pejoratively as an adjective (as in "he *is* compromised"). Overcoming those difficulties was already hard enough when the political center of gravity in the Democratic Party had shifted into the trade-skeptical camp, and the generally pro-trade Republicans enjoyed the luxury of unified government only once in a not-so-blue moon. Even those verities disappeared when the supposed party of free trade elected the most protectionist president in more than eight decades.

The only certainty to emerge from the 2018 midterm election was a return to divided government. With Democrats retaking control of the House of Representatives, the opposition party is once more in a position to frustrate any administration plans that require congressional approval. It is far from certain, however, just how strongly Democrats will fight Trump on trade – or if they will fight him at all. Even if they did, he could continue to take full advantage of the broad powers that Congress has granted to presidents in this field.

The future state of the trading system may depend more on the Republican Party than on any other factor, as the incomplete evidence for the reemergence of pro-trade sentiment in the Democratic Party's base – as well as some of its office-holders – may prove to be more of a mirage than a leading indicator. Unless and until some major Democratic figure exerts the same influence on that party that Trump did on Republicans in 2016, but in the opposite direction, it may be safely assumed that contenders for the Democratic presidential nomination and other party honors will remain beholden to labor unions (notwithstanding the decline in unionization since the 1980s)[18] and other core constituencies. The trade-skeptical skew in that party also takes energy from people whose post-materialist and sociotropic instincts lead them to view globalization with deep suspicion. The pro-trade wing of the party might well be needed to deliver votes in specific conflicts, especially if it must counterbalance a rising level of protectionism in the Republican caucus, but we should not be surprised if it remains a minority faction for years to come.

The struggle within the Republican Party may depend in no small measure on what happens to Donald Trump, but that will not be the sole factor. Trump won the Republican nomination, and then the presidency, in part by recognizing and exploiting the economic loss, social alienation, and political disenfranchisement of those on the losing side of globalization. He could do so only because the rest of the political field overlooked this rich source of votes. No matter when or on what terms his presidency comes to an end, contenders in both parties will covet the support of that base. There is a serious risk that this could set off a race to the bottom in both parties, with candidates for Congress and the presidency competing over who may appeal to the least common denominator in the trade-skeptical quarters of the electorate. The danger is that Yeats' words of a century ago will prove prophetic: "The best lack all conviction, while the worst/Are full of passionate intensity."[19]

How might the pro-trade sentiments of the Republican Party be reinvigorated? Two principal sources come to mind. One is the rural base of this party, many of whose members depend on access to foreign markets. The spirit of Physiocracy lives on in the Senate and the Electoral College, where the rural and Republican-leaning states still enjoy disproportionate representation. To the extent that Trump's confrontations with US allies and adversaries undermine agricultural export interests, especially through counter-retaliatory responses to US trade restrictions, the rural vote may sour on this president. The White House hopes to tamp down any such rebellion against its trade policies by compensating farmers with side-payments, but that does not sit well with the party's fiscal hawks. The interests of other globalized sectors of the US economy may also come into play, especially those that rely on relatively open movements of goods, capital, and people. This would mean organizing the more traditional core of the Republican Party business

---

[18] The share of American workers represented by unions rose from 5% in 1933 to 22% in 1945, plateaued for a time, and then fell from 23% in 1983 to 12% in 2015. U.S. Department of Commerce (1975), p. 178, and Bureau of Labor Statistics data at https://data.bls.gov/pdq/SurveyOutputServlet.

[19] William Butler Yeats, "The Second Coming" (1919).

establishment. And while the only area where this group enjoys a numerical advantages is in campaign contributions, that could be a critical consideration in any future tussle over the party's presidential nomination.

The broad outlines of these partisan struggles can be described, but it is far too early to foresee which side may have the advantage. The outcome will depend on several unpredictable elements, chief among them the state of the economy, the consequences of the international confrontations over trade and other matters, the political and legal fate of the president, and the willingness of other Republicans to stand up for core issues of their party orthodoxy. Those are a great many moving parts. The only things that can be said with absolute confidence are that the stakes are enormous, both for the United States and its partners, and that the outcome is unpredictable. Smith and Schattschneider could prove to be right after all.

Annotated Bibliography

TREATIES, DIPLOMATIC CORRESPONDENCE, PRESIDENTIAL
DOCUMENTS, AND CLASSIFIED MATERIALS

I have followed the standard practice of restricting the source citations for treaties to the
title and (where appropriate) the relevant article number. Readers who wish to find the
original texts of these treaties may look to www.wto.org/english/docs_e/legal_e/legal_e
.htm for World Trade Organization (WTO) agreements; to https://ustr.gov/trade-
agreements for current US trade agreements; to Bevans (1968–1976) for older,
perfected treaties of the United States (whether or not they are still in effect); and to
Wiktor (1976–1994) for unperfected US treaties (i.e., those not submitted to Congress
by the president, not approved by Congress, or otherwise not ratified by the United
States and/or its partners).

References to documents in the State Department's Foreign Relations of the United
States series are cited as FRUS with the corresponding year (also in italics) and the
volume number. The following are the titles of the FRUS volumes cited in this book:

1933, Volume II: *The British Commonwealth, Europe, the Near East
and Africa*
1945, Volume VI: *The British Commonwealth, the Far East*
1945–1950: *Emergence of the Intelligence Establishment*
1947, Volume I: *General; the United Nations*
1948, Volume I, Part 2: *General; the United Nations*
1948, Volume IX: *The Western Hemisphere*
1949, Volume IV: *Western Europe*
1949, Volume IX: *The Far East: China*
1950, Volume I: *National Security Affairs; Foreign Economic Policy*
1952–1954, Volume IX, Part 1: *The Near and Middle East*
1961–1963, Volume XIII: *Western Europe and Canada*
1961–1963, Volume IX: *Foreign Economic Policy*
1964–1968, Volume VIII: *International Monetary and Trade Policy*
1964–1968, Volume XXXIII: *Organization and Management of Foreign Policy;
United Nations*

1969–1976, Volume IV: *Foreign Assistance, International Development, Trade Policies, 1969–1972*
1969–1976 Volume E-11, Part 1:   *Mexico; Central America; and the Caribbean*
1969–1976, Volume XXXVI: *Energy Crisis, 1969–1974*
1977–1980, Volume III: *Foreign Economic Policy*
1981–1988, Volume XLI: *Global Issues II*

Public Papers of the Presidents are shown as *PPP* and the year covered by the volume, such that (for example) *PPP* 1977 means the volume in that series covering the first year of the Carter administration.

Presidential directives have gone by various titles in the years since the creation of the National Security Council (NSC) in 1947. They were simply identified with sequential NSC numbers in the Truman and Eisenhower administrations, as in NSC-68, but in later administrations they went by such names as the Nixon administration's National Security Study Memoranda and National Security Decision Memoranda, the Carter administration's Presidential Review Memoranda and Presidential Directives, etc. All citations of documents going by those names, or the many small variations on the theme, can be found in either or both of two types of online resources. For the official sources, see the websites of the presidential libraries (e.g., www.reaganlibrary.gov/sites/default/files/archives/reference/nsdds.html). The alternative and unofficial repositories of these documents are maintained by the Federation of American Scientists at https://fas.org/irp/offdocs/direct.htm and by George Washington University's National Security Archive at https://nsarchive.gwu.edu/.

I have relied on two additional sources for materials that had originally been classified (some of which remain so). Any memos, reports, or other documents cited as coming from the Central Intelligence Agency (CIA) for which my footnotes provide the titles and dates but without any further identifying numbers are available via the CIA's very user-friendly Freedom of Information Act Electronic Reading Room at www.cia.gov/library/readingroom/home. That same source yielded up some documents that were originally produced by other agencies (e.g., Office of the US Trade Representative [USTR]). In some cases the CIA redacted those documents so as to suppress specific passages, portions of the title, or the name of the person who wrote the document or delivered the speech. Where appropriate, I have inserted the term "[deleted]" to indicate such redactions. In addition to this official source, I have also relied on WikiLeaks (https://wikileaks .org/) for the texts of other classified but hacked materials, primarily in the form of State Department cables. Citations of those documents include the identifying alphanumeric that WikiLeaks has assigned as the "canonical ID" to each item on its site. Listings such as 02ROME5323_a or 1974TOKYO04568_b may be taken to indicate that WikiLeaks is the source.

OTHER GOVERNMENT AND INTERNATIONAL ORGANIZATION DOCUMENTS

Bevans, Charles, ed. 1968–1976. *Treaties and Other International Agreements of the United States of America, 1776–1949.* Washington, DC: U.S. Government Printing Office.

Congressional Research Service. 1984. *Treaties and Other International Agreements: The Role of the United States Senate.* Senate Print 98–205. Washington, DC: U.S. Government Printing Office.

Contracting Parties to the General Agreement on Tariffs and Trade. 1970. *Basic Instruments and Selected Documents.* Seventeenth Supplement. Geneva: General Agreement on Tariffs and Trade.

Hamilton, Alexander. 1791. "Manufactures." In Henry Cabot, Lodge, ed. 1903. *The Works of Alexander Hamilton.* New York: G. P. Putnam's Sons.

International American Conference. 1890a. *Reports of Committees and Discussions Thereon,* Volume I. Washington, DC: U.S. Government Printing Office.

——— 1890b. *Reports of Committees and Decisions Thereon,* Volume IV: *Historical Appendix: The Congress of 1826.* Washington, DC: U.S. Government Printing Office.

International Bank for Reconstruction and Development. 1955. *The Economic Development of Syria.* Baltimore, MD: The Johns Hopkins University Press.

International Monetary Fund. 2016. *Russian Federation: Staff Report for the 2016 Article IV Consultation.* Washington, DC: IMF.

Jefferson, Thomas. 1793. *Report of the Secretary of States on the Privileges and Restrictions on the Commerce of the United States in Foreign Countries.* Reproduced in Walter Lowrie and Matthew S. Clarke, eds. (1832), *American State Papers,* Volume I. Washington, DC: Gales and Seaton.

League of Nations. 1942. *Commercial Policy in the Interwar Period: International Proposals and National Policies.* Geneva: League of Nations.

Lodge, Henry Cabot, ed. 1903. *The Works of Alexander Hamilton.* New York: G. P. Putnam's Sons.

Lowrie, Walter and Matthew S. Clarke, eds. 1832. *American State Papers,* Volume I. Washington, DC: Gales and Seaton.

Maddison, Angus. 2003. *The World Economy: Historical Statistics.* Paris: Organisation for Economic Co-operation and Development.

Moss, Alfred G. and Harry N. M. Winton. 1979. *A New International Economic Order: Selected Documents 1945–1975.* UNITAR Document Service Number 1. New York: United Nations Institute for Training and Research.

Robinson, Chalfant. 1911. *History of the Reciprocity Treaty of 1854 with Canada.* Senate Document Number 17. Washington, DC: U.S. Government Printing Office.

United Nations Conference on Trade and Development. 1964. *Towards a New Trade Policy for Development.* E/CONF.46/3. New York: United Nations.

——— 2004. *Beyond Conventional Wisdom in Development Policy: An Intellectual History of UNCTAD, 1964–2004.* UNCTAD/EDM/2004/4. Geneva: UNCTAD.

U.S. Bureau of the Census. 1973. *Congressional District Data Book: 93rd Congress.* Washington, DC: U.S. Government Printing Office.

U.S. Bureau of Statistics. 1896a. *Commerce of the United States with Asiatic Countries, 1821–1895*. Washington, DC: U.S. Government Printing Office.

1896b. *Commerce of the United States with European Countries, 1790–1896*. Washington, DC: U.S. Government Printing Office.

U.S. Department of Agriculture. 1968. *Preferential Trade Arrangements of Foreign Countries*. Washington, DC: U.S. Government Printing Office.

U.S. Department of Commerce. 1975. *Historical Statistics of the United States, Colonial Times to 1970*. In two parts. Washington, DC: U.S. Government Printing Office.

2001. *The Effect of Imports on the National Security: Investigations Conducted under the Trade Expansion Act of 1962, as Amended*. Washington, DC: U.S. Department of Commerce.

U.S. Department of Homeland Security. 2011. *Yearbook of Immigration Statistics*. Washington, DC: U.S. Government Printing Office.

U.S. Department of Justice. Immigration and Naturalization Service. 2001. *2000 Statistical Yearbook*. Washington, DC: U.S. Government Printing Office.

U.S. Department of State. 1934. *Policy of the United States toward Maritime Commerce in War*. Publication 331. Two volumes. Washington, DC: U.S. Government Printing Office.

1949. *Postwar Foreign Policy Preparation, 1939–1945*. Publication 3580. Washington, DC: U.S. Government Printing Office.

U.S. Department of Transportation. National Highway Traffic Safety Administration. 2009. *Consumer Assistance to Recycle and Save Act of 2009: Report to the House Committee on Energy and Commerce, the Senate Committee on Commerce, Science, and Transportation and the House and Senate Committees on Appropriations*.

U.S. Department of Veterans Affairs. 2017. "America's Wars." Available at www.va.gov /opa/publications/factsheets/fs_americas_wars.pdf.

U.S. Executive Office of the President. 1991. *Response of the Administration to Issues Raised in Connection with the Negotiation of a North American Free Trade Agreement*. Washington, DC.

U.S. House of Representatives. 1918. *Papers Relating to the Foreign Relations of the United States*. 62nd Congress 2nd Session, Document Number 114. Washington, DC: U.S. Government Printing Office.

Committee on Foreign Affairs. 1994. *U.S. Trade Policy*. Washington, DC: U.S. Government Printing Office.

Committee on Ways and Means. 1973. *Trade Reform* Part 15 of 15: Summary of Testimony. 93rd Congress, 1st Session.

Committee on Ways and Means. 1979. *United States-China Trade Agreement*. 96th Congress, 1st Session, November 1–29.

Committee on Ways and Means. 1980. *Approving the Extension of Non-discriminatory Treatment to the Products of the People's Republic of China*. 96th Congress, 2nd Session, Serial Number 96–733.

Committee on Ways and Means. 2002. *To Explore Permanent Normal Trade Relations for Russia*. 107th Congress, 2nd Session, April 11.

U.S. International Trade Commission. 1980. *Certain Motor Vehicles and Certain Chassis and Bodies Thereof.* Investigation TA-201–44. USITC Publication 1110. Washington, DC: United States International Trade Commission.

1994. *Effects of the Arab League Boycott of Israel on U.S. Businesses* Investigation 332–349, USITC Publication 2827. Washington, DC: United States International Trade Commission.

2010. "Import Injury Investigations Case Statistics (FY 1980–2008)." Available at www.usitc.gov/trade_remedy/documents/historical_case_stats.pdf.

U.S. Office of the Trade Representative. 2000. "The Arab League (Boycott of Israel)." In 2000 *National Trade Estimate Report on Foreign Trade Barriers.* Washington, DC: United States Office of Trade Representative.

2003. "The Arab League (Boycott of Israel)," in 2003 *National Trade Estimate Report on Foreign Trade Barriers.* Washington, DC: United States Office of Trade Representative.

2016. "The Arab League (Boycott of Israel)." In 2016 *National Trade Estimate Report on Foreign Trade Barriers.* Washington, DC: United States Office of Trade Representative.

U.S. Tariff Commission. 1919. *Reciprocity and Commercial Treaties.* Washington, DC: U.S. Government Printing Office.

Wiktor, Christian, ed. 1976–1994. *Unperfected Treaties of the United States of America, 1776–1976.* Dobbs Ferry, NY: Oceana Publications.

World Trade Organization Appellate Body. 1998. *United States – Import Prohibition Of Certain Shrimp and Shrimp Products* (AB-1998–4). WT/DS58/AB/R. Geneva: WTO.

2012. *United States – Measures Affecting the Production and Sale of Clove Cigarettes* (AB-2012–1). WT/DS406/AB/R. Geneva: WTO.

JOURNAL ARTICLES, MONOGRAPHS, AND WEB POSTINGS

Aizcorbe, Ana. 2007. "Japanese Exchange Rates, Export Restraints, and Auto Prices in the 1980s." *Monthly Labor Review* (February).

Allison, Graham. 2015. "The Thucydides Trap: Are the U.S. and China Headed for War?" *The Atlantic* (September 24). Available at www.theatlantic.com/international/archive/2015/09/united-states-china-war-thucydides-trap/406756/.

Ardanaz, Martin, M. Victoria Murillo, and Pablo M. Pinto. 2013. "Sensitivity to Issue Framing on Trade Policy Preferences: Evidence from a Survey Experiment." *International Organization* Volume 67, Issue 2.

Atwood, Margaret. 1990. "The Art of Fiction No. 121." *The Paris Review.* Available at www.theparisreview.org/interviews/2262/margaret-atwood-the-art-of-fiction-no-121-margaret-atwood.

Baker, James. 1988. "The Geopolitical Implications of the U.S.-Canada Trade Pact." *The International Economy* (January/February).

Baker, Stewart A., and Richard O. Cunningham. 1983. "Countertrade and Trade Law." *Journal of Comparative Business and Capital Market Law* Volume 5.

Barry, Colin M., and Katja B. Kleinberg. 2015. "Profiting from Sanctions: Economic Coercion and US Foreign Direct Investment in Third-Party States." *International Organization* Volume 69, Issue 4.

Berry, Steven, James Levinsohn, and Ariel Pakes. 1999. "Voluntary Export Restraints on Automobiles: Evaluating a Trade Policy." *American Economic Review* Volume 89, Issue 3.

Biglaiser, Glen and David Lektzian. 2011. "The Effect of Sanctions on U.S. Foreign Direct Investment." *International Organization* Volume 65, Issue 3.

Bradley, Curtis A. 2007. "Unratified Treaties, Domestic Politics, and the U.S. Constitution." *Harvard International Law Journal* Volume 48, Number 2.

Brownstein, Ronald. 1988. "Losing Its Grip?" *National Journal* (February 6).

Buckel, Sonja and Andreas Fischer-Lescano. 2009. "Gramsci Reconsidered: Hegemony in Global Law." *Leiden Journal of International Law* Volume 22, Issue 3.

Buzan, Barry. 1984. "Economic Structure and International Security: The Limits of the Liberal Case." *International Organization* Volume 38, Number 4.

Carbaugh Robert J. 2011. "NAFTA and the U.S.-Mexican Trucking Dispute." *Journal of International and Global Economic Studies* Volume 4, Number 1.

Chase, Kerry A. 2006. "Multilateralism Compromised: The Mysterious Origins of GATT Article XXIV." *World Trade Review* Volume 5, Number 1.

Churchill, Winston. 1939. "The Russian Enigma" (broadcast of October 1). Transcript available at www.churchill-society-london.org.uk/RusnEnig.html.

Cobden, Richard. 1848. Untitled letter published in the *Morning Chronicle* (January 4, 1848).

Crandall, Robert W. 1987. *The Effects of U.S. Trade Protection for Autos and Steel*. Brookings Papers on Economic Activity. No. 1. Washington, DC: Brookings Institution.

Crowther, Bosley. 1945. "'Three Caballeros,' a Disney Picture, with Actors and Animated Characters, in Debut at Globe Theatre." *The New York Times* (February 5, 1945).

Dahl, Robert A. 1957. "The Concept of Power." *Behavioral Science* Volume 2, Number 3.

Dardis, Rachel and Susan Decker. 2005. "The Welfare Loss of the Voluntary Export Restraint for Japanese Automobiles." *Journal of Consumer Affairs* Volume 18, Number 1.

Davidson, Carl, Steven J. Matusz, and Douglas R. Nelson. 2010. "A Behavioral Model of Unemployment, Fairness and the Political Economy of Trade Policy." Available at https://editorialexpress.com/cgi-bin/conference/download.cgi?db_name=MWITFall2010&paper_id=5.

Diebold, William. 1994. "Reflections on the International Trade Organization." *Northern Illinois University Law Review* Volume 14, Number 2.

Drake, James D. 2010. "The Defining Relationship." *Diplomatic History* Volume 36, Issue 2.

El País. 2007. "Acta de la Conversación Entre George W. Bush Y José María Aznar – Crawford, Tejas, 22 de Febrero de 2003" (September 26, 2007).

Fisher, Allan G. B. 1933. "Capital and the Growth of Knowledge." *The Economic Journal* Volume XLIII, Number 171.

    1939. "Production, Primary, Secondary and Tertiary." *The Economic Record* Volume XV, Number 28.

Førland, T. E. 1990. "Economic Warfare and Strategic Goods: A Conceptual Framework for Analyzing COCOM." *Journal of Peace Research* Volume 28.

Gallagher, John and Ronald Robinson. 1953. "The Imperialism of Free Trade." *Economic History Review Second Series* Volume VI, Number 1.

Gamberoni, Elisa and Richard Newfarmer. 2009. "Trade Protection: Incipient but Worrisome Trends." Available at www.voxeu.org/index.php?q=node/3183.

Gawande, Kishore and Bernard Hoekman. 2006. "Lobbying and Agricultural Trade Policy in the United States." *International Organization* Volume 60, Number 3.

Grennes, Thomas. 2017. *An Economic Analysis of the Jones Act.* Arlington, VA: Mercatus Center at George Mason University.

Grossman, Gene M. and Elhanan Helpman. 1994. "Protection for Sale." *The American Economic Review.* Volume 84, Number 4.

Guisinger, Alexandra. 2009. "Determining Trade Policy: Do Voters Hold Politicians Accountable?" *International Organization.* Volume 63.

Hahn, Michael J. 1991. "Vital Interests and the Law of GATT: An Analysis of GATT's Security Exception." *Michigan Journal of International Law* Volume 12, Number 3.

Healey, Timothy. 2011. "Will Clayton, Negotiating the Marshall Plan, and European Economic Integration." *Diplomatic History* Volume 35, Issue 2.

Hillmann, Henning and Christina Gathmann. 2011. "Overseas Trade and the Decline of Privateering." *The Journal of Economic History* Volume 71, Issue 3.

Hiscox, Michael. 2006. "Through a Glass Darkly: Framing Effects and Individuals' Attitudes toward Trade." *International Organization* Volume 60.

Jensen, J. Bradford, Dennis P. Quinn, and Stephen Weymouth. 2017. "Winners and Losers in International Trade: The Effects on US Presidential Voting." *International Organization* Volume 71, Issue 3.

Kalat, David. ND. "The Three Caballeros." www.tcm.com/this-month/article/107477 0%7Co/The-Three-Caballeros.html.

Keynes, John Maynard. 1933. "National Self-Sufficiency." *The Yale Review* Volume 22, Number 4.

Kholodilin, Konstantin A. and Netsunajev, Aleksei. 2016. Crimea and Punishment: The Impact of Sanctions on Russian and European Economies. DIW Berlin Discussion Paper No. 1569.

Kinder, Donald R. and D. Roderick Kiewiet. 1979. "Economic Discontent and Political Behavior: The Role of Personal Grievances and Collective Economic Judgements in Congressional Voting." *American Journal of Political Science* Volume 23.

Krasner, Stephen D. 1976. "State Power and the Structure of International Trade." *World Politics* Volume 28.

Krisch, Nico. 2005. "International Law in Times of Hegemony: Unequal Power and the Shaping of the International Legal Order." *European Journal of International Law* Volume 16, Issue 3.

La Croix, Sumner J. and Christopher Grandy. 1997. "The Political Instability of Reciprocal Trade and the Overthrow of the Hawaiian Kingdom." *The Journal of Economic History* Volume 57, Issue 1.

Lampe, Markus. 2009. "Effects of Bilateralism and the MFN Clause on International Trade: Evidence for the Cobden-Chevalier Network, 1860–1875." *The Journal of Economic History* Volume 69, Issue 4.

Lewis, Justin. 2013. "Veiled Waters: Examining the Jones Act's Consumer Welfare Effect." *Issues in Political Economy* Volume 22.

Lowi, Theodore J. 1963. "American Business, Public Policy, Case-Studies, and Political Theory." *World Politics* Volume 16.

Mansfield, Edward D. and Diana C. Mutz. 2009. "Support for Free Trade: Self-Interest, Sociotropic Politics, and Out-Group Anxiety." *International Organization* Volume 63.

Marceau, Gabrielle. 1997. "NAFTA and WTO Dispute Settlement Rules: A Thematic Comparison." *Journal of World Trade* Volume 31.

Marchetti, Juan A. and Petros C. Mavroidis. 2011. "The Genesis of the GATS (General Agreement on Trade in Services)." *European Journal of International Law* Volume 22, Issue 3.

Marcus, Daniel. 1983. "Soviet Pipeline Sanctions: The President's Authority to Impose Extraterritorial Control." *Law and Policy in International Business* Volume 15, Number 4.

Mastanduno, Michael. 2016. Hegemony in International Law. Available at www .oxfordbibliographies.com/view/document/obo-9780199796953/obo-9780199796 953–0141.xml.

Mazzetti, Mark and Matthew Rosenberg. "Michael Flynn Misled Pentagon About Russia Ties, Letter Says." *The New York Times* (May 23, 2017), page A1.

McDonald, Judith A., Anthony Patrick O'Brien, and Colleen M. Callahan. 1997. "Trade Wars: Canada's Reaction to the Smoot-Hawley Tariff." *The Journal of Economic History* Volume 57, Issue 4.

Meardon, Stephen. 2008. "From Religious Revivals to Tariff Rancor: Preaching Free Trade and Protection during the Second American Party System." *History of Political Economy* Volume 40, Issue 5.

2014. "On Kindleberger and Hegemony: From Berlin to MIT and Back." *History of Political Economy* Volume 46, Supplement 1.

Morabito, Robert E. 1991. "Maritime Interdiction: Evolution of a Strategy." *Ocean Development and International Law* Volume 22, Number 3.

Morkre, Morris E., Dean Spinanger, and Lien H. Tran. 2008. "Are Unfair Import Laws Unfair to Developing Countries: Evidence from U.S. Antidumping Actions 1990–2004." Social Science Research Network Working Paper Series.

Owen, Erica and Noel P. Johnston. 2017. "Occupation and the Political Economy of Trade: Job Routineness, Offshorability, and Protectionist Sentiment." *International Organization* Volume 71, Issue 4.

Palen, Marc-William. 2015. "Free-Trade Ideology and Transatlantic Abolitionism: A Historiography." *Journal of the History of Economic Thought* Volume 37, Number 2.

Pelc, Krzysztof J. 2010. "Constraining Coercion? Legitimacy and Its Role in U.S. Trade Policy, 1975–2000." *International Organization* Volume 64, Issue 1.

Pierce, Justin R. and Peter K. Schott. 2012. "The Surprisingly Swift Decline of U.S. Manufacturing Employment." NBER Working Paper No. 18655.

2016. "Trade Liberalization and Mortality: Evidence from U.S. Counties." NBER Working Paper No. 22849.

Pop, Valentina. 2014. "Multi-Billion Losses Expected from Russia Sanctions." EU Observer. Available at https://euobserver.com/economic/125118.

Rappaport, Armin. 1981. "The United States and European Integration: The First Phase." *Diplomatic History* Volume 5, Issue 2.

Roberts, Adrienne and John D. Stoll. 2018. "Toyota Plant Puts Foreign Car Makers on Path to Pass Detroit in U.S. Production." *Wall Street Journal* (January 11, 2018).

Robertson, Horace B. 1991. "Interdiction of Iraqi Maritime Commerce in the 1990–1991 Persian Gulf Conflict." *Ocean Development and International Law* Volume 22, Number 3.

Russett, Bruce. 1985. "The Mysterious Case of Vanishing Hegemony; or, Is Mark Twain Really Dead?" *International Organization* Volume 39.

Safire, William. 2000. "The Biggest Vote." *The New York Times* (May 18, 2000).

Samuelson, Paul A. 1954. "The Pure Theory of Public Expenditure." *The Review of Economics and Statistics* Volume 36, Number 4.

Schmeisser, Peter. 1988. "Is America in Decline?" *The New York Times Magazine* (April 17, 1988).

Shagaida, Natalia, Natalia Karlova, Vasily Uzun, and Renata Yanbykh. 2014. "Russian Agriculture: The Impact of Sanctions." Moscow: Russian Presidential Academy of National Economy and Public Administration.

Shain, Yossi and Aharan Barth. 2003. "Diasporas and International Relations Theory." *International Organization* Volume 57, Number 3.

Snow, Nicholas. 2010. "If Goods Don't Cross Borders . . . ". Foundation for Economic Education. Available at https://fee.org/resources/if-goods-dont-cross-borders/.

The New Republic Staff. 1986. "'Worthwhile Canadian Initiative': Can You Top This?" *The New Republic*.

The New York Times. 1959. "Obituary: Dulles Formulated and Conducted U.S. Foreign Policy for More Than Six Years" (May 25, 1959).

VanGrasstek, Craig. 1997. "Is the Fast Track Really Necessary?" *Journal of World Trade* Volume 31 Number 2.

Wade, Nicholas. 1988. "The Ascent of Books on Decline of U.S." *The New York Times* (April 10, 1988).

Wallace, Don Jr. 1983. "Extraterritorial Jurisdiction." *Law and Policy in International Business* Volume 15, Number 4.

Watson, Richard A. 1956. "The Tariff Revolution: A Study of Shifting Party Attitudes." *The Journal of Politics* Volume 18, Number 4.

Whitt, Richard S. 1987. "The Politics of Procedure: An Examination of the GATT Dispute Settlement Panel and the Article XXI Defense in the Context of the U.S. Embargo of Nicaragua." *Law and Policy in International Business* Volume 19, Number 3.

Zaucha, Jerome J. 1983. "The Soviet Pipeline Sanctions: The Extraterritorial Application of U.S. Export Controls." *Law and Policy in International Business* Volume 15, Number 4.

BOOKS AND CHAPTERS

Abramson, Paul R. and Ronald Inglehart. 1995. *Value Change in Global Perspective.* Ann Arbor: The University of Michigan Press.

Acheson, Dean. 1969. *Present at the Creation: My Years in the State Department.* New York: W. W. Norton.

Adler-Karlsson, G. 1967. *Western Economic Warfare 1947–67: A Case Study in Foreign Economic Policy.* Stockholm: Almquist & Wiksell.

Ahrari, Mohammed E., ed. 1987. *Ethnic Groups and U.S. Foreign Policy.* New York: Greenwood Press.

Allison, Graham. 2018. *Destined for War: Can America and China Escape Thucydides's Trap?* New York: Mariner Books.

American Federation of Labor-Congress of Industrial Organizations. 1961. *AFL-CIO Looks at Foreign Trade . . . A Policy for the Sixties.* Washington, DC: AFL-CIO.

Arpan, Jeffrey S., José de la Torre, and Brian Toyne. 1982. *The U.S. Apparel Industry: International Challenge, Domestic Response.* Atlanta: Georgia State University Business Publishing Division.

Baldwin, Robert E. 1985. *The Political Economy of U.S. Import Policy.* Cambridge, MA: The MIT Press.

Bailey, Thomas A. 1980. *A Diplomatic History of the American People,* 10th edition. Englewood Cliffs, NJ: Prentice Hall.

Bard, Mitchell. 1987. "Ethnic Group Influence on Middle East Policy – How and When: The Cases of the Jackson-Vanik Amendment and the Sale of AWACS to Saudi Arabia." In Mohammed E. Ahrari, ed., *Ethnic Groups and U.S. Foreign Policy.* New York: Greenwood Press.

Bauer, Raymond, Ithiel de Sola Pool, and Lewis A. Dexter. 1963. *American Business and Public Policy: The Politics of Foreign Trade.* New York: Atherton.

Beard, Charles A. 1915. *The Economic Origins of Jeffersonian Democracy.* New York: The MacMillan Company.

Bemis, Samuel F., ed. 1958. *The American Secretaries of State and Their Diplomacy.* New York: Pageant Book Company.

Berger, Peter L. 1976. *Pyramids of Sacrifice: Political Ethics and Social Change.* Garden City, NY: Anchor Books.

Bhagwati, Jagdish and Hugh T. Patrick, eds. 1990. *Aggressive Unilateralism: America's 301 Trade Policy and the World Trading System.* Ann Arbor: University of Michigan Press.

Bond, Ian, Christian Odendahl, and Jennifer Rankin. 2015. *Frozen: The Politics and Economics of Sanctions against Russia.* London: Centre for European Reform.

Bourgin, Frank. 1989. *The Great Challenge: The Myth of Laissez-Faire in the Early Republic.* New York: Harper & Row.

Bovard, James. 1991. *The Fair Trade Fraud.* New York: St. Martin's Press.

Browder, William. 2015. *Red Notice: A True Story of High Finance, Murder, and One Man's Fight for Justice.* New York: Simon & Schuster.

Brown, Sherrod. 2004. *Myths of Free Trade: Why American Trade Policy Has Failed.* New York: The New Press.

Brown, William A., Jr. 1950. *The United States and the Restoration of World Trade.* Washington, DC: The Brookings Institution.

Buchanan, Patrick J. 1998. *The Great Betrayal: How American Sovereignty and Social Justice Are Being Sacrificed to the Gods of the Global Economy*. Boston: Little, Brown and Company.

Burton, Theodore E. 1958. "Henry Clay." In Samuel F. Bemis, ed., *The American Secretaries of State and Their Diplomacy*. New York: Pageant Book Company.

Byers, Michael and Georg Nolte, eds. 2003. *United States Hegemony and the Foundations of International Law*. Cambridge: Cambridge University Press.

Cafruny, Alan W. 1987. *Ruling the Waves: The Political Economy of International Shipping*. Berkeley: University of California Press.

Carter, James. 1982. *Keeping the Faith: Memoirs of a President*. New York: Bantam Books.

Choate, Pat. 1990. *Agents of Influence: How Japan Manipulates America's Political and Economic System*. New York: Simon & Schuster.

Churchill, Winston. 1949. *The Second World War, Volume II: Their Finest Hour*. Boston: Houghton Mifflin.

Cline, William R. 1982. *"Reciprocity": A New Approach to World Trade Policy?* Washington, DC: Institute for International Economics.

Cohen, Warren I. 1990. *America's Response to China: A History of Sino-American Relations*, 3rd edition. New York: Columbia University Press.

Congressional Quarterly. 1974. *Congressional Districts in the 1970s*, 2nd edition. Washington, DC: Congressional Quarterly.

1993. *Congressional Districts in the 1990s*. Washington, DC: Congressional Quarterly.

2003. *Congressional Districts in the 2000s*. Washington, DC: Congressional Quarterly.

Corwin, Edward S. 1957. *The President: Office and Powers*, 4th edition. New York: New York University Press.

Cottier, Thomas and Krista N. Schefer. 2017. *Elgar Encyclopedia of International Economic Law*. Cheltenham: Edward Elgar.

Curzon, Gerard. 1965. *Multilateral Commercial Diplomacy*. New York: Frederick A. Praeger.

Dadush, Uri. 2009. *Resurgent Protectionism: Risks and Possible Remedies*. Carnegie Policy Outlook. Washington, DC: Carnegie Endowment.

Davey, William J. 2012. *Non-discrimination in the World Trade Organization: The Rules and Exceptions*. The Hague: Hague Academy of International Law.

De Melo, Jaime and David Tarr. 1992. *A General Equilibrium Analysis of US Foreign Trade Policy*. Cambridge, MA: The MIT Press.

Destler, I.M. and Marcus Noland. 2006. "Constant Ends, Flexible Means: C. Fred Bergsten and the Quest for Free Trade." In Michael Mussa, ed., *C. Fred Bergsten and the World Economy*. Washington, DC: Peterson Institute for International Economics.

De Vattel, Emmerich. 1758 [1883 republication]. *The Law of Nations: Or, Principles of the Law of Nature, Applied to the Conduct and Affairs of Nations and Sovereigns*, translated by Joseph Chitty. Philadelphia: T. and J. W. Johnson and Company.

Diebold, William. 1941. *New Directions in Our Trade Policy*. New York: Council on Foreign Relations.

Dobson, Alan P. 2002. *US Economic Statecraft for Survival 1933–1991: Of Sanctions, Embargoes and Economic Warfare*. London: Routledge.

Dorfman, Joseph. 1946. *The Economic Mind in American Civilization, 1606–1865*. Two volumes. New York: The Viking Press.

Drezner, Daniel W. 1999. *The Sanctions Paradox: Economic Statecraft and International Relations*. Cambridge: Cambridge University Press.

Drysdale, Peter and Ross Garnaut. 1989. "A Pacific Free Trade Area?" In Jeffrey J. Schott, ed., *Free Trade Areas and U.S. Trade Policy*. Washington, DC: Institute for International Economics.

Earle, Edward M. 1943. "Adam Smith, Alexander Hamilton, Friedrich List: The Economic Foundations of Military Power." Reprinted in Peter Paret, ed. (1986), *Makers of Modern Strategy from Machiavelli to the Nuclear Age*. Princeton, NJ: Princeton University Press.

Elliot, Jonathan. 1836. *The Debates in the Several State Conventions on the Adoption of the Federal Constitution*. Five volumes. Washington, DC: N.P.

Ellis, Howard S. 1945. "Bilateralism and the Future of International Trade." Reprinted in Howard S. Ellis and Lloyd A. Metzler, eds. (1949), *Readings in the Theory of International Trade*. Philadelphia: The Blakiston Company.

Ellis, Howard S. and Lloyd A. Metzler, eds. 1949. *Readings in the Theory of International Trade*. Philadelphia: The Blakiston Company.

Ellis, Lewis Ethan. 1939. *Reciprocity 1911: A Study in Canadian-American Relations*. New Haven, CT: Yale University Press.

Feiler, Gil. 1998. *From Boycott to Economic Cooperation: The Political Economy of the Arab Boycott of Israel*. London: Frank Cass.

Ferguson, Thomas. 1995. *Golden Rule: The Investment Theory of Party Competition and the Logic of Money-Driven Political Systems*. Chicago: University of Chicago Press.

Fine, Morris and Milton Himmelfarb, eds. 1973. *The American Jewish Yearbook 1973*. New York: The American Jewish Committee.

Fischer, Stanley, Dani Rodrik, and Elias Tuma, eds. 1993. *The Economics of Middle East Peace: Views from the Region*. Cambridge, MA: The MIT Press.

Fisher, Louis. 1985. *Constitutional Conflicts between Congress and the President*. Princeton, NJ: Princeton University Press.

Fleming, Denna Frank. 1930. *The Treaty Veto of the American Senate*. New York: G. P. Putnam's Sons.

Fortune. 1945. "Fortune Survey." Extracted in Robert E. Summers, ed. (1945), *Dumbarton Oaks*. The Reference Shelf Volume 18 Number 1. New York: The H. W. Wilson Company.

Frank, Dana. 1999. *Buy American: The Untold Story of Economic Nationalism*. Boston: Beacon Press.

Friman, H. Richard. 1990. *Patchwork Protectionism: Textile Trade Policy in the United States, Japan, and West Germany XE "Germany"*. Ithaca, NY: Cornell University Press.

Gerschenkron, Alexander. 1962. *Economic Backwardness in Historical Perspective*. Cambridge, MA: Harvard University Press.

Gershman, Carl. 1975. *The Foreign Policy of American Labor*. Beverly Hills, CA: SAGE Publications.

Gibbs, Nancy and Michael Duffy. 2013. *The Presidents Club: Inside the World's Most Exclusive Fraternity*. New York: Simon & Schuster.

Gilpin, Robert. 1981. *War and Change in World Politics*. Cambridge: Cambridge University Press.

1987. *The Political Economy of International Relations*. Princeton, NJ: Princeton University Press.

Goldstein, Judith. 1993. *Ideas, Interests, and American Trade Policy*. Ithaca, NY: Cornell University Press.

Gomaa, Ahmed M. 1977. *The Foundation of the League of Arab States: Wartime Diplomacy and Inter-Arab Politics, 1941 to 1945*. London: Longman.

Goodwin, Crauford D., ed. 1991a. *Economics and National Security: A History of Their Interaction*. Durham, NC: Duke University Press.

1991b. "Introduction." In Crauford D. Goodwin, ed., *Economics and National Security: A History of Their Interaction*. Durham, NC: Duke University Press.

Green, Mark J., ed. 1973. *The Monopoly Makers: Ralph Nader's Study Group Report on Regulation and Competition*. New York: Grossman Publishers.

Haberler, Gottfried. 1933. *The Theory of International Trade with Its Application to Commercial Policy*. London: William Hodge.

Handoussa, Heba and Nemat Shafik. 1993. "The Economics of Peace: The Egyptian Case." In Stanley Fischer, Dani Rodrik, and Elias Tuma, eds. *The Economics of Middle East Peace: Views from the Region*. Cambridge, MA: The MIT Press.

Harding, Harry. 1992. *A Fragile Relationship: The United States and China since 1972*. Washington, DC: The Brookings Institution.

Harris, Nigel. 1986. *The End of the Third World: Newly Industrializing Countries and the Decline of an Ideology*. Middlesex: Penguin Books.

Hartz, Louis. 1955. *The Liberal Tradition in America*. New York: Harcourt Brace & World.

1964. *The Founding of New Societies: Studies in the History of the United States, Latin America, South Africa, Canada, and Australia*. New York: Harcourt, Brace & World.

Haus, Leah A. 1992. *Globalizing the GATT: The Soviet Union's Successor States, Eastern Europe, and the International Trading System*. Washington, DC: The Brookings Institution.

Heilbroner, Robert L. 1986. *The Worldly Philosophers: The Lives, Times, and Ideas of the Great Economic Thinkers*, 6th edition. New York: Simon & Schuster.

Hero, Alfred O. Jr. and Emil Starr. 1970. *The Reuther-Meany Foreign Policy Dispute: Union Leaders and Members View World Affairs*. Dobbs Ferry, NY: Oceana Publications.

Hirschman, Albert O. 1945. *National Power and the Structure of Foreign Trade*. Berkeley: University of California Press.

Hofstadter, Richard. 1948. *The American Political Tradition and the Men Who Made It*. New York: Vintage Books.

ed. 1958. *Great Issues in American History: From the Revolution to the Civil War, 1765–1865*. New York: Vintage Books.

Homans, J. Smith, Jr. 1857. *An Historical and Statistical Account of the Foreign Commerce of the United States*. New York: G. P. Putnam and Company.

Hubbard, Charles M. 1998. *The Burden of Confederate Diplomacy*. Knoxville: The University of Tennessee Press.

Hufbauer, Gary C. and Kimberly Ann Elliott. 1994. *Measuring the Costs of Protection in the United States*. Washington, DC: Institute for International Economics.

Hufbauer, Gary C., Jeffrey J. Schott, and Kimberly Ann Elliott. 1990. *Economic Sanctions Reconsidered: History and Current Policy*, 2nd edition. Washington, DC: Institute for International Economics.

Irwin, Douglas A. 1996. *Against the Tide: An Intellectual History of Free Trade*. Princeton, NJ: Princeton University Press.

2017. *Clashing over Commerce: A History of U.S. Trade Policy*. Chicago: University of Chicago Press.

Jackson, John H. 1989. *The World Trading System: Law and Policy of International Economic Relations*. Cambridge, MA: The MIT Press.

2000. *The Jurisprudence of GATT and the WTO: Insights on Treaty Law and Economic Relations*. Cambridge: Cambridge University Press.

Jackson, John H., William J. Davey, and Alan O. Sykes, Jr., eds. 1995. *Legal Problems of International Economic Relations*, 3rd Edition. St. Paul, MN: West Publishing Company.

Jarvie, Ian. 1992. *Hollywood's Overseas Campaign: The North Atlantic Movie Trade, 1920–1950*. Cambridge: Cambridge University Press.

Jefferson, Thomas. 1784. *Notes on Virginia*. Extracted in Richard Hofstadter, ed. (1958), *Great Issues in American History: From the Revolution to the Civil War, 1765–1865*. New York: Vintage Books.

Jerome, Robert W. 1990. *U.S. Senate Decision-Making: The Trade Agreements Act of 1979*. New York: Greenwood Press.

Johnson, Emory R., T. W. Van Metre, G. G. Huebner, and D. S. Hanchett. 1915. *History of the Domestic and Foreign Commerce of the United States*. Two volumes. New York: Burt Franklin.

Jones, Joseph M. 1955. *The Fifteen Weeks: February 21–June 5, 1947*. New York: Harcourt, Brace and World.

Kaempfer, William H. and Anton D. Lowenberg. 1990. "Analyzing Economic Sanctions: Toward a Public Choice Framework." In John S. Odell and Thomas D. Willett, eds. *International Trade Policies: Gains from Exchange between Economics and Political Science*. Ann Arbor: The University of Michigan Press.

Keck, Margaret E. and Kathryn Sikkink. 1998. *Activity beyond Borders: Advocacy Networks in International Politics*. Ithaca, NY: Cornell University Press.

Kennedy, Paul M. 1976. *The Rise and Fall of British Naval Mastery*. London: The Ashfield Press.

1987. *The Rise and Fall of the Great Powers*. New York: Vintage Books.

Keohane, Robert O. 1984. *After Hegemony: Cooperation and Discord in the World Political Economy*. Princeton, NJ: Princeton University Press.

Keynes, John Maynard. 1935. *The General Theory of Employment Interest and Money*. New York: Harcourt, Brace and Company.

Kindleberger, Charles P. 1970. *Power and Money: The Economics of International Politics and the Politics of International Economics*. New York: Basic Books.

1973. *The World in Depression, 1929–1939*. Berkeley: University of California Press.

Kreider, Carl. 1943. *The Anglo-American Trade Agreement: A Study of British and American Commercial Policies, 1934–1939.* Princeton, NJ: Princeton University Press.

Kuhn, Thomas. 1970. *The Structure of Scientific Revolutions*, 2nd revised edition. Chicago: University of Chicago Press.

Lake, David A. 1988. *Power, Protection, and Free Trade: International Sources of U.S. Commercial Strategy, 1887–1939.* Ithaca, NY: Cornell University Press.

Lande, Stephen and Craig VanGrasstek. 1986. *The Trade and Tariff Act of 1984: Trade Policy in the Reagan Administration.* Lexington, MA: Lexington Books.

Langer, William L., ed. 1972. *An Encyclopedia of World History*, 5th edition. Boston: Houghton Mifflin.

Laski, Harold. 1940. *The American Presidency: An Interpretation.* London: George Allen & Unwin.

Lenin, Vladimir I. 1916 [1965 reprint]. *Imperialism, the Highest Stage of Capitalism.* Peking: Foreign Languages Press.

Lippert, Kevin. 2015. *War Plan Red: The United States' Secret Plan to Invade Canada and Canada's Secret Plan to Invade the United States.* New York: Princeton Architectural Press.

Lippmann, Walter. 1943. *U.S. Foreign Policy: Shield of the Republic.* New York: Pocket Books.

Lipset, Seymour M. 1979. *The First New Nation: The United States in Historical and Comparative Perspective.* New York: W. W. Norton.

LTV Corporation. 1983. *Congress and U.S. Trade Policy.* An LTV Forum, Dallas.

MacArthur, John. R. 2000. *The Selling of "Free Trade": NAFTA, Washington, and the Subversion of Democracy.* New York: Hill and Wang.

Maclay, William. 1988. *The Diary of William Maclay and Other Notes on Senate Debates, March 4, 1789-March 3, 1791.* Edited by Kenneth R. Bowling and Helen E. Veit. Baltimore: The Johns Hopkins University Press.

Madison, James. 1787. "Debates in the Federal Convention of 1787." Reprinted in Charles C. Tansill, ed. (1927), *Documents Illustrative of the Formation of the Union of the American States.* House Document Number 398. Washington, DC: Government Printing Office.

Malloy, Michael P. 1990. *Economic Sanctions and U.S. Trade.* Boston: Little, Brown and Company.

Malmgren, Harald. 1983. "A Historical View of Congress' Impact on Trade Legislation and Negotiation." In LTV Corporation, *Congress and U.S. Trade Policy.* An LTV Forum, Dallas.

Mander, Jerry and Edward Goldsmith, eds. 1996. *The Case against the Global Economy.* San Francisco: Sierra Club Books.

Marvin, Winthrop L. 1902. *The American Merchant Marine: Its History and Romance from 1620 to 1902.* New York: Charles Scribner's Sons.

Mastanduno, Michael. 1992. *Economic Containment: CoCom and the Politics of East-West Trade.* Ithaca, NY: Cornell University Press.

McCoy, Drew R. 1980. *The Elusive Republic: Political Economy in Jeffersonian America.* Chapel Hill: The University of North Carolina Press.

McCusker, John J. and Russell R. Menard. 1991. *The Economy of British America, 1607–1789.* Chapel Hill: The University of North Carolina Press.

McNaught, Kenneth. 1988. *The Penguin History of Canada*, revised edition. London: Penguin Books.

Mendershausen, Horst. 1940. *The Economics of War*. New York: Prentice-Hall.

Milward, Alan S. 1979. *War, Economy and Society: 1939–1945*. Berkeley: University of California Press.

Moran, Daniel. 2002. "The International Law of the Sea in a Globalized World." In Sam Tangredi, ed. (2002a). *Globalization and Maritime Power*. Washington, DC: National Defense University Press.

Muñoz, Heraldo. 2008. *A Solitary War: A Diplomat's Chronicle of the Iraq War and Its Lessons*. Golden: Fulcrum Publishing.

Murphy, Sean D. 2008. "The United States and the International Court of Justice: Coping with Antinomies." In Cesare Romano, ed., *The Sword and the Scales: The United States and International Courts and Tribunals*. Cambridge: Cambridge University Press.

Mussa, Michael, ed. 2006. *C. Fred Bergsten and the World Economy*. Washington, DC: Peterson Institute for International Economics.

Nader, Ralph, et al., eds. 1993. *The Case against "Free Trade": GATT, NAFTA, and the Globalization of Corporate Power*. San Francisco: Earth Island Press.

Nader, Ralph and Lori Wallach. 1996. "GATT, NAFTA, and the Subversion of the Democratic Process." In Jerry Mander and Edward Goldsmith, eds. *The Case against the Global Economy*. San Francisco: Sierra Club Books.

National Opinion Research Center. 1945. "Public Trend toward World Order." Extracted in Robert E. Summers, ed. (1945), *Dumbarton Oaks*. The Reference Shelf Volume 18 Number 1. New York: The H. W. Wilson Company.

Nau, Henry R. 1990. *The Myth of America's Decline: Leading the World Economy into the 1990s*. New York: Oxford University Press.

North, Douglass C. 1966. *The Economic Growth of the United States 1790–1860*. New York: W. W. Norton and Company.

Nye, Joseph S. Jr. 1990. *Bound to Lead: The Changing Nature of American Power*. New York: Basic Books.

Odell, John S. and Thomas D. Willett, eds. 1990. *International Trade Policies: Gains from Exchange between Economics and Political Science*. Ann Arbor: The University of Michigan Press.

Olson, Mancur. 1982. *The Rise and Decline of Nations: Economic Growth, Stagflation and Social Rigidities*. New Haven, CT: Yale University Press.

O'Rourke, Kevin H. and Jeffrey G. Williamson. 1999. *Globalization and History: The Evolution of a Nineteenth Century Atlantic Economy*. Cambridge, MA: The MIT Press.

Padover, Saul, ed. 1958. *The Mind of Alexander Hamilton*. New York: Harper & Brothers.

Paine, Thomas. 1776. "Common Sense." In Gordon Wood, ed. *Common Sense and Other Writings*. New York: The Modern Library.

Paret, Peter, ed. 1986. *Makers of Modern Strategy from Machiavelli to the Nuclear Age*. Princeton, NJ: Princeton University Press.

Patterson, Gardner. 1966. *Discrimination in International Trade: The Policy Issues, 1945–1965*. Princeton, NJ: Princeton University Press.

Petty, Sir William. 1676. *Political Arithmetic*. London: Robert Clavel.

Piketty, Thomas. 2014. *Capital in the Twenty-First Century*. Cambridge, MA: Harvard University Press.

Pitkin, Timothy. 1817. *A Statistical View of the Commerce of the United States of America*. New York: James Eastburn and Company.

Prestowitz, Clyde V. Jr. *Trading Places: How We Allowed Japan to Take the Lead*. New York: Basic Books.

Puttnam, David and Neil Watson. 1998. *Movies and Money*. New York: Alfred A. Knopf.

Radosh, Ronald. 1969. *American Labor and United States Foreign Policy*. New York: Random House.

Rappaport, Armin, ed. 1966. *Sources in American Diplomacy*. New York: The Macmillan Company.

Rodrik, Dani. 1997. *Has Globalization Gone Too Far?* Washington, DC: Peterson Institute for International Economics.

2018. *Straight Talk on Trade: Ideas for a Sane World Economy*. Princeton, NJ: Princeton University Press.

Romano, Cesare, ed. 2008. *The Sword and the Scales: The United States and International Courts and Tribunals*. Cambridge: Cambridge University Press.

Rosencrance, Richard. 1990. *America's Economic Resurgence: A Bold New Strategy*. New York: Harper & Row.

Rossiter, Clinton, ed. 1961. *The Federalist Papers*. New York: New American Library.

Rutland, Robert A. and Charles F. Hobson, eds. 1977. *The Papers of James Madison* Volume II. Charlottesville: University Press of Virginia.

Schattschneider, Elmer E. 1935. *Politics, Pressure, and the Tariff: A Study of Free Private Enterprise in Pressure Politics, as Shown in the 1929–1930 Revision of the Tariff*. New York: Prentice Hall.

1960. *The Semi-Sovereign People: A Realist's View of Democracy in America*. New York: Holt, Rinehart and Winston.

Schlesinger, Stephen E. 2004. *Act of Creation: The Founding of the United Nations: A Story of Superpowers, Secret Agents, Wartime Allies and Enemies, and Their Quest for a Peaceful World*. Cambridge, MA: Westview.

Schott, Jeffrey J., ed. 1986. *Free Trade Areas and U.S. Trade Policy*. Washington, DC: Institute for International Economics.

2004. *Free Trade Agreements: US Strategies and Priorities*. Washington, DC: Institute for International Economics.

Schumpeter, Joseph. 1954. *History of Economic Analysis*. New York: Oxford University Press.

Seldes, George. 1967. *The Great Quotations*. New York: Pocket Books.

Shoch, James. 2001. *Trading Blows: Party Competition and U.S. Trade Policy in a Globalizing Era*. Chapel Hill: The University of North Carolina Press.

Sick, Gary. 1991. *October Surprise: America's Hostages in Iran and the Election of Ronald Reagan*. New York: Crown Publishing.

Skidelsky, Robert. 2000. *John Maynard Keynes: Fighting for Britain, 1937–1946*. London: Macmillan.

Smith, Adam. 1776. Edited by R. H. Campbell and A. S. Skinner, 1981. *An Inquiry into the Nature and Causes of the Wealth of Nations*. Glasgow edition of the works and correspondence of Adam Smith. Indianapolis: Liberty Classics.

1790. *The Theory of Moral Sentiments*, 6th edition. Edited by Sálvio M. Soares. MetaLibri.

Stairs, Denis and Gilbert R. Winham. 1985. *The Politics of Canada's Economic Relationship with the United States*. Toronto: University of Toronto Press.

Steil, Benn. 2013. *The Battle of Bretton Woods: John Maynard Keynes, Harry Dexter White, and the Making of a New World Order*. Princeton, NJ: Princeton University Press.

2018. *The Marshall Plan: Dawn of the Cold War*. New York: Simon & Schuster.

Summers, Robert E., ed. 1945. *Dumbarton Oaks*. The Reference Shelf Volume 18 Number 1. New York: The H. W. Wilson Company.

Tangredi, Sam, ed. 2002a. *Globalization and Maritime Power*. Washington, DC: National Defense University Press.

2002b. "Globalization and Sea Power: Overview and Context." In Sam Tangredi, ed. (2002a), *Globalization and Maritime Power*. Washington, DC: National Defense University Press.

Tansill, Charles C., ed. 1927. *Documents Illustrative of the Formation of the Union of the American States*. House Document Number 398. Washington, DC: Government Printing Office.

1943. *Canadian-American Relations, 1875–1911*. New Haven, CT: Yale University Press.

Tarbell, Ida M. 1911. *The Tariff in Our Times*. New York: The Macmillan Company.

Taussig, Frank. 1931. *The Tariff History of the United States*, 8th edition. New York: G. P. Putnam's Sons.

Thucydides. 400 BCE [1952 Richard Crawley translation]. *The History of the Peloponnesian War*. The Great Books of the Western World, Volume 6. Chicago: Encyclopædea Brittanica.

Toder, E., N. Cardell, and E. Burton. 1978. *Trade Policy and the U.S. Automobile Industry*. New York: Praeger.

Tumlir, Jan. 1985. *Protectionism: Trade Policy in Democratic Societies*. Washington, DC: American Enterprise Institute.

Twain, Mark [Samuel Clemens]. 1883 [1917 edition]. *Life on the Mississippi*. New York: Harper and Brothers.

VanGrasstek, Craig. 2013. *The History and Future of the World Trade Organization*. Geneva: WTO Publications.

2017. "Mercantilism." In, Thomas Cottier and Krista N. Schefer, *Elgar Encyclopedia of International Economic Law*. Cheltenham: Edward Elgar.

Viner, Jacob. 1950. *The Customs Union Issue*. New York: Carnegie Endowment for International Peace.

Weintraub, Sidney. 2004. "Lessons for the Chile and Singapore Free Trade Agreements." In Jeffrey J. Schott, ed., *Free Trade Agreements: US Strategies and Priorities*. Washington, DC: Institute for International Economics.

Whidden, Howard P. 1945. *Preferences and Discriminations in International Trade*. Washington, DC: Carnegie Endowment for International Peace.

Williams, Ernest Edwin. 1896. *Made in Germany*. London: Heinemann.

Wolman, Paul. 1992. *Most Favored Nation: The Republican Revisionists and U.S. Tariff Policy, 1897–1912*. Chapel Hill: The University of North Carolina Press.

Womack, James P., Daviel T. Jones, and Daniel Roos. 1990. *The Machine that Changed the World: How Japan's Secret Weapon in the Global Auto Wars Will Revolutionize Western Industry*. New York: Harper Perennial.

Wood, Gordon, ed. 2003. *Common Sense and Other Writings*. New York: The Modern Library.

Wu, Yuan-Li. 1952. *Economic Warfare*. New York: Prentice-Hall.

Yergin, Daniel. 1991. *The Prize: The Epic Quest for Oil, Money, and Power*. New York: Simon & Schuster.

Zakaria, Fareed. 1998. *From Wealth to Power: The Unusual Origins of America's World Role*. Princeton, NJ: Princeton University Press.

FICTION

Alighieri, Dante. c. 1306 [2002 translation by Robert and Jean Hollander]. *Inferno*. New York: Anchor Books.

Clarke, I. F., ed. 1995. *The Tale of the Next Great War, 1871–1914*. Liverpool: Liverpool University Press.

Condon, Richard. 1959. *The Manchurian Candidate*. New York: New American Library.

Crichton, Michael. 1992. *Rising Sun*. New York: Ballantine Books.

Danson, David. 2012. *Faultline 49*. Toronto: Guy Faux Books.

Doyle, Arthur C. 1892. "The Adventure of Silver Blaze." In *The Strand* (December, 1892).

Hobart, Alice T. 1933. *Oil for the Lamps of China*. New York: Grosset & Dunlap.

Kelly, Walt. 1953. *The Pogo Papers*. New York: Simon and Schuster.

Lewis, Sinclair. 1925 [1980 paperback edition]. *Arrowsmith*. New York: New American Library.

Moorcock, Michael, ed. 1976. *Before Armageddon*. London: Wyndham Publications.

Prindle, Tamae K., ed. 1989. *Made in Japan and Other Japanese "Business Novels."* London: M. E. Sharpe.

Rohmer, Richard. 1973. *Ultimatum*. Toronto: Clarke, Irwin & Company.

Rohmer, Sax. 1936. *President Fu Manchu*. New York: Doubleday, Doran & Company.

Shimizu, Ikkō, ed. 1996. *The Dark Side of Japanese Business: Three "Industry Novels"*. London: M. E. Sharpe.

Vaughan, Brian K., Steve Skroce, and Matt Hollingsworth. 2016. *We Stand on Guard*. Berkeley: Image Comics.

Index

CPSIA information can be obtained
at www.ICGtesting.com
Printed in the USA
LVHW021621190720
661032LV00013B/250

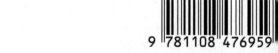